DATE DUE

MAR 1 0 1986	
April 14	
MAY 1 2 1986	
MAY 9 1988	
MAY 1 1989	
MAY 2 7 1991	
OCT 2 6 1992	
MAY 1 6 1994	

CHILDREN AND LANGUAGE

DORRIS M. LEE
Professor Emeritus
Portland State University

JOSEPH B. RUBIN
Assistant Professor
University of Arizona

CHILDREN AND LANGUAGE
Reading and Writing,
Talking and Listening

Wadsworth Publishing Company
Belmont, California
A Division of Wadsworth, Inc.

Education Editor: Roger Peterson
Production Editor: Connie Martin
Designer: Penny Faron

Library of Congress Cataloging in Publication Data

Lee, Dorris Mary Potter, 1905–
   Children and language.

   Bibliography: p.
   Includes index.
   1. Language arts.   2. Children—Language.
3. Communication.   I. Rubin, Joseph B., joint author.
II. Title.
LB1575.8.L43   372.6   78-27256
ISBN 0-534-00686-8

Text Credits (Page numbers are given in parentheses.)

Charles M. Galloway, *Teaching Is Communicating: Nonverbal Language in the Classroom*, 1970; used by permission of the Association of Teacher Educators (21–22).

Yetta Goodman and Carolyn Burke, *Reading Miscue Inventory Manual: Procedure for Diagnosis and Evaluation*, 1972; used by permission of Yetta Goodman (300).

David W. Johnson, *Reaching Out: Interpersonal Effectiveness and Self-Actualization*, 1972; used by permission of Prentice-Hall, Inc. (14–15).

Elizabeth M. Pflaumer, "Listening: A Definition and Application," 1972; used by permission of Elizabeth M. Pflaumer (94–95).

Huberta V. Randolph, "Measuring the Unmeasurable," in *Evaluation in Reading*, 1972; used by permission of the International Reading Association (295).

Hilda Taba, Samuel Levine, and Freeman F. Elzey, *Thinking in Elementary School Children*, 1964; used by permission of San Francisco State University (46).

Photo Credits
Chapter 1: © David Powers.
Chapter 2: © Elizabeth Hamlin/Stock, Boston.
Chapter 3: © Daniel S. Brody/Stock, Boston.
Chapter 4: © Elizabeth Crews/Jeroboam.
Chapter 5: © David Powers.
Chapter 6: © J. Berndt/Stock, Boston.
Chapter 7: © David Powers.
Chapter 8: © Elizabeth Crews/Jeroboam.
Chapter 9: © David Powers.
Chapter 10: © Elizabeth Hamlin/Stock, Boston.
Chapter 11: © Julie O'Neil/Stock, Boston.
Chapter 12: © Norm Hurst/Stock, Boston.

To Helen Dunis,
a precious friend, a keen analytical mind,
a true humanist, who spent her last years
planning for a better world for children

CONTENTS

315   EPILOGUE—THE LANGUAGE ARTS PROGRAM IN ACTION

318   12   Putting It All Together

335   Appendixes

FOREWORD

Language is the most uniquely human of humanity's many remarkable attributes. It enables human individuals to link their minds in such a way that a common social mind is formed as people communicate their experiences, thoughts, needs, feelings, insights, and aesthetic reactions.

Language is, at once, social and personal. Language is possible because we can think symbolically, and so it becomes the medium of learning and of thought itself. The very act of expressing a developing idea to someone else through language is a major aspect of human learning. Further, we can express our thoughts through language to ourselves, thus synthesizing new concepts and advancing our knowledge of the world.

Language becomes an almost infinitely expandable medium of human communication. We can use it to deal not only with the familiar, but also with new experiences never encountered by humanity before.

Language is wonderfully varied. It is a universal gift to all people; we never lose our power to create language, so it is constantly shifting and changing as we use it. The result is that languages, English included, are families of dialects different in minor and major ways from each other. Differences develop among groups of speakers separated by space, time, age, interest, values. Our language is not quite the one our grandparents spoke, nor will the language of our grandchildren be quite the one we now speak. And that is good because the language must grow and change to meet our changing needs.

The role of schools in language development has not always been in tune with these linguistic realities. Schools have not always accepted and built on the remarkable language achievement learners bring with them to school. Schools have not always capitalized on the universal human ability to learn and create language. Schools have not always cherished linguistic variation. Too often school curriculum has had the mistaken objective of imposing arbitrary constraints on language use. Too often instruction aimed at teaching correct, proper language has stifled language and inhibited growth. Too often language has been treated in school as a restraint on human communication rather than its flexible medium.

Here is a book that cherishes language and language development. Here is a book that sees the role of the school as building on language strengths of children, seeking to help them expand their language, to increase its scope, to add to their flexibility and adaptability to meet new needs. Here is a book that redirects the teacher to work with the children as they grow linguistically. Here, in this book, is an invitation to glory in the marvel of human language and take pride in helping it grow.

Kenneth S. Goodman
University of Arizona

PREFACE

Children and Language: Reading and Writing, Talking and Listening is a text about language, about how children learn language and how teachers can help children to build their communication skills. We believe teachers need an understanding of how language and communication develop *naturally* in children, and we want to provide teachers with guidelines and strategies for helping children develop those natural skills even further. *Children and Language* has taken into account the latest findings in psycholinguistics about the language processes of listening, talking, writing, and reading. We believe these processes are inseparable. We believe that each child is an individual and that teachers need to understand children as individuals, but we also believe that teachers need to have a rationale for helping children to acquire knowledge and skill. We believe that teachers can make constructive decisions and children can become self-confident learners.

We hope to challenge teachers to become acquainted with children, so that they can learn from each child the best ways to help that child, for each person is different—each teacher, each child. We hope that teachers will encourage independence and initiative, so that children will become self-directing, responsible individuals. Deep personal involvement and commitment on the part of the teacher to what the learner values results in long-term, life-related learning.

The *Introduction* provides the rationale for our ideas about children and language. The section on *How to read this book* gives suggestions for implementing those ideas.

Our first expression of appreciation goes to Helen Dunis, now deceased, who discussed with us for many hours the plans, the philosophy, and the theory on which this book is built. We only wish she could have lived to see students and teachers come to understand the significance of her contribution. Next, we want to thank Marie DeCarlo and Zola Dunbar for their critical review of parts of the manuscript, their invaluable insights and suggestions. Others who helped with critiquing special sections are Bea Dusenbery and Freeman Anderson. We extend much appreciation to Sharon Barnes, the typist who cheerfully saw us through revision after revision, and Barbara Wiegele, who came to our rescue with additional typing when deadlines were too close.

We appreciate the support of Wadsworth's Editorial Director, Richard Greenberg, and of the Education Editor, Roger Peterson, who secured the reactions of people in the field and made many useful suggestions for our writing.

Those reviewers included Carol Lynch-Brown,

Florida State University; Dorothy Watson, the University of Missouri; Marilyn Buckley, the University of California, Berkeley; Judy Lea Smith, the University of Idaho; Merri Schall, Arizona State University; Mary Kay Stickle, Ball State University; and Ruth Gallant, the University of North Dakota. We also thank Sheryl Fullerton, Wadsworth's pre-production editor, for her helpful work, and Carol King for her assistance with the writing.

Dorris M. Lee
Joseph B. Rubin

INTRODUCTION

Helping children develop competence in communicating through language involves far more than knowing some lessons to teach. Teaching is not just practicing ready-made procedures according to given directions. Rather, it is an art-science in which knowledge of basic principles—about children and about concepts and skills to be developed—provides the secure basis for day-to-day, hour-to-hour decisions in the classroom. Although preplanning is necessary, much actual teaching is spontaneous response to the individual child in the immediate situation. The way teachers relate to children has more effect than the facts they impart. The atmosphere in the classroom makes more difference than any required activity.

John Goodlad* once said that a teacher carries a knapsack containing a rich lore of understanding about children, the world, and the processes of communication and learning. Working with a child in a specific situation, the teacher can reach into that knapsack for whatever content and process is recognized to be most useful at that time. It is our hope that we can add further understanding to the knapsack you are filling.

*Dean, Graduate School of Education, University of California at Los Angeles (in a professional discussion).

The four aspects of communication—talking, listening, reading, and writing—develop together all day, every day, and not separately, each at a set time in the schedule. When teachers and children recognize this interrelationship, learning is easier and more certain. By the time children come to school, their use of oral language is well-developed, automatic, and a very personal part of themselves. Increasing numbers of preschoolers have begun to read and write, but no two children have the same competencies in any of the four aspects. Therefore, children learn best in a child-centered program that recognizes individual differences.

We believe that, in order to be effective, teaching should be based on a consistent rationale. In the writing of this book, the authors have been guided by a rationale based on the following assumptions about children and how they learn:

Children learn much from others and through experience, without instruction.

All children can learn and want to learn whatever they perceive as interesting and valuable for themselves.

Children do whatever seems to them at that moment to be best for them.

Children learn in proportion to their confidence that they *can* learn.

Children internalize understanding by using facts and information for their own purposes.

Children at all ages, and especially in early childhood, learn intuitively through concrete experience.

Since involvement is the essence of learning, children learn more by taking responsibility for their own learning.

Children learn when they identify what is important to them and establish their own purposes.

Children learn when the learning meets needs they recognize and is relevant to their out-of-school lives.

Children learn when they are psychologically comfortable.

Children learn what they discuss in their own words.

These recommendations, based on sound, current research, make maximum use of children's natural learning. Findings from recent research distinguish between short-term learning, which is memorization of information with minimal understanding, and long-term learning, which is the understanding of concepts internalized for the child's own purposes. Long-term learning occurs when concepts are discovered through experience—with or without teaching—and developed through the child's rational thought.

When today's children leave school, they will enter a world quite different from the world of their parents and teachers. They will need knowledge, of course, but their fast-changing world will also demand the ability to learn continuously and independently in order to keep abreast of new and necessary information. Even though audiovisual communication will increase, reading, writing, and face-to-face communication will become more important than ever before. As population in-

creases and concentrates in urban areas, all the human-relations skills will become essential, and communication is the most important of those skills. The schools should not be expected to teach *more* information, but to teach different kinds of information, such as updated understanding about ourselves and about physical, political, and social characteristics of the world we live in.

That world is, and will continue to be, very different from the one that traditional schools served so well. Therefore, new goals and new procedures are necessary, and many schools are already moving to answer the challenge. Some educators, who feel that the learning they experienced as children was adequate, are reluctant to try anything very different. Some schools are "innovating" either with token change or with procedures previously tried and discarded, such as ability grouping (now called "continuous progress") or departmentalization, now carried out in certain kinds of team teaching. Some schools attempt to mechanize children's learning as if children were objects on an assembly line.

Other well-meaning educators have broken the unity of learning into bits and pieces labeled "behavioral objectives" and developed accountability procedures based on "objective" tests that have little relationship to the child's ability to use skills in life situations, or to the current goals of education. We believe that learning can be evaluated significantly only as it is demonstrated in real life.

Critics of the schools point out that today's graduates are unable to perform adequately in life situations. From kindergarten on, therefore, school learning must be more closely related to the individual's needs in the out-of-school world, and evaluation also must be life-related. Reading to pronounce words correctly, and spelling to get 100 percent on Friday's test, are totally inadequate objectives in today's world.

The cry of "back to the basics" recognizes the need for a different kind of education—but the "basics" have been defined in various ways. Guided by the rationale we have set forth, we define basic skills in the language arts as follows:

Listening with more perceptive understanding

Talking so that the message is clear, accurate, and effective in accomplishing its purpose because it has taken its listeners into account

Reading with understanding so that the implications of the material read are clear, and the reading process is both habitual and enjoyable

Writing clearly and succinctly with the reader's needs in mind

Communicating on the basis of clear and appropriate thought processes

Accepting personal responsibility for one's own learning

School should not be a do-as-you-please place, but it should hum with the activity of children who want to learn, who understand the purpose of their learning and are able to adopt purposes of their own. If learning is an exciting and satisfying experience, children will become life-long learners. Thus, teachers need to develop each child's creativity, independence, involvement, cooperation, and self-direction. Children need the ability to recognize purposes important to themselves and the ability to evaluate their accomplishments realistically.

Although much has been written about new goals and new approaches, only a few authors have tried to describe a unified program that is internally consistent and makes use of new knowledge about how children learn. This we have tried to do. Teachers may find that our procedures are incompatible with the programs advocated by their schools. A teacher who is hesitant to put our program into effect should gradually begin with aspects that seem most important and can be implemented with least disturbance. The first essentials are a positive attitude toward children and a trusting relationship with them. When the program is developed gradually, the teacher's greatest concern should be to maintain or increase the children's confidence in their ability to learn and to maximize their natural way of learning.

The results of a successful program can be documented by children's positive attitudes toward themselves and their learning, demonstrations of competence in real-life tasks, and ability to use language with steadily increasing effectiveness.

How to read this book

The rationale for our program is based on new knowledge of how children learn. Consequently, the teacher who wishes to implement this program will find many of our guidelines inconsistent with procedures recommended in a more traditional approach to teaching language arts. You will need time to integrate this new knowledge with your present understanding. As you read this book, ask "What does this new insight mean to me? How will it affect the way I work with children in the classroom?" Continue to explore these questions as you observe children, read books and articles recommended at the ends of chapters, and discuss teaching procedures with your peers.

This book does not provide prescriptions or recipes for teaching *all* children because each child is unique and each child's needs are different. Equally important is the fact that *you* are unique. Each teacher's way of working with others is different. Teachers must work out their own ways of using the ideas and procedures suggested in this text.

This book is divided into four sections. The first section sets the stage for effective communication by describing how meaning is conveyed and interpreted. It focuses on young children by examining their thinking processes and the developmental stages through which language is acquired. The second section deals with oral language, both listening and talking. The third section analyzes the producing and consuming of recorded language, both writing and reading. The final section, the Epilogue, describes the plans, organization, and implementation that enable you to put our program into operation. (The reader who needs an overall view of the program might benefit from reading the last chapter first.) Each chapter ends with practical suggestions for teachers.

Suggested Learning Experiences for Prospective Teachers. The experiences recommended in these sections can help you understand some of the major points in the text. They provide first-hand knowledge that you can apply to your responsibilities with children. For those currently teaching, the learning experiences provide challenging ideas, questions, and procedures to consider and perhaps try out with children.

Suggested Readings. We have listed useful books and articles with comments explaining how each fits into our program. We suggest you choose the references that meet your own needs; you may want to skim some, read some in depth, make notes from others, and ignore some entirely. The choices are yours. Bibliographical references are placed at the end of the book, and each reference can be identified by author and date given in the text.

Strategies for Children's Learning. These activities can help children to understand and use skills especially appropriate to the topic of the chapter. Many strategies can be applied to concepts developed in other chapters as well. They may be adapted to a range of ages, as suggested in each strategy, but should be fleshed out and modified as approprite for any particular group of children.

I

COMMUNICATION:
THE PURPOSE
OF LANGUAGE

All the interactions and interrelationships of mankind are influenced by communication. Yet the development of competence in the use of language has been taken for granted at the elementary school level. Recently, however, emphasis has shifted toward greater attention to communication, toward increasing awareness of the exchange of meaning, and toward developing adequacy in expressing and interpreting a message.

The quality of the individual's thinking is the most important factor that affects communication. Although the misuse of words or syntactic structures can lead to inadequate communication, meanings can be clarified when the thought processes are clear. In most cases the syntactic structure of language is learned intuitively. The semantics of language is acquired merely by living in a verbal community, such as a family, neighborhood, or school. But the messages that are the heart of communication depend on the thought processes that generate them. Like the information that is the content of thinking, the thought processes can be developed and extended through both experience and teaching.

By analyzing communication, thought processes, and language development, the first three chapters of this text provide background information needed throughout the remainder of the book. The opening chapter, which deals with effective communication, will help the reader both as a person and as a teacher.

Chapter 2 examines the thought processes that underlie all human activity, especially learning. Even though our thoughts are made known to others through our actions, we are often unaware of our own thinking. Helping children learn to use various thought processes consciously is an essential teacher task throughout the school day.

Chapter 3 provides information about language. Understanding how language develops and how it operates at various stages enables teachers to help children develop their language skills.

COMMUNICATION

Communication is the main avenue through which people establish relationships with others. Whether public or private, communication is always interpersonal. Most communication is the expression of one individual to another or to any others who may be aware of it. But communication may also be the expression of a group of people to an individual or to another group—perhaps a nation. It may take such forms as drawing, painting, sculpturing, singing, playing musical instruments, or dancing. But since this book is concerned with the language arts, our discussion is confined to the art of verbal communication.

Verbal communication is the interchange of thoughts, feelings, and ideas through words, either oral or written. Although it is characterized by words, there are almost always nonverbal influences. Communication through language is produced by a writer or speaker and is received by a listener-observer or reader.

This chapter is concerned with each individual's communication, with what affects it, what effect it has on others, and why understanding sometimes breaks down. We will use the words *we*, *us*, and *our* to refer to all people, not just to the authors or the readers, because communication problems are common to all, and understanding our own communication problems is essential to helping others

with theirs. How do we come across to others? How can we "read" another's meaning more accurately? What part do perception, experiencing, trust, and nonverbal cues play? We will look at how well we understand others and how well we understand ourselves. All individuals need to become more self-aware in order to develop effective interpersonal relationships. Self-awareness will help teachers, prospective teachers, and other adults to develop good relationships with children through improved communication.

Verbal communication

Oral communication occurs when someone speaks and someone else listens—on any scale from private conversation to public broadcasting. But communication has *not* occurred unless an intended message is accurately received and reacted to, either overtly or covertly. Overt reaction is not necessarily speech, but may be any physical action or behavior change, such as smiling, looking incredulous, handing an object to the speaker, or turning one's back. Covert reactions are nonverbal, may be difficult or even impossible for another to read, and may range from feeling empathy to thinking of retaliation.

Miscommunication

Miscommunication has occurred when the message received is not the one the speaker intended. Why should such distortion occur when both individuals speak the same language? Many interferences, sometimes called "noise," can prevent the listener from receiving the intended message. Just as environmental noise can prevent normal conversation, factors in the communication process can result in a discrepancy between the message intended and the message perceived. What are some of these interferences that all too often distort communication?

Probably misunderstanding results most frequently from the fact that words mean only what each speaker or listener believes they mean. Meaning is in people, not in words, because understanding is based upon the individual's previous experience. Language differs from group to group—from one occupation to another, for example, or among various socioeconomic groups. The wider the difference between the life experiences of speaker and listener, the greater the likelihood of miscommunication. Implicit assumption by one or the other is often the basis of the problem. A teacher may ask children to write answers to certain questions but criticize those who write only the necessary words rather than complete sentences even though this requirement was not specified.

Among people in many kinds of groups, the *connotative* or implied meaning of certain words may be quite different from the dictionary definitions, their *denotative* meaning. People in different careers and professions, or in close-knit social groups like the teenage society, are almost certain to have special meanings for many ordinary words. If the implied or connotative meanings have emotional overtones, they carry a stronger message than do the more factual denotative meanings. In the past, for example, a *skirt* or a *frail* sometimes had the connotative meaning of a *woman*—the emotional overtones are obvious. Such meanings not only may result in misun-

derstanding, but also may create a social distance that is hard to bridge. An important implication for teachers is that they should avoid using professional terminology when talking with people from different backgrounds.

Some people say the opposite of what they mean and expect nonverbal cues or the trend of the conversation to carry the real message. This practice is especially dangerous when it occurs in the form of sarcasm. First, sarcasm is nearly always intended to belittle someone or something, a motive most detrimental to interpersonal relationships; and, second, those who do not recognize the sarcasm will surely misinterpret the meaning.

Although less serious, teasing is another questionable use of reverse meaning. Teasing will damage a relationship unless there is genuine understanding between the teaser and the object of teasing, and even then, results may be negative if teasing is prolonged. The expression "Smile when you say that" illustrates the importance of nonverbal cues to clarify real meaning.

Self-doubt is another kind of problem that creates misunderstanding. Persons who doubt their own competence or desirability may misinterpret requests for help or offers of assistance or companionship. If they suspect that friendly gestures are made out of compassion rather than true interest, they may withdraw in the hope of getting reconfirmation. A family that spent many evenings reading aloud began asking their ten-year-old to take her turn at reading. Although she was delighted at first, she soon became dissatisfied with her ability to read material she had not seen before. The second time she was asked to read, she demurred without explaining why and was scolded for being unwilling to take her turn. This misunderstanding, which was never resolved, created unhappiness that the girl remembered for the rest of her life.

The need for confirmation is illustrated by this commonplace incident: Lisa offers to help Betty, but Betty responds, "Oh, I don't want to bother you." Lisa feels rejected. Betty wants confirmation that Lisa is motivated by genuine interest, not by a

COMMUNICATION: THE PURPOSE OF LANGUAGE

sense of duty. Both feel let down and their relationship suffers. Teachers need to be aware of the harm that can result from this type of misunderstanding and of the need to offer reassurance.

Such illustrations show how important it is to understand what a person means, rather than only what words say. Speaker and listener share a responsibility to be aware of emotional tone, an aura that inevitably surrounds all communication. A question as simple as "Where are you going?" can indicate anger, fear, curiosity, disapproval, or a request to go along.

Procedures to clarify meaning To *paraphrase* means "to reword the thought or meaning expressed in something that has been said or written before." As a literary device, paraphrasing enables us to summarize another writer's point of view in our own words, thereby avoiding plagiarism. As an oral device, paraphrasing enables us to summarize another speaker's point of view in our own words, so that the speaker can either correct our interpretation or assure us that we have captured the true meaning. The usefulness of oral paraphrasing is most apparent when the subject is controversial and several points of view are represented. To paraphrase, ask "Do you mean . . . ?" and interpret in your own words.

When we paraphrase a single statement, rather than an entire viewpoint or position, the procedure is called a *perception check*. Suppose you have been discussing a new program offered in education. A listener asks, "Do you mean the program doesn't have much appeal?" You have the opportunity to clarify your feeling about the program.

Used consistently, these techniques can prevent "talking past each other" and the arguments that develop unnecessarily because one person misinterprets another. We can also develop a feeling for the true meaning by observing nonverbal cues.

Nonverbal cues

The least consciously recognized form of communication is the ubiquitous nonverbal. Nonverbal cues include tone of voice, facial expression, and position and movement of various parts of the body. Consistently ignoring a person in a group or a topic of conversation is a nonverbal cue that conveys a negative message either with or without intention. Others may or may not receive the nonverbal message. If they receive it, they may or may not interpret it correctly.

Nonverbal cues are subtle factors that affect communication in many important ways. Learning to become more aware of them, use them more effectively, and interpret them correctly is an essential part of improving communication. It is tragic that this sensitive area, so important in all interpersonal relations, has not received more attention.

Words may or may not be the most important part of oral communication. The tone of voice, varied emphasis on different words, rate of speech, and pauses and hesitations all tell us a great deal about what a person means. We can receive these messages whether we are talking face to face or over the phone. Besides these messages, there are still others we can receive when we can see our communicator. A frown, a quizzical look, twisting fingers, or a look of joyful anticipation may support or deny the message expressed in words. Many of those in the field of communication estimate that about 65 percent of our encounters with others are nonverbal.

Written communication

Interpersonal exchange of written messages may seem simpler than oral interactions because words on a page lack the extra input derived from hearing and seeing a speaker. Nonverbal cues are expressed in punctuation marks, underlinings, italics, and the like. But if communication is to be accurate, the receiver must be aware of much subtler cues, like choice of words and, even more important, what is left unsaid. Because readers are freer to put their own interpretation on the message, there is a hidden danger. To guard against unwarranted interpretation, we can consider how consistent our perception of the message is with what we know about the writer. Are we reading only what we hope—or fear—that the writer will say?

One advantage of written communication is that we can reread if we feel we have failed to get the message. Because we can create it over a period of time, writing tends to take on more regulation and more formalism than speech. Writing can be studied, revised, and repunctuated, and these changes can be reviewed and rereviewed, while speech can be revised only when it is tape-recorded, and then only to a limited extent.

The communication process

We have said that communication is *a mutual understanding of a message sent and received*. Let us now explore more specifically the steps that must occur in order for communication to take place. First, a message is conceived in our thoughts; second, we encode* the message in the language to be used and produce the sounds or the symbols needed; third, another person must hear or see these symbols; and, fourth, the receiver must decode† them to produce an approximation of the original message. Two-way communication requires a re-

*Encode means to put thoughts, feelings, ideas, or messages into a written or spoken form so that someone else may perceive them.

†Decode means perceiving audible or visual forms and interpreting from them the thoughts, feelings, ideas, or messages of the sender.

sponse that goes through the same procedures with sender and receiver reversing roles.

Even though all these steps are taken with care and precision, however, communication may not result. Why not? The above formula leaves out perception, the essential ingredient that caused all the interferences we have discussed. Since our knowledge of anything is, and of necessity must be, limited to our personal perception of it, a message can be understood only to the extent that we can relate it to our previous understanding. In order to communicate, two people must have some matching or similar perceptions. The greater the overlap of these perceptions, the greater the opportunity for communication. When this factor is unrecognized, people may carry on lengthy conversations yet achieve a minimum of communication because the words they use and the thoughts expressed mean different things to each person. We sometimes say they are "talking past each other" or one is "going over the other's head." The diagram shows the communication process with the effects of perception added.

Although this diagram is simplistic, it represents the main structure of attempted communication. We shall now take a brief look at the complexities of this process as specialists see it.

In recent years communication has been the subject of research and theory development in some twenty different disciplines. Sereno and Mortensen (1970) have proposed that "communicative behavior cannot be considered as something completely distinct from the general determinants of behavior: perceptions, learning drives, emotions,

---

Sender conceives message, $\rightarrow$ encodes it in language or movement, $\rightarrow$ makes it public. $\rightarrow$

Receiver hears or sees message, $\rightarrow$ decodes message, $\rightarrow$ searches for common perceptions, $\rightarrow$

conceives response from relevant perceptions, $\rightarrow$ encodes it in language or movement, $\rightarrow$

makes it public. $\rightarrow$ Receiver (previous sender) hears or sees message, $\rightarrow$ decodes message, $\rightarrow$

searches for common perceptions, $\rightarrow$ conceives response from relevant perceptions, $\rightarrow$ and so on,

for the rest of the conversation.

COMMUNICATION: THE PURPOSE OF LANGUAGE

attitudes, beliefs, values, decoding-encoding, meaning, messages, and social situations" (p. 4). They describe various kinds of systems or models of communicative behavior. The mathematical model indicates that communication occurs when "a *source* or *sender transmits a signal* or *message* through a *channel* to some *destination* or *receiver*" (p. 7). However, the social science models include "such factors as the *nature* of the interaction, the *response* to the message, and the *context* in which the *interaction* occurs" (p. 7).

Colin Cherry marvels that

> human communication works at all, for so much seems to be against it; yet it does. The fact is that it depends principally upon the vast store of habits which each of us possesses, the imprints of all our past experiences. With this, we can hear snatches of speech, see vague gestures and grimaces, and from such thin shreds of evidence we are able to make a continual series of inferences, guesses, with extraordinary effectiveness (Cherry, 1966, p.12).

Obviously each individual's perceptions play a significant role. Let us now examine how we acquire these perceptions.

Experiencing

Three people stand at Times Square in New York. One says, "Aren't the bright lights exciting?" Another says, "Look at all the energy going to waste!" A third grabs his companion by the arm and mutters, "Let's get out of this dirty mess and go where it's quiet." In a forest an ecologist thinks, "How peaceful! A retreat for the harried people of the world!" A lumber prospector thinks, "What fine trees for cutting! I'll try to buy them for our company." And a young child, separated from hiking companions, thinks, "These trees all look alike! How can I ever find my way out?"

Experience can be defined as (1) anything observed or lived through, or (2) individual reactions to events and feelings about them. To distinguish between these two meanings, we will use *experience* to mean being present in a particular setting, such as Times Square or a forest, and the word *experiencing* to call attention to internal reactions. In this sense, the ecologist, the lumber prospector, and the child had the same experience, but their experiencing of it was entirely different.

A child's internal experiencing of feelings and reactions to events is far more significant than the experience itself. It is these reactions and feelings that build children's perceptions and attitudes, modify their thinking, and change their understanding of the world. Some children's experiencing of school is positive and self-fulfilling, while that of others in the same classroom may be negative and defeating.

Perception

Our perception is based on experiencing, either firsthand or vicariously. Conversely, relevant perceptions affect experiencing. The same task may be perceived as fun by one child and as a threat by another child. The teacher may say, "Now, each of you write a story about your pet." Evelyn's perception of herself as a storywriter is good; she has consistently experienced approval of her writing. Tom, however, has usually found red marks and critical comments on his stories. His perception of himself as a storywriter is defeating.

Bobby, who has been having fun with his new beagle puppy, perceives the task as an opportunity to tell about satisfying experiences. But Sarah, who has never had a dog or a cat, perceives the task as threatening. Her friend Susan, seeing Sarah's dismay, suggests she write about her goldfish. Sarah is still puzzled, and asks, "But doesn't a pet have to be a dog or a cat or something like that?" What Susan perceived as a pet, Sarah did not, although both had experienced the goldfish. Different perceptions of common experience often cause communication to break down (see Tiger's perception of constellations and stars). Communication depends not only on similar experiencing, but also on common perceptions that produce common meanings.

©*King Features Syndicate, 1975.*

Shared experience can produce different meanings because each person draws not only on immediate perceptions, but on past experiencing as well—past experiencing that may or may not be based on shared perceptions. A conversation may focus on the common perceptions or on the unshared perceptions. When two people disagree, they need to explore the bases of their differences in a calm and rational way. They should begin by searching for perceptions, or beliefs, that are held in common, thus narrowing differences, clarifying bases for thought, and perhaps even reaching agreement. When total agreement is impossible, at least the areas of disagreement, lack of common experiencing, or different perceptions of a mutual experience become evident so the participants can deal with them.

Communication is improved through increasing the number of shared experiences, discussing these experiences to arrive at common perceptions, or exploring previous experiences that led to different perceptions.

The effect of social meanings In spite of common experiences and the opportunity for discussing them, many serious gaps in perception can be traced to social meanings. Social meanings develop within groups: Groups are characterized by age difference, social class, race or ethnic background, and other distinctions, and there are a variety of subgroups in each category.

For example, the word *baby* is warmly accepted when it refers to an infant but rejected when it refers to an older child. One may speak quite differently to first graders and to sixth graders. Failure to make the distinction may result in the older children "not hearing" what we say, or the younger children not being able to understand because we are "talking over their heads." As another example of social meaning, consider the difference between informal and formal speech. Two extremes might be "C'mon—chow time" and "Shall we dine?" Either might communicate acceptably in a certain situation. Formality or informality determines the form of address one person uses for another and the social meaning each form has. Words perceived as inappropriate tend to set up a communication barrier that may be difficult to overcome.

Another kind of barrier is erected when two people of the same nationality speak the same language in different dialects. Everyone speaks one dialect or another. Dialects develop partly through close association with racial, national, or ethnic groups, particularly within an area where the population is fairly stable. But a dialect may also represent a cultural or professional level. When a dialect represents a socioeconomic level, too often it is labeled as unacceptable, while an equally different one spoken by those of a higher level is well accepted. Communication is impaired whenever lack of acceptance decreases the desire

COMMUNICATION: THE PURPOSE OF LANGUAGE

and effort to understand others. (Dialects are discussed in greater depth in Chapters 3 and 5.)

Beyond language and dialect, each person has an *idiolect*, a unique way of using voice and language. A person's idiolect may combine elements of two or more dialects picked up from those heard and modified by the idiolects of those loved or admired. It is part of what makes a person's voice identifiable over the telephone. Communication is more difficult for a person whose speech is highly idiosyncratic.

Selectivity of perceptions   In every situation at all times, there are so many possible perceptions that no person can attend, even partially, to all of them. Therefore all perception is selective. This selection is affected by our immediate needs and interests and by the extent to which various perceptions seem relevant or valuable to us.

Our interpretation of these perceptions depends on expectancies that are based on past experience. We see writing a story as threatening if past experience resulted in red check marks and low grades. We see the storywriting assignment as rewarding if previous experience led to recognition for successful work and assistance where needed. In either case, we are reacting to perceptions of which others are unaware. When certain skills have proven valuable, we will pay attention to related skills. We tend to ignore those we have not perceived as valuable for us. The implication for children's learning is enormous.

Earl Kelley explains the basis of selectivity of perceptions:

> The choices seem to be on the basis of experience and unique purpose. We all have a background of experience upon which perception is in part based. We cannot see that which we have no experience to see. . . . The additional element which appears to determine perceptive intake is *purpose* (Kelley, 1962, p. 14 [italics added]).

What we perceive in our environment may be accurate or distorted. Of various influential factors, the most important is confidence in, and acceptance of, ourselves as worthwhile persons. Self-confidence increases not only the accuracy of our perceptions, but their breadth and depth as well.

Implications for teachers   Successful teaching depends largely upon recognizing the effect of children's varied perceptions and making constructive use of this factor. The greater the difference in people's backgrounds, the less likely real communication—the mutual understanding of shared thoughts—can take place. All people need to explore for common ground and build from there.

Because a gap inevitably exists between adulthood and childhood, communication between adults and children is more difficult than most people realize. The words used and the way adults organize their sentences may be part of the problem, but by far the greater part is the difference between the way adults view things and the way children do. Being far more experienced than children, adults know more alternatives and can judge which ones are acceptable. Being in a position of authority, adults hold responsibility that they too often refuse to share. Rightly or wrongly, the children may feel there are many things they cannot or should not say to teachers, and some questions they may not ask. Too often both teachers and children think in "we/they" terms that build barriers.

Teachers are too apt to generalize, to think of and talk to "the group," ignoring the uniqueness that affects communication. Being aware of each child's feelings is essential for improving communication. Since everyone, adult and child alike, needs to feel accepted in order to function effectively, real respect for each individual is necessary for good communication. Because perception is uniquely individual, and people can react to any situation only as they perceive it on the basis of past experience, each child's perceptions need to be considered in every learning situation if all children are to have equal opportunity to learn.

Trust as a factor in communication

Another factor that hinders communication is lack of mutual trust. Without trust, we are unwilling to expose ourselves by expressing our true thoughts and feelings. As relevant thoughts occur to us, and we suppress one after another, what we finally say may be so bland and devoid of significance that it is valueless for communication. Our evasions may trigger like responses from others, both now and well into the future. Although early contacts with strangers call for some reticence, ongoing relationships need to develop mutual trust to be of value.

Openness is necessary for real two-way communication, and openness depends largely on trust. When we feel perfectly comfortable, we do not need to put up defensive barriers. However, if the situation evokes fear of failure, demands performance we do not feel capable of, or entails some other threat to our selfhood, we may be able to take in only a small part of what is said. We may misinterpret the message entirely or hear it as threatening, even though it is not. Thus, those of us already the least successful may be the ones least able to take in needed information. Before we can really "hear," we must believe beyond question that the speaker is "on our side," believes in us, and will not betray us.

We will not be able to say what is really on our minds or express our real feelings unless we trust our listeners and expect their acceptance of us as persons. The lack of mutual trust, which leads to mutual fear, may exist between peers, between teacher and child, between teacher and administrator, between teacher and parents, as well as between cultural groups and nations. Open communication can be initiated only by someone with enough faith in others and a commitment to the necessity of communication.

Any adult, so committed, can initiate openness with children. Being more mature, more experienced, and more knowledgeable, and having greater responsibility for the outcome of the interchange, adults are in an ideal position. Teachers can establish a trust relationship that builds on and promotes real communication, not only between themselves and the children but also among the children. In general, the younger child is more trusting, and if nothing is done to undermine this natural trust, it can be extended easily.

Building trust Acceptance of individuals *as they are* is essential for building a trust relationship. People will feel comfortable with us if we show sincere interest in their intents, desires, and expectations for themselves, and then offer to help them attain their own goals. In other words, we can extend to others the right to make their own decisions. If we raise questions about issues they have not considered, and help them seek alternatives when they are not satisfied, they can trust us to be helpful without imposing our decisions on them. Providing relevant information and expecting others to make decisions is far more helpful than giving advice. Both taking others seriously and exhibiting supportive behavior help to build a trusting relationship.

Supportive behavior involves intensive listening to what others wish to tell us, responding appropriately, and perhaps reflecting their feelings as we perceive them. Personal interaction with individuals in a caring way, talking about things together, if only for a moment, builds far more trust than devoting that time to the entire group. Small groups are more effective than large ones but not as useful as one-to-one conversation.

When trust is low, many important things are left unsaid. We too often bury our feelings beneath the surface of awareness when they become uncomfortable or when we feel they have been belittled by others. "Forgetting" them may put us out of touch with ourselves—a serious but common mistake.

The surest way to lose another's trust is to prove untrustworthy. If we find someone has made a significant statement to us and a contradictory statement to someone else, we stop trusting that person's word. When we have given information in confidence and later discover that our confidence has not been honored, all trust is lost. But the recipient of important confidential information often faces a moral dilemma. It may be possible to handle the problem without involving the other person, or to work out a solution between the two of you. If neither of these approaches is feasible, then try to persuade the person to report the information to someone who can help, and assure the person of your support.

Trustworthiness applies to actions as well as words. Promises made are promises to be kept. If something interferes, we need to explain to the other person as soon as possible and arrange for an alternative action. Forgetting, either real or as an excuse, tells children and adults they are not very important to us and should not count on us.

Freeing and binding responses

The teacher does more than set an atmosphere for open discussion or for keeping personal feelings to oneself. With each separate statement, the teacher either binds the child to a pattern of conformity to adult direction or frees the child to develop values that can be relied upon for self-evaluation. In a democracy, it is hardly necessary to stress the importance of developing citizens who are aware of their own values and confident that they can use their values to make generally valid decisions. Yet many of our statements are binding or controlling responses through which, either intentionally or unintentionally, we manipulate children.

Expressed and implied expectancy   One kind of binding statement that can be very restricting is the way expectations are expressed. When a teacher says "I know you will want to cooperate" to a child trying to express a difference of opinion, it leaves the child only two options, submitting or rebelling. In either case the teacher-child relationship has deteriorated. "I like boys and girls who _____" tends to force conformity or builds feelings of hostility at being forced to comply without a hearing.

Using what might be called stereotyping, the teacher might say "Good citizens always _____"

and name some desired behavior or characteristic. These statements put pressure on a person in such a way that any type of protest or even questioning is virtually unavailable. Stereotyping creates a vague and pervasive anxiety in children too young to understand what is happening and great frustration in those who are aware but feel trapped. In addition, it prevents children from doing critical thinking in evaluating their own actions. These behaviors in teachers are ways of manipulating children, and manipulation is for things, not people. Teachers who believe in developing self-directing, self-confident children who understand themselves need to avoid this use of language.

The teacher's expectations may be implied, rather than stated explicitly. "When you have read five library books" implies that each listener *will* read five library books. If such action has not been agreed upon, the statement implies expectancy and may be disturbing. "If you should decide to read five library books" changes the impact. The essential difference is acknowledging another's right to make decisions.

Praise and recognition   Contrary to the opinion of many teachers and other adults, praise can be at least as damaging as punishment. In fact, punishment is often more honest. Praise is usually given when children do what *we* want them to. Under these circumstances it would be better to say so—"Now, that's what I wanted you to do."

Even though teachers sincerely want to encourage children to continue and expand what they are doing, praise may have a different effect. Usually praise is too general: "That's fine" or "You're being so good today." How can children interpret statements that do not specify what it is that is "fine" or "good"? Such praise is binding because it encourages children to try to figure out what the teacher approves and to seek further evidence of approval. Instead of providing a basis for decision making, this procedure encourages children to depend on the teacher to tell them what they should or should not do. Because their own judgment has been downgraded, they look to leaders for direction. Judgmental statements nearly always limit the options of the recipient.

General expressions of confidence in another's future accomplishments are another aspect of subtle pressure. "I know you'll do better next time." Sometimes teachers use this strategy deliberately in the belief that it will be truly helpful; but any temporary gain is minimized if the child still feels incompetent or tries and fails. The child will no longer trust the judgment of an adult whose appraisal and expectancy appear to be unrealistic. Specific small tasks agreed to by both teacher and child are more likely to succeed.

Except in seriously hazardous situations, we can free children to make their own decisions and be responsible for them. We can raise questions to help them evaluate their actions and recognize the effects of their behavior. "What do you think you should do? Why? What do you think will happen if you do this?" Such questions tell children that they are able to make decisions and that they are expected to make them. This kind of response increases the children's self-confidence and places upon them greater responsibility for their own actions. If ways of living together have been thoroughly thought out by the group, then praise for carrying out these procedures means that the teacher really did not expect the children to succeed, rather than assuming that of course they would and simply recognizing the fact. Thus praise often leads to a breakdown in children's following through with their planned procedures.

Recognition differs from *praise* because it acknowledges accomplishment, rather than making a judgment. Praise says "Your handwriting is good." Recognition says "This week your *r*'s and your *n*'s are easier for people to read." Or praise says "You've been a good boy today" while recognition says "You were very helpful to Jimmy by explaining his math problem" or "I appreciated your taking care of the gerbils when Sarah was absent."

Listening and response styles Johnson, in his book *Reaching Out: Interpersonal Effectiveness and*

Binding	Freeing
General praise	Recognition of specific accomplishment
Threatened punishment	Request for child's plan for alternative future actions
Teacher-desired specific expectations	Expectation of child's initiation and success
Manipulation	Opportunity for child's point of view and decision making
Reaction from teacher's perception	Attention to child's perception
Evaluation of persons	Child's evaluations of results of actions
Evaluation of happenings	Discussion of happenings
Judgmental, evaluative statements	Development of criteria so child can evaluate

Self-Actualization (1972), talks about listening and response styles. He reports that Carl Rogers, the noted psychologist, conducted studies to find out how people respond to each other. Rogers identified five types of responses: evaluative, interpretative, supportive, probing, and understanding in this order of frequency; that is, evaluative was the most frequent. He also found that when a person responded a certain way 40 percent of the time, others saw him or her as a person who always responded that way.

Johnson discusses each of these responding styles and the intention that underlies it:

Evaluative (E): a response that indicates the receiver has made a judgment of relative goodness, appropriateness, effectiveness, or rightness of the sender's problem. The receiver has in some way implied what the sender might or ought to do.

Interpretative (I): a response that indicates the receiver's intent is to teach, to tell the sender what his problem means, how the sender really feels about the situation. The receiver has either obviously or subtly implied what the person with the problem might or ought to think.

Supportive (S): a response that indicates the receiver's intent is to reassure, to pacify, to reduce the sender's intensity of feeling. The receiver has in some way implied that the sender need not feel as he does.

Probing (P): a response that indicates the receiver's intent is to seek further information, provoke further discussion along a certain line, question the sender. The receiver has in some way implied that the sender ought or might profitably develop or discuss a point further.

Understanding (U): a response that indicates the receiver's intent is to respond only to ask the sender whether the receiver correctly understands what the sender is saying, how the sender feels about the problem, and how the sender sees the problem (Johnson, 1972, p. 125).

You will notice that the understanding response is paraphrasing.

While each type of response may be appropriate in certain situations, the understanding response is most likely to make the receivers feel you are really listening and interested in them as persons and to encourage them to go on and explore their problems further. Since no one else can solve our problems for us, we often need to take further steps to understand them and explore ways of solving them.

Since judgmental statements, either approving or disapproving, are apt to be barriers to mutual understanding, we need to minimize them. They limit the options open to people. If others do not follow our advice, they may feel guilty. The amount of pressure depends on the relationship, the extent of the authority of each, and their internal strength.

On the other hand, an implementing response, such as "How do you think you might work at the problem?" or "What do you think you might do first?" or "What might be a tentative solution?" helps people see ways in which they might act constructively.

Intrapersonal communication

Solving problems is more difficult for those who have not learned to communicate with themselves. There are many problems that we hide from ourselves because admitting them would damage our self-esteem; and there are many solutions that we ignore because recognizing them would require difficult action. Lack of intrapersonal communication enables us to use self-deception as a shield.

Being unaware of our true feelings, we might pretend that we "love football" only because we might "lose face" if we admitted that we really hate this popular sport. Or we give devoted but confining care to an invalid in the belief that we love this person so much that we could not do otherwise; we deny that we are beginning to hate the invalid for all the time-consuming, menial tasks that prevent us from meeting our own needs. No solution to such problems is possible without awareness of our true feelings. Recognizing our feelings enables us to stop punishing ourselves by watching football and to arrange for someone else to share the invalid's care.

Some teachers support the traditional "stay in your seat and keep quiet" discipline because they unconsciously fear they will not be able to "control" children otherwise or that they will be criticized by other teachers and the principal. Being unaware of their true feelings, they continue to defend their procedures as those that produce the most learning. In a graduate class, the lecturer suggested that grades are sometimes used as a way for the teacher to "get even." A teacher exclaimed with mingled astonishment and conviction, "That's right! I remember saying to myself, 'That D will teach you to talk back to me!'"

Being in touch with their true feelings and motivations is extremely important for teachers and anyone else who is responsible for the growth and development of others. Without self-awareness it is easy to adopt self-serving procedures that may do great harm. Most teachers have a sincere desire to help children and could not accept doing otherwise, but when self-awareness is limited, they are very likely to use methods that protect their own insecurities but damage children. For example, Mr. Cox, without being aware of it, needed to feel that people depended on him in order to feel self-worth. Thus, he worked with children in a way that created such dependence, which undermined the children's self-confidence and self-direction.

Values and self-awareness Everything we do, every decision we make, every plan we devise is based on our own particular values. These values may be explicit; that is, we may be fully aware of them and able to verbalize them clearly. Or they may be implicit; that is, we may be totally unaware of the basis for our decisions. The pace and complexity of modern life may confuse us in deciding what is more valuable to us and what is less so.

Many express a dedication to equality of opportunity for individuals. Yet all around us there are examples of discrimination against blacks, Indians, women, the uneducated, and the poor. What have we expressed to these people through our actions or words? Our actions are the result of how we perceive the issue and ourselves. Therefore, a value is made clear by the action we take or fail to take in relevant situations.

Many people's intrapersonal communications are not clear, they may truly feel they believe in nondiscrimination, and yet be unable to relate discriminatory acts to this belief. They protect their self-image by keeping this discrepancy below the conscious level. It takes strong and self-confident persons to admit, even to themselves, that other, perhaps less noble, values may take precedence. To be as deeply aware as possible of what our operating values are, we need real in-depth communication with ourselves.

The relationship of the self-concept and communication

The self-concept is a composite of all the ways we see ourselves. A good or healthy self-concept, or self-esteem, has no relationship to egotism, or being cocky, or tooting one's own horn. In fact, these characteristics usually indicate that people feel inadequate and need to convince themselves and others that they are worthwhile. Since the self-concept affects communication both within the self and with others, as well as all learning, let us review some of its most important features.

How is the self-concept developed? The development of the self-concept starts as soon as children become aware of themselves as separate persons. Positive or negative coloration results from their perceptions of themselves as they interact with others and read others' reactions. Pleasant, loving attention develops good feelings about oneself. Negative reactions create unhappiness, both with oneself and with those reacting negatively.

Another factor affecting the way we see ourselves is our success—or lack of it—in attempting to meet our needs. Occasional failures have little effect, but when failures come more often than successes, a pattern begins to emerge. If we continue to be ignored when we have signaled our needs over and over, we begin to feel powerless and inadequate.

Guidelines for improving a child's self-image include the following:

Provide opportunities to demonstrate successes.

Accept each child unconditionally and optimistically.

Be enthusiastic about what you and the children are doing together.

Consider each mistake a learning situation.

Encourage self-direction and self-evaluation.

Look for and find something to give positive recognition for.

Appreciate all children as equally valuable individuals.

The self-concept develops and is modified throughout one's life. As time goes on, however, the main core of it becomes increasingly firm and hence more difficult to change substantially. People vary in the extent of agreement between the way they see themselves and the way others see them. The more positive the self-image, the more realistic it tends to be; that is, the way we see ourselves compares more closely with the way others see us.

What is the effect of the self-concept? The self-concept is extremely complex, being affected by nearly every kind of activity we participate in. The more we care about the activity, the greater its effect. A boy may see himself as a son, a brother, a participant in family decisions, a student, an athlete, a pal, and so on. The effect of each of these facets of life on the self-concept varies in relation to its importance to the child and his friends.

For instance, it may not bother Steve that he cannot play football very well, for he really excels at baseball and his classmates always choose him first for their team. He concentrates on baseball at every opportunity, reads the sports page and remembers the standings of teams in the major leagues and the batting averages of his favorite players. Yet, in school, Steve sees himself as a poor reader since it seems to him his teacher is never satisfied with his oral reading and is always correcting him. He avoids reading at every opportunity since it always makes him feel uncomfortable. The less he voluntarily works at reading, the greater becomes the pressure from his teacher, so that the effect becomes circular. The more the teacher tries to help with explanations, the less he is able to "hear," and his teacher's concern adds to his own perceptions of himself as inadequate. Since he approaches his reading tasks with a feeling of incompetence, which prevents an active, confident approach, he fails as he expected to. He does not even realize that if he can read the sports page he might be able to read other things as well.

Steve is unable to express his specific needs for help, either because he fails to recognize the op-

portunity or because he feels that the teacher would not accept them. He becomes increasingly unaware. Since he is convinced he cannot read and avoids thinking about it, he has no way of finding out what his specific needs are. Thus, all three aspects of communication—giving and receiving messages and self-awareness—are hindered. Although his self-concept suffers in the classroom, his confidence in his ability to play baseball will help him to be increasingly successful at the game and probably at other related activities.

Writers such as Purkey (1970) believe that our concept of our own competence in a certain field aids accomplishment more than any other single factor, perhaps more than all other factors combined. Self-confidence makes a difference in what children attempt and how well they perform. It makes a difference in their social interactions. When their communication frequently breaks down or is ignored, they begin to feel less accepted than others and may react in various ways. They may observe themselves in action to see if they can identify and correct negative factors. They may redouble their efforts at contact and become demanding of attention to the point of making a nuisance of themselves. They may continue the pattern throughout a lifetime, always pushing and struggling for attention and finding that others avoid them more and more. Another response is to withdraw, partly or wholly, from social contacts. Those who withdraw, the loners, sometimes present serious problems for themselves and for society. Criminals and suicide victims are frequently described as loners. Other loners, of course, are constructive members of society.

Do self-concepts change? Self-concepts change continuously as individuals get feedback from others and experience day-to-day successes and failures. But strong negative feelings, especially in areas important to them, are most difficult to change because they create an underlying expectation of failure. In fact, those who succeed by others' estimates may still see their attempts as failures. Perhaps it is threatening to prove that one's self-evaluation was wrong. Perhaps their definition of success represents such a high standard that it would be impossible to reach it. Therefore, it is easier to prevent children from developing negative self-concepts than to reverse such concepts after they have developed.

Nonverbal communication

Nonverbal communication is a relatively new field of study. The topic is extremely complex and what various researchers include or exclude varies greatly. One consistent finding is the importance of its impact on the messages people convey.

Various investigators of nonverbal communication believe that from 50 percent to 80 percent of the meaning a person receives comes through nonverbal cues rather than the spoken words. People react to nonverbal cues without being aware of why they respond as they do. Because these cues have such an important impact on the messages people convey, anyone who works with people of any age needs to be constantly aware of these effects.

Nonverbal cues include both *body language*, or position and movement of the body, and *paralanguage*, which embraces all aspects of speech beyond words and their arrangement. The most obvious aspects of body language are facial expression, interpersonal distance and touching behavior, and movement of head, feet, and hands, including gestures. Paralanguage includes vocal cues such as tone of voice, loudness, pacing, points of emphasis, and voice quality. No one of these factors operates alone; any one of them may color any of the others.

The message that words convey is further affected by body shape, color, smell, hair, clothes, adornments, and general attractiveness. For instance, an attractive, athletic person using a strong, relatively loud voice will be accepted quite differently from an unattractive, thin, stooped person using the same voice characteristics. Or a

small, sour-faced, whining individual will affect people differently from an equally small person with a smile and a cheerful voice.

Between people who know each other, reactions are complicated by previous experiences, extent of familiarity, and mutual acceptance. We may feel empathy for a complaining friend, but feel irritation when a person we do not like expresses the same complaint.

How do we use nonverbal communication?

How can we use nonverbal communication to increase our own effectiveness? Some factors, such as body shape, are largely beyond our control— except that we can try to maintain a state of good health, physical stamina, and normal weight. But dressing and caring for hair and skin with thoughtfulness can indicate our own self-esteem, how well we like ourselves. We cannot expect others' reactions to us to be more positive than our own. We can keep ourselves nice-to-be-near by cleanliness, the addition of a fragrance, or elimination of an undesirable odor, such as stale tobacco smoke.

Body language is also within our control.

> Various body movements can communicate like or dislike for another, status, affective states or moods, intended and perceived persuasiveness, approval seeking, . . . interpersonal warmth, and various interaction "markers" to accompany certain spoken behaviors (Knapp, 1972, p. 113).

Birdwhistell (1967) discovered that certain movements, called *kinesic markers*, accompany specific oral language. For example, downward head, eyelid, and hand movements accompany the end of a statement, but their rise accompanies the end of a question. Gestures are usually, though not always, intentional and helpful. In giving directions, reinforcing verbal statements, and adding emphasis, they improve communication. When too frequent, gestures can become distracting and annoying. Sometimes gross shifts in posture mark the point of view a speaker expresses. Warmth is shown by a shift of posture toward the other person, direct eye contact, a smile, and concentration on what the other is saying or doing. A negative attitude is expressed by leaning back or away from the other person.

Touching can be very important, especially with children, when it is used to express tenderness, encouragement, and emotional support (Montagu, 1971). Communication is usually improved by a gentle hand on a shoulder or back. We need to be alert for children's reactions, however, since a few children are made uncomfortable by the touch of someone not yet completely trusted. The way we touch also makes a difference. When we want a child to come with us, offering a hand carries a far different message from grabbing a wrist. Any touch in anger or for punishment creates more persistent negative feelings than words, expression, or tone of voice.

The way we touch ourselves also has significance. Wringing hands and twisting fingers are usually recognized as signs of nervousness or anxiety. Using our hands or arms to cover, protect, or hide our faces or bodies also shows anxiety and defensiveness, while open positions indicate relaxation. Hairstyles that partly hide the eyes or face may be an attempt to follow fashion, a defense adopted by those who feel more comfortable with some protection.

Paralanguage is generally more easily read than body language. We have learned the meaning of various tones of voice, the volume appropriate for each situation, and various kinds of emphasis. In fact, children learn their meaning very early, perhaps even before they learn the meaning of words. When we are self-aware, we realize that we can express annoyance through paralanguage, mainly tone of voice or loudness of speech, for reasons other than annoyance with those present. Frustration with our own behavior, like losing or forgetting something important, can make us speak in a way that may seriously disturb others. To clear the air and reestablish good interpersonal relationships, it is important to explain our prob-

lem and reassure our listeners, particularly when they are children.

When nonverbal cues contradict verbal ones, others are confused about which to believe. It is interesting and perhaps disturbing that people tend to believe the nonverbal rather than the verbal. If one student sees that another needs help on an assignment but offers to help with a kiddingly sarcastic tone of voice, the help will probably be refused because the nonverbal cue—the sarcasm—contradicts the verbal one.

Intentional deception, on the other hand, is sometimes expressed by overreaction as a too vociferous "yes" or "no," too much laughter, or too sad a face. When reflecting real feelings the face is most expressive, the hands next, and the feet and legs least. When trying to deceive, the order of most expressive features is reversed, and there is usually excess movement because of anxiety.

Significance for working with children

Teachers who wish to be honest and open with children must be certain that what they say and the way they look, sound, and act are congruent—that is, match—so that the children feel that they can trust their teachers. Raymond (1973), working with preservice teachers during student teaching, confirmed that a significant proportion of their communication in the classroom is nonverbal. Galloway (1970) found that children were more likely to believe the nonverbal clues if the verbal ones were difficult to understand or confusing. Developing interpersonal relations through both verbal and nonverbal behavior is important for all individuals, especially those working with others, and is of greatest importance for those working with children. Being less mature, less experienced, and therefore less sure of themselves, children can suffer more serious damage when they feel they have poor relationships with people important to them. Communication may decrease or break down, which means that learning is minimized.

Children's learning is influenced by the type of

room and seating arrangements that affect pupil participation and status (Sommer, 1967); by the "action zone," where those sitting near the teacher and within easy eye-contact range are more likely to participate (Adams and Biddle, 1970); and by teacher expectations (Braun, 1976). A teacher's enthusiasm is a significant factor that "produces comprehension gains, increases recall, improves attitudes, lessens anxiety, and increases divergent thinking" (Rosenshine, 1970).

The trust and perception that influence communication are also essential for learning. Teachers need to express acceptance, warmth, and confidence in children if the children are to feel accepted, trusted, and capable and if they are to develop the positive self-concepts and self-confidence essential for effective learning. Acceptance does *not* mean that all of the child's *behavior* is accepted, but that the *child* is accepted. Teachers need to trust children to make good decisions when the children are led to face a situation realistically. They may not always follow through on promised actions. (Does anyone?) But responsibility grows gradually as children have the opportunity to exercise it. We do not learn what we are not allowed to experience.

Evaluation of communication

Evaluation focuses on the questions "How am I doing? What have I accomplished so far? What are my next steps?" Although the process is continual, at certain times it should become the main focus of our attention. Evaluation of our communication is an essential step for anyone involved in interpersonal relationships.

The teacher's own evaluation

In order to evaluate the effectiveness of our own communication, it is necessary to discuss it and get feedback from others. In addition, records should be kept of problems, of progress in overcoming

them, and of useful procedures to continue or initiate.

For verbal communication In evaluating your verbal communication, you may find it helpful to consider the following questions.

As a speaker

Are most listeners able to respond to the meaning I try to convey?

Does my contribution to a discussion make a difference?

Do I recognize how the perceptions of others differ and am I able to help them recognize these differences?

Do others frequently misinterpret or misquote me?

Do others tend to ignore what I say?

Am I frequently interrupted before I have completed my thought?

Do others tend to reinterpret the point I was trying to make?

Do others often ask me to react to or summarize what has been discussed?

Do I counter self-depreciating statements with comments expressing confidence?

Do my comments consistently help people think more positively of themselves?

Do I show my confidence in others by helping them analyze their situation and see alternatives, and then expect them to make their own decisions?

As a listener

Am I usually able to understand the meaning others express?

Do I frequently find myself in argumentative discussions about what someone has said?

Do others show that they consider me trustworthy by sharing information or feelings that they wish kept confidential?

Do others indicate confidence in me by bringing me their problems?

Do I listen intently so as to raise pertinent issues that are not a part of their thinking?

Do I accept, without expressing judgment, others' problems, concerns, and queries, so as to help them make their own decisions?

As a self-communicator

Can I listen to my own real feelings so that I can understand myself better?

Am I usually aware of the true reasons for what I do and say?

Am I able to face feelings I have but disapprove of, and am I able to deal with them constructively?

For nonverbal communication Galloway (1968) constructed a scale of seven categories for observing a teacher's nonverbal communication. Three of the categories were considered as encouraging communications, and three were considered as inhibiting. The neutral category of *pro forma* was considered as neither encouraging nor inhibiting.

Encouraging communication

1. *Enthusiastic Support.* A nonverbal expression implying enthusiastic support of a pupil's behavior, pupil interaction, or both. An expression that manifests enthusiastic approval, unusual warmth, or emotional support; being strongly pleased.

Facial expression. Any facial expression that connotes enjoyment, pleasure, or satisfaction with the pupil or the topic.

Action. Any movement or action that portrays enthusiastic approval and active acceptance.

2. *Helping.* A responsive act which suggests a detection of expressed feelings, needs, urgencies, problems, etc., in the pupil. A communicative act that performs a function which helps a pupil or answers a need.

Facial expression. An expression that implies "I understand" or "I know what you mean," which is followed up by some kind of appropriate action. An expression that is consistent and sensitive to the pupil's need.

Action. The action of the teacher is consistent with the need expressed by the pupil. Any action that suggests understanding and assistance.

Vocal language. A vocal utterance that is acceptant and understanding. The voice may be tender, compassionate, or supportive, or it may be a laugh or vocalization that breaks the tension.

3. *Receptivity.* A nonverbal expression that implies a willingness to listen with patience and interest to pupil talk. By paying attention to the pupil, the teacher exhibits an interest in the pupil, and implicitly manifests approval, satisfaction, or encouragement.

Facial expression. Maintains eye contact with pupil in a systematic fashion, exhibiting interest in pupil, pupil's talk, or both. Facial expression indicates patience and attention.

Action. The teacher's demeanor suggests attentiveness by the way the total body is presented and movements used. Teacher may be paying attention to pupil talk, even though eye contact is not established. A gesture that openly or subtly encourages the pupil to continue.

Vocal language. An utterance indicating "yes-yes" (um-hm), "go on," "okay," "all right," or "I'm listening." Although, in a sense, the utterance can be characterized as an interruption, it in no way interferes with the communication process; indeed, such a vocalization supplements, and encourages the pupil to continue.

4. *Pro forma*. A communicative act that is a matter of form, or for the sake of form. Thus, the nature of the act, whether it is a facial expression, action, or vocal language, conveys little or no encouraging or inhibiting communicative significance in the contextual situation; a routine act.

Inhibiting communication

5. *Inattentive*. A nonverbal expression that implies an unwillingness or inability to engage attentively in the communicative process, thus indicating disinterest or impatience with pupil talk.

Facial expression. Avoids eye contact to the point of not maintaining attention; exhibits apparent disinterest, or impatience.

Action. An expressional pose or movement that indicates disinterest, boredom, or inattention. Postural stance indicates preoccupation with something else. Either a moving or completed hand gesture that suggests the teacher is blocking pupil talk, or terminating the discussion.

Vocal language. A vocal utterance that indicates impatience, or "I want you to stop talking."

6. *Unresponsive*. A communicative act that openly ignores a pupil's need, or that is insensitive to pupil's feeling. Display of egocentric behavior or a domination of communication situation by interrupting or interfering in an active fashion with the ongoing process of communicating between pupils, or from pupil to teacher. A failure to respond when a response would ordinarily be expected by ignoring a question or request.

Facial expression. An expression that is troubled, unsure, or unenthused about the topic in question. An expression that threatens or cajoles pupils; a condescending expression; an unsympathetic expression; or an impatient expression. An obvious expression of denial of feeling of pupil, or noncompliance of a request.

Action. Any action that is unresponsive to or withdrawing from a request or expressed need

on the part of the pupil. An action that manifests unacceptance of feeling, tension, or nervousness.

Vocal language. A vocalization that interferes with or interrupts ongoing process of communication between pupils, or from pupil to teacher.

7. *Disapproval*. An expression implying strong disapproval of a pupil's behavior or pupil interaction.

Facial expression. The expression may be one of frowning, scowling, or threatening glances. Derisive, sarcastic, or disdainful expression may occur. An expression that conveys displeasure, laughing at another, or that is scolding. An expression that "sneers at" or condemns.

Action. Any action that indicates physical attack or aggressiveness, e.g., a blow, slap, or pinch. Any act that censures or reprimands a pupil. A pointed finger that pokes fun, belittles, or threatens pupils.

Vocal language. Any vocal tone that is hostile, cross, irritated, or antagonistic to pupil. The vocalization is one of disappointment, depreciation, or discouragement. An utterance suggesting unacceptance.

Others including McDaniel (1974) developed procedures for observing teachers' classroom behaviors, such as enthusiasm, which they found could be rated consistently by different reviewers. Collins (1976) has identified eight behaviors that constitute teacher enthusiasm. She then developed a program that significantly increased those behaviors. She lists them under the headings of vocal delivery, eye contact, gestures, body movements, facial expression, word selection, acceptance of ideas and feelings, and overall energy level.

A summary of research related to evaluation of teachers' nonverbal communication and their awareness of the messages they send supports the following practices:

(1) Educators should make themselves conscious of the messages they send their students by using the available observation procedures and by asking students what messages they received; (2) administrators should work with teachers to develop awareness of their nonverbal messages and ways of deliberately including nonverbal messages in their teaching; (3) teachers should plan to have their "action zone" move about the room and to expand its size; and (4) teachers can become conscious of the proximity and eye-contact aspects of nonverbal communication and use them in instruction (Kachur and Goodall, 1977).

Evaluating the communication of children

Many of the teacher-evaluation questions will be useful in helping children become aware of the effectiveness of their communication. In addition, two special skills are needed: (1) the ability to recognize the reason for a child's problem with communication, and (2) the sensitivity to know the kind of help a particular child will be able to accept at any time. The teacher should keep records on the children's communication problems and progress, and encourage the children to keep their own records.

The main thrust will be one of increasing their awareness of what creates problems and then providing opportunities for self-evaluation. Although no specific action is required of the child, those who feel free to comment on their own shortcomings and/or solutions will help others to attempt similar analysis.

Summary

Effective communication is important for many purposes. Common perceptions and trust are positive factors in arriving at mutual understanding, and these factors can be developed through awareness and effort. Though many are unaware of the often inadequate nature of intrapersonal communication, improving communication can enhance one's own development as well as relationships with others. We have tried to show the importance of the self-concept for communication and interpersonal relationships, and have touched on its effect on learning.

Suggested learning experiences for prospective teachers

The learning experiences suggested below are for a teacher's own personal growth in the improvement of communication. These experiences may be carried out in connection with a class in teacher education, either in or out of class, with interested friends and acquaintances, or with family members. We hope that experienced teachers also will find some challenging ideas and activities among the suggested experiences, and will try them in the classroom and discuss them with other teachers.

Suggestion A

1. Work with a group of three or four others. Each one serves as observer on a rotating basis.

2. Start discussing some topic of interest to all. Anyone may start by making a statement or asking a question.

3. Someone responds by first restating the *meaning* of the first speaker's statement or question in different words, then making a response. This *perception check* may start with "Do you mean_____?" or "Are you saying that_____?"

4. Someone then responds to either of the speakers, again restating the meaning of the earlier communication.

5. Continue this procedure for several minutes.

6. Ask the observer how accurately comments have been restated, and ask each speaker to evaluate how well *meanings*, not just words, were restated.

7. Evaluate the experience. Were some speakers more able than others to restate in their own words the essence of another's contribution?

Suggestion B

1. Work with a group of three or four others and agree on a topic of interest to the group at the moment.

2. One speaker states a position on the topic in three or four sentences, and a second speaker paraphrases it. *Paraphrasing* is giving the essential meaning or position of another person in different wording. It is similar to a perception check on a topic except that it involves a longer communication, usually of a position.

3. The first speaker agrees with the paraphrase or disagrees, restating the position.

4. Another in the group paraphrases until the first speaker is satisfied. Some helpful beginnings are "I hear you saying _____," "Do you mean _____?" or "You feel that _____." The observers must ensure that the reflected statement is put into the paraphraser's own words and that the first speaker is satisfied.

5. Another in the group takes a position on a topic and others paraphrase. Continue until each member of the group has made an initial statement, and each has paraphrased another.

6. Evaluate how closely initial speakers held paraphrasers to the original meaning. Discuss causes of problems any of the paraphrasers may have had and ways of avoiding them. Are people willing to say "That's not quite what I meant" when the paraphraser misinterprets slightly?

Suggestion C

1. Plan ahead a three-minute presentation. Orga-

nize it and plan how to illustrate or demonstrate to make the presentation as meaningful as you can.

2. Plan to set up the context for your talk. First, tell what you will be talking about and why, what the current situation is, and any needed background. Lead your audience through logical steps to your conclusion.

3. Be conscious of the use of all the channels: words, paralanguage, nonverbal cues. Your demonstration may also include written illustrations or labels. (Use this presentation before any class or group of students or adults, or out of school.)

4. Plan an appropriate way to discover how much of the content of your presentation the group remembered, how much they understood.

5. Which parts of the presentation did they understand best? Which part was least understood? Can you explain why, in relation to how you presented your material? Did you learn something of value?

Suggestion D

1. Secure the cooperation of two or three classmates or friends.

2. Find or make a series of slightly complicated abstract line drawings.

3. First, arrange a barrier between yourself and the other participants. Give each one paper and pencil. Tell them you will give them directions for a drawing they are to make, but they are not to ask questions, make any comment, or look at each other's papers.

4. Position yourself where they cannot see you. Give directions for making the drawing; for example, "Start near the upper left-hand corner of the page. Draw a four-inch diagonal line," and so on, until the drawing is finished. Compare with the original drawing.

5. Now remove the barrier, and repeat the exercise with a similar drawing. You may use normal

nonverbal communication. Are these drawings more like the original?

6. Next, repeat the exercise, but allow participants to ask questions you can answer yes or no. Are these drawings still more like the original?

7. Repeat the exercise for the last step, but permit any desired communication except showing the master drawing.

8. What are your conclusions about communication from this experiment?

Suggestion E

1. Test your ability to read nonverbal communication. Whenever you see people talking together but cannot hear what they are saying, see how much you can infer by observation. If possible, find out later whether your inferences were correct.

2. When you see people talking, hear their voices, but cannot tell what they are saying, what can you gather from the paralanguage? Check later, if possible, to see if your inferences were correct.

3. Repeat both experiences until you become aware of body movement, gestures, and facial expressions as communicating factors, as well as pace, volume, and intonation. How do body language and vocal cues work together? Do they ever give conflicting messages?

4. Select material from the Suggested Readings to help interpret what you see.

Suggestion F

1. Form a group of three or four. Refer to the discussion of Carl Rogers' responding styles (pp. 14–15). Read over the illustration and five responses below. Work together to identify each of them as evaluative, interpretative, supportive, probing, or understanding.

"I've lived in this town all my life, and in the same house for seven years, but I don't know anybody. At school I just can't seem to make friends. I try to be nice to the other kids, but I feel uncomfortable inside. And then I tell myself that I don't care. People aren't dependable. Everyone is out for himself. I don't want any friends. And sometimes I think I really mean it."

a. "Listen, here's what we can do. You can join this club I belong to. Our group is small and we want more members. We go horseback riding and things like that, so even if you are afraid to make friends at first, at least you can have fun."

b. "When you first meet someone, how do you act? What do you say to them?"

c. "It's gone on so long it almost has you convinced. Is that right?"

d. "Maybe your not wanting friends is just to cover up for something else."

e. "It's pretty hard to be without friends. I would really work on that. There are lots of things that you could do to learn how to make friends, and the sooner you start, the better."

2. Put yourself in the position of the person in the illustration. How would you react to each of the responses?

3. In your daily living, notice types of responses others give. Notice your own. Are you more aware of how you respond? Are you beginning to minimize your evaluative responses and increase the ones that express understanding? Do you notice the difference in the follow-up responses you get?

Suggested readings

References that increase our awareness of human relations and interpersonal interaction are Dan and Frank Millar's *Messages and Myths: Understanding Interpersonal Communication*, delightfully written; David Johnson's *Reading Out: Interpersonal Effectiveness and Self-Actualization*, containing planned activities; Thomas Faix's article "Listening as a Human Relations Act" with key principles, factors, and related activities; Rothwell and Costigan's *Interpersonal Communication*, helpfully suggestive; Joseph Luft's *Of Human Interaction*, dealing with self-awareness, group interaction, and leadership; and Richard and Jeri Curwin's "Building Trust: A Starting Point for Clarifying Values," giving ten classroom activities to help build mutual trust. Dorothy Hennings clarifies the role of the teacher in the giving and receiving of messages in *Mastering Classroom Communication—What Interaction Analysis Tells the Teacher*. Courtney Cazden and others explain *Functions of Language in a Classroom*.

To help in understanding the self-concept, its development and importance, basic books are Kenneth Gergen's *The Concept of Self* and Kaoru Yamamoto's *The Child and His Image: Self-Concept in the Early Years*. Two other references explain the relationship of the self-concept to school learning, LaBenne and Greene's *Educational Implications of Self-Concept Theory*, and William Purkey's *Self-Concept and School Achievement*. Articles to help teachers develop children's positive self-concepts are Simon and O'Rourke's "Every Child Has High Worth—Prove It" and Marianne Simon's "Chasing Killer Statements from the Classroom."

While everyone uses and reads nonverbal communication, people have had very little help in using it effectively. Some very helpful sources are Mark Knapp's *Nonverbal Communication in Human Interaction*, Albert Mehrabian's *Silent Messages*, and Julius Fast's *Body Language*. This last is focused mainly on adults. Archer and Akert let you test yourself in "How Well Do You Read Body Language?"

The effect of cultures on nonverbal messages, important for all, but especially for people who deal or expect to deal with those whose culture is different from their own, is Edward Hall's *Beyond Culture*, as well as his earlier *The Silent Language* and *the Hidden Dimension*. For direct help with children in the classroom, James Thompson's *Beyond Words: Nonverbal Communication in the Classroom* and Dorothy Hennings' *Smiles, Nods, and Pauses: Activities to Enrich Children's Communicative Skills* are especially useful. Paul and Happie Byers' chapter in Cazden, John, and Hymes' *Function of Language in the Classroom* describes significant implications, and Charles Galloway's booklet *Silent Language in the Classroom* provides many suggestions.

Strategies for children's learning

Strategies at the end of each chapter are to use with the children in your own classroom. These are not ready-made lessons for you to teach without planning and adaptation. Such lessons would fit only an assumed group, and since all groups are different, plans need to be adapted or modified according to the needs, age, and experience of the children. You can insert specific content that is relevant to the individual child or the group at that time, guided by firsthand knowledge of the students' problems, interests, and capabilities. Strategies listed at the end of one chapter may also be useful in connection with learnings relevant to another chapter as, for instance, the last strategy for this chapter is also useful for writing, as described in Chapter 8.

Making a perception check

Purpose. To check one's understanding of what another has said.

Appropriate level. Eight years and older.

Participants. All children.

Situation. When people assume incorrectly that they know what another person means, communications "go past each other" or arguments develop. Children can learn early how to recognize and avoid these useless and frustrating experiences.

Teacher role

1. To be constantly aware of discrepancies in meaning between teacher and child and between one child and another.

2. To use perception checks routinely with children when any possibility of misunderstanding occurs.

3. Encourage children to use perception checks with other children or with the teacher when this might help.

Procedures

1. When a misunderstanding occurs or you are uncertain about a child's meaning, say "Are you saying that _____?" or "Do you mean_____?" The child's response should clarify the matter.

2. If it would not embarrass the child, explain your perception check to the group. Explain that a misunderstanding might have led to unfortunate results.

3. Ask children to recall previous misunderstandings. Have each volunteer state what he or she might have said to clarify the matter.

4. Ask children to make statements they feel others often misunderstand. Have another child ask for a clarification.

5. Be continually aware of your own or children's misunderstandings and encourage the use of perception checks.

Evaluation. Are you more frequently using perception checks that prevent misunderstandings? Are the children? Are there fewer arguments and frustrations?

Paraphrasing

Purpose. To clarify the overall meaning or conclusion of a series of statements.

Appropriate level. Nine years and older.

Participants. Those who use the simpler perception check successfully.

Situation. Often a report or stated position does not end in a clear statement of the reporter's conclusion. The meaning is ambiguous.

Teacher role

1. Be aware when the conclusion of a report or stated position is ambiguous.

2. Use and encourage children to use paraphrasing as a means of clarification.

Procedures

1. At the end of a child's report, say "I hear you saying that _____," giving a conclusion that could be taken from the report. "Is that what you mean?"

2. Accept the child's response, but if it is just a "yes" or "no," ask the child to restate the conclusion.

3. After demonstrating and discussing paraphrasing, ask volunteers to paraphrase the conclusions of another report.

4. Discuss and create other situations to help children recognize the need for paraphrasing.

Alternate Procedure

1. During a class meeting or any group discussion of a problem, when a child states a position that may be interpreted differently by different children, paraphrase the position.

2. Discuss the procedure you used and its results.

3. Ask each child to paraphrase a statement before responding to it. They might say "I hear you saying that_____. Is that what you mean?" When they get a positive response, they may go ahead with "I believe_____" or "I want to say_____."

4. After all children have used paraphrasing and responded to it, only ambiguous statements need to be paraphrased.

5. Use paraphrasing frequently yourself to (1) prevent your own misinterpretations, and (2) encourage clear and more precise statements by the children.

Evaluation. Are the children acquiring the habit of paraphrasing your statements, as well as the statements of other children? Are misunderstandings occurring less frequently? Are you and the children making positions, explanations, and other statements more precise?

Organize for communication

Purpose. To help children prepare reports that communicate more effectively.

Appropriate level. Nine years and older.

Participants. All children.

Situation. As children work independently or in small groups on phases of a larger problem, they share their findings with the others. The more children consider the criteria for communication in preparing their reports, the greater the learning of both reporter and listeners.

Teacher role

1. To make children aware of the factors that improve communication.

2. To help children implement them in their reporting.

Procedures

1. Discuss planning reports at a time when children are beginning to prepare them. Elicit ideas on how to present information so others will understand and remember. Record these on the chalkboard.

2. Raise issues that the children have not mentioned. See that the following are included:

State the context of the report, that is, the topic and how it fits into the larger study.

Organize the main points in some logical fashion. Ensure that all subpoints are under their proper headings.

Plan to use more than one communication channel. (These will vary according to the topic but may include one or more of the arts in a demonstration; or a visual listing, on a chart or overhead projector, of the main points, including any compared statistics.)

If the rest of the children are to be actively involved, plan to give directions for their actions clearly and in the order they will be carried out.

Emphasize the main result or conclusion from the study.

3. Record the agreed-upon main points for planning (on a chart or section of the chalkboard that will be available for a period of time).

4. Arrange for children to give the reports as they are ready and in a useful sequence.

5. Conduct an evaluation session following each report. Make comments positive or as suggestions for improvement.

Evaluation. Do the children see the reports as more interesting? Are they learning more from them? Do the children follow their guidelines on the next report they make?

Building interpersonal relations

Purpose. To help children establish good interpersonal relationships.

Appropriate level. All levels.

Participants. All children; or children mature enough to benefit.

Situation. The school's failure to help children develop interpersonal relationships, one of the most basic skills in each person's life, has resulted in rejected and rejecting children, who are thus less able to learn.

Teacher role

1. Accept all children as individuals worthy of respect.

2. Encourage children's mutual acceptance by making them aware of the specific contributions and positive attributes of each child.

3. Lead discussions of factors that improve interpersonal relations.

Procedures. All children.

1. Discuss at the beginning of each school year how the group wants to live and work together. Elicit suggestions from all children about what they can do to make each one more comfortable in the group and, therefore, more productive. Bring out any important ideas children do not. (Points all children can deal with are: being courteous, being pleasant, being constructive, giving positive feedback when it is due, and being helpful. With younger children, discuss these points in separate sessions.

2. When children do not carry out agreed-upon ways of communicating, ask questions like "What did you forget?" or "How else could you say that?"

3. Carry out your role consistently and with frequent positive and appreciative comments. A model means more than words.

Procedures. Older children.

1. Early in the year, discuss the characteristics that make a person likeable. Elicit children's suggestions and record them on chart or chalkboard. Supplement as necessary. (Include characteristics of children who are friendly, trusting and trustworthy, cheerful, positive thinkers, accepting, and interested in others' activities.)

2. Ask children to think what, specifically, they might do to confirm present friendships and develop new ones.

3. Once or twice a week, choose one characteristic for in-depth exploration. For instance, raise questions about behavior that creates or destroys trust. Encourage children to give illustrations of trust-developing actions of group members. Anonymous examples from outside the group should be used for trust-breaking actions.

4. Give recognition freely for what children say or do that builds good interpersonal relationships.

5. Follow all suggestions in both sets of procedures, both as a model and as a subtle reminder.

Evaluation. Are relationships developing positively? Is the classroom a more pleasant place to work? Is most action constructive? Is group morale and solidarity developing?

Self-concepts are important

Purpose. To improve children's self-concepts through increased awareness.

Appropriate level. Ten and eleven years.

Participants. All children.

Situation. A positive self-concept and a resultant self-confidence may do more than all other abilities and factors combined to increase school learning abilities. Many self-concepts are too negative. Remember that the cocky braggarts are trying to convince themselves and the world that they are worthwhile. The self-confident person does not need to brag. Although teachers can help children from kindergarten on, children can begin to analyze self-awareness only at the preadolescent stage.

Teacher role

1. Make children aware of all of their positive abilities and characteristics.

2. Enlist the help of all through their awareness of their feelings and the feelings of others.

Procedures

1. Conduct a series of discussions on such questions as "What kind of person am I? What do I like most about myself? What do I like least about myself?" To the last question add "What can I do about it?" Ask the class "What can we do about it?"

2. Keep the discussions constructive. Show the relation between self-concept and accomplishment. For instance, we all try harder when we think we can do something. We do not waste as much time and energy worrying about the outcome. When we think we can, we pitch right in.

3. After considerable discussion, suggest that the children write about themselves in an exploratory way. Explain that this is personal writing that will not be shared with anyone unless the writer wishes to share it.

4. Following such writing, conduct another discussion. Ask "Did this writing help you to understand yourself better? Did it help you to discover positive things about yourself?"

5. Ask volunteers to tell anything a member of the group did or said that made them feel good about themselves, or made it easier to work at some school task.

6. Monitor your own behavior to be certain you give positive, or at least constructive, feedback. Help children take a long look at accomplishments to see their progress.

Evaluation. Do children feel better about themselves? Are they more enthusiastic and active in their learning? Are those who were discouraged gaining more self-confidence? Do the boasters no longer need to promote themselves so vigorously?

THINKING:
ITS DEVELOPMENT

Thinking determines communication. Talking is the oral expression of selected portions of a person's thoughts, and listening depends on the thoughts a speaker triggers in our minds; writing and reading are similar responses to written language. Without thought there could be no meaningful communication. The adequacy of the thought involved determines the quality of the communication and of learning. Thus, the thinking process becomes an essential factor for teachers to consider. Helping children develop those thinking skills most appropriate for various purposes becomes a top priority.

In this chapter we will first present some of the more recent and important findings about thinking and discuss their relevance for teachers. Next, we will describe the developmental levels of thinking and some specific thought processes. On the basis of this information, we will suggest useful ways for teachers to develop children's thinking.

What is thinking?

Thinking is a process of the mind that is ongoing through all our waking hours and, some now believe, during sleep as well. The phases of thinking we will explore are those that help a person be-come more aware of the meaning of things, more effective in dealing with the world, and more able to have an enjoyable, enriched life. The content of thinking is made up of each individual's experiencing, that is, that person's perceptions of the world, interactions with it, and to a great extent, the feelings thus engendered.

Most means of understanding mental activity are indirect and limited. Science cannot explain how thought is produced, but some findings from current brain research provide information that appears important for the teaching profession.

What does brain research tell us?

For centuries, culture has recognized a dualism between the yin and yang of the ancient Chinese, between religion and science, the imaginative and the factual, the intuitive and the logical. Since 1864 neurologists and surgeons have been finding evidence that the two sides of the brain physiologically control different functions: The left brain controls the right side of the body and the right brain controls the left side. Now we know that left brain thinking is logical and symbolic, the right, comparative and relational; the left, verbal and mechanical, the right, spatial, musical, and integrative; the left, analytical, sequential, logical, and linear, the right, imaginative, holistic, and intuitive. There is communication and cooperation between the two halves through their neural connections. When one half is damaged, in many cases the other half can take over.

Fincher comments on the attitudes of our society toward the functions of the two brains:

> Our society . . . especially in the fields of science and education, is inherently prejudiced against the intellect of the right, or nonlanguage, hemisphere. It is the linguistic, the abstract side of ourselves we test and educate and reward—and by such powerful social stratagems catapult to an overarching prominence in the human scheme of things (Fincher, 1976, p. 73).

This preference for one category of abilities has had a tremendous effect on our public school education. Many believe that we are embarrassed by intuition, that security rests in conscious, rational thought because only that is socially acceptable in our culture. Yet intuitive thinking, largely unrecognized, plays an important part in all of our lives. Many scientific achievements, the scientists themselves say, started out with a hunch.

Psychologists are finding the many effects imagination has on other factors. Pulaski (1974) and other experimenters have studied children's use of fantasy. In life situations, fantasy develops cognitive and creative skills that help people endure temporary deprivation while working toward long-term goals. For instance, such skills helped American prisoners endure torture in the Viet Nam war.

Researchers found that the ability to daydream and make believe is a cognitive skill that helps children be more creative and more flexible in solving problems, and it improves their capacity to postpone immediate gratification for future aims. Children who have vivid imaginations can sit quietly longer than less imaginative youngsters. This discovery raises the question whether development of the ability to fantasize might help the hyperactive child (Singer, 1973). Several studies indicate that low fantasizers tend to be more aggressive and physically active than their highly imaginative peers.

Psychologists believe that a child's natural ability to fantasize may be well formed by the age of five. However, they have also found that those who have lost the ability can recapture it, at least through elementary school. Some of the most effective items used to help children have been pipe cleaner people, Playdoh, blocks, and Tinkertoys. With these, children can act out small plots and engage in make-believe adventures. The adult starts the storytelling but, as children catch on, their stories become spontaneous and original. Two months after such experiences, children show greater imagination and improved verbal communication, are more spontaneous, and have increased attention spans (Freyberg, 1973).

In another study, elementary and junior high school children were shown an abstract film, which the experimenter interpreted in an imaginative way. They were then shown another and asked to make their own interpretation. The elementary school children showed a significant increase in the amount of fantasy they used, but not the junior high children (Gottlieb, 1973). Perhaps the older children found it more difficult to recapture imagination.

Another factor important for developing children's imagination is having adult models play with them imaginatively, which also helps children develop language skills through verbal communication and interaction. Children also need privacy and time to themselves to think over and replay their experiences. Teaching children to pantomime, use sign language, and play charades also are useful (Pulaski, 1974).

Other functions of the right brain that are getting more attention are those related to the arts, the esthetic, the divergent, and the spatial. One center exploring the connection between art and learning is the Mead School in Byram, Connecticut, where children devote a considerable but variable amount of time to art. During the 1976–77 school year each grade was performing at or above Standard Achievement Test norms in every subject. "Important new evidence shows not only that the arts are beneficial in themselves but also that their introduction into a school's curriculum causes marked improvement in math, reading, science, and other subjects that the educationists pronounce 'essential'" (Williams, 1977, p. 11). Art seems to stimulate children's natural curiosity, their whole-body thinking, the right brain's visual-spatial abilities. Many other schools and school systems are using the arts extensively, apparently accepting the researchers' conviction that, without art, children are being systematically cut off from most of the ways they can perceive the world; in many ways they are being de-educated. As educators study the issue further, watch for other ways in which conscious development of the right brain will affect children.

Research dealing with brain injury provides additional information. Cases of stroke, which damage only very specific areas of the brain, allow an accumulation of data about the functions of various portions of the brain. When a certain area is damaged, what functions are impaired?

One special relationship the researchers are studying is that of thought and language, which has been argued extensively over the years to no final conclusion. Followers of Benjamin Lee Whorf, an American linguist, believe that all thought processes are shaped by language (Carroll, 1956). On the other side of the issue, those who follow Vygotsky (1962) and/or Piaget (1959), a Russian and a Swiss psychologist respectively, believe language and thought develop separately. But brain research reveals "quite clearly the inadequacy of both extremes," leading to the conclusion that language and thought are mutually developmental (Gardner, 1975, p. 28).

Delgado is investigating the mechanisms of awareness and personality, and thus our behavior now and in the future. He believes that new technology allows scientists to explore the "thinking brain" that produces the unique qualities of human behavior. He has demonstrated strikingly that monkeys roving freely in the wild are much *less* susceptible to brain control (via electrical stimulation of the brain) than they are when cooped up in laboratories. On the basis of his studies he states, "There seem to exist critical periods when the brain can be decisively influenced by environmental factors as diverse as the adequacy of the diet or the permissiveness of the schools" (Restak, 1975, p. 25).

The implications seem to be (1) that an adequate diet is even more important than we have believed, and (2) that when children feel "cooped up" in school they may be more susceptible to "brain control," or manipulation, than when they feel freer, more self-directed, and more responsible, though not left without guidance.

How do theories help us?

Another approach to understanding thinking is through theories built on experimentation, observation, and extensive records of what subjects do and say under controlled conditions. In this century two theorists, in particular, have done much creative and innovative work with children, mainly with those in their early years, and have arrived independently at quite similar conclusions. The work of Vygotsky (1962), who died at age thirty-eight, was published posthumously. Jean Piaget is still working, writing many books, and stimulating others to write about his work and theories. Both Vygotsky and Piaget deal largely with verbal thought, that is, thought as expressed in language. Remember, however, that much thought occurs without words, in the form of symbols, visual imagery, ideas, or insights that are difficult to express in words.

Piaget's theory of cognitive development While Piaget is concerned with the development of language, he is more concerned with the developmental levels of children's thinking. He has posed four stages of cognitive development. These stages are based on how children are able to manage their thinking at different maturity levels. One level merges into another gradually and inconsistently over a period of time. Since children differ in their rates of maturation, the ages Piaget uses are merely approximations and convenient reference points.

The *sensory motor stage* extends from birth to about two years. During this time infants build a basis for their thinking by developing their perception and their ability to manipulate objects, through experience with the surrounding world.

The *intuitive* or *preoperational stage* covers approximately the years two to seven. During this time children continue to explore the world and try to make sense of it, to find out how it works. Most learning during these years is not logical but intuitive, a product of right-brain activity. Children make many deductions and arrive at some level of understanding but cannot explain what they know. When pressed for an explanation, they give some related factor, not a causal one. The response to "How do you make your tricycle go around the corner?" might be "'Cause I want it to."

What does Piaget mean by *preoperational*? The term refers to children's limited ability to operate their thoughts in the absence of firsthand experience with concrete objects. For example, they cannot look at themselves as others see them or put themselves in another's shoes. This is not the time to develop empathy by asking "How would you feel if you were Johnny?" The child cannot recognize another's feelings. It is an egocentric time, which means that children see the world only from their own point of view. For instance, it is easy for them to say "You are my mother," but not "I am your child."

Neither can children in the preoperative stage reverse actions mentally. If Sally is shown two equal balls of clay, she will be able to tell the experimenter that they are the same size. When the adult rolls one of the balls into a long slim roll and asks her which one now has more clay, or if they are the same, Sally always thinks the long roll has more clay. She cannot mentally put the roll of clay back into a ball and see that the amount has not changed. Thus, "the thought processes, representing actions, are not yet reversible. Consequently

the child's knowledge is not yet systematized" (Almy, 1966, p. 17). She cannot yet operate her thoughts.

Almy has interpreted Piaget's ideas more clearly than many other writers. She explains that the third stage, *concrete operations*, involves children from about seven to eleven or twelve (1966, p. 18). These children can begin to work *mentally* with thoughts about concrete experiences, without actually manipulating the materials themselves. They no longer act and respond only intuitively. Piaget calls these *concrete* operations to distinguish them from the *formal* operations of the next stage. The implication is that virtually all the way through elementary school, children's learning must be based on firsthand experience, or on vicarious experience that is firmly based on direct experience. Otherwise, children are unable to understand, and if they "learn," it is only through rote memory.

The fourth stage, *formal operations*, is one that only a portion of the more mature children reach in elementary school. It involves truly abstract thinking wherein the adolescent can construct theories and make logical deductions without the need for empirical evidence.

Piaget's position on cognitive development is probably the most widely accepted explanation of children's thinking today. Later discussion will apply it to types of learning activities appropriate to various age levels. But first, let us look at issues that are appropriate to all thinking.

Nonverbal thought

Long before children develop language there is evidence of thought. The deaf child who has no verbal language certainly thinks and demonstrates thought continually.

Other convincing information comes from adults. Do you recall suddenly remembering something that you need to do? You may think a key word or two, but what you are going to do and the reason for it are just an awareness with no words attached. Another and even more useful illustration occurs when you have a sudden insight, perhaps a solution to a problem or comprehension of a previous discussion. All at once you know, you see the solution, or have the understanding! But then comes the difficult task of putting the insight into words. You may have trouble finding the exact words to express it. Forcing ourselves to put thoughts into words is helpful when it requires us to be more specific, but hinders when it "jells" our thinking too soon and prevents consideration of alternatives.

When children seem unable to express thought, they need time to find the right words. Teachers may suggest that they think about what they want to say and tell it later. Or they may help children by asking open questions that do not influence the child's thinking. A "hurry up and answer" attitude interferes with the child's attempt at clarification.

The growing edge

Each child needs to operate mentally at his or her own *growing edge*, a level high enough to be challenging but not beyond the child's capacity to understand. In this way children are continuously developing, expanding their abilities, and finding excitement in learning. Both lack of challenge and lack of understanding may result in loss of their attention and involvement.

If teachers push children into responding in ways they cannot understand, they will feel less capable, less self-confident, and more doubtful about their ability in comparison with others. They will make no attempt to comply or will try to meet the demand by rote memory. Rote memory without understanding is never useful and may prevent or delay understanding. Piaget and other writers describe *pseudo-development*. When children feel the teacher expects them to respond in a certain way, they will try to say the "right words" by imitating other children or the teacher. For instance, many can produce intuitively what sound like thoughtful, well-understood answers. The same sort of verbalizing can be deceptive with the

ten- or eleven-year-olds, who may respond to abstractions in terms of associated experiences without understanding the significance of the abstraction. Such pseudo-responses prevent development because children believe that they understand and no longer seek clarification. On the other hand, if the teacher's expectations involve thought processes already mastered, little development will occur, and the child will become inattentive.

To discern a child's growing edge, the teacher should watch behavior and listen to responses, being careful to avoid prejudgments.

All teachers need to be aware of *individual differences*, including (1) differences between children, (2) differences within a child from one situation to another, and (3) differences within a child from one time to another. For instance, a child may write a word correctly in a story, but not be able to tell either the parent or teacher how to spell the word on request. Or the child may respond well in a situation that is mainly successful, poorly when things are not going well. Therefore, we cannot expect all children in a group to be able to understand the same levels of thinking at the same time. As long as no child is required to respond in any particular way, the responses of more mature children can help the less mature to develop perception and understanding. Such experiences are most effective for developing thinking skills. In light of the above discussion, teachers need to be well aware of the developmental levels of thinking in the children they teach.

Developmental levels in school children

Most elementary schools work with children from five years old, or possibly four, up through eleven or twelve. Referring to Piaget's stages, we will discuss two groups, the fours to sevens and the sevens to elevens. The first group are in nursery school, kindergarten, and first and second grade. Since the range of individual differences is considerable, this group may not include all second graders and may involve some third graders. Those who have interpreted Piaget's theory generally assume that the level of thinking at these ages is intuitive, egocentric, and preoperational. For the effective development of children, the school must match their learning experiences to the growing edge of their level of thinking.

The second group consists of children who have developed their thinking through the preoperational period and into concrete operations. These children can consciously manage (operate) their thought processes as long as the content is actually present, the experiences are firsthand, or the content can be easily and validly related to their firsthand experiences.

This group will include an occasional first grader probably in the latter part of the year, some second graders, most of those in the third grade, and those in grades four through six. Some of the sixth graders may be moving on to abstract thought, called *formal operations*. These mature sixth graders may be able to "construct theories and make logical deductions as to their consequences without the necessity for empirical evidence" (Almy, 1966, p. 18).

Piaget (1964) attributes the transition from one stage to the next to four factors: The first is the increasing differentiation of the nervous system, or *maturation*, which develops more rapidly in some children than others. The second is the child's *experience* in the physical world. The third depends on interaction with people, particularly in a learning-teaching relationship, or *social transmission*. And the fourth, *equilibration*, is bringing into balance or harmony the world and the child's view of it, or *accommodation* and *assimilation*, which we discuss a little later.

Further studies point to additional factors that affect development of thought. Piaget presented children with situations and tasks of *his* choosing. When we examine the uninhibited, natural, and free-flowing thought that comes from children in a situation of *their* choosing, it may be more advanced and complex at the same ages. Observation of free play is significant in understanding each child's level of thinking at any particular time.

Intuitive thinking of the fours to sevens

By age four most children can arrange things in order by size, height, length, or weight. They can classify according to obvious characteristics, such as things to eat, things to play with, plants, animals, and people, but can consider only one characteristic at a time. Having separated plants and animals, only then can they classify different kinds of animals. They can compare the *size* of different breeds of dogs, or the *kind of hair* they have. They can put pictures from a story in a correct time sequence. They can distinguish likenesses and differences as long as fine discriminations are not required. They can begin to identify the main idea in a short story or paragraph, particularly if it is one they have composed.

Children need to be more mature in most cases before they can generalize or form inferences. They will definitely need to be older before they apply a generalization to a specific situation. In most cases they are ten, eleven, or twelve before they can reason logically and at least that old before they can deal verbally with abstractions, that is, at someone's request. They are more likely to reason logically or speak in abstract terms when dealing with their own projects and concerns.

Early learning is mostly intuitive. Children are beginning to make sense of their world largely by the compare-contrast procedure and through simple categorizing. They are not yet ready to explain reasons. If we ask why the ball bounces, the child might respond, "That's so I can catch it." Things "are" the way the child sees them; for example, when scattered blocks have been gathered together, most children at this stage will say there are now fewer blocks.

The learning that becomes useful to children in the preoperational stage is done intuitively as it relates to them personally. This realization will change the way teachers work with five-, six-, and even seven-year-olds. The teacher's main role is to be aware of the kind of thinking the children are doing, and to set up a variety of situations that invite and stimulate discussion and thought.

Teachers can provide children the opportunity to handle various materials from nature. Now is the time for collections. Children bring in flowers, leaves, seeds, and nuts and sort them according to those categories. This is not the time to try to convince children that some of the pretty flowers are really bracts, a kind of leaf, and that the flower itself is inconspicuous. Nor is it the time to set up experiments to prove that nuts are really seeds. For eight- or nine-year-olds, however, planting a filbert or some other nut that sprouts easily can be an intriguing experience. Asking "How did it start to grow?" and "What else starts the same way?" helps children relate what they have believed in the past to the reality they are observing in the present.

Verbal explanations "proving" the children's earlier perceptions were wrong still do not make sense to them or teach them anything useful; the children simply verbalize the concepts back to the explainer. To be useful, concepts must develop through insight and understanding. They cannot be taught. The teacher's responsibility is to provide experiences and ask questions compatible with the child's ability to think.

By taking their cues from the children themselves, teachers can avoid putting children under pressure to discuss concepts they are not yet mature enough to understand. For example, young children can respond to the meaning of words in the context of a sentence before they are able to identify specific likenesses and differences in the words themselves. When the more mature children begin to comment on these similarities and differences on their own, the less mature increase their perceptions gradually, although they may not discuss the concept directly. For instance, a child may comment, "See, drink and dinner begin with the same letter as dog." Later, another child may say, "Billy's name and Bobby's name begin the same, but mine is different."

The bases for new concepts should be available to children of all ages, but children do not need to verbalize them. Since young children learn intuitively—and to considerable extent, older ones as well—they may not be able to put into words what they understand, how they have learned it, or what the implications are. The child provides evidence of a new concept by using it, not by explaining it. Once the child gives evidence of the initiation of a concept, the teacher may encourage—but not require—the child to talk about it. At this point, talking helps to extend and clarify the concept; and such discussion provides nonpressuring, nonthreatening information that the less mature children can assimilate.

The intuitive, egocentric aspect of their thinking sometimes causes children to confuse imagination with reality. Stimulated by the story, a child may identify with Jack and insist, "Once I saw a giant beanstalk and climbed all the way to the top of it." The teacher may choose to give a noncommital response ("Oh, you did?") and continue with the business at hand. Avoid a challenge unless the child's insistence requires impossible or undesirable action. Later the teacher may introduce a comparison of real and imaginary events; but the individual child's experiences should not be the content for such discussion. Rather, discuss the difference between fiction stories and news stories. Give examples and ask which stories could be true and which could not. You can stimulate right-brain activity by showing that you appreciate imaginative themes and by encouraging children to tell stories.

Thinking as concrete operations

Concrete operations develop gradually in most children over the years seven to eleven. Scattered blocks still look like more blocks than the same blocks grouped close together. But now children count, move blocks back and forth, and understand that no matter what the arrangement, it is still the same number of blocks. Later they understand this concept without seeing or manipulating blocks. When a child has developed this ability through experience, without teacher pressure, grouping procedures and sets can be used to advance mathematical understandings, to further both the thought process and the language to express it.

By third grade most children can really understand that nuts, peach pits, and beans are all seeds. By now children can be thoroughly aware of separate letters in words—though they often are not. By association, they have discovered, perhaps more intuitively than through instruction, the relationships between letters and the sounds they represent. Through association and compare-and-contrast, they become aware of similar words and parts of words before they are able to analyze the similarity. On occasions they need this kind of help in reading, especially if the relationships of letters and sounds was emphasized too early, out of context, thus so confusing them that understanding has become more difficult.

Children still need to deal with concrete objects to develop concepts. These concepts are built on the way things look or feel or work. As adults accustomed to thinking in generalizations and abstractions, teachers are easily fooled by what Vygotsky calls *pseudo-concepts* (1962, p. 66). Sorting shapes of cardboard, the child puts a triangle with other triangles, and the adult says, "Ah, he has abstracted the concept triangle!" In reality the child thinks only that this piece looks more like the triangle sample than like the other samples. It may become obvious that the child doesn't understand the concept when he attempts to classify a shape such as the one in the illustration.

If the teacher stops using concrete objects or specific statements about concrete objects that children have experienced, the child will not understand. To the extent children can use rote memory to give back abstractions, they have failed to acquire usable learning, and may find it more difficult to do so later. Let children touch, feel, and manipulate objects to sense the concepts they need. The real understanding and concepts they develop will enable them to make and operate verbal generalizations and abstractions.

Toward the end of this period, complex thinking may occur. Expressing cause and effect in concrete terms, identifying qualifications and restrictions, coming to conclusions, and making and defending decisions are some of the thought processes children begin to use as they enter the formal operations or abstract thinking stage.

Assimilation and accommodation Piaget's concepts of assimilation and accommodation relate to incidents of development from one stage or substage to another. Maturation, experience, and learning through contacts with others, all have a place in children's development. The process of facing new situations and coping with them requires an *assimilation* of new concepts into children's thought structure, a reorganization of their understanding about the world. The "nuts are seeds" experiment may change their previous thinking and beliefs, or it may extend them. At first they may reject new concepts or respond adequately in one instance and then return to their original position. But as time goes on and experiences are repeated, the structure of their thinking reorganizes to integrate new understanding. At this point we can say children have *accommodated* the new way of thinking and in so doing have advanced a step in their thought development. Thus, the development of thinking throughout childhood, and throughout life, is a series of assimilations and accommodations. We can say children—all people—have new experiences, leading to new insights that in time become an integral part of their thought processes.

Gottlieb sees the relationship of fantasy to the development of assimilation-accommodation in children's thinking.

There is assumption that symbolic and make-believe play contribute to the development of representational thinking; it is pure assimilation, repeating and organizing thinking in terms of images and symbols already mastered. On the other hand, imitation is accommodation to external reality, an adjustment made to the external world. Intellectual development is related to the active waxing and waning and interchange between assimilating and accommodating and culminates in equilibrium. For Piaget, both symbolic and make-believe play as well as imitation are part of normal development and go through similar stages of maturation (Gottleib, 1973, pp. 158–159).

Children impose their perceptions on the environment and in return receive feedback that tells them whether these perceptions are accurate. *Disequilibration* exists when children experience a mismatch between their perceptions and this environmental feedback. *Equilibration* exists when feedback verifies the accuracy of the child's representations of the world.

Specific thinking processes

Writers who list, classify, and organize kinds of thinking often rank daydreaming as the least useful level. Adults may see daydreaming as wasting time since the child is not following instructions and keeping busy. The child who uses daydreaming too frequently to escape from reality may need help. But daydreaming usually results in seeing ourselves as stronger, more clever, or more capable than we believe we are. We overcome our "enemies" and score tremendous successes that bring us acclaim. Such thoughts may have a positive effect on our self-image. An invention, a story, or some other creative work that starts as wishful thinking may result in real success.

Reminiscing might also be regarded as a low level of thinking, but it too results in positive values. We may see past happenings in a different light and begin to understand them better. We may become aware of solutions to problems or think of more effective ways to relate to others.

Our choice of candidate for low-level thinking is memorizing by rote. Certain things need to be memorized, as all children need to know their telephone numbers and addresses. But rote learning is no substitute for understanding and may prevent or delay understanding. As Frank Smith says, "Facts can make no sense to a child until they have been integrated into other knowledge that the child has already acquired and tested" (1975a, p. 140). We see no justification for rote learning in any of the four basic language arts, with the possible exception of spelling certain words.

Memory brings to mind, almost automatically, knowledge frequently needed but learned through understanding. Through memory we are able to express an idea without being aware of choosing words, read by using minimal cues of meaning and syntax, write words with little or no conscious attention to letters, and know immediately the answers to number combinations. Recalling specific information is certainly a necessary thinking skill. But better than memory based on rote learning are the reconstruction of a situation, the associations related to desired information, and other thought processes more broadly useful.

Fincher provides a broad look at memory by saying, "Memory is the indisputable matrix of the mind. Without it, there can be no learning, no thinking, no creating, no intelligent behavior as we know it." He then distinguishes between long-term and short-term memory in that the latter "retains the sequence of sounds or syllables in a spoken or written sentence until their meaning can be extracted, then banishes them from our consciousness. . . . Without the full-time filtering of sensory priorities that short-term memory gives us, consciousness would be chaos" (1976, pp. 31–33).

By failing to distinguish between long-term and short-term memory, educators have required the retention of much information that is only temporarily useful. Moreover, they have too often evaluated on the basis of verbatim response rather than essential meaning. This expectation has contributed to the rote learning of minutiae rather than the understanding of basic concepts that become useful long-term memory.

COMMUNICATION: THE PURPOSE OF LANGUAGE

Studies on the recall of connected discourse "show that memory for prose involves a reconstructive process from an abstract representation of the substance of the passage" (Sulin and Dooling, 1974, p. 262). When one has understood what one has heard or read, the main ideas are stored. On retrieval or recall, these ideas can be stated in appropriate words, including some of the original words and some paraphrasing.

Another study found that when a series of unrelated sentences was heard, one noun was as useful as another to prompt recall. When the sentences constituted a paragraph with a theme, however, a noun related to the theme prompted much greater recall than other words in the paragraph (Perfetti and Goldman, 1974).

A similar study compared recall from seventeen unrelated sentences and seventeen sentences in a story. Those recalling the story remembered significantly more words and sentences and made more theme-related word substitutions in both immediate and long-term recall (de Villiers, 1974).

These studies indicate (1) that people remember more when they understand what they hear, when it makes sense to them; (2) that it is the idea or theme of the material that is retained; and (3) a theme-related word triggers the idea, which calls for specific words to express it. Both Fincher's understandings and the findings of research on the recall of connected discourse are consistent with concepts about children's reading developed in Chapters 9 and 10.

Certain kinds of thinking can be described by pairs of opposites. One such pair is the intuitive-reasoning pair.

Intuition and logical reasoning Reasoning or logic is a left-brain activity, while intuitive thinking—knowing without reasoning—is a right-brain activity. Adults say of intuition, "It's off the top of my head," and the more knowledgeable and understanding they are, the more accurate and useful their intuitions can be. A scientist working in cancer research uses intuition more effectively than a well-educated person in another field. Teachers need to encourage intuitive responses, followed by a logical reasoning process when the problem being solved is a significant one. Logical reasoning, the process of forming conclusions, judgments, or inferences from facts or premises, plays a critical role in people's lives. The curriculum, especially when related to the out-of-school world, provides almost unlimited opportunities to develop logical thinking.

Prior to third grade, few children are able to do any significant reasoning. During intermediate grades, children begin to reason by manipulation of concrete objects and consideration of actual experience with them. By sixth grade some children are able to think logically using generalizations and abstractions based only on verbal experience. Before leaving elementary school, all children need to use logical reasoning habitually in appropriate situations.

Analysis and synthesis The contrast between analysis and synthesis is focused on the opposite tasks of taking apart and putting together. Analyzing is the critical examination of a subject to bring out its essential elements, while synthesizing is combining elements to make a unified whole. If the problem is simple and involves concrete objects or experiences with them, some children can use these skills with understanding at least by third grade. Children can use these thinking skills profitably to analyze a problem they are experiencing and synthesize a solution. With most children aged eight to eleven, the process requires direct experience, or at least vivid vicarious experience, with a problem related to direct personal experience. They may not have been through starvation themselves, but if they have experienced a day without food with no assurance of getting any soon, a film about starving people can have more impact on them than on those who have not had that experience. Consistent and frequent use of these skills prepares children for more effective learning and for problem solving throughout their lives.

Many reading programs attempt to use either

analytic or synthetic phonics. Prior to and perhaps even during second grade, children can learn such procedures by rote, without understanding, but are seldom able to use the procedures appropriately. Although they may verbalize the relationships, they are not likely to use them effectively, and real understanding may be long delayed. It is also possible for children to gain these understandings intuitively on their own.

Classification and categorization   To classify is to arrange in groups based on some common factor. Categories are the groups into which things are classified. The actual thinking processes involved are recognizing likenesses and differences on a certain basis, which must be clear enough in the child's mind so that there is consistency to the classification. Those in the intuitive stage can keep only one basis or set of categories in mind at a time; in other words, they can sort buttons for either size or color but not for both size and color. Neither will they be able to note small differences, say, in color. As children mature they are able to discriminate into more than one set of categories at a time and also to discriminate finer and finer differences.

Induction and deduction   Induction is deriving a generalization from a series or group of particulars. For example, children might find out by experimentation that plants grown in darkness weaken and die, and the same kinds of plants grown in the sunshine grow strong and healthy. If other factors affecting the two sets of plants are the same, children can then generalize that these plants need light to grow.

Deduction, on the other hand, starts with a generalization and applies it to a specific situation. For example, starting with the generalization that an industry needs ready sources of power and means of transportation, children can consider where we might expect industry to locate in their state.

Because most children through seven years of age are still at the intuitive stage, they are not able to use either of these processes. These children might say that a plant should be in the sunshine "because that is the way mother does it and she has nice plants." The answer "So it will grow" could be interpreted as a generalization, whereas in reality it is more likely a repetition of their mothers' direction.

Making generalizations and deductions, mental processes very similar to *making inferences*, is quite difficult if not impossible for most third graders and begins to be generally useful only in fourth grade and above, as Taba (1964) found in a social studies project. Younger children in particular tend to overgeneralize, that is, to make generalizations that go beyond the evidence. However, the study showed progress at all levels as children gained experience with this type of thinking.

Cause and effect   By the time they are eight years old, children can begin to understand cause and effect, but they still give some answers based on intuition because they have not yet matured enough to manage their thinking with consistency. Children can use cause and effect with understanding at some point in the concrete operations stage if the specific concepts in the problem deal with concrete objects or experiences. It is important for everyone to have experience and gain competence in using this skill accurately. Too many adults interpret without justification the concurrence of two factors as a cause-and-effect relationship. They may say, "I walked under a ladder just before I broke my leg. I'll never walk under a ladder again."

After an undesirable event, teachers can lead children to question why it happened, and to attempt to identify the factors that caused it. Deciding on the effect of various actions or lack of action can help children make decisions about their own behavior. Questions like "What would happen if _____?" or "What if I_____?" when they are asked frequently during each classroom day, become an automatic basis for evaluating group and

COMMUNICATION: THE PURPOSE OF LANGUAGE

individual actions in advance of need. With added maturity, children can extend thinking of causes and effects to happenings in the wider community.

Divergence and convergence Situations call for convergent thinking when individuals need to agree on solutions to problems or accuracy of information. *Convergent thinking* is useful when only one answer can be right, such as in solving problems in mathematics and science, or in recalling the facts of history. *Divergent thinking*, however, calls for exploring possibilities, finding alternatives, and trying different approaches to solving a problem. These thinking skills again illustrate the difference between left-brain (convergent) and right-brain (divergent) thinking.

Both kinds of thinking skills are useful, but difficulties arise when the wrong skill is applied or when either skill is used exclusively. A serious problem in school is the overuse of convergent thinking, representing the overbalanced development of the left brain. Too often when children see alternatives, another way to solve a problem, or a different approach, teachers "put them down" as wrong because it is "not the way we do it" or it is "not what the book says." Even if, through experience, you have learned that one procedure is more efficient than another—at least for you—children should have the opportunity to find out for themselves. In fact, children need to be *encouraged* to figure out and compare different approaches and procedures in order to discover their own best ways.

Young children in the preoperational or intuitive stage seem to excel at divergent thinking unless the school teaches them they are supposed to look for only one right answer. At least, a few minutes each day should be devoted to finding different ways of looking at things.

Creative thinking Creative thinking is thinking that is done independently and leads to an idea that is new to the producer of the thought. The process combines divergent thinking with various other thinking skills to develop an idea, a product, or a solution. Also creative thinking underlies originality in speech, writing, drama, art, and dance. Creativity shows up in human relations and even in finding new ways of thinking about concepts in mathematics, science, and social studies. To encourage creative thinking, a teacher needs to involve children in solving a problem they see as real and important. Children need assurance that whatever thoughts they offer will receive serious consideration and respect.

Problem solving Problem solving is a process that may utilize any or all of the thinking skills. The procedure begins with identification of the problem, which is often the most difficult step. Once the problem has been identified, the solution may be obvious.

The most important problems for children to consider are not the contrived problems in mathematics, social studies, and science texts, but practical problems that children see or can learn to see in their daily living. Problems using mathematical computation, if they are to be useful later in life, should be derived from the children's real experience of the moment. A child can write out problems for other children to read and solve, which provides immediately accountable experience in reading and writing, as well as in problem solving and computation. The same procedure can be used in science and other curriculum areas.

Children can consider problems involving human relations between individuals or groups in the school. For the older children, community issues discussed in newspapers or other media provide a purpose and motivation for problem solving. In many cases, school projects have been a means of involving adults in the community.

A real problem to solve may stimulate critical thinking, creative thinking, and thinking about values, both one's own and the community's. Critical thinking is evaluative and raises, implicitly or explicitly, the question of values.

Decision-making and evaluation Children are actively making decisions and evaluations long before they attend school. They make decisions on impulse, based on their perceptions and feelings: "I want to do this," "I don't want that," "I like you," "That doesn't taste good." The role of the school is to involve the child in the consideration of decisions on the basis of judgment. The school can begin the process early by offering choices of activities. At first some children will be unable to deal with more than two choices. Group decision-making can begin with simple, clear-cut alternatives.

Older children need to be pressed to state the bases for their decisions. They need to become aware of alternatives and learn to analyze how various alternatives serve their own purposes. When creative thinking is a consistent classroom experience and teachers treat their alternatives seriously, children learn to predict the results of different approaches and make decisions that are reasonable and effective. Teachers who are open to new ideas also may gain insight from such activities. Group decision-making procedures develop cohesiveness and morale as well as securing commitment to carry out decisions.

As children mature, they begin to use evaluation to establish criteria for making decisions. Children gradually develop the ability to evaluate by asking and answering the question "why?" Why is one choice better than another? When a young child can say only "because," the teacher should not press for a complete response. The child will make more progress by listening to more mature children cite reasons for their choices.

Anyone who makes an evaluative or judgmental statement may be asked to state the criteria on which it is based. Children should feel free to ask for an explanation of decisions that affect them. Such explanations help children to understand procedures that otherwise seem arbitrary—and may occasionally prompt teachers to reconsider their decisions. More important, however, such explanations help children to evaluate their own decisions more consistently.

Self-evaluation is an important aspect of the evaluative process. If children are put on the defensive and made to feel inadequate by negative criticism or belittling comments, they cannot afford to be open and self-aware. When others criticize, they feel they must defend themselves in any circumstances. But when self-evaluation begins early, children become aware of their capabilities and able to judge their own work. A teacher's repeated admonition to "do your best" is counterproductive for children may set goals or adopt standards that are unrealistic. More important is the child's recognition of the progress that takes place between the initial effort and the final product.

Critical thinking In all but the youngest children, intuition needs to be checked by critical thinking, a combination of many thought processes. Critical thinking always involves analysis and evaluation, often involves determining a cause-and-effect relationship, and frequently leads to decision-making. All the thinking skills must be developed so that children can learn how to analyze and evaluate in the critical thinking process.

The taxonomies, a different framework

A different approach to various types of thinking is organized in the *Taxonomy of Educational Objectives, Handbook I: Cognitive Domain* (Bloom, 1956). A group of educators, working over a period of time, attempted to classify thinking skills in ascending order of development: knowledge, comprehension, application of knowledge and comprehension to specific real situations, analysis, synthesis, evaluation. Although each category consists of skills appropriate at the adult level, children seven to eleven can exercise them at their own levels. A companion volume, *Taxonomy of Educational Objectives, Handbook II: Affective Domain* (Krathwohl, 1964), analyzes the kinds of thinking involved in affective educational goals: receiving (attending), responding, valuing, organization, and characterization of a value or value complex. These two taxonomies are useful to teachers because they provide reminders of various kinds of thinking children need to use in a conscious, deliberate way. They also indicate, generally at least, the order in which these skills can be developed.

Concept development

The development of concepts is an essential part of the experiencing that occurs throughout life. Concepts develop gradually, extending and deepening as individuals are involved in related activities and discussions. Schools supplement this natural development.

"Concept" has had many definitions and interpretations. Klausmeier defines a concept as

> . . .ordered information about the properties of one or more things—objects, events, or processes—that enables any particular thing or class of things to be differentiated from and also related to other things or classes of things. . . . Definitions vary apparently for three reasons: The number of entities called concepts is very large; there are real differences in the nature of concepts both across and within disciplines; and an individual's concept of the same thing or class of things changes markedly with increasing maturation and learning (Klausmeier, 1974, pp. 4–5).

A growing child's idea of a dog can be used to illustrate a simplified definition: A *concept* is whatever one understands about a particular subject at a particular time. A baby's concept of a dog may be a fairly big, furry, active, sometimes noisy "something." As the child grows, so does the concept. Jeanne now calls the "something" a dog, and it has a name, Tammy. There are lots of kinds and sizes and colors of dogs. Jeanne's dog is black, a kind called Scottish terrier. Dogs can be mommies or daddies. Tammy had babies, called puppies, so she was a mommy dog, but then she had an operation, and now she cannot be a mommy dog any

more. And so the child's concept of that dog grows, and differentiates, and deepens.

Concepts can be as simple as a concept of a chair as something to sit on. Limiting it and clarifying it can be quite complex. Is the floor a chair? Or the curb? Or the bed? Or the davenport? The question is, Could all agree on a fully developed, adequately limited concept of something as simple as a chair? Then take a concept like democracy! It is easy to see how misunderstanding and misinterpretation create problems. Just ask the question, "What is your concept of a good school?"

The child learns to limit the concept and to clarify it through differentiation. Cats and dogs have many attributes in common, but a cat is not a dog. Great Danes, French poodles, and Chihuahuas are included in the concept of dog. Since concepts develop through the experience of living in the world, the child's concept of dog will continue to grow, even with no special teaching. But how does her concept of dog agree with that of another child? How does it differ?

Unless key concepts are clarified, and their meanings are agreed upon, group problem solving is impossible. What is your concept of a "good school"? The inclusion or exclusion of a particular school as "good" is based on value judgment as well as philosophy. What is your concept of democracy? The answer will probably be political as well as conceptual. The larger the group and the more abstract the concept, the more difficult it is to arrive at consensus. When agreement is assumed but not tested, misunderstanding and misinterpretation interfere with problem solving.

When children are engaged in group thinking, one of the first responsibilities of the teacher is to help the group establish clear concepts. The group should consider and agree on the terms they are using in the discussion. When consensus seems impossible, the group may be able to arrive at a tentative definition, to be used in this discussion only, or to substitute other terms upon which all can agree. There is no point in continuing a discussion in which people have significantly different meanings for the same concept.

How are concepts developed?

Concepts develop primarily through concrete experience, such as the actual handling of objects or other firsthand encounters. Vicarious experience becomes useful only when we can relate it to something reasonably similar from our own experience. We can read words, memorize them, and repeat them verbatim, but without previous experience as a basis for understanding, we have no use for them. Consider this statement: READ (1,6) NUMSTU, KLASS. If you have had experience with a computer language called FORTRAN IV, you might use that statement as part of a computer program. But if your past experience encompasses neither computers nor FORTRAN IV, the statement would make no sense at all. The same principle, learning from experience, holds true for children, except that their experience is far more limited than yours. Elementary school teachers must provide opportunities for the kinds of concrete experience upon which children can build the concepts they need. We will now look at the procedures and the implementation of research which have direct bearing on the teacher's role in developing the skills of thinking.

The school's role in developing thinking

Among those who have contributed much to the conscious development of thinking in the classroom is Hilda Taba. In order to begin an implementation program in the public schools, Taba established an exploratory program in twenty classrooms in the Contra Costa, California, county schools. The teachers were given special preparation and a curriculum outline. The study focused on three general thought processes:

1. Grouping and classification of information
2. Interpretation of data and the making of inferences
3. The application of known principles and facts to explain new phenomena, to predict conse-

quences from known conditions and events, or to develop hypotheses by using known generalizations and facts (Taba, 1964, p. 30)

As a specific illustration of concept development in a particular study, they defined the thinking skills involved as:

1. The differentiation of the specific properties of objects or events, such as differentiating the materials of which houses are built from other characteristics of houses. This differentiation involves the process of analysis, in the sense of breaking down the global complexes representing objects and events into specified properties.
2. Grouping, or a process of assembling specific properties across many objects and events, i.e., grouping together hospitals, doctors, and medicine according to some semi-intuitively identifiable basis such as representing something to do with health, or the fact that their availability serves as an index for the standard of living.
3. Labelling or categorizing; i.e., explicitly identifying the basis for grouping and subsuming the items under some label or category (Taba, 1964, p. 31).

Most surprising was the relatively low relationship of the level of children's thinking to their intelligence, achievement, and reading comprehension test scores, or their social class. This finding may have serious implications for our traditional tests and evaluation procedures. It may also indicate that children have not been helped to develop their thinking abilities to near optimum level. Studies indicate that

when there was an emphasis upon thinking, the behavior of the experimental children changed during the work of one semester . . . children in the classes in which thinking was stressed, made more than average (subject matter) gains achieved by several previous classes at the same level of instruction (Raths et al., 1967, pp. 304–305).

This result seems to be typical of situations in which, with a reasonable understanding of the thought processes, teachers have helped children develop their thinking and learning.

The main purpose of the learning situation in the Taba program was to enable each child to develop the ability to use the designated thinking skills. In developing these autonomous thought processes, the teacher's main role was not one of giving information, or even of having children know the information, but of helping children think about the content in specific ways. Thus, the role of questioning became crucial as it set the direction and guidelines for children's thinking.

The importance of questions

Questions serve various purposes according to the ways in which they are worded. A question is either closed or open; that is, there is one correct answer or there may be more answers than have yet occurred to anyone. Closed questions are necessary when asking for recall of facts or information: How much is six times nine? What is the name of that plant? Which countries are represented on the United Nations Security Council?

Closed questions help to introduce a discussion in which other questions may be open. For instance, what plans did we make for our last field trip [closed]? What other plans will we need to think about this time [open]? During the discussion resulting from the second question, the teacher might ask, "What did our principal say about using a school bus for transportation [closed]?" The purpose of closed questions here is to bring relevant information into the discussion.

If an important goal of teaching is to develop children's thinking, closed questions should be limited to specific needs. The majority of questions then will be open ones. Too many closed questions lead children to look for "the right answer" based on authority rather than possible alternative answers based on rational judgment. Through frequent opportunities to respond to open questions, children develop the skill and confidence to deal with them.

An *open question* that has a focus permits children to think actively about the content under discussion without trying to decide what answer the teacher wants. Exploratory thinking broadens each time a comment suggesting an alternative is offered from the group. The discussion is at the level of the child's thinking, the only starting point for growth. Open questions can stimulate any of the thinking skills.

Questions of evaluation require criteria as a basis. These questions may ask children to rank items as to their importance for certain purposes, rate procedures as to their usefulness, or determine whether their written stories have shown improvement. Children need to participate in the establishment of such criteria so that they understand them and recognize their importance. Without usable criteria, their only recourse is to guess what the teacher wants or to search for some authority to give them the "right" answer.

Values and thinking

People's values develop, either implicitly or explicitly, out of their experience. The valuing process uses critical thinking to deal with personal attitudes and feelings. The first step is thoughtful consideration of the consequences of each alternative. The most important step is making a choice (Raths et al., 1966). Evidence of success in the valuing process is the person's pleasure in the choice, willingness to talk of it openly, and inclination to act on the choice consistently.

Many people hold values that are not a result of critical thinking, and some are not even aware of their values. Individuals who lack clearly established values may be unpredictable, show little interest or direction in life, feel uncertain what to do, and be overconforming, using others' decisions as guides to making their own.

Helping children to develop the valuing process does *not* mean telling them what to value, persuading or trying to convince them, limiting their choices, or establishing rules and regulations. Rather, it means providing a free choice among alternatives, each of which children analyze for its consequences. When the children have made a choice, they accept the responsibility for following through and living with the consequences. The experience helps the child to make even better future choices.

Children's maturity must be considered in extreme cases. No one would permit a two-year-old to choose to play in a busy street, but a two-year-old is not able to consider alternatives and their consequences. Laws such as a minimum age for driving cars are compromises that provide enforceable limits to potentially serious behavior. In less extreme cases, however, school rules prevent children from developing their own values, such as consideration for others. Children are better off without those rules *if they are learning the process of valuing in their own groups*. Children discover the consequences of alternatives by carrying them out and then evaluating them. A teacher needs to intervene only in case of serious danger, physical or psychological. As children make decisions and expect to be responsible for them, they become more responsible people.

Valuing can be a part of nearly every decision-making process. We know that how a child feels about a situation or a task has at least as much effect on learning as any other factor. Valuing is related to the commitment that we will deal with in later chapters.

The content of thinking

The teacher may take time in connection with any content to talk about thinking, the specific thinking skills, and ways to develop and improve them. Teachers do not need a special class in which to teach thinking. The discussion may focus on a mathematical process or a problem on the school grounds. Both thinking and language competencies are developed through use with any significant content.

Because of the relationship between language use and thinking, the development of one is essential to optimum development of the other. Teachers can help children increase their thinking skills through listening and talking, writing and

reading. At the same time, children increase their competency in each of the language areas through development of their thinking skills.

Evaluation of thinking

Various tests of thinking are available, but the validity of most tests is questionable. Any significant evaluation relates to the child's ability to use thinking skills in a natural life situation. The best evaluation of the level and effectiveness of a child's thinking is made through observation and making notes during a small group discussion in which the child is involved. In the larger group some children hesitate to speak up or try to tailor their remarks in light of their relationships with others.

A tape recorder makes the discussion available for later evaluation. Arrange a group of five to fifteen children so that all voices can be recorded. The teacher listens and monitors the discussion, mainly through open questions, to keep it constructive and on target. On a specially prepared sheet listing the names of the children, the teacher records the level of each child's thinking by using a code for the various thinking skills. The teacher then focuses on a few children on each occasion, and makes notes for each child at one- or two-month intervals. The patterns that emerge indicate the range, level, and progress of each child's thinking. In addition to providing a useful evaluation, this procedure shows the teacher which thinking skills need emphasis with individuals and groups.

Summary

Developing children's thinking skills is an important responsibility because thinking underlies not only development of all the language arts skills, but also understanding in all other curriculum areas. Direct attention to thinking skills can maximize children's development in problem solving and decision-making, and hence increase their effectiveness both now and throughout life.

COMMUNICATION: THE PURPOSE OF LANGUAGE

In order to develop thinking skills, a teacher can

Ask open questions to stimulate thinking

Be aware of the levels of thinking that are normal to each age group

Provide experiences and concrete materials that invite the development of appropriate concepts and thinking skills

Be able to identify the more common and important thinking skills that children are using

Be alert during discussions for disagreements occasioned by different concepts for the same words

Help children clarify differing concepts or substitute other terms on which they can agree for use in discussion

Keep children moving forward on the growing edge of their thinking through appropriate questioning without requiring an answer from those not yet ready to respond

Provide children time and, when needed, assistance in expressing their thoughts

Treat each child's offering with respect, even when it's inadequate

Let each child modify his or her offering with acceptance, as the thinking of others helps to clarify it

Take advantage of opportunities to extend children's thinking at any time with any content

Provide opportunities several times a day for divergent thinking, since the usual school program requires convergent thinking

Seek out true problem-solving situations, then give children the opportunity to reach a logical conclusion with necessary guidance but without direct help

Set up many decision-making situations, in which children understand the boundaries and assume the responsibility for the decision they make

Provide opportunities for evaluation, at the end of each day and each week, and self-evaluation at teacher-pupil conferences in any skill or content area

Monitor his or her own question-asking, using closed questions as needed, and open questions for focusing, extending, and raising the children's thought processes

Set up a procedure whereby the teacher identifies, and records at appropriate intervals, the thinking skills used by each child.

Suggested learning experiences for prospective teachers

Suggestion A

1. Listen to teachers at various grade levels as they talk with their students. Analyze the questioning strategies used with the youngsters.

2. Analyze the kinds of questions teachers raise during instruction and discussion. Are these questions ones that require yes or no answers? Are they open-ended? Or closed? Which types of questions are used in which setting?

3. When questions that require critical thinking are asked, are they addressed to all of the children

or only to those who are exceptional in some way? If the latter, why are these children chosen?

4. Plan a variety of learning experiences to help youngsters ask questions that require critical thinking.

Suggestion B

1. Observe groups of children at different grade levels in a school setting.

2. Ask permission to record discussion for at least two grade levels.

3. Later listen to the tapes and decide what thinking skills were used by each child.

4. Compare the kinds of thinking done at the different age levels. How did their thinking compare with Piaget's findings?

5. Did older as well as younger children use intuitive thinking? Were the older ones challenged to support it with more rigorous thought?

Suggestion C

1. Ask permission of their teacher to work with two older children (fifth or sixth grade) either in or away from a school setting. Determine their abilities to distinguish relevant from irrelevant information as one aspect of critical thinking.

2. Ask the youngsters to decide whether a particular piece of material or an idea is pertinent to the topic at hand. Make sure your own knowledge of the subject is adequate, and that the topic you choose is important to you and to them.

3. Compare the reactions of the two children as you determine their individual abilities to choose the appropriate from the irrelevant.

4. Ask questions such as, "How does this idea relate to the topic? Is this piece of material applicable to our subject?"

5. What thinking skills were these children using?

Which ones were they not using that would have been helpful?

Suggestion D

1. In a fourth, fifth, or sixth grade, introduce a concept the children do not have: "Most people in the world are poor," or "In the sea horse species it is the male that bears the young."

2. Plan questions in advance to stimulate children's thinking and provide information they can use as a basis for conversation and discussion.

3. Have children respond using the three thought processes from Taba's study as given in the illustration: differentiation, grouping, and categorizing.

4. Ask children how well they think they have done the tasks. Are they able to evaluate their own accomplishments?

5. How well do you feel the children were able to carry out these thinking tasks? What questions did you find most helpful to the children? Why? Do you feel the children developed new concepts?

Suggestion E

1. Form the habit of tape-recording your discussions with children whenever possible and use these recordings to evaluate your own effectiveness in eliciting group participation and using open and closed questions appropriately.

2. Were you able to focus, extend, and raise children's thought processes?

3. Can you identify the kinds and levels of thinking children are doing? Are these appropriate for their level of maturity?

4. What did you do to raise children's levels of thinking?

5. Arrange with someone who is also tape-recording discussions with children to critique each other's interactions constructively. Suggest alternatives each of you might try.

6. Continue the tape-recording in the Learning Experiences suggested in the following chapters. Compare and note improvements.

Suggestion F

1. Look again at the summary of the teacher role.

2. Select at least one item and develop a strategy to use with children to carry out that role. (See Chapter 12, "Strategies for children's learning," for suggestions on how to develop a strategy, and study the strategies at the end of this chapter.)

3. If possible, get permission to carry out the strategy with a group of children of the appropriate age.

4. Were you able to accomplish your objective? What did you learn from the experience?

Suggested readings

Basic references on thinking include John Dewey's *How We Think*, as useful today as when it was published in 1910; Lev Semenovich Vygotsky's *Thought and Language*; and numerous publications by and about Jean Piaget. Chapter 5 in Frank Smith's *Comprehension and Learning* is especially useful. Articles dealing with many aspects of thinking are Henry Cole's "Process Education and Creative Development: Retrospect and Prospects," which considers process as ways of thinking, and McCay Vernon's "Relationship of Thought, Language, and Non-Verbal Communication to Reading."

The split-brain studies are attracting wide attention. One of the most substantive references is Jack Fincher's *Human Intelligence*. Articles with implications for the classroom are David Galin's "Educating Both Halves of the Brain" and Robert Samples' "Are You Teaching Only One Side of the Brain?"

Clarifying Piaget's influence in the development of children's thinking is a book coauthored by Piaget and Bärbel Inhelder, *The Psychology of the Child*. Richard Evans produced an illuminating book, *Jean Piaget: The Man and His Ideas*, by interviewing Piaget and clarifying many of the concepts. Part II, "Stages of Cognitive Development," is especially useful as is David Elkind's introduction. An interview by Eleanor Duckworth, "Piaget Takes a Teacher's Look," interprets some of his ideas for the classroom. Other educators interpreting Piaget's ideas are Millie Almy in *Young Children's Thinking: Studies of Some Aspects of Piaget's Theory*; Brearley and Hitchfield in *A Guide to Reading Piaget*; Molly Brearley by editing *The Teaching of Young Children: Some Applications of Piaget's Learning Theory*; Furth and Wachs in *Thinking Goes to School: Piaget's Theory in Practice*; Lawson and Renner in "Teaching for Thinking: A Piagetian Perspective"; and Schwebel and Raph in *Piaget in the Classroom*.

Others making significant contributions to understanding and developing thinking are Hilda Taba in her *Teaching Strategies and Cognitive Functioning in Elementary School Children*, which she wrote as a result of the experimental teaching project she directed that was based on the belief that "Today, developing the cognitive potential of students is considered to be central to education"; Louise Berman in *From Thinking to Behaving*, in which Part Two, pages 19 to 63, suggests activities in the "Development of the Thoughtful Person"; and Louis J. Rubin by editing *Life Skills in School and Society*, which develops practical implications for our changing times. Chapter 4 deals specifically with productive thinking.

In "Changes in Mean Levels of Thinking in Grades 1–8 through Use of an Interaction

Analysis System Based on Bloom's Taxonomy" Irwin Willson shows that as teachers raise the level of their questions, the level of the pupil's thought processes increases. Several others have dealt with more effective questioning. Jack Frankel, in *Helping Students Think and Value: Strategies for Teaching the Social Studies*, provides many ways thinking can be developed through social studies content and focuses on teacher questions and their effect on student's thinking; Francis P. Hunkins in *Questioning Strategies and Techniques* emphasizes process and new goals in effective questioning and discusses both Taba's and Suchman's questioning strategies; Norris M. Sanders in *Classroom Questions: What Kinds?* discusses questions to trigger many kinds of thinking, especially for "more than memory." See also M. D. Gall, "The Use of Questions in Teaching"; Melvin Silberman et al. (eds.), *The Psychology of Open Teaching and Learning: An Inquiry Approach*; and Robert Sund, "Growing through Sensitive Listening and Questioning"; Nash and Torrance, "Creative Reading and the Questioning Abilities of Young Children."

Concerned with critical or evaluative thinking, Jimmy Cook wrote "I Can't Believe I Ate the Whole . . ." about the bombardment of advertising, and Daniel Dieterich edited *Teaching about Doublespeak*, both with suggested classroom activities.

Stimulating creativity concerns many authors, among them Angelo Biondi, who edited *The Creative Process*; Gabriel Jacobs who wrote *When Children Think*, based on children's journals about new experiences; Sydney Parnes with "Idea Stimulation Techniques"; and Treffinger, Speedie, and Brunner, who reported "Improving Children's Creative Problem Solving Ability: The Purdue Creativity Project." Edward de Bono added *Children Solve Problems*.

Authors who have written general books on teaching to develop creativity include E. Paul Torrance with his *Encouraging Creativity in the Classroom*; Torrance and R. E. Myers, *Creative Learning and Teaching*; and Vivian and Virgil Logan in their *Design for Creative Teaching*. Another approach is *Values and Teaching: Working with Values in the Classroom* by Raths, Harmin, and Simon.

Strategies for children's learning

Reading pictures

Purpose. To help develop children's picture reading skills.

Appropriate level. Five- and six-year-olds.

Participants. All children.

Situation. Children have been looking at pictures for several years before coming to school. What they see in pictures is often not what adults see. Reactions to pictures is one of the subtests in an individual intelligence test, perhaps because it is closely related to thinking skills. The first level is naming of items only; next comes some evidence

of the relationship of the items, and the third level is an interpretation of the picture.

Teacher role

1. Provide opportunity for children to react to pictures by thinking carefully about what is represented.

2. Present learning experiences that develop a sequence of picture reading abilities.

Procedure

1. As children volunteer comments about pictures, determine (a) their level of thinking in

relation to the picture, (b) how accurate and comprehensive their comments are, and (c) whether they are using the picture as a basis for creative story building.

2. When needed, try to expand and extend the child's thinking. If comments are minimal, you might say "Yes, that is a_____. Can you tell me more about the picture?"

3. If only further enumeration takes place, try to extend the child's thinking by asking questions like "What do you think the_____is doing?" Be certain your question does not limit the child's response. The request "Tell me what you see in the picture" has drawn detailed listing from intelligent adults. The better question is "What can you tell me about the picture?" or simply "Tell me about the picture."

4. If you get only description from a child, your questions might be "Why do you think_____?" or "What do you think might happen?" When children do not seem able to respond to these extending questions, the questioning should be postponed until later.

5. Include one or two less mature children in a small group of children whose thinking is more advanced. They may or may not respond at a higher level than before, but whatever they say, accept their responses.

6. Present in random order a series of four pictures that illustrate an incident. Ask the child to arrange the pictures in a time sequence. Or ask the child to draw a series of pictures indicating a time sequence. The latter may be easier since the sequence is in mind prior to the drawing; however, it requires initiation of the incident.

Evaluation. Do children volunteer to tell about pictures? Do they enjoy the experience? Are they progressing in the development of their thinking skills as they relate to pictures? Recording characteristics of children's responses at intervals is a useful basis for evaluation.

Solving problems

Purpose. To help children learn verbal problem solving.

Appropriate level. All levels from kindergarten through elementary school.

Participants. All children, or, at times, those involved with the problem.

Situation. Interpersonal difficulties often erupt as self-directed programs begin, and frequent problem-solving discussions may be needed. When such discussions start with the problem as each sees it, children can recognize another child's misperceptions and the problem may be solved quickly. If not, they may recall relevant previous decisions that they can apply or modify. When all feel they have guidance for their functioning, the discussion ends. Gradually, the need for these discussions lessens, but it will not disappear. As they arise, new problems call for analysis and solution.

Teacher role

1. Help children to identify a specific problem, determine its causes, and find solutions.

2. Provide opportunity for both group and individual problem solving.

Procedures. Encourage children to discuss any problem they experience in the classroom. When the problem is interpersonal, bring the children involved together, and say, "I see we have a problem. What do you think the problem is?" Allow each child who wishes to give an explanation to do so without interruption. If the explanation is confused and wordy, reflect a condensation in a clearer statement. If any of the children do not agree, ask them to restate the problem as they see it until a reflection of it is acceptable to them. When the problem is agreed on by the group, ask what they think they could do to solve it. Any solution they agree on can be tried and then evaluated, modifying as necessary.

Make suggestions only when necessary, for the children must choose the solution if they are to learn to depend on themselves, rather than on the teacher. Continue to raise factors children must take into consideration, until the suggested solution includes them. Gradually, when procedures for problem solving have been consistent, children learn to manage most of their own problems without the teacher's help.

Different levels. The younger children may solve interpersonal problems more quickly, but will tend to have more problems to solve. Older children who have learned to expect the teacher to make these decisions will take longer to learn how to handle their own problems, but should be able to develop these abilities effectively.

Other problems. Use the same procedures with problems related to classroom or school procedures. Some situations may involve one child in the classroom or any number up to the total group. Others may involve people outside the group who are not able to participate. If the problem involves your decisions, it is important to model the behavior you want children to use. Listen without being defensive, ask the children for alternatives, and suggest some of your own. If some situations cannot be changed, understanding the reasons can bring acceptance, even though reluctant.

Evaluation. Are children solving their problems more quickly as they learn what needs to be considered and become aware of various procedures? Are they beginning to solve problems among themselves without needing teacher help? Are they tending to prevent problems from occurring? Notations on the records of children can indicate how they handle problems.

Let's reason

Purpose. To develop inductive and deductive reasoning.

Appropriate level. Most appropriate for ten- to twelve-year-olds.

Participants. All those who need help with reasoning.

Situation. Inductive and deductive reasoning are the main thought processes by which children achieve understanding in the various curriculum areas. Forming generalizations from a number of specific instances, and applying a generalization to specific situations, are basic to the thought processes in all areas. Generalization requires analyzing a number of relevant situations, recognizing similarities and differences, and summarizing common factors.

Teacher role

1. Provide learning experiences in which youngsters can reason inductively and deductively.

2. Develop children's thinking through reasoning.

Procedures. Select a generalization from any content field the children are studying. Help the children develop the generalization and then apply it to a specific situation within their experience. The following is an illustration from social studies:

1. Raise the question of why cities were built where they are. Get general discussion that you accept, but treat all comments as something for them to explore—not as answers.

2. Bring in relevant material from school and school district libraries and perhaps the city, county, or state libraries as well.

3. Provide a time for children to explore the materials to get an overview and ideas to pursue.

4. Help the children to organize the topic so that small study groups can concentrate on any aspect for which they volunteer. (This organization could be by cities of different sizes, in different parts of the country, in different geographic situations, or any other categories the children agree on.)

COMMUNICATION: THE PURPOSE OF LANGUAGE

5. Each group organizes for work and researches the aspect they have chosen. As you work with each group, continually raise the question of evidence for their data and the validity for that evidence. Encourage further analysis as necessary and the recording of likenesses and differences.

6. Set up a time when each group can present its summarized report to the whole class. Record the headings (terrain, waterways, natural resources, climate, and the like) on a chart or the chalkboard and list the findings of all the groups.

7. Raise the question of what generalizations they can make, taking into account both likenesses and differences.

8. Have them apply their generalizations to their own city. It is important that children recognize that generalizations or conclusions need to be tentative until all pertinent factors have been taken into account, a situation seldom attained.

Evaluation. Do children's comments indicate conscious use of the various thinking skills stressed? Do they ask each other for evidence? Are they more tentative and guarded when drawing conclusions?

Think—how?

Purpose. To help children distinguish between situations requiring convergent or divergent thinking.

Appropriate level. All levels.

Participants. All children.

Situation. A most important area of schooling is that of goal setting and learning ways to implement goals. While some goals will be quite individual, many are common to all. A common situation is following school regulations. Children are more likely to follow rules when they are aware of the purpose, think them through to an agreed-upon (convergent) basis, and then are challenged to think of alternative ways of accomplishing the same purposes.

Children have had excellent experience in thinking about purposes and various ways of achieving them in their life out of school. Also, children can think of many reasons why it is important to be relatively quiet and orderly when moving through the hallways. They can also think of alternative ways of accomplishing this purpose. Most may feel they can do this on their own. Some may feel it safer to have a partner who will remind them when necessary. Others may suggest reasons for running, such as the one who reaches the playground first gains some privilege in a game. Ask for suggestions to solve such problems.

When the goal is to be able to use certain mathematical procedures effectively, alternatives lie in the way a child works at the goal and the way success is identified. Another goal may be to gain more pleasure from reading. Ways of accomplishing this goal will vary. One child may want to have several periods of ten to twenty minutes each day to read; another wants at least an hour to get thoroughly involved. One prefers a short story, another a book. One wants to read fiction, another science material.

Teacher role

1. Provide learning experiences in which children can use both convergent and divergent thinking.

2. Help children distinguish which kind of thinking is more appropriate in a specific situation.

Procedures

1. Identify day-to-day situations in which custom has expected all to do the same thing, in the same way, at the same time.

2. In each situation, ask "Is there something we all need to agree on?" "Is there one right answer?" or "Are there different ways?" "Do we need to look at alternatives?"

3. Lead discussions to distinguish needs for

convergence or divergence in both thought and actions.

4. Follow through with a group self-evaluation. How are we doing? What problems are there? How can we solve them within our agreed-upon framework?

Evaluation. Is there an increasing self-awareness among children as they are asked to decide on alternatives that are most useful *for them*? Are children becoming more aware of what is convergent, what divergent? Are they more aware of what they really *want* and *need* to do? Are they taking responsibility for doing what is important to them in situations where they are free to select?

Relevant or not?

Purpose. To develop critical thinking by identifying relevant information.

Appropriate level. Nine-year-olds and up.

Participants. All children.

Situation. Analyzing promotional or persuasive type materials, and selecting materials for reporting.

Teacher role

1. Develop children's ability to select relevant material in relation to a specific topic or task.

2. Assist children to be able to reject irrelevant material and/or reasoning.

3. Use appropriate instructional strategy to develop critical thinking skills.

Procedures

1. When children are analyzing any type of advocacy materials, ask them to consider whether statements are relevant to the particular point in question or whether they have been included to affect general reaction.

2. Lead children, in preparing a report, to question the relevance of each piece of material in terms of the purpose for the report. The child's peers may challenge the relevancy of any point made.

3. In any discussion, be alert to what is relevant at each point. Raise the question of "How does this relate to the topic?" to help children think along these lines.

4. Bring in appropriate materials containing irrelevant statements for the children to identify, and also suggest that all listen for such statements in any reports made by the other children, and on radio and television.

Evaluation. How effectively do the children identify irrelevant material in various situations? Note relevant comments of children on their records.

LANGUAGE DEVELOPMENT

When Timmy, age eight months, had eaten the last bite of his lunch, he said "awgone." Although Timmy had often heard his mother say "all gone," she could not be certain on the basis of one incident whether Timmy had said his first word or only chance sounds that meant nothing about his language development. That same evening Timmy sat in his high chair and watched his grandmother eat ice cream. As she scraped her dish and ate the last spoonful, his eyes followed her motion, and again he said "awgone." Apparently "awgone" expressed a thought, which Timmy applied not just to himself but also to a situation. Perhaps it referred to the empty dish, or to scraping up the last bite. Whatever it meant to Timmy, it was intentional speech. Vocalizing becomes speech when the sounds that the infant can produce are consistently associated with some specific person, thing, or action.

By observing children between birth and the age of five or six, we can see how language begins and gain some understanding of the factors that affect its development, both positively and negatively. This understanding provides a sound basis on which to build a program for continuing development during the school years. In this chapter we will describe how speech begins and how its development continues as children make language work for them in various ways. We will note the close relationship of language to thought and the place of language in the development of concepts. Finally, we will look at ways in which language development can be evaluated.

The beginnings of speech

Infants' early sounds occur without intention as a natural result of comfort or discomfort. Soon babies become aware of the sounds they make, and that they can control them within limits. Lefevre notes that intonation precedes infants' ability to produce all the range of language sounds and the formation of a vocabulary (Lefevre, 1968, p. 297). They pick up the cadence and the melody of the language they hear and integrate it into their language learning. In exploring what they can do, they babble and experiment with sound. Fond parents listen for the first "da-da" or "ma-ma," easy sounds that most infants make naturally. If the respective parent always responds in some positive way, the baby learns to make a particular sound in order to get the response, and this sound becomes the first intentional vocalizing.

All intentional speech is expressed thought. The sound may be only "ma-ma" but the baby's tone of voice, facial expression, and other nonverbal cues express the thought. The baby is really saying "Ma-ma, take me" or "Ma-ma, I hurt" or "Ma-ma, I'm hungry," and any attentive mother understands which it is. Infants both use and respond meaningfully to intonation, tone of voice, and other nonverbal cues well before they respond to speech itself.

These behaviors raise the question of when thought begins. An automatic response to a physical condition cannot be considered an expression of thought. When the infant intentionally makes a sound to bring about a desired response, however, it is intended behavior, and that intention can be considered thought.

The one-word sentence

A sentence is often described as the expression of a complete thought. How then can one word be a sentence? Without a context, of course, it could not be. Just as the above sentence depends for its meaning on the previous ones, one word may express a thought in certain contexts.

We can interpret the thought when a baby says "wa-wa" or "bye-bye" or "cookie" by relying on gesture, location, intonation, or some other context to give it meaning. "Bye-bye" means one thing if the baby is waving to a departing parent, and another if the baby is using a questioning tone and dragging a coat or a stroller.

Lefevre confirms the idea of one-word sentences when he writes

> Soon [the baby] says recognizable "words," many of them actually *sentences as defined by intonation and by what the baby intends them to mean*. . . . These early sentences, using only intonation patterns and single referent words, communicate fairly effectively in the total situation (Lefevre, 1970, p. 47).

A one-word answer to a question is a sentence because it is meaningful in context, although the context assumed by the child is not always obvious to the adult. The question "Who gave it to you?" may be answered by "Boy," even though there are several boys present. And the sounds children make are not necessarily words as we think of them. Rather, the child is consistently expressing a certain meaning through sound. As Halliday said, "Learning language is learning how to mean" (Halliday, 1973, p. 24). If a single sound conveys meaning, can we then assume that a sound is the basic unit of language?

The expression of meaning

Various units of meaning have been proposed by students of language. Some contend that the smallest linguistic unit is the *morpheme*, a word or part of a word, such as a prefix or suffix, that has relatively stable meaning. Vygotsky believed that the word is the smallest unit of meaning. Frank Smith points out that the meaning a speaker or writer intends to convey is largely determined by the syntax of the expression within a specific context: "We need to know the meaning of the sentence before we can decide anything about the meaning of individual words" (Smith, 1971, pp. 86–91).

Halliday goes beyond Smith when he says, "The basic unit of language in use is not a word or a sentence but a 'text'; and the textual component in language is the set of options by means of which a speaker or writer is enabled to create texts—to use language in a way that is relevant to the context" (Halliday, 1970, pp. 160–161).

It is *syntax* that gives different meanings to the word *fast* in *You can run fast* and *You can make the boat fast to the dock*. Is *cement* a noun or verb? No one knows until it is used in context. Smith uses four sentences to illustrate that the meaning of words cannot always be determined even by sentence structure:

Mother is cooking in the kitchen.

Father is cooking in the kitchen.

Meat is cooking in the kitchen.

Cabbage is cooking in the kitchen.

Does *cooking* mean the same in all four sentences? We could say that mother and father are cooking in the kitchen, or that meat and cabbage are cooking in the kitchen. But what happens if we say that mother and meat are cooking in the kitchen? Context is essential to the meaning of any word. In the sentence *Racing cars can be exciting*, is *racing* a verb or an adjective? Is the thought one of action or of appreciation?

Many of our most common words have a large variety of meanings. The word *dog* is usually a noun that refers to a pet of a particular species, but it can also mean a worthless person or an ostentatious style (putting on the dog). *Dog* can even become a verb (to dog one's footsteps). Many common words are used as different parts of speech. *Right* can be a noun, a verb, or an adjective. The way words are combined in sentences determines the intended meaning of the sentence and of the word. In order to read a sentence meaningfully, one must first understand its meaning, which in turn indicates the meaning of the words. If the sentence is spoken, one must also be aware of both verbal and nonverbal cues in order to hear it meaningfully.

Meaning, then, depends on getting enough cues to interpret the thought of the producer of language. Cues include intonation, other nonverbal cues, words (obviously including the morphemes of which they are composed), syntax, and all types of context clues, such as physical setting, the language setting, and the sense the sentence makes.

The syntax of sentences

Gradually children not only expand their vocabularies but acquire control over a variety of sentence patterns. Many of these patterns are common to children of similar age. Some students of language development now believe that these patterns are not an attempt at imitation of adult patterns, but a succession of grammars that evolve as children gain increased insight into how they can make language work for them. By the time most children are about three their sentence patterns closely approach those of adults, but the children's sentences are often their own creations. That is, the child has never before heard those particular sentences spoken.

Tommy, who had just turned three, followed his father out into the yard. Preparing to make some repairs on the garage, his father said, "Tommy, will you please tell Mommy I need the hammer?" Tommy trotted off feeling the importance of his mission, and on finding his mother, said, "Mommy, Daddy wants da hammer." Tommy did not repeat verbatim what his father had said, but took the meaning and restructured it into a different statement with a different verb. The sentence is structured correctly with subject, predicate, and object, and with the third person singular ending for the verb. This process involves gaining meaning from what someone says and later expressing that meaning in a different form with different words. The structuring requires not only the necessary ordering of words, but also the selection of the forms required to show the desired relationships.

Toddlers chatter all day, making surprisingly few statements with confused syntax while expressing innumerable relationships. During the first three years of life, children progress from zero knowledge at birth, to recognizing themselves and others as separate individuals, to having thoughts, to knowing there is such a process as communication, to recognizing specific sounds and intonations, to learning several hundreds or even thousands of specific sounds we call words, to understanding how relationships between these words are expressed. They can then internalize the meaning of a series of these words and their relationships and reorganize them in appropriate ways for adult understanding.

Many linguists have questioned how most children, during their least mature years when they have so much to learn, are able to accomplish this complex task. Some see it as the most difficult task any individual will ever accomplish. Two factors may help to explain: First, the *potential* for learning and using a language in all its complexity is present in all human beings, unless this potential is negated by injury or disease. Second, listening focuses on the meaning of what is heard, which is then interpreted in speech at the level of competence with which children are able to speak their own thoughts. Research indicates that people retain a message they understand as an idea without words and then express it later according to their current ability to communicate.

How children develop their language

Among those who have proposed theories of language development is B. F. Skinner (1957), a behavioral psychologist, who advocated the imitation-reinforcement theory. Briefly, Skinner proposes that children learn their language by imitating the speech of those around them and continue to use language that people react to in a positive way. This theory fails to explain how children build sentences they have never previously heard, which constitute much of their early speech. It also fails to account for growth in the use of language that is increasingly unique and closely related to the child's immediate situation.

In the Skinnerian sense, the positive reaction of adults is *reinforcement* that rewards children for behaving or speaking in a particular way. People tend to repeat whatever behaviors are consistently rewarded and to abandon those behaviors that lead to negative results. In response to Skinner, other observers of language development point out that reinforcement is not always given, and that whatever reinforcement children receive from their parents depends on whether their meaning is understood, not on the maturity of their language. It seems clear, however, that further communication is stimulated by the extent of verbal interaction with adults who show interest in what the child is saying. Adult interest is positive reinforcement; correct use of language by children is gradually "shaped" by such interest.

Although theories of language development dif-

fer, all theorists recognize the importance of children's experiencing of language. Children learn to speak the language they hear. If children hear two languages, they learn both; after some initial confusion, they quickly learn to keep the two languages separate and to use the appropriate language with specific individuals. Deaf children speak no language unless they receive very special and extensive help.

Children discover how language works

An alternative theory, proposed by Noam Chomsky (1968) and supported by others, is that the child *discovers how language works*. Chomsky proposes what he calls "linguistic universals," which are in the broadest sense the basic meanings people express or the commonalities of all language. He also proposes that language is innate, which we interpret to mean that humans are innately able to develop and use a symbolic language. Further, our knowledge of children tells us all children wish to express their thoughts. By experiencing the language used by those around them and having thoughts and meanings of their own, children gradually but relatively quickly discover how the language works to express them.

Evidence for Chomsky's theory can be observed in some common grammatical errors that young children make. The child who says "He gived it to me" or "I goed outside" is attempting to express past tense by adding the *-ed* sound to a verb. The child who says "I saw two mouses"—or "two sheepses"—is attempting to form a plural by adding the *-es* sound to a noun. Even though the child cannot verbalize the rules of grammar, such usages are evidence of overgeneralization.

In *Child Language and Education* (1972a), Cazden discusses the child's use of forms never heard in adult speech, including questions like "What he wants?" and "Why he can't open it?" Such departures from adult speech indicate that the child is developing language based upon understanding. Children move toward more mature speech through greater differentiation of linguistic expressions and integration of understanding into longer and more complex sentences.

Probably the best evidence of understanding is the child's command of syntax to the point of being able to apply it in a situation never experienced before. Berko presented children four through seven with a series of nonsense words, such as *bik*, *wug*, *gutch*, and *spow*. Each nonsense word was written on a card that was read to the child. For example, the *wug* card read, "This is a wug. Now there is another one. There are two of them. There are two_____." Most children responded correctly whether the word required only an added -*s* or an added -*es* sound (as in *gutches*). To use nonsense words as verbs, Berko presented sentences such as "This man knows how to spow. He is spowing. He did the same thing yesterday. What did he do yesterday? Yesterday he_____." The children were able to give the appropriate form for a past tense. Other cards called for formation of possessives and adjectives (Berko, 1958).

Another indication of progress is increasing freedom from dependence on the nonverbal context. The child who can say "I want a cookie" does not have to point to the cookie jar. However, there is evidence that children can put into words a complex sentence that conveys a thought they want to express more easily than they can repeat that same sentence later. This ability seems to indicate the importance of thought for language, and that it is the thought that is retained rather than the words to express it.

Children use the subject-verb-object sentence pattern before they use the passive form, which reverses this order. They also use and understand sentences in which phrases and clauses are sequenced in a natural order. The child's recognition of sequence indicates that teachers need to give directions in the order in which they are to be carried out.

Discovery is a normal way of learning All day long children are busy exploring this new and fascinating world they have come to live in. As soon as they begin to handle objects, they try to find out what they can do with these objects and how they work. As soon as they begin to "handle" words, they try to find out how words "work" and what can be done with them. Their discovery of the way language works is consistent with their other behaviors.

It would be impossible to catalogue—or even to guess—everything a three-year-old has learned through this method of discovery. Behaving as highly motivated people, children make these discoveries on their own, with little or no "teaching" by adults, other than answering their questions and occasionally rescuing them from difficulties caused by their curiosity. And all of these observations apply to their discovery of the way language works.

Early growth summarized The growth of language from birth through age three or four has been researched and documented by many investigators. These studies are extremely useful in planning programs for preschoolers. The generalizations can be summarized as follows:

Earliest intentional speech is mostly one-word sentences, given meaning by context and nonverbal cues.

Two-word sentences combine key words, but their relationship still depends largely on context and nonverbal cues.

As utterances expand, regular syntactic structuring becomes evident and more meaning is conveyed through words.

By age three most children have adequate use of sentence structure and from then on become less dependent on immediate context for communicating.

By three or four years, speech approaches adult level, communicating thoughts with adequate structure and meaning.

Handicaps to language development Significant handicaps that prevent normal development are lack of regular social interaction, impairment of hearing, severe emotional problems, or severe retardation in mental development from any cause. Adults can retard the child's language development by overcorrection of early speech, or by oversolicitous attention, which makes talking unnecessary. However, the ability to use language still may develop at a near-normal rate so that when children need to talk, their language may be nearly normal.

By age five or six, nearly all children have a command of most of the basic ways of (1) expressing their thoughts in the oral language of their communities and (2) interpreting the expressed thoughts of others. Many teachers and researchers working with so-called deprived children would disagree with this statement, but current studies tend to confirm it. Let us explore the differences of opinion.

The United States has many subcultures among its population. Some groups of recent immigrants still use their mother tongue exclusively or at least as the basic language in home and neighborhood. More have moved to the use of English while retaining a dialect and many of the attitudes and expectancies of their own culture. Still more have, for a variety of reasons, developed a regional dialect based on English but including idiosyncrasies peculiar to their area or group. Black English, Brooklynese, and the Boston accent are examples. Besides these groups, there are individuals whose experiences affect the way they communicate—such as those who have learned that it is safer to keep quiet than to venture expressing their thoughts. They have learned to speak only when some response is demanded and then in the fewest words possible. All of these situations affect the language children bring to school and their ability to perform as they are expected to in the usual school program.

When these culturally or individually "different" children enter a classroom with the "typical American child," their use of language is certain to set them apart. But research shows that their *competence* in the use of language is not nearly as inadequate as their *expression* of it.

Studying the language of school children

When Piaget first described the stages of cognitive development in 1926, he concentrated on the close relationship between language and thought. But in a more recent book, *The Child and Reality* (1973), he draws new conclusions from the study of intelligence during the sensorimotor period, before language. From further study of the stages of child development, he had found that children can operate on a level above that on which they can use language. Even more important for school programs was Piaget's discovery that when a child does not already have a concept, he or she cannot gain it through language (Piaget, 1973, pp. 118–121). If concepts cannot be taught through purely verbal activities and the giving of information, then the child's use of concrete materials is essential.

In *The Language and Thought of the Child* (1959), Piaget explores the egocentric thinking of children below age seven. When they carry on conversations, they seem to be sharing ideas, but each is talking mainly about his or her own actions and thoughts. Real collaboration and a meeting of minds does not occur. For this reason, teachers need guidelines that emphasize individualized instruction for children under eight. While younger children can understand and carry out many activities and interactions, children benefit from receiving individual instruction about their own roles and responsibilities, rather than interpreting it from general instructions to the group.

Furthermore, Piaget found that the young child "is incapable of keeping to himself the thoughts which enter his mind. He says everything. He has no verbal continence." This finding explains those who, in spite of punishment, still burst forth with talking when talking is forbidden. The repression these children experience during school hours may explain many disciplinary problems both in and out of school. Much inadequate learning may result from the attention the child must give to keeping quiet and the inner turmoil it creates.

Until seven or eight, Piaget found, children

make no attempt to be consistent in their opinions. And they are unable to be accurate and objective in reporting what another child has said. Younger children are not inaccurate intentionally, but because of their high egocentric concerns, they do not pay close attention to what others say (Piaget, 1959, pp. 137–138). This finding should affect the way teachers talk with children and plan learning procedures at this stage. It is important for children to express in their own words what they need to do and their responsibility for doing it. Thus, learning procedures based on teacher-pupil planning can be more effective and result in more learning than those based on teacher-made assignments.

A seven-year longitudinal study Loban (1963) reported one of the most comprehensive studies of language development in school-age children. The longitudinal study followed children from kindergarten through sixth grade. He started with 338 regular kindergartners, 30 kindergartners rated exceptionally high in language development, and 24 rated exceptionally low (at least two standard deviations above or below the mean). The children were selected on the size of their vocabularies and the combined score of all teachers' ratings. In 1966 Loban published a continuation of this study through the high school years.

All children increased the number of words spoken each year and increased their effectiveness in speaking. The group starting out with better language ability maintained its superiority, increased complexity of sentence structure, and added vocabulary until it was about double that of the low language-ability group. (Change in viewing dialects would modify his early analysis.) The three groups used an equal number of words that have the highest frequency of use, but the high group used more of the less common words. The high group was most fluent, the randomly chosen group next most fluent, and the low group least fluent. Once handicapped in speaking, children in a regular school situation seem to become increasingly less able in comparison with the more capa-

ble children. The difference could be the result of school practices, since the children who speak well and fluently are the ones who get the most opportunities to talk, while those less ready with words and less assurance are sometimes ignored.

In their structuring of speech, the low group used many more partial expressions, such as sentences incomplete as to meaning. The high group used more of the linking verb patterns, that is, some form of the verb be as the only verb (The book is red). Otherwise structural patterns of the two groups differed little. However, the skill with which the high group used elements within the sentence, such as moveable elements, and nominals as subject or complement, was superior. The high group used infinitives and clauses to function as nouns, as well as the nouns and pronouns used by the low group.

In other words, Loban noted that maturity in language usage includes a greater variety of sentence structuring. He further noted that tentativeness in what was said also distinguished the effective users of language. That is, these children tended to express hypotheses or possibilities subject to change. Loban recommended less use of workbook drill and more emphasis on using speech to express ideas, attitudes, and values of concern to the learners. Rather than drill in usage, he suggested working with the individual to achieve coherence and organization in talking.

Ruth Strickland considers "the best measure of the maturity of a child's language . . . to be his ability to expand and elaborate basic sentence patterns and to use them with a high degree of flexibility" (1971, p. 391).

Measures of language maturity Many researchers sought ways to measure language maturity in children. Loban used "a communication unit," while others used such means as length of sentences, length of clauses, ratio of subordinate clauses to independent ones, and numerous others. Hunt introduced the *T-unit*, which he described as consisting of "one main clause with all the subordinate clauses attached to it" (1965, p.

20). Thus, a simple or complex sentence would be a T-unit, but a compound sentence would be measured as two T-units. The average length of all T-units in a child's speech (or writing) has become the most common means of rating that child's language maturity.

The T-unit measure of maturity is influenced by an increase in the number of sentence-combining transformations, that is, the number of ideas combined in a single sentence through *embedding*. First, modifiers are embedded; instead of saying "My sister is big. She took me to the store," the child says, "My big sister took me to the store." Embedding then progresses to phrases and clauses. Instead of saying "I lost a book. Now I found it," the child says, "I found the book that I lost." The transformation increases the length of the T-unit from an average of four words to seven and indicates increased linguistic maturity. (See Appendix C.)

Language structures learned later In an extensive study involving thirty-six youngsters, kindergarten through fourth grade, Carol Chomsky (1969, 1972) found several sentence structures that these school-age children misinterpreted prior to a certain stage of development. Five of these proved to be acquired in a sequence that reveals developmental stages because children always acquired them in the same order, although the rate varied greatly.

The first of these misinterpretations developed around the word *see*. A doll that closed its eyes when lying down was laid on a table. Children were asked, "Is the doll hard to see or easy to see?" Then the doll was placed out of sight under the table, and the same question was asked. All children under five and a half said the doll was hard to see in both instances, when its eyes were closed and when it was out of sight. Beyond this age some children began to interpret the question correctly and by age nine all children did.

A second problem involved confusion of *asked* and *promised* as used in these sentences: (1) John asked Bill to leave. (2) John promised Bill to leave.

All children understood the meaning of *promised* in other types of sentences. In the above sentences, however, all children before 5.6 years interpreted *promised* the same as *asked*, by nine years all interpreted it correctly. Another possible meaning of the first sentence, which none of the children recognized, is that John asked Bill (for permission) to leave. Only context can provide the basis for interpreting this meaning.

A third problem, again involving the word *ask*, is even more confusing at times. When the children were told, "Ask Bruce what to feed the dog," they most often responded, "What do you want to feed the dog?" or "What are you going to feed the dog?" Only one-third of the group gave the correct response, "What should I feed the dog?"

A fourth problem pertained to referents of words in certain structures. In "Mother scolded Gloria for answering the phone and I would have done the same," many children thought "the same" meant "I would have answered the phone" rather than "I would have scolded Gloria."

As a fifth problem, in the same sentence as the one above, when *although* was substituted for *and*, only four children of the thirty-six, the most advanced, made the correct distinction. When the less familiar concept of *although* was added to the uncertainty of the referent for *same*, difficulties increased.

A similar type of study by Bormuth (1970) involved written items containing certain syntactic structures. Some fifty-five structures were tested at the fourth grade level and the percentage correct for different structures ranged from 28.1 percent to 88.3 percent; this was further evidence of the need to check, rather than assume, children's understanding of what they hear and read.

Carroll (1970) studied children's comprehension of words with multiple grammatical functions. The list of some 600 words considered grammatically ambiguous included 468 words that can be nouns or verbs (such as badger, bridge, hedge, mix, snake, voice), 64 words that can be nouns or adjectives (absolute, deep, minute, principal, standard), 52 words that can be nouns, verbs, or adjectives (boring, express, front, lead, right, uniform), and 23 words that can be verbs or adjectives (best, long, secure, warm). Carroll asked 1500 children in grades three, six, and nine to write sentences illustrating 240 of the words. He concluded that learning to understand grammatically ambiguous words is a slow process, far from complete by grade nine.

Another study identified other types of ambiguity that confused children aged six, nine, twelve, and fifteen years. These ambiguities included: phonological—different words with the same sounds, as in "The doctor is out of patience [patients]"; lexical—same words but with different social meanings, as in "He did not have enough dough [money]"; surface structure—"He laughed at the school [to laugh at or where he laughed]"; "They are visiting sailors [with *visiting* a verb or an adjective]." There was little understanding of ambiguities of the last type before a child was twelve (Shultz and Pilon, 1973).

While other investigators study the child's developing ability to understand various grammatical structures, Halliday (1973) has analyzed beginning speech in terms of the uses to which children put it. From the sociolinguistic point of view, Halliday suggests a tentative system of development that begins with the words "I want_____" representing the *instrumental* use of speech. In the order they evolve, the seven functions, and examples of each use of speech, are as follows:

Instrumental	I want
Regulatory	Do as I tell you
Interactional	Me and you
Personal	Here I come
Heuristic	Tell me why
Imaginative	Let's pretend
Informative	I've got something to tell you

Children use *regulatory* speech to persuade others to do what they want them to, and the *interactional* to develop interpersonal relations. Another use children make of language is the

personal, a way of developing self-awareness, of recognizing characteristics of their selfhood as separate from that of others and separate from their environment. Along with this use of language, they develop what he calls the *heuristic* use with which they explore that nonself environment. They ask questions—What? How? Why?—and others' responses become exceedingly important for children's mental growth. When questions are answered sincerely and in ways that encourage children to think further or, when appropriate, to marshall their present relevant knowledge, children develop in understanding and self-confidence.

A sixth use of language by young children is the *imaginative* by which they build worlds of their own, separate from the world of reality they are trying to understand, through linguistic play. Halliday then lists a final use for children's language, the *representational*, or a way to communicate about things. Because it is the last to develop, the child uses it least and is least able to understand others' use of it. This fact may explain why children in kindergarten and first grade may not respond adequately when teaching is mainly telling children what teachers want them to know. The child must develop a concept before using representational speech to describe it.

Developing concepts and semantic understanding

Piaget and others believe that the thought, concept, or understanding must be present in a child's mind before words can be more than imitated sounds. Children conceive an idea or thought before they are aware of the words to express it; then, as the words become part of the situation, the words have meaning. Teaching the words and demonstrating a concept like classification before children have conceived the idea of classifying, does not lead to their understanding of the concept. An exception might occur if a child were close to the point of understanding classification.

Then the discussion and terminology might trigger understanding.

An important implication for working with elementary school youngsters is that if teachers take cues for learning experiences from children, they can be fairly sure that the basic concepts are already in their thinking, even though not explicit. Further exploration of the ideas can perhaps clarify these concepts and develop related ones that children only partially understand or that are below a child's level of awareness. In other words, the child was ready to develop those ideas but would not have been likely to do so at this time without relevant exploration and discussion.

Billy had learned in rote fashion to count to ten but had no clear idea of what the number words meant. He had also learned by imitation to spread out one hand and say, "I'm five years old." He began piling up blocks and saying, "I make eight, nine, ten stand up." But Sam, his partner, would say, "No, you don't, you only have seven." When Billy objected, Sam would defend his contention by counting the blocks and pointing to each as he said the number. Billy then "counted" but did not stay with the one-to-one concept. Each day he challenged Sam with the number of blocks he could pile up. After several days of similar interchange, Sam grew tired of Billy's lack of understanding. Putting a finger on each block in turn, Sam very deliberately counted to eight. Billy imitated but put in some numbers between blocks and came out with ten. Sam said, "No, look!" He took Billy's finger and put it on each block as he said one number at a time. Then Sam said, "Now, you do it."

Since Billy's experience with block building and counting had been going on for some time, he already understood that there was some relationship between the words and the number of blocks, but he did not know quite what it was. The days of piling and "counting" and having Sam correct him, along with his gradually maturing understanding of many other relationships, enabled Billy to make the next connection. If all of these factors had not been present, he still would not

have been able to follow through. Soon on his own he was counting many things. He had a birthday and to his spread-out-hand he added one finger from the other. "Now I'm six, one more than five." He had taken another step.

Billy had been using words that did not express thought until the specifically needed experience made the words meaningful. His rote learning and verbalizing may have delayed understanding. For the child who is not yet ready and able to develop a particular concept, an experience like Billy's can be a necessary preliminary one. It can do no harm *as long as* children are never put in the position of feeling they have failed to meet the teacher's expectations. Productive learning situations provide opportunities for as long, and only as long, as children wish to explore them. In this way children's concepts and understandings, and their ability to express them in language with meaning, can progress from each child's own developmental level, without the fear of failure.

These procedures for developing concepts and understanding may involve five minutes or five weeks. They may involve one child or several or the whole group. If children wish to explore areas in which the teacher does not feel competent, they can extend the teacher's own learning. Such activities create self-confidence and valuable opportunities for decision-making on the part of children, who acquire considerable satisfaction and self-confidence from knowing something the teacher does not. In the process, the children are putting language to work for their own personal growth as individuals.

How language works

There are four major ways to examine how language works. The first is grammar, which includes the relationship of words in a sentence, the structuring of the sentence, and the forms of words.

The second perspective is the way individuals put language to work. A child learns much in general understanding, in attitudes, and in beliefs through testing them out linguistically. The child—or adult—attempts to express a thought or feeling in order to find out what kind of response the listener will give.

The third way language works is through its role in human relations. The words and the way they are used can convey more than the surface meaning of the communication.

The fourth perspective considers the effect of the social situation on communication. In addition to the immediate situation, both life-style and social class put constraints on language.

How language works grammatically

Grammar has long been a threat to both teachers and children, largely because it was the wrong kind of grammar. Until recently, with the impact of *structural linguistics* and later *transformational generative grammar*, most grammar was a formal and immutable structure. It set forth rules to be learned and applied. It was mechanistic and its use was based largely on rote memory of prescriptive rules. Teaching of this grammar remained general school practice more than twenty years after a summary of more than 200 research studies unanimously found that knowledge of the rules of grammar made no difference in a person's speaking or writing. Its only value was to help students do better on grammar tests (Green, 1947)!

Grammar has been, and perhaps still is, one of the most confusing of all the misunderstood areas of the language arts. New approaches and aspects are still being suggested and fought for. Nothing at present indicates an end to this movement toward a more complete understanding of how to produce effective communication. (See Appendix A.)

Grammar according to the linguists *Linguistics*, which has been called a theory of the nature of language, came to the fore as a different way of thinking about language. A group of linguists had for some time been considering the structure of

language and developing understanding of its use. They were called structural linguists and their field of knowledge, structural linguistics. They were primarily concerned with spoken rather than written language and worked mainly on a system for the classification of parts of speech. They defined the total linguistic meaning of language as the lexical meanings of the separate words, plus the structural meaning of the sentence.

Out of structural linguistics developed the field of transformational grammar supported by a group of linguists led by Noam Chomsky. This group's goal was to explain the way language is used. They worked mainly with language in its ideal form, dismissing for the time being variations in the language by special groups speaking other than a standard dialect. They studied what is called the standard speech of adults and particularly the way children develop their spoken language from their first intentional expression to near adult usage. By examining language as it is, they devised rules by which to explain the various constructions. The rules they propose are not arbitrary procedures to be followed explicitly, but rather ways language accomplishes various functions or purposes. They say, this is the way users of standard English speak and write, rather than, these are the rules you must use.

Transformational grammar

Noam Chomsky has for many years been a leader in exploring how language works, introducing the concept of transformational generative grammar (1957). He followed this idea with various extensions and modifications explained in his *Aspects of a Theory of Syntax* (1965). He produced a simplified version in a periodical (1968) hoping for wider understanding of his ideas. He has emphasized *linguistic universals* as the basic elements of the thought to be communicated: what the communication is about and what the person wishes to say about it. The speaker can then expand on these two elements.

This grammar is almost entirely descriptive. It describes the various ways a "string of utterances," a sentence, can be transformed into other related sentences, that is, how these other sentences are generated. For example: (1) John saw Sally. (2) Sally was seen by John. (3) Did John see Sally? (4) Was Sally seen by John? These are the simplest of the transformations, and as the sentences grow longer and more complex so do their transformations.

Halliday (1970) has analyzed the various functions of language on three bases: (1) the expression of the ideational, or cognitive, meaning; (2) the interpersonal, or interactions between people; and (3) the textual component, or thematic structure. His approach is evident in the title of one of his publications, *Learning How to Mean: Explorations in the Development of Language* (1977). In relation to the grammatical use of subject-predicate-object, he finds that the grammatical, the logical, and the psychological subjects may be different in any one sentence.

Other proposed modifications center on the inclusion of the semantic as well as the syntactic in generative theory. A doctoral study (Maxwell, 1972) deals with semantic relationships that were proposed as logical and relational but not transformational (for example, kill-die, enjoy-amuse). Perfetti (1972) also discusses the semantic conception of syntactic relations, syntactic semantics, and semantic features as components of lexical meaning.

Schank and Wilks (1973) join those who say that linguistic theory must deal with the ways humans use language, such as understanding in context, and the use of inferential information. They feel that Chomskyan generative linguistics is for the purpose of generating sentences that satisfy some criterion of correctness. Thus they raise the issue of the way language *can* be used versus the way it actually *is* used.

Surface and deep structure The concept of surface structure and deep structure also developed. *Surface structure* is the order in which words are combined when they are spoken or written. *Deep structure* is the idea, the thought being expressed. The surface structure is the same in the two similar sentences *Mother told Mary to buy some shoes* and *Mother promised Mary to buy some shoes*. But the deep structure differs because in the first, Mary will do the buying and in the second, Mother will. In order to understand language, one must be able to understand the deep structure or what the real meaning is. Some people who have studied the thought processes believe it is the deep structure, the meaning, often without words, that is stored in the memory.

Some of the more important specifics of grammar are the basic structures of sentences, such as noun phrases and verb phrases; that is, nouns with their modifiers and verbs with their modifiers. Noun phrases include (1) the subject, or what we wish to talk about, and (2) usually an object, direct or indirect. Verb phrases include an action (*makes*), linking (*is*), or relational (*belongs*) word that expresses the relationship between the subject and the object.

Form and structure words On another dimension we have two basic categories of words, *form words* and *structure words*. The form words, sometimes called class words, include nouns, verbs, and modifiers such as *red* and *softly*. Structure words or function words are the words that show the relationships of parts of the sentence—the connectors, like conjunctions and prepositions, and what are called *markers*. Markers may be words such as *an* and *the*, other modifiers such as *this* and *these*, and also endings to words, like those that indicate verb tense. For example, *the* consistently acts as a noun marker and *-ed* as a verb marker. They are called markers because they mark words as nouns or verbs and may identify them as singular or plural, or determine the tense of the verb. Markers are added to the young child's vocabulary later than the form words. We find they are also recognized later in the reading process. They seem to be picked up incidentally on the basis of meaning, for adults seldom discuss them with children. Children seem to be unaware of their own use of markers even into school age.

Phrase structure The structural linguists devised a way to illustrate structure in somewhat the way traditional grammarians did with their sentence diagramming. These illustrations are called "trees." NP is a noun phrase and VP is a verb phrase; the trees are produced in a series of steps.

Rules:

1. S (sentence)   NP + VP

2. NP (noun phrase)   T + N

3. VP (verb phrase)   V + NP

4. T (article)   the

5. N (noun)   boy, ball

6. V (verb)   hit

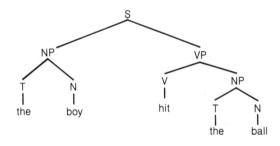

Here is an illustration of phrase structure grammar. Questions arose about other forms of the sentence, such as *What did the boy hit?* In the subject-verb-object form it would read *The boy did hit what?* So *ball* and *what* have the same function in the sentence. In the diagram, the right side would show *did hit* in place of *hit* and *what* in place of *the ball* directly under the NP. The rule, then, for forming the question is to replace the word *ball* with a question word and move it to the beginning of the sentence. This is a very simple illustration of what

is meant by transforming sentences, or transformational generative grammar. The term *generative* is added to indicate that the basic sentence can, through various transformations, generate a number of different sentences.

Teachers need to have a deep understanding of the basic principles of grammar as a description of how meaning is communicated by the form and order of words. Beyond this, they need to be able to use these generalizations to make their own speech and writing more effective and to gain more precise meaning from listening and reading.

How much grammar will teachers need to teach children? Certainly no rules to follow or diagrams to make! Rather, as teachers recognize the grammatical problems of individuals, they need to ask children how others will understand their talking and writing, and how they think they might express their thought differently so people can understand more easily. In doing this, teachers will want to take into consideration several factors: (1) the maturity of the child; (2) the current stage of the child's language development and dialect; (3) the relative importance of the problem in relation to other principles of grammar; and (4) perhaps the most important, the relative significance at that time of a change in talking or writing in relation to the child's developing concept of self as a successful communicator. Maintaining feelings of competence is more important than any single change in language at any particular time.

How language works for the individual

While the linguists find out how language works by studying the language as spoken, the psycholinguists attempt to find out how people deal with language mentally to make it serve their purposes. Scholars in the field admit they are only at the threshold of understanding the nature of language and thought and their interrelations.

Children's early development of oral language is stimulated and influenced substantially by their speech environments. They learn how to make their needs and desires known, how to get some of the information they want and need, and how to relate to others in many ways through speech. They extend and refine this tool as they continue to use it for many purposes.

Self-talk, either with or without listeners, is a way of learning to think about things. As children hear themselves echoing or passing along others' suggestions or commands, they react by building these expressions into their own behavioral controls. In order to learn, children need to put new knowledge in their own words.

Older children and adults are more capable of silent self-dialogue and directed thinking. Yet, if we are aware of our own speech and that of other adults, we recognize how frequently we work out our positions on issues, reaffirm or modify our beliefs and behavioral controls, absorb and integrate new knowledge, and test different ways of thinking about things through talking. Since children must do most of these tasks through overt speech, it is essential that the child have many such opportunities.

As children progress, other linguistic tasks they must master are:

Ordering information when giving directions or explanations so listeners can follow

Taking account of the discrepancy between their own informational position, background, and experience and that of their listeners

Shifting their style of speech according to their listeners or their purposes

Being aware of their point of view so as to be consistent and change only by intention

Analyzing their information in relation to the problem to be solved

How language works in human relations

While linguists explain how language works, other researchers are building on their findings to come closer to the heart of the communication process. These investigators are *sociolinguists*, those con-cerned with the way language actually operates in interaction in the everyday world.

Linguists deal mainly with language as an expression of meaning, in the sense of giving information. Sociolinguists are concerned with the interpersonal and social meanings of language. They deal with the relationship of language and people in a society, with how language is used, and what effect it has. They study not only the patterns of language but more particularly the patterns of usage that underlie communication. Each of us communicates in a complex physical environment with its own unique social and cultural background.

Constraints School is an environment that influences all communication that takes place within it. Many teachers see their role as one that restrains their natural feelings and impulses. When they feel they must play a role not entirely natural to them, they are vulnerable to reactions of peers as well as to those of the children. Children anticipate or "read" expectations of teachers that put severe constraints on their communication, limiting and modifying it. Children respond with an eye to the reactions of their peers also and often are caught in a dilemma between the two. How each child responds depends on his or her self-concept, the relationships already established with teacher, peers, and people in general, previous experiences in any similar situation, conception of what school is, and cultural and family background.

Children often adopt resisting behaviors that are puzzling and disturbing to teachers. One boy read mechanically in a monotone because he felt reading with expression was "sissy." Another group adopted two strategies: Either keep your mouth shut in class, or if you give the right answer, counteract the "fink effect" by sprinkling your response with stigmatized language (Shuy, 1974).

Teachers need to be aware of cultural differences and their effect on children's reactions to the school situation. For instance, many cultures have an oral tradition in which reading and writing have little part. When children sense a lack of understanding or respect for their culture, they may feel that the dominant society is imposing its own culture through the requirements of the school. Thus, mutual distrust may build so that learning is minimized. It is important, therefore, that teachers try to avoid actions, words, and non-verbal signals that children may interpret negatively. Also, the way a school program is planned and carried out can help children to see school as an important and enjoyable experience.

The topic discussed and the function of that discussion also put restraints on a person's response. We are all aware that there are some subjects we discuss only with family and close friends, and some we discuss only with one friend. Some feel more constraints than others, but probably few ever feel completely free of any restraint past early childhood.

The way we express ourselves may be as restricted as the topic. Most of us have command of several language levels, including what has been called the "homey" or informal, "company" language, and perhaps formal speech for those who speak to groups in either prepared or spontaneous situations. Children quickly learn the difference between playground talk and classroom talk, between talking with peers and talking to the teacher. Whether these differences should exist and to what degree is a question deserving serious consideration and requiring an in-depth look at how the school creates this environment.

How what one says is received by others depends on many factors: the connotative as well as the denotative meaning of the words (do the words have special meanings to people because of past incidents?); the intonation, emphasis, and timing; other nonverbal aspects such as facial expression and body position and action; and the relationship already established between individuals involved.

How language is affected by social context

The social context of various cultural and economic groups affects children's communication in a number of ways since they speak the language they hear. We hear casual talk, the more careful speech of the better educated, and talk affected by the cultural mores, the language, and the speech patterns of ethnic groups. American Indians, particularly the children, are known for reticence, while the communication of some other cultures is marked by great volubility. Two resultant language characteristics will be mentioned briefly here.

Dialects   As these speech communities develop, the language they use is referred to as dialects. Because dialects vary in speech communities, communication between different groups is hampered. When poverty is also a factor, people tend to be less accepting of the dialect. As educators saw the devastating effects of poverty on children, particularly in groups with a nonstandard dialect, they labeled them as "culturally disadvantaged." Many school people saw the speech of the "culturally disadvantaged" as undeveloped and inadequate, and even as an indication of lack of ability to learn. Their children's culture and the language they grew up with were blamed. However, Gumperz documents that injustice.

> Recent systematic research in the inner city has successfully disproved the notions of those who characterize the language of low income populations as degenerate and structurally underdeveloped. There is overwhelming evidence to show that when both middle-class and non-middle-class children, no matter what their native language, dialect, or ethnic background, come to school at the age of five or six, they have control of a fully formed grammatical system (Gumperz, 1972, p. 84).

Restricted speech   Restricted speech is speech that can be understood only by people with relevant shared experience. Studies of the speech of certain groups in England called attention to the issue. Working on the sociology of language, Bernstein (1971a) found that the children of the working class frequently used restricted speech inappropriately.

Everyone uses restricted speech. People living and/or working together use sentences like "I sent that off today and he should receive it by Monday" or "Do you think it will work?" or "Why don't we let her do it?" If the first restricted statement were elaborated, it might become "I mailed my job application to Mr. Johnson today, and he should receive it Monday." The person to whom these messages are addressed usually understands them perfectly. This type of interchange is *context-dependent* and may be called *particularistic*. When meaning does not depend on shared experiences, speech is called *elaborated*, *context-independent*, or *universalistic*.

When individuals use restricted speech with those who do not know the context or background the speaker has in mind, the message is meaningless. Many young children from all social groups use restricted speech inappropriately, but those who have limited experience beyond their families and immediate neighborhoods need special help in learning when to elaborate.

Evaluation of language development

Evaluation, as always, needs to be related to goals. The most important goal is *continuous growth in the effectiveness with which each child uses language*. Under this heading we can ask various questions:

Is the child increasingly comfortable and self-confident in using the language that he or she brought to school?

Is the child increasingly able to make himself or herself understood by both peers and adults, adapting natural speech as necessary for better communication?

Is the child increasingly showing evidence, in speech with peers and adults, of using language to internalize new knowledge, attitudes, and feelings?

Is the child increasing the maturity of his or her language as indicated by T-units or other means?

Is the child increasingly able to understand, through context, the ambiguous use of words and constructions in others' speech or writing?

Is the child increasingly aware of personal point of view and position on issues so as to be internally consistent and aware of any change?

Is the child increasingly able to change or modify speech to make it more appropriate to the purpose and situation?

Is the child increasingly able to use language to improve relationships with others?

Is the child increasingly using and developing thinking skills along with language?

In evaluation of language development, the important aspect is each child's own growth, not a comparison of his or her language with that of others. The most useful tool for evaluation is observation of children interacting with one another in both formal and informal situations. Teachers' conversations with them, both individually and in groups, provide useful data. Tapes children make for other purposes also can be used to provide evidence of growth in some areas of evaluation.

The most useful tool is the child's self-evaluation when purposefully established. Just as we must know our goals for children before we can begin to evaluate, so each child must be aware of what he or she wants to accomplish. Group and individual discussions near the beginning of the year can set the stage for both learning and subsequent evaluation. As children set their own goals, they are thereby making a commitment toward those goals. Such commitment is the most effective motivation possible for learning. As each child periodically evaluates progress toward those goals, the commitment is renewed.

In discussing self-evaluation with the child, the teacher can ask how the child feels about learning and what causes these feelings. If the response is too general, the child needs help in looking at specific instances. Some children look only at their successes, which may be a valuable experience for

Basic principles for developing language competence

In these first three background chapters, we have formulated ten basic principles for the development of children's communication skills. In the chapters that follow, we will apply these principles to the four areas of language development—listening, talking, writing, and reading—and suggest guidelines for their use in helping children to develop competence in each of these areas. The principles are equally appropriate for all the areas because of extensive interrelationships and mutual interdependence.

1. Communication occurs to the extent that one's thoughts and feelings are understood by another.

Whatever does not convey meaning, does not communicate. Just as we cannot assume the listener or reader understands what we have said or written, we cannot assume that children understand the words they speak or write. Only other evidence of understanding can prove attainment of meaning by either giver or receiver.

2. Communication develops through constructive experiences that promote the child's self-confidence as a communicator.

By our reactions to children's talking, we need to encourage them to continue, for it is obvious that children cannot develop their talking ability without talking. The same is true of the other aspects of language use—listening, writing, and reading. Even as mature adults, we seldom voluntarily put ourselves in a position where we expect negative reactions and criticism. Nor will we usually put forth much effort to accomplish

something if we have little confidence or expectation of success.

3. Children discover how language works through communication with peers and adults.

Children discover how language works; they develop the ability to use a very complex language with little or no direct teaching. By developing their ability to listen, they learn to use the language they hear. To a considerable extent, they also discover how to write and how to read.

4. Children's own language is most useful as a basis for growth and development of communication skills.

All children come to school with a well-developed oral language, with the exception of those few severely handicapped by deafness, extreme mental deficiency, or other disabilities. Since children have grown up in families and communities with widely differing speech and word-usage patterns, each child's speech is unique. The child's unique experience determines what is meaningful. Skills and knowledge must begin on an individual basis with the speech and meanings that each child uses at that time.

5. Children's communication develops through their need to understand others' thoughts and have others understand theirs.

Just as children's language skills developed from infancy because of an overwhelming need to understand and be understood, so they continue to develop through frequent and free exchanges with peers and adults. This need for mutual understanding ensures that children will work intuitively at ways to achieve it. Suggestions provided by others will be put to use only as children feel they are useful.

6. Children learn only through experiencing and internalize the learning through their own verbalizing of it.

Before children are seven or eight, concepts can be achieved only through concrete manipulation. For most children concepts need to be expressed in terms of a concrete experience until they are about twelve, after which they can begin to deal meaningfully with verbal logic. Before that time children need to explore concretely and put their findings and observations into their own words to make them their own. Concepts put into words by others are either repeated by rote memory with little understanding, or are really meaningless.

7. Children learn much intuitively and often cannot explain how they know.

Before children are seven or eight, most of their learning is intuitive. Intuitive learning is the ability to respond in ways that individuals have never been taught, an ability developed below the level of consciousness. Such learning may include concepts and information previously "taught" but not understood until they are discovered through experiencing.

8. Each child's development and experiencing is unique; no two have all the same learnings at the same time.

Since children have learned different things at various times because of different experiences, children's needs at any one time are different. Total group teaching of skills inevitably involves trying to teach what some children already know, what others are not ready for, and what only some may need and find appropriate. Since we learn only what we can bring relevant meaning to, teaching requires individualization, not always in a one-to-one situation, but at least in specifically identified temporary groups.

9. Children extract meaning, the core of the communication, and express it in language natural to them at that time.

Thoughts and meanings are conceived through experiencing, by sensing interrelationships of previous understandings, or their relationship to current situations. Children may become aware of these concepts either without words or with only key words. They may then express the thought in their own language without conscious selection of either words or structure.

10. Children's learning occurs through involvement with materials and activities they perceive as valuable.

Children easily become involved with materials and procedures that have personal meaning for them. While teachers have some basis for choosing such materials and procedures, they can never be sure of the validity of their choices. To ensure personal involvement, each child needs to be able to choose from a wide selection. When the learner is not involved, learning is negligible.

These broad, comprehensive principles will become increasingly meaningful as their effects on instructional decisions in all the language arts areas are described in the following chapters. As teachers use them in making decisions about instructional procedures, these principles take on ever increasing significance.

those who are less sure of themselves, as long as they are making reasonable progress. If they are not, the teacher needs to question whether the learning attempted is appropriate to their maturity, their previous learning, and their perceptions of its value for them. If it meets these criteria, perhaps they need help in knowing how to accomplish it. The teacher can ask how they think they might go about this learning, and offer suggestions if they need help. They may then select a procedure to which they can make a commitment.

More of the children will minimize their progress than overestimate it. By asking them to think of specific gains, and reminding them of progress they do not recognize, the teacher can give them a basis for knowing what to look for, provide support, and make a small contribution toward their self-confidence.

Summary

In this chapter, we have considered the beginnings of speech in the very young child, the development of language throughout the elementary school years, and studies of the way language develops at various stages.

We next explored how language works. How language works grammatically is a useful understanding for teachers but has more indirect than direct relevance for children's learning. At the elementary level language development is more effectively accomplished in terms of the purpose and effect of what children say, rather than the abstract logic of grammar. We next considered how language works for the individual and how it works in human relations. Finally, we looked at the effect of the social context on children and their language. We established basic principles that will provide guidelines for children's learning in each of the language areas. We then provided a basis for evaluating language development.

Suggested learning experiences for prospective teachers

Suggestion A

Become aware of children's ability to use language before they come to school. Arrange to talk with one or more children four or five years of age. If possible, tape their conversation either with you or with their peers. Later transcribe the conversation. Note the maturity of the sentence structure and the breadth of vocabulary. Consider the following questions:

1. Is there evidence of a dialect different from your own? Does this affect your understanding of the child's meaning? If so, how and why?

2. What evidence do you have that the language recorded is typical of children of that age?

3. Do you feel different about young children's language as a result of this experience? Why?

Suggestion B

Using T-units, determine the maturity of a child's talking and/or writing.

1. Read Hunt's discussion of T-units.

2. Ask an elementary school child of any age to tell a story and give you permission to tape-record it.

3. Transcribe the tape and apply the T-unit measurement. Do you have questions about its use? If so, raise them with your group or your instructor.

4. Ask permission of children who can write to use some of their written material. Apply the T-unit measurement and compare the results with those of oral language. Is there a significant difference? Why?

Suggestion C

Become aware of language structures children may not yet understand.

1. Involve one or more children seven or eight years old. Use some of the sentences discussed in the section Language Structures Learned Later or some from the article by Bormuth. Ask the children what these sentences mean.

2. Since most of the illustrative sentences are not typical of classroom discussion, write some sentences that you might use with children.

3. Revise these statements so that you feel sure all children would understand them.

Suggestion D

Increase your awareness of the interpersonal or social meanings of language as they differ from the common dictionary meanings (connotative vs. denotative). In your own conversation with other adults or in conversations you overhear, note meanings dependent on special situations. Listen for use of language that, without direct statement,

1. Builds or implies a close relationship

2. Indicates race or sex bias

3. Excludes one or more members of a group talking together

4. Implies a "put down"

5. Indicates feelings of superiority

Suggested readings

Recognized authorities on children's language include Noam Chomsky, Carl Lefevre, Mario Pei, Jean Piaget, and Lev S. Vygotsky. Materials for getting acquainted with their thinking are Chomsky, "Language and the Mind"; Lefevre, *Linguistics, English, and the Language Arts*; Pei, *Language Today: A Survey of Current Linguistic Thought* or his older but revised *All About Language*; Piaget, *Language and Thought of the Child*; and Vygotsky's *Thought and Language*. Dell Hymes' introduction to Cazden, John, and Hymes' *Function of Language in the Classroom* provides an overview of the structure and use of language. Other background materials include Dan Slobin's *Psycholinguistics*, which explains complex theories; Kellogg Hunt's *Syntactic Maturity in School Children and Adults*, which describes the maturing structure of the language; and Halliday's *Learning How to Mean: Explorations in the Development of Language*.

The way children acquire and develop their language is explained in James Britton's *Language and Learning*; in Hopper and Naremore's *Children's Speech: A Practical Introduction to Communication Development*; in Courtney Cazden's *Child Language and Education*; and in Walter Loban's research report, *Language Development: Kindergarten through Grade 12*. Mary Lorton provides many illustrated activities to help kindergarten primary children develop language skills in *Workjobs: Activity-Centered Learning for Early Childhood Education*.

Since dialects of school children have become an issue, teachers need a background for the discussion. Three valuable books are Maehr and Stallings (eds.), *Culture, Child, and School*; Staten Webster, *Knowing and Understanding the Socially Disadvantaged: Ethnic Minority Groups*; and Dell Hymes' introduction to Cazden, John, and Hymes, *Function of Language in the Classroom*.

Strategies for children's learning

Structure and the marker

Purpose.   To help children use markers in understanding language.

Appropriate level.   Nines through elevens.

Participants.   All children.

Situation.   As children begin to think about how language conveys meaning over and above the meaning of separate words, they can become aware of what markers indicate.

Teacher role.   To set up a situation in which children use their intuitive knowledge of language structure to (1) identify various markers, and (2) to figure out what they indicate.

Procedures

1. Provide each child with a copy of "The Jabberwocky" from Lewis Carroll's *Alice in Wonderland*.

2. Ask the children to find a nonsense word that is a noun, the name of something. Ask how they know it is a noun. As children find many other nouns, encourage them to generalize about noun markers.

3. Proceed in the same way with verbs, adverbs, and adjectives. Encourage group discussion and ask open questions if necessary to refocus.

Evaluation.   Do children show evidence of being aware of markers in material they read? Are they consciously using them to help interpret material somewhat difficult for them? Record any significant learning or what needs to be learned.

Giving directions

Purpose.   To help children learn to give clear directions.

Appropriate level.   All ages.

Participants.   Those who have not yet learned to give clear directions.

Situations.   From early childhood on, all people need to give directions on occasion. As children are permitted more responsibility in the classroom, they will need to give directions more often.

Teacher role

1. To help children decide on ways to give directions that can be followed easily and accurately.

2. To provide situations in which children experience giving directions.

3. To encourage evaluation of direction giving.

Procedures

1. Encourage group discussion of the purpose of giving directions in a specific situation, and what it is that those directed are expected to accomplish.

2. Discuss the sequential nature of effective directions, beginning with where the directed person(s) is in location or understanding.

3. Provide opportunities for a number of children to decide on directions they want to give, give them, and have the directed child or children evaluate their effectiveness, along with the rest of the group.

Directions a child might give include: where to find a needed article, how to use a piece of equipment, how to produce a certain paper sculpture or artistic effect, how to revise writing for more effective communication, or how to play a game.

Evaluation.   Evaluation is most effective when it comes from those directed. Any such comments can be useful feedback. Record results when a child gives directions; indicate improvements and what needs yet to be learned.

Special occasion talk

Purpose. To help children plan appropriate speech for special situations.

Appropriate level. All levels as needed.

Participants. All children.

Situation. Guests, expected or unexpected, from within or outside the school, and special occasions provide excellent learning situations for this kind of language learning.

Teacher role

1. To raise the issue of how to handle situations involving people outside the classroom.

2. To help children plan and role-play various ways of responding on a variety of occasions.

Procedures

1. Using a past or projected occasion as a basis, encourage children to suggest the following: individual responsibilities; what to say and do; and the role of each child in the group during the specific occasion. For instance, who responds when someone comes to the door—a particular child or whoever is closest? How does one talk to an expected visitor, to an unexpected or unknown visitor? Under what circumstances does one child handle the whole situation? When does one refer the visitor to the teacher? What is the responsibility of others in the group? With five- and six-year-olds, initial discussion would involve one specific situation. With eleven-year-olds, one discussion at the beginning of the year might cover all likely situations. Follow-up is needed if planned procedures break down, or a special situation requiring different guidelines is anticipated.

2. After identification of specific situations, several children take turns role-playing different responsibilities.

3. When no more alternatives are offered, the group evaluates those presented and settles on guidelines to be used.

Evaluation. The first assessment relates to children's effectiveness of carrying out planned interchanges. A more important evaluation occurs as we observe the appropriateness and spontaneity of student responses in related impromptu situations. Identify to what extent children have internalized the essence of using language effectively for their own purpose. Record the effectiveness of the responding child and note any improvement or behaviors yet to be learned.

Appropriate talk

Purpose. To help children learn that talk needs to be appropriate to a situation, especially when dealing with private information.

Appropriate level. All ages.

Participants. All children.

Situation. Sometimes children give private or personal information to others inappropriately. Children are likely to divulge family matters or reveal personal information about others, especially those with whom they are angry.

Teacher role

1. To help children establish guidelines as to what is and what is not appropriate to say to whom and under what circumstances.

Procedures

1. Initiate discussion of the difference between public talk and private talk; include family information, information about others, and details about oneself.

2. Help children develop guidelines for making decisions; for instance, happy situations are safer to report than problems. When the information involves others, usually find out if they object to having it known. When it involves oneself, the decision is one's own. Here the teacher needs to be alert to the child who is implicitly asking for help by frequently being disparaging.

3. Discuss tattling and help children see: (1) that broadcasting negative comments about others may be unfair; (2) complete details are seldom available and people's perceptions differ widely; (3) insignificant incidents are best ignored; (4) a harmful or dangerous matter should be reported to *those who can do something about it*. Unwillingness of adults to get involved in such reporting may be partially the result of children being told "Don't tattle." Teachers have a responsibility to help children distinguish between tattling and reporting hazardous conditions to authorities. Examples of incidents or situations that should be reported are behaviors that are likely to cause serious physical harm, malicious gossip that can create serious problems in personal relations, or destruction of public property or that of others.

Evaluation. Are children internalizing the guidelines? Are children reporting serious situations to proper authorities, but refraining from discussing them publicly? Record incidents that indicate positive actions and those that indicate more understanding is needed.

Language changes

Purpose. To develop the concept that language change is constant and normal.

Appropriate level. Nine-year-olds and older.

Participants. All children, but probably not to the same extent.

Situation. Writers of earlier periods used words and phraseology different from that used today. Also, children may hear older people use expressions that are no longer common usage. New words are constantly being added to the language in newspapers, periodicals and books, and on radio and television.

Teacher role

1. To develop children's understanding that language and its use change as conditions and situations change.

2. To rouse children's curiosity about word origins.

Procedures

1. As children read books written in the nineteenth century (*Moby Dick* and *Twenty Thousand Leagues under the Sea* are illustrative of this type of book), suggest a child or a group of children select particularly difficult passages, rewrite them in their own style, then share the two versions with the entire group. Useful discussion of a variety of ways of expressing ideas can follow.

2. Encourage children to find words that are newly coined, used in a new way, or transformed into a different part of speech. (Note the current trend toward making verb forms from nouns and adjectives, such as *to pencil, to finalize*.) Suggest that the children explore how and why the word or use developed.

3. Help children develop ways of discovering word origins and recording their information. This activity can extend to words in common usage.

Suggest children use resource books to find where particular words originated. Suggest they start, on a chart or a bulletin board, a list of interesting words with their origins. (For example, *sandwich* was named for the fourth Earl of Sandwich in the eighteenth century. He was a great gambler. In order not to take time out from card playing, he invented a meal that could be eaten by hand without a dinner table or fork. It became known as the sandwich.)

Have children look for books with words, phrases, and language usage from another period, and suggest they share them with the group. (See Chapter 15, "Language in Flux," in Farb's *Word Play*.) Date of origin is roughly indicated by the year of publication of the first dictionary to include the word.

Evaluation. How rapidly does the children's recording of word origins grow? Is the involvement limited to a few, or do others show interest even though they do not contribute? Does children's writing give evidence of the awareness of new words and constructions? Record significant happenings.

II

ORAL COMMUNICATION: TALKING AND LISTENING

As adults, we usually talk, listen, then respond with no conscious thought of the words we use or the ways we combine them. Our attention is fixed on our purpose, rather than on the words we select as a means of attaining it. As teachers, however, we must focus attention on some vital questions about the communication process: How do individuals develop facility with oral language? Are all people equally competent in developing it? If not, why not? How does language work, and what do we need to know about it in order to use it more effectively? How can we help children to become more effective in both expressing and interpreting oral language?

Are we helping children to become more effective in expressing their feelings, their desires, their needs, and their concerns?

Are we helping children to interpret more accurately the feelings, desires, needs, and concerns of others, even when expressed indirectly or nonverbally?

Are we helping children to develop the ability to give and receive information more accurately, recognizing the effects of perception on communication?

Are we helping children to develop oral language as a more useful tool in dealing with all aspects of human living?

Oral communication has no content of its own but develops through the use of any and all content. A frequent error in the schools is to be aware of developing oral language competence only during "language period." Rather, such awareness needs to extend throughout the school day whenever a message is communicated.

The further development of thought processes is an essential part of all learning situations. Oral communication is particularly useful for the task because it provides immediate feedback on meaning. When listeners misinterpret our statements, we examine the thinking that produced them.

This section on the development of oral language skills deals with the use of language for both listening and talking. We explore the concepts, the problems, and some of the procedures used to increase children's skill in the give-and-take of oral language. Chapter 4 focuses on listening, and Chapter 5 on talking. Chapter 6 describes experiences that are interesting and fun for children, and at the same time extend their effective use of language.

LISTENING 4

Since children learn to speak the language that they hear, listening is the basis for learning all the skills of verbal communication. But hearing and listening are not the same thing. Hearing is a physical process dependent upon the function of the eardrum. Listening is a mental process dependent upon paying attention to what we hear. Our attention is selective. Since we could not possibly pay attention to all the sounds around us, we process an estimated 50 percent of the sounds we hear (Lundsteen, 1971). We select sounds we perceive to be important to us, but we ignore other sounds unless they become too persistent—like the incessant barking of a neighbor's dog.

There is more to listening than just hearing and paying attention. Listening provides the basis for response. Unless we react mentally to what we hear and pay attention to, we cannot say we are listening. We must understand (bring meaning to the sounds) and then respond through acceptance, rejection, or some other reaction. When we are puzzled by a noise we cannot identify or by a statement that does not make sense, we react by attempting to understand. Undoubtedly, the key to listening is understanding, or attempting to understand, what we hear.

But listening differs in one respect from the other communications skills. Listening is an ability we all utilize during every waking hour, yet the only evidence of listening is indirect. Consequently, researchers have been able to learn relatively little about the listening process, and no developmental stages of listening have been determined.

Although we will be focusing on listening, remember that it is only one facet of the whole of communication. We have all learned more than we realize through listening. Listening to different types of music may affect how we feel. Listening to thoughts expressed in literature modifies one's speech and writing, and may influence further reading. Effective listening promotes clear thinking and is essential to the comprehension of oral language. In this chapter we will examine the research findings that are available and consider what schools can do to improve the ability of children to listen effectively.

Comprehension of oral language

Both the speaker and the listener contribute significantly to the comprehension of oral language. The speaker must choose words that are familiar to the listener and place them in a coherent syntax. The listener's experience provides the background for understanding. In addition, the listener must pay attention, use thinking skills effectively, and feel confident of being able to understand.

Comprehension is most likely to result when all words are familiar and used in the way listeners themselves use them. However, a word may be familiar to the listeners in one context but not in another. When someone talks about riding the *coach*, for example, children may be reminded of the football coach at the weekend game on TV. Unless they can pick up useful context cues, meaning may be completely lost. When words used are completely unfamiliar, the listeners' only recourse is to use the context cues in the comment or the situation.

A second factor in comprehension is the listeners' ability to understand the message provided by the syntax. What meaning is signaled by the structure of the sentence, the series of sentences, the discourse? What is indicated by the order and arrangement of the content words and the function words? How simple or complex a statement can listeners understand?

The listeners' experience background provides a meaningful framework for what they hear. What concepts or ideas are available for integrating new knowledge? Comprehension will be slight if listeners have not developed a framework to hang new concepts and information on. Little learning will result, for instance, when children are asked to add fractions before they have internalized what the two numbers in a fraction really mean.

Comprehension is affected by a desire to pay close attention or a lack of interest in what listeners hear. Children listen more attentively to instructions for a field trip to the beach than to instructions for completing a work sheet. Their relationship to the speaker makes a difference, for they are accustomed to the way their friends or associates speak. Friends are likely to use the same words and have experiences and thoughts in common. When listeners think highly of the speaker, or tend to identify with him or her, comprehension is likely to increase.

The listeners' ability to use thinking skills effec-tively improves comprehension. Especially involved are the skills of inference, deduction, and problem solving, as well as memory.

The ever-present and often overriding factor is the listeners' confidence in their ability to understand what they hear—their self-images as listeners. If experience leads them to expect to understand, listeners usually monitor their comprehension and know when they do not. They will ask questions if they are given the opportunity and made to feel comfortable, and their efforts to understand will prevent difficulties that might arise later. Lack of comprehension is probable when listeners do not expect to understand.

Listening and talking

Listening is the reverse of talking in that one is the receiving of messages and the other is the sending of messages; however, one is not the mirror image of the other. Talking happens when experience and knowledge promote expression. Listening happens when sounds occurring externally elicit meaning from internalized experience.

Infants listen and experiment with their voicing equipment. Listening is experiencing that forms associations between certain sounds and specific people, things, or actions. Infants begin to internalize meanings relevant to certain sounds. When they want to express a meaning, they learn to produce a close approximation to the associated sound. When people begin to interpret their meaning correctly, children have made progress in learning to talk.

Children learn their paralanguage—rhythm, pitch, stress, and other aspects of intonation— from listening to others talk. They also learn the pronunciation of words from the speech of people around them. However, in both language and paralanguage, and in the attaching of language to meaning, each child is unique.

Listening and reading

Listening and reading are both intake processes in which people attempt to understand the thoughts and meanings of others. In both, the receiver is processing another's language in order to understand it, and there is a continual prediction of the forthcoming message. (Notice how often you can finish the sentence a speaker has started.) But comprehension is affected by significant differences between listening and reading. Time is more pressing in listening because unless it is possible to ask the speaker to repeat, the listener receives the message only once. Reading can be repeated as often as necessary. Aids to interpreting speech include intonation, emphasis, and the time-spacing of words into meaningful units. In reading, one must understand the meaning in order to group words and identify points of emphasis. A speaker's gestures, facial expressions, and other nonverbal cues help to provide meaning. Statements that are not clearly expressed are more likely to be interpreted correctly from speech than from the printed page.

Listening and communication

Oral communication is an exchange of spoken messages that contain information, feelings, and ideas. Receiving the message and understanding what is spoken may lead to an overt response, either verbal or nonverbal. We can say that listening is an *attempt* to get the message, just as speaking is an attempt to give a message. Either may or may not be successful.

The most important aspect of listening is the individual's personal reaction to the message. Though we may take in messages all day long, listening has no value if we do not understand so as to react in some way, sort the messages as to their importance, respond to the more important ones, and decide what if any action to take. Hence, thought processes triggered by listening must be considered an integral part of listening itself.

Purposes of listening

People listen to become aware of what is being said and what is going on. We "tune in," but whether we continue to pay attention depends on the messages we get. If they are important to us for any reason, we continue to listen. But we "tune out" if our experiences provide no basis for understanding, if the message is not relevant to our interests, if we are getting nothing out of it for ourselves. We will continue to hear (as the sound waves impinge on our eardrums), but our minds are no longer dealing with the ideas and information expressed.

When we try to force ourselves to listen because we "ought to," our attention is divided between listening and reminding ourselves to listen. Or we may continue to hear sounds but refuse or be unable to deal with the concepts that the words express.

The main purpose of listening is to find out information of importance to us, not only facts but also the feelings and perceptions of others. This kind of listening provides much of the data on which we operate.

As a society, we have neglected one of the most rewarding reasons for listening—listening for enjoyment and appreciation. People who are concentrated in large cities have ready access to orchestras and choral groups, and nearly everyone has easy access to radios, television sets, and record players. But many people have not learned to listen appreciatively. Because of our hectic lifestyle, we turn on a television program and then ignore it as we concentrate on something else. People turn on the radio when they are uncomfortable about being alone with their thoughts. Stereo provides the background "noise" that makes conversation unnecessary or impossible. In our noisy big-city environments there are many people who seldom have the opportunity to listen to birds singing or streams tumbling over rocks. In our own preoccupation, we have neglected to share with children the rewards of listening for enjoyment.

Research reports on listening

Less research work has been done in the field of listening than in other language arts areas. Lundsteen (1971) reports that 90 percent of the research in listening has been done since 1952, and less than 1 percent of the content of textbooks was devoted to listening lessons by 1967. Three reasons for the lack of research are (1) the implicit nature of listening, (2) the lack of agreement on a clear definition for listening, and (3) the nearly impossible task of isolating listening for testing purposes.

Units of meaning

The most important research, which explores how we understand language, has led to the conclusion that we do not understand language as a series of separate words. Rather, we understand it in meaningful units, phrases, or "chunks of meaning." This discovery is consistent with much that we already knew, for example, that intonation patterns are based on units of meaning. One-word utterances can be sentences in the situational context, but otherwise isolated words are meaningless, for meaning is generated through the relationships of words.

Interest in units of meaning grew out of research using compressed speech to find how "fast" people can listen. Ralph Nichols proposed that we can listen "faster" than a person can talk. Investigators were unable to test this hypothesis by speeding up a record because when a record is speeded up, the pitch is raised and the material becomes unintelligible. The solution was to delete tiny sections of the recorded material and then to introduce time-spacing between various units (Aaronson and Markowitz, 1967).

In transferring the spacing procedure to natural language, Martin (1968) found that placing a space after every word in a sentence *reduced* the accuracy of recall. It is easier to remember a sentence spoken in natural phrasing than a sentence spoken word-by-word. Other studies by Wales and Marshall (1966) and Anglin and Miller (1968) confirmed the importance of phrasing. Friedman and Johnson (1969, pp. 39–40) found that natural spacing served as an organizing function for the lis-

teners so that the entire string of discourse became easier to recall without error.

The structure of language

If the listener must recognize the structure of a sentence in order to understand it, then perhaps slight pauses between phrases facilitate recognition of the underlying syntactic structure. This recognition of relationships is really a confirmation of the nature of language, as Lenneburg notes.

> Virtually every aspect of language is the expression of relations. . . . For instance, in all languages of the world, words label a set of relational principles instead of being labels of specific objects. . . . Further, no language has ever been described that does not have a second order of relational principles, namely, principles in which relations are being related, that is, syntax in which relations between words are being specified (Lenneburg, 1969, pp. 640-641).

Friedman and Johnson add

> There are relationships among sentences also, as attested by the fact that readers can identify paragraph boundaries in unindented prose passages . . . and can reduce the content of a paragraph to summary form. . . . *Comprehension as a process can be understood, then, as the recognition of relationships, within and between sentences.* . . . it seems plausible to suppose that an important aspect of selective listening involves the directing of attention to relational cues (Friedman and Johnson, 1969, pp. 77–78 [emphasis added]).

Two levels of selective attention in listening for relational cues are (1) listening for cues that identify the "core-meaning unit" within the sentence, and (2) listening for cues that identify the independent element in a group of sentences, the topic sentence. Friedman and Johnson suggest the following generalizations:

> 1. Whether a listener is decoding a single sentence or a well-formed text, the act of understanding is intricately associated with the process of selective attention: to identify the "core-meaning" of the message, as distinguished from its adjunct components (i.e., qualification, modification, comment, etc.).

2. In the identification of the "core-meaning," the listener is guided by structural cues: syntactic markers within the sentence, hyper-syntactic markers between sentences.

3. The perceptual processing of these structural cues requires time at critical junctures: temporal intervals at phrase boundaries for syntactic-semantic analysis within the sentence, temporal intervals between sentences for integration of each sentence with the portion of the text which preceded.

4. There is an implied hierarchy of processes: the evaluative judgments about the relative importance of elements within a sentence must be completed before that sentence can be evaluated for its relative importance to the text in which it occurs (Friedman and Johnson, 1969, p. 80).

First one must understand the "core-meaning" of what one hears, either one sentence or a longer unit, by using the structural cues as well as key content words. Spacing by units of meaning helps convey the "core-meaning," and one decides on the relative importance of the elements before deciding on total meaning. These decisions must be made almost instantaneously, which is a reason for "temporal intervals," or pauses. The process is a far cry from the traditional assumption that listeners arrive at understanding word-by-word as a message is produced. This study seems to explain how we understand language and to describe the process of comprehension in listening.

Another finding is that the listener does not need to hear or understand every word or every part of each word in order to understand the message, if the portion missed is not a key element. We all miss or disregard much that we hear. We often know our reactions or responses before the speaker has finished a statement, although we may sometimes guess the ending incorrectly. Thus, listening becomes a sampling, predicting, confirming process.

Because these studies show how people understand language, they also suggest ways of helping children to listen more effectively. For example, teachers need to consider how much of a new concept children need to hear in order to grasp the "core-meaning"—to find out what the concept is about. Then as teachers go over the concept, they need to provide time-spaces, or pauses, that children can use for fitting the new ideas into their understanding. We can use the # symbol to illustrate how a teacher might present the concept of addition: "Today we are going to talk about adding (drop voice, pause). When we add, # we put things together # to find out how many we have all together (drop voice, pause)." At each unit of meaning, the teacher allows time for children to internalize their understanding.

Since young children understand only what they have experienced concretely, the teacher will not describe addition until they have had experience with "putting things together" (such as blocks) and counting to see "how many we have all together." But when the process is verbalized and named, *adding*, the children need time to make the mental connections that seem so obvious to adults.

The teacher's own speaking needs to have rhythm, emphasis, and variation in pace and tone. Such clues help to indicate the important elements of a sentence and their relationships. These clues would be lacking in a dull monotone. When teachers model speech that is easy for others to listen to, children understand more accurately, develop an expectancy to understand, and adopt a more effective way of speaking, since they tend to speak like those they respect.

With the more mature children, teachers can discuss the importance of meaningful phrasing. As children make tape recordings or give oral reports, they can listen for their intonations that indicate the "chunks of meaning," the phrasing most helpful to the listener. By becoming more aware of structure and meaningful units, children will gain more meaning from both listening and reading.

Improvement of listening

A number of studies have tried to see whether listening could be made more effective among elementary school children. Since studies used different concepts of listening, different purposes for listening, different procedures for developing those listening skills, and different means of evaluation, any general conclusion is impossible. Among the listening skills various researchers tried to develop are:

Simple memorizing

Recalling facts

Recalling in series

Analyzing

Analyzing critically

Analyzing commercial propaganda

Analyzing and judging arguments

Following directions

Identifying main idea

Identifying sequence ambiguities

Identifying mood

Discriminating sounds

Distinguishing fact and opinion

Developing vocabulary

Hearing organizational pattern

Listening creatively

Listening for a specific purpose

Detecting speaker's purpose

Inferring purpose

Inferring main idea

Inferring connotative meanings

Practicing inference

Perceiving relationships

Predicting sequence

Reinstating sequence

Remembering story sequence

Organizing ideas

Noting details

Noting cause and effect

Judging logical validity

Judging propaganda

Applying standards

Providing examples

Increasing visualization

Generalizing

Interpreting

Concluding

Understanding

Appreciating

Enjoying

Conversing

This list of forty-one items came from relatively few studies and is included here to demonstrate vividly the lack of agreement about what listening is. The same items are important for the improvement of reading, and all are relevant to thinking. If teachers attempted to teach each skill in a specific instructional lesson for that purpose, only unimaginable confusion and inefficiency could result. We cannot build listening, reading, or thinking by piling up a multiplicity of minute items. Rather, children need to consider total meaningful experiences that have immediate significance. This consideration involves thinking and aids in developing oral language skills.

Procedures that increase test scores

One study used an eighteen-item listening response test (Steen, 1969). Each day for four weeks experimental groups were given a lesson emphasizing remembering, recalling in order, and analyzing what was heard. The control group had no particular listening experiences. Test scores for the experimental and control groups indicated significantly greater gains for the experimental group. There was no testing of carry-over to regular classroom situations.

In another study (Thompson, 1970) the Metropolitan Achievement Test was given to eighty-five first graders and fifteen second graders in the experimental group and to sixty-nine first graders and twenty second graders in the control group in December and May. The Wepman Auditory Discrimination Test and the Durrell Listening-Reading Series were given in February and April. The experimental group used the listening equipment in the project room. Children chose tapes from the available supply and listened in small groups under the supervision of an adult. The results indicated that the experimental group improved reading, auditory discrimination, and listening, but not word knowledge or discrimination. Both teachers and parents described the enthusiastic interest of the children in the experimental group. Since the experimental groups were small, had the use of the project room, and made their own selection of tapes to listen to, one must question what increased their interest and what part that interest played in the learning reflected by the test results.

There is some indication that fifth graders can improve their ability to follow oral directions (R. Rogers, 1969). After a period of specific attention to following directions, noting important factors, and analyzing instructions, they achieved considerable progress. They maintained the improvement for at least a month. Since there was no improvement in general listening, indications are that the children had learned what to pay attention to in certain situations, and how to identify a particular kind of information.

A study attempted to find out if listening skill instruction was more effective when given by a teacher or by a tape (Kranyik, 1972). The two experimental groups had four weeks of training, one group by a teacher, the other group by a tape, and each child marked an activity sheet each day. A control group had none of these experiences. No difference was found between the success of the two methods, but both experimental groups showed significantly better scores on test sheets than did the control group. Had the experimental groups learned to listen better, or to mark sheets?

Increasing racial integration of schools raises the question of differences in speech patterns and characteristics among teachers. Minnie Rogers (1972) found that differing speech patterns did not affect the listening comprehension of third grade children. Perhaps exploration should be extended to first graders, and to children who have had virtually no previous contact with a different dialect. Also, would the *extent* of difference in the dialects and speech characteristics of teachers make a difference?

One implication of these studies is that new experiences enable children to carry out any activities related to those experiences more effectively. Results may also indicate that when these activities are stimulating and self-selected, the learning is greater. When reading such research, it is essential to evaluate critically whether children learned to listen better or whether higher test scores were merely a serendipitous result of the study. For instance, does filling out activity sheets help children to fill out testing sheets more effectively? Are children better listeners or better test takers?

Developing critical listening

Some educators and other citizens are becoming particularly concerned about children's ability to think critically about advertising and propaganda. Children need to analyze whatever they hear, rather than accept it unquestioningly. Lundsteen (1963), who has carried on some of the more significant research on listening, explored this question. She studied such abilities as detecting the speaker's purpose, analyzing and judging propaganda, and analyzing and judging arguments. She attempted to develop critical listening through the process of examining spoken materials in the light of related objective evidence, comparing the ideas with some consensual data, and summarizing or acting upon the judgment made.

Using a specially devised test, Lundsteen found evidence of related but separate critical listening abilities that are part of a general listening ability, a part that can be tested and improved. A year later Lundsteen (1965) found that the children had maintained the gains they had made but had not increased their scores during the previous year. She cites the possibility that the group had approached the test ceiling so further growth would be difficult to measure with that particular test.

In a similar study Cook (1972) used sixteen forty-five-minute lessons to help ten-year-olds learn to identify such propaganda techniques as Band Wagon, Card Stacking, Glittering Generalities, Name Calling, Plain Folks, Testimonials, and Transfer. Testing showed marked improvement in identifying propaganda techniques. Teachers noted that the children transferred their new skills to reading and to conversations concerning advertisements in newspapers and comic books.

These two studies focus on developing critical thinking concerning material presented orally. Success with the younger age group raises the question of how early such a program can be effective. Perhaps children could develop such concepts gradually from an even earlier age. Children could acquire habits of examining many factors in their world and learn procedures for each analysis.

How teachers improve their own listening

One study (Lundgren, 1972) put teacher interns through a training program, "Effective Listening," prepared by the Xerox Corporation. The teachers were then videotaped while conducting discussions, which were not identified as related to the listening program. Listening tests before and after the program showed significant gains. On the videotapes, evidence that the interns were hearing student input included repeating, rephrasing, paraphrasing, advancing, elaborating or otherwise building on input, referring to earlier input from

students, and summarizing. Interns with higher pre- and postlistening test scores made better use of student input during classroom discussion.

A quite different approach to listening helps individuals become more self-aware by analyzing what they do when they listen (Pflaumer, 1972). The program would be appropriate for preservice or inservice teachers. Four dimensions of personality are organized from data secured in answer to the question, "What do you do when you listen?" Positive and negative listening characteristics of the "ideal personality" are described as follows:

Positive learning characteristics

Keeps an open mind

Is curious

Listens for new ideas everywhere

Integrates what he hears with what he already knows

Is unwilling to blindly follow the listening crowd

Is conscious of what is going on

Listens to the essence of things

Looks for ideas, organization, and arguments

Is open-minded; knows no two people listen the same

Is mentally alert; outlines, objects, approves, adds illustrations of his own

Has the capacity and desire to critically examine, understand, and attempt to transform some of his values, attitudes, and relationships within himself to others

Listens to the speaker's ideas

Focuses his mind on the listening

Listens with feeling and intuition

Realizes that the speaker's intent is not always correctly interpreted

Notes the effect of that which he hears upon him

and also notes that this knowing how he is being affected affects him

Categorizes facts

Maintains total awareness in receiving fine details in the total picture

Can empathize easily

Looks for possible distortions, misinterpretations of information and facts

Negative listening characteristics

Avoids personal involvement in listening, preferring to remain detached

Is seldom introspective in listening

Sometimes allows pressures or conflicts to enter into the listening situations

Is satisfied without undue demands of further proof or evidence

Listens to details rather than overall essence generally

Is content to receive the message

Seldom catches what other people do not say

Will let conflicting affections hinder the intake of the intended message

Listens only to what the speaker says literally

Keeps his personal feelings and reactions to himself

"Gets" the message without worrying about ideas, organization, arguments, or other isolated facts and the like

Insists that generalizations are indefensible

Accepts words at their face value with their usual connotations

This study shows how our personalities influence our ability to listen effectively. Positive characteristics emphasize openness to what is heard,

active involvement with ideas, the relation of these ideas to previous thinking, and a continuing awareness of self as affected by what is heard. Certainly these are desirable characteristics for any teacher and may be taken as guides for continuing self-development.

The school's role in improving listening

We are now ready to suggest a definition that can be useful to teachers: Listening is paying attention to spoken language in such a way that the individual gains meaning efficiently and deals with it effectively. Teaching listening means providing a situation in which children find listening a rewarding experience and learn to use the content in ways that are relevant to their purposes at that time. Thus, teaching listening needs to include helping children establish purposes for listening, which implement the goals of education, self-development, and human relations.

In general, there are no nice, neat ways to *teach* listening. Children *learn* to listen intuitively in situations that are stimulating, rewarding, helpful, and make them feel good about themselves and their accomplishments. They *learn not* to listen, again intuitively, in situations they perceive as dull, without significant purpose, negative, belittling, or punitive. Further, they learn what they are expected to do with what they hear: Regurgitate it, ignore it, or think about it in any of various ways. The expectation is set not only by what the teacher wants them to do but also by the implicit, unvoiced confidence in what they will be able to do. While teachers can and should discuss listening directly with children, it is probably better to make listening one of the purposes of most lessons, rather than have lessons in listening. Since no one can or should attend to all they hear, the school's most important role in developing good listening skills may be to help children develop habits of selective listening. They will learn to select whatever they find is consistently of value to them.

Basic principles and guidelines applied to listening

The basic principles in the acquisition of communications skills that we developed in Chapter 3 can be applied to listening through the following guidelines:

1. Listening involves understanding a spoken message.

Check the effectiveness of children's listening by having them comment on what they have heard in their own words. Check on your own listening by responding in a way that enables the child to indicate any misunderstanding you may have.

2. Children need to develop self-confidence as listeners. Emphasize the portion of what they have heard that they understood correctly. Repeat any information not received correctly by the child who was trying to listen.

3. Children improve their listening by talking with their peers frequently and with purpose.

Set up small groups to work together for various purposes and conduct discussions in which children have the opportunity to listen to each other. Follow suggestions in Teacher Roles when expecting children to listen.

4. Children improve their listening for meaning by listening to the standard dialect, to their own dialect, and to dialects of their peers.

When one child does not understand another who speaks a different dialect, ask what he or she thinks the child means, what the main topic is, and is the other asking something or telling something? Help the listener look for nonverbal cues as well.

5. Children work at listening when they feel they need to know what others are saying.

Since this implies a need for cooperative activity, make as much of such activity available to children as possible. Involvement increases the need to know what others are saying. Establish a climate that stimulates involvement of all children.

6. No one can tell another how to listen.

Provide as many as possible of the useful experiences that develop listening. Particularly, establish purposeful oral communication between peers and stand by to assist in successful listening.

7. Children listen intuitively.

Do not ask children to explain how they listen, for they cannot. Only some ten- to twelve-year-olds will be able to talk about it in a meaningful way, and the attempt may do more harm than good. Rather, provide situations in which the child sees listening as very important.

8. Since no two children have the same experience or understanding at any one time, all children will not be able to listen with equal effectiveness to all topics or in all situations.

Help children identify problem areas and do what is possible to build these areas.

9. Children listen to meaning rather than words, so paraphrasing is a natural feedback.

Utilize this tendency in order to identify

what is not understood as children try unsuccessfully to repeat the words or misstate some aspect of what they believe they understand.

10. Materials and activities children perceive as valuable to them increase their involvement, which in turn increases their desire to listen.

Be selective in providing such materials and activities to increase successful listening.

Factors affecting listening

In a classroom teachers probably feel that children "should" listen to whatever the teacher says to them. Why don't they? A number of studies have shown that teachers talk a large percentage of the time, giving directions, asking questions, answering questions, presenting information, explaining procedures, and scolding children, either for misbehavior or for failure to learn.

Weaver (1972) found that the extent of children's listening seems to decrease through the school years. If a teacher stops talking and asks each listener to indicate what the talking was about, the percentages of people who could respond correctly were 90 percent for the first grade, 80 percent for the second, 43.7 percent for junior high school, and 28 percent for high school. This decrease may result from lack of attention or from lack of comprehension. Does the teacher talk so much that children increasingly "tune out," or talk so that they cannot understand? Teachers may forget that students are intensely involved in their own lives and may be unable, or perhaps unwilling, to lay their concerns aside at the schoolhouse door.

Some of the factors that affect the listening of children are important to keep in mind.

1. Many things hold children's attention in the classroom. They may be involved in reading or other school work. They may be watching a close friend, interacting with this friend nonverbally, or observing the friend's interaction with someone else, wondering if the other child is "making points." They may be remembering a conversation at home that raised an already high anxiety level. They may be figuring how to avoid the bully on the street as they go home, or avoid the "little kids" who want to tag along. All these are normal, understandable involvements that keep children from listening when the teacher expects them to.

2. If what the teacher wants children to hear is relevant to them, involves what they want or need to hear, and holds personal meaning for them, they are more likely to listen.

3. To the extent that children recognize the value to them of what the speaker is saying, they will listen. Teachers need to make their purposes clear so that listeners can recognize and identify with them. Better yet, teachers can involve the children in establishing these listening purposes so that the recognition of value is ensured. When children are directly involved in the discussion, their listening increases significantly.

4. When children feel they already know what the teacher is going to say, or know that the information is otherwise easily available to them, they may keep their attention on something they feel is more important.

5. The more often children find it doesn't really matter whether they listen or not, the less they will pay attention.

Improvement of listening

How individual teachers attempt to improve listening depends on their definitions of listening. If listening is paying attention to a speaker, we all want to listen when it obviously is to our advantage. Children may listen because of the negative, even punitive, measures used by some teachers, or because what they are listening to has intrinsic value. If children feel that listening means *following directions*, doing as they are told, they listen when the incentive, negative or positive, is great enough. However, under these conditions the long-term results are usually negative.

If teachers think listening means *memorizing facts* for later reproduction on a test, this kind of listening can be improved with various mnemonic devices within the limits of each individual's ability for rote memory. Any factor in the material or the way it is presented that increases personal meaning for the child will increase this type of listening effectiveness. Thus, memorizing poetry by meaningful units, rather than line-by-line, produces better results.

If teachers believe listening includes a *deep appreciation* for arts such as music, poetry, and drama, that kind of listening can be acquired through positive and frequent experience with each of the art forms to develop appreciation. These experiences can be offered but should never be forced, because negative feelings are quickly attached to whatever is forced. When appreciation is the goal, evaluation should be achieved by some means other than testing.

Often teachers hope that listening means *increasing understanding* of oneself, of others, and of the world so that each may live more effectively. To accomplish such purposes, each child needs to see value in what is listened to, and be encouraged and challenged to use all the appropriate thought processes in relation to it. Long-term learning, the kind that affects people's lives, is not accomplished by a mere intake process. Learning must be judiciously integrated into one's own understandings, feelings, values, and purposes as a basis for intentional action.

Purposes of listening Of the many available lists of listening skills, one of the best is by Lundsteen

(see Appendix B). Her list includes purposes, specific skills, and procedures to improve listening. Some procedures require maturity beyond that of the elementary school child, but are useful for teachers and other adults.

Probably a teacher's most important contribution is to provide situations in which children develop habits of listening for a specific purpose. We all are more effective when we are working toward a purpose we have established or at least accepted. To be effective in stimulating listening, the teacher needs to help the children pinpoint a specific purpose in each case. For instance, "We need to listen for directions to know how to play the new game." "How is it like games we know." "How is it different." Such tie-ins evolve out of everyday experiences in the classroom.

Some purposes and requirements for listening are as follows:

Listening to follow directions—requires understanding of directions and need to follow them.

Listening for needed information—requires recognition of need for information.

Listening to evaluate content or procedures—requires understanding of the basis for evaluation.

Listening to recall related information or understanding—requires recognition of need for information.

Listening for new words to expand vocabulary—requires a real purpose for extending vocabulary.

Listening to discussion so as to participate in it—requires mental involvement.

Listening to enjoy literature, plays, and music—requires some preliminary appreciation.

This list, modified by one's own desired inclusions, can be kept available and checked daily by teachers to ensure an adequate program.

Weaver (1972, p. xvii) has suggested various ways of increasing listening capacity and evaluating what is heard. To Weaver's procedures below, we have added our own illustrations:

Increasing your capacity to listen

You can reflect the message to the talker.
Are you saying that _____? Do you mean _____? You mean that _____.

You must guess the talker's intent or purpose.
What does she want me to understand or do?

You should try to determine whether your referents for the words of the talker are about the same as his.
When you say _____, do you mean _____?

You should try to determine your purpose in every listening situation.
What should or can I get from this?

You should become aware of your own biases and attitudes.
I don't like to hear about spiders, but I need to know about them anyway; or I didn't like Steven's talk, but I guess it was because it was about skiing, which I'm afraid to do.

You should learn to use your spare time well as you listen.
How does that fit with what I know about the topic? If we carry out that suggestion, what would we do?

You should analyze your listening errors.
I guess I did not understand what you meant. Was it because I didn't like the way you were saying it? Why?

Developing your ability to evaluate what you hear

You should get the whole story before evaluating it.
I don't see how you could do that, but I'll listen to see if you can tell me how it could be done.

You should be alert to mistaken causal relations.
Just because those things both happen, does it mean one causes the other? If so, which causes which? Or are they both the result of something else?

You should ask yourself whether the opinions you hear are sound.
I like what he says, but what basis does he really have for saying it?

You should judge how much the speaker's biases are affecting the message.
I know she really wants that to happen. Is she considering all the results?

School programs for improving listening Before the late 1960s any substantial emphasis on the development of listening ability in curriculum guides and school programs was hard to find. The listening skills to be "taught" were mostly in the service of the other curriculum areas. That is, listening was a way of learning whatever else was taught in the schools.

A publication of the Akron Public Schools (1956) suggests that teachers play an important role in children's listening if each teacher—

1. Regards what the child has to say as important

2. Helps the pupil choose content suitable to the interest and maturity of the group

3. Plans with the children so that they sense the purpose for which they are listening in a given situation

4. Helps the group set up standards for listening

5. Provides many opportunities for child participation by answering, questioning, adding to, and discussing what they have heard

6. Makes provision for children to participate in follow-up experiences in drawing, dramatization, telling, constructing, and writing

7. Guides children to judge the value of what they have heard

8. Plans seating arrangements so that the children may face one another

9. Adjusts the length of listening time to the maturity of the group

Bracken (1969) suggests that teachers first determine which children need a specific listening skill, that they use attention getters and good motivating devices, give specific instructions and use examples, and stimulate critical thinking. Children should have the opportunity to check themselves and evaluate their progress.

Listening in improving human relations The ability to listen for what the other person really means is a key factor in good human relations. One procedure that can be used to develop this ability is resolving disagreements between children. It is probably better to start with only a small group, including the disputants and a few others. As children become accustomed to this procedure and greater mutual trust develops, everyone in the class might be involved. Indeed, there is much for all to learn.

Dick and Sam were in a serious quarrel one noon. Their teacher, Mr. Bailly, let each participant in the disagreement state his case without interruption. Then he asked Paul, one of the other children, to restate Dick's position as he understood it. It is easier for a person not involved in the controversy to state the position objectively. Mr. Bailly explained that Dick must accept Paul's statements as to what he meant, or Paul must modify them until they are acceptable to Dick. Then Sam stated his case and had it interpreted to his satisfaction. When both positions had been restated acceptably, the group analyzed the difference in the perceptions of the two.

Children's disputes may result from misunderstanding of facts or information, or simply a difference in the way each perceives the actions, words, or intentions of the other. When it seems better not to involve others, each of the children involved can restate the other's understandings and feelings to that child's satisfaction. Whatever the problem, the procedure requires each child to listen to the other and recognize that perceptions differ. The procedure uses thoughtful listening and communication to sharpen or change perceptions. A situation is only what people perceive it to be, and all they can act on is their own perceptions. For this reason the only significant way to change behavior is to clarify each person's perception of it and the situation that elicited it. The rationale for this procedure, as explained by Combs (ASCD, 1962), is that every person does what seems to him at the moment he does it to be best for him. If he can perceive either the situation or his behavior differently, he can then see the need to respond differently.

While children listen for and reflect perceptions and feelings of others, the teacher is able to focus on the perceptions children are operating on. Over and above the settling of a dispute, these values are very important. The procedure also provides experience in listening for feelings, which is a most neglected area.

The teacher's role is to set up situations for exploring problems, monitor the procedures, but stay out of any substantive discussion. As differences in perceptions are resolved, there need be no moralizing, only recognition of how perceptions are formed and how they are changed.

Gradually, boys and girls begin to see that others' perceptions may differ from their own and that perhaps the truth—reality—lies somewhere in between. The teacher can model this kind of concern by listening to understand every child's meaning and the intended but often unexpressed message. "What is it the child really wants me to know?" Teachers need to look for ways in which they may be misperceiving. Another benefit is learning to listen well enough to state another person's perceptions accurately without necessarily agreeing with them.

Teacher roles in developing listening

Indirectly, teachers develop children's habits of *not* listening in several ways. As a teacher, you will need to check yourself on the following points.

First, are you sure that what you have in mind needs to be said, and said now, and said to the whole group? If it is something you just remembered and are afraid you will forget, make a note. If only some need to hear, ask the chairperson to gather that particular group. If it is time for orchestra practice and no one has noticed, catch the attention of one musician and point to the clock, so that child can alert the others. In other words, there are many ways to avoid much of the usual "teacher talk," many of them excellent procedures for developing children's responsibility.

Second, when children are busy with their own thoughts or activities and you have decided it is essential to have their attention, you need to ask for it. To avoid more talk that they may not heed, use a cue for this purpose. It may be a piano or a harmonica. A quiet but successful cue, when children are moving around and conversing, is a raised hand to be imitated by all as they become aware of it.

Third, when you have the children's attention, you will need to help them focus their thinking on the matter at hand. Try to think from their point of view. Will *they* see your topic as relevant to their purposes? Will *they* be able to bring personal meaning to what you say? If they cannot, there will be little communication. Will they be glad to do what you ask of them? If not, your request may be inappropriate for one of two reasons: The children see no point in doing it, or they feel they cannot be successful at it. If either situation exists, very little learning will result.

By individualizing activities, you can avoid requesting work that some children believe they cannot do successfully, and others find too easy to be of value. There is nothing all of us are less apt to "hear" than a request to do something we see no value in doing or that we are sure we cannot do.

When you feel there really is a reason for them to listen, then it is worthwhile to explain it. When it is a requirement over which you have no control, explain just that. If you ordinarily do not ask them to do things in which they see no purpose, they will probably accept your explanation.

Fourth, if you give children information they already have, or read directions to them that they can read for themselves, they will find little reason for listening. On the other hand, if most of their school work is the result of discussion among the group, guided by teacher questions, there will be little need for assignment and direction giving. You can get commitment by asking who will be responsible for group-determined tasks, or by asking guiding questions.

When children ask questions already answered, it may mean they really did not understand the discussion and hesitated to say so in the group. They need further help to clear up their concerns, rather than to be told "You weren't listening!" However, when it is obvious they were not listening, establish this fact clearly, then ask what they think they might do about it. Unnecessary repetition encourages more nonlistening.

When pressure is brought to bear on children to make them feel they *should* listen, docile, conscientious children may develop habits of listening to everything, whether they need to or not. Children who are self-directing will continue to make their own decisions about whether to listen. Many develop very effective shields, making eye-contact with the speaker, looking interested, and smiling or laughing when the group does, so that they may carry on mental activities that seem more important. Habits of not listening are hard to break. In fact, school experience may develop the kind of selected listening that tunes out teachers. Therefore, your responsibility as teachers is not to try to control children's listening, but to help them develop effective self-directed listening habits. It becomes very important to make a continuing and careful analysis of what you say and how you say it in the classroom. You can enhance children's listening habits by using appropriate procedures, so that children will find it helpful and rewarding to listen and will know that their questions and responses will be treated with respect.

Direct influence is mostly carried out in connection with other subjects. Teachers need to be aware of the listening factor whenever oral communication is going on, and frequently make children aware of it too. But listening should seldom be "a lesson" as such. Since listening in natural situations always deals with other content, its skills are best learned in that way. And since reacting to any oral message is an essential part of listening, teachers need to lead children to use and develop their thinking skills when discussing such content. Teachers need to realize that they can only give children information and express their feelings about it. Children will not gain knowledge from the reception of the literal message, but from their thinking about the significance of it.

Whatever material teachers present orally for children's listening should stress phrasing to make the underlying syntactic structure easier to recognize. Phrasing places the emphasis on the relation of one group of words to another, and pauses allow time for children to relate new information to what they already know. Since this process is essential for an effective use of new input, it greatly increases the likelihood of desired action.

The concept that *listening is a language process*, rather than a mechanical process, has had fresh confirmation. As talking is not just voicing words, but expressing thoughts and ideas through the implicit use of the structural nature of language, so listening is gaining understanding of those thoughts and ideas through the intuitive understanding of that structure. It is an internal, subjective process that is difficult, if not impossible, to make evident to others.

Teachers need to be aware that this subjective process is affected by visual cues. Motion catches our eye, either to gain or distract our attention. People's faces may tell us how important it is for us to listen. If their eyes do not include us, we can assume we are not a necessary part of their audience; if we have no other reason for listening, our attention drifts away. Demonstrating, writing on the chalkboard or on charts may help to focus attention and increase listening. The attractiveness of displays related to the subject also enhances listening.

Teachers need to keep records of how well each child is listening. Simple procedures for record keeping are discussed in Chapters 2, 5, and 6.

Evaluation of listening

Valid and reliable testing in listening is difficult because listening cannot be seen or measured but can only be inferred from some overt reaction that may be impossible to interpret. Listening ability has no significant content or information to be learned. Because listening and speaking are in the oral realm, written material is not appropriate. There is no obvious product for either reading or listening as both are intake, receiving activities. And since the input for listening is oral, it is seldom available as a basis for evaluation.

Children need to be aware of the various purposes for listening—enjoyment of a birdcall, learning directions to play a game, finding out how others feel. They can set goals that involve listening for certain things or for specific purposes. Other desirable goals are greater selectivity of what to listen to, and more sensitive interpretation of its meaning. Teachers can encourage children and then observe and listen for the extent to which they have accomplished their purposes. Teachers will become aware of progress through sensitive observation and listening to children they have come to know well. They need to record instances of such growth because no paper-and-pencil test will give such information.

There is no generalized listening skill. All the language arts competencies are communication skills, and in the last analysis their evaluation depends on the accuracy and adequacy of that communication, which is interaction. Based on life situations, they depend on affective as well as cognitive factors. Since listening depends on the development of language and thinking abilities, it matures as the listener matures and clearly sets more purposes for listening.

Criteria for all school evaluations

Evaluation in a child-centered program has been a stumbling block for many educators in all types of positions. The problem grew out of initial reaction to the idea of providing for the needs of individuals. "If we don't test the whole group, how will we know what they have learned?" "If children are doing different tasks or working on different competencies, how do we know whether they are making progress—progress equal to that of the rest of the group?"

These concerns are based on misconceptions: (1) that a group test, standardized or teacher-made, gives a valid answer to "how much a child has learned"; (2) that children must be compared with other children, even though all learning takes place at different times, at different rates, and may be expressed in very different ways; and (3) that what is important is how children respond in the school setting in a teacher-directed situation—which is quite irrelevant to what they will do on their own in an out-of-school situation now or later.

Under the traditional system there is a minimum of record keeping other than grades or test scores. Little is known about the specific understandings and abilities of individual children. It is only teachers who recognize the importance of such knowledge who make the extra effort to record such information.

Therefore, even sketchy records of what each child has done, in terms of tasks selected and carried out, and some comment on the extent of accomplishment, is more useful evaluative information than grades on any number of recitations or tests. We do not recommend that records be sketchy, however; they need to be as comprehensive and detailed as a teacher can reasonably make them. It never will be possible to know "where every child is in each area," or even in any one area. Humans are too complex for such simplistic concepts.

At best, we can keep a continuing record of specific successes and accomplishments on tasks chosen in terms of a child's specific need. Need is recognized when the child is unable to accomplish some portion of an important activity adequately for his or her stage of development; when a child wants to move ahead of normal expectancy; when children are dissatisfied with their progress in any ability. The task itself may be as simple as a six-year-old not making legible *r*'s or a ten-year-old not understanding how to embed run-on sentences. In teacher-pupil conferences, the children's evaluation of what they can do and what problems they have is an essential element for determining next steps. When children are not subtly, or openly, rebelling against inappropriate, imposed tasks, they operate with the same needs and desires that produce extensive learning in preschool and out-of-school situations.

Evaluation is one of the most important factors in learning and development. It must meet the following criteria:

1. It must be continuous.

Following the accomplishment of each activity, and sometimes along the way, learners ask themselves, "How am I doing?" Such evaluation depends on the learners' awareness of what they want to accomplish (purposes) and what their expectancies are.

Teachers are consistently looking for each child's new accomplishments and successes, no matter how small, and reflecting them to the child. Without pressure, the teacher-child interaction is a normal response to every individual's natural desire to be capable. At appropriate intervals, learners look back over long periods—months, terms, and school years—to see major progress.

2. Evaluation must be carried out primarily by the learner with the assistance and awareness of the helping person, the teacher.

The individual learner knows better than anyone else how simple or confusing a task is and what has been accomplished. If teachers do not take advantage of this fruitful source of evaluation but arbitrarily impose their own judgments, children may soon learn to discount their own evaluation and feelings. The result is lowered self-esteem, less basis for self-direction, and decreased learning. Children's self-evaluations can go on no matter what else the teacher is doing. However, teachers can often identify causes of problems or stalemates, open new avenues for progress, and suggest additional directions and possibilities. Have you thought about_____? Have you tried_____? Did you see (or read or hear)_____? Would you like to try it? Might it help?

3. Evaluation must be related to immediate purposes that are consistent with long-range goals.

Evaluation needs to be focused on specific details as well as on larger issues, for the way the specifics are carried out largely determines the overall progress. However, the specifics must be related to the long-term goals to which they contribute. Often school practices interfere with long-range goals. For instance, development of more effective thinking skills is a universally accepted goal.

However, children often have most decisions made for them, are given conclusions to be "learned" rather than thought through, and are handed solutions to problems they should be solving for themselves. Such procedures not only do not contribute to the development of more effective thinking, they actually prevent such development by suggesting that children are not able to think for themselves.

4. Evidence of progress is what the learner accomplishes—not what the learner can be required to do under imposed conditions.

School learning has been disappointing to the public. Complaints are that children and young people cannot read, write, or spell, and lack competence in the world outside of school. The truth is that too often school learning and evaluation are not applicable to long-term life skills, but only to contrived school situations.

5. Evaluation's main purpose is feedback, the basis of planning by and for the learner.

Too often evaluation has meant paper-and-pencil testing. One of the main reasons for the widespread use of such tests is the numerical score that results. Numerical scores can be arranged in a series to rank children in the order of their ability to take the test. Ranking scores forces comparison of each child with all the others on a basis built on questionable assumptions. It also provides an easy way to assign grades. We believe this practice has been first a misinterpretation of evaluation, and second a most unproductive use of the results. The usual feedback from such evaluation is a grade on the paper with certain items checked as wrong. It provides little or no information to the learner as to how to proceed to further learning. On the other hand, planned or informal teacher-pupil conferences can examine and mutually evaluate any results of daily activity, explore the child's thinking about it, and help discover any misconceptions and needs, thus providing a basis for further learning.

One of the most damaging of the current practices is the way schools are interpreting behavioral objectives. No one questions the desirability of seeing the major objectives of education evidenced in the behaviors of learners. In a mistaken attempt to make the objectives explicit, however, school districts have broken them down and spelled them out into literally thousands of minutely detailed statements with specified behaviors for each. These procedures ignore the fact that children do not learn effective ways of dealing with life situations by acquiring a collection of bits and pieces that they must then put together in some useful way of their own devising without guidance or assistance. Evaluation, usually testing, indicates how many of these details a child has collected at any particular time, not how well he or she can meet a normal life situation.

Schools have been able to put these behavioral objectives into classroom instruction by a process called "accountability." All teachers worthy of the name want to feel responsible for the development of the children with whom they work. But accountability is being based largely on the results of paper-and-pencil tests of behavioral objectives. Children's response to these may—or may not—give some evidence of what children *can* do, but the tests provide little or no evidence of what they *will* do as citizens in our society, now or later. Evaluation based directly on these requirements has little validity. Such methods of evaluation are counterproductive in a democracy, where the goals of society and the schools are to develop citizens who can perform effectively with self-direction and responsibility, to enrich their own lives and the lives of others. Schools have limited the child's responsibility to doing assignments and following orders, without understanding or accepting the purpose of the school's requirements.

Evaluation criteria applied to listening

As stated in criteria for all school evaluations, the evaluation of listening needs first to be continuous. During the day's activity, teachers can comment frequently on evidence of good listening on some child's part, and ask if children listened for specific directions suggested earlier.

The second criterion refers to self-evaluation, which is appropriate in teacher-pupil conferences, group evaluations at the end of the day, and at any other time evaluations are taking place. Since teachers are always on shaky ground when they say "You weren't listening," it is better strategy to

ask "Were you listening? If you were, then what did ____ mean?"

The third criterion which involves purposes for listening, has implications for the teacher as well as for the children. Teachers need to be certain when there are valid purposes for children's listening and that the children understand the need to listen at that particular time. Since children need to develop selective listening, they need bases to consider such decisions.

Teachers need to be certain immediate purposes are consistent with long-term goals. For instance, teachers should ask children to listen to the discussion so they can react to others' comments, as this is one aspect of the long-term goal of group decision-making. Teachers should not ask them to listen because "I tell you to" or because "I will grade you on your listening." Following orders (except in an emergency) is not a long-range goal in a democracy, and acting only to get a grade defeats the major goals of education. Evaluation, then, considers the extent children are aware of and have internalized valid purposes for listening.

The fourth criterion evaluates listening as it affects all of learners' lives, what they do now and will continue to do on their own. Teachers can evaluate the kinds of things children listen to on their own. Perhaps seven-year-old Sherri consistently stops her own activity to listen to her peers' conversation, or nine-year-old Tom is unwilling to listen to another's discussion of feelings, or eleven-year-old Alan does not want to listen to any music except the most current popular songs. These characteristics indicate lack of development of some of the long-term purposes for listening and are likely to have significant effects on the children's lives.

The fifth criterion is that evaluation of listening should provide feedback to each child and give support and guidance in planning for additional learning. When Sherri recognizes that she needs to be more selective in her listening, she and her teacher can work out a plan to bring it about. Tom may need considerable help in recognizing that his own anxiety may prevent him from listening to other people's feelings. He and his teacher can discuss this possibility and so may agree on ways to reduce his anxiety in the classroom. Alan can accept the fact that there are many kinds of music, but he has heard very little besides the currently popular songs. He and his teacher can begin to broaden the range of music he enjoys. Popular songs based on classical music, Gilbert and Sullivan's *Pirates of Penzance*, or Grofe's *Grand Canyon Suite* may be helpful. Planning a willingness to listen to other music is often acceptable in exchange for an opportunity to share the kind children already enjoy.

The teacher's role in evaluating listening

Teachers' first responsibility is to see that each child has a hearing acuity test across the entire range of the human voice. If such testing is not possible, teachers should try to locate any children that give evidence of hearing problems and refer them for testing. Children who are subject to frequent earaches or severe nasal congestion may need follow-up testing. Teachers need to be aware, however, that affective factors may prevent listening in the classroom even though children do well on a hearing test. When the child finds it more comfortable not to listen for any reason, the problem is not inability to hear, but lack of desire to listen.

Many of the methods teachers have used to evaluate listening are invalid because they test factors other than listening. Asking children to repeat what was said could test the ability to imitate or replicate sounds, with or without understanding. Asking children to operate mentally with the spoken message could test their thinking ability and previous understanding. Evaluation should focus upon how listening affects the children's understanding, how it makes them feel, and what they do because of it. For example, does the child analyze better when a problem is presented orally or in writing? Evaluation should be related to the goals we have set for listening: Is the child increasingly able to put in his or her own words what others say? Is the child increasingly reacting in some useful and relevant way to what others say?

Although various tests to measure listening have been published, what these instruments actually measure is generally questioned. Carroll (1972) calls them a "hodge-podge" and reports that the intercorrelations of various listening tests are no higher than their correlations with reading or intelligence tests. The validity and reliability of some tests have been considered inadequate, and the relationship between test results and regular classroom behavior is questionable. Test results can be distorted by the material in the test, the

ORAL COMMUNICATION: TALKING AND LISTENING

means of presenting it, the pressures exerted by the testing situation itself.

The most effective evaluation seems to be the teacher's observation and the child's self-evaluation. Working closely with the children, the teacher can gather much information about what each has gained from listening in the classroom. In children's self-evaluation, they need to offer specifics. "How do you know you are listening more effectively? What evidence do you have?"

Summary

Listening is paying attention to spoken language in such a way that the individual gains meaning efficiently and deals with it effectively. The most significant research has documented the importance of the concept that listening is a language process and so, like talking, reading, and writing, is based on the nature and structure of language and not on separate words as such. Although the question of whether listening can be taught is uncertain, we know that it is learned, can be modified, and that the child's perception of the situation and what is to be listened to is an essential element. Studies of specific aspects of listening with clear and limited goals, such as critical listening to detect propaganda, show more defensible and positive results. Listening is the most difficult aspect of the language arts to evaluate.

Suggested learning experiences for prospective teachers

Suggestion A

1. You have been taking college classes for some time now. Under what circumstances do you listen with involvement, intensity, and good later recall?

2. Are there times something in class triggers a thought that intrigues you and blocks out other happenings for a while? Do you sometimes feel this diversion was more productive than continued listening?

3. Are there occasions when it seems impossible to keep your attention on what is happening in class?

4. Think about these situations and decide why you reacted the way you did.

5. If children in your class reacted this way, what would it tell you?

Suggestion B

1. When you are a teacher, children will need to listen to you. How well do you enunciate? Phrase statements so meaning is clear? Utilize pace and tone of voice to communicate most effectively?

2. Use a tape recorder and a cassette to record your speech, first as you are preparing to talk with children, and later as you are actually talking with them.

3. Recall the children's responses, both verbal and nonverbal, as you replay the tape. Can you identify any use of your voice that seemed to produce more intent listening?

4. What characteristics of your speech do you want to extend and expand? Is there something you hope to minimize?

Suggestion C

1. One of the more effective ways of developing children's habits of listening is indirect—the teacher's own talking. How effective is your talking?

2. How likely are people to follow up on a topic you have introduced? Or how likely are people to listen with little response and then change the subject?

3. In a group discussion start a tape recorder. Later play it back and listen for (1) how much you talked in relation to others, (2) how much of your talk was "I" oriented, (3) how many times you picked up someone's idea and explored possibilities or potential advantages, and (4) how often you showed interest or concern for another's reported experience.

4. Set up a situation in which you discuss a planned or unplanned topic with children. Tape it and later play it to discover how you handled the discussion and how children responded to you. What characteristics of your talking do you want to emphasize and which do you want to minimize?

Suggestion D

1. Ask permission to observe a classroom while the teacher is actively working with the whole group.

2. Make a rough chart of the seating with a circle representing each child. Observe what you consider evidence of intent listening and not listening. Place a small check in the circles of children showing evidence of good listening and a cross in those of children showing poor listening. Continue observing and marking for fifteen or twenty minutes.

3. Select the child whose circle has the most checks, the one with the most crosses, and one whose circle has no marks at all. Ask permission to talk with each of these separately. Ask each questions about what was said and what it meant, both as to specific topics and as to the general purpose and results of the session. Ask how well they feel they were listening and why.

4. How well did their responses confirm or contradict your expectations? What insights did you get from the experience?

Suggestion E

1. Ask permission to discuss listening with a small group of children, preferably those nine to eleven.

2. Talk with them for a few minutes about any appropriate topic.

3. Raise the question of listening with questions such as "Bob, what did you hear Sarah say about_____?" If his response is inadequate or distorted, ask others. Or "Norma, what do you think Sam meant when he said_____?" If others had different opinions, encourage them to express them.

4. Suggest what you and the group have been talking about is how well people listen. Ask different ones what they do when they listen, under what circumstances they listen best or least, and when they feel listening is important or not important.

5. What have you learned about these children's attitudes and abilities for listening?

Suggestion F

1. Decide on the age of children you will feel most comfortable working with.

2. Check "How to Develop a Strategy" in Chapter 12, "Strategies for children's learning."

3. Decide on your purpose, and in terms of that, on your procedures.

4. Carry out the strategy with the children.

5. Evaluate the results. What did you learn from the experience?

Suggested readings

Any of Sara Lundsteen's writings on listening are useful, particularly her "Critical Listening—Permanency and Transfer of Gains Made during an Experiment in the Fifth and Sixth Grades" and *Listening: Its Impact on Reading and the Other Language Arts*. (See goals taken from this booklet in Appendix B.)

Carl Weaver's book *Human Listening: Process and Behavior* is also useful. Recent articles about listening include Holly O'Donnell, "Are You Listening? Are You Listening?"; Harry Sheldon, "Wanted: More Effective Teaching of Oral Communication"; John Stammer, "Target: The Basics of Listening"; Robert Sund, "Growing through Sensitive Listening and Questioning"; and Daniel Tutolo, "One Approach to Teaching Critical Listening." Jimmy Cook's article "I Can't Believe I Ate the Whole Thing . . ." also deals with critical listening.

Strategies for children's learning

Settling disagreements

Purpose. To help children understand the difference in perceptions of an incident through listening.

Appropriate level. Nine-year-olds and older.

Participants. At least those involved in the disagreement, often others, or the whole group.

Situation. Children, and often adults, perceive a situation only from their own viewpoint, affected by their needs, desires, and self-concept. Everyone's ability to consider the situation from another's point of view is important.

Teacher role

1. To bring together those who have a serious disagreement they are not able to resolve by themselves.

2. To set up a situation in which they listen thoughtfully to each other's position.

3. To stay out of the substance of the discussion except perhaps to raise relevant issues not brought out by others.

Procedures

Alternative A. When the procedure is unfamiliar or the content is better kept private, only those in the disagreement should be involved.

1. Bring the two or three together where others will not hear. State that each will be given the opportunity to speak without interruption.

2. When the first child is finished, ask the other to express in his or her own words the perceptions and feelings of the first child. If not satisfied with the statements, the first child indicates what is wrong or missing. The second child then amends his or her statement. When the first child is satisfied with the statement, they reverse roles.

3. After they have accepted each other's perceptions, if there is still disagreement as to the solution, refrain from any decision-making but attempt to have them compromise by raising questions as to possibilities.

Alternative B. When the procedure is known and the subject not sensitive, a few other children aware of the disagreement can become involved.

1. The other children restate both positions to the satisfaction of those disagreeing, and also may become involved in reaching a solution, but only by raising possibilities.

Evaluation. Children's ability and willingness to listen consistently for differences in perception shows up in their interrelationships, their comments, and the ability of at least some to settle their own disagreements without help from peers or teacher. Evidence of progress in this type of listening should be recorded.

Critical listening

Purpose. To increase children's ability to consider the validity of oral statements.

Appropriate level. Nine-year-olds and older.

Participants. All children.

Situation. Children, as well as adults, are confronted frequently with judgmental, self-serving statements by radio and television advertising, store clerks, and peers.

Teacher role

1. To raise the issue in any appropriate situation.

2. To make such situations available to children.

3. To refrain from evaluative statements so that children will make the evaluations on their own.

Procedures

1. Take advantage of self-serving statements children have heard and role-play some situations such as advertising, political speeches, or some more personal situation.

2. After students have clarified what actually was said, raise the question, "Is that true?" then, "Are there other questions that need to be asked? Are there other aspects to be considered?" Encourage the students to deal with these questions to the extent their perceptions allow.

3. Raise any further questions you have for their continuing discussion.

4. If appropriate, ask them to make generalizations about under what circumstances they need to raise questions, and any typical questions they need to ask.

Evaluation

1. Did the group sense the need for considering the validity of statements?

2. Were their questions useful ones?

3. Are there other factors of which they need to be aware (to be raised at another time)?

The experience can be evaluated also in questions children raise in future situations. Record individual instances.

Developing appreciation of music

Purpose. To increase children's appreciation and enjoyment of a particular piece of music.

Appropriate level. Any level.

Participants. All children.

Situation. Many children have little opportunity to hear music other than the most popular music of the day. We all tend to enjoy what is familiar and heard in comfortable situations and to reject distinctly different kinds or music heard in uncomfortable circumstances.

Teacher role

1. Make music easily available at various times and for various purposes, such as concentrated listening, relaxing, stimulating, or as background making incidental sounds less distracting.

2. Provide or involve children in providing appropriate records or tapes to meet and extend current interests.

3. Involve children in discussion of the music as they indicate interest and suggest other kinds of music as an exploration.

Procedures. Alternative procedures according to the purpose of listening and the musical sophistication of the group or some of its members.

1. For background music, start a quiet record or tape at a time when all are quietly involved. Note any reactions but delay any discussion till later. If children accept it without comment, no discussion is needed. If children offer to bring records or tapes of their own, involve them in discussion of the kind of music desirable for the purpose.

2. After music has become an acceptable part of the classroom situation, provide music appropriate for that group's concentrated listening. Talk with them about the piece, maybe how and why it was written. Ask children to listen for some particular purpose relevant to that music, and discuss it with them later.

3. When children become more familiar with music as a part of the classroom situation, provide relaxing music and stimulating music. When the group has been active and needs to calm down, say "Here is something that may help us all to relax" and put on that record or tape. Or if the group is in the doldrums, use stimulating music, such as "The Stars and Stripes Forever." The children may want to get up and march briskly around the room, and be more ready to tackle the next task.

Evaluation. The extent to which children ask for and contribute to music is one means of evaluation that can be continuous. Another is the extent to which the music they ask for is appropriate to the situation at the time. Keep records of significant comments.

Listening for specifics

Purpose. To help children focus on kinds of information they need.

Appropriate level. Five-year-olds through elevens.

Participants. All children, also small groups for various purposes.

Situation. Listening to helpful information or directions.

Teacher role

1. To raise the question, prior to the time the information is given, about what children need to listen for.

2. To follow up the information-giving with questions to find out if they heard what they needed.

Procedures. This activity needs repeating regularly in many different kinds of situations until children learn to think about what they need in advance and so recognize it when they hear it. Teachers, also, need to remember to alert children before giving directions.

Illustrations

Kindergarten. "Today we are going to make the stick puppets for our story about the Little Red Hen." (Children already have their pictures drawn, colored, and cut out from construction paper.) "What do you need to listen for now?" After the children respond, the teacher then gives that information. Early in the year you may need to have the children give back that information. Later, let them go ahead, checking to see who has and who has not understood, and why.

Eight-year-olds. "Today, as you know, is our field trip." On previous days they had decided on the purpose of the trip, what they want to find out, and the specific children who will assume responsibility for reporting certain information. "What, especially, will you be listening to find out?" Remind them also to be listening for any additional or unanticipated information. On returning, provide an opportunity for each to report on his or her own responsibility. "What was it you were especially listening for?" Then when all have reported, ask "What else did you hear that interested you?"

Eleven-year-olds. These children have been studying their state government. The legislature is now in session. The PBS station presents a televised portion of the day's deliberations each evening and repeats it the next morning. One of the group's concerns is the way the state supports education. The teacher finds that this topic was discussed during the evening broadcast and alerts the children the next morning. They quickly identify the specific issues they want information on and decide to find out what other issues and points of view were discussed. Following the program, they report which of the specific issues were discussed and what positions the legislature took. They also find there was discussion about issues they had not considered.

TALKING

5

Talking follows listening as the second language skill children develop. By the age of five, nearly all children have a well-formed language quite comparable to that of an adult, and can use it with varying effectiveness to accomplish their purposes and meet their needs. There is no need to teach the average child to talk or *how* to talk. But in order to help children develop their talking, teachers need to know what to expect of children and what factors have influenced their speech. In addition, teachers need to learn to recognize the very unusual child who needs special diagnosis and care.

When others have difficulty understanding what a child says, the teacher can continue to accept that youngster as a person and provide help only if needed. If eight-year-old Linda still has trouble sounding her *l*'s, she needs the help of a skilled person. But if Sara cannot sound her *s*'s because her front teeth just came out, all that is necessary is to wait for new ones to grow.

Through interaction in the home and in the neighborhood, each child develops an idiolect, a personal way of self-expression that is comfortable and useful in most situations. Teachers know the importance of accepting and valuing the differences in people. Pedro, coming into a fairly homogenous speech community from another area of the country, can experience rejection by his peers because of his accent or dialect. But teachers can use Pedro's dialect to help children learn to value an individual for what the person is, rather than for superficial characteristics. Children who feel accepted will work at modifying their dialects when others have trouble understanding them. Those who do not understand will modify and improve their listening ability when it becomes important to them. It is essential to help all children accept others for themselves and the contributions they can make.

Before children come to school they have, through listening, developed competence and skill in using language to express their thoughts and feelings. Continued interaction, based on listening and talking, continues their language development. They soon record their thoughts, and the maturity of their writing roughly parallels the maturity of their talking. Hearing and reading their own thoughts as they put them into oral then written language, and then the thoughts of others, they gain meaning through the structure of the language they have learned to speak.

In this chapter we will explore children's speech and the factors affecting it through the elementary school years. On the basis of school practice and research, we will examine a variety of ways in which teachers can help children talk more effectively. We will look into dialects—what they are and what teachers can, should, and should not do about them. We will suggest ways to implement many of the goals listed in the evaluation section of Chapter 3 and suggest guidelines for implementing the basic principles. Although we will focus on talking, you should be continually aware of the extensive interrelationships with all other areas of communication through language.

Using language: Competence or performance?

A difference of emphasis exists between the linguists as represented by Noam Chomsky, and the sociolinguists as represented by Dell Hymes. The issue is one of *competence* vs. *performance*. Chomsky (1965) has used the term "linguistic competence" to mean the implicit knowledge every speaker has of his or her native language. This knowledge enables one to speak an infinite number of grammatical sentences and to understand those spoken by others. Performance, then, is the actual production of these sentences. Many workers in the field of linguistics express a difference of opinion on the competence vs. performance dimension of language. Halliday believes competence, or idealized knowledge, should include communicative ability, which he analyzes as ideational, interpersonal, and textual uses of language (Lyons, 1970, p. 140). According to Hymes (1971) performance may be due to various factors of custom, social and cultural group usages, appropriateness, and motivation.

These two groups differ in their purposes. Chomsky is attempting to make explicit *linguistic competence*, that is, all the ways language is implicitly structured—a task no one yet has been able to accomplish. On the other hand, the sociolinguists focus major attention on *communicative performance*: how people use language, for what purposes, and how effectively.

So, when considering a person's talking, we need to think not only about the structuring and the grammar, but even more important, about the effectiveness of the communication. How well did listeners understand what the speaker intended to convey?

Communicative ability

The ability to communicate the thought one wishes to, effectively and efficiently, is generally considered *communicative ability* or *competence*. While this ability seems simple and straightforward, it is affected by many complexities, such as the appropriateness of what is said, the situation, the values of the community, whether or not the affective or feeling aspect is included, and whether the more usual patterns of usage are heeded.

Appropriateness Limitations on speech are imposed by the situation, the context in which it takes place, and the speaker's perception of various constraints. Whether one is talking with a close personal friend, a teacher, or an understanding parent makes a difference. Hymes lists seven factors affecting the language the individual will use: the sender, the receiver, the channel, the message form, the code, the topic, and the context of the communication. In other words, these factors affect what you feel you can say:

1. How you see yourself
2. How you perceive the person or persons to whom you are speaking (for instance, whether you feel that what you want to say would be unacceptable)
3. The means of communicating (for example, a private telephone line or a loudspeaker)
4. Whether the message is a statement, or poetry, or a song
5. Whether you are talking face-to-face or sending a written message
6. Whether you are discussing politics or religion—two topics avoided in most social gatherings—or talking about the weather
7. Whether the context is formal or informal, in a familiar group situation or a group of strangers (Hymes, 1962, p. 25).

Whether to say "I shall be pleased to come to dinner" or "Sure, I'll be there" depends on a person's relationship to the host or hostess and the formality of the affair. Those who can use either response in the appropriate situation are sensitive to word patterns in various social contexts. Sensitivity promotes both better communication and better human relationships. Teachers need to strive toward the goal of promoting sensitivity and appropriateness as they help children to use their language more effectively.

Hopper points out that grammatical competence does not include the child's "ability to apply his linguistic knowledge in a functionally appropriate and predictable manner in many different communication situations" (Hopper, 1971, p. 31). He believes that language serves a function, and feels schools have not done enough with the functional aspect of language. He suggests that the best way to teach grammar is indirectly, by putting more emphasis on helping children use their language more effectively to perform certain common functions in society.

Therefore, children need to have much firsthand experience and frequent opportunities to use language for such purposes as to offer or request help, make one's position known without belittling that of others, make recommendations and respond to those offered, express empathy, and express appreciation. Any situation that does not go smoothly needs individual and/or group consideration focused on how it might have been handled more sensitively and effectively.

Another influence on a person's way of saying things is the cultural values of a community. Hymes says, "One and the same sentence, the same set of words in the same syntactic relationship may be now a request, now a command, now a compliment, now an insult, depending upon tacit understandings within a community" (Hymes, 1972, p. xxix). Both teachers and children need to be aware of the effect of community values on language and alert to discrepant reactions to what they say.

The affective use of language   One of the functions of language is to express feelings and emotions—something children do naturally unless they have learned not to. Such expression is important because of its effect on our feelings, on our interactions with others, and on our accomplishments, and because intrapersonal communication is facilitated by the open expression of relevant feelings. Further, our enjoyment and appreciation of others, and of the natural world, is greatly enhanced as we become more aware of our affective reactions by expressing our feelings.

To increase sensitivity, we need to help children clearly distinguish between personal feelings and private feelings. Personal feelings are those we do not mind sharing with people we trust. Private feelings are those we would share with no one or only with certain people, or those that involve others who would not want the feelings shared.

Our schools have done little to enrich children's lives by helping them become aware of the pleasant feelings that derive from relationships. Such satisfactions might minimize the need for stimulation through drug abuse and violence.

In light of current trends in interpersonal communication, Weaver (1973) feels that we must work toward four goals in the way we use language:

1. Establishment of a climate of trust

2. Encouragement of open expression of emotions

3. Persuasive expression of interpersonal needs

4. Provision of an environment for individual discovery of self-originated emotions and the creative expression of those emotions through use of the whole range of oral and bodily communication modes.

A climate of trust must be created before much significant language development can take place, particularly in the affective areas. In such an atmosphere children will be able to express emotions and explore the way they feel about themselves, their relationships with others, and various aspects of their school life. But first we, as teachers at all levels, need to make it very clear that such discussion is important.

Teachers can start by expressing their own feelings in less sensitive areas. Noting a lack of enthusiasm in the group, Mr. Gray might say, "A cloudy, rainy day like this makes me feel like crawling back into bed! How does it make you feel?" The group may express both agreement and disagreement. "It's a cozy feeling. I want to stay in and read." "It makes me feel sad." "I don't pay attention to it. I just do what I would anyway." If several express feelings of depression, the teacher may take the next step. "Some of us are bothered by this kind of day. What can we do to make us feel better?" Suggestions may include lively music or a favorite group activity. Two things are accomplished—an awareness and acknowledgement of feelings, and the setting of a happier and more productive tone in the classroom.

As appropriate situations arise, teachers can use them to extend such discussions. Feelings about nature, flowers, trees, streams, and animals are other topics useful for initial building of affective language and expression. Therefore, teachers need to be alert for opportunities to develop affective expression through what children initiate or what they themselves introduce. Such discussion is better kept positive as much as possible, though children's expression of negative feelings about themselves may provide insights that can be used to build more positive feelings. Negative feelings about other individuals need to be ruled out or expressed as constructive suggestions, usually in general terms. Particularly, negative feelings about home and family have no place in any group discussion. However, sharing family experiences that all have enjoyed may be suggestive and helpful.

Negative feelings toward people should be expressed, but in a different situation. One occasion is illustrated in Chapter 4, where children are learning to listen for feelings and for different perceptions, under a teacher's guidance. Here they can learn to express negative feelings so as to clear the air.

Another situation is expressing negative feelings toward the teacher, as in "That's not fair!" The teacher can respond, "You feel that's not fair? Why do you feel that way?" The issue can be discussed quietly, clarifying both the child's and the teacher's perceptions. This expression of feeling should always be available to children but will usually only occur when a deep feeling of trust has been established. One small move of retaliation or defensiveness and the trust vanishes. When children are permitted and encouraged to express their negative feelings, they can learn more effective ways of expressing them. When a child is consistently feeling negative toward a variety of things and people, the teacher needs the help of an expert in relieving the internalized hostility that so affects the child's life. As children find acceptance in expressing their true feelings, the threshold of submerged feelings lowers and with it the intensity of the complaints.

Language usage

Broadly, *language usage* refers to the form of expression of the language user, or what people do with their language—the choices of words and structure in speaking and writing. In different social situations people adjust the usage so that the language varies according to its purpose, content, and intended audience. Thus, *usage comes to mean what is acceptable in specific situations*.

In the traditional school where the emphasis on language learning was mainly on "correctness," the term *usage* often was narrowed to mean the "proper" form and enunciation of words. A child's talking was measured against the rules of the older grammar and the use of the standard dialect, regardless of its appropriateness to the situation. Most adults today learned under this type of schooling. Obviously, many did not adopt the speech that was "taught," partly because of its lack of meaning and appropriateness in their out-of-school world, and partly because of isolated drill-type instruction. Children who imitate the speech of these adults show many of the same frowned-on usage patterns.

"Acceptable" and "unacceptable" forms of speech Certain usages that are part of any child's speech may interfere with communication. We find what is called "slovenly" speech: careless speech, confused expression, and incomplete meanings. (Incomplete sentences may have complete meanings in a verbal exchange.) All of these aspects of usage need attention. All people can improve their speech by making it more exact, more concise, and more vivid. They can eliminate patterns that are disturbing or confusing to their listeners. Therefore, helping children move in all these directions is a continuing responsibility of the school.

Pooley, an authority in the field of grammar and usage, lists speech forms that should or should not be a part of usage teaching in the elementary school. He comments that "the wise teacher will not attempt to teach all the items of this list but will select for concentrated attention those of the greatest social penalty and greatest utility in the community" (Pooley, 1974, p. 183). Further, he suggests the wise teacher will not "teach" by drill or criticism, but rather by modeling and by discussions of how we can express our thoughts more effectively for better communication with specific listeners.

If teachers follow Pooley's recommendations, in communities that have accepted *ain't*, its usage in school does not become an issue. Where Black English is widely spoken, both the double negative and the redundant ("my brother, he") are used for emphasis. These usages probably would not be selected for more than casual mention, except with those children actively trying to move to the standard dialect.

Pooley gives examples of forms that deserve at-tention. Teachers can approach the expression *"learn me a song"* by asking, "Who will do the learning? Then what does the teacher do?" The use of the auxiliary verb *have* or *has* can be clarified to avoid *I have did* and *I done*. Verbs like *brung*, *drug*, and *clumb* can be checked in the dictionary. Verb forms that can be accepted include either *dove* or *dived*, *dreamed* or *dreamt*, *lighted* or *lit*. Pronouns like *hisself*, *yourn*, *hern*, and *hisn* also can be checked in the dictionary. However, the use of the objective case, *me*, *him*, or *her*, after *it's* is so common in informal speech generally that any serious attempt to change it is doomed to failure.

"Careless" speech, including dropping the *g* from *-ing* and running words together (like *gonna*), is generally acceptable in informal speech, and much classroom talk needs to be informal. By insisting on formal English we will not change children's language in their out-of-school hours. We will only increase their feeling of the irrelevance of school and discourage them from talking. We will prevent the development of aspects of language far more important than what little might be gained.

Like all other learning, usage should serve the individuals' needs. A child who already has a command of good usage can still improve communication by making it more effective. Each child might select one change he or she wishes to make and concentrate on it until it is accomplished. Children may identify these on their own or in discussion with peers and/or teachers. Teachers may want to participate also, perhaps by asking children for suggestions. The purpose in all cases is more effective communication. The changes to be emphasized depend on community values, each individual child's needs, and what is likely to succeed under the circumstances. Pressure for more than can be accomplished has negative results.

When the class is planning an event, such as hosting an important visitor, all children can discuss and practice what to say and how to say it so that it will be *appropriate* and make their guest feel comfortable. Other events that lend themselves to this purpose are:

Intergroup visiting within a school for sharing various projects, experiments, informal dramatic presentations

Field trips on which children will want to ask questions

Interviews with school personnel, community workers, city or town officials, people in business

Discussions for which both leadership and auxiliary responsibilities are identified and planned in advance

Thus, the eventual goal in language competence is to acquire the flexibility of several levels of language usage and to be able to use each as it is appropriate. Children need their home usage to communicate with family and neighborhood friends. They need an informal usage understood by peers and teachers. They also need at least the beginnings of more formal usage for special situations. Communicative competence is the *ability to make language accomplish what we want it to.*

Effects of home and community on language

The social, cultural, and economic contexts of families and communities have a major effect on language and communication. People tend to cluster in areas (and communities) where they find acceptance and congenial surroundings. Often they find it impossible to move into other areas, either because of outright social rejection or because of economic conditions they are unable to meet. Thus, cultural and language differences tend to be maintained throughout the speech community. Many of these groups have two major sources: immigrants and their descendants, and those persons of low economic status from various racial groups, including native whites.

Speech of inner-city children

In the mid-1960s people became more and more aware of the educational problems developing in the inner cities, partly because of rapid urban growth. More and more inner-city children were failing to meet the school's standards, and language differences were often seen as a main cause. Educators called children "culturally deprived" and said they were without adequate language. "They don't know what to call anything—they don't even know their names!" Yet Labov, who worked extensively with many such children, writes, "The concept of verbal deprivation has no basis in social reality; in fact, black children in the urban ghettos receive a great deal of verbal stimulation, hear more well-formed sentences than middle-class children, and participate fully in a highly developed verbal culture" (Labov, 1975, p. 64).

The myth was spread by those school people who believed all children should speak the same way—*their* way—and all should conform to the same standards. Children's being different had to be corrected! Since many teachers did not understand the effect of culture, the language difference provided a "legitimate" basis for their negative reactions to these children. Feeling unaccepted, the children tried to protect themselves by clamming up, a behavior which confirmed the teachers' diagnosis. The way schools received and responded to these children created many of their problems and ours.

Blacks, Chicanos, and Puerto Ricans are the largest minority groups with "different" dialects. These groups have moved into previously established areas in large numbers, thereby creating changes in living patterns. Each group has become a part of the labor force under circumstances that put most of them in the working class at a low socioeconomic level. Therefore, the two factors of dialect and social class are inevitably confused.

Children of these groups have experienced difficulty in schools and communities for various reasons. Since they "look different" they are highly visible and easily identifiable. They are often uncertain how to respond to the expectations of another culture, with the result that their reactions are frequently interpreted as lack of ability. Teachers have treated their speech differences as "bad grammar" and slovenly speech, without recognizing that each ethnic group has its own dialect, a consistently spoken version of English. These basic dialects have been modified in different areas, so that Black English in the South differs from that in the inner cities of the North. Whatever the variety of speech used, we must ask, "Do we appreciate the uniqueness of the rhythm and tone quality? Can we view the speech as having a difference, rather than a deficit?"

What is a dialect?

We all speak dialects, and each of us has our own special variety. One of the most common dialects, seldom designated as such, is the speech pattern of teenagers in each generation. Parents sometimes feel they must learn a new language to converse with their teenagers. Here is one of the places we can become aware of the change in living languages.

Whether standard or nonstandard, dialect is *not* an indicator of *the ability or competence of a person*. Speakers of all languages and dialects occasionally—or consistently—speak carelessly and inadequately. But the way a person uses language does not indicate anything significant about either intelligence or achievement in other areas.

The most widely accepted dialect is called "standard English" or the *standard dialect*. (The second is a better term because it emphasizes the fact that everyone speaks a dialect.) The standard dialect has been defined as "a socially unmarked variety of American-English used as a reference point in school language instruction to increase the individual's repertoire of important and useful ways of communicating. This variety of American-English is often heard on network radio and television newscasts" (Horn, 1970, p. 4). Good-

man (1968) says standard English is nothing more than the speech of the group with the highest social status in the region. The standard dialect is the best point of reference, but *certainly not a goal for which all should strive.*

The British can identify our standard English as a dialect since our sounds, cadences, and intonations are different from theirs. A number of words are unique to each nation. When we discuss cars, we talk about a *windshield* instead of a *windscreen* and use *trunk* and *hood* instead of *boot* and *bonnet*.

Within the United States there are regional dialects. Many of us can identify those from the deep South, from Brooklyn, Boston, or Texas. Experts, amateur or professional, can often place the state, or even the city, where a person has grown up. One day in the Orient two Americans met. After a few words but no exchange of identification, one said, "You are from Charleston, South Carolina, aren't you?"—and he was right!

A regional dialect develops among people who have lived for several generations as a stable group in a particular geographic area. Since they talk mainly with each other, rather than with people from other areas, they tend to develop similar voice and speech characteristics. Vocabulary is likely to differ; depending on the area, one fries eggs in a *frying pan*, a *skillet*, or a *spider*. One may go wading in the *crick* or in the *branch*.

A dialect becomes the characteristic speech pattern of the group when immigrants from the same country learn to speak English together and/or from one another. Each language has its own particular sounds, intonations, and rhythms, which are carried over into the delivery of English. We recognize the speech characteristics of someone, say, from Germany, from Italy, or from Japan. The Puerto Rican and the Chicano can be identified by their speech. American Indians have their tribal languages and often several dialects of each. Thus, each language group has its own dialect, a variety of English spoken by those with a common group or national background.

Black English represents a type of dialect. While it is built on the English language, its grammar varies from that of the standard dialect. Its pronunciation, rhythm, and typical syntactic patterns developed from interaction between southern whites and blacks whose speech was influenced by African languages.

Within these groups, each individual develops his or her own idiolect. Within our mobile population, we experience a variety of dialects. One may identify with certain individuals and either consciously or unconsciously take on some of the characteristics of their speech. Thus do idiolects develop and change.

Both teacher and children need to accept all idiolects and make the effort to understand them. For example, they need to respect Black English as highly as a broad Scottish dialect. Carroll sums up a statement on language and thought:

> I would emphasize the incorrectness and fallaciousness of the apparently widespread belief that speaking a non-standard dialect is somehow a sign of a deficiency in thought or in mental development. There may be some connection between language and thought, but it is not exhibited in non-standard speech. Our children who are speakers of non-standard dialects— whether they be blacks, Puerto Ricans, or Chicanos, are not the victims of underdeveloped language codes. Their languages have principles and rules similar to those that govern any language (Carroll, 1973, p. 184).

A black inner-city boy was asked to repeat, "I asked him if he did it, and he said he didn't do it." The child said, "I asks him did he did it, and he said he didn't did it" (Laffey and Shuy, 1973, pp. 22–23). This example is evidence that what one hears is retained as a thought, mostly without words, and then expressed in the person's own language. The child reconstructed the sentence into his own language pattern, his grammar. Such reconstructions may be perceived inaccurately by teachers as errors, rather than as children's remarkable display of ability to process and translate a form of language different from their own while maintaining the meaning.

A study made in Texas compared black and white, middle and lower class, four- and five-

year-olds on oral language comprehension. Apart from the socioeconomic level, race did not affect the level of performance (Jones, 1973). In other words, socioeconomic conditions rather than race may be the major factor in determining children's facility with oral communication.

In light of these findings, the most useful attitudes seem to be (1) to accept and respect each child and the child's language, (2) to help all children understand each other's words, ways of using them, and intended meaning, and (3) to learn to understand and interpret the nonverbal messages important for mutual understanding.

Restricted and elaborated speech

All people use both restricted and elaborated speech. *Restricted* speech is the context-dependent speech that we use with close friends and co-workers when details are unnecessary to communication. For example, we often use a pronoun without first mentioning the noun that it refers to: "Do it the way he did" or "There, you did it!" When a newcomer enters the discussion, however, it is necessary to expand such statements by adding background information and related details. Precise, detailed statements that anyone can understand are called *elaborated* speech. It is context-independent. We use restricted speech when we ask, "Will they follow through with it?" We use elaborated speech when we ask, "Will Congress pass the president's energy bill?"

Restricted speech, which all children tend to use inappropriately, causes one of the greatest difficulties teachers have in understanding what children are saying. Such speech might be understood by anyone who has shared the child's experiences in the home or neighborhood, but the statements are unintelligible to those who do not know the context. Here is an extreme example that illustrates the teacher's frustration:

"She told me no." "Who told you?" "My ma." "What did she tell you?" "She told me no." "No what?" "Not to." "Not to what?" "Not to come."

All speakers need to recognize which people

have the background to understand what they are saying. When children use restricted speech inappropriately, teachers need to make them aware of the need for more elaborated statements. After the teacher or peers have asked questions to elicit the information they need, they can then ask the child to "start over" and tell them about it. The more elaborated the speech patterns a person is able to use, moving easily from one to another, the more social roles the person may fill effectively.

Roles affect language Bernstein relates language to roles a person plays and believes "that unless a child has the opportunity to act a certain role he may not be able to learn to use the appropriate code which that role involves; and that the range of roles, which a child learns, may enhance his ability to use language" (Bernstein, 1971b, p. 71). In the classroom, children can take turns carrying out many roles that contribute to a broad, enriched program and require communication. Various helpers are needed:

The chairman at the day's beginning

The rolltaker and reporter

The school lunch and milk money collector

The messenger to the office or to other rooms

The telephone answerer

The custodian of materials, such as paints, paper, and equipment

The person in charge of each of the learning centers, (a) to see that all is in order at the day's end, and (b) to pass on to the teacher requests for needed materials

Other helpers unique to the operation and age level in a classroom

Another factor is that "the form of the social relationship acts selectively upon the meanings to be realized, which, in turn activate specific grammatical and lexical choices" (Bernstein, 1971a, p. 14). In other words, the relationship between people, whether it is between peers, between adult and child, or between controller and controlled, affects the meaning people get from a statement. Each of these relationships also affects the way the message is worded and expressed.

Teachers need to consider what adult-child relationship they wish to project by the way they use language. When they hope to develop responsibility, creativity, and initiative on the part of children, the expressed relationship cannot be generally one of controller, a "do-as-I-say" relationship. Teachers have final authority in many matters, but by taking the role of controller they lose the cooperation and sense of responsibility the children need to develop, and make their task far more difficult than necessary.

Perhaps the most useful relationship for a teacher to express is that of a more mature and experienced co-worker. This relationship can be demonstrated by requests rather than orders, by suggestions rather than commands, by asking children to help solve their problems rather than by imposing solutions, by securing commitment based on children's thought-out purposes and choices rather than making demands.

Further, teachers are responsible for helping children become aware of the relationship implied by the language they use with each other. The "bossy" child often loses friends and attracts only those who want someone to fight their battles for them. Children who speak tentatively and hesitantly are apt to be ignored and do not secure fair treatment, develop adequate communication skills, or contribute thoughts and suggestions to the group. For the development of effective human relationships, children need to be aware of the language they use and the way they use it.

The school's role in developing children's speech

The school's overriding goal in developing children's speech is to help them communicate more effectively with everyone they contact. The message, the meaning with its aura of feelings, must be conveyed so that it is interpreted as the speaker

Basic principles and guidelines applied to talking

1. The primary goal children have for developing their talking is to talk so others listen and understand what they mean.

   Therefore, listen and respond specifically to what children say. When uncertain of their meaning, paraphrase by saying "You mean _____?" and persist until you or someone else understands. "Tell me more about it" or "Show me what you mean" are other ways to increase understanding. Establish an atmosphere in which children listen to each other.

2. Children need the opportunity to talk, to be listened to with interest, and to be helped through interaction to feel more confident and accepted.

   Therefore, provide many opportunities for every child to interact verbally on a one-to-one basis with peers and a variety of adults. Do what is necessary to ensure that children feel themselves and their talking accepted. Only by feeling comfortable will the child be able to develop effective talk. Arrange for pairs who accept each other to work and talk together for various tasks.

3. Opportunities for talking with others, peers and adults, provide motivation for improving communication skills.

   Therefore, provide such opportunities, particularly where children are involved in content important to them. When children need to have their thoughts understood, they will strive to be understood, and thus communicate better.

4. Children use their own natural language as a base, adding and modifying as they find new ways to talk so they can communicate more effectively.

   Therefore, recognize that each child has a well-developed, unique language pattern. Accept it as it is and help the child develop additional ways of talking that communicate more effectively.

5. Children discover more effective ways of talking through interaction requiring communication with peers and adults.

   Therefore, establish active listening and constructive responding by children and teachers. The less well-developed a child's communication skills, the more opportunities are needed. Ask questions so as to help children expand their thoughts. Provide a wide variety of situations and purposes for talking with many different people.

6. Children internalize knowledge and understanding when they deal concretely with concepts and information in their own words.

   Therefore, provide situations in which children talk with their peers about what they are learning, explore meanings and applications, and express the new learning in their own words in a variety of ways. Committees and learning centers help.

7. Talking is almost entirely an intuitive process in which words and structure are modified only a little by conscious selection. Most changes come in response to another's need for clarification, which is also handled intuitively.

   Therefore, providing opportunities for

children to experience the need for expansion, clarification, and more exactness of expression is more effective than directed teaching and drill.

8. Children's talking develops through interaction in their own environments, and thus no two have exactly the same competencies at the same time; often the differences are great.

Therefore, note and record the accomplishments and needs of each child. On this basis provide opportunities for each child to have the experiences most likely to further the particular development needed.

9. Children have a thought or response in mind with few if any words, and express it in language natural to them at that time, usually with no conscious selection of words or structure.

Therefore, as children talk about information given them orally or read in books, encourage them to express the ideas in their own words, their own language patterns. Thus, misunderstandings are more easily identified and greater understanding is assured.

10. When children identify activities and materials as significant to them, they become actively involved, which increases their talking about the activities, hence internalizing their learning and developing their speech.

Therefore, ensure positive motivation and learning through the child's self-selection of materials and activities to the greatest extent possible. These choices lead to greater involvement and hence more discussion by providing needed opportunities for more effective talking.

intended. This process involves far more than saying the "right" words. The basic principles for language development (pages 74–75) provide direction in terms of children's talking.

How to implement the guidelines

Methods accomplish their purposes to the extent that they are based on what we know about children and how they learn. Since these guidelines represent important knowledge about children and how they learn to use their language more effectively, we will refer to them frequently. Three generalizations derived from these findings need to be kept in mind as teaching is planned.

1. Since virtually all children have developed language of their own that is effective in some degree,

instruction should build on the current language of each child, which is seldom possible with a ready-made lesson given to all.

2. Specific skill development should be used only with children who are ready for it but have not already achieved it.

3. Significant long-term learning occurs most effectively through individual experimentation and discovery as children interact verbally with others, putting concepts in their own words.

General guidelines to learning The implementation of the above generalizations implies learner-centered instruction, either on a one-to-one basis or with small temporary groups who need the same kind of help and stimulation at the same time. It also implies opportunity for children's informal interaction. We need to check each contemplated procedure against guidelines derived from the understanding of basic factors affecting children's learning (see page 317).

Remember that oral communication—people talking together, no matter who they are—is seldom totally "correct" in grammar or syntax. Sentences may end in midair, and words may be repeated. Reliance upon restricted speech becomes evident as we listen to tape recordings of conversations or group discussions by people of any social or maturity level. To refine grammar and syntax, written language is far more useful than speech. As these modifications become habitual in writing, they often transfer to speech.

Grammar rules not helpful While it is very important for *teachers* to understand how language works, including the descriptive rules of grammar, this linguistic lore is quite unnecessary for children. It is also virtually impossible for them to apply, except intuitively. Most children must be nine or ten before they can be expected to apply a generalization, like a rule, to a specific situation, like something they are saying. Even beyond age ten, ways of talking are so automatic and unconscious as to specifics that an externally applied rule has little influence.

Children can learn to use the terms *noun, verb, modifier,* and perhaps *marker* by the second or third grade, mainly in connection with editing their own papers and using context clues in reading. The terms need not constitute a lesson, but can be used and picked up through familiarity. In editing, a teacher might say, "Is there another verb you might use to describe the boy's action more clearly?" or "What modifier might give a more vivid picture of what she saw?" In context, as a child attempts to identify an unrecognized word, the teacher could say, "It's a noun, isn't it, because of the marker *the*. What noun might fit the sentence?" It may or may not be useful to introduce the concept of the grammatical *subject-predicate-object*. Questions such as "What (or when) are we talking about?" "What are we saying about it (or them)?" help children analyze meaning. Gross errors in usage can be explored by asking "How else might we say that?" "Which way do most people say it?"

Learning to use language orally can be compared to learning to ride a bicycle. There is a difference between knowing the mechanics involved and being able to get on one and ride. Instructors in bicycle riding must recognize when the learners' strategies are not working and do whatever is needed to help them be more successful. Language learning is much the same. When the child is focusing on some specific skill to improve speech, the understanding of specific language information may prove helpful. If so, the teacher can make available as much as is immediately useful. We all learn quickly and easily what is useful at the time of need. In the elementary school, language learning is largely comparable to bike riding—increasing the effectiveness of the daily use of language for the real purposes of thinking, learning, and communicating.

Effects of correction and drill Correction and drill are likely to do more harm than good. A long-term change will be made only if the child feels the need to change in order to communicate more effectively. "To hope, by means of grammatical formulations, to shortcut through the deep, cumulative learning that comes from speaking is to indulge in wishful thinking" (Moffett, 1968, p. 168). Children prevented from making "errors" or criticized for making them may be reluctant to try out new ways of speaking. If they stay within the limits of the speech they have found approved, development is delayed or cut off. Many educators think verbal drill runs counter to all that is desirable in the education of children.

Rather, we need to help children extend, clarify, and amplify their own basic sentence patterns. Talking can be an ongoing and integral part of most classroom experiences. While children engage in any purposeful pursuits, teachers have the opportunity to help each one express thoughts more effectively. Teachers can stimulate thinking with questions of "then what" and "why," and encourage children to explore various choices of words for more vivid and exact meaning. Through open questions, teachers can help children to grapple with ideas—"What different points of view can be identified?"; to elaborate and extend ideas—"What else may we want to consider?"; to foresee consequences—"What might happen then?"; to learn to follow through with a thought or purpose—"How do you see that related to the problem?" "What do you know now that you didn't before?"

To develop effective language, the child needs a room full of interesting things to talk about and the freedom to exchange ideas with others, both teacher and peers, with mutual respect. Children hear specific patterns that they can use as models for their own speech as they recognize the effectiveness of those patterns. As teachers listen, they can interact, particularly by raising questions to extend and clarify the children's thinking and ways of expressing their thoughts.

Opportunities that children need

Having established an atmosphere conducive to free expression, we next need to provide a wide range of opportunities that stimulate and facilitate children's talking. The classroom should be a communicating place where children talk with one another for many purposes. Teacher and children together can establish procedures for talking in ways and at times that do not disturb others involved in their own activities.

The classroom should be a place where the teacher is readily available to individuals or small groups much of the time, for discussing problems, meeting needs, stimulating thinking, helping children find their own solutions, and facilitating long-term learning in many ways. Organizing this type of classroom and establishing a comfortable, accepting, and stimulating atmosphere are main themes in Chapter 12.

Informal and planned talking Informal talking is valuable within the classroom. In order to utilize our learning, we all must talk about it in a relevant situation and say it in our own way, so as to internalize its meaning for us. Another value of informal talking is that, when communication is not successful, the teacher and children can discuss the problem on the spot. Why didn't the interchange work better? What was said? Did it show respect for the other person? Did it ask more than the other was willing to give? Was there a problem in the way the request or statement was made? In such situations children learn to modify their interactions so they can more effectively accomplish what they intend. They can explore alternatives in relative safety. Each can develop a unique and more effective way of interacting.

Beyond the casual, informal talk, planned opportunities for talking should be provided.* Each opportunity should have its own built-in evaluation, in the form of feedback without negative impact. Since talking is for communication, the question is always "How well was the meaning of what you said understood by those listening?" First the listeners comment on what they like best about what was said, and note any improvements over previous occasions. Perhaps they suggest what the child might work on next, such as giving more background, displaying something to "show what you mean," or talking more slowly or loudly so all can understand. Any suggestions should be in the direction of more fully developed communication that takes the listener into account.

Planning an oral presentation is useful in a different way from off-the-cuff talking. Perhaps Sammy, a ten-year-old, has been using a potter's wheel at home and has made several pieces of pottery. The other children's requests to see the pottery and find out how he makes it are the bases for planning a presentation. The teacher can

---

*Additional opportunities for planned talking are presented in Chapter 6. Strategies at the end of Chapters 5 and 6 provide more suggestions.

listen in advance to what Sammy plans to tell about and raise questions to help him round out his explanation.

Sammy's preplanning with the teacher, parents, or friends is a key element in developing his talking. The other children's questions during and after his talk give him an opportunity to think on his feet and respond in ways that satisfy the curiosity of the questioner. An evaluation can identify positive aspects of the experience and give feedback on clarity of explanations and the extent to which the audience understood the message.

Sammy's oral presentation may be expanded by many kinds of follow-up activities. Peers may ask Sammy to write out his information so that others can use it. Sammy, the teacher, or another listener may recommend books about making pottery. Perhaps another child has access to a potter's wheel but has never used it before. Now the two children may develop a mutual interest, become fast friends, and carry on long discussions of many of the issues involved. Similar results can come from any out-of-school interest. An oral presentation may be taped for various purposes.

Using a tape recorder If the program is flexible, two or three tape recorders are adequate for a group of twenty-five to thirty children, and these recorders will be more useful than some of the more expensive equipment that is put into classrooms. A tape recorder can be used for many purposes. The child can use it to prepare a talk or a report. By playing it back, the child perceives what others will hear and modifies the talk until it is satisfactory. A small group of children can record their ideas for some future activity, then listen to the tape and select the most useful suggestions. If their discussion breaks down, the children can use the tape to discover why. They will need the teacher's help until they have had considerable experience identifying the cause of communication problems.

To use the recorders most effectively, each child needs a cassette tape. The child uses one side of the tape to record, listen, and erase, but saves the other side for long-term use, for example, to record the child's language ability early in the year as a basis for comparison and evaluation later on. Teachers, parents, and the children themselves find real satisfaction in noting progress. The comparison also may identify next steps for accomplishing what the child has not yet learned.

Literature and talking Both informal and planned talking occur as children choose material to read. Their choices are influenced by comments and recommendations of their peers. When several have read the same book or story, they can gather to share their reactions. Did they like it? Why? How do they feel about the characters? Do they seem like real people? If not, why not? Is the plot realistic? Does it hang together? If any have read another book by the same author, how does it compare? Each child may see some new aspect of the book that makes further reading more significant.

Taking care not to dominate or control these discussions, the teacher can ask open questions designed to help the children think more deeply about the story and about the comments they make concerning it. Judgments can be challenged by "Why do you think that?" "How might the action line in the story have been developed differently?" and "What else could have happened?" Identification with the author can develop through questions such as "Why do you think the author chose this setting [this action, these situations]? What does the story tell us about the author?" Such questions also help children in the writing of their own stories. With experience, groups can later carry on these discussions by themselves. One frequent outcome is the suggestion of other stories with similar situations, plots, or incidents, which in turn leads to more reading.

With more mature children, the examination of writing style, characterization, and story line raises their awareness of these aspects of fiction and enriches their reading. It can also help children in the development of their own writing. Books, articles, or stories based on fact, such as historical novels, can stimulate children to check on their accuracy. Such involved discussions stimulate more precise use of language.

An ever-present advantage of discussion and planning is the involvement of many of the thinking skills. No useful oral presentation or follow-up can happen without related thought; different situations require different thinking skills. As teachers are aware of the kind of thinking required, children can also become aware of it. When "thinking" is brought out into the open, children begin to recognize what they are doing with ideas and relationships.

A serendipitous advantage is that almost inevitably what children read will affect the way they talk to some extent, although both the child and the teacher may be unaware of such effects. Over a period of time, however, reading is one means of helping the child develop more mature speech patterns.

The question of linguistic differences

We have described linguistic differences such as restricted speech and dialects and some of the relevant issues involved. But how can the school effectively improve children's communication and opportunities for acceptance into the wider community without doing violence to their self-concepts, their family and neighborhood relations, and their right of personal choice?

Dealing with restricted speech Early and frequent experiencing of situations in which listeners need more information may help those who need to expand their speech. Also being with others who naturally use expanded speech provides helpful models for talking. Although every person frequently uses restricted speech, these children are not aware that others who do not share their experiences cannot bring meaning to their context-bound talk. Our suggestions call for children whose restricted speech causes problems to be

with children from different backgrounds rather than being grouped together in compensatory programs. Here they would have models of more effective speech rather than hearing only speech like their own. Criticism and correction only do harm, sometimes serious.

Our understanding of children's learning indicates that we should set up experiences in which children recognize the need to make changes. A useful procedure is to ask children with this problem to explain some of their experiences to classmates. When the listeners want to understand, they will ask questions. Gradually children can learn to relate necessary information. Helpful activities include advance planning about what they will need to tell a particular group (their own class, other classes, or parents) and role-playing various situations in which the child is explaining something to a newcomer. Because the role-playing situation should be as real as possible, preparing for a visitor is one way to stimulate talk about what to tell and how to say it. As various ones try out ways of expressing the information, the other children can decide whether their guest would understand. Under any circumstance, it is important to encourage children to talk as freely as possible. Feeling valued and liked as a person enables the child to accept suggestions and work at the business of being understood.

Robinson describes a program, "Use of Language," that is "aimed to improve and expand the range and type of grammatical and lexical categories available to the children, . . . and so equip the children with an increased awareness of new ways of describing and discussing the world. In terms of Bernstein's theory, the aim could be summarized by saying that the objective was to provide an opportunity for children to develop an elaborated code" (Robinson, 1971, pp. 58–60).

Some of the tasks involved are to analyze their own attributes and those of relatives, friends, and objects, to devise their own categories and discuss the results, to describe to another child the nature of unseen objects, to develop vocabulary and the syntax of questions and statements, and to develop an inferential and hypothetical approach to stories. This last item means that in discussing stories the children read, we need to lead them to think of what can be inferred from various parts of the story, what the author means. Also, we need to ask "What if _____?" questions to lead the children to think beyond the actual words of the story.

Dealing with dialects Improving communication has become a serious issue in areas where the dialects of the community, and hence of the children, vary widely. Those whose speech is closer to the standard dialect have often insisted that other groups adopt their speech.

Of many factors that deserve consideration, the rights of the individual come first. We have the right to use the language of our families, our friends, and our community. Our language is a very personal part of ourselves, of our thinking as well as speaking, of our deep ties to loved ones and associates, of our lives from our earliest recollections. It is implicit and automatic. To have it rejected is to feel ourselves, our family, and our friends rejected. Anastasiow asserts, "When a teacher tries to directly change a child's language, he is inadvertently trying to change the child's thinking processes—which is to deny the reality of the child's self-concept and usually causes withdrawal and apathy, symptoms which Coleman and others have demonstrated to be widespread among inner-city youth" (Anastasiow, 1973, p. 25).

Hymes feels that "the concern [with dialect] is not with something that is cognitively necessary to the child's intellectual growth, but with something that is considered socially necessary. When one teaches a variety of language to children for whom it is not a normal variety, one is engaged, not in logic, in reasoning, or cognitive growth, but in social change" (Hymes, 1972, p. xxxi).

Hymes says many programs for children speaking dialects "imply a lesson that is terrifyingly simple. If one rejects a child's speech, one probably communicates rejection of the child. In reject-

ing what one wishes to change (or to which one wishes to add), one probably is throwing away the chance of change. In accepting what one wishes to change (or to which one wishes to add) for what it is to the child, one probably is maximizing one's opportunity for change" (Ibid., p. xxxiii).

On another side of the issue, all persons should be helped to modify their speech or adopt another language if and when *they decide they want to*. If we decided to live in France, Mexico, or China, we probably would want to learn how to speak French, Spanish, or Chinese as well as we are able. Likewise, if black children speaking Black English decide they want to communicate more effectively with people in the white community, they may wish to learn a white dialect. Just as we would not give up our own speech when we learned one of the other languages, neither should we expect black children to give up their language. They need it to keep in touch with people important to them. That language deserves respect, but we need to provide opportunities and assistance to those who wish to adopt a second language. We can encourage the addition of a white dialect, but if we try to force it, we may set up a resistance that defeats our goal.

Various reasons exist for wanting to adopt the language of the majority. One is that communication improves in proportion to understanding. Because this is so, businesses hiring employees who must meet the public or supervise a staff have a legitimate reason for selecting those who will communicate well. Because economic factors loom large, many students find increased motivation to learn to speak the standard dialect, or the dialect of the community in which they wish to work. Many black leaders are encouraging young blacks to learn to work effectively in the white community since most opportunities for economic advancement lie there.

Early one May, a group of sixth graders, three-fourths of whom were black, discussed the possibility of finding summer jobs. Various ones told of experiences their older brothers and sisters had had and of the attitudes of white employers. Interest was intense, and one in the group, quickly joined by many others, suggested they really concentrate on modifying their speech during the next month. They could choose at any particular time which dialect they wished to use, but when they were trying to use the local white dialect, they wanted the teacher to listen closely and suggest needed changes. Here were the ingredients for effective change!

Fifth grade children, who were studying dialects in their language work, invited a student's Scottish grandmother to talk with the group. Several of the children tried to imitate her dialect. Then a man with a different dialect was invited. During the project a variety of dialects were imitated by the youngsters. The next step was to explore the dialects within their own group, with each trying to learn another's. When speech differences were made interesting rather than "bad," children found that they could learn to use a number of dialects to some degree, and their respect for all ways of speaking increased.

Dorothy Strickland (1973) participated in a study to test the possibility of adding some of the standard dialect to the speech of lower socioeconomic area black kindergartners. Children in an experimental group listened daily to selected children's books and took part in oral language activities such as creative dramatics, choral speaking, puppetry, and role-playing. They did much imitation and repetition of the language patterns used in the teaching of English as a second language. All activities involved the children in active dialogue. The control group experienced the same daily oral reading of children's literature, but their follow-up activities did not include oral language participation by the children.

The procedures with the experimental group proved a successful way to expand the language repertoire of these linguistically different black five-year-olds. They began including more of the standard dialect in their normal speech, an expansion of language rather than a substitution. They did so at a faster rate than did the children in the control group, and the kindergarten level proved to be an effective age at which to begin the project.

While this study was limited to five-year-olds, it seems that an extension of such a program through the grades would continue to produce gains in children's use of the standard dialect without requiring loss or discrediting of their own. Since reading to children and involving them in active dialogue are advocated for many other reasons, both devices seem particularly useful.

People generally believe that children develop their language through imitating the language they hear. However, while general imitation certainly exists, it seems to depend greatly on the child's identification with certain adults. We tend to talk like the person we want to be like. Further, imitation very often fails when an adult tries to correct the child's way of speaking. McNeill (1966) gives the following example:

Child: Nobody don't like me.

Mother: No, say "Nobody likes me."

Child: Nobody don't like me.

(eight repetitions of this dialogue)

Mother: No. Now listen carefully; say "Nobody likes me."

Child: Oh! Nobody don't likes me.

There is irony in the mother's concern for "correct" form rather than for the child's feelings! However, this illustration has particular significance. Apparently the child had in mind the thought she wanted to express and was using her current facility with language to say it. This example may be further evidence that children listen for the message and are not consciously aware of the words that are used, just as they express a message giving no conscious thought to selecting words. Practice in the form of repeating a phrase or sentence that a teacher requests, has little chance of being internalized and used.

Compensatory education   Some educators have attempted the task of helping children expand and modify language to meet traditional school expectancies through what they have called *compensatory education*. Bernstein raises the issue of the implications of any "compensatory" program. First, such children are publicly identified as not up to the expected standard of performance, and such identification sets up a self-fulfilling prophecy* in the minds of both teachers and learners.

Second, if a child is "culturally deprived," then his parents are presumed to be inadequate. The result is that he must either reject school or feel that what was meaningful and purposeful outside school is no longer significant or valuable. Thus, such programs may progressively drive a wedge between the child's imposed school experience and his family, friends, and community. The alternative is minimal learning because the child rejects the program.

Third, such programs distract attention from inadequacies in the larger community. These programs assume without question that the goals and procedures of the regular school programs, as presently *implemented*, are the most desirable. They evaluate all children against those whom that program designates as "successful," and thereby maintain a *status quo* that recognizes few of the new understandings about the needs of children (Bernstein, 1971a, Chapter 10). Considering current awareness of increasing problems in our changing society, change in our basic educational procedures is both desirable and inevitable. Most compensatory programs now attempt to change children's dialects to the standard dialect, to expand their restricted speech, and teach the traditional approach to "reading readiness," which may be more confusing than helpful.

Fourth, compensatory programs group together children who have problems, thus isolating them

from children who could become models both for talking and for other desired development.

Constructive procedures for change

As children become aware of more effective ways of expressing their thoughts through listening and participating in conversations and other oral language use, they consciously or unconsciously change their ways of talking. Also, they may adopt speech patterns of those whom they want to be like. In fact, their language is constantly developing if they have not become self-conscious about it, or hesitant to express themselves lest they be criticized, or resistant because of pressure to change.

Present knowledge of speech development projects six constructive procedures. First, children need models. The model may be the teacher or one or more of the children whom they respect and like. These are "in the flesh" models. Another kind is the speech of those heard on tapes or records, radio or television. These secondary sources have various values but, unless used specifically to call attention to ways of speaking, are usually not as effective as the firsthand models with whom children can form good relationships. An exception may be someone on radio or television with whom the child identifies, such as an athlete or Mister Rogers.

Learning from models does not mean children will model themselves totally from one person. Rather, various people they contact demonstrate characteristics and behaviors that fit their perception of an ideal self, what they wish to become. They use their contacts with these people to help accomplish this goal, whether or not consciously aware of what they are doing. If children like their teachers, admire and respect them, then they will acquire speech patterns that are more appropriate and an improvement over earlier speech.

Second, teachers need to look primarily for the thoughts and ideas a child is expressing, rather than for the child's way of expressing them. Often they can understand at least a portion of what a

---

*"Self-fulfilling prophecy" is a term made popular by Rosenthal and Jacobson's *Pygmalion in the Classroom* (1968). They found that when certain learning accomplishments are predicted and expected, the very expectation itself increases the likelihood of the predicted result.

child says, or means, and so can respond constructively with interest and concern. If teachers need more elaboration, they can ask questions about the thought until it is clear. If the child seems unable to explain, teachers can involve another child or two, because children can nearly always communicate with one another more effectively than with adults. Children may then pattern their speech after that of peers who communicate more effectively with the teacher. Looking for the thoughts that are pertinent and meaningful to children is an important task for teachers. Once they can identify these ideas, they can work to help youngsters clarify, explain, and interpret them more clearly.

Third, children's talking develops through use of thinking skills. At any age teachers can encourage children to respond intuitively by using questions such as "What do you think would happen?" or "What might it be?" Asking "Why?" will bring out reasoning in some second grade children and in most children from fourth grade on. Consistent expectation of a reasoned response helps children develop both thought and the language useful in expressing it, including the complex sentence.

Classification and categorization lead to expressions of likenesses and differences, to qualifying language (alike in some ways but not in others), and to concepts of more and less and other comparative words such as *brighter* and *brightest*. Thus, classification and categorization encourage more exactness of speech while they develop the thinking skills.

Divergent and creative thinking bring in tentativeness of expression as well as of thought. *Might* and *maybe* and *what if* help children learn to deal verbally with imaginative thought. Such ways of talking help to unleash children's exploratory thinking while keeping both children and their listeners aware of its relationship to reality.

Fourth, teachers need to provide situations that encourage more effective speech for many purposes. Speech, of course, is developing all through the school day—in fact, a child's every opportunity to talk about ideas is important. Group work provides many opportunities in which three, four, or five children are deciding on purposes, planning procedures, organizing their findings, and making their presentations. Learning centers allow an ever-changing group to explore, discuss, and follow up on ideas and operations suggested.

Fifth, children need opportunities to talk about new concepts in all content areas, explain them to others, and put them in their own words, because these are primary means of internalizing the concepts. Such opportunities not only help children fit new concepts in with their relevant previous understanding, but also provide the content for many of the thinking processes. As children discover, see relationships, and defend or argue against ideas and ways of organizing, they are developing many abilities that they will need and use for the rest of their lives. Content varies in its relevance and permanence, but ways of using language are always essential in exploring, testing, accepting, rejecting, organizing, and explaining ideas.

In order for children to have such opportunities they need to work in independent small groups in which they are responsible for making decisions and carrying them out. Larger group discussions also are useful.

Sixth, there are invaluable learnings in human relations: being convincing without being overbearing, disagreeing without being disagreeable, being open to consideration of viewpoints or conclusions different from our own while maintaining a well-thought-out conviction, and not letting a persuasive leader or a "best friend" push aside our own thinking. These learnings can only be acquired when children have the freedom to exercise all these thinking skills in verbal interaction.

Beyond granting this freedom, the school has the obligation to provide situations in which much of this type of verbal interaction is an integral part of the program. Evaluation of work sessions, class meetings, and other discussions of problems and concerns of the children provide such opportunities. Continuous constructive evaluation of the effectiveness of these skills can be a major factor in their development.

Evaluation of children's talking

Evaluation of children's talking is valid to the extent that (1) it is in terms of the basic goal of communication of meaning and of the specific competencies that contribute to it; (2) it considers progress from each child's previous ways of talking; and (3) that many opportunities have been provided relevant to that child's specific needs.

Consider progress on various dimensions

The broad sequence in the development of children's talking may be described as follows:

0 to 2 years—Experiments with sound producing and sound modifying through lips, tongue, vocal cords, and body muscles controlling intake and exhalation of air. Use of one- or two-word sentences, made meaningful through intonation, context, and nonverbal cues.

2 to 5 years—Extends meaningful speech from the key words in context to that very close to those adult speech patterns consistently heard. Intonation continues intuitively.

5 to 7 years—Increases length and complexity of utterances. Relates meanings expressed orally to those expressed graphically by self and others. Uses increasingly mature syntax to express thoughts.

7 to 9 years—Continues to modify speech according to that consistently heard. Hearing and reading effective speech and well-written thoughts lead to more mature expression.

9 to 11 years—More concepts and concerns develop through listening and responding; writing and wide reading increase fluency, accuracy, and maturity of talking. Literature listened to

and read increases awareness of possibilities and leads to higher self-expectancy, thus increasing and enhancing oral expression of ideas, relationships, organization of thoughts, and self-evaluation as a communicator.

While there is general progression of competence in all areas of the language arts, the sequence of the more specific abilities may depend more on personal opportunities, perceptions, and experiences than on any predetermined sequence. Further, the sequence depends more on the maturity of children's thought processes than on age or instruction. Those who have not reached the maturity nor had the opportunity to develop critical or evaluative thinking in concrete situations will not be able to evaluate a report they hear a classmate give, talk about their own evaluation of their progress, write an evaluation of advertising material, nor judge the values of a book they have read. Their obvious need is for experience with critical and evaluative consideration of concrete situations. However, sequence is evident as sentences of two or three key words precede a well-organized summation of the results of a project or an effective, reasoned request for new procedures.

In general, we can expect

Short simple sentences before complex sentences

Statements of action before description

Description before a reasoned position

Reporting before criticizing

Shorter prepared talks before longer ones

More restricted speech before more elaborated speech

More rambling talking before better organized talking

Children of any age may be found in any of these stages. Kellogg Hunt's (1970) criteria for language maturity may be useful in identifying progress. The time limits for progress to the later stages depend largely on thought development, which depends on age, experiences, and teachers' encouragement through appropriate questions. As teachers raise questions leading children to respond at higher levels of thought, and some are able to succeed, those not yet ready to respond will have a useful experience if they do not feel inadequate or "put down" because they have not yet reached the more advanced level.

Questions to ask about Jim's* talking:

Do others now understand more of what Jim means when he talks with them?

How often do they misunderstand?

What opportunities has Jim had to work directly on this competence?

How often does Jim volunteer to prepare a presentation to a group? More or less often than before? How is his presentation received? What help has he had in this area?

Does he use restricted speech appropriately?

Does he recognize situations in which more elaborated speech is needed? What has helped him in this area?

Does Jim's particular idiolect interfere with his communication with the teacher? With all, many, a few, or none of the other children?

If it does interfere, what has he done about it? What help has he received and which procedures seem most useful?

Is there evidence of the effect of Jim's reading on his ways of talking? Of his writing?

The following are questions for children with a dialect difficult for most to understand.

*In order to emphasize the individual nature of evaluating in terms of progress, a child's name has been used. Each child needs to be considered in turn, using some of the above questions and others specifically related to that child's learning.

Is Rosita gradually adjusting her communication to the speech of the school community so that she is understood more easily?

Is Bill, by the intermediate grades, becoming aware of the social and economic values of supplementing his speech with the dialect of the larger social and business community?

These evaluative questions are suggestive of those that may be used in various ways. Some questions may involve group evaluation following a specific contribution by the child. Some may be part of a pupil-teacher conference during the child's own self-evaluation. Others focus on the teacher's self-evaluation. These questions emphasize awareness of the individual child's needs and progress, and the extent and kind of help offered to meet these needs.

The most effective means of evaluation is a conference between teacher and child in which together they explore the progress the child has made toward purposes mutually established at the beginning of the term. One very useful procedure is to tape each child's oral presentations at intervals on the side of the cassette reserved for that child's long-term use. Then the whole tape can be played and improvements noted. In many cases both teacher and child may be surprised and pleased at progress neither had been aware of.

Evaluation criteria for children's talking

We can think about evaluating children's talking by referring to the five criteria for evaluation presented on pages 103–105. First, evaluation needs to be continuous, so teachers need to raise the issue of effective communicating with the children daily, giving recognition of growth whenever warranted. Since much evaluation should be self-evaluation, teachers need to provide such opportunities after oral participation in a small group or the total class, as well as in teacher-pupil conferences. As children set up specific purposes for talking, these should be consistent with long-term goals. Evaluation can be in terms of how well each one accomplishes these purposes in the ongoing activity. What evidence can the child or others in the group cite that progress was made? Such discussion along with the conference provides the child with excellent feedback.

The long-term goals children will be working toward include increasing their ability to:

Communicate their thoughts more effectively

Express their thoughts more precisely

Use affective language more freely and effectively

Develop and improve human relations through language

Use imaginative and colorful language

Participate, neither too much nor too little, in all group discussions

Adjust their speech to their audience

Move gradually, but only to the extent they desire, toward acquiring the majority dialect of the community without losing their native speech (for those with dialect differences)

Summary

This chapter has examined the language children bring to school, what they can accomplish with it, ways we need to consider it, and what influences, develops, and changes it. Since talking with others is the means of developing and maintaining relationships throughout life, attention to its use for this purpose is a primary concern. We believe that appropriateness, from various standpoints, is important and that affective as well as cognitive expression needs to be developed. Children's language varies according to the usage they hear in their homes and communities.

Children need an atmosphere that encourages them to experiment with new and different ways of expressing their thoughts; offers them a variety of opportunities to talk with individuals and in large and small groups; and provides them the stimulation that develops curiosity, interest, and enthusiasm for learning. Emphasis on the communication of meaning helps children to develop more effective and appropriate ways of talking.

Suggested learning experiences for prospective teachers

The main purpose of the following experiences is to help you as a future teacher translate the information and suggestions in this chapter into actual classroom activity. Since these procedures will be helpful in planning your work with children, we suggest that you file the results and your reactions for reference.

Suggestion A

1. Observe three maturity levels within the elementary age range, in a school setting if possible.

Provide a focus for children's talking, such as a pet, an appropriate artifact, or an exciting picture.

2. Ask permission to tape the informal talking of one or more children or a small group at each level for two to five minutes each.

3. Analyze these three recordings as to sentence structure, use of appropriate restricted or elaborated talk, idiolect (most like what dialect?), thinking skills, and effectiveness of communication, how well you and/or others understood what the children meant.

4. What do you feel you learned from this experience?

Suggestion B

1. Observe the informal talking of children at a grade level of your choice, either in sessions set up by the teacher, or in response to some stimulus as in Suggestion A.

2. Select one student you consider an effective communicator and another who is less effective. Ask permission to tape-record about five minutes of their informal speech as they talk with you or one of their peers.

3. Analyze the recordings as to structure, elaboration, idiolect, and the thinking evidenced in what each said. Explain, if possible, why one subject's talking seemed more effective.

4. Think about what kind of experience or which of the Talking Strategies would be most useful for the less effective communicator, and why. In general, what kinds of experiences do you feel are most important for developing children's talking?

Suggestion C

1. Determine the difference in a child's talking with you and with peers, if this difference exists. Try to be as unobtrusive as possible where children are talking together.

2. Try to discover whether other children exhibit this difference. Identify which children demonstrated greatest flexibility based on appropriateness for the situation.

3. Decide what experiences or which Talking Strategies would be appropriate for those children

showing least flexibility, and why you would choose them. You may want to explore experiences suggested in Chapter 6.

Suggestion D

1. Obtain permission to work with a group of children to increase their appreciation of some aspect of the natural environment, such as an animal, the beauty of nature, or an ecological concern.

2. Determine to what extent different children are able to use affective language.

3. If you were to continue working with this group, what experiences or which Talking Strategies would you use with then   and why?

Suggestion E

1. After you have become familiar with a group of children, decide which child's talk bothers you most.

2. Analyze your reaction. What part do these factors play: the child's appearance or general behavior, your inability to understand what the child says, the child's use of unacceptable speech forms, a dialect of a lower-class group? Do you find it difficult to accept this child in other ways because of the speech usage? What would you do if this child were in a group for which you were responsible? What experiences or which Talking Strategies would be appropriate?

3. Decide whether your concept of specific youngsters has a direct influence on how you react to their talking.

Suggested readings

For an overall look at the use of language by children and adults, read Postman and Weingartner's delightfully written *Linguistics: A Revolution in Teaching* or James Moffett's equally important *Teaching the Universe of Discourse*. In Peter Farb's *Word Play: What Happens When People Talk*, chapters on "The Language of Children," "The Spoken Word," and "Making Combinations" are directly related to our purposes.

James Britton describes specific ways of helping children develop effective talking in Chapters 4 and 5 of *Language and Learning*. In Chapters 6 to 10 of *Child Language and Education*, Courtney Cazden discusses the effect of the environment on communication styles and the role of language in thinking. In *They All Need to Talk: Oral Communication in the Language Arts Program*, Wilma Possien suggests ways of making children more aware of a variety of words and more able to use them effectively. Glen Dixon's "Investigating Words in the Primary Grades" tells how to excite children's curiosity about words. Harold Longman tells the story of thirty-nine words and how new words replace old ones in *What's Behind the Word?*

Sheila Fitzgerald gives help on "Teaching Discussion Skills and Attitudes" and Barbara Olmo on "Teaching Students to Ask Questions." Somewhat broader areas are treated by Marvin Klein in his *Talk in the Language Arts Classroom*; by Joy Moss in "A General Language Arts Program in an Informal Classroom"; and by Barbara Wood in "Implications of Psycholinguistics for Elementary Speech Programs." Margaret Brown, in "A Practical Approach to Analyzing Children's Talk in the Classroom," gives examples of factual and interpretative reporting, of reasoning and the expression of feelings.

Children with "different" dialects are the subject of Charlotte Brooks in *They Can Learn English*, which deals with the everyday problems of teachers, and of William Labov in his article, "Academic Ignorance and Black Intelligence," as well as several chapters in De Stefano's *Language, Society, and Education*, in which Labov tries to put the dialect of the black child in realistic perspective. Robert Granger discusses "The Nonstandard Speaking Child: Myths Past and Present," saying the goal to focus on is every child's ability to use effectively whatever idiolect the child brings to school. Dorothy Strickland suggests "Expanding Language Power of Young Black Children: A Literature Approach," while Isenbarger and Smith ask "How Would You Feel If You Had to Change Your Dialect? Using a Simulation Game to Show the Effects of Forcing Language Change."

De Stefano edited *Language, Society, and Education: A Profile of Black English* in which leaders of various specialties discuss related problems. In *English in Black and White* Robbins Burling deals with all dialects, with Black English, and then makes constructive suggestions. Cazden, John, and Hymes in *Functions of Language in the Classroom* discuss Indian, Hawaiian, and black dialects; William Labov in *The Study of Nonstandard English* provides a better understanding of nonstandard dialects. And Roger Shuy in *Discovering American Dialects* provides a vocabulary checklist that can be used to point out dialects in any group.

Three delightful books that children can use to explore origins and derived meanings of words are Sam and Beryl Epstein's *The First Book of Words: Their Family History*, Charles Ferguson's *The Abecedarian Book*, and Mitford Mathew's *American Words*. They list words alphabetically, give their origins and various derivations.

Strategies for children's learning

Important steps for teachers to take toward helping children talk more effectively are:

1. Make each child feel comfortable about talking to teachers and peers, both one-to-one and in small or large groups.

2. Model talk appropriate and desirable for children's use, that is, adequate but informal, easily understood, and responsive to the audience.

3. Be aware of children's talking in all situations throughout the day, and raise questions about its effectiveness as needed.

The talking strategies that follow are useful to enrich learning experiences for children. They may be used directly or scanned for ideas for developing more effective talking among children. As teachers become aware of problems, looking through the purposes of the various strategies can help locate ways of dealing with individual difficulties. As consistent problems are noted, teachers may want some children to continue working within a specific strategy framework for a greater depth of understanding.

Be clear!

Purpose. To help children develop ability to use clear and specific speech.

Appropriate level. All children.

Participants. All, but particularly those with more restricted speech.

Situation. One child describes an object to someone who cannot see it, so that the object can be identified. Several procedures can be used: Two children sit across a table from each other with a screen between them; the object is placed in a bag; walkie-talkies are used by a child in the room and another outside; or one child describes the object

and the whole group tries to identify it. Ask the group to evaluate guesses. What information already given was disregarded when the guess was made?

An alternative: One child presents a problem to be solved. The group will try to solve it by using the information given, but may ask for more information. The goal is to give all needed information when setting up the problem. Evaluation notes how much added information is required.

Ask children to identify what information was not needed. Are children able to identify and ignore irrelevant information?

Teacher role

1. Set up a learning situation asking children to suggest or select details of the procedures.

2. Record performance of those who have participated as describer and as identifier.

3. Invite (but do not force) participation by children who do not volunteer, particularly those who need it most.

Procedures

1. Organize by total group or small groups those children who are ready for and can profit from the situation to be used. Conduct the activity leaving as much as possible to the children involved.

2. Make notes for evaluation purposes of individual children's thought development, especially analysis of all available, relevant information. Also note children needing further development of clear and organized expression.

3. Help children to use correct, precise words through group discussion. "What statements were confusing?" "How else could the describer have said it?" Probe for a variety of expressions and get group evaluation of their usefulness.

ORAL COMMUNICATION: TALKING AND LISTENING

Evaluation. Which children take advantage of wrong guesses? Do they improve on subsequent opportunities? Which children express problems more clearly? Which need most help? What improvement is evident since previous similar activities? Record significant successes and needs.

Consider the audience

Purpose. To help children modify their speech to communicate better with those with whom they are talking.

Appropriate level. All levels, procedures varying with the maturity of the group.

Participants. All children, but particularly those whose natural language is difficult for others to understand.

Situation. A visitor to the classroom: (a) an author who will talk about writing books; (b) someone who speaks a different dialect; (c) a community helper; or (d) a resource person from business or industry. An alternative: The group will visit or be visited by (a) younger children; (b) older children; (c) people in a place of interest on a field trip.

Teacher role

1. Set up a situation or take advantage of one in which children will be talking with someone not a part of their group.

2. Plan with the children what they may want to say or to ask.

3. Help children become aware of any specific problem that may arise in communicating.

Procedures

1. Plan with the children in each situation how to handle any particular problems in communicating.

2. If children normally use a dialect different from that of the person or group they will be talking with, ask them to consider what, if any, modifications they will need to make in order to be under-

stood. (Most important, perhaps, is to talk at a moderate pace and enunciate each word clearly.)

3. Ask them how they will need to modify their speech when the other group is younger. Let children with younger brothers and sisters discuss their problems and make suggestions.

4. When the group decides that some kind of modification or awareness is needed, have children participate in role-playing, one or more children taking the role of the group and others the role of the outsider. The remainder of the class evaluates what is said and asked, and how it is said. Will the other person or group understand? Will they get the information they want? Will they feel comfortable? What else can be done to improve any aspect of the situation?

Evaluation. Are children becoming aware of the speech, needs, and feelings of others? How readily are they able to identify the need for changes in vocabulary or dialect under specific situations? Record significant progress and needs.

Elaboration

Purpose. To help children elaborate their speech.

Appropriate level. All levels.

Participants. All, but more often those children whose language tends to be barren of color or detail.

Teacher role

1. To help children elaborate a kernel sentence.

2. To encourage children to expand their speech through elaboration.

Procedures

1. Talk with children about making their talking more interesting and informative.

2. Suggest a kernel sentence, for example, *Monkeys climb*. Write it on the chalkboard. Ask what

else they would like to know about it—what kind of monkeys, what did they climb, where, and why? Make all suggested additions, perhaps developing several alternate sentences as the children add words, phrases, and clauses, always checking whether it makes sense and sounds like language someone would use.

3. Suggest for those able to write that each take a kernel sentence and expand it. Results can be shared with the group. The extent of elaboration will depend on the age and language development of each child.

Evaluation. Has the experience affected the elaboration of any of the children's talking? Does referring to the experience bring expansion? Record any significant instances.

Question asking

Purpose. To help children learn to ask significant questions.

Appropriate level. All ages.

Participants. All children at times; those who especially need it, more often.

Situation. During exploration, discovery learning, and discussion in all content and skill areas.

Teacher role

1. To set up experience in questioning appropriate to the age and competence of the children involved.

2. To bring together those children whose question-asking ability needs development and plan appropriate experiences with them.

3. To recognize progress in any situation that indicates development.

4. To model effective questioning appropriate to a purpose.

Procedures for less mature, less experienced children

1. Begin a group discussion by asking, "What question would someone like to ask Tommy to find out more about his new pet?"

2. If appropriate when the questions stop, ask "What else can we ask about the pet?"

3. Gradually have children become aware of the kinds of questions that more effectively elicit desired information.

From this beginning, question asking can be developed gradually over the years as children's maturity and experience suggest. Some useful experiences are:

Asking follow-up questions after a report

Listing what children want to know about a topic in any content area as they embark on a new project, then deciding what questions would most effectively get this information

Surveying a list of questions suggested by the group, combining some, breaking down others into more specific ones, and adding any new ones someone raises

Becoming aware of the difference between open questions and closed questions and the purpose for each

Determining the purpose for their questions— to get information, to get opinions and reactions, or to get further suggestions—and deciding how to frame questions for each purpose

Considering various ways questions can be worded to gain the cooperation of those persons asked to respond and contribute

Evaluation. Following any discussion in which children were asking questions, have them evaluate the questions asked, pinpoint particularly effective ones, and explain why they proved useful.

Note and record incidents in the growth of ability and understanding of each child (1) in asking more effective questions and (2) in evaluating questions asked by others in terms of their purposes for asking.

Awareness of dialect

Purpose. To develop awareness that many dialects exist for a variety of reasons and that all are acceptable.

Appropriate level. In some form at all levels, mainly eight-year-olds and older.

Participants. All children or those who volunteer.

Situation. In many places, a single group speaking a certain dialect may form a significant portion of the children in school. Where this group also has a low socioeconomic status, and/or the dialect differs from that spoken by teachers and those of a higher socioeconomic level, the concept develops that the different dialect is simply "poor speech" and so must be eliminated.

Teacher role

1. To provide experiences to develop positive and constructive attitudes toward types of dialects.

2. To set up situations in which children can become aware of the variety of dialects and reasons for them.

Procedures

1. Bring into open discussion language differences within the classroom, putting no value judgment on any.

2. Starting with children whose speech is closer to the standard dialect, ask several why they speak the way they do. Then ask some whose speech is different. Continue until children begin to realize that there are many dialects, some more similar than others.

3. Ask children to generalize about why each person talks differently.

4. Focus on one type of difference.

Alternatives. There are four main causes of dialects: (1) national origin, (2) region, (3) community, and (4) occupation or hobby. The first category includes Puerto Rican, Chicano, American Indian, Black English, Scottish, Irish, Polish, Germanic, French, and the like. All these dialects, based on different languages, are also affected by the region in which the families live. The regional influence produces Brooklynese, Bostonian, the Texas drawl, and so on. Community influence develops when a group of people live consistently in one area (center city, low-income housing, farms, middle-class suburbs, or the exclusive areas of the wealthy).

The effects of occupation or profession, hobbies or sports, are usually observed only among older children and adults.

These alternatives can be introduced in any order depending on the particular need in a school. However, generally the order listed above starts with areas most evident to children. At any rate, beginnings need to be as nonthreatening as possible.

Procedures for studying dialects based on national origin

1. Start with those dialects represented in the classroom. Listen for speech affected by the less frequently occurring languages and bring them in as a similar kind of dialect to those more often noted.

2. Demonstrate acceptance of all dialects as adding variety and interest to speech. All people need to have pride in their heritage so that self-esteem is not destroyed.

3. Establish small groups around the dialects children elect to study. Be sure to include the dialects that have no stigma.

4. The groups can explore (1) different words with the same meaning, (2) different pronunciations of the same words, and (3) different syntax for expressing the same meaning. Children may de-

velop charts to make this information available to all as a step toward better communication.

Procedures for exploring regional differences

1. Start with those dialects represented in the classroom. There may be less awareness of differences here, and some may be surprised that others consider their speech a dialect.

2. Demonstrate acceptance for all dialects as adding variety and interest to speech.

3. Establish small groups around the dialects children elect to study.

4. The groups can explore and list (1) different words with the same meanings: *pail* and *bucket*; *blinds* and *shades*; *green beans*, *string beans*, and *snap beans*; *carry* and *tote*, and many others; (2) different pronunciations for the same word: *tomāto*, *tomäto*, and *termāter*; (3) different phraseology: *at some distance* and *a fur piece down the road*. The groups can then share and discuss their findings.

Procedures for exploring community differences

This may be the most sensitive of all dialectal differences since it is so largely based on personal economics. In some situations it may be better to leave it untouched. If the group has learned to accept differences without disparagement, however, it could lead to greater intergroup acceptance.

The main point to learn is that these language differences occur because of fairly closed communities, and that attitudes of other groups and what many see as self-protection are the main contributing factors. *The language one speaks does not indicate the kind of person one is!*

Procedures for exploring occupational or hobby dialects

These dialects tend to be characterized by specialized vocabularies, different words with the same meanings as more commonly used words, and somewhat different syntax patterns. The topic is probably better suited to the ten- and eleven-year-olds than to younger children.

1. Raise the issue with the group until all recognize some of these dialects, which include professional talk by lawyers, doctors, or educators, who usually limit such dialect to communication with colleagues or discussions of professional topics. The category also includes various occupational groups, such as computer operators and auto mechanics, and hobbyists such as skiers and baseball fans.

2. Let each child or small group of children explore any of these areas, compile translations of words and phrases, and share them with the total group.

Evaluation. All meaningful evaluation considers attitudes of acceptance of speech differences, and also of those who use different speech. This acceptance can take many forms but indicates appraisal of others on evidence of personality and character, rather than on the language they speak.

EXTENDING ORAL
LANGUAGE SKILLS

6

The purpose of this chapter is to suggest and describe specific uses for oral language, both speaking and listening, and some of the many ways of developing such use in the classroom. Effective learning procedures involve thinking skills. One child's talking provides an opportunity for another to sharpen listening skills, and considering the needs of the listener sharpens talking skills. What others "hear" can be used to evaluate both the talker and the listener. Often, writing is a follow-up experience, and reading is a basis for talking. All of these observations emphasize the close interrelationship of the language areas.

Developing interpersonal relations

An important use of oral language is the establishment of relationships between persons. Largely through oral language we come to know each other, know what others are like, how they react to people, things, and situations, and how they perceive and respond to us. Oral interchange is a means of resolving conflict, clarifying intended meanings, and arriving at compromise. Such experiences provide feedback that enables us to modify our reactions through new insights, in order to become more effective in human rela-

tions, and so to lead lives that are productive and comfortable.

People's effectiveness depends largely on their ability to establish good relationships. One of the more serious problems of people in business and industry is the inability to relate to others constructively. Happiness depends largely on friendships and comfortable relationships with others. For all these reasons, helping children develop more effective interpersonal relationships should have a high priority.

In nursery school, kindergarten, and first grade, opportunities for oral language are available throughout the day in many forms, such as block play, sand play, water play, homemaking, dressing up, and playground activities. All these encourage informal talking between children, and listening to each other increases the satisfaction in participation.

The teacher's first role is to establish an accepting and stimulating environment with appropriate ground rules. A second role is to listen and learn as much as possible about each child. Solving minor difficulties is a useful language experience for children, and it provides valuable insights to the teacher who is listening unobtrusively. A third teacher responsibility is to be aware of children who are not participating actively. After observing that Billy is standing alone but watching a particular activity, the teacher can ask if he would like to be a part of it. If he agrees, the teacher can take the child's hand and introduce him into the group. If he denies interest in the group, the teacher may ask what he would like to do, and if possible, see that he is included in another group or involved with one accepting child. Teachers cannot force group participation, but need to encourage it because interaction is an important basis for oral language development, through both talking and listening, as well as for social development.

The value of informal talking

Children gain much from a "talking time" in either large or small groups. Children talk about what they have been doing, reflect on it, recall their feelings about it, evaluate it, and generalize meaning and conclusions. Listeners who participate vicariously may decide to try the activities they hear about.

As children mature, their activities change, but they still need informal verbal interchange in natural situations, such as exploring, discovering, and speculating together in learning centers. Other opportunities include committee work, cooperating on group or class projects, and discussing books or stories they have read. Conversing person-to-person, they will occasionally share thoughts or worries unrelated to school activities.

Children need a special time when they can talk about whatever they wish, including the events and problems of their out-of-school life. The teacher needs to be available for observing, listening, and providing guidance. Appropriate questions help children to think through their concerns and plan direction for ongoing activity. Relationships deepen and mutual trust builds through such interaction. The interest stimulated by such discussion may initiate a whole new project.

When informal talking is the first activity of the morning, children can deal with their concerns and then lay them aside in favor of the day's activity. Suppression of the child's personal concerns

can produce worry and frustration that interferes with learning for the rest of the day—or even for days to come. Learning is more durable when it is attached to the learner's concerns. Child-initiated discussion increases involvement, which is essential for long-term learning. In fact, involvement largely explains the extensive learning that occurs during out-of-school hours.

Interchanges among children who are deeply involved increase their ability to communicate effectively. By observing the natural interaction of children involved in constructive activities, teachers can see the human relations problems that develop and help children recognize what is causing them. When ineffective communication occurs, the teacher can work with boys and girls on ways to use language to help, not hinder, their relationships. Without such help, ineffective communication can make children afraid to express themselves or drive them to incessant talking in their struggle to get feedback or to make themselves understood.

The teacher's procedures

As Miss Adams quietly moves around her classroom, she notes (in mental or penciled notes) which children are providing leadership, remaining on the sidelines, making statements that need clarification or expansion, or having successes that could be shared with others. She has observed that other children are sometimes hostile to Brenda. She notes that Brenda often moves into a group without permission and tries to change what the group is doing. Although many of Brenda's ideas are good, other children are becoming more and more resentful.

When Miss Adams hears loud voices, she moves over to Brenda's group and asks quietly, "Having a problem?" All start to defend their own perceptions, but Miss Adams explains she can listen to only one at a time. After asking questions to probe for feelings, Miss Adams asks if anyone can suggest a solution. "She should ask instead of doing things to mess up our project." "She should stop being so bossy." Miss Adams asks Brenda how she might find out what the others are planning and how she might make suggestions that they would welcome rather than resent. Brenda attempts to suggest new ways, and the others offer suggestions. Miss Adams ends her intervention by asking Brenda to try some of the alternative ways, and asking the group to help her remember other ways to communicate her ideas. Now the children have focused on ways to handle verbal interchange cooperatively, and all have new understandings about the effects of both the words and the tone of language.

At another learning center a boy picks up his books and papers and moves away in disgust. Miss Adams watches a moment, then inquires about the problem from the remainder of the group. Two children look chagrined, while two others look unhappy and accusing.

Finally Connie says, "We were being silly. I guess we shouldn't have teased Bob, but I didn't think he would get so mad."

One of the children chimes in, "I told you to cut it out, didn't I?"

"I'm sorry. I won't do it again," Connie promises.

"What do you think you might do about it?" Miss Adams asks.

A long pause, then hesitantly Connie says, "I guess I could go tell him I'm sorry and I won't do it again."

"Do you think he might come back and continue working with the group?" suggests Miss Adams.

"I don't know, but I could ask him to."

Slowly Connie gets up, her face a picture of mixed feelings. She has already learned that she will feel a lot better when she has straightened out a relationship. But it is hard to say "I'm sorry," and perhaps Bob will still be mad at her. She looks back at the group that is watching her and waiting. She walks slowly to where Bob is sitting. He looks up.

"I'm sorry I said what I did, Bob." When he does not answer, her lip begins to quiver. "I won't do it any more, honest. Will—will you come back—please?"

"Okay," and again he gathers up his papers. As Bob approaches the group, he says, "If you want to tease me, do it some place else. I want to get on with the project." Miss Adams turns away. No need to say anything more. Everybody has learned something about communication.

Not too many weeks before, Bob would have exploded with unforgettable words and might even have hit Connie. But he has learned that when he moves away without saying anything, things work out much better. Connie has confirmed a recent discovery—that in the long-run she feels more comfortable after she has said "I'm sorry." Before she was able to do this, she tried to cover her hurt and only made things worse.

As Miss Adams joins another group, she is thinking, "It's interesting that they learn most from the difficulties they get into. I'm glad they have the freedom to work together here. When they create problems, they have help to think clearly what to do about them."

Such illustrations point up one of the important reasons for using language—to improve human relations. This purpose is seldom listed among the goals of education, and when it is, suggestions for "teaching" it usually provide impersonal illustrations or rules that are irrelevant, for they are not related to the children's feelings. The chance of changing behavior under such circumstances is near zero. Changes occur when children carry out effective procedures under the impact of real situations.

Developing group discussion skills

In this era of group action, effective discussion skills are even more important than understanding the structure of language and having a large vocabulary. If we cannot state our position clearly and support it with relevant information and logical argument, we fail in a very important aspect of communication. Schools have the responsibility to help children increase their skill in effective group discussion.

In group discussion, each speaker needs to be aware of the feelings, needs, and desires of others concerning the topic at issue. To deny and belittle these feelings produces immediate hostility. Each member of the group must listen well, not only to words, but also to nonverbal cues that reveal the feelings and needs of the speaker. Both speaking and listening require sensitivity.

When members of the group differ, the speaker must seek an alternative, a middle ground that all can accept. The alternative may be found by considering action to deal with a problem, analyzing relevant issues, or identifying what the problem really entails. But caring about others is as important as analytical thinking.

In order to state the point clearly, comments should focus on the issue, state a position, and explain the reasoning behind it. Occasionally the reasoning or rationale precedes the stated position. Practicing this ability can be the main purpose of certain classroom discussions. When a child has stated a position, the teacher or another child can ask the speaker to summarize the main point and rationale in one sentence: "I believe [or suggest or recommend]____because [or since, or when]____."

Each speaker needs to recognize the contribution of previous speakers. The more supportive each person can be of previous speakers, even when advocating a different point of view, the more likely that a group can reach consensus. Children can develop this competence by restating a previous speaker's position to the latter's satisfaction prior to expressing their own. Also, they can recognize any portion of another's position, or intent, that they can support.

Relevancy of statements should be considered. A useful approach is to ask Tommy how his statement is related to the topic, rather than to declare it irrelevant. This procedure puts the responsibility on the child to defend its relevancy or withdraw the statement. It provides an opportunity for Tommy to explain instead of feeling "put down." Asking a pertinent question can help children consider points they have ignored because of personal desires or missed because of lack of information. Teachers can help children by asking, "What question do we need to ask to help us understand our problem more clearly?"

When we realize how seldom these skills are used by adults, we recognize the importance of helping children to develop them early. Controversy in both private and public life could be reduced through mutual respect, an accurate recognition of the other's position, and a clear statement of our own position supported by reasons. Agreeing to some portion of an opponent's position can spark further agreement and suggest alternatives acceptable to all.

Until the age of seven or eight, when children are basically egocentric, they can see a subject only from their own point of view. Conversations are not so much a meeting of minds as parallel talk. Gradually, children learn to perceive others' concerns and sense how others feel. When such issues are raised and empathy is discussed, children's progress is hastened. Without this experience some people never develop an ability to see how another person perceives an issue.

Group problem solving

Classroom discussion should focus on a real-life issue of the type children encounter either in or out of school. The topic should be an open-ended question or issue with no one "right" answer. It should be a real, significant topic that the group has expressed concern about. Children need to understand the purpose for the discussion, and any action proposed as a result of the discussion must have realistic limits that are clearly recognized and understood by each member of the group. Such action can be tried out to see if it is a good solution, one for which the children are willing to accept responsibility.

The participants themselves should decide how the group will operate. Getting acquainted and building trust are two important factors in the beginning. If trust and self-direction have been an inherent part of classroom operation, the process will be simplified. The teacher's role depends on the size of the group and its experience in self-direction and group work. Some large-group talk provides useful experience, but more will be accomplished in small groups with the teacher offering questions that focus and extend the discussion. As the group matures in discussion skills, the larger group becomes more useful.

Both teacher and children need to be aware of the various kinds of thinking involved in the discussion. A variety of thinking skills centers on problem solving. Identifying the problem is the first step. The group can evaluate the relevance and importance of all later comments on this basis. Other thinking involves stating hypotheses, providing data as evidence, stating reasons, arriving at tentative conclusions, and seeking verification.

Members of the group should feel free to take any position they believe they can defend. All should feel free to change their positions, without loss of face, as more information is brought out. The difficulty arises when a child changes position without realizing it or making others aware of it. Younger children quite often express two opposite points of view without recognizing their inconsistency. Some people never overcome this problem. Some adults sincerely express one belief but operate on another, unaware of the inconsistency. Therefore, it is important to help children learn to recognize inconsistencies in their thinking, at least by the intermediate grades.

In the sense that William Glasser (1969, Ch. 10–13) uses the term, class meetings are a special type of group discussion, useful for oral language development as well as for personal growth. Speaking is impromptu but not without guidelines that require responsible thinking. The dual purpose is largely to help children understand themselves as individuals and as a group, and to explore feelings in an atmosphere that is supportive, honest, and open. Children should be encouraged to think before they speak so that what they say accurately expresses their opinions.

The teacher can introduce the first meetings, but as quickly as possible the group should assume responsibility for initiating them and carrying them out. The content is whatever the group feels the need to discuss. The group may be working toward a long-term goal or solving an immediate problem. The teacher's role is to encourage the children to take responsibility for keeping the discussion focused, for ensuring that comments are constructive, and for carrying out any decisions made. More and more, the teacher becomes an observer, and there is much to observe and learn about the development of each individual's communicative competence.

Procedures for group discussions

The teacher will help in the initial stages of setting up the group, while the children determine their purposes and procedures. Later the teacher can become just another group member, or perhaps only an observer. As long as the group is progressing and handling problems with reasonable success, they should remain on their own. If discussion breaks down the teacher may intervene, not with criticism but with questions. What is happening? Why? What can you do about it? What responsibility does each individual have?

Several procedures should be talked about and understood by the group. Each group member needs to

1. Take responsibility to participate, to stay on the topic, and to show feelings of respect for all other members.

2. Recognize the value of every contribution, what its relationship is to previous contributions and to the topic under discussion.

3. Be aware, before making a contribution, of what position a statement is supporting or disagreeing with, or whether it is an alternative, a new and different idea. One may state its relationship while expressing it.

4. Be aware, as far as possible, of the extent of agreement within the group, and be able to state it when it would be helpful.

ORAL COMMUNICATION: TALKING AND LISTENING

5. Listen to each contribution carefully enough to reflect its main point or points to the group.

6. Recognize different roles that are useful in a group discussion, such as

a. *initiator*—one who starts new approaches and raises new questions.

b. *clarifier*—one who asks for additional information and for definition of terms, or who offers an explanation of a confused or confusing contribution.

c. *summarizer*—one who brings the group up to date on where they stand on the issue and points out areas of agreement and disagreement.

d. *evaluator*—one who points out what is delaying progress or promoting it toward solving the problem.

The discussion ends with a general evaluation under the leadership of the teacher. Each individual may identify what he or she did better than the last time and choose what to work on next time. No general comparison should be made between children, though they may want to point out techniques of individuals who are particularly helpful. They can identify problems for the group as a whole to work on and discuss possible ways of implementing better procedures. Like any evaluation, it should be positive, or at least constructive through identifying needs and ways of meeting them.

Developing language through creative dramatics

Unlike formal drama, in which actors learn lines created by a playwright, creative drama is built on the insights, feelings, and interpretations of the participants, either as individuals or in groups. Creative dramatics may involve one actor or many, spontaneous reaction or planned action, pantomime or dialogue. While such activities can be used profitably by any age group, they are especially useful at the elementary school level.

Playing a story

Playing a story is a way of enjoying it more and understanding it better. Kindergartners can play stories that have been read to them. In the early grades children can play stories that several have read or books that the whole class has read. One child may write a story and persuade friends to help present it to the group.

If the group has not experienced creative dramatics previously, the teacher will need to introduce the activity. The introduction should include an overall look at the story or the part of the story to be played. Younger children can enact the story spontaneously. As children mature, they begin to express deeper meanings as they recognize the author's purpose and how it is made clear through character development.

The group decides on the part of the story they want to play, the events they will need to portray, and the characters they will require. Usually children volunteer for these parts, but occasionally the group recognizes that one of their classmates is "just right" for a particular role and persuades him or her to try it.

The longer and more complicated the story, the more planning it requires. The group may set up acts and even scenes within the acts, but no script is written and no lines are memorized. The actors decide on the essential meaning that should be conveyed through action and characterization. Each participant must convey certain ideas to the audience through interaction with other characters, but each child is free to improvise a role. When several children have read the story, they can meet together to consider how each character feels in a certain situation. How can they show these feelings? How does a person look when confused, or afraid, or overjoyed? The children take turns at demonstrating such responses.

Children can create spontaneous stories through the "let's pretend" approach, which results in creative thinking and acting through "the serious business of make-believe" (Woods, 1970). A spontaneous story might evolve from an idea, a classroom incident, or even a prop. (A box of props can be kept in a corner of the classroom.) An old lace curtain transforms a little girl into a fairy, and the addition of a pointer makes her a fairy godmother. As other children respond, a play springs into being.

Spontaneity is the essential ingredient. Children's inner selves are released as they throw off conventional classroom behavior. Through improvisation they can express their own thoughts and feelings in words and actions, while the experience of being somebody else places responsibility on the character, rather than on the actor. When a repressed child portrays an angry mother, the role may provide much needed catharsis. A boy who had stormed and roared as the North Wind in "East of the Sun and West of the Moon" commented afterward, "I'm glad I was the North Wind. I really needed that!"

Usually this type of play is rehearsed only once or twice and presented only once, before the participants' own group. Occasionally the children want to present it to other groups. An upper grade group played a portion of *Tom Sawyer* first before a few groups at school and then before parents at various club meetings. No two performances were alike. In each performance someone introduced a new element that the group had to deal with on the spot. The values of such experiences include not only improvising speech and actions, but also careful listening in order to respond appropriately. The children learn to express themselves in an impromptu way, within an agreed-upon framework.

Using puppets

Many different kinds of puppets are useful as characters in creative dramatics. Stick puppets are children's pictures of the characters, fastened to sticks that hold them high enough to be seen easily. Children can sew hand puppets in the classroom from scraps brought from home. The faces of people or animals can be painted, colored with crayons, or embroidered.

At the other extreme of complexity are marionettes, or figures manipulated by strings. These vary from a solid figure moved around by one string to completely jointed figures with many strings fastened to two or more crossed sticks. Great skill is involved in creating the almost human movement of the most complex marionettes. Some children may be willing to experiment and practice until they become proficient.

Puppets are designed to be characters in a story. The story may be read or told by one child while the others carry or manipulate their puppets to fit the action, or the children may talk for their own puppets. Sometimes the children are hidden from view by a "wall" such as a divider or a sheet hung on a wire, and the stick puppets or hand puppets appear above the "wall." Or the children may build a stage from appliance cartons placed on tables so that they can work from below, with the characters appearing just above the "footlights." With marionettes the children are hidden from view but work from above, nearly always on some sort of stage. Often the children arrange curtains that may be opened and closed to indicate the different scenes.

The less mature children mainly use stick or hand puppets. Someone to read or tell the story relieves the shy child of the necessity to speak before the group. Working behind the barrier may give a child the anonymity needed in order to speak for the character. Children who do not need this protection may prefer to play their parts in full view of the audience. Focusing on the puppet and its movements helps to eliminate stage fright.

Using pantomime

Pantomime, also called *mime*, is the art of conveying a message or feelings through body movement without words. Like all nonverbal communication, pantomime is more directly related to thinking, listening, and feeling than to talking. It has many purposes and can be a part of many procedures.

An easy way to start with almost any age group is by reading a story and asking the children to show how they think the story characters feel. "How do you think the children looked and acted when they were happy?" The story continues and listeners demonstrate until a repertoire develops. When children have become adept at pantomime, they may try a variation in which one child exhibits a certain feeling and others try to interpret it. Eventually the children are "telling" long stories, including complex activities and emotions, by gesture and body movement. Two or three children may create a presentation that requires close attention and involvement for understanding. Pantomime can be used also in response to music. Even very young children sense the rhythm, pace, and feeling of music and respond with free movement expressing their reactions to it. Groups can become trees swaying gently in the breeze or tossing wildly in a storm.

A goal of all creative dramatics and particularly of pantomime is for children to lose themselves in becoming whomever or whatever they are portraying at that time. Expressing the feelings of characters in a story requires the understanding of those feelings, which increases understanding of the story. As children learn to interpret pantomime, they also learn to interpret real feelings more accurately, which is essential to improving human relations. Pantomime can increase recognition of one's own feelings and how one is expressing them. As children mature, so do their perceptions and insights into ways of interpreting feelings.

Role-playing

Role-playing is a natural form of creative dramatics for most children: "Let's play store. I'll sell things. You can be my helper and keep putting food on the shelves. We'll get Terry and Carla to come and buy." Children use make-believe to try out and

clarify the roles they see. Through role-playing, teachers can help children transcend their egocentric viewpoint and begin to see through the eyes of others.

Role-playing is particularly useful in preparing for new situations, such as the field trip in the following example.

A new house under construction three blocks from the school was a potential hazard for the children, who were curious about the building and eager to gather blocks of wood and other "treasures." The contractor had been ordering the children to get out, partly because they got in the workmen's way, and partly because a suit might result if some child were hurt. The teacher had arranged a walking trip to the building site, and the contractor had agreed to answer the children's questions.

The day before the trip, the children chose partners and planned to walk by twos. They discussed crossing the streets and waiting on the sidewalk until Mr. Woodbury, the contractor, came out to talk with them. They made a list of the questions they wanted to ask, then planned how they would follow Mr. Woodbury and gather around quietly while he took them through the house.

After this planning, they chose Fred, who lived next to the new house and had explored it with his father, to play the role of the contractor. Fred took his place at the front of the room to wait for the group. Partners joined hands and walked around the room, commenting on things they might see on the way. Somebody "saw" a wild flower and left her partner to pick it. When they came to Fred, several began asking questions. Fred said, "Hey, I can't hear you that way. If you can't talk one at a time, you better go back to school." This had its effect, and the children asked questions in turn. Sometimes the "contractor" would ask, "What do you mean?" and the questioner would try to phrase the question differently. Then Fred led the group in and out among the furniture in the classroom, warning those who bumped into anything. When they got back to the starting point, the children thanked him and, still with their partners, "walked back to school."

When they were back in their places, they evaluated the experience. Many disapproved of the girl who left her partner to pick a flower and decided no one should leave the group for any reason. They remarked about how much better it was to ask questions one at a time, and decided they would be careful where they stepped as they followed Mr. Woodbury around. They all learned to use his name, and somebody suggested a better way to thank him for his help.

As a result of this preparation, their field trip was a great success. The children learned when and how to ask questions and how to word questions effectively to obtain information. They also began to understand why workmen do not want children to play around building projects or enter buildings under construction. They learned to express the feelings and concerns of a person they had not understood before.

Role-playing human relations problems Planning field trips is only one of the many ways role-playing can be useful. Another is in solving problems or disagreements between children or groups, which can take a number of forms. If two children are each accusing the other of some misdeed, the teacher may say, "Can you show us what happened?" If one objects to what the other says or does, the teacher can then suggest, "How about changing places? You each pretend you are the other and show us what happened." If this still does not bring agreement, observers of the situation may volunteer to play the parts. This whole experience is an excellent demonstration of how people see problems differently depending on their "stake" in the situation.

Another problem-solving procedure to be role-played is when individuals or groups disagree on positions to take on questions or issues. Again those with differing positions reverse roles and must argue for the opposite point of view. This

procedure does not necessarily change opinions but it usually increases understanding. There is also a valuable experiencing of alternatives and differing viewpoints, an excellent situation for developing thinking.

There are two most useful little books, *Role-Playing the Problem Story*, and *Role-Playing for Social Values* (Shaftel and Shaftel, 1952 and 1967), that provide a number of situations and discuss ways to deal with them. The stories develop a problem and then stop, leaving the group to attempt to solve the problem. Volunteers can take the various roles in the story and carry out their ideas of what to do about the situation. They can play it over as many times as there are different solutions that individuals can see. With all the various alternatives laid out, discussion has a much sounder base. A group that has worked through several of these stories may want to tackle a real problem in which individuals in the group are personally involved. The careful thinking that must be done in this kind of situation, and the clarity with which they need to express their thoughts, are invaluable. Another important learning involves experience in seeing things from the other person's point of view.

Role-playing is useful in many curriculum areas of the school program. History comes alive and is better understood when role-played. Role-playing can explore international issues and the various roles of government—administrative, legislative, and judicial—at the national, state, and local levels. Real-life problems involving quantitative thinking can make mathematics a useful tool rather than a dry exercise. People out of the past become living beings when children role-play their accomplishments, whether as scientists, political leaders, or authors. Children may play the roles of candidates for political office or sponsors and opponents of ballot measures, and can begin to understand issues before the city council and the school board.

In each of these areas children feel the necessity

of getting information from people, books, and other publications, thus learning many sources of information. Perhaps an even more important learning is that every issue has at least two legitimate points of view.

Choral speaking

A group of children may wish to learn a favorite poem or prose passage and interpret it through choral speaking. This activity might begin with ''Mother Goose'' and progress through the years to rhymed poems, such as ''Paul Revere's Ride'' and ''The Highwayman,'' and unrhymed poetry, such as selections from John Ciardi's ''You Read to Me and I'll Read to You.''

Choral speaking requires interpretation as well as memorization. Thus, children will read and re-read the material, discuss the meaning of the entire selection and the meaning of each phrase, and reach agreement on the best way to say the lines. They must reach a consensus on pace, rhythm, emphasis, and tone quality, and decide whether pantomime will be used. The need for consensus often entails compromise that must be worked out verbally.

More mature, experienced groups will make finer discriminations and see more possibilities in choral speaking. For example, they may choose specific voice qualities for certain portions of the selection. Some parts call for light, high-pitched voices, some for heavy, emphatic voices. The selection may be divided among solo voices, small groups, and the large group. In some selections, only the chorus is spoken by the total group. Such decision-making requires a meaningful and rather demanding use of language and listening for the meanings and feelings others express.

The teacher's role is to introduce possibilities the children have not experienced and to offer a minimum of guidance, exercised mainly through giving encouragement and asking pertinent questions.

Developing ability to talk before a group

Talking before a group, with or without preparation, is a skill much needed in a democracy, which cannot function adequately without the expression of thoughts, feelings, and beliefs by its citizens. Schools are responsible for helping the child make significant progress in speech skills each year through direct and specific attention to speaking before a group.

Sharing time

A time-honored procedure, which has more or less fallen into disrepute, is sharing time, or ''show-and-tell.'' Often sharing time degenerates into a sort of busy-work, anything-goes activity to keep children involved while the teacher makes out lunch, milk, and attendance reports. The value some teachers saw in it was letting children get personal concerns off their chests so they could pay attention to the ''important'' work of the day. But sharing time should be seen as an opportunity for improving language effectiveness, and an activity that calls for evaluation.

In a classroom where all are interested in each other as persons, each child can be a learning resource for someone else. A well-planned sharing time can be a time of learning and of increasing interpersonal respect and solidarity. As with all classroom learning experiences, both teacher and children need to be involved in the planning. The teacher needs to set the overall framework based on long-term goals, and with this assist children to plan by raising questions and suggesting alternatives. The decisions at this point should be the children's, as this period is uniquely their own. Some guidelines for the framework may include the following:

1. No child should ever feel required to share something at any particular time.

2. The teacher becomes one of the audience and models appropriate listening behavior.

3. Purpose is a requisite for sharing or reporting experiences because it provides the framework within which the planning takes place. The purpose one has in speaking determines the selection of topic, thoughts, and words to be used in communicating with others.

4. Special longer sharing experiences should be planned in advance to allow for adequate preparation on the part of the sharer and perhaps of the audience.

5. Every sharing period is followed by evaluative comments by the listeners. Bases for evaluation are those purposes for which children have planned to work and listen.

The following are some of the values, and hence purposes, that sharing times provide:

1. Children develop the ability to stand before a group and express themselves. Facing an audience is easier when children are talking about something they really want to tell.

2. Children learn more about classmates and their special interests. Such knowledge may trigger new friendships and increase effectiveness of communication between children.

3. Children learn to plan what they want to say, to emphasize the main points, and to state their views if their listeners ask questions.

4. Children learn to consider the background and experience of the audience as it affects content and ways of expressing it. What needs to be explained? This aspect is particularly important for children with inappropriately restricted speech.

5. Children modify their presentations according to audience response, by cutting short the sharing if the audience does not seem interested, or expanding and responding to questions and comments when interest is high.

6. Children learn to evaluate their presentations

and their progress, and to use the constructive comments of their peers in planning their next sharing.

7. Listeners learn to relate what is said to what they already know, to identify points that are not clear, and to think of questions that might clarify the subject.

Content for sharing A wide range of content is appropriate for sharing. It is in this area that children make the decisions. They may make few decisions at first, but group evaluations will gradually set guidelines. What the group appreciates and enjoys will affect future sharing. Evaluations can include content and procedures, and can call attention to sharing that is innovative or has other special values. As a group member, the teacher can give positive feedback for unusually desirable features children may miss, thus opening new opportunities.

When children report an experience they enjoyed, they should be able to express and explain these feelings. This type of reporting, which is common with younger children, can deteriorate unless listeners probe for meanings. Why was the experience interesting? Why was it funny? Why did the experience make you feel good? Such questions lead to discussion on, for instance, what makes us feel good about ourselves, and what we can do to help other people feel good about themselves. Or the questioning may help children broaden or deepen their knowledge. What else do we know about _____? How can we find out?

When children wish to report on TV programs or movies, the purpose of the report should be discussed by the group. Would the story be more appropriate at a storytelling time? Did the program illustrate a special point previously discussed by the group? Have the other children already seen the program or movie? Perhaps others are planning to see it and do not want to know the story in advance.

By the time some children are reading the newspaper and/or watching news programs, important news items can be shared. These reports often lead into discussions or even long-term study. Certain days may be designated for different aspects of news: international, national, state, local, and human interest stories. Children can bring clippings for bulletin boards. If several children bring the same clipping, each should have an opportunity to express feelings about it or reactions to it.

Another very useful sharing involves hobbies. Children can bring their hobby or samples from it and tell what it means to them, what they are getting out of it, and how someone else might get started with it. In areas where only a few children have hobbies, teachers particularly need to encourage sharing hobbies and to explore with the children what other hobbies might be available to them.

Children may wish to bring favorite records or tape recordings. Some may be suitable for playing softly during quiet work periods in the day, as well as during sharing time. Book sharing is an integral part of any personalized reading program, rather than a part of the sharing period.

Teacher roles   A teacher has very important roles in developing a valuable sharing time.

1. Provide opportunity for the children's discussion and decision-making about questions of what, how, and when to share.

2. Provide for their determination of purposes both for procedures and for content in planning what they will present.

3. Provide for evaluation each period. Keep comments constructive.

4. As a member of the audience, raise questions and issues that broaden, extend, or clarify ideas and information, and encourage such questions from children.

Teachers need to be aware of the developmental characteristics of the age group involved. Because the fives, sixes, and some of the sevens are still egocentric, much of their conversation consists of describing personal experiences related to any subject that is mentioned. Although this tendency can be recognized in some adults, it usually gradually diminishes through the grades. Questions help children consider whether further reporting would add significantly. Evaluation helps children to plan future sharing and increases the value of their contributions.

Teachers need to be aware of the inability of young children to distinguish between actual happenings and their own thoughts, including daydreams, wishes, fears, or worries. These thoughts that seem real to youngsters should not be labeled lies, for they are not intentional untruths. When reality must be made clear, we can say, "That's what you hoped [or were afraid] would happen, isn't it?" When it does not particularly matter, the reporting can be accepted without comment. At another time, perhaps when stories are read, emphasis can be placed on distinguishing between reality and imagination.

Oral reporting

A report is a summation of the results of a study by a group or an individual with specific demands to meet. If a group is making the report, the work of individuals must be combined or coordinated to make a coherent whole. The group needs to select, plan, and organize the content for the presentation. Children can learn to time the report and allow time for questions and comments. Limiting the content to stay within the time limit is valuable experience.

Speakers must consider what the audience knows about the topic. What is new and of interest? What background needs to be built? Reporters need to feel they understand the material well enough to answer questions from the audience. At least, each reporter should be able to say where the answer might be found, or why it would be difficult to find. The audience has a responsibility to be certain they understand the report, and to ask questions either for clarification or to challenge the relevance of any portion.

The level of language used requires attention when older children are reporting to younger ones. Speakers should neither talk down to, nor over the heads of, their audience. The children themselves will think of ways to check their language, perhaps trying it out on younger brothers and sisters, or enlisting the advice of the younger children's teacher. Suiting language to the audience involves appropriateness as well as level and complexity. Some children are just beginning to learn about the appropriateness of language when they begin school. The finer distinctions may puzzle adults all their lives. A teacher can help by raising the issue so that children can think and talk about it.

Using a tape recorder   Taping tryouts helps children prepare for oral presentations far better than writing them out. Writing encourages rote memorization. A tape provides feedback that includes voice, oral emphasis, and pauses, as well as the need for clarification. Since retaping automatically erases the tape, rote memorization is not encouraged. Using notes as reminders leaves the speaker freer and more spontaneous. The experience of taping and playing it back, with retaping if desired, provides a basis for self-evaluation and promotes confidence.

Ordering information   In both sharing time and giving reports, one of the goals is organizing information in a logical sequence. In addition to chronological order, there are many other ways of organizing. The deciding factor is how the audience will best understand.

Several procedures can help children with the organization of their talks. First, encourage listeners to ask questions if they do not understand. Such feedback illustrates the importance of sequence. Second, encourage each speaker to plan what to say in advance. When each child has identified a competence to develop or improve, the child focuses particularly on that aspect in planning. Third, provide special group planning when

visitors are expected or the children will go to another room. Speakers will need to explain the background of their program, their purposes, and perhaps some of their experiences. In the group's planning with the teacher, they need to discuss the question of sequence or ordering of ideas. They may suggest various alternatives with a rationale for each. When one is chosen, all can be aware of the basis for the decision. This type of planning becomes effective after age eight, but can be discussed with younger children also.

Ways of keeping records

Each teacher will choose his or her own means for keeping records on each child's accomplishments. If you choose a loose-leaf binder, we suggest using a tab divider marked with the first name of each child, for easy access to that child's page. Provide a column for the date and add any other headings of your choice. Some teachers may want a separate page for each subject area. We suggest keeping all the language arts areas on the same page because of their close interrelationship. When a page is filled, it can be filed and replaced by a fresh page. Each entry should be dated. You may prefer to keep records on five-by-eight-inch cards in a file box with a tab divider card for each child.

Either plan allows the teacher to make notes in the binder or on a handful of blank file cards while walking around the room observing activity or sitting in a group. Notes, brief but translatable, can be made on the spot. Only occasionally, when involvement in the ongoing situation is too great to allow note-taking, will a teacher need to recall and record after the children have left. Like all other activities of being a teacher, note-taking will become easier with time and experience.

Children's self-evaluation and much of teacher evaluation will take place in the teacher-pupil conference. Notes can be made during the conference. Permitting the children to know what the teacher records makes children more aware of their accomplishments and also builds trust.

Evaluation of talking and listening skills

We use our goals to decide what we need to evaluate. In addition to the principles listed in Chapters 3, 4, and 5, the following guidelines are important. Again, we are using a child's name to indicate the individualized nature of evaluations and the term "increasingly" to indicate that *progress* is the goal.

Is Sally becoming increasingly aware that what she says and the way she says it make a difference in the feelings and reactions of others?

Is Sally increasingly able to use discussion skills effectively?

In group discussions, does Sally take an increasing part and in other ways indicate heightened involvement?

Does Sally increasingly monitor her group participation so that she does not monopolize the discussion? Are her contributions increasingly useful? Does she build up rather than lower the self-esteem and confidence of others?

Is Sally increasingly able to participate in role-playing effectively?

Is Sally increasingly able to use her imagination and creativity in devising skits, plays, and other dramatic activities, and to involve others in them, or to become a part of such an activity initiated by others?

Is Sally increasingly capable of talking before various kinds of groups for a number of purposes?

Does Sally continue to develop and use her thinking skills in talking and listening?

No tests can give us answers to these questions. Making notes on observations of children in various situations is more useful and significant. Notes should indicate the extent the child initiates, participates eagerly or reluctantly, or resists involvement in various relevant situations. Tape recordings should be made of each child's sharing, reporting, and participation in creative dramatics at the beginning of the year and then at key times during the year. Both teacher and child become more aware of change by listening to the tapes than by trying to recall general evidence of progress.

The single most important way to evaluate is through the child's self-evaluation. Children can be made aware of goals appropriate for their stages of development, their competencies, and their problems with talking and listening. Out of these each child can select those that seem most important. At appropriate intervals (shorter with younger children and those with greater problems) a teacher-pupil conference is most useful. Specific signs of success in meeting goals can confirm progress and stimulate further development.

Summary

In this chapter we have looked at a variety of opportunities for the development of talking and listening, the oral language skills. Any use of oral language, incidental or planned, should emphasize the importance of thinking. Such emphasis can be an integral part of the development of interpersonal relations, group discussion, creative dramatics, and any situation calling for talking before a group. Both planning and spontaneity are important. Each child's competence in these areas can be recognized by the group, by the teacher, and most importantly, by the child.

Suggested learning experiences for prospective teachers

Suggestion A

1. Observe in a classroom at the level where you feel most comfortable.

2. List situations that cause children to lose time or are substantial distractions from their constructive activities.

3. In one or two of the situations determine the basic cause of the problem, as you see it, and who might most profitably role-play it to bring out the cause, with each child free to express true feelings.

4. Can you now mentally put yourself in the place of a disturbing child to role-play acceptable (to the child and others) alternatives?

5. What do you understand about the situation now that you did not in the beginning?

Suggestion B

1. Observe in a fifth or sixth grade classroom.

2. Identify a topic of interest to five or six of the children. Ask permission to set up a discussion group with these children on this topic.

3. Raise the issue with them and note the way they deal with it. Do they follow the group discussion procedures described in this chapter?

4. Select one they are not following and discuss it with them. Get their feelings about it. Let them continue the discussion of the topic. Note whether raising their awareness of the procedure makes any difference.

5. Did this experience help you become more aware of discussion procedures? What cues did you notice?

Suggestion C

1. Observe in a fifth or sixth grade classroom.

2. Again identify children who are interested in a certain topic or question, and ask permission to work with them.

3. Raise the issue for their discussion. This time note which children take the roles of initiator, clarifier, summarizer, and evaluator.

4. Discuss with them the various roles and how they can be carried out. Observe if, in the continuing discussion, any are being used. If so, which ones?

5. Does this experience make it easier to recognize the taking of these roles? What cues are you aware of?

Suggestion D

1. Whenever you are in or observing a discussion (in class, at home, or with friends), remember the specific procedures on roles for discussion. Which are being exercised? Which not? Which are most needed?

2. If possible, enter the discussion using the procedure or role most needed. What is the result?

3. Later in the discussion tell the group what you did and why. Ask for their reactions. If they say it was helpful, ask them to explain why. If it was not helpful, ask why they feel it was not.

4. Was your attempt to take a role a learning experience for you? What did you learn?

Suggestion E

1. Observe in a primary classroom where self-direction is stressed at least to some extent.

2. Bring a few props that may stimulate imaginations. Ask for permission to work with a small group.

3. Show the children the props. Ask "What do these things make you think of?" After some free discussion, ask if they can make up a story to play using some of the props. Observe quietly from a little distance.

4. Did they invent a story they could play? Which props did they use? Was this result what you had expected for those props?

5. What did you learn from this experience?

Suggestion F

1. Observe in a third or fourth grade. Bring a poem you think the children would enjoy. Choose a poem that has repetitive lines and needs to be read with much expression. Ask permission to work with the children in choral speaking.

2. Read the poem through to them. Suggest they join you in the repeated lines. Read these lines, then have the children repeat them, first with you and then by themselves. Now read the poem again and signal them when to join in. Direct them as you would in music.

3. If their lines could be spoken differently in different stanzas, let them practice this, always keeping their voices together. As a variation, the soft voices could repeat the lines at one time and the stronger voices at another. Continue exploring alternatives within your time allotment as long as the children are having fun.

4. Was your choice of a poem a good one? Had these children done choral speaking before? If so, could they have handled more advanced procedures?

5. What did you learn about choral speaking? About your ability to develop it? What more do you need to learn?

Suggestion G

Write a strategy following the general format of those at the end of this chapter or at the end of Chapter 12.

1. Select a group of children whom you have been observing or working with.

2. Decide on a specific concept or skill you feel this group needs and is ready for developmentally, in some aspect of using oral language. Recognize the part thinking skills will play as the children carry out the strategy. Plan to strengthen thinking skills, along with the oral language skills, by the questions you will ask.

3. Determine the purpose you have for this strategy and your role in carrying it out.

4. Plan procedures needed. It is useful to consider alternative procedures to provide the flexibility that may be needed for the immediate situation.

5. Plan ways to evaluate (not test) the learning that has occurred. For example, do the children demonstrate a greater understanding or competence—mentally, emotionally, socially, physically—in the area of the strategy? What notes could you record that would demonstrate progress?

6. After the strategy has been developed to your satisfaction, carry it out with the group for which you planned it and evaluate their learning. In light of this experience, revise your strategy or write a new one.

Suggested readings

William Glasser's *Schools without Failure* describes class meetings, their purpose, how to start, develop, and conduct them. Gene and Barbara Stanford suggest *Learning Discussion Skills through Games* and provide many important ways to help children carry on more useful discussions. Joe Nathan illustrates how group discussion and planning can result in a worthwhile project in his article, "Can Kids Improve Their Community? You Bet." Two other articles emphasize activities and values in developing oral communication: William O'Bruba's "Promoting Oral Communication As the Basis for Reading and Writing," and Manuel Darkatsh's "Improving Oral Language Activities," which stresses social courtesy. Marlene Glaus in her booklet *From Thoughts to Words* has many ideas for enriching vocabulary and expanding imagery and imagination.

Two booklets give practical suggestions for ways to carry out creative dramatics: Emily Gillies' *Creative Dramatics for All Children*, and Charles Duke's *Creative Dramatics and English Teaching*. Bob Everle asks "Does Creative Dramatics Really Square with Research Evidence?" and answers by explaining some of the reasons to use this activity.

Providing ideas for content and procedures for creative dramatics, Albert Cullum has written three most encouraging, helpful, and ageless books, *Push Back the Desks, Shake Hands with Shakespeare*, and *Aesop in the Afternoon*. The first, particularly, illustrates ways of making school learning exciting. Mable Wright Henry gives specific help for younger children in her *Creative Experiences in Oral Language*. Dorothy Hennings' *Smiles, Nods, and Pauses* describes nonverbal activities and provides other ideas. Margaret Woods, in addition to "The Serious Business of Make Believe," has produced *Wonderwork: Creative Experiences for the Young Child*, and with Beryl Trihart, *Guidelines to Creative Dramatics*, the "why, how, and with what" of creative dramatics for young children. Eloise Hayes, in "Expanding the Child's World," and Ross and Roe, in "Creative Drama Builds Proficiency in Reading," provide different approaches.

Dan Cheifetz suggests "Improvisation: A Basic Skill for Living." Ruth Carlson writes of "Raising Self-Concepts of Disadvantaged Children through Puppetry." Eileen Divone in "Puppets, An Educational Experience" talks about using puppets the children have made from "junk." In "Puppetry for School Children" D. Currell explains about writing scripts and building theaters for puppets and marionettes, in grades one through six. When dramatics call for masks, Capparell and Suid provide not only illustrated directions for making them but also colored pictures of several different kinds.

Role-playing has various purposes, procedures, and values. Fannie and George Shaftel, in *Role-Playing for Social Values*, have provided a deep and rewarding understanding of its rationale, as well as suggestions on how to develop it and materials for using it. Their earlier book, *Role-Playing the Problem Story*, is shorter and focuses mainly on that one aspect.

The Suggested Readings for Chapters 4 and 5 are appropriate here also.

Strategies for children's learning

Developing discussion procedures

Purpose. To increase children's ability in group discussion.

Appropriate level. All children, but procedures vary with age, experience, and the size of the group.

Participants. All the class together or in small groups.

Situation. Although some total group discussion is necessary for children at all levels, small groups are more suitable for the younger children. Coming together for almost any purpose, a group may need to discuss purposes, goals, procedures, materials and resources, sharing ideas and information, and other topics.

Groups with more experience. Groups who have had more experience with discussions may have accomplished, partially at least, some or all of these tasks: establishing or recognizing the purpose of the discussion, its goal, and general procedures; discussing without acrimony, speaking one at a time, everyone listening, recognizing need for resources and reasonable preparation for the discussion.

Teacher role. To act as moderator until procedures are clear and children are fairly successful in operating on their own. Leave the group for short periods, and stay away as long as things are going reasonably well and the children are solving their own problems. Ask a child to be temporary moderator.

When problems develop, stop the action and encourage the children to make needed decisions. Help the children identify the problem, its cause, and what each of them might do to prevent or solve the problem.

Procedures

1. Establish with children the purpose of the group and what they hope to accomplish.

2. Establish or review how they will operate. The fewer rules and restrictions the better; do away with raising hands for permission to talk. Most five- and six-year-olds can learn to take turns talking, and not to interrupt the person speaking.

3. Whenever necessary, help children understand and practice various group service roles, such as group leader or moderator, recorder of agreements, one who helps keep the group on target, and so on.

4. Help children analyze the discussion as they recall it or by playing it back from a tape recorder.

5. Play a lessening role as rapidly as the children can assume responsibility.

6. Move from moderator to participator on the same basis as any group member while a child takes over the moderator role, to an observer and resource person, to finally, an occasional short-time visitor. In general, the smaller the group the more quickly that last role can become operative.

Evaluation. Group self-evaluation, with the teacher asking omitted but pertinent questions. Is the group becoming more effective? Do some individuals need more experience? Which skills are still needed by the group? By individuals? Are the children able to identify needs and suggest ways of meeting them?

Solving problems

Purpose. To use role-playing to work out ways of living together and solving problems that living together incurs.

Appropriate level. All levels; simple with young children, more complex with older children.

Participants. All children in general situations, or those who have special problems.

Situation. At the beginning of the year, children and teacher need to agree about how they will live together. As some of these ways break down, role-playing can pinpoint causes and suggest solutions so that all can understand and thus are more likely to follow through. When a problem involves only a few children, these children can analyze the situation and agree on acceptable alternatives through role-playing.

Teacher role. To identify a problem that persists. To use role-playing to increase children's awareness of its causes and solutions, thus providing a more comfortable and satisfying situation for all children.

Procedures

1. Identify for children the situation that is at variance with earlier agreements and that seems to persist.

2. Let children volunteer to role-play the situation either to highlight the cause of the problem or to illustrate a possible solution.

3. Discuss with the group the causes and solutions thus suggested, and attempt to gain consensus on future procedures.

Evaluation. Was the problem solved? If not, can children now identify causes or suggest solutions? Can they identify the causes of some children's discomfort or lack of satisfaction through further, more insightful role-playing?

Preparing for visitors

Purpose. To role-play to identify situations requiring careful speech, specifically when visiting or receiving visitors.

Appropriate level. All levels for appropriate situations.

Participants. All children, particularly children who wish to modify or upgrade their speech.

Situation. At classroom doors, visitors range from children from other rooms to adults from outside the school system.

Teacher role. To use role-playing to develop attitudes and competency for meeting people at the door. To help children establish guidelines and provide practice in carrying them out. To extend experiences to being a guest, and to role-play what is expected of guests.

Procedures

1. Help children recall recent visitors who came to the classroom door and list the categories into which they fell. These might include a child from another room, another teacher, the principal, a student's mother or father, an invited guest, or a stranger.

2. Discuss with children available alternatives, whether or not to invite the person in, and what to say under either circumstance; also what the children should say when they themselves are visitors.

3. List important essentials, such as courtesy, clear speech, either fulfilling the visitor's request or staying with the visitor until someone else takes over.

4. Ask volunteers to be responsible for answering knocks—one child each day with another as alternate, who may then take over responsibility the following day. (When such a program is established, request the cooperation of any school personnel who usually just walk in.)

Evaluation. Are children improving the clarity of their speech as they meet people at the door? Are they becoming more sensitive to the feelings of visitors? Are they stating requests more clearly

ORAL COMMUNICATION: TALKING AND LISTENING

when they go to other classrooms? Is there any evidence this improvement is carrying over to out-of-school situations?

Understanding the past

Purpose. Role-playing to understand incidents and situations of the past.

Appropriate level. All levels, but most useful from eight years on.

Participants. All children or small groups.

Situation. Episodes in history and living conditions of the past are difficult to understand, particularly for children. Role-playing can bring a measure of reality to many incidents and situations in the social studies curriculum.

Teacher role. To check each child's understanding of a historical incident or situation. To suggest playing it if there is lack of understanding. To raise questions or use children's questions to stimulate interest and curiosity that will lead to exploration in depth as children plan and prepare for the reenactment. To make materials and resources available for such exploration.

Procedures for younger children

1. Limit the concepts for children to develop to a few significant ones, not the superficial ones often emphasized. For instance, at Thanksgiving a group may focus on the way the first settlers got their food, in contrast to how we get ours.

2. Discuss the difference with the children and begin planning with them how they will play it.

3. Stimulate them to check the pictures and text of books about the food of these early settlers, and to discuss the details of food acquisition and preparation. Try to bring out and correct the children's misconceptions.

4. Raise the question of how people felt on that first Thanksgiving Day, how our families would feel if we were unable to buy food. Have them compare what the early settlers were thankful for with what we have to be thankful for.

5. Discuss with them their final plans for role-playing, taking advantage of the specifics that have interested them, and keeping it focused on the one issue of acquiring food.

Alternatives for older children

1. Pick up on questions, misunderstandings, and curiosities of children in learning about incidents and situations of the past.

2. Help them pinpoint their questions and discuss what situations they might role-play for clarification.

3. Make as many resources of information available as possible.

4. Help them follow up on their questions and misunderstandings.

5. Discuss with them their plans for playing the incident.

Suggested subjects

1. At Thanksgiving this age group may focus on the relationships between Indians and colonists. Those interested in following up the issue may study relationships between Indians and whites up to the present.

2. Show how the Declaration of Independence was written and adopted.

3. Set up a congressional, state legislature, or city council debate on an issue past or current.

4. Reenact the Boston Tea Party to show why it occurred and who took part in it.

Evaluation. Was enthusiasm generated for finding out more about the event explored? Did children read more to seek information they needed? Did the impromptu playing of the situation develop more fluent, communicative speech? Did understandings deepen?

What are different jobs like?

Purpose. Role-playing for exploring occupations.

Appropriate level. Ages concerned with different occupations. Younger children are mainly interested in community service roles (police, fire, telephone, postal, electrical, sanitary) and clerk roles in various kinds of stores. Older children are likely to be concerned with a broader range of occupations. The role-playing technique is especially appropriate in connection with career education.

Participants. All children or groups particularly concerned.

Situation. The situation may arise in various ways, including teacher initiation, children's questions, a school or class visitor, or a community incident. Whatever the source, explore it through role-play only if some children show interest in finding out more about it.

Teacher role. To recognize a group interest and further it through questions. To encourage children to do all of the planning they can; both the thinking involved and the special use of language for this purpose are highly desirable developmental processes. To use questions to open areas children are not aware of. To recognize that children's ideas may lead in a different direction from the one you have in mind. To provide resources and encourage their use.

Procedures

1. Discuss with the children the workers involved, the situation or situations where their work takes place, and what their functions are.

2. Assist the group in planning how to carry out the role-play for a day or two or for a longer, in-depth study.

3. Make both human and printed resources available and encourage the exploration of the selected careers through these resources.

4. Discuss with the children how they will carry out their role-playing, who will be involved, and a clarification of these roles.

Evaluation. The first and most important evaluation at all levels is the children's self-evaluation of their project. Did we accomplish our purpose? What did we learn beyond our original plans? Which parts of the project were done best, were most useful? Which the least useful? What have we learned that will help us with some other project? What have we learned about interpersonal relations?

Further evaluation can be done by teacher observation. Have some children made unusual progress in reading? In writing? In interpersonal relations? In use of language in communication? In broader friendships? Is there greater group morale and cohesiveness? A greater interest in school in general? All of these benefits and others have been noted following successful projects.

Developing choral speaking

Purpose. To improve various aspects of speech through choral speaking.

Appropriate level. Eights and older.

Participants. All children.

Teacher role. To acquaint children with the various approaches to choral speaking, to make it a fun time for enjoyment and appreciation. To encourage children to modify their voices, making them louder or softer, and to speak at the same time and pace, as a beginning of vocal control for effect.

Procedures

1. Read a poem, new or familiar, to the children.

2. Decide on an appropriate way to arrange the choral speaking and carry it out, either according to one of the suggestions given below, or some plan that seems better suited.

a. Read the poem with children joining in the refrain at the end of each stanza. For younger children "This Is the House That Jack Built" is a possible choice.

b. Read the two-stanza poem, "The Bear Went over the Mountain." Divide the group into thirds, each saying a line, then either the whole group or a strong solo voice saying "To see what he could see."

c. Read James Whitcomb Riley's "The Raggedy Man" at a time when dialects are being discussed. Have children come in on the last two lines of each stanza. The poem also illustrates a life-style of people in one part of the country a number of years ago.

d. Read Rose Fyleman's "Fairies" to children to help them retain their enjoyment of the imaginary world. Children can come in on the last line of each stanza.

3. Increase and diversify the children's participation as they become more familiar with choral speaking. Have different groups say each stanza or couplet. Certain lines can be spoken solo for various effects. Choose groups so that the voices are balanced, or divide lines between lighter voices and stronger voices to achieve effects.

4. Plan with children how to speak a poem as soon as they begin to understand the procedure.

5. Encourage children to find poems they would like to say together and plan how to present them.

Evaluation. Do children often ask to do choral speaking? Do they bring in poems to work out? Do groups get together to plan and produce choral speaking before the rest of the children? Do they show evidence of more vocal control than before?

Telling stories

Purpose. To develop storytelling through a series of pictures.

Appropriate level. Sixes and older.

Participants. Any child or small group that wants to tell a story using a series of pictures.

Situation. Storytelling can be a part of sharing time or a separate period in the weekly schedule. Both developing the story and choosing pictures to illustrate it are useful experiences. Compared to written notes, pictures lend more spontaneity, which improves the telling.

Teacher role. To suggest or help children develop the idea. To lend necessary assistance to any construction. To provide time and opportunity for preparation and presentation. To encourage similar activities by others through appreciation of the project.

Procedures

1. Conduct a discussion of storytelling and ask children to think of various ways of making the telling more interesting for the listeners.

2. Suggest, if children do not, making a "movie" of it.

3. Work out with the children ways it could be done. (One way is to take a substantial carton, cut a window in one side, fasten vertical rollers in either end, and roll up the strip of pictures, glued together in sequence, on the right-hand roller, beginning with the end of the story. Then the first picture can be fastened to the left-hand roller. As the left-hand roller is turned, the pictures are seen in sequence through the window. (In one school the custodian became interested and built a substantial box that was used to illustrate many talks.)

Alternative. If making a movie is too difficult, a child may make a series of pictures, stack them in

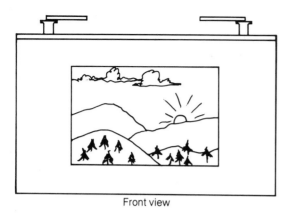

Front view

Movie box—front view

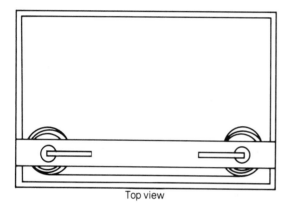

Top view

Movie box—top view

order face down, and set them in the chalk tray. Then the storyteller or an assistant can turn the pictures one at a time as they are needed in the story.

Evaluation. Does some scheme using pictures as props encourage more storytelling? Are the children more aware of sequence in telling stories? Are members of the audience better listeners?

Fact or fancy?

Purpose. To help children distinguish fact from fancy.

Appropriate level. Five to eight years.

Participants. All children, especially those having difficulty in distinguishing fact from fancy.

Situation. Stories provide nonthreatening material to illustrate both fact and imagination.

Teacher role. To raise the issue with stories read to or by children. How can we tell if it really happened? In identifying fanciful material, be careful not to downgrade it.

Procedures

1. Raise the issue of reality versus delightful or amusing unreality, for instance, in a story in which animals talk. Children may explain how the animal really expresses these thoughts or intents.

2. Contrast this type of story with one about people that could be real even though it is fiction. The question of whether the story is true and accurate is another issue, as in a factual account or a biography. Consider these same distinctions in a child's account of happenings, what could be as opposed to what is. Make no issue of it unless it poses a serious problem.

3. Do not press the issue of believing certain things are true that are not, for some children may not yet be ready to deal with reality, for instance, the reality of Santa Claus. Drop the matter at signs of resistance or anxiety.

Evaluation. Observe the extent a child recognizes the distinction between fact and fancy and still enjoys the fanciful. Are children beginning also to recognize the difference between fiction and nonfiction? Do they question the accuracy of nonfiction?

Reporting results of interviews

Purpose. To gain information through interviews.

Appropriate level. Eight years and older.

Participants. All children at appropriate ages.

Situation. In any area of learning, a question may

arise concerning what others do or what others think about some issue. The best way to find out is to ask. When one or more children are excited about a book they have read, they may want to find out whether other readers enjoyed it too. They may interview others, either members of their own group or other children they see on the playground or after school. Certain issues can be explored by interviewing teachers in the building and/or the principal. The ten-year-olds and older children, concerned with community problems, may interview families in their neighborhood, public officials, city librarians, businessmen and women, and many others. Some children may want to find out how people in different careers use mathematics or what kinds of material they read and write. In exploring careers, children may want to find out how people feel about their work and its advantages and disadvantages.

Teacher role. To introduce the idea of interviewing, if children do not suggest it, and to help them analyze and plan each aspect of the interview. To listen to any problems that arise and help the child solve them. To plan with children how to conduct good interviews and interpret them reasonably.

Procedures

1. Plan with children procedures for the interview, the purpose as they will state it to those interviewed, and who will be interviewed (for younger children, people in the school and at home; for older children, people whose answers would contribute most).

2. Plan with children geographic areas, vocations, or other classifications for the interviewers, so that no one is interviewed by more than one child.

3. Help children decide whether appointments are needed, and plan questions to ask so that the interview will be well organized and no longer than necessary.

4. Discuss sensitivity to interviewee's feelings about the interview as a basis for cutting it as short

as possible or allowing it to continue when the person wishes to extend it.

5. Help children plan ways of recording essential information quickly, perhaps by using a checklist, a one-word response, or quantitative data.

6. Help children plan an appropriate ending to the interview, including a statement of appreciation.

7. After the experience is over, help children organize, analyze, and draw defensible conclusions from the data.

Evaluation. Each interview should be considered individually. What reactions did each child get? What does each feel contributed to the reaction? What would they do the same way next time, and what differently? What new guidelines would they establish? Would they change the guidelines they used? Both the self-evaluation of each child and evaluation by the group should be considered. What, if any, changes are noticeable in the child's oral communication skills?

Improving oral reports

Purpose. To help children devise ways of making talks or oral reports more interesting and effective.

Appropriate level. All levels.

Participants. All children.

Situation. Any, but not every, time a child is making a talk, explaining a hobby, or giving an oral report.

Teacher role. To raise questions about how to make a talk clearer and easier to follow when the children listening had difficulty understanding it.

Procedures

1. Raise the issue of why the talk was hard to understand.

2. Discuss how it could have been more easily understood. Since seeing usually gives more in-

formation than just hearing, a series of drawings or cartoons might help to carry the theme. A puppet could be used to illustrate a point. Masks representing each character in a story could be held up in front of the face to indicate which character was speaking. Children could start with two masks and increase the number as their powers of storytelling grew.

Evaluation. Consider the reactions of the audience. If children actually gain more understanding rather than just entertainment, the graphics and demonstrations are successful. Therefore, it is very important to discuss audience reaction during the group evaluation.

ORAL COMMUNICATION: TALKING AND LISTENING

WRITTEN LANGUAGE: RECORDING AND RETRIEVING THOUGHTS

O pinions differ about the ways we learn to use oral and written language. Some educators feel that learning to use oral language must be a natural or innate ability since all humans (except the severely handicapped) learn to talk; but written language is contrived, they contend, and so difficult that many people can never learn to use it effectively for either reading or writing. Recent research findings about the learning process may change such beliefs.

Those who think of written language as contrived should realize that oral language is equally symbolic and therefore equally contrived. Yet when children are exposed to the interchange of ideas through oral language, they learn to use the language quickly and easily.

We have only recently become aware that children may learn written language in much the same way—through experiencing its use. The prerequisites are competency in oral language and physical maturity in eye development and coordination. Today many preschoolers learn to read and write from older brothers and sisters, from television, from books that others read to them, from signs and labels and many other sources. When schools provide the same kind of experience, children can learn to read and write easily and quickly—unless they are handicapped by negative feedback and confusing procedures.

Writing and reading—the recording and retrieving of thoughts—are closely related, but the schools' treatment of them as separate "subjects" has made both reading and writing more difficult. Interrelating them can help children learn to read and write more effectively.

We have dealt with writing first, in Chapters 7 and 8, because a thought must be written before it can be read. In Chapters 9 and 10 we find that children's writing, which begins in the form of drawing pictures, is the most useful "text" for teaching reading.

Before they come to school, many children start writing in some form: scribbling, printing their names, or copying words from books, newspapers, or television. Since they understand what they record, they obviously can read it. Even the scribbling has a meaning that they can put into words. They receive and express meanings within their own experience and at their own level of concept development. And meaning, or comprehension, is the first objective in teaching all areas of communication.

When children start writing, their oral capability has reached a stage approximating that of adults. Writing involves acquiring the mechanics and dexterity for graphic recording of the language that they use. But their first efforts to write may be less rewarding than the first attempts to talk. Children are encouraged to talk by the interest and understanding of people around them. Yet teachers often feel compelled to correct the child's first writing, instead of waiting for changes to develop through experience and maturity.

The information about writing that children require is not found in textbook rules memorized by rote, or in fill-in-the-blank exercises, which children complete only to fulfill an assignment. In the process of learning to write, children need to read and hear well-written prose and poetry in a wide variety of styles. Through such materials the child can internalize a foundation of ideas, acquire expectancies for writing, and become aware of language patterns and relationships. The next most important step toward effective writing is for children to write frequently, with involvement and enthusiasm, whatever they care enough about to choose to put into words. The long-term goal is for children to develop their writing so that it communicates with increasing depth and accuracy.

As they extend their recording through dictation and familiarity with the dictation of others, children extend their reading ability; and, as their ability to read increases, they become familiar with ways to record further meanings. Here is the intrinsic interrelationship of various aspects of communication. All aspects are enhanced when they are interrelated and diminished and hindered when they are not.

In this chapter we discuss ways of identifying and developing each child's readiness for writing through involvement in the day-to-day living in the school environment and through developing a pride in authorship. When each child has gained confidence in an ability to express thoughts in writing, growth and development come through the process of polishing. We suggest a number of ways children can use writing as an integral part of each school day. We then interpret basic principles in terms of writing and suggest guidelines for teachers' roles in helping children develop writing competence. We forecast some bases for evaluation, which we develop further in Chapter 8.

Writing in historical perspective

Written language developed later than oral language in all cultures. Prehistoric evidence indicates that the first recorded messages were pictorial representations of situations and events. Gradually signs and symbols were added that were not directly representative. Recent archeological findings in France seem to show that as early as 40,000 B.C. men were carving a sort of time record on bone, perhaps a lunar calendar, an intentional symbolizing. The Cro-Magnon period, 40,000 B.C. to 10,000 B.C., produced periods of major art, some of which was representational but some seems definitely symbolic. Also, pictures continued to tell stories of events. The transition from representative to symbolic recording continued until written languages were developed, such as the Egyptian with its *hieroglyphs* and the Chinese and Japanese with their *ideograms*. In each of these written language systems, a symbol, representing a concept or idea, may have no relationship to the sound of the spoken concept but rather to its meaning.

In a further development, Semitic languages used a *syllabary*, a system of written characters representing spoken syllables rather than ideas. This system began the tie between a written symbol and sound. The Greeks extended this syllabary concept to an *alphabetic* system in which each character represents a separate sound. These symbols could be combined to form words, and words could be arranged in sequence to express a thought. The original series of Greek symbols went through various transitions until in one area the Arabic alphabet emerged, and in another, the Roman. This latter series of characters, each symbolizing one or more sounds, is in general use today in all languages in the western culture. (See Claiborne, 1974, pp. 10–15, 20.)

However, even today a majority of the world's languages do not have a visual form, and many that do are *pictographic* rather than *phonographic*; that is, the pictographic is composed of stylized symbols of objects, while the phonographic is made up of symbols related to spoken sounds. The languages without visual symbols belong mainly to primitive peoples with relatively small populations who are so closely knit that there has been little need to communicate over distances. Traditionally, they impart their culture orally to children in each family group through the folktales involving their more distant past. This custom has met the need to communicate over time.

Written language is an essential factor in the culture of any country and of the world. It is the means of transmitting and retrieving ideas, knowledge, and information across time and across space, even across cultures with different languages. It can be as trivial as a shopping list, written only for our own immediate use. Or it can make available for retrieval for all time the fundamental beliefs, values, and wisdom of all the cultures that devised or used some system of writing.

While the alphabetic principle has proved useful, it also creates problems, more in some languages than in others. The alphabet used in the English language has presented many problems in the field of written language, both in reading and writing. Scholars of the English language and individuals attempting to use the sound-symbol relationship have long recognized its variability and inconsistency. The more knowledgeable one becomes in the field, the more variations become apparent. Children taught to read and write mainly on the basis of the sound-symbol relationship thus face considerable difficulty.

Beginning to write

When are children ready to begin writing? The answer depends on the child's personal experiences, involvement with oral language, and access to paper and pencil. When children regularly participate in conversations and see adults or older children engaged in writing, they often start to write early.

A three-year-old had been busy with paper and pencil. She asked her father, "Want to hear my story?" Being assured he did, she "read" two well-formed sentences while looking at her marks on the paper. Several hours later she repeated the sentences exactly as before to her mother. This child had experienced a rich verbal environment in which she frequently saw things written and then read.

Many preschool children develop an understanding of what reading and writing are all about. These children have been getting satisfaction from their scribbled stories for a long time. Then on entering school, they may be limited to "reading readiness" activities and denied the opportunity to write much more than their names for most of a school year! But other children have had less than adequate preschool experience with recorded language. All programs must have the flexibility to meet the needs of both the advanced child and the inexperienced child, so that all children will be stimulated to make progress, whatever their current competence levels.

Almost universally, children's first recorded thoughts are expressed in the form of pictures. These pictures are their first "writing," and when encouraged they can tell what the pictures mean to them. Most children produce these drawings or paintings before they come to school, sometimes as early as two or three years of age.

Kindergarten provides time and materials for children to record thoughts in pictures, in clay, or in building blocks, and talk about these thoughts with their peers and their teacher. When children express ideas in these ways, they are ready for the teacher to write a few key words the children say about their ideas. Teachers should obtain permission before writing on a child's picture. An alternative is to write the caption on a strip of paper that can be displayed along with whatever the child has made. Some children will want to copy the caption on their pictures. They may remember what the writing says, or ask to have it read, then tell it to others. And thus begins the writing-reading process, the idea that writing is putting a thought on paper, and that reading is recovering that thought.

When children show no interest in this type of activity, they are not ready to profit from it, but being aware it is going on around them may stimulate such interest. When a child seeks this type of experience, encouragement is helpful, but the child should not be required to participate.

When writing and reading emerge from children's representation of their own experiences, there can be no question that it has meaning for them. This procedure is the *only* way one can be sure that each child has the background and perception that make writing and reading meaningful. Since purpose is essential to communication, we need to ensure from the very beginning that these less familiar processes of written communication are meaningful.

Through the natural experience of participating in language interchange, the child develops a fairly clear impression "of what language is and what it is for. Much of his difficulty with language in school arises because he is required to accept a stereotype of language that is contrary to the insights he has gained from his own experience. The traditional first reading and writing tasks are a case in point, since they fail to coincide with his own convictions about the nature and use of language" (Halliday, 1973, p. 11).

When children first come to school, they are eager to share their experiences. They may begin to develop the concept of a *unit of meaning* by telling "the most important part" of a particular personal experience, such as a trip, a hobby, or an event. This one-sentence idea is a unit of meaning, which the teacher records just as each child says it. For example, the most important idea Mary wants recorded is "My dog he sleep in my bed." The statement is her way of communicating, representing her present development. At this stage Mary needs to see her own talk written down just as she says it. If the teacher rearranges the words to make them grammatically "correct," the expressed thought is the teacher's, and not Mary's.

Another way a teacher may help children start recording their thoughts is by using the concept of "Who am I?" The idea of authorship can start very early, in the first grade or in kindergarten for some children. Each can make a book about herself or himself. All children can draw pictures of themselves and their families. Some can write their own names on their pictures and write or dictate other information. Children can make pictures about the classroom, their out-of-school world, their pets, or about "What Is Around Me?"—perhaps a store, park, or firehouse. In this way, children draw meanings from their own background. The child's own language is used to make learning more meaningful.

Thus, children's first "writing"—recording of thought—should be a representation of their own experiences in the form of pictures, crafts, or dictation for the teacher to write. In dictating, they can learn to identify the most important thought as a unit of meaning.

Making books

When children are using picture books from which to tell stories or obtain information, they can begin making their own books on various topics, such as animals. Most five- and six-year-olds enjoy making pictures of animals following a trip to the zoo. If the group lacks facilities for a field trip, some children can bring well-behaved pets to school for a day. The subject of pets can be broadened to include goldfish, turtles, or even imaginary or wished-for pets. Some children may want to make books about their pets by "writing" several picture stories on successive days. At the child's dictation, the teacher can write the animal's name on the picture. These pictures may form several books as children classify the animals into categories. Production of books on the children's pets has the advantage of bringing the home and the school closer together.

The children write or copy their names on their pictures and dictate the title to the teacher. As these pictures are bound into books, the teacher needs to emphasize that the children are now authors and illustrators of picture books. The books can be covered with bright construction paper, finger paintings, or the children's illustrations, then fastened with staples, raffia, or yarn. The children may want to add their names to the covers.

Books take on many forms as the children increase their ability to write, or to copy the dictation that the teacher has written for them. From picture books the child progresses to books that include one-line stories with the illustrations. The child then titles the book and signs the cover as author and illustrator.

At first the books are the size of the paper used at the easel. Gradually, the books become smaller in overall size or take on shapes indicative of the contents. Stories about the signs of fall may have a leaf-shaped cover, or stories about fishing may be cut into the shape of a fish. The teacher can prepare in advance a few plain pages stapled into bright covers. A stock of these empty booklets, easily available to children, is a great incentive for recording their thoughts in both pictures and words.

Thus, children can begin making their own books very early, even in kindergarten, and progress through various stages as they mature and develop competence. Teachers need to stress authorship from the beginning and develop pride in accomplishment. The children may want to take their books home or to leave them in the reading center for others to read.

"Talk written down"

In the beginning stage, children's writing is "talk written down." To be the children's own, it should be written as they say it, because children see their own idiolects as part of themselves. Using their language enhances their feelings of self-worth and is an essential part of "accepting the child as he is." Differences in pronunciation resulting from dialect can be written in standard spelling—write *here* even when Charlestoners say *hair*—but the characteristic grammar differences and sentence structures should be maintained as the child uses them.

The early stage focuses on one idea—a unit of meaning—which the child dictates. At first, the thought may be just a label, such as "zoo animals," or "the fire truck." From the children's other talking the teacher can decide when they are ready to extend the thought. "What do you want to say about the fire truck?" When the teacher has written a child's thought, it is important to read it back to the child. The child may or may not choose to read it alone.

If a child responds in *mazes* or *garbles*, that is, in confused, partial thoughts, or in volumes of information, a teacher may help by suggesting the child focus on the *one most important thing* he or she wants to say about the picture. This suggestion may help the child to respond with one unified thought, a unit of meaning. As clearer thinking develops, clearer expression results.

Constructively helping children, rather than correcting them, enables them to feel comfortable about expressing themselves freely, which is essential for effective language development. Instead of fearing that children will continue to make "mistakes," adults should remember the changes, the language development, that the child has already accomplished without correction. The less self-conscious children are about their talking, the more likely they are to pick up the more mature speech that they hear. Gradually over the years, children recognize the need for more "correctness" in both speaking and writing.

Learning to write by writing and talking

Children acquire knowledge about writing from their own participation in writing—not from instructions. When teachers want children to write, they need to set up real purposes and possibilities for writing. Children's actions and the motivation for these actions are their own ongoing interests. Piaget has stated:

> True interest appears when the self identifies itself with ideas or objects . . . and they become a necessary form of fuel for its activity. When the active school requires that the student's effort should come from the student himself instead of being imposed, and that intelligence should undertake authentic work instead of accepting predigested knowledge from outside, it is therefore simply asking that the laws of all intelligence should be respected (Piaget, 1970, pp. 158–159).

Teachers can help children to identify themselves with ideas or objects and think and write about them. Teachers need to focus on children's identification with their own writing and their ability to write, and to see that writing is a satisfying accomplishment for each child, regardless of the stage of development.

Teachers can increase children's confidence, identification, and pride of accomplishment in their own writing in several ways. They can recognize each small step of progress. An attempt, whatever the result, is progress over no attempt. "You're trying and soon you will_____." Teachers can display whatever writing children wish displayed, letting them substitute "better" writings as they produce them. During an evaluative "talking time," the teacher and the children can point out what they especially like (keep it positive!) about displayed writings, particularly about progress they have noted. Of course, the child's name appears clearly on each piece of work displayed. Teachers need to prevent any comparison by reminding children that each person can do something better than others do it. If Sarah is comparing her work as "better" than someone else's, the teacher can ignore the comparison but specifically mention some positive gain Sarah has made, thus legitimately giving her the recognition she needs. A simple statement of some positive aspect of the other child's writing may follow.

Discussing a topic among those interested in it, either with or without the teacher, stimulates thoughts and opens up ideas to explore for writing. Shanahan (1977) uses discussion, both preceding and following writing, for developing concepts and hypotheses from third grade on. He also sets up writing marathons in which all write whatever they choose, nonstop. If no new thoughts come, they copy the preceding sentence, but children seldom need to repeat a sentence more than once. Mechanics of spelling, punctuation, and grammar are not of concern during this time.

To provide direct assistance, the teacher can ask questions concerning the *meaning* expressed. When Jack is obviously dissatisfied with his product, the teacher needs to find out why, without evaluative comment. Help is most effective when it is offered in response to the child's concern. Thus, with stimulation and encouragement to write, and help when the child feels the need for it, children's writing improves and increases through experience in writing.

Providing resources

As soon as children begin writing on their own, they will want to write words that they do not know how to write. A child comes to the teacher and says, "I need a word." One way to help is to provide little slips of paper, which children may take to anyone who can write the word for them—the teacher, an aide, an older helper-child, or one of their own group whose writing is more advanced. The resource person then writes the requested word in manuscript writing on the slip.

Another resource is all of the stories—pictures with sentences—on display around the room. Perhaps Paul recalls that Betty used a particular word in her story the day before, so he finds the story and the word. As more children write, begin to write longer stories, and bind their stories into books, their own books become a resource.

Children often write about various family members and so may need to write *Mother* or *Mom*, *Dad* or *Daddy*, *aunt*, *uncle*, *cousin*, and other such des-

ignations. A chart labeled "Our Family" might then list all the titles for relatives. Holidays call for writing about pumpkins and witches, or turkey and dressing. Seasons suggest falling leaves and nuts or snow and sliding. Each of these occasions can generate a chart.

When children need many words, they can start their own word banks. Milk cartons can be used to hold words written on slips of paper. Children can cut off the top (two or three inches above the bottom), rinse the inside clean, and use their imaginations in decorating them. The teacher cuts slips of paper slightly shorter than the width of the carton and about one-half inch wider than the carton is high. Each child is given a number of these slips, which stand up in the little box. When Dianne needs a word, someone will write it for her on one of these slips. After copying the word in her story, she can file the word in her bank and find it whenever she needs it.

Eventually the child has collected so many words they are hard to find. Now the teacher cuts twenty-six cards per child, to use with the slips in the word bank. On the top of each card the child writes a letter of the alphabet—using the ubiquitously posted alphabet—and files each of the collected words in its proper place. This procedure is a rational way for the child to become familiar with the alphabet. By filing many words, children quickly learn whether a letter is near the beginning, the end, or the middle of the alphabet, and which other letters are near it, before and after.

When children are accustomed to using these devices, and a child asks for a word that is readily available, the resource person can ask, "Couldn't you find that word? Where did you look? Where else do you think you might look?" By this means children are made responsible for their own use of resources, and they become increasingly independent. Of course, words not readily located are still provided.

With this background of experience, encouragement, and opportunity, children write longer and longer stories and books. Gradually, the pictures are emphasized less and the writing grows longer. Children begin making more elaborate covers as their pride in their stories increases (Wexler, 1975). These books can have a special place on the room library shelves. Often they are read more than any other books in the room.

As children move on in their reading, they become aware of more formal writing. Through such concepts as sentence structure (making what they write sound like spoken language), form (statements, questions, and exclamations), capitalization, and punctuation, the child's writing becomes more than "talk written down." The teacher's role is to know where each child is in learning about writing, and to raise questions that help children to evaluate their own written work. In this way children move toward becoming their own diagnosticians.

Involvement in writing

Teachers, particularly in the later grades, often complain that their children do not want to write. The one sure reason is that children are not getting satisfaction from their writing. There may be a variety of causes for this lack of satisfaction. First, the school may not provide enough stimulating experiences that challenge their thinking and thus their interest in writing. Second, if there are too many stipulations to meet too early, children may feel writing is not worth all that effort. Third, when children have been told what to write about—often subjects of little interest to them— they have not had the opportunity to explore their own interests through writing or to develop confidence that topics they think of will be acceptable. Fourth, children may lack recognition of progress they believe they have made, or feel the presence of too much negative feedback. Any of these conditions may cause them to invest their effort in activities in which they seem to be more successful. A child with little self-confidence may feel it is better to do nothing than to put effort into work

that is only criticized. When children do not want to write or say they do not know what to write about, they are not deeply and comfortably involved in their school experience.

Let us examine one way of encouraging involvement in the writing process. We will "walk" through a situation that is typical of a group of six- to seven-year-olds.

The school is situated near the ocean in a fishing town on the Oregon coast. The involvement began when children came to school on a bright spring day discussing a huge Oregon crab they had found on the beach the previous day after school. When they were playing outside, they showed Mrs. Roberts where they had seen the crab. Because of their questions, the teacher arranged an excursion to fulfill the children's recognized need to learn more about life along the seashore.

In preparation for the excursion, Mrs. Roberts planned *with* the children about gathering information. She proposed questions about what kind of information they wanted, how they might use the information, and how they might report it. The children decided to use a chart on which to list plants and animals they might find. Someone remembered that it is against the law to remove from the beach anything living. It is all right to collect shells and any skeletons of sea creatures but anything alive must be left where they find it, including plant life. (Teachers should always check with local authorities before going on such field trips; laws regarding collecting may vary from state to state.) They selected equipment to take along for collecting and recording. Some decided to work in pairs or small groups. They planned how they would gather and record their information.

At the beach, each group (or child) set out for a different area, having in mind things to look for. They all returned with specimens to further their study, and sketches of what was not collectable.

On their return to the classroom there was much excited talk about what they had found. Some had many different shells, one had the hard shell or exoskeleton of a crab, another some bones of a bird wing. Several had picked up interesting rocks including what they discovered were barnacles broken off from rocks or ships and washed ashore, and three had found agates. All had drawn pictures of living animals found in tide pools. Questions were listed on a chart so that answers could be discovered later. Mrs. Roberts suggested putting their ideas into a painting or drawing, and for those who wished, writing a story about it. Some children decided to model some forms of sea life out of clay. When the children were ready, either individually or in small groups, they explained their pictures or models. For children who were not yet writing, Mrs. Roberts wrote the idea the child expressed just as the child dictated it.

By recording words for the child, the teacher provides a transition from talk to writing. The children choose what to put into these pictures or models, and they also choose what to write for the "story." Jerry, who has not been writing, may copy the words Mrs. Roberts wrote and find that what he says, he can write down. And so Jerry begins to build the relationship between reading and writing. With the children's permission, their pictures and models may be shared with the class, put on the bulletin board or display table, or bound into a book. Hence, Jerry receives recognition for his first writing.

One of the most significant ways to help children clarify their ideas for writing is to encourage them to discuss their experiences and their thoughts, and to ask questions. After the trip to the seashore, each child would be given an opportunity to offer ideas, usually in a small group. The total group would assemble from time to time when the teacher felt it was important for all to share information or make decisions. As a follow-up, one group might decide to make a model of the seashore, another to start a saltwater aquarium. These experiences would involve much discussion, as well as many drawings and stories. Various ways of displaying the children's work would be discussed and accepted. The children, together or individually, begin to learn how to look for information in the books in the class reference library. They study the pictures and scan the print for clues to information they need.

Thus, such a project can stimulate children's interest, powers of observation, development of oral language abilities for planning and reporting, and ways of recording thoughts and information through both pictures and writing. Using books extends their competence in obtaining needed information, as well as a deeper understanding of the situation they have explored. Quantitative concepts can also develop naturally.

The seashore exploration was set at the school beginners' level, but the same basic plan can be implemented at any age and in any place when children's concerns are recognized and stimulated. Procedures vary with the children's maturity and competencies, but the same level of involvement occurs.

It is the creative teacher who envisions some way to intrigue children's curiosity and develop interest when the natural environment is bleak. Where leaving the school or even the classroom seems impossible, the teacher must enlist the children's aid in enriching and enlivening that classroom environment so that learning and teaching do not become dreary. Experiences like the seashore excursion are the kind Piaget recommends for balanced development of right and left brain.

> The principle goal of education is to create men who are capable of doing new things, not simply of repeating what other generations have done—men who are creative, inventive, and discoverers. The second goal of education is to form minds which can be critical, can verify, and not accept everything that is offered. The great danger today is of slogans, collective opinions, ready-made trends of thought. We have to be able to resist individually, to criticize, to distinguish between what is proven and what is not. So we need pupils who are active, who learn early to find out by themselves, partly by their own spontaneous activity and partly through material we set up for them; who learn early to tell what is verifiable and what is simply the first idea to come to them (Duckworth, 1964, p. 175).

Pride in authorship

Teachers' positive attitudes and constructive ways of working with children can generate pride in all children for their accomplishments. It is this pride that builds motivation for increasing one's competence. The idea of authorship is introduced when children put together their very first "books" with their names on the covers as authors. Follow-up procedures can be used to increase their pride in authorship.

An effective way to stimulate authorship is to invite an author into the classroom. The guest may be any person who writes books, articles, or newspaper stories for publication, and also relates well to youngsters. For children who are just beginning to produce books, the experience should be kept simple and guided by comments and questions from the children. Children and teacher plan in advance what they want to say and how they want to say it—an excellent time for developing oral communication skills.

Later, when most children have developed confidence in their ability to write, authors can tell how they decide what to write about, how they get started, and how they revise. They may talk about reading the material over, perhaps to a friend, to see that every sentence makes sense. If the friend does not understand what the author means, this section is revised for clearer communication. Then probably the author checks the spelling of difficult words and makes a clean copy of the manuscript. The author may tell about any initial drafts that were thrown away because they were not worth spending the time and effort to revise. Each author will indicate different procedures because the writing process is unique for each person, although the basics remain the same. The children's questions will indicate the level of their maturity and therefore the amount of detail the author should disclose.

Listening to authors encourages children to talk about first drafts they are revising so they can be proud of the finished product. Children also have the right to discard without changing writing that they feel is not worthwhile. Some insecure children may not be satisfied with any of their first drafts. They need the support of the teacher and/or some of their peers. The teacher can ask to read their drafts or suggest showing them to a special friend, one who will be supportive. When the child feels someone really likes the ideas in the first draft, minor changes can be suggested, and the polishing will proceed. Children should understand that *all* writing, including the writing of adults, can be improved.

Therefore, it becomes especially important to point out specific values and progress in the finished product. A small number of finished products, which the children revised until they were satisfied, can develop better writing than many papers written hastily and copied over, using spellings and punctuations supplied by the teacher.

Teachers must be careful at all stages of writing not to let their own preferences in styles or content influence their reactions. Some years ago, a college English professor, who was highly critical of a student's story, handed back the paper and said, "Now, try rewriting that and see if you can produce something acceptable." The student took the paper, paused a moment, then responded, "I'm sorry, sir, but I don't think I will rewrite it. You see it has already been accepted by the *Saturday Evening Post*." Although the story did not appeal to the professor's personal taste, the writing was professional in quality.

Teaching children to polish writing

Many teachers have found that correction via the red pencil does little to improve children's writing, but is more likely to make their writing as short and infrequent as possible. Yet many teachers continue to believe that students' work will not improve unless it is corrected. These teachers should be reminded that all children have tremendous implicit knowledge of the structure of their language demonstrated by their use of it in talking, and that research has been unable to identify any significant improvement of writing brought about by instruction in formal grammar. When assigned by the teacher, corrected by the teacher, and evaluated only by the teacher, writing becomes a task done *for* the teacher with little personal involvement. A few try their best to please the teacher, but most students see no reason to care much about their writing or to do more than is required.

The solution is *involvement* and *pride of authorship*. Involvement produces a desire to talk and write about their own activities, and pride of authorship creates the desire to do it as well as possible.

When does polishing begin? Certainly not until children have gained confidence in their ability to express themselves in writing. Acceptance of their writing as it is and recognition of progress are more important in the beginning. The appropriate time and circumstances to suggest changes and revision depend on the individual child. When the child recognizes mistakes and shows concern, the opportunity to revise may be offered. When a number in the group begin to indicate this readiness, a professional writer can be invited to describe revision. The polishing process then develops gradually.

Editing for the child with different speech patterns

Children who speak an idiolect that varies widely from that of standard written English will need special and sympathetic help. They have started their writing by having the teacher record their speech as they say it. The spelling is conventional, but sometimes word order is changed or words are added, deleted, or combined. Perhaps the child says and writes *gonna*. When the child's confidence has developed enough for editing to begin, teachers can say "People who write books write *going to*." They then provide a well-written sample

for the child to copy. When the child has mastered one change, the teacher can introduce another.

Any child may have these changes to make where the natural speech varies from basic writing patterns. The greater the speech differences, the more extensive the changes needed in writing. The essential factors that make this instruction effective are the acceptance and valuing of the child's writing as a whole, carefully paced suggestions for change, and recognition of the child's success in following them.

Other children may note and question the different written forms derived from a dialect. The comments of other children are effective if the writer is not embarrassed by them. If the writer shows disturbance or the amount of writing diminishes, the teacher needs to intervene.

Developing skills

First the children learn that what they are writing must be important enough to spend time on, that a trivial or valueless idea, polished to shining splendor, is still valueless. Second (through small group discussion under the guidance of the teacher), they gradually learn how to review for clarity the larger overall meanings, and then alternatives for organizing, sequencing, adding or deleting ideas to sharpen and clarify the focus. Third, they check spelling and punctuation, then fourth, make a final copy with attention mainly to neatness and handwriting. Any other order results in a waste of time and effort. When children are aware of their purpose for writing, they are more involved, will work harder at it, and have a better basis for evaluating it. They can decide whether what they have started is worth continuing and revising, or whether to discard it and start again.

When children have a first draft that they feel is worth polishing, the revising process begins. First, they read it over to see if it really says what they want it to say. Then they ask someone else to read it, react to it in terms of purpose, and make suggestions. A small group may read the material and reflect interpretations by putting the ideas in their own words. The children may also respond directly by saying, "You mean that_____." Teachers also sit in on these groups and raise questions. As the children become more competent in reflecting interpretations and raising questions, the teacher's presence is less and less necessary. The maturity of structural changes depends, of course, on the maturity of the children's writing skills.

When the rewriting is finished, the child goes over the paper for mechanical errors, like mistakes in spelling and punctuation. When satisfied, the author copies the paper neatly and makes it available according to the original purpose. Anything that is going to other rooms or the school library should be checked by the teacher before the final copying, and questions should be raised about any serious errors still needing correction.

The product of this type of polishing is worthy of pride, not only the author's but the teacher's and classmates' as well. Polishing brings far more growth and development of writing competence than a new assignment every day. However, such polishing is not appropriate for daily writing in a journal or diary. In fact, over a period of time a diary, seen only occasionally by the teacher and never submitted for "correction," may be a significant evaluation instrument, reflecting the development of writing competence.

Choosing editors Another procedure that may develop out of the polishing process is the designating of editors for the group. These may not be the most competent writers in the group, but they are writers who are competent and also effective in helping others become aware of what needs polishing. Would-be editors who want to make the changes themselves need help in understanding that only the author makes changes in his or her work. If the editor raises issues and points out problems, the writer can provide solutions. The writer decides how to express a thought by considering how the reader will best understand it.

As the writing process advances through the grades, the writers feel more competent in judging and polishing their products. With the kind of writing opportunities recommended throughout this chapter, children usually achieve competence expected only at more advanced levels. They also begin to know what helps them most to recognize needed changes. They may read their writing aloud to a chosen friend, ask the friend to read it to them, or read it into a tape recorder and play it back.

An outline Do writers need to outline? The answer varies with length and complexity of the writer's material. Beginners have in mind what they want to say. As children grow older and their writing becomes more extended, they need to do more preplanning, but writers differ in their methods. Some make a list of major points and choose the sequence as they write. Even with a familiar topic the author has thought about for some time, the preliminary planning must allow for changes and modification as the writing takes shape. James Britton says, "What is written takes its own shape. . . . The shape expresses, and arises from, the movement of thought . . . shaping at the point of utterance" (Britton, 1970, p. 33).

When older children are writing up the results of a study, an outline becomes more important. They can use an outline as a list of ideas or topics, then write under each of these topics a few words reminding them of points they wish to make. Perhaps the most useful way for children to recognize the organization of effective writing is to outline a piece of well-written, published material. Hassid (1977) describes novels of many chapters that sixth graders write and "publish" for their peers. These children develop a list of chapters and the necessary ideas to be included in each one.

Is an outline really necessary? We must say that the answer depends on what type of preplanning the writer finds most useful. Procedures must be flexible enough to accommodate new perceptions that modify preliminary plans. The first criterion is, "Can the reader easily follow the intended meaning?"

The "right" word   In the polishing process, more varied, exact, and colorful words replace the routine, global, and banal ones used in the first draft. Colorless words that children use routinely include *said*, *goes*, *get*, *have*, and *went*. Children can list replacements for these words on charts. They can fill a bulletin board with exciting words, along with the definitions, as they run across them in their reading. Colorful words or phrases that help the reader build a mental picture make description more vivid and interesting. The addition of colorful words is also a way of elaborating.

Restricted and elaborated writing   Inappropriately restricted writing results from minor omissions, such as the use of pronouns without clear antecedents, and major omissions, such as the lack of necessary background information. The journalists' list of who, what, where, when, why, and how can be used to round out an incident so all may understand.

Children like to experiment and discover how language works. They need a great deal of experience and stimulation in building sentences from the *kernel* sentence to its expanded form before any formal study of grammar begins. A simple sentence like "Dogs run" leads to elaboration step by step:

1. Big dogs run.

2. My cousin Sally's big dogs run.

3. My cousin Sally's big brown dogs run down the road to meet her after school.

Obviously this development would take place over a period of time, and some children would move much faster than others. Children may be helped most by asking a small group to elaborate one of their own restricted sentences. Each child might search his or her own writing for such a sentence to offer to the group. On the basis of all elaborations offered, the child can rewrite the sentence so that it is true and fits into the paragraph. Such personalized learning experiences promote more lasting change.

Tightening writing   Attempts to elaborate can result in wordiness. "Tightening" means reviewing the writing to see what can be omitted, what clauses can be shortened to phrases, what phrases can be reduced to single words. *Embedding* of sentences as clauses or phrases can be part of this tightening (O'Hare, 1971). Although most writers from age eight or nine on can understand elaboration, tightening becomes useful a year or two later, depending on the maturity of the writer.

Many kinds of sentences require tightening. One of the most common is the run-on sentence in which several independent clauses and/or sentence fragments are connected. This problem can be dealt with in the middle or upper grades if the children still write sentences like this: *Nancy ran down the hill, she fell down*. This sentence can be corrected by the addition of a conjunction: *Nancy ran down the hill, and she fell down*. But subordination results in a better sentence: *Nancy fell when she ran down the hill*. The word *and* is overworked in children's sentences: *It was twelve o'clock and I ate my lunch and I got jelly on my shirt*. Telling children to stop using "ands" without helping them to say what they want to say does not further learning. With help, they can learn to use subordination and embedding: *I got jelly on my shirt when I ate my lunch at twelve o'clock*.

Another common problem is the use of a series of short, jerky sentences: *It rained. I got wet. I went home*. As a first step toward improvement, the child might write: *It rained. I got wet so I went home*. A more effective solution is: *When it rained, I went home because my clothes were wet*. The sentence can easily be made more vivid: *All drenched and shivering, I ran into my house, out of the downpour*. Since a number of embeddings are possible, the writer's main idea becomes the independent clause.

Insistence on "correctness" for its own sake labels the child's writing as "wrong" and may discourage further writing. But children are willing to learn about connectors or run-on sentences when a teacher puts the parts on the chalkboard and encourages them to find other ways of saying the same thing. Children who frequently write either run-on sentences or short, choppy sentences may meet to work on the problem. They can choose such sentences from their own writing and ask the group to suggest ways to embed the ideas into more mature sentences. Since this capability may be related to a child's total maturity, we can make children aware of possibilities but should not put on pressure to carry them out. However, the ability to identify immature construction in their own writing is essential before children can make progress.

Word order Children can improve the clarity of their writing by considering the order of words within sentences. Usually the straightforward sentence—subject-predicate-object—is most effective, though various arrangements should be explored for their effect. The more modifiers involved, the more important their arrangement is. The placing of modifiers should leave no question about what they refer to. For instance, in the sentence "Mary saw the boy walking toward the railroad station," who was walking? The sentence could be clarified by writing "Walking toward the railroad station, Mary saw the boy," or "Mary saw the boy, who was walking toward the railroad station."

Connecting words Because reading is largely making sense out of written or printed material (Smith, 1975a, p. 9), the writer can help the reader by using connecting or relational words. For instance, *because* can be used to show the logic or reason for an action. "Because it was getting late, I decided to wait until morning." Other words that can be used for this purpose include *although, however, nevertheless, so,* and *when*. Such words estab-

lish a relationship between the thoughts in two clauses, such as "It was getting late" and "I decided to wait until morning." The dependent clause is another example of embedding.

Word meaning Another consideration is whether all words or phrases will be understood by the reader. Whether connotative meanings will communicate is sometimes uncertain, especially when the audience is unknown. The wider the range of readers, the more elaborated the writing must be. For instance, if Ron had received an ocarina he might write: "I received a musical instrument for my birthday. It is called an ocarina and you blow into it to play a tune." However, a more interesting approach, which would make use of the reader's prior understanding less directly, could be: "Dad gave me an ocarina for my birthday." (What's that?) "I can play a tune on it" (must be a musical instrument), "but I get out of breath before long." (An ocarina is a musical instrument you blow into to play a tune.) Readers now have used their prior knowledge to make sense of what Ron wrote, to bring meaning to a previously unknown word. This writing illustrates normal *redundancy* that Frank Smith defines as *"Information that is available from more than one source. . . . Prior knowledge on the part of the reader permits redundancy to be used"* (Smith, 1978, p. 242).

Redundancy, which is a usual part of talking and listening, is a factor in writing and reading, too. When children learn to use it in their writing as a means of elaboration, it becomes a more effective tool in their reading through their greater awareness of its effect. When older children write material for younger ones to read, there is an excellent opportunity for using redundancy consciously and intentionally.

Paragraph development Logical organization of a paragraph is another help to the reader. A first sentence that sets the stage for the rest of the paragraph increases understanding. Sometimes a paragraph lends itself to a summary or concluding sentence also. Limiting a paragraph to one topic or one aspect of a topic is important.

As children give more thought to their readers, the organization of their writing improves. Reminding children of the reader is far more useful than simply telling them, "You need to organize your writing better." As always, a specific purpose that the child understands and accepts is more effective than any set of rules. In fact, the purpose suggests other ways to improve communicative effectiveness. Children need to be continually aware that the main guideline for all writing and revision is, Does it communicate better with the audience for whom it is intended?

Developing style

Between third and fifth grade, the child begins to show an individual style of writing. Children's style comes from writing on subjects of their own choosing and developing self-evaluation through feedback from teachers and peers. The books they read and their discussions of books undoubtedly influence their style. Also, listening to people whom they admire will have an effect.

The teacher may bring up style as the group discusses a book by a favorite author. When someone mentions a characteristic section or episode, the teacher might raise the question, "What about this book might tell you who wrote it if you did not already know?" "Are there other things that might tell you?" If there is scant response, the teacher might follow up with "Let's listen for cues that are characteristic of the author's style." Each day, following the reading time, the group could discuss the style of the book and compare it with other books by the same author and books by different authors.

Children who are most perceptive of style could take another step. At the reading conference, as Lloyd identifies an episode in the story he is reading as exciting, or funny, or noteworthy for some other reason, Mrs. Duncan might ask him to find that section. She could then ask him how the au-

thor made it attention-getting. Together they may analyze it for one or two major points. Then Mrs. Duncan could suggest that Lloyd may wish to try writing a story using these techniques.

Lloyd may then use this general procedure with the material of another author, and another, and another. As a writer, he will actually be trying different techniques for achieving writing style. Some he will reject outright as not for him. But through the analyzing, the writing, the evaluating of many different ways to create effects, including poetry, he will be consciously developing a style of his own. By the time several of the children are working toward this goal, a great deal of discussion can be going on among them, and gradually others will become interested and join.

Teachers can help children develop characters in their stories by asking questions about people in the stories they are reading: "Does this character seem like a real person?" "Do you think you might sometime know such a person?" "Is she the kind of person the author intended her to be?" "Is the character predictable, in other words, consistent in her behavior?" "Does the character's action stay within the normal bounds of the story?" Children can then evaluate the characters in each other's stories. All of the ways of working at their writing, of course, increase awareness and enjoyment of the materials they read.

Writing activities

Authoring books, as we have described, can be the main emphasis in the development of the ability to communicate in written language. In addition to sharing them with their peers, children can offer their books to other groups of children of the same age and younger, as they provide easy but interesting reading material and may stimulate others to write similar books.

When the children's books are included in the school library, they provide material that is often more relevant to children in the area than published books are. They may also stimulate writing among children who do not have such opportunities in their own classrooms. Perhaps the greatest value is to the self-concept of the child who authored the book. Where these books are included in the school library, librarians report that they are checked out more frequently than most published books.

Besides the writing of stories and books, a whole range of shorter, planned or incidental writing activities are useful and significant to children. Practical writing includes notes to parents, telling them about the projects children are working on at school, or inviting them to come to see some special activity. Children can write letters to their friends who have moved or who are ill, and to friends or relatives who live far away. After they have learned some poetic forms, they can write poetry. They can make a collection of jokes or riddles. The creative teacher will think of innumerable possibilities to suggest, and the children will, too.

Journals

Daily writing in journals can be a most substantive writing procedure. Each child should have a blank booklet or notebook that is a personal possession to be shared only by choice. The idea and materials can be introduced to several children who are writing on their own. Others can start theirs when they are ready. Such journals can be used effectively all through elementary school. Some children will make a commitment to write in their journals every day. One teacher asked the children to write in their journals on any five days each week, which encouraged out-of-school writing. What they write is their own choice. They often wish to share what they write with their friends and usually, though not necessarily, with the teacher. A general sharing time provides an opportunity to talk about what they like best of what they have written, thus encouraging children to

evaluate their own writing and broadening the range of possibilities perceived by all the children.

Class and school newspapers

When responsibility for the class or school paper is largely carried by teachers, children are deprived of significant learning experiences. A small paper published by the class every week or two is better than a larger paper that appears less often, particularly in the primary grades. The newspaper staff will include a general editor, copy editors, reporters, layout personnel, printers, and distributors. These positions can be shifted until all children have been involved in as many positions as feasible.

The general editor makes the final selection of material for any one issue and may also suggest themes for special issues. The editor also presents ideas to the group for their consideration and decision. All children are free to make suggestions. The copy editors are the class editors whose function has been described. Reporters check the principal's office, the Parent-Teacher Association's secretary, the student council president, and other sources for announcements of future events and the results of the previous week's activities. Reporters then write up this information for the paper. The layout personnel fit the contributions on the pages; the printers make copies on the duplicator, and the distributors hand them out.

The ditto machine is probably the least expensive method of printing. Very young children can copy their final drafts onto ditto masters. The effect is more personal than typing, and it provides strong motivation to improve handwriting. Typed copy can be used if children can do their own typing. (Ditto masters can be cut and reassembled with cellophane tape.) Under the watchful eye of the school secretary, young children can run the ditto machine with little assistance. If the children are too young, helpers from higher grades can assist.

Basic principles and guidelines applied to writing

The basic principles provide guidelines for teaching written expression.

1. Children strive first of all to write so that others understand their meaning.

Arrange opportunities for feedback to help children revise their writing so that others understand it.

2. Children write more, and more effectively, if they are aware of progress and success in writing.

Provide feedback from both yourself and the children, focusing on specific areas of progress.

3. Children continue to discover how language works when they write frequently and for various purposes.

Provide opportunities for children to use their writing to explore alternative ways of expressing thoughts.

4. Children use their natural language when they begin to write their thoughts.

Accept all of children's writing until they are confident they can write, then gradually introduce polishing to modify the written expression toward the dialect standard in your area.

5. Children modify their writing so as to be more easily understood as feedback from peers, teacher, and other adults indicates the need.

When children are ready to begin polishing, provide opportunities for feedback from others.

6. Children learn only through their own experiencing and internalize the learning through writing it in their own words.

Provide opportunities for children to select, organize, and express information so that this knowledge becomes part of their understanding.

7. Children learn much of their ability to write intuitively.

Provide opportunities for children to watch others write, to copy their dictation, and to become aware of the writing of others as a main means of developing their own.

8. Because children's writing development and experiencing is unique, no two have all the same learnings at the same time.

Provide help to individuals or small groups of children who need the same specific learnings when they are ready for them.

9. Children acquire meaning of all aspects of their world from their experiencing, and express it in language natural to them at that time.

Provide a wide range of opportunities for exploring many aspects of their world, including the writing of many others, as a basis for their own writing. Accept these writings and, when appropriate, encourage polishing.

10. Children become more involved in materials and activities important to them and thus are more likely to write because of their stimulating effect.

Provide opportunities for children to choose materials and activities within reasonable limits, as a means of securing their greater involvement in writing.

Teacher's role in developing children's writing

With the concurrent development of writing and reading, *teacher-pupil conferences* take on an important role, for both learning and evaluation. Important guidelines for individual teacher-pupil conferences are:

They are voluntary; children sign up for them as they are ready.

Their frequency and duration depend on the needs of the child.

They focus on the child's expressed concern, need, or desire for sharing.

Teachers record significant progress or need in any specific aspect.

The end result of each conference is positive and supportive.

The early informal interaction with children about their writing will change in time to planned teacher-child conferences. Children sign up when they feel a conference would be helpful. The teacher can be ready to recognize progress and raise questions for the child's guidance and consideration. Until children are ready for such conferences, they continue to have teacher interaction informally whenever it is appropriate.

The positive approach develops a feeling of *I can*. Teachers must exercise caution, however, not to convey the impression that quality is unimportant. Such feedback is false. On the other hand, criticism and correction can lead children to feel they can never write anything acceptable. A more successful approach is for Mrs. Anderson to find out how Daryl feels about his production. If he feels pleased with it, she can ask what he likes best about it. His response may help her see what he is attempting and that he has made a beginning in a desirable direction. After giving positive recognition to his attempts, she might offer a suggestion for a next step. If, however, he does not feel satisfied with his work, she can ask what particularly bothers him about it. By talking about it, he may see a way to make it more satisfying or perhaps she can help by an open question.

Another approach to children's writing is to search for some aspect that has shown improvement over previous attempts, so that the teacher can make a specific positive comment about the progress. Teachers should not give either general praise or criticism, for both can be equally harmful. General praise creates dependency and tends to make children look for outside approval rather than developing their own judgment. Negative comments sap their confidence in their ability to succeed. The teacher's purpose is to strengthen children's confidence in their own ability to evaluate and make decisions.

The guidelines rather directly suggest what a teacher does and, by implication, does not do in this role. Some supplementary suggestions are:

Provide a stimulating classroom, with a wide variety of things to explore, experiment with, look at, and listen to.

Read to children daily at all levels of the elementary school from well-written, stimulating books.

Provide a room collection of good books of many types, in a wide range of concept difficulty and areas of interest.

Raise children's awareness of the world around them and how they can gain understanding of it by the use of their senses.

Make it possible for children to get feedback from other children easily and informally as a help in recognizing any problems of communication. This procedure is more effective than teacher evaluation and leads to self-evaluation.

Provide experience in writing various forms of poetry as a means of increasing children's confidence in using poetry and including it in their personal writing.

Develop consistent expectancy to polish whatever they wish to make available to others.

How do children develop these polishing procedures? Polishing is a gradual process starting in a small way with a few of the most mature writers near the end of first grade. It develops until, by sixth grade, all children have gained some competence in the polishing process.

Many older children have not experienced polishing their writing because their papers have been corrected by their teachers. These students need encouragement to write about what is important to them. For these children, the teacher makes available a wide selection of topics, which they can use if they need suggestions. Teachers next help each child to identify writing worth polishing and to utilize those aspects of polishing most needed and most likely that the child can manage.

When children have written a first draft, teachers need to help them to think about their purpose for writing: "That sounds like an interesting idea. Do you have a special reason for writing it?" or "What do you plan to do with it when it is finished?" Group discussions can identify various purposes, such as to share with other children, to add to the reading center, or to give to one's family. As children mature, they may plan their writing to give to children in earlier grades, to put in the school library, to tell more about a topic the class has discussed, and an even more mature purpose, to increase their own understanding of some thought or idea. "I just like to think about it. I want to keep it" is a thoroughly justifiable purpose.

"Correctness" does not develop by doing exercises in language books nor by correcting errors marked by the teacher. Children's writing becomes more effective when they struggle to make clear some thought important to them. The children who have problems with writing have had unfortunate experiences, such as low expectations, little opportunity to write, or red-marked papers with little or no feedback as to the content.

Resultant attitudes may be hard to overcome, but can be changed through the kinds of experiences that develop writing ability in the younger child. It will take time, particularly time to develop a feeling of confidence in self and trust in the teacher.

Perhaps the most important factor in the development of children's writing is *pride in their accomplishments*. When children feel proud of at least some aspect of their writing, their attention and effort increase amazingly. When this pride is not counteracted by negative comments and criticisms, they will strive to improve all aspects of their work, and will seek constructive help. Appreciative comments should be honest and reasonable because insincerity can backfire badly. But in most work produced by children, there is something worth valuing. The most important comments are those related to aspects we hope to develop.

Evaluation of children's writing

Evaluation deals mainly with basic writing skills, which improve with the frequency with which the child chooses to write and/or the length of the writings produced. The volume of children's writing is measured by individuals, not by comparing children. The amount of writing they do is less significant than their progress in interest and satisfaction.

Improvement in the quality of children's writing can be gauged informally by comparing their current writing with that produced at the beginning of a term or year. If each child has a folder or file, children can put their first writing of the period in the file, add any they wish, and select a recent production to compare with their first at their teacher-pupil evaluation conferences.

A more definitive evaluation can be made in terms of syntactic maturity as explained by Kellogg Hunt (1970). This technical procedure becomes manageable with study and practice and is effective in judging increasing maturity of writing. (See Appendix C.)

Summary

In this chapter we have shown how children learn to write their thoughts and suggested procedures useful to that development. We have indicated the importance of involvement and pride in authorship. Polishing is a basic procedure that enables children to improve continuously. Through polishing, children can learn how to increase the effectiveness and maturity of their writing. We have presented various projects and activities useful to encourage writing, and basic principles and guidelines to develop writing. There is a more extensive evaluation of children's writing at the end of Chapter 8.

Suggested learning experiences for prospective teachers

Suggestion A

1. Observe in a middle grade classroom when children are writing. Try to find out how many revise or rework their expression before making it available for others to read. How much time do children spend polishing their recorded statements? What procedures are followed?

2. Determine whether the craft skills of writing (grammar, spelling, punctuation, and so on) carry over to children's personal writing and into writing in other subject areas.

3. Select one or two youngsters who proofread and revise their papers before turning them in for teacher perusal. Ask how they like writing and why they are preparing their papers carefully. Think about reasons why other children do not.

4. Determine if the teacher helps students to discover that one's audience should be considered when writing. Should others be considered when we write for ourselves? When writing for others, is revising and proofreading important?

5. Think about your own writing. Do you write for various purposes? Is your personal writing differ-

ent from your public writing? What can teachers do to develop children's concern with both the craft and content of writing?

Suggestion B

1. Determine in a primary classroom how many children understand the concept that one's "talk written down" becomes material for reading. Ask permission of the teacher to meet with several youngsters for this purpose.

2. Direct their thinking to the basic principles of natural learning. "What I think about, I can talk about. What I say, I can write down. What I write, others can read." Discover what these principles mean to each individual.

3. Help youngsters to feel free to write by assuring them that each can be a writer and provide reading materials for others.

4. Observe how children react to one another's thoughts and ideas when put down on paper.

5. Decide what ideas you hold that you would like to record either for your personal use or to share with others.

Suggestion C

1. Observe teachers while they are providing learning experiences for developing children's written expression. Determine if and how children's writing is shared with other children.

2. Share a piece of literature with a group of youngsters for their enjoyment and instruction. Choose literature that you like and that children could use as a model for their personal writing. Follow your reading by leading a discussion that includes awareness of author style.

3. Later give these children an opportunity to write and observe whether your selection has influenced their writing.

4. Analyze what resources the teacher uses as examples of writing. What kind of carry-over, if any, do you find?

5. Focus upon a piece of writing that you like. Under what circumstances would your selection influence your own written expression?

Suggestion D

1. Think about the importance of writing in today's society. What, in your opinion, should schools do to improve children's writing abilities?

2. Focus upon occasions when you have wished to make your writing more effective. Have you ever felt that you could not put your thoughts in writing? Why? Could your schooling have helped you to be freer and more skillful?

3. Look for articles that criticize children's writing abilities. What are the public's main objections to our schools' accomplishments in basic communications?

Suggestion E

1. Think of some of your favorite writers. What characterizes their written expression? What literary devices do they employ to capture audience attention?

2. Examine your own writing style. Has it been influenced by any of these authors? Would you like to be able to use some of their techniques in your own writing style?

3. What experiences have helped to formulate your attitude toward writing? Is writing easy or difficult for you? Do you like the way you write?

Suggestion F

1. In a middle or upper grade classroom, ask permission to provide a stimulating experience appropriate to the age and situation of the group.

2. Read or tell the beginning of an exciting story, but do not reveal how it ends (or provide some other experience that creates high expectancy and stops before curiosity is satisfied).

3. As the experience is halted, say "Now what do you think happens?" If a number of the children have ideas, ask who would like to finish the incident by writing an ending for the story. Those who do not want to write may choose some other activity.

4. After those who chose to write have finished, read or tell the rest of the story or experience.

5. What proportion decided to write? Why do you think others did not? Ask the children if they will share their writing with you. Consider their writing on the basis of imagination, consistency of ideas, and the kinds of help each of these children would need to polish their writing.

Suggested readings

The National Council of the Teachers of English publishes much useful material about developing children's writing. A volume edited by Ouida H. Clapp, *On Righting Writing*, contains more than thirty articles describing how to make writing an enjoyable learning experience for elementary school children; a book edited by Eldonna L. Evertts, *Explorations in Children's Writing*, includes a helpful chapter by James Britton; George Hillocks' *Observing and Writing* helps to increase the students' specificity as observers and recorders of sensory experience; Iris M. Tiedt's *Individualizing Writing in the Elementary Classroom* describes writing centers and activities. Sara Lundsteen's *Help for the Teacher of Written Composition: New Directions in Research* provides recent discoveries about children's writing. The council's periodical for elementary schools, *Language Arts*, previously called *Elementary English*, publishes many useful articles. See "Focus 2" in the May 1976 issue.

In John Dixon's *Growth through English*, Chapter 7, "Implications for the School," is especially helpful; and Richard Larson's *Children and Writing in the Elementary School: Theories and Techniques* includes articles by many respected authors. Responding to the back-to-the-basics movement, Ross Winterwood writes "A Teacher's Guide to the *Real* Basics." Herbert Kohl, in Part I of *Math, Writing & Games in the Open Classroom*, describes happenings in groups of culturally different children.

Several articles focus directly on experiences of children. Linda Dinan in "By the Time I'm Ten, I'll Probably Be Famous" shows that when children think of themselves as writers, they write better and are better evaluators of writing. Charles Stallard in "Writing Readiness: A Developmental View" says, "It is the act of writing that enables the mind to invent or conceptualize a message." Mimi Schwartz in "Rewriting or Recopying: What Are We Teaching?" and Charles Suhor in "Linda's Rewrite" deal with the teacher's response to children's writing.

Mauree Applegate wrote *Freeing Children to Write*, an easy-to-read book with ideas for helping children write both prose and poetry creatively. Alvina Treut Burrows, Doris C. Jackson, and Dorothy O. Saunders wrote a much used book, *They All Want to Write: Written English in the Elementary School*, now in its third edition, that emphasizes children's individual differences. Hennings and Grant's *Content and Craft: Written Expression in the Elementary School* extends many points made in this chapter. Hughes Mearns wrote *Creative Power: The Education of Youth in the Creative Arts* in 1929. The revised edition, describing his experiences inspiring children to write prose and poetry, is equally fresh and useful today.

Two simplified thesauri for elementary school use help to enrich writing—and speaking— vocabularies. *In Other Words: A Beginning Thesaurus* was developed by W. Cabell Green and others and *The Clear and Simple Thesaurus Dictionary*, by Harriet Wittels and Joan Greisman.

Strategies for children's learning

Talk and written expression

Purpose.   To help children discover that talk is important to written expression.

Appropriate level.   All levels.

Participants.   All children.

Teacher role

1. To help children learn that talking about their experiences helps to develop, clarify, and extend those experiences.

2. To provide opportunity for children to represent their thoughts on paper.

Procedures

1. Explain that we can write about anything we can talk about, and that when beginners write, it is their "talk written down," which others can then read. More experienced writers usually express their thoughts more carefully than when they talk. But at any age, people expand and clarify their thoughts by talking about them.

2. When working with *kindergartners* and *first graders* who are not yet writing, use a book with pictures and related quotations. As you show a picture and read what the character is saying, help the children discuss what the character thought about and said, and what the words look like. Copy the quote on a chart or chalkboard and read it aloud. The children will become increasingly aware of the relationship between thought, talking, and writing.

3. After children are writing comfortably, usually beginning in *second* grade, ask children to find partners and discuss an idea they would like to write about. If some children do not have ideas, suggest several. Such suggestions may stimulate

the child's own ideas. The more mature writers may prefer to work alone and write out ideas previously discussed. Under any circumstances, children need to write independently, and to polish if the child is confident enough and the first draft warrants it. Call attention to the fact that talk is not edited, but writing nearly always requires editing.

Evaluation.   Do children more often discuss, clarify, and expand ideas before writing? Does each child have a greater awareness of the relationship between oral and written communication? Are they aware that the opportunity for polishing is an advantage of writing?

I am a writer

Purpose.   To help children become writers by representing ideas on paper.

Appropriate level.   Any beginning readers.

Participants.   All children.

Situation.   At beginning reading levels, children's pictures and other graphic representations can provide a basis for language development. The concept of "What I think about, I can talk about" leads directly to putting "talking" on paper. Children first draw or paint pictures about something they think about. Children's personal experiencing is the basis for written expression and enables every learner to become a writer.

Teacher role

1. To provide materials and opportunities for children to create pictures to talk about.

2. To use these pictures to tie together the child's thoughts, oral expression of them, and their written form.

Procedures

1. Lead a discussion encouraging children to recall interesting activities in and out of school.

2. Provide opportunity for children to record in a picture whatever they are interested in and thinking about.

3. Bring four or five children together to talk about their pictures.

4. Record the one thought—unit of meaning—each wants recorded about the picture. The teacher writes what the child dictates. Later children can copy or write their own thoughts. Develop in each child the concept "I am an author."

5. Do not discourage exploration if a child consistently makes pictures only to experiment with color and line. Occasionally ask "Can you tell me about your picture? What were you thinking about?" Such questions can lead children gradually to become aware of their thinking as they paint and be able to verbalize their ideas.

Evaluation. Are children representing their ideas on paper? Are they eager to talk about them? Do they view themselves as writers?

Preparing writing to share with others

Purpose. To develop revision and polishing skills.

Appropriate level. Third grade and beyond.

Participants. All children.

Situation. It is important for children to understand the value of polishing writing that is to be read by others. Once they establish their purposes, each student becomes an editor of his or her own writing. Children can learn these editorial skills in small groups or individually, but it is unlikely that all members of a class will need the same help at the same time. Students can share their writing with one another for suggestions on how to improve what they have said on paper.

After much experience in writing and polishing their writing, children will be able to write at a much more mature level than we usually expect. Helping others improve their writing requires knowing how to help without criticizing.

Teacher role

1. To teach proofreading and polishing skills.

2. To encourage children to revise and polish until they are proud of their product.

Procedures

1. For beginners at editing, develop with them three procedures to use. *First,* read what they have written to see if it "sounds like language" and "makes sense." *Second,* check questionable words with some resource to correct spelling. *Third,* check the basic use of capitals and periods.

2. With more advanced writers, develop additional procedures for checking variety and effectiveness of words and appropriately elaborated sentences. Children will be ready for various kinds of polishing, so work with a small group who want help with one particular skill.

3. Help the most mature writers at upper grade levels to consider relevancy of the content, logical sequencing, development of style, or any of the polishing suggestions in this chapter.

Evaluation. Are children able to revise and polish their shared writing? Do they use their editorial skills? Are class papers better prepared because of carrying out this strategy?

Making books

Purpose. To develop children's ability to make books.

Appropriate level. All levels.

Participants. All children.

Situation. The making of class books can begin with primary students. Together, children and teacher plan the purpose and theme of the book. Possible topics are fish, fairy-tale castles, favorite foods, things that are round, or "Things I'd Like to Be." These beginning books should include both drawings and writings dictated, copied, or written by the students. The books can become part of the classroom library. Some youngsters may want to make individual books. If their books are considered personal, the authors may decide whether or not to contribute them for general use.

Books made by older children may include few, if any, illustrations. All topics close to the lives of young people are suitable. Possible subjects are poverty, the plight of the elderly, hobbies and sports, air pollution, love, divorce, and antiestablishment movements. Children need to discuss negative feelings, but constructive suggestions should be included. Magazine and newspaper photos help the more sophisticated thinkers to create an exposé or attack on some negative aspect of society and to recognize positive aspects.

Teacher role

1. To stimulate creative expression.

2. To help children compile drawings and writings on a selected topic into book form.

Procedures

1. Provide increasingly extended projects as children move through the grades. Expect children to carry out only those projects they can see as interesting and valuable. Do not expect all children to work on the same project.

2. Encourage children to write successive papers related either to the project or to ideas of their own.

3. Help children plan and make a book format to contain their related or continued stories. One child who develops an attractive book to share stimulates others to follow suit.

Teacher evaluation. Are children developing their abilities to make books? Are they becoming more involved in projects in or out of school? Is there a direct connection between their books and their personal reactions and feelings about their world?

Expanding written expression

Purpose. To help children learn to add meaning to what they write by expanding sentences.

Appropriate level. All levels beyond second grade.

Participants. All children.

Situation. Many children can improve their writing through expanding sentences in various ways to communicate more meaning.

Teacher role

1. To teach sentence expansion through classroom learning experiences.

2. To develop children's abilities to write with clear meaning.

Procedures

1. Form a small group of five or six children, either those whose written sentences need expansion, or preferably a heterogeneous group so the more mature writers will demonstrate new possibilities. Choose a sentence from one of the children's papers or one the group suggests based on their common experience, for instance, "Mopsy had babies." Write it on a chart and ask what someone not in our room would need to know in order to understand it.

2. Lead discussion, helping the children decide on changes and additions. With younger or less mature writers, encourage children to ask "Who is Mopsy?" "When did she have babies?" "How many?" Their sentence might become, "Mopsy is our rabbit and yesterday she had five babies." After mature children have suggested additions, the sentence might read, "Yesterday Mopsy, our

white rabbit, gave birth to five tiny, white baby rabbits with bright pink ears and noses."

3. Lead each child to choose a very simple sentence and go to the writing center to expand it independently.

4. Suggest watching for interesting, well-formed sentences to share with the group or at the next reading conference.

5. Lead the more mature writers to try embedding by combining two or more simple sentences into one well-expressed statement, or to tighten a long, wordy one.

6. Help all children to realize that sentences need to vary in length and complexity for interest and emphasis. Work with the group, each using a different book, to explore this aspect of author style.

Evaluation.   Are children adding meaning and expanding sentences on their own? Are they more aware of needing variety in their sentences? Have their writings improved because of the learning experiences the teacher provided?

Outlining

Purpose.   To become familiar with outlining through materials read.

Appropriate level.   Tens and older.

Participants.   All children.

Situation.   Outlining is useful in both writing and reading. Children can learn what an outline is by outlining material that they read. When they are familiar with outlining, it will be helpful in their writing if it is used flexibly, as a guide but not a control.

Teacher role

1. To help children identify the main topics and subtopics of a series of paragraphs and to understand the physical arrangement of an outline.

2. To suggest children develop and use an outline

in their writing, as an aid to clarity and sequencing, not as a rigid formula.

Procedures

1. Bring a group together, each with a copy of an appropriate book or a few pages of duplicated material. The book or material should be fairly difficult and well written so outlining can be developed.

2. Ask the children to read the first paragraph silently, then decide what its main topic is. Ask them to write this topic, as a phrase or sentence, at the top of a blank sheet following the Roman numeral I.

3. Next have them reread the paragraph to identify ideas about that topic. If they decide on two, have them write the first of these following a capital A indented under I.

4. Have them reread to find what is said about that idea. If three points are made, have them place these on separate lines, again indented, and following Arabic numbers 1, 2, and 3. If there are subheadings under any of these, which is unlikely in one paragraph, these topics are indented following small letters a, b, c, and so on. (Paragraphs may not have points beyond the A, B level.)

5. Have the children return to the second main point, indenting B the same as A. When the paragraph is outlined, have the children reread the paragraph to see that all significant information is included. They then proceed to the following paragraphs. Children should use this procedure only to help them understand difficult material.

Evaluation.   Can children understand difficult material better by making an outline of it? Does it help them keep in mind all the important points? Do some children try making an outline in advance of their own writing? (It should be simpler than one they would make of someone else's material.) Does this process clarify their writing?

Develop the framework on a chart or chalkboard
and discuss its common variations.

I.	I.
A.	A.
1.	B.
2.	II.
B.	A.
1.	1.
2.	2.
3.	*a)*
II.	*b)*
	B.

THE WRITING PROCESS

Writing—putting ideas, thoughts, and feelings on paper—cannot exist apart from thinking, talking, listening, and reading. It is an individual activity that depends on the writer's total experience. Language helps children to clarify their experiences and consider what they mean for future action. Printed words are symbols for spoken words, and spoken words are symbols for thoughts. Through symbols, children can deal with objects and events to extend their thinking, or knowledge, to what is outside their immediate perception but still within the area of their understanding.

Teachers often view writing only in relation to the end product. When writing is thought of as a process rather than a product, however, teachers are able to consider what happens before and during the time children are recording what they want to say. Through many different approaches, researchers and theoreticians are attempting to describe what we all do mentally when we write. Some have built models consisting of writer, subject, and audience. Walshe (1977) adds technique to this model.

D'Angelo (1975) presents a theory of rhetoric, the study of effective use of language. He maintains that the rhetorical categories are "dynamic organizational processes, symbolic manifestations of underlying mental processes, and not merely conventional, static patterns" (p. 57). A third approach describes "Stages of the Composition Process" in three segments: prewriting, writing, and postwriting (Koch and Brazil, 1974, p. xi). Prewriting includes experiencing that leads to a desire to write, discovering or identifying a topic and an audience, choosing a form of writing and a form of organization. Writing includes using the form selected, making language choices, and the process of carrying out the language choices. Postwriting involves criticizing and proofreading.

In Chapter 7 we attempted to paint a clear picture of the development of writing by considering experiences that encourage and improve it. In this chapter we will look at the writing process itself. We will examine additional factors that affect children's writing, specific purposes and forms for writing, and the mechanics of writing, such as spelling and handwriting. Record keeping and evaluation of writing also are included in this chapter.

Preparation for writing

Sensory awareness is the basis for all communication. The more children are aware of themselves—their feelings, thoughts, and values—and the more they are aware of the world around them, the more thoughts they have to communicate and the greater their desire to communicate. Teachers need to recognize the importance of developing sense experiences for children. Given the opportunity to observe, hear, feel, smell, touch, and talk about their experiences, children acquire the raw material for understanding the world and themselves more clearly.

Given the opportunity to observe a snowflake, feel it, taste it, talk about it, and perhaps "become" a snowflake through spontaneous drama, the child learns sensitivity to feelings and awareness of self as well as awareness of the environment. This kind of experiencing is more likely to lead to imaginative, exploratory writing than work that is purely factual or descriptive.

Since the development of concepts is the effective means of expanding vocabulary, children need varied experiences with people, books, and happenings so that new words can be related to experiences and become concepts with meaning, not just sounds. Thus, extensive oral language experiences are essential to writing at all levels of the elementary school. Talk provides the stepping stones between what is thought about and what is written. After a new and interesting experience, we "talk our thoughts" before we write them. In addition to inner speech, we may involve others as listeners in order to explore and organize our thinking for ourselves. In the classroom, talking not only extends and clarifies thinking, but also increases children's confidence that they have something to say on paper and some specific ways to express it.

Before they begin to write, children need to talk about the substance of their writing with their peers, individually or in groups. Discussion increases interest, requires thought, and develops ideas beyond those in the writer's mind originally. The teacher's next step is to help the writer focus thoughts and language on the topic. But teachers should not let the children exhaust the topic in discussion; rather, at the peak of interest they can

say, "Each of you has so many thoughts, why don't you write them so we all can know them?"

In addition to providing sensory experiences and the opportunity to talk about them, teachers can help young writers by making them aware of the audience for whom they will write and of their purposes for writing.

Writing and audience

Whenever and whatever we write, we write for an audience, even if the audience is only ourselves. The audience puts constraints on what writers say and the way we say it. In addition, we tend to feel we can talk with a person in confidence about things we would hesitate to write about. Teachers need to realize that, no matter who the audience is, most children will feel some constraints to their writing.

Teachers may introduce the concept of "sense of audience" (Rosen, 1973) in kindergarten or first grade when the whole class is writing a request for information or material on a project. The teacher may ask, "Who can help us?" "Whom do we want to write to?" When children begin to write stories, the question is, "Are you writing this to take home to your family? Or is it for the other boys and girls to read here?" The child's awareness of audience usually makes a difference in the writing. Teachers can mention this basic factor again and again as the need arises. All writing is for the purpose of communicating with someone.

The four main categories of audience Rosen deals with are: (1) self as audience, (2) teacher as audience, (3) another known audience, and (4) an unknown audience.

Self as audience can be very broad or very limited. In the broad sense, much that people write for others is written for themselves as well, perhaps to bring joy by recalling and retelling happy incidents, or to think through a problem and find a solution. In the limited sense, most of us write ourselves reminder notes on shopping lists intended only for temporary use. Children at one time or another may use all of these forms of writing.

In school children direct most of their writing to the *teacher as audience*. In traditional classrooms teachers assign the topic, designate the time, require children to write a report on Japan, a paragraph of description, or do some "creative" writing. Consciously or unconsciously, most children write the way they think the teacher wants them to (Rosen, 1973, pp. 180–182). Since they are not formulating and developing their own preferences, there is little relationship between their own thoughts and what they write. When their purpose is pleasing the teacher, children do not get as personally involved, find little satisfaction in writing, and thus do as little writing as possible.

Personal letters are written to a *known audience* (Rosen, 1973, pp. 182–186). When an older child is writing stories for younger ones, the audience is known. The writing may be a report stating a position on a topic to be discussed by the school planning committee, the all-school council, or some other known group.

Each of these cases calls for different language. The personal letters might be quite informal. Stories for younger children to read would require simple vocabulary and sentence structure. Reports on special topics would be more formal and well polished. Writers need to identify their audience so they can adjust their writing to the form and manner that will most effectively convey their thoughts to the reader.

The known-audience category is appropriate for much of elementary school children's writing. Writing for an *unknown audience*, which Rosen calls a "public audience," is most appropriate for the more mature writers. Stories written to be placed in the school library come under this category. Such stories need more careful editing by the writer, sometimes with the help of the group.

Purposes for writing

Children need to be aware of the purpose for anything they write. When they write without pur-
pose, writing becomes a routine exercise with little value. We cannot defend a teacher's purpose of "finding out what a child knows." School activities are for children's learning, not for teachers', so both teachers and children need to express purpose from the child's viewpoint. "Would it help you understand and organize your thinking if you made a list of important points and then explained each point?" A child might say, "Mr. Williams [a local author] helped me so much when he was here. I want to write a story for him to thank him," or "I want to write a letter asking Aunt Mabel to visit our class to see what we can do."

Purpose creates involvement, which motivates effective learning. The less the teacher's direction, the greater the children's involvement and the more they care about the outcome of the writing. Involvement also stems from an enriched environment, a wide variety of materials of real interest to children, and freedom to explore and discuss them with their peers. In other words, involvement and purpose occur when children find their school experiences exciting and enjoyable.

Two broad purposes for writing are practical writing and personal writing. Practical writing is the routine kind, used largely in the other curriculum areas and in the everyday world. Personal writing, which expresses feelings and reports on personal experiences, includes creative writing.

Practical writing Practical writing for our own information sometimes consists of abbreviations, short phrases, or only key words. The writer must learn, however, to make notes complete enough to serve as reminders later. A telephone number or address without a name is of little help. Writing for others requires more care, including proofreading, correction of mechanics, and often rewriting.

Memoranda and reports must be accurate, clear, and understandable to the audience for whom they are written. In business letters the writer needs to be as concise and specific as possible; children can bring letters their parents have received as examples of forms for such letters. Even personal letters are practical writing when they merely report needed information.

One specific goal for all writing is to say what one means. Children need to learn as quickly as possible that writing communicates only what the reader receives from it. The teacher might say to the child, "Suppose the reader knows nothing about this subject. Will he understand what you are writing?"

Perhaps the most difficult aspect of practical writing is making it significant to the child. When information is to be shared in written form, the writer needs to share it with an audience beyond the teacher. This audience may be another class, families and friends, a community group, or the school council. Undoubtedly other audiences will occur to children as they study issues relevant to them in the various content areas of the school curriculum.

In social studies children can write to government officials to request information. Younger children can investigate matters of concern to their own neighborhoods, while older children investigate community problems or state and national issues. Children can write reports of their study and present them to whatever community groups are also concerned. Letters to other classes, individual friends, or relatives tap a rich source of information about other parts of the country, and the response is far more meaningful than information found in textbooks. Accuracy can be checked in texts and reference books.

Science offers many opportunities. Writing for younger children, a group may create science puzzles or describe simple experiments as a basis for demonstration projects. Children's questions can be addressed to older science classes. If no adequate answer is available locally, the questions can be submitted to a university or to other scientists throughout the state or nation. Communicating on this level requires much writing, critiquing by the group, and rewriting before everyone is satisfied that it meets all criteria. This procedure for developing writing skills is demanding and exciting enough to involve all who are concerned with the problem. The response to such a request is the big payoff!

Sixth graders involved in a history project discovered that information written by one historian differed significantly from other writers' accounts of the same events. After comparing all the available sources, they wrote to the author whose material differed. They were careful not to say that this author was wrong, but instead gave careful documentation to all the differing sources, then asked for the basis of the historian's information. Human relations were woven into the project as they discussed how the author might feel and tried to choose the best way to word their request. The historian's equally courteous reply thanked the group for calling the issue to his attention. Everyone had learned!

Personal writing   Through the personal and private world of children's thoughts, when they are willing to share them, teachers can come to know and understand children better. But sometimes personal writing involves private thoughts that a child is unwilling to share. This privacy should be distinguished from the hesitancy of the child who fears negative comments or ridicule, but under no circumstances should teachers require children to share their writing when they do not want to. Their privacy must be respected.

Much personal writing is in the form of narrative, descriptive, or analytical prose. It may be expressed with awareness, sensitivity, or imagination, but the one constant factor is that the personal thoughts, feelings, wishes, or ideas of the writer are involved. Personal letters are often in this category, and long distance telephone can never entirely replace the pleasure children gain from writing and receiving letters. Correspondence provides one more type of writing to broaden their experience.

Personal writing may take the form of a play in which one character represents the child's beliefs and desires while other characters oppose them or help to plead the child's case. Another purpose for this form of writing is to explore and clarify under-standings or feelings about an event or a relation-ship. Such interaction might take the form of a cartoon strip in which the nonverbal supplements the verbal.

Personal writing may be just for release, for clar-ification of how one feels, or to communicate these feelings to others. Based on sense experience, it conveys the *impression* things, people, and events have made upon the writer. Children may express their feelings through poetry, expressive prose, or imaginative writing.

McPhee (1971) suggests that the writing process may be less important than developing children's awareness of themselves, their feelings, and their world. He lists six goals to strive for in work with children: (1) deeper awareness and understanding of themselves; (2) deeper and wider sympathetic understanding of others; (3) a fuller understanding of their own position in time and space; (4) a fuller awareness and understanding of nature; (5) a more highly developed and refined aesthetic awareness; and (6) the ability to express these feel-ings and concepts appropriately.

Conversations about feelings help children de-velop the vocabulary needed in affective writing and make it acceptable to talk and write about feelings. Competency in expression of thoughts and feelings develops gradually through this proc-ess. Material of this type should be read to chil-dren and made available for their reading.

Much of the so-called creative writing we have seen in schools is not what we believe creative writing to be. Assignment of creative writing for children to complete and hand in between 1:00 and 1:20 each afternoon shows lack of understand-ing. Creative writing comes from within, when the individual in interaction with the outside world has developed relevant thoughts to the point he or she can express them on paper.

Children are curious, eager, and imaginative. The world is still so new to them that everything is interesting, and a sensitive awareness can create sensitive writing. They may choose to write in the form of poetry, story, or drama, for versatility be-comes part of children's thinking when they find these forms are acceptable and appreciated. Young children share their own thoughts in school far more easily than does the older child, as any sur-vey of young children shows. (Could it be that older children have learned not to?) The begin-ning-to-write child is not a poet, yet has a fresh-ness, a quality of language that may be poetic and a source of delight to adults and other children. Furthering this quality in a positive environment will help the child discover how to write better. If children experience encouragement from their early attempts on through the grades, they main-tain an openness to experience that provides them with new thoughts to express and new ways to express them.

When some creative writing appears, have the author, if willing, tell about it and share it with the group. Since it is the process we are mainly con-cerned with rather than the product, ask the child to tell how he or she started thinking about the topic and putting it down on paper.

Unique, personal ways of saying things may occur at any time. Even if it is only a phrase, recognition and appreciation of its effectiveness encourage further attempts. Concern with cor-rectness will inhibit creative effort, but if the child produces something he or she is proud of, there is good reason to polish it.

Poetry is personal writing, but children seldom think of using poetry to express themselves be-cause it does not occur to them that rhyming, metered lines are within their capability. The var-ied patterns now being used make writing poetry seem more feasible. Rhyming is not necessary, nor is meter as long as the lines flow smoothly with a natural rhythm.

Poetry has become increasingly difficult to de-fine. In her *Poetry in the Elementary School* (1970, pp. 18–21) Virginia Witucke writes that poetry is experience; poetry is emotion and thought; poetry is noticing; poetry is sensation; poetry is original; poetry is compressed; and poetry is rhythm. Poetry is also a variety of forms, and the most effective way to help children write poetry is to help them become happily familiar with many kinds and many forms of poetry.

Children can begin with one-line poems. For example, after reading Charles Schulz' *Happiness Is a Warm Puppy* (1962) to introduce it to children, one can suggest they make up their own definitions of happiness. The experience creates and extends an awareness of a variety of feelings. Suzanne Heller's *Misery* (1964) can be another catalyst. From here children can move to poems of several lines and more specific forms.

The *limerick*, popularized by Edward Lear in the nineteenth century, consists of three long lines that rhyme and two short lines that rhyme. Many children can write humorous verse in this form:

> There once was a girl of Kildare
> Who wore ribbons on curls in her hair.
> The showers came down
> As she went to town.
> Oh, how sad she did look at the fair!

Another form of humorous verse is composed by adding an original ending to the first two lines of a nursery rhyme.

> Mary, Mary, quite contrary,
> How does your garden grow?
> With crawling bugs and slimy slugs,
> And ugly weeds all in a row.

Japanese verse has provided a popular form that is easy for children to use and lends itself readily to personal writing. *Haiku* has three lines and seventeen syllables distributed 5-7-5. The subject matter often deals with nature and expresses feelings either directly or indirectly.

> The warm sun rises,
> Dew drops reflect its bright rays,
> Flowers greet the morn.

Tanka is similar but longer, having five lines in which syllables are distributed 5-7-5-7-5. Like haiku, it often paints a picture of nature but can deal with any subject.

> The bright river flows,
> White water breaks the surface
> Where rocks hide beneath.
> Salmon jump, splash in the sun.
> Then all is quiet.

Another form of verse children use easily is *cinquain*. This form has five lines; the first is one word, a noun; the second, two words describing the noun; third, three words tell what it does; fourth, four words tell how it makes you feel; and fifth, one word, either the noun repeated, or a synonym. Cinquain has been used successfully by first and second graders as well as older children.

> Kittens
> Fur balls
> Chasing each other
> They make me laugh
> Kitties

Some children who find satisfaction in these simple forms will want to write more sophisticated poetry, either rhymed or unrhymed. Children should be encouraged to use free verse.

Thus, creative writing is a special kind of personal writing that can be encouraged and stimulated but not required. Some children may produce a considerable amount and others none, in spite of the teacher's best efforts. Usually creative writing is produced irregularly, none for weeks or months, then perhaps something every few days. Because creativity lies in the process, not in the product, the quality of the writing should be judged by the extent to which the writing is unique to the child. In order to write creatively, children need stimulation of their thinking and feeling. They need to read and hear a wide variety of good writing. From this experience they learn new forms and internalize expectancies and possibilities. They need freedom from pressure to write and time to record ideas before they are forgotten.

Then when the thoughts have been captured, children need support and encouragement to polish them so that they can experience the pride of authorship. Pride in accomplishment provides strong motivation for all learning, but especially for creative endeavors, which are a portion of children's private, unique selves.

Feedback on writing

It is difficult for everyone, particularly children, to consider what they write from the reader's point of view. Material that seems perfectly clear in terms of the writer's experience may make no sense to readers with different backgrounds. Since all "public" writing is written to be read by others, awareness of this problem and ways to deal with it are important. For this reason, as well as others, feedback on writing is essential to children.

Feedback should be prompt, genuine, and meaningful to the writer. When children know that someone really cares about their writing, their desire to write increases. If no one reacts, however, the drive to write may diminish or be directed into other channels. Feedback should come both from the teacher and from other children. When the writing is too restricted, when it does not convey meaning to readers, peers can raise questions that show what additional information they need. This type of feedback is most useful at all ages and stages of writing development.

But children do not solve their writing problems as a result of red pencil marks or negative comments in the margins of their papers. Such feedback tells the writers that they cannot write well, and consequently they become less able to write.

Let's suppose Ralph has brought the teacher a piece of writing that is bad by all standards of usage, punctuation, and spelling. Should the teacher mark the errors on the paper? Should Ralph be required to rewrite it? Perhaps the inaccuracy was due to Ralph's carelessness and indifference, but negative response from the teacher might increase Ralph's don't-care attitude. Instead, the teacher can look for something positive—a valuable thought, an ordinary thought well expressed, or even a word Ralph has recently learned to spell correctly.

After positive recognition, teacher and child might talk about Ralph's purpose for writing this material and what he is planning to do with it. If he expresses a thought about this, the teacher can comment, "Then you will want to polish it. Do you need help, or can you do it by yourself?" If he looks doubtful, the teacher can suggest that he start polishing and ask for help when he needs it. Such a procedure reestablishes expectancies, leaves the responsibility in Ralph's hands, but offers help after he has done what he can. Children should feel responsible for improving their writing within limits they can accept, and they should enjoy writing while gradually improving the quality. The basic priority is having them *want* to write.

The teacher's feedback must be realistic but constructive and focused on progress. Carol's concept of herself as a writer has more effect on her success than any other single factor. The teacher starts with a sample that seems to be representative of Carol's present capabilities. If the writing is not legible, the teacher asks Carol to read it aloud. Carol may recognize some of her own errors or omissions, which she can then correct on her own. The teacher can ask what she might have done to make these changes earlier. The conference can end with a recap of progress, evidence of her interest in the content, and confidence in Carol's commitment to developing her writing ability.

Another approach can be used when the teacher feels that the low quality of the writing was due to lack of interest and concern. As the teacher, you might lay the paper aside, invite Don to sit down beside you, and open up the problem. You might reflect your understanding of his feelings by saying quietly, "I feel you didn't think this writing was very important to you. Is there something else that would be more important for you to write?" The purpose is to establish open and honest communication, show interest in Don's concerns, and assure him that in developing writing competence, one topic can be as useful as another. Since progress is largely dependent on involvement, the concerns and interests of the writer provide the most useful topics. Perhaps Don chooses to do investigative and factual reporting rather than narrative writing. The crucial task at this point is to revive his desire to write. Without interest in writing, there is little hope that he will make progress.

Perhaps Don believes he will never have any purpose for writing. His father is a mechanic, and Don wants to be one too. His father never writes anything. Don's mother writes all the letters written in the family, and he expects to have a wife to do the same. Don will not need to write to finish high school because he plans to drop out as soon as possible. That the world is changing and no one knows what skill may be needed in the future is beyond his current perceptions.

Since force breeds resistance, perhaps tentative agreement with him at the moment will minimize his resistance. Then watch carefully for him to contribute from his areas of interest. If teacher and peers recognize his interests, he may wish to expand on his contributions. He may need to read related magazines or books, which will deepen and expand his interest. If he can now see a real purpose for writing, progress may be on the way.

Feelings about a task affect one's perception of it, and perception of a task determines what one expects to be able to accomplish. Writers know intuitively what they can write about effectively, in what forms they can best express their thoughts, and when and where they can write best. Some professional writers can discipline themselves to write in an office from nine to five, but most people write best at their own times and places. Some teachers will be reluctant to turn over to the child the responsibility for selecting the time, place, and content for writing. But removing the element of personal choice curtails the learner's motivation as well as the ability to think and write effectively.

Changes take place when teachers keep the pressure off and opportunities for success and recognition open. When the classroom environment is stimulating but nonthreatening, and when their writing is accepted and respected, children will develop their sense experiences and relate them in expressive ways that are necessary for continued growth.

The conventions of writing

Conventions of writing include certain generally accepted rules, such as writing English from left to right, indenting, capitalizing, punctuating, and paragraphing. Such consistencies have made writing a more effective communication process. Conventions change, however, because language is constantly changing. Many of today's adults, for example, were taught never to begin a sentence with *and* or *but*, or to end it with a preposition. But a preposition is occasionally a very functional word to end a sentence with. Today some of our finest authors violate such "rules."

Language always changes over generations and sometimes changes within a few years. "Drive Slow" is a common sign, even though *slowly* is the adverbial form. In speech, people commonly substitute *who* for *whom*, as in "Who do you wish to speak to?" The distinction between *can* and *may* is becoming obliterated through usage. Although purists object, many writers are making verbs out of nouns (*prioritize*) and adjectives (*finalize*), and some believe that the tendency is enriching, simplifying, and clarifying meaning. Children who were corrected for saying "Me and Sally are going to school" grew up to be adults who overcorrect and say "The gift is from Sally and I." Many people use *than* after *different* (Your book is different than mine), even though *different from* is still preferred in formal writing (Pooley, 1974, pp. 163–167). Another type of change is the coining of new words through acronyms, such as *wasp* for "white, Anglo-Saxon Protestant."

In working with children, we should not make an issue of changes in informal speech that are part of the current vernacular. But as children's writing matures, we should encourage them to follow the examples of today's more highly respected writers. As children write and identify with authorship, they can refer to books they are reading for guidance in writing.

Punctuating and paragraphing

Written language is arranged spatially, English being ordered from left to right and top to bottom in successive lines. White spaces separate the patterns of letters we call words, and successive patterns of words are separated from other patterns by marks called *punctuation*.

Punctuation is a set of signals that indicate how to read a sequence of words as a speaker would say them. These signals work much like traffic lights. They tell the reader when to stop, go, and pause. The writer tries to convey meaning to the reader through the use of signals, such as commas, colons, semicolons, exclamation marks, periods, question marks, apostrophes, and quotation marks. These marks link, separate, and enclose sentences and parts of sentences to help bring meaning to the written thought.

Punctuation in writing is related to intonation in speaking. The relationship is not exact, for punctuation marks cannot show all the intonations in our speech. But just as there is some general sound-letter relationship between spoken and written words, so there is some matching of graphic signals with voice variations.

Children often are not aware of intonation as a clue to punctuation, and learning "rules" for punctuation seems purely mechanical, rather than a help in understanding written material. Periods to separate thoughts, question marks to indicate questions, and exclamation points to show emphasis are the main punctuation marks needed at first. Children can try out different punctuation to discover the effect: "The fire is out." "The fire is out?" "The fire is out!" However, we do not always raise our voices at question marks. For

example, we might drop our voices following "What time is it?"

When a teacher raises these questions, children experiment with punctuation and soon become aware of the patterns of intonations and their relation to meaning. Children need to think about punctuation as signals to a reader from a writer, to help convey meaning. In this way children will have less difficulty with punctuation in writing and will be able to see its relationship to the syntactic structure as well as to the meaning.

Paragraphing varies with type of material. Newspapers and other narrow-column publications use very short paragraphs of one, two, or three sentences. Paragraphs are longer in wider columns. The format can be considered when children discuss topic sentences and the number of paragraphs needed on a topic. In all written material, one essential stands out—all sentences in a paragraph must have some meaningful relationship with one another. Consistency of thought within paragraphs, with bridging words or phrases between them, is a guide to easier reading.

The place of grammar in writing

We are still besieged with the myth that teaching grammar (knowledge of facts and rules of grammar) will increase the child's syntactic competence. Since grammar is the way language is structured or put together to convey meaning, all children use it very early and quite well by the time they come to school. This use is intuitive, and unconscious, internalized from years of verbal interaction. Is it important to bring this competency to the level of awareness? If so, when is it most useful to do so? To what extent? And how? Traditionally teachers thought that only when children understood the grammar of their language could they learn to speak and write effectively. However, much research and observation of children has shown that studying grammar as formal subject matter does not improve the ability to read or write. Strickland writes:

> Over the past century, grammar has been taught in thousands of classrooms but with little appreciable effect upon the written or spoken language of many pupils. Perhaps it was naive to expect it, in terms of what we know today about the language learning process (Strickland, 1964, p. 16).

Hundreds of research studies of the effectiveness of formal grammar for improving writing have consistently shown no effect. Studies of children's learning demonstrate that the application of generalizations to specific situations, especially when the two are taught separately, seldom happens. On the basis of the studies in both grammar and learning, we are convinced that in the first six grades of schooling, children should be experiencing grammar rather than learning grammar by prescription.

Grammar too often has been narrowly conceived as largely having to do with proper word forms, verb tense and mood, and some very specific and rather abstract rules concerning usage. Instead, grammar really has to do with the total organization and structuring of sentences to indicate relationships of words and phrases clearly in order to express the intended meaning. It is hard to explain what difference, if any, being able to label the subject and object would make in a child's talking or writing. A two-year-old may say "Me eat candy" but never "Candy eat me." And, with no direct teaching, the *me* changes to *I* long before schooling begins.

Children have discovered the proper arrangement of word forms to show their mutual relationship within a sentence, in keeping with regular grammatical usage in their own dialect, standard or otherwise. They have also learned intuitively that certain English words, and/or word parts, function as pattern markers. Words such as *an*, *the*, *was*, and *her*, and inflectional endings like *-ing* and *-es* form the base for patterns. These markers

alone do not give meaning, but the appropriate use of these markers makes meaning possible. For instance, when children see "An____fell from the____," they know that both spaces should be filled by names of things. And when they see "The weather was____," they know that some descriptive word is needed.

We must caution those who would generalize that we advocate or approve exercises in "patterns of writing." Exercises using sentences irrelevant to their thoughts cannot help children express their own thoughts more clearly. Teachers need to pay attention to the technical and mechanical aspects of a writing program, but these aspects must never be given priority and used as a foundation for the program. Grammar is most effectively considered in reference to a particular piece of a child's own writing. Where several children are having the same difficulty, they can come together and explore the difference certain structural or pattern-marker changes could make in their writing.

The difference between effective and noneffective users of language, in either speaking or writing, does not appear to lie in their control of the knowledge of grammar rules. Far more important are (1) increased experience in talking for a specific purpose, followed by feedback on how effectively the child talks; (2) wide reading of many authors and many types of books; and (3) much experience in writing of kinds and on topics of their own choice, and then polishing that writing. As children construct sentences, and read and listen to a great variety of well-formed sentences, they internalize many possibilities. This approach to learning is consistent with Piaget's ideas of learning through firsthand experiences.

The mechanics of writing

To keep the various aspects of written language in proper perspective, we discuss spelling and handwriting under the heading of "the mechanics of writing." Handwriting and spelling are not unimportant, but they have only superficial relationship to written language, which is the recording of thought. If the recording is indecipherable and the selection and arrangement of letters are unconventional enough to delay the retrieval of meaning, the usefulness of the recording is greatly lessened. But the essentials are there, even when the translation is difficult.

Some have classified punctuation as one of the mechanics. This classification can be defended only when punctuation is taught as arbitrary rules. When it is viewed as the graphic expression of intonation—pitch, stress, and pause—that clarifies or even determines the meaning of the spoken language, punctuation is far more than mechanics. It is an important factor in the effective expression of the thoughts and feelings of the writer.

Spelling

Most authorities agree spelling has been one of the most ineffectively taught areas of the curriculum. If this is so, it certainly means we must change the way we teach spelling. But some of the recent changes have not proved too successful. To understand why, let us first look at some of the basic factors involved in spelling.

Until the dictionary was developed in 1755 by Samuel Johnson, words were spelled according to familiar patterns or as people heard them. Any word might have a variety of spellings, which apparently created few problems. But since that time, there have been right and wrong ways to spell a word. What is more, anyone, regardless of other abilities, can "know" whether or not a word is spelled correctly, if he or she can find the word in a dictionary. This factor underlies public attention to spelling, which is one of the less important areas of the curriculum.

The main issue is that what one writes, others need to read easily. However, the substitution of letters in many words is scarcely noticed when the material is read for meaning. After material is set in type, several people proofread it to pick up

errors. Even so, virtually everyone has at one time or another found a misspelling in published material. People tend to see what we expect to see, and we are not aware of every letter when we are reading. So the importance of perfect spelling in material made available to others is social and political. Therefore, for the children's sake—and our own—it is important to help them produce *final copy* as correctly spelled as feasible.

Spelling programs Most spelling programs are based on the logic of adults who analyze words and the spelling of them, but ignore the way children learn. They ignore children's interests, needs, and concerns, the transitory nature of rote memory, the difficulty that children have applying what they learn in one situation to a different situation, and the limits to the amount of new information that children can absorb in a period of time. They ignore the fact that when children have no real desire to spell certain words, their only motivation is negative—fear of what will happen if they do not.

The typical spelling program has organized from 2,000 to 5,000 of the most commonly used words in children's and adults' writing into a spelling series. This series usually extends from grade two through grade eight, includes some thirty-two to thirty-six lessons per year, and incorporates from fifteen to fifty words per week. The program usually includes a review of words most often misspelled.

There have been arguments about how many words a series should include altogether. Studies have shown that the 2,800 words most commonly used by adults include 97.2 percent of the running words each person needs in adult writing. The rest of adult writing includes names and words specific to people's living situations and means of livelihood. If the 4,000 most common words are taught, the percentage increases to 98.3.* The addition of

*This data is based on material in Ernest Horn, *Basic Writing Vocabulary*, published in 1926. The actual words might vary some today, but the generalizations would undoubtedly be similar.

1,200 words to be learned seems unjustifiable, especially if only 1.1 percent of these words are needed by adults, and some are never used by children. However, the finding has had little effect, and most series still include far too many words.

Fitzgerald tried to concentrate instruction on a smaller number of words. A selected list of 2,650 words makes up 95 percent of the running words used by children and adults in their writing. He selected from these a list of 449 most useful spelling words and a supplementary list of 521 words almost as useful. These two lists, 970 words, constitute about 85 percent of the average person's writing vocabulary (Fitzgerald, 1951, p. 53). It does not seem particularly efficient to triple the number of spelling words to be learned at elementary level, to gain an increase of only 10 percent in usage.

Instructional patterns One basic pattern of spelling instruction has been followed by most programs for years. A list of words is introduced on Monday; children study them on Tuesday, take a trial test on Wednesday, study words they missed on Thursday, and take a final test on Friday. One variation on this plan is a pretest on Monday so that children will need to study only the words they miss, rather than the whole list. This procedure encourages longer lists so children will "have enough words to learn."

Other variations in spelling programs include having different lists for the more able, the average, and the less able spellers. In any grouping of this sort, the "low" group generally accepts the label and their attempts at learning become more feeble and less confident. Children in the "high" group do not need a spelling program, but could more profitably spend their time on other activities.

Another approach attempts to individualize the program by having children choose from a comprehensive list the words they want to learn to spell. While this procedure may create interest, it is seldom interest in spelling written work correctly, which is the only real purpose of spelling. A procedure that holds more promise is doing away with the midweek and final tests and having two children work together and test each other. Children benefit when this procedure is used to correct words they have misspelled in their own writing, but usually a prescribed word list is used for all students.

The value of pretesting is questionable. Isolated words are out of context, which is never the way a child will need to write them, and thus may eliminate clues from associational memory. A second problem is that when words are written in a dictated list, the child gives full attention to each, whereas in actual writing the child's attention is on the thought being expressed, not on the spelling of each word. Still another problem is that a one-time writing may be a lucky guess, which does not ensure correct spelling later in written work.

Using a dictionary to learn how words are spelled has been overemphasized. Before trying to use a dictionary, children need to acquire the skill of guessing the first two or three letters of the word they want to find. By the time children are able to use a dictionary, they have usually developed a fairly reliable sound-symbol relationship, especially for initial consonants. Vowels may be harder to identify, and homonyms can be a problem. Children and teachers need to be aware that many words are nearly impossible to find without fairly good clues. What about *aisle*?

Most of the analysis of the spelling process has been of words to be spelled rather than of children's spelling of them. The most monumental such study was Project 1991 under the direction of Paul Hanna (1966). The study analyzed the phoneme-grapheme relationships of all phonemes in more than 17,000 words and showed that many factors affect the spelling of words. While it is a fascinating study, its utility in helping children to spell seems dubious.

Pronunciation may help in ways other than the phoneme-grapheme relationship. One-syllable words with a single medial vowel having a long vowel sound usually end in a silent *e*. Syllabification has implications for spelling. A long vowel usually occurs in an open syllable (one ending in a vowel) and a short vowel in a closed syllable (one ending in a consonant). The latter situation frequently indicates double consonants, as in *cater* and *batter;* and *committee* must have two double consonants or it would be pronounced cō•mī•tee. However, it is not hard to find exceptions to these generalizations, and Zuck (1974) questions the value of syllabification as an aid to spelling. A practice to be avoided is teaching mnemonic devices like put *a rat* in *separate* or use *lice* to know that with *ei* or *ie, i* follows *l* and *e* follows *c.*

The purpose of correct spelling The only purpose for knowing how to spell is to be able to write words correctly in any material that will be read by others. This purpose provides a number of guidelines for a spelling program.

Each child needs to learn the words he or she wishes to write at the time that child wants to write them. Words children need to learn to spell are those they spell incorrectly in their everyday writing. And the only real test of whether children have mastered a word is whether they consistently spell it correctly in their writing.

Spelling programs should be differentiated for children on the basis of need. If children do not misspell words, they do not need to study spelling. If they only occasionally misspell words—and it is impossible to predict which words they will misspell—they need only to learn to spell the words they miss.

It makes no sense for children to learn to spell a word that is not in their speaking or writing vocabulary. There is no point in teaching children to spell words that they are unlikely to use in the near future. When a class is discussing crustaceans, the children do not need to learn to spell *crustacean.* The teacher can display the word on a chart or chalkboard for the duration of the project so that children can copy it in their writing. Some children will undoubtedly learn to spell it, but there is no need to burden all of the children with the requirement of learning such terms.

Introducing new words to children as spelling words

does not increase their vocabulary significantly. Words that become meaningful are those tied to personal experience—not just experience with the word, but experience with that which the word symbolizes. If children have only looked at pictures and read and talked about crustaceans, most children will forget the word very quickly. They will remember the word and want to use it only if the word has become theirs through experience: finding some crabs, comparing them with lobsters they have seen in the meat market, handling crabs and feeling their firm shells, trying to pull barnacles off the rocks, trying to think of other sea life that belongs in the same category. If children want to write the word *crustacean*, they will learn how to spell it. The words that need to be learned must be related directly to each child's own writing.

Selection of spelling words There is no list of words that all children need to learn to spell. There are many words that each child already knows how to write correctly, and some words that it would be helpful for the child to learn to spell. Often children realize that they are unsure how to write a certain word every time they need it. Learning how to spell it would be easier than looking it up or changing what they want to say to avoid using the word.

As soon as children start writing on their own, each child can keep a list of words he or she wants to write but does not know how to spell. The list might be on slips in a box as described in Chapter 7, or in a notebook especially made for this purpose with twenty-six pages, one for each letter. Susie may take a slip or her list to whomever can write the words she needs—the teacher, a helping adult, or another child. The helper can write the requested word on the slip or on the page headed by the letter the word begins with.

When Susie has to look up a word many times and is still uncertain how to write it, she is encouraged to focus on it. When she can write the word without checking, the word is discarded or crossed out. Having words readily at hand until they are mastered can prevent spelling problems. The key is for Susie to care enough about her writing so final drafts, at least, are correctly spelled. Pride in accomplishment is the only reason children—or adults—will continue to write correctly. The point is that spelling is only for the purpose of writing correctly whatever it is one wants to write.

Spelling problems Perhaps a third to a fourth of all elementary school children have no trouble with spelling, nor would they if they never had a spelling lesson. If they have seen a word, they know how to write it. If they make a spelling error once and become aware of it, they will probably never make that error again. The time that these children spend on spelling lessons is wasted. Another third to half of a group can easily approach 100 percent on spelling tests with a reasonable amount of time devoted to studying the words. If we read the writing of this middle group, however, we will undoubtedly find words misspelled that they have previously spelled correctly on a test. Almost any teacher will confirm this observation. But about one-fourth of a class will probably never be able to score well on any spelling test under most current spelling programs, nor to produce any written work correctly spelled without much revision.

Why do these children have trouble with spelling? The answers are almost as numerous as the children involved. Sometimes children become anxious about spelling because an issue has been made of spelling too early and too critically. Afraid they will misspell, children think of alternative spellings and choose the wrong one. Anxiety is related to forgetting (Lighthall, 1964, pp. 20–22).

In some children, poor spelling and low reading competence go together and probably have one or more common causes. Perhaps reading and writing were not tied together closely so children could understand the relationship. Or it may be that children had difficulty with reading because of an instructional approach that prevented their making sense of it. These children learned they weren't very good with words, and this expectancy transferred to writing. Another possible

cause is an overemphasis on phonics. Many words, particularly in early reading and writing (*was, one, come, does*), are not spelled phonetically. Too much emphasis on the letter-sound relationship hinders both reading and writing. An early and consistent emphasis on the left-to-right progression in reading can help prevent trouble by having the child always look at a word in a consistent way.

When children have arrived in the intermediate grades with many spelling problems, teachers should play down the importance of spelling and play up the value of the thoughts expressed. When children feel their thoughts are important and others may wish to read them, their spelling usually improves automatically. The child's own feeling of uncertainty or the polishing process helps each child to identify two or three words that most often cause trouble. Teachers can work out with the child ways to master them once and for all. Then the child can select another two or three.

Research on the troubled speller has shown that the more words he studied, the fewer he learned (Lee and Lee, 1941). This would imply that only a few words should be studied at any one time. But the poor results of spelling instruction puts pressure on teachers to teach even more words, not realizing they are defeating their own purposes. Most children do not misspell a large number of words in their writing, but repeatedly misspell a relatively small number of words. Many words are never misspelled. If children would gain lifetime control over just one word each week, most spelling problems would be solved.

One way to develop a positive approach to writing, when children have a great deal of trouble spelling, is to count the number of words correctly spelled in each piece of original writing. The practice of emphasizing the number of errors tends to create more. Another way is to emphasize the number of correct letters in any misspelled word.

How spellings are learned All children are more or less consciously aware of words and letters in our very verbal environment. Some people doubt there was ever a child in the world who could not read *Coca-Cola* before going to school! Most children learn the writing of many words implicitly, as they learn many other things about their world, through experiencing. At the beginning they usually copy the word, writing it letter-by-letter until they become aware of the sequence and internalize the way of writing it.

Another intuitive aid is the way the word sounds. Almost universally, children make some connection between meaning and the way the symbols look and sound. Many children who learn to read on their own devise their own understanding of this relationship. Since the initial consonant sounds have the most consistent *phoneme-grapheme* (sound-to-letter) relationship, the child can often start a word on that basis. The initial letter is one more cue, one more nudge to memory.

To date, no one has studied what a child does when learning to write, in the sense of either composing or spelling—and it was only within the last fifteen years that studies from this point of view were begun in reading. Until such studies are conducted, we can only guess at the process. Our best guesses will be based on what we *do* know about how children learn—and much of this research has been based on the learning of meaningless symbols or words. Such research has almost no relevance for the implicit internalizing based on experiencing.

Sometimes it seems that rote memory is needed to learn to spell some words, but usually this is not entirely so. Let us think about how we write as adults. We decide on the thought we want to express, then the sequence of words to express it. As we think of one word after another or say them to ourselves, our fingers automatically write them. We do not say the letters except in words we have not yet learned. We see what we write and accept it if it looks right. If it does not look right, we stop and make corrections.

This process is what we are aiming for as children learn to spell. They will need to write the word to fix it in their *kinesthetic* system. Then they need to evaluate its correctness visually. The writing of a word 10 times or 100 times violates the procedure because there is no need to evaluate, and because an isolated word is not tied to its use in recording thought. Saying the word aloud or spelling it aloud is not part of the process. In the normal course of spelling, we do not need to say the letters. We say the letters only when people ask us to spell a word for them. Even then, it is far better to write the word on a scrap of paper, because it is the appearance of the word, not the sound of individual letters, that we hope they will learn.

In the same way, children can learn the two or three words that are bothering them most at any one time. They may write the words in bright color on a card and tape it to their desk or table, where they will see it hundreds of times a day. When they need to write it, they can either copy it or try to write it without looking at it. In either case, they check it against the card. After they have been able to use the word in their writing correctly several times, they may decide to put a book over the card. Then when they need to use the word, they write it, and if they decide it looks right, go ahead with their writing. On reading over what they have written, they check the word against the card. They will soon have confidence they can always write the word correctly. They may then select another word to learn.

There are some pronunciation consistencies that aid spelling, but few can always be depended upon. Note that the *e* in *vowel*, the *o* in *occurs*, the *a* in *syllable*, the *i* in *generality*, the *u* in *focus*, and the *ou* in words ending *-ous* all sound the same. The sound is called a *schwa* and is designated by ə. It is the sound of any vowel in an unaccented syllable.

Pointing to the need for research on how children learn to spell, Charles Read says, "We can no longer assume without study that children categorize the sounds of English precisely as in a traditional phonemic analysis" (Read, 1973, p. 37). Children need to give a reasonable amount of attention to the relationship between letters and sounds, but the very best way to learn to write correctly is to move directly to the use of the word—copying, writing from memory, checking—so as to be able to pick up misspellings because "they don't look right."

Evaluation of spelling competence Testing spelling competence by asking children to write words in a list is neither fair nor reliable. Since the only reason for spelling is to write one's thoughts correctly so others can read them easily, spelling should be evaluated in that context.

Probably the "spelldown" is the most damaging way to test spelling. Those who use it rationalize that the child who misses just goes to the end of the line, or the one who spells the word correctly makes points for the team. When teachers say, "It's just a game, and no one takes it seriously," they indicate their insensitivity to children's feelings.

One teacher thought everybody liked spelldowns until he checked carefully and found that the good spellers liked them, while the others only acquiesced in silence. Still he tried it. On the second round of words, a husky ten-year-old was the first to miss a word. The boy sat down. The teacher's back was to him as he pronounced the next round of words. Then as he turned, he saw the boy, head down on the desk, shoulders heaving. That was the last spelldown the teacher ever gave.

Handwriting

Most things we learn to do, we learn largely through imitation and experimentation, giving special attention to the more troublesome aspects. We usually arrive at our own personal adaptations and idiosyncrasies. Handwriting can be learned the same way.

Many children learn to write their names and perhaps much more before they come to school. In school, each can have a card with his or her name on it in good, clear manuscript writing, so that it is readily available for copying. When children begin dictating sentences for the teacher to write for them, they will soon want to write for themselves. Thus begins their first significant writing "lesson."

The teacher can write the sentence in good, clear manuscript on a strip of paper the appropriate length for the child's picture. The child takes both the strip and the picture to the writing center, places the strip just above the blank space reserved for the sentence, and copies the sentence directly below the teacher's writing.

When this procedure is repeated many times and combined with discussion during dictation, no other writing "lessons" are needed. When a few children have difficulty with a certain letter, the teacher can group these children for a few minutes, explain the problem, and provide a good model for them to copy. They can solve the problem quickly by keeping this model in front of them as they write.

Teachers must be aware that there is a great difference in the small muscle coordination of children of this age. When a child is trying, the writing must be accepted with appreciation for progress, regardless of imperfections. If it is really illegible, perhaps larger writing—or smaller writing—would help.

Teachers have long thought that little children should have large pencils and crayons and write on wide-lined paper. Recently more teachers have been using regular, fairly soft-leaded pencils and regular lined tablet paper—which most children used before they came to school. The writing of whole classes of children who have been using these for the first year shows very satisfactory results. In some classes children write on unlined newsprint. Their teachers make two points: learning to make the letters is difficult enough without worrying about the lines; and having no lines gives children freedom to write whatever size letters seem easiest for them. At an appropriate time, children move to lined paper.

Manuscript writing Close to 100 percent of school children use manuscript writing, at least the first few years. This writing is often called

ABCDEFGHI
JKLMNOPQR
STUVWXYZ

abcdefghijklm
nopqrstuvwxyz

Manuscript alphabet

printing, but it is much simpler than type used in books and newspapers. The letters are made of straight lines and circles or parts of circles. Manuscript looks enough like type for children to easily make the transition to reading books. All teachers expecting to work with children in kindergarten and the primary grades need to perfect their own use of manuscript, particularly for writing on the board or on charts.

On some published manuscript alphabets, arrows indicate where one starts a letter and the direction for each line of each letter. This practice provides guidance for the teacher's own writing but is more confusing than helpful to children. Children learn how to write the letters by watching the teacher write them many times. If children find it more satisfactory to do it their own way, there is no defensible reason why they should not, as long as the result is clearly legible.

Italic writing   In a few communities an interest in italic writing is developing, stimulated largely by educators in the British schools. When well done, italic is an attention-getter and may help children develop pride in the finished product.

The process requires the use of pen and ink, which may be difficult for some children. Ink, which is not easily erasable, poses problems in the writing of final drafts. Watching a group of sixth graders writing with ink, discarding sheet after sheet of paper as they make one uncorrectable mistake after another, seems convincing evidence that ink should be used for final copy only, and then only if the child wishes to use it. Guidelines indicate children will need manuscript, or at least the very similar letter forms of the italic alphabet, but written in pencil. If offered, italic writing should be an alternative for those children who wish to use it.

Cursive writing A number of years ago, adults insisted that after the primary grades, manuscript must be abandoned for cursive, the only "real" writing. They predicted that signatures in manuscript would not be legal, and believed that manuscript was much slower than cursive. But as it was used over a period of years, manuscript signatures took on characteristics as individual as those of cursive. When children used manuscript consistently through the sixth grade, they could write as fast as children brought up with cursive. A main difference is that, in time-pressured writing, manuscript results in greater legibility.

Most people use cursive, and if children wish to learn it, as many do, there is no reason why they should not. Some districts require it, but we hope this custom will be modified to make it optional. One solution is to continue to allow use of manuscript writing under any circumstances, which offers children the option of using it or not, depending on the purpose for which they are writing, and keeps it operational for out-of-school or later school use.

Cursive writing is more difficult to make even and legible but still can be mastered easily by children with good fine-muscle coordination. If children at any time wish to learn it, samples should be made available, and the children should receive help. Their desire to learn cursive, along with self-evaluation of their success, provides the best possible learning situation. When a group of children wish to learn cursive, they can come together to discuss problems they are having. Three factors largely determine legibility: the form of each letter, a consistent slant, and spacing. Children can compare the form with models provided. They can check the slant of letters by moving a straightedge along the line of their writing. The preferred angle is indicated in the second example. However, backhand, vertical, and forehand are equally legible if the slant is consistent. Children's preferences as to direction of slant should be honored.

Slant Slant Slant

Many writers are not aware of the effect of spacing. For legibility, letters should be moderately close together, and adequate space should be allowed between words.

write write write

Permitting individual children to move into cursive as an option may be the easiest way to interest all children. When some succeed, others will want to try. Children who lack adequate small muscle coordination but use manuscript legibly should be permitted to use manuscript in all situations.

Writing problems Most problems in writing occur during the stage of development of coordination. The difficulty of writing tends to increase tension which may result in too tight a grip on the pencil, which in turn makes writing more difficult as well as more tiring. Teachers can help by encouraging a more relaxed hand and arm without going to the extreme of writing entirely by "arm movement." When both arm and fingers are relaxed and provide needed motion, writing can be continued comfortably over a longer period. The more comfortable the writing process, the more likely the child is to do more writing.

When a child is definitely left-handed, no change should be made. The recommended procedure is simply to reverse the process of the right-handed writer. The paper should be slanted the same as for right-handed writing, but in the opposite direction. The pencil should be held the same way but in the left hand. The problem of the hand covering what has been written is alleviated by holding the pencil farther from the point—a good practice for right-handers as well.

Most sloppy papers indicate lack of interest. The only way to counteract indifference is to ensure that children care about their work. We all care most when we are doing something we have chosen to do.

Teachers need to think about the quality of their

own writing in different situations. When do you use your "best" handwriting? What governs the quality of your writing? We should not expect more of children than we expect of ourselves.

The mechanics of writing—spelling and handwriting—should be kept in a realistic framework. Because they are the most noticeable aspects of writing, compulsions have grown up around them. Final products can be made acceptable and deserving of the author's pride without undue attention to mechanical factors.

Evaluation of children's writing

Writing can be evaluated in terms of the objectives, and in terms of each child's progress. First let us review the goals: Children will increasingly

1. Find satisfaction in writing

2. See a variety of purposes for writing

3. Communicate thoughts, feelings, and information effectively

4. Expand their use of varied sentence patterns and their vocabulary

5. Take into account their audience with its implications

6. Expand the audience for their writing

7. Develop a more complex sentence structure through combining elements and tightening appropriately

8. Develop their own style, build plot and characters in storywriting

9. Develop ability to express themselves poetically in a variety of forms

10. Use a wide range of resources for both specific skills (spelling, punctuation, information) and general purposes (author's style, form, purposes)

The degree of accomplishment of the first two goals largely determines the extent the others may show gains. Thus, when a child shows little progress in goals 3 to 10, progress in 1 and 2 should be evaluated very carefully.

Evaluation criteria and procedures

In writing, as in other skills, there are five major criteria for evaluation. The first is that evaluation is continuous. In the beginning progress is usually quite evident and children are quite aware of it. The teacher's recognition of progress in comments to the child is productive. When children start polishing their writing, evaluation is inherent in the process.

The second criterion is that evaluation must include the child's own self-evaluation. Third, the daily use of writing should be consistent with long-term goals. Teachers can check both teaching and evaluation practices against the goals listed above.

The fourth criterion examines whether children write on their own initiative. Do they write outside of school? Do they write more than a token amount in journals, or stories, or reports?

And the fifth criterion is that evaluation should be used consistently as feedback for the pupil's progress. Polishing procedures and teacher-pupil conferences are recommended forms of feedback on writing.

The only valid material to be evaluated is the writing the child produces. No verbalizing of rules and procedures can tell us how well anyone can write. In fact, when children verbalize rules but do not demonstrate them in their writing, they do not really understand the rules.

In evaluating children's writing, the content, the thoughts, are most important, then the way the thoughts are structured. Syntax and style come next, along with the choice of words to express meaning more adequately. At this point children need to check the spelling of words they are not sure of. The rough draft should be kept reasonably legible but attention should not be focused on penmanship until the final copy is written. Neatness and good penmanship require adequate letter form, a consistent slant, and even, relatively close spacing of letters in any style of writing. Left-hand margins should be straight and paragraphs indented.

Since evaluation must deal with the child's writing on an individual basis, we suggest three major procedures: comparison of each child's writing over a period of time, self-evaluation by the child, and teacher-child evaluation conferences.

Comparison of each child's writing over a period of time   After the children have been in school a week or two, teachers can initiate a discussion of the evaluation of progress. The framework might be "What do we want to learn to do this year?" and "How can we know what we have accomplished?" During these discussions, children will set some goals and realize they need something tangible to evaluate.

Each child can place the next piece of writing in a file, then add other examples at his or her discretion. Teacher and child can evaluate progress by comparing these in chronological order, along with some current writing. Obviously, all the goals and purposes of developing writing competence should be part of this evaluation.

In addition, the teacher can take notes at teacher-pupil writing conferences. Notes will include any observations of special involvement with writing, any significant amount of writing in out-of-school situations, and the child's concern with producing a well-polished final copy. The number of pages written or the amount of time spent writing are not necessarily positive signals.

Journals and other unrevised writing provide a useful basis for evaluation because the natural writing of a child shows increasing maturity over a period of time.

If a file is available, use a drawer at a convenient height for children. If not, a cardboard carton can be decorated and used as a file. Whenever Kay wants to check progress, she can compare her current papers with her first-of-the-year writing. She need not share her reactions unless she

wishes to, but what she sees can provide real motivation.

Child's self-evaluation   Necessary both for evaluation and for continued growth are the child's perception of gains made and satisfaction with that progress. These perceptions need to be requested frequently, particularly at the completion of a writing project. More extensive, in-depth self-evaluation is needed at intervals through the year.

In preparation for the more substantial self-evaluations, the teacher and the group can discuss procedures well in advance. Obviously, this decision-making discussion will vary with the maturity of the group. With fives, sixes, and some sevens, discussion will be limited but still very important for setting expectancies and starting the self-evaluation process. Questions such groups might want to consider are:

Am I writing more now than I was before?

Do I like most of the stories I hear?

What have I written besides stories?

Do I know more of the words I need?

Can I find more of the words I don't know yet?

When children are ready to begin polishing, they may add questions considering the choice of words, avoiding overused words and selecting words that are more exact and colorful. As they become aware of the structures, plots, and characters of stories, and of the authors' purposes, they can consider these aspects of their writing. Children who prefer nonfiction writing can evaluate in terms of what they see as important to them in their writing. Those ready to become aware of their own style may evaluate their progress toward achieving it.

When polishing begins, another question for self-evaluation concerns awareness of audience. Do I think about who will read what I write? Will readers understand what I mean? Those working at the more mature levels of writing, some ten-, eleven-, and twelve-year-olds, need to begin to evaluate their paragraph organization, their use of connecting words to build a flow of thought, the length and organization of their sentences, and any tightening or embedding that would increase readability.

As children discuss evaluation with the teacher, questions they need to consider are recorded on a chart. Teachers should make very clear the fact that all children in a group will not necessarily use all questions. This recognition of individual differences and needs is a most important concept for all children to develop—not that some are "better" than others, but that each is a unique person, different but as worthwhile as any other. The self-evaluation questions that are useful for all can be starred.

During evaluation all children will compare their baseline papers with recent projects they have been satisfied with on the questions they see as appropriate for themselves. Over the next few days, the children will then write out their responses to the questions they have selected. These responses are made available to the teacher for their teacher-child evaluation conference.

Teacher-child evaluation conference The next step is a conference in which teacher and child talk together about progress the child has made. The teacher has prepared for the conference by reading the child's self-evaluation and by going over recollections and any notes made regarding that child's progress.

Many teachers find a conference notebook or a file of five-by-eight-inch file cards useful for keeping records. Each child may have a page or a card with his or her name on an index tab. Anything significant the teacher notices about the child can be recorded and considered in the teacher's evaluation.

The child's feelings about writing also should be recorded. The most desirable attitudes are realistic appraisal of progress and awareness of needs. Children's feelings, of course, should be evaluated in terms of progress. A pride in accomplishment may be thoroughly justified by immature writing that shows significant improvement. Some children downplay their writing only to elicit confirmation from the teacher. Such confirmation should stress specific areas of improvement and help the writer make a realistic self-evaluation.

When they are ready, children sign up for their conferences, which are held in the order of their signing. Because this procedure is too valuable to be rushed, conferences with the whole group may be distributed over two weeks or more. Duration of the conference varies with the maturity of the child. Younger children will require less time, but their conferences should be held more often. On the average, conferences take five to fifteen minutes.

The teacher's purpose in the conference is to be supportive, constructive, and specific, and to help the child set next steps in the progress toward goals. Specific tasks with individual children may be to encourage by documenting progress, relieve anxiety by helping a child modify expectancies, reassure the discouraged child by focusing on specific progress and setting a single small step as an immediate goal with promise of early review. It is essential to keep all children making at least a little progress with some measure of self-confidence.

Summary

In this chapter we have considered factors related to children's writing. We have discussed the importance of considering the audience for writing, and of writing for specific practical and personal purposes. We believe creative writing is one kind of personal writing, and the teacher's approach should be quite different from the usual classroom practice. We consider spelling and handwriting to be mechanical aspects, affecting the legibility of writing but having no other intrinsic relation to it. We have provided basic guidelines and summarized the teacher's role in carrying them out and in evaluating children's writing.

Suggested learning experiences for prospective teachers

Suggestion A

1. Think about how much writing you do. How much do you write that you are not required to? Can you explain your answer?

2. Turn to the list of goals under Evaluation of Children's Writing. How many of these writing goals have you met? How many through instructional experiences? How many independently? Are your answers related to the first item above?

3. How much have you used writing to clarify your own problems? If there is any problem on which you are uncertain of your position, but will soon need to make a decision, try writing out all the issues. Does it help? This is personal writing for oneself and need never be shared.

4. What implications for teaching do you see in your answers to these questions?

Suggestion B

1. Ask permission to work with a group of fourth, fifth, or sixth graders at least twice.

2. The first time, with no preparation, ask them to write a story about a boy or girl stranded on a desert island. Collect their papers after twenty minutes.

3. The second time provide some firsthand experience, in or out of the classroom, that will raise their awareness through use of their senses. Get them to talking among themselves about their feeling and reactions. As interest and involvement rise, suggest each write about it. Let them give you their papers whenever they finish.

4. Compare the two papers from each child as to amount written, the quality of the writing, and the involvement that is evident.

5. What implications do you see? If this were your classroom, could you provide even more provocative experiences?

Suggestion C

1. Ask permission to work with any group from third grade on.

2. Select a form of poetry easy for children to write.

3. Explain and illustrate it, working through several examples with the children until they all understand.

4. Suggest each write a poem in this form. Circulate around the room, noting progress but making no comment except to answer questions.

5. When most children have finished, ask volunteers to share by reading what they have written.

6. How do you feel about the results? How did the children feel? Would you do anything different next time? If so, what?

Suggestion D

1. Ask a teacher for a set of first-draft writings from a class, or set up a writing experience for them and indicate they will have a chance to correct (polish) their writing later.

2. Take their writing and, without putting marks on their papers, copy the misspelled words, listing those from each paper separately. Is there a difference among the papers? Can you note any consistent problems in any one child's misspellings? Can you guess at a cause?

3. Are the same words misspelled by more than one child? Does the section on spelling in this chap-

ter help to explain why those words were mis-spelled? How could you help these students?

4. If this were your classroom, what procedures would you initiate to improve spelling? Do all the children need to work on spelling? (Keep the papers for Suggestion E.)

Suggestion E

1. Using the papers you collected for Suggestion D, go through each one for structural writing problems, such as run-on sentences or a series of very short sentences, restricted writing that needs elaboration, improper paragraphing or lack of it, lack of smooth follow-through of ideas, and incorrect word forms or usage.

2. Organize these problems by type and note how many children have each problem.

3. Do some children have more problems than others? Do some have few if any problems?

4. Plan how you might work with children in the group if it were your classroom.

5. Ask permission to work with four or five children who have the same problem.

6. After your group meeting, return the unmarked papers to all the children and thank them for their cooperation. What did you learn? How successful was your work with the small group?

Suggestion F

1. Select an area of writing that you are uncertain how to handle in working with children.

2. Think about it, read various authors, and talk with various teachers about it.

3. Work out a strategy for dealing with the problem in a classroom of your own.

Suggested readings

Various authors have provided guidance for that rather confusing activity, creative writing. Joy Moss, Nilsen and Greenwell, Jacqueline Jackson, and Leah Wilcox suggest either listening to or reading literature as a way of developing creative writing. Kantor and Perron believe children can write creative exposition and argument as well as description and narration.

Samuel Perez suggests ways to improve personal letters; Bingham and Dusenbery ask teachers to take a second look at some writing rules; and Sue Brandt has written a little book to help children write a report.

A wealth of material is available for guidance in the writing of poetry. Kenneth Koch has written two books, *Wishes, Lies and Dreams*, and *Rose, Where Did You Get That Red*? To understand some of the debatable issues of modern poetry, Myra Livingston asks "But Is It Poetry?" and Richard Western writes "A Defense of Kenneth Koch." Others suggesting various approaches are Mauree Applegate, Barbara Ebsensen, Nancy Larrick, Richard Larson, and Carrie Stegall. Most of these books are for working with children eight or older. Joanne Rukavina has suggestions for the beginner, while Hall, Moretz, and Stantom have explored preschool writing.

"Focus 3" in *Elementary English*, February 1975, presents a collection of articles about spelling by authors including Dunkeld and Hatch, George Manolakes, Jay Monson, Florence Roslier, and Leo Schell. Another article that gives insight into the spelling process is "Invented Spelling in Kindergarten" by Rhea Paul. The children she worked with figured out ways to write words that they—and usually grown-ups—could read. Ronald Cramer expressed a similar point of view in "The Write Way to Teach Spelling," in which he advocates accepting early spelling "as best they can," as we accept "baby talk." Hanna, Hodges, and Hanna have interpreted some of their findings to help the more mature child solve spelling problems.

"Focus 2" in *Elementary English*, February 1975, is a series of articles on handwriting. Especially useful are Leona Foerster's "Sinistral Power! Help for Left-handed Children" and Kuipers and Riccio's "From Graphomania to Graphophobia." In "An Approach to Writing for Kindergartners," Georgia Peterson expresses the value of the child's sense of accomplishment in doing "real writing." The Halpins' "Special Paper for Beginning Handwriting: An Unjustified Practice?" reports there is no advantage to using inch-wide lines for children instead of the normal half-inch ones used by adults.

Strategies for children's learning

Writing letters to friends

Purpose. To broaden the range of letter writing so each child has at least one special person to write to.

Appropriate level. Eights and older.

Participants. All children.

Situation. For children whose families have moved, letter writing is the most feasible way of keeping in contact with friends at a distance. For children who have no acquaintances at a distance, correspondence with individuals as suggested below adds a dimension to their lives. For all children it provides an important writing experience.

Teacher role

1. To stimulate and record suggestions of the children, add any that are feasible, and then make necessary arrangements for letter writing.

2. Provide time and encouragement for children to write and polish their letters and address the envelopes, including a return address. (The child's home address is usually best for this type of letter.)

3. Help children make their own envelopes if necessary.

4. Provide a supply of stamps to sell or give to children. (If letters are to be sent overseas, aerograms can be purchased at the post office for less than stamps. They will be delivered anywhere in the world for the same cost.)

Procedures

1. Plan with the whole group.

2. Start with a personal letter received by anyone in the group, including yourself.

3. Raise the question, To whom might each of us write? When one child has an idea, it will trigger other suggestions. Some ideas that the children or you may suggest are:

A child in another school, another city or town, another state, another country, whom they know or with whom they can make contact as a pen pal.

Friends or relatives in other places as sources of information about those places.

People in retirement or nursing homes, whom they know or whose names and addresses they can obtain.

Children in hospitals for extended periods of

time, whose names, ages, and condition they can obtain.

Children in another country to gain information and understanding of their country and culture. Teachers who have visited schools in other countries can make this arrangement with teachers or heads of schools whom they have met.

4. See that each child has selected a correspondent and has obtained the full name and address. Provide names and addresses for those who wish to write to an unknown person, in a hospital, nursing home, or overseas.

5. Discuss with the group what would be appropriate to say in different circumstances.

6. Discuss the acceptable form for personal letters.

7. Have children polish and prepare their letters for mailing. If feasible, they can take them to the post office or a neighborhood collection box. If not, they can take them to the school office for the postman to pick up, increasing their awareness of the school's use of the mails.

8. The letter writing and mailing may be an introduction to a visit to the post office and study about it. Different age groups will be concerned with different aspects of the study. Third graders, for instance, will be interested only in the major aspects and in talking with a mail carrier about his or her work and the more common problems in the job, including what each person might do to make the job easier. Sixth graders can become interested in the more complex functions of the postal service and its employees.

Evaluation. Are children's interests broadening as they get information from wider areas and receive responses to their letters? Are their own letters becoming more interesting? Are they gaining and retaining enthusiasm? Is the polishing of their letters producing results in other writing they are doing?

All kinds of practical writing

Purpose. To encourage various types of practical writing.

Appropriate level. Nines and older.

Participants. All children.

Situation. Children need to learn to write for various purposes beyond creative writing and letter writing. It is essential that such writing have a real purpose in the minds of the children.

Teacher role

1. To initiate discussion and generally monitor the process.

2. To raise questions to help the children express their thoughts as clearly and effectively as possible.

Procedures

1. Take advantage of every situation that could lead to children's meaningful personal writing.

2. Ask the children to suggest writing activities. Some possibilities that the teacher may suggest if the students do not are:

a. Write up travel guides for people who are going on a trip. Include various means of transportation with relative costs and travel time needed, what they might see while traveling or on a stopover, places of interest at their destination, and the like. The children may obtain this information from various resources, such as libraries and travel agencies. A research project has many advantages besides developing writing skills.

b. Write to authors for more information about topics covered in their publications, either in books or in periodicals. If the authors' addresses are unknown, address letters in care of the publisher. Most authors will reply to a single, well-written letter, asking for a reasonable amount of information or a source for further information relevant to the material published.

c. Write letters to a newspaper's Letters to the Editor section when the group is concerned about a community, state, or national issue. After discussion, any children who are interested may make a first draft of such a letter. The group can agree upon a composite of main points and select one child to rewrite. Under these circumstances the class is stated as author. However, when an individual child expresses concerns, writes, polishes, and sends in such a letter, the child's name and home or school address is given.

d. Write up reports of special studies or research on issues or problems. When individuals or small groups have completed a study, they need to summarize their findings in a report to the group. If they make an oral report, a written report should be available for reference.

Evaluation. Do children discuss more current issues? Do they carry these discussions home? Do they think of writing to more people about pertinent questions? Do they do more reading and research?

Tall tales

Purpose. To encourage imagination in writing.

Appropriate level. Nines and older.

Participants. All who wish to take part.

Teacher role

1. To stimulate interest in writing tall tales.

2. Assist in making them available to others, when polished.

Procedures

1. Read children some tall tales.

2. Suggest all those who wish might write a tall tale. The one requirement is that it could not possibly be true.

3. Work with those who wish to polish their stories for sharing. Reading some completed stories may stimulate others to write. Some children may write several stories.

4. Set up various ways of circulating these stories. Each child can write and "publish" a story as a book for the classroom, to share with another classroom, or to place in the school library. Authors (eight or older) could read them to classrooms of younger children or read them into a tape recorder and share the tape.

Evaluation. Are the children dreaming up impossible but humorous situations? Is their interest in writing increasing?

The *e* that makes a difference

Purpose. To increase awareness of the effect of the final silent *e* so that children can use the pronunciation of words as a cue to spelling.

Appropriate level. Eights and older.

Participants. All children at least once and some more often as needed.

Situation. In a one-syllable word or in the last syllable of a polysyllabic word, the vowel is long when the word or syllable ends in *e* and short when it does not.

Teacher role

1. To set up the situation as a fun experience.

2. Work with groups and express satisfaction at their success, watching particularly the small group activity of those least active in the total group participation.

Procedures

1. Put two words like *pin* and *pine* on the chalkboard and ask how to say them.

2. Ask if they know other pairs like that. Suggest that volunteers come up one at a time, put such a pair on the board, and say them. Sooner or later someone may write a pair, one of which is not a word.

3. If the child says it correctly, call the group's attention to it. What does it mean? Did the one who wrote it say it correctly?

4. Ask if they can think of similar pairs that are really not words. Volunteers will again suggest pairs, which will undoubtedly be pronounced correctly. Use *fon fone, gaf gafe, kem keme,* or any others you think of, and see if the children can pronounce them correctly.

5. Set up groups of four taking turns thinking of pairs of either words or nonwords and pronouncing them.

Evaluation. In their writing, do children spell correctly most words that fit this pattern? Does it help some children in their reading?

Making crossword puzzles

Purpose. To help children become aware of how words are spelled by constructing crossword puzzles.

Appropriate level. Nines and older.

Participants. Any who wish to take part.

Teacher role

1. To set up the situation for making crossword puzzles.

2. Provide opportunities for those who wish to work on it.

3. Give enthusiastic encouragement as progress is made.

Procedures

1. Bring in some simple crossword puzzles. Some children will be familiar with the procedures for solving them.

2. Encourage children to work the puzzles as a refresher or to become acquainted with them.

3. Suggest they might like to try making some crossword puzzles, and discuss what is necessary.

4. Suggest they start with a piece of plain white paper, a ruler, and a ballpoint pen, draw ten or fifteen parallel lines as long as they wish about three-eighths inch apart, then the same number of perpendicular lines to make boxes three-eighths inch square.

5. Suggest they start filling in words with pencil, being sure they spell a real word both across and down, and putting an *x* in the space at the end of each word. They will need to number the squares that contain letters.

6. Suggest they wait till they are satisfied with the completed puzzle before they write out the cues for solving the puzzles.

7. Suggest they exchange puzzles, keeping the key but making copies of the blank puzzle and cues.

Evaluation. Are children becoming more aware of the spelling of some words? Do they become aware of meanings as they write out the cues for solving the puzzles?

During all our waking hours, we read whatever is within our perception. We read the environment—the weather, the time of day, the time of year. We read our companions—their feelings, purposes, and concerns. We read their expressions, posture, movements, tone of voice, pace of speech, the phrasing and emphasis of their statements and questions. Obviously, we also read signs, labels, maps, newspapers, magazines, and books. We read what we write and what others write.

Is there a basic difference between reading a person's actions and reading a person's written thoughts? In both, we give attention to what we read, bring to mind our relevant experiences, and relate them to the immediate actions or writing. In both, our purpose in reading is to answer the question, What does it mean? How well we succeed depends on the relevant experience we can bring to the reading, and on the relationships we perceive between the reading and ourselves. When we know the person well and the action is appropriate, we understand far more than when the person is a stranger and the action bizarre. Likewise, when the content of written material is strange to us and its way of expression unfamiliar, we understand far less than when it refers to something we have experienced and is couched in familiar terms. So the desire to find meaning, and the factors that assist us, are the same, no matter what we are reading.

Reading written language can be defined as *understanding an author's recorded thoughts as well as our own experience enables us to perceive them.* Furthermore, reading includes integrating our reaction to these thoughts into our own understanding. In this chapter we will look at various reading programs to see how well they accomplish this integration of language and understanding. We will see how reading is currently taught, some of the underlying assumptions, and the problems involved in choosing a reading program. We will next explore a different approach to learning to read, based on what we know about children's thinking, their language development, and their natural ways of learning.

Learning to read

The fact that reading is a language process means that learning to read is learning to process language. It means that children can learn to read in basically the same ways they learn to talk and to listen. These procedures differ greatly from setting forth a series of specific skills to be learned and then applied. Too often the specific skill programs are designed to enable the reader to pronounce words. When teachers view reading as a language process, their procedures enable the reader to deal with ideas in the written material. And dealing with ideas is what we mean by *reading*.

Anyone who reads *meaning* uses a thinking process that allows for understanding the author's thoughts and relating these thoughts to one's own. Without some significant understanding of the author's thoughts, relating these thoughts to personal experience, and responding in some way, the person is not reading, but is just "saying words." Reading cannot occur without thinking.

Many educators try to separate reading from thinking. These people spend considerable time and effort teaching children to name words. As children sense that naming each word correctly is important to teachers, they focus their attention on it. Such a focus minimizes children's thinking by distracting them from the essential process of following the author's thought. Thus, reading becomes less interesting and less valuable, and children read no more than is necessary.

Various sources, such as the Chicago non-oral reading program, speed reading programs, and miscue research, provide proof that saying words, even to oneself, is not necessary to reading. Saying words, implicitly or explicitly, slows reading to the rate of speech. Thus, a teacher's goal must be to enable children to read without saying words. This process should begin as early as possible so that children quickly learn that meaning can come directly from sight.

Among the general public, reading is not thought of as a mechanical skill of recognizing individual words. Rather, people consider reading a way of dealing with language in order to gain understanding of recorded thoughts or information. As they read a letter or a magazine, they think about how the writer's ideas are modifying, extending, or confirming their present understandings. In reading either literary or nonliterary material, their real concern is the *experiencing* that the message stimulates. If they do not have such experiences, they are certainly not reading in the sense most people use the term.

There are those who believe learning to read is basically a different process from reading. Perhaps these people think of oral reading as evidence of ability to read—although oral reading is very poor evidence of understanding the meaning. Perhaps they ignore the implications of the reading behavior of many preschool children. Without instruction, these children gain meaning from what they read whether or not they name the words. They may read signs, labels, titles of books and stories others have read to them. From these successful experiences, they have discovered enough about how reading works to read material they select but have not seen before. Both children learning to read and literate adults look at print and gain understanding of the thought expressed.

Reading since 1850

Let us look at reading programs in our schools to find out what people in the field believe about the reading process. A first impression is that many points of view exist, since we find a large assortment of programs. On analyzing their rationales, however, it becomes apparent that the differences in most cases are in the specifics rather than the basic premises.

Many years ago children developed reading ability through the reading of whatever books were available. During the 1800s books were developed for the purpose of teaching children to read. The procedures used were very similar to those used in most books published for the same purpose today. These books contained stories, very short for beginners and increasing in length as children grew older. Most had a controlled vocabulary for the first few years; that is, each story contained only words previously taught plus new words for each lesson. Children were first taught the sounds and the names of the letters, usually those embedded in the words that were introduced. Children were expected to sound out words they did not recognize. Many books included a list of new words for each story, and instructions to teachers were added to each lesson. In addition, some readers quite early used markings to indicate some twelve "elocution rules" to be used in reading, as virtually all school reading at that time was oral.

Today, what do we find? Graded books from primer through sixth or eighth grade, short stories gradually increasing in length through the grades, beginners learning the names and sounds of letters so they can blend the sounds to identify unknown words, a controlled vocabulary at least in the primary grades. The new words introduced in each story are listed in the manual of instructions for teachers, but there are no elocution rules!

There have been some changes in children's books. Much color has been added, as pictures have increased in number and importance. The stories are more childlike, though whether more interesting is sometimes questionable. During the last ten years or so, however, the quality and appeal of the content has increased significantly over that of several previous decades.

The teacher's manual is another change that has had both positive and negative results. It provides many suggestions for teaching a particular reading program. However, the suggested detailed procedures have made teachers less confident about making changes to meet specific needs of individual children. A number of manuals have put more emphasis on the development of oral language since its importance for reading has been established.

The basic rationale underlying a reading program has changed very little over the last 150 years. If nearly all children were learning to read successfully under this program, few would question it. But parents, teachers, and other educators are disturbed about the number of children who have difficulty learning to read, and about the large numbers who can read but choose not to. Virtually all schools, even secondary schools and colleges, have remedial reading programs. Communities, states, and even the federal government have proposed programs intended to increase children's reading ability. Therefore, since results of the program are not acceptable, let us examine the underlying rationale.

Most programs for teaching reading have been based on "common sense" assumptions, rather than research to find out how children learn to read. Those purportedly based on research have only added or changed specific aspects of the same basic procedures. In *The Torch Lighters Revisited*, Morrison and Austin take note of the lack of a theoretical basis for programs:

> It is regrettable that so many of our students are engaged in hit or miss activities when more often than not they have only minimal understanding of the "why" of what it is they are doing. If the present theme in public schools is "back to the basics" we have to begin with some theoretical basis, and I am afraid that too many of our students are not receiving this kind of instruction (Morrison and Austin, 1977, p. 54).

The first of these "common sense" assumptions, and certainly a necessary one, is that, since written language is built on oral language, there is a close tie between oral language and reading.

Second, since words are made up of letters that indicate sounds, many assume children must know the sound of each letter in order to say the words. Thus phonics is required for beginning reading. Some hold that children should have a basic sight vocabulary of 50 to 125 words before they start phonics. Through exposure to one or two words at a time with related pictures, children generally learn to recognize the words. When they have learned these words, phonics becomes a separate part of the program for teaching reading.

A third assumption is that if children can say the printed words one after another in a sentence or paragraph, they understand the meaning. Further, since each word is important to the meaning of the sentence, and children must recognize each word in the order given, it is considered essential that a child say each word correctly without modification of the printed text.

A fourth assumption is that all children must be

taught each word. They must read each story in the order presented, for planned repetition has been carefully built into the material, not only repetition of words but of many specific word recognition skills.

A fifth assumption is that the teacher's manuals should provide specific instructions for each lesson so that teachers will know how it should be taught and how to follow planned procedures sequentially.

Basal reading programs

The above rationale is the basis for nearly all of the materials prepared to teach children to read. Each program has its own unique aspects and variations, but their concept of the reading process is basically the same. Such *basal reading programs* include a series of readers, teacher's manuals for each book, and in most cases supplementary materials such as workbooks and/or ditto masters, particularly at the primary levels.

One feature of nearly all basal programs is a *controlled vocabulary*. From the beginning, words are introduced slowly, and no word is used that has not been introduced. Derived from the above assumptions, the belief that reading is a process of identifying individual words further assumes that children cannot recognize any word that they have not been taught. As children learn the words taught each day, they should be able to progress through the series with little difficulty and become successful readers.

They also assume that if a child cannot read—or say—a word in a list of words, that child does not know the word. However, we have known for some time that children consistently read correctly words in context before they can read them in a list (Goodman, 1965).

The content of basal readers is mainly short stories, most of which have been planned by the series' authors to incorporate the skills they wish to teach. Increasingly books intended for intermediate and upper grades are now including ex-

cerpts from children's literature and other material of a variety of types.

Teacher's manuals for each series explain the way the series has been developed, the authors' concept of the reading process, and a sequence of specific skills that should be taught. Often the manual suggests the actual wording for teachers to use in each of the lessons, and also suggests dividing the class into groups according to reading ability, three groups being the common practice.

The children's books consist of one or more for each grade, with the larger number at the beginning levels. The "top" group starts a book before the others are ready for it, and finishes in time for the "middle" group to start it, who in turn finish it so the "low" group can use it. Thus, each group can use the same materials successively. Some series provide several different books for each grade level for the exclusive use of different ability groups.

"Look-say" readers The greatest difference between programs is the way phonics is handled, the way the letter-sound, or *graphophonemic*, aspect is developed. Some reading series begin by introducing one or two words a day with picture associations. Children learn to recognize the words as wholes. Gradually words are introduced a little faster, and most children soon build a word-recognition vocabulary of 50 to 125 sight words. At this point the program begins to include phonics, the sounds indicated by separate letters. Children are expected to recognize unknown words by blending these sounds. Some programs start with sounds indicated by vowels, and others, with consonants.

Phonics programs *Phonics* is defined as the use of elementary phonetics in teaching beginners to read or enunciate. *Phonetics* is described as the branch of language study dealing with speech sounds, their production and combination, and their representation by written symbols.

Some reading programs start by teaching each letter, its name, and the sound it represents, beginning with either vowels or consonants. In some programs children begin reading words composed of the letters already taught, but most programs teach all the letter-associated sounds prior to any significant reading. Procedures then emphasize the "sounding out" of words not recognized. These programs are likely to be more strictly controlled than others.

Linguistic programs In the early 1960s some linguists became interested in the contribution their field could make to the development of all aspects of children's language. They have contributed much to the understanding of language structure. One early by-product, a somewhat different rationale for the reading process, is exemplified in "linguistic readers." Their authors believed that learning to read was learning to respond to contrasting spelling patterns by saying words. Their interpretation of phonics skills was that the child intuitively transferred the sounds indicated by letters in one word to the same letters in a similar word. Words with similar patterns were built into "stories" with as few other words as possible, such as "The fat cat sat on a mat" and "Dan can fan the man." Presumably, children should be able to "decode" these words from their knowledge of word patterns with no clue from other sources. By *decoding* the authors meant that, by looking at the word and being aware of words with similar spellings, children would be able to pronounce it. Since the method depends on only one linguistic factor, spelling patterns, and ignores other more significant aspects, the term *linguistic readers* is really a misnomer.

The first linguistic material had no pictures. When this material was not well received by children or teachers, publishers added pictures that were entirely irrelevant to the content of the story. The rationale was that if children had no clue except print, they would learn to read the print sooner. By teacher demand, today most of the linguistic readers are illustrated, and some of the pictures relate directly to the contextual meaning.

i.t.a. Recognizing the inconsistency in the sound-letter relationships in our language, one program initiated a new forty-four-character alphabet, called the initial teaching alphabet or *i.t.a.* Each character represents a single speech sound, and together these are supposed to represent all the main sounds in the English language. This phonics program was intended to include the large number of nonphonetic words in our everyday language.

One limitation of this program was the lack of material for children to read. Some i.t.a. approaches used children's writing, already a part of some other programs, to augment basal readers, and it became an integral part of this program. In addition, some children's story books were translated and reprinted in i.t.a.

Initial teaching alphabet

WRITTEN LANGUAGE: RECORDING AND RETRIEVING THOUGHTS

thu boi iz plæeiŋ with æ littl træn hee baut at thu toi ſhop. tω him it iz æ trezuer. thu gerl iz reediŋ æ bωk and eetiŋ an egg sandwich. thæ bœth thiŋk thæ ar haviŋ fun.

Story written in i.t.a.

Another problem with i.t.a. is the transition to traditional orthography (*t.o.*), which usually takes place sometime in the second or third year of reading. Although some children accomplish this easily, others find more difficulty in the transition to t.o. in spelling than in reading.

Different approaches to reading

Different formats for basal reading programs have been developed, some with the use of electronics. Computer programs have used closed circuit television and other "hardware" to present reading programs. Programmed reading often permits individuals or selected groups to progress at their own rate through these materials, and the computer-assisted instruction provides both self-pacing and immediate feedback. Other new programs use printed materials in the form of booklets, workbooks, and ditto masters. In most of these programs, the format is new, but the rationale is essentially the same. There are, however, programs that entail a different rationale.

A non-oral reading program As long ago as the late 1930s and early 1940s, the Chicago Public Schools began a non-oral reading program. Buswell reports that more than 70,000 people were taught reading in these experimental classes after 1935. In the first and second grades no oral reading was permitted at any time, although much oral language was used. The essential purpose was "to enable children to get the meaning of the printed page directly from the visual symbols without the intervention of oral pronunciation and without employing inner speech" (Buswell, 1945, pp. 1–2). Instruction was carried on through picture dictionaries, pantomime, and other ingenious activities by which the meaning of words might be made clear without saying the word. The visual symbol went directly to meaning, not *symbol* to *spoken word* to *meaning*. The evaluation of the program was summed up thus:

> The evidence derived from the present investigation warrants the conclusion that the non-oral method has achieved results which certainly are as good as those achieved in the schools employing the usual method of teaching reading. Furthermore, in certain respects such as lip-movement, progress in school, and scores on reading tests, the evidence indicates not only that the non-oral method is as effective as the method which it replaced but that it is somewhat better (Buswell, 1945, p. 32).

These results were obtained with teachers trained in a short inservice course in the non-oral method. The project was given up not because of dissatisfaction with it, but because it was impossible to find or prepare enough teachers competent in the method.

Individualized reading Individualized reading is a general term that covers a wide range of programs. Basically it means that *each child in a classroom is planned with and for individually*. The material children read takes into account their general stage of reading development, interests, and desires. Therefore, each child chooses materials to read from among those available. A teacher or school using this program must provide materials with a wide range of difficulty, content, and format. The child's progress is noted and any needed instruction provided either in specific instructions to small groups with common needs, or during the teacher-pupil reading conference. The frequency of conferences varies with the stage of development and the particular needs of each child, from four or five times a week to once each week or two.

Three factors began to modify the original idea. Schools did not have a wide range of materials because their supply had been limited through purchase of many sets of thirty-five or forty copies of the same books, rather than fewer copies of more different books. Many teachers had not learned to work with children when lack of texts made it impossible to say, "Take out your books and turn to page 67." A third factor was the teacher's lack of confidence that children could learn without direct instruction. "How can they know it if I don't teach it? And I just don't have time to teach it to each one separately."

Programs have been modified in various ways. Some schools continue their basal program but use individualized reading as a supplementary library program. Some use the basal readers but allow the "good" readers to read ahead as fast as they can and in any sequence they wish. Another procedure developed; each child used the same materials in the same sequence and carried out the same assignments in the same way, but each moved along the path at his or her own rate. The problem was that some children rather quickly finished the tasks—and no one knew what to do with them.

As the concept of individualizing gained popularity, publishers jumped onto the bandwagon and marketed extensive sets of material keyed to tests. Each child was plugged into the materials at the point indicated by test scores. From here on, children worked at their own rate and, because of the volume of material available, were kept busy throughout the year. The program, called IPI, Individually Prescribed Instruction, met the needs of teachers and offered a number of advantages over the textbook teaching approach. Few recognized that IPI violated all but one of the basic principles originally established for individualized instruction, the rate of going through the material. The implicit assumption, often unrecognized, was that the more capable the child, the more of this type of material the child needed to cover.

Language experience approach A true language experience program is built on the child's natural ways of learning—through experience. The basic premises are expressed by the child's conceptualization that "What I think about I can talk about. What I can talk about I can express in painting and writing. What I write I can read" (Lee and Allen, 1963).

The language experience approach to the teaching of reading is an individualized program that began in the late 1930s and early 1940s with experience charts. At first these were all group charts. Then it was discovered that children were more interested in their own personal charts and learned more from them. As the interrelationship of all aspects of the language arts became more evident and teachers were more aware of the importance of children's own experiences to their learning, the language experience approach developed.

The program encourages each child to record a personal experience in paint. After the children talk about what they have painted, each child dictates a statement that the teacher records. After a number of painting, talking, and dictating experiences with a small group of peers, the children can read back the sense of the stories. Soon they begin writing by themselves using many resources available around the room. They can read their own stories as well as many of their peers'. They begin to find they can read some of the books in the room library. Written language skills are extended by a continuous process of reading and writing alternately, along with further development of oral language through conversations with peers, and an increased reading of published books.

Through self-direction, decision-making, and choice, children assume responsibility for their own learning. Since the reading and writing are chosen by the children rather than by the teacher, the approach is virtually a no-failure program. When children do not succeed with a self-appointed task, they have not failed to do what someone expected them to; they just decide to try something else. Therefore, this situation builds positive self-concepts and self-confidence, two factors essential for effective learning.

Misunderstanding has resulted in modification of the program. Sometimes only group dictation is used and everyone copies it. Sometimes a dictated story is then taught with all the rigor and mechanics of a basal program. Some expect children to work alone having no interaction with other children and books, reading only what they themselves dictate or write. Children are often limited in their choice of reading material, except during library period. Occasionally children are grouped on the basis of achievement.

In contrast, when one teacher using the language experience approach was asked how on earth she was able to teach an immature Jimmy to read in first grade, she responded, "He never found out he couldn't." Perhaps the most common misunderstanding is that the program is only for getting started in reading. Actually the rationale is equally useful on through the grades—or even into graduate school.

Selecting a program

Reading series have always been profitable for the educational publishers who produce them, as well as for the authors. Because of the nationwide concern about reading and the Right-to-Read movement, new programs are in demand today. Companies who have not traditionally had a reading program are now publishing them and promoting some unique aspect of each program. Publishers are revising previously published materials in line with popular ideas, such as more colorful illustrations, better written material, or a variation on phonics teaching.

The task of selecting a program from this welter of material, with each program promoted commercially, is overwhelming. Additional choices are the programs that use only library materials and children's own writing and hence have no materials for publishers to advertise. Too often the "newness" of the material, the cost, or the effectiveness of a salesperson determines the selection. The true handicaps to judgment are that there are no hard data to use in choosing programs; there is no consistent rationale, and hence the basis for decision-making has not been clarified.

School people have looked to research to provide information as a basis for their choice of materials. But after much research on various methods of teaching reading, the net result is that no "method"* or materials stand out as consistently better than others. The teacher often is indicated as the most important factor, yet no specific characteristics of successful teachers are generally accepted beyond the fact that their children are successful. How well a child learns to read—whatever the "method"—depends on many factors.

An often unrecognized variable that invalidates much research is the variety of interpretations different teachers put on a "method," since the assumptions underlying programs are not clearly stated by the authors. More valuable research would result if (1) goals or outcomes for teaching were specified by each group; (2) all procedures inherent in each approach were specified; (3) teachers were selected on the condition that they use only the specified procedures; (4) evaluation instruments were selected and/or devised to determine the extent of accomplishment of each of the goals specified; (5) the results were reported in terms of the degree of success of each program in meeting each goal.

Educators have the responsibility for critically questioning the validity of all reported research.

*We are putting the word *method* in quotes because it means different things to different people. Each method is built on a basic theory of the reading process (whether recognized and identified or not) and the belief that certain procedures will implement the theory.

We will never be able to resolve the question of which "method" is best for teaching any subject by *instructional* research. The question is too clumsy and global. Rather, we must know what processes we want children to learn to use. Then, without trying to fit in past procedures, we need to take a fresh look at each process and explore the experiences that help children learn it.

Researching the reading process

For many years a few educators have questioned the assumptions on which basal reading programs are built, but ideas that differed so widely from those usually expressed were largely ignored. Edmund Burke Huey (1968) was one of these critics. His book, *The Psychology and Pedagogy of Reading*, first published in 1908, expresses many ideas about the reading process that are consistent with the foremost thinking of today. For instance, Huey believed that reading is a thinking process, a language process dependent upon the structure and relationships of language, rather than a process of naming words. As a procedure to teach reading, he recommended that parents and teachers hold children comfortably, read to them, and talk with them about the story and the way it is expressed. Through their experiences with children, Lamoreaux and Lee (1943) found that stories children dictated were easiest for them to read. In a revision, Lee and Allen (1963) extended the program to include substantial use of individually dictated stories, writing, and self-selected reading.

Sylvia Ashton-Warner (1963) developed a program based on a similar rationale. In New Zealand, working with Maori children, she used an individualized program with a "key vocabulary." This vocabulary was unique to each child because it was developed from the one word that each child most wanted to know each day. Dr. Ashton-Warner wrote each of these words on a card and found that when the word was truly important to the child, it was never forgotten. She

also emphasized creativity and ways in which children could initiate their own learning. Similar points of view and reactions against the formalisms and mechanical aspects of learning to read have surfaced from time to time.

A basic research project

By far the largest and most productive recent study is one started in 1962 by Kenneth S. Goodman and his associates (1969; *see also* Smith, 1973, pp. 158–176). Goodman has avoided the pitfall of trying to deal with methods of instruction. Instead, he focused on the reading process itself by discovering *what children do when they read*. A number of investigators are extending this research by developing new and confirming data.

Goodman's (1977) research is based on psycholinguistic theory, which deals with the psychological development and use of all aspects of language. Some of the most important findings are as follows.

Reading is a language process, an interaction between thought and language. When it is recognized that gaining meaning is the only defensible purpose for reading, the interaction of thought and language becomes essential. Language, of course, is not a series of separate words but the organizing and structuring of words into a thought. Meaning is not available unless and until the reader understands and reacts to the author's thought, expressed in language.

The language structure, including pattern markers, is most important for communicating meaning. The reader pays attention to the structuring of the language as the most important key to meaning. One is aware of the significance of the order of words—*The dog bites the man*, or *The man bites the dog*. Any user of language is implicitly aware of pattern markers. For instance, because of *the*, a noun marker, one knows that the last word in either sentence will tell *what* is bitten, not *how* one is bitten, as in *The dog bites viciously*. The arrangement of the words into a structure, whether it is

WRITTEN LANGUAGE: RECORDING AND RETRIEVING THOUGHTS

simple or complex, is the only way in which a reader—or a listener—can understand the thought expressed.

The reader's ability to recreate meaning depends on his experiences and ability to associate them with the language. Even when the reader can recognize the structuring of a thought and when all the words are familiar, the reader may not be able to understand the meaning. If we can find nothing in our experience that we can relate to the language we are reading, we cannot get the meaning. For example, we find little meaning in material from a highly technical and unfamiliar field. When colloquialisms or dialect differences are outside our experience, we can bring little or no meaning to the reading.

Reading cannot be considered to be a series of word perceptions but must be understood in relation to the grammatical structure of language and the structure of the meaning being communicated. When attention is focused on each separate word, recognizing the structure of the thought is far more difficult. This procedure is called "naming words" or "word calling." If the intention of the reader is to look for and recognize phrasing and structure, the thought comes through more readily. When beginning readers have dictated the sentences on their pictures, they recognize one or two cues and read the sentence. Although they scarcely see some of the words, they recognize the thought and can express it in language.

Three types of information are used simultaneously, not sequentially: graphophonic, syntactic, and semantic. Readers see recorded symbols and notice some of the symbol groups representing concepts or words they have come to associate with them, one way or another. Simultaneously they are aware of the structure or syntax of the sentence. For instance, with words like *read*, or *envelope*, or *permit*, pronunciation and meaning cannot be known until their functions are determined. What is more, readers cannot begin to phrase the sentence, with any normal intonation, until they sense the structure. And the phrasing, pitch,

stress, and pauses must be sensed—whether or not the sentence is spoken, overtly or covertly—before they can know the meaning. The third factor, semantics, stops readers if what they have tentatively put together does not make sense. The material must sound like language and must make sense. If it does not, then and only then do readers need to reconsider the graphophonic aspect of the material. They look back until they see their misinterpretation. When they have corrected it, the language and meaning fall into place and make sense, and they proceed with their reading.

Reading, like listening, is a sampling, predicting, confirming process. It is quite unnecessary and undesirable to *pay attention* to every word, and certainly not to every letter, when we read. Such minute examination obscures the meaning and takes far too much time. Sometimes material with many words omitted can be easily read, particularly if the reader is well into the content of the selection. The reader samples the material, selects important parts, and on the basis of the overall context, predicts what will come next. All of this, of course, is implicit and below the level of consciousness.

Frank Smith (1975b) calls prediction the "prior elimination of unlikely alternatives." Perhaps putting it the other way around is more useful. Predicting is selecting the more likely alternative or alternatives. If we are reading about farm machinery and see the word *cat*, we think of a Caterpillar tractor rather than an animal or any of the other nineteen meanings for *cat* in the dictionary. Or if we are reading about a meeting and see *chair*, we expect it to function as a verb, and we structure the sentence accordingly.

As Smith says, words are multiply ambiguous. In reading that sentence, did you read *multiply* as a verb? If so, you are word reading and not predicting adequately. *Are multiply* is not an acceptable verb form. If your eyes are ahead of your voice, you note that the next word is an adjective, a description of what words are. The reader does not reason this out but senses it intuitively in a fraction of a second and on the basis of long-term use of language. Therefore, *multiply* is not a verb but an adverb, and so its meaning and pronunciation are different.

The smaller and more common the word, the more likely it is to have multiple meanings. Prepositions, for instance, take up extensive space in the dictionary, yet when we hear or read language, we are almost never in doubt about their meaning because we can easily predict it from context.

For various reasons, a large proportion of the words read cannot be determined through phonics alone. Venezky (1967) says that there are more than 300 spelling-to-sound correspondence rules. Smith gives a fascinating example. How should a word beginning with *ho* be pronounced? Smith says the answer depends on whether the *ho* is followed by -t, -ot, -ok, -rizon, -rse, -pe, -use, -ney, -ist, -ur, or -nest (Smith, 1975b, pp. 305–306).

Obviously, the reader must use some strategy for gaining meaning other than phonics, or at least in addition to it. That strategy is the structure of language, the basic factor that determines meaning. "I will give you my address." "The man will address the group from the stage." "Please address the package to my home." No one can know the meaning or the function of *address* except through the structure of the sentence.

The importance of meaning has been corroborated in another way. In one study various arrangements of letters were displayed for one-tenth of a second, about the length of time a reader looks at any one point while reading. When the thirty letters were arranged in random order in a line, readers could identify only four or five. If these letters were arranged in a series of words, a reader could identify two or three of the words, which is two or three times as much as with individual letters. But when all thirty letters were arranged in a meaningful sentence, most readers could identify it all. *Therefore, we do not read by identifying letters.* It would be impossibly slow, and it would be only slightly faster if we were to read by identi-

fying each word. The meaningful thought expressed in language structure can be understood in one glance.

You can test out the extent your mind "predicts" ahead of actually seeing the print. To do this read the two or three lines at the bottom of any right-hand page (that does not end in a period) and predict what the next few words will be. You may not be entirely correct but you will be close, unless the words to be predicted, or the thought expressed, cannot be related to your previous experience.

This "guess," based on both semantic and syntactic cues, depends on the experience and prior knowledge of the reader and also on the effectiveness of the author's writing. (Material is difficult to read when the writer uses an unusual or cumbersome structure. Prediction is gained more easily and accurately when the receiver of meaning can anticipate the next words. For this reason, children can more easily read sentence patterns like their own.)

Silent reading is a very different process from oral reading. We have been describing the process of silent reading. When children are asked to read orally, they do one of two things. They may look at each word in succession and say it, which is *recoding*, that is, changing from the written code to the oral code directly. Or they may use their silent reading skills to gain meaning (decode), and then put that meaning into oral language, that is, *encode* it. In the first situation they "read" accurately but often fail to use their voices with expression to interpret meaning, for they may have little understanding of the material. In the second situation the meaning is interpreted, but when the material is new to the child the reading may be uneven.

In the recoding process, the child's attention is needed first for saying the words, second for the proper expression, and last for obtaining the overall meaning. The monotonous, expressionless oral reading of so many children documents this procedure. These children are unable to pick up the syntactic cues that tell them how to phrase correctly and read with expression. If they are not decoding (getting meaning), they cannot explain the sentences they have read aloud. When one boy was asked to tell about what he had read, he replied, "I don't know. I wasn't listening."

When children are able to decode meaning while reading aloud, they must then encode this meaning into the oral code. They gain far more understanding of the thoughts expressed, but their encoding often varies from the graphic code. Goodman calls this type of "error" a *miscue*. The reading may sound halting and uneven because the sampling, predicting, and organizing process does not necessarily move evenly. Even good readers may not orally encode all the meaning they gain. Or they may include evidence of their own thoughts as they integrate the author's thoughts and their own reactions to them. Someone following the text may report many "errors" and lack of smoothness in reading. Thus, the really good readers may be designated poor readers in an oral reading situation.

In order to read well orally, the readers' eyes and attention must be ahead of their voices, taking in the meaning through identifying the structure and picking up other context clues. Or the reader must have read the selection in advance. The better readers are at predicting, and the more meaningful the material is to them, the better they read.

Reading, then, is an active process by which the reader selects the fewest and most effective cues in order to understand the author's thoughts. The more efficient the readers, the fewer cues they need to get meaning. They are able to select cues important to the concepts, so that the meaning is not distorted. In longer selections, there is sufficient natural *redundancy*, the building of one thought on another, so that misinterpretations are recognized. When readers understand what they are reading, a word or phrase that seems inconsistent alerts them that something is wrong. They then recheck until the passage makes sense and sounds like language. The longer the selection, the more information is available for checking consistency of meaning.

This fact argues for reading whole stories or sections of stories rather than paragraphs or pages.

Self-correction

Instead of picking up cues that accurately recode the print, the oral reader often picks up miscues. Some miscues distort the meaning more than others. When there is no problem with meaning, readers seldom correct themselves, nor should teachers correct them. When either the meaning or the structure of the sentence does not seem right, however, most readers correct themselves if they are reading with comprehension. Goodman (1969) found this was true over the grade range studied, the second through the sixth grade.

In related and confirming research, Clay, who studied emergent reading behavior of one hundred five-year-olds in New Zealand, concluded that "there is evidence that the error behavior of the children was guided by the syntactic framework of the sentences read rather than by the phoneme-grapheme relationships in the words" (Clay, 1968). In other words, the miscues children made were the result of their attempts to make their reading sound like language and make sense. These errors were not unsuccessful attempts to pronounce words as separate entities.

In another article, Clay (1969) summarizes evidence of self-correction behavior in five-year-olds who are making good progress in reading. These children apparently develop an efficient information-processing strategy while they are still at the stage of intuitive thinking. Clay found that five-year-olds use an effective process of gaining information that includes self-correction of miscues when the first attempts do not make sense or sound "right."

The child's ability to correct miscues is derived from the considerable redundancy in language, which builds meaning, especially in longer selections. When instruction emphasizes meaning over phoneme-grapheme relationships, children expect what they read to make sense, and they need to correct it when it does not. When children can speak their thoughts with relative fluency, they reject that which does not "sound like language." This third factor was documented by Clay when she found that "words in sentence structures which mirror the syntactic and semantic forms of the language which the child speaks fluently will increase the child's opportunities to detect errors and develop error-correcting strategies." This statement argues strongly for reading material as close as possible to each child's idiolect (Clay, 1969, p. 55).

Weber (1970b) also found that first graders brought their knowledge of linguistic structure to bear on the identification of words. Both strong and weak readers demonstrated that they did not need to be taught this competence.

Studies of these kinds corroborate Goodman's research results and form a basis for an understanding of the reading process. Goodman expresses it thus:

> The reading process (what a reader must do to attain meaning) does not change. Readers vary rather in their ability to integrate graphic, semantic, and syntactic information to get meaning. The proficient reader gets the most meaning with the least effort. It is the progress toward this ability to maximize comprehension while minimizing effort which our studies have documented (Goodman and Burke, 1973b, p. 326).

Future reading programs

Undoubtedly in the years to come educators will gain more insights into the reading process. Meanwhile, we are ready to take a new look at reading instruction based on our understanding of the learning process and child development and research on the reading process itself. The early assumptions of language experience, built on what seemed like logical common sense at the time, served a useful purpose. Let us see how valid they still are and what additional understanding the new research has produced.

Acquiring reading skills The primary skills needed for reading are not word attack skills, but skills that depend on implicit knowledge of linguistics and semantics—sounding like language and making sense. How much of the graphic representation is used, and what part of it we pay attention to, depend on many factors: the individual's experience, prior knowledge, understanding and recognition of certain language patterns, the length of the selection, and how far the reader is into the selection. Thus, familiarity with both the content and the language that expresses it provides the individual's main cues. Taylor (1977) suggests that when readers do not recognize a word, they should substitute a word that makes sense. The reader uses phonic cues to identify a word with a meaning and syntax that fits, rather than to "sound out" the word. "Sounding out" is helpful only when meaning of the sentence or paragraph is unclear or outside the reader's experience.

So while phonics is still an aspect of the reading process, it plays a much less important part. Its value in the past has never been verified; its use in instruction has swung from pole to pole. In the late 1930s and early 1940s, because reading specialists had recognized children's slow rate of reading and poor comprehension, phonics became a "bad word," and a whole generation of children grew up with little or no instruction in it. Interestingly, there seem to be as many competent and avid readers in this group as in any other.

How meaningful or significant can the rote learning of isolated letters and sounds be for six-year-olds? How feasible is it as a learning task for children at the stage of intuitive thinking? When children are trying to make sense of their world, anything as divorced from meaning as isolated letters and their arbitrarily determined sounds, is not likely to make sense.

Furthermore, the large number of words that are not phonetic, especially the little words common to nearly all communication, can make emphasis on sound-symbol relationship confusing to children. Words like *was, come, walk, talk,* and many others are easily identified through meaning and natural language structure but confusing when one tries to pronounce them phonetically. Some educators believe that as many as 85 to 90 percent of the phonics rules are more confusing than helpful. (See Appendix D.)

In the *natural process* of learning to read, children use personal understandings to explore thoughts in written form. In a very real sense, they discover how to read. As they search for cues they begin to notice similarities and differences between words or phrases. With more and more experience, children gradually develop intuitively, and nearly always below the level of awareness, certain sound-symbol relationships that they add to their store of cues for gaining meaning. These relationships enable them to identify unrecognized words for which the meaning context and the language structure do not provide adequate cues.

Some may say that since children use the sound-symbol relationship, why not teach it to all? There are several reasons. Children need and use such understandings at different times, in different ways, and with different perceptions. It is impossible for anyone to plan a program that would be useful to all, or even many, children. Since their early learning is intuitive and their perceptions unique and virtually unknowable, the usual phonics instruction is likely to do more harm than good. What can help is making children aware that there often is a sound-symbol relationship that they can figure out if and when they need it. The more they read, the more they discover all kinds of useful cues.

To ignore the sound-symbol relationship completely is as serious a mistake as considering it the only way to learn how to read. Teachers need to use it in a reasonable way: with those children who have not discovered it on their own, at the time they need it, and in direct and immediate relation to the point of need. All agree that phonics has no value for its own sake, that its value lies in the extent to which it helps children read. Since children learn in their own individual ways, an awareness of sound-symbol relationship will be helpful to some, make no difference to some, and be seriously confusing to others.

The problem has been documented by adults looking back at their own process of learning to read. For instance, one said, "I can remember reading and feeling successful at it, and then we would have a phonics lesson and I could do that. But I can remember wondering what it was for. I was an adult before I ever tied phonics to reading."

The numbers of children who learn to read on their own, with no *conscious* knowledge of the sounds indicated by letters, makes it obvious that instruction in phonics was not necessary for them. *Children learn the phonics they need intuitively by reading.*

Recognizing words There are many words that we cannot define out of context or without knowing the structure of the sentence in which they are used. There are many we cannot even know how to pronounce, for example, *read. Therefore, the sentence, not the word, is the smallest unit of meaning.* (By sentence we mean a word or group of words that expresses a thought in context.)

A *morpheme* is, by definition, the smallest meaningful grammatical unit, a word or part of a word. For example, in the word *helplessly*, *help*, *-less*, and *-ly* are morphemes. *Help* carries various meanings, and its specific meaning in a sentence could vary widely. The suffix *-less* certainly has a different meaning here than in *sugarless*, for *helpless* means "not being able to help oneself," not "without help." The suffix *-ly* is a syntactical marker indicating the word relates to a verb or another modifier. So while each morpheme adds its bit of information, one cannot be certain of the thought expressed without knowing the whole word. One cannot be certain of the meaning of a word without knowing the whole sentence:

I saw wood the right way.

I saw a woods off to the right.

You can know the meaning of *saw*, *wood(s)*, and *right* only through the sentence in which they are used. The sentence gives the words meaning as much as the words give the sentence meaning.

Do children need to be taught each word? The belief that they do documents a lack of understanding of the tremendous learning all children do on their own. Denying children opportunities for finding out things for themselves is especially harmful. By presenting all words that children will encounter in their reading, we are telling them subtly, but very effectively, that we do not think they can find out what they are for themselves. Or they are told to "sound out" the word, a task they really do not understand, rather than to try to figure out from the rest of the sentence (syntactic and semantic cues) what the word might be. Instead of trying to find out for themselves, children then ask someone, or if that becomes too much of a chore, they give up.

Many reading programs teach phonics so children can identify unknown words, then teach all words introduced in each lesson. Theoretically there should be no unknown words in their readers, none to practice on! The only logical explanation for this contradiction is that the authors do not really believe children can use phonics to sound out unknown words.

Teachers' manuals To help teachers select materials, manuals should give the rationale and purposes of the program, how it was constructed to accomplish those purposes, and suggestions for a variety of ways the materials can be used with children. If some concepts and/or skills truly do depend on others, this information needs to be given. Beyond this minimum, sequencing should be determined by the uniqueness of each learner, rather than by the material. Also, how much and what can be included in a lesson depends on learners and teachers. When manuals actually put words in teachers' mouths, that is the ultimate put-down!

Materials for new reading programs

To teach different skills, teachers need materials that are different, too. We no longer need word

recognition skills built into the material. This change eliminates the tight vocabulary control of basal readers and puts the emphasis on content written in language and sentence patterns familiar to children. Content should focus on children's interests. Material should include good literature, to provide models and to extend knowledge and understanding of this great, wide, and diverse world that children are entering. In other words, the material should be valuable in its own right, not as just a tool.

Children need both the right and the expectancy that they will explore this literature and choose material that interests them and meets their needs. The goal is an individualized program with self-selected materials. Since any child's reading skills develop in a unique way and in a unique sequence, an individualized program is essential for that reason, too.

Libraries are a key resource whenever stimulating children's reading is at stake. The room library or reading center should be replenished frequently with books related to major topics of interest to small groups or the whole class. The books should provide a wide range in the maturity of concepts as well as in areas of interest. Teachers need to check frequently to eliminate books that are no longer being used in order to save space for other books of current interest.

Besides published books, the reading center should include books written by the children in the room. Expressive photographs and art work executed by both teachers and students can stimulate the writing of books for use in the classroom. Thus, reading materials created by children can become a valuable part of a library collection. Such materials can provide the art program with a rationale for book illustrating, binding, and production.

Most schools have hundreds, perhaps thousands of reading textbooks. All classrooms can share reading texts of each indicated grade level and mix them with other fiction on the room library shelves. As they become available for selection, many children may find some of the stories interesting, particularly in the more recent editions. Also, the short stories fit into any time slot the child has available.

Other books already in the school are textbooks in the various content areas. Although no one text should ever be utilized as the only source of information, texts should be resources used in a variety of ways. Children need to learn that each title or series presents one point of view, while others may differ. Children can learn to recognize such differences and to report such information.

Newspapers and magazines belong in every classroom. A daily or weekly newspaper, widely read in the community, can stimulate reading and the habit of keeping up with world and local events. All nines and older, and some children as young as six, can get much information and satisfaction from newspapers. In addition a weekly children's magazine is important.

The school library is most helpful when it is available to any child at any time, not as a place to sit and read, but as a source of reference material. The library should be as well stocked as possible, with books organized by subject and author, no matter what the maturity level of the book.

Group visits to public libraries, both main libraries and branches, familiarize children with them and encourage their use. When children know both the personnel and the procedures, the library is no longer a formidable place. Often parents can be enlisted to take their own children or groups who might not otherwise have access to the library.

When children come from homes where reading is accepted as a worthy use of time, teachers and librarians can add to their experiences by advising, sharing, and appreciating books. For youngsters who have not yet identified books as a useful source of entertainment and information, the role of school personnel is even more important. Teachers and librarians should read to all children regularly, but even more frequently to those particular children, so that books become a center of communal enjoyment. When children find delight and satisfaction in books, they develop reading competence and continue a lifetime of reading for enjoyment.

Sharing books   An integral and essential part of any successful reading program is the regular sharing of books and materials the children are reading. Such sharing provides natural opportunities for children to talk informally but purposefully before the group, requires children to organize thoughts and feelings about their reading, and encourages other children to read the material.

Often teachers feel that the sharing process is most valuable as part of the whole-class activities at the beginning of the morning. Sharing is voluntary. The teacher or a child chairperson asks if anyone has a book to share. When children enjoy reading, particularly where a warm group relationship has been established, several children respond each day.

The reporter holds up the book, names the title and author, describes the general content, recounts an incident or shows a picture, then asks if anyone wants to read the book. Usually several hands go up and one child has the privilege of reading it next. Such sharing epitomizes the atmosphere of a stimulating, cooperating classroom where enjoyment of reading is a developing and unifying force.

Summary

In this chapter we have briefly examined the most widely used current reading programs or types of programs and have stated the basic assumptions and rationales evident in their procedures. Research documenting what the reading process is—that is, what we do when we read—indicates the need for different assumptions and a new rationale. Research also shows that the process of gaining information is used intuitively by five-year-olds who are learning to read. Implications of the process indicate the need for new procedures and different kinds of material.

Basic principles and guidelines applied to reading

These guidelines provide a basis for choosing procedures to help children learn to read and to evaluate their success.

1. Reading involves understanding of written thoughts.

To find out how well children read, ask them to tell you about what they have read. Ask follow-up questions in terms of the purpose for which they were reading.

2. Children need to develop self-confidence as readers.

When children select their own reading materials and can talk about what they have read, they experience success. When helping children who have difficulty, emphasize how much they were able to understand on their own.

3. Children discover how reading works through dictating, seeing their words written, and hearing them read back.

They continually extend their discovery as they read what they and their peers have said and written, and discuss the reading and the writing.

4. Children need to see the direct relationship between what they say, what it looks like written, and how it is read back.

Therefore it is important to record dictated statements in the child's natural language.

5. Children will work hard at reading whatever is important to them.

Self-selection of reading materials helps to ensure this importance.

6. Children learn to read by reading.

At first they may understand the thought and express it in somewhat different words. As they continue reading, gradually they become more accurate. As they experience the process and talk about it, it becomes clearer to them.

7. Since learning to read is largely intuitive, as most learning is at this age, explanations, directions, and direct teaching may do more to confuse than to help.

After children have established successful reading processes, they can discuss ways to gain greater depth and evaluative ability.

8. Each child's development and experiencing in reading is unique.

Since no two children have all the same learning at the same time, listening and responding to them individually, in small groups, and in teacher-pupil reading conferences is more useful than group instruction.

9. When children read effectively, they understand the meaning but may or may not report it in the exact words of the print.

As long as they do not seriously distort meaning, teachers should make no issue of it. If there is distortion, teachers should allow time for children to self-correct. If children do not question the meaning of the distorted sentences, teachers should raise the question of meaning.

10. Children learn to read most effectively when what they read is important to them.

When children choose their own reading material, it is automatically more important to them than what might be assigned, and they want to find out what it says. They concentrate on getting the meaning.

Suggested learning experiences for prospective teachers

Suggestion A

1. Ask teachers for permission to discuss with youngsters what they read. Try to determine what they prefer to read. Do they all like to read the same books? Are they using basals as well as library books? Do magazines and newspapers comprise part of their reading materials?

2. Survey children to determine how many (a) do not read on their own initiative, (b) cannot read well but still try, (c) do not try or seem to care. Much of this information can be given to you by the teacher.

3. Plan experiences for children who are in need of additional reading help. Does the preceding chapter have any suggestions for you? What key points should be considered when dealing with children with reading problems?

Suggestion B

1. Think about children's concept of the reading process in comparison to that of the teacher. Do you feel the teacher's concept influences the class reading program? Can you determine what influences the teacher's concept?

2. Find out whether children view reading as part of a language process or as a word-attack or "decoding" program. If this were your class, what changes could you make in their reading program that would put the emphasis on the communication of meaning through syntactic-semantic cues?

3. Think about what reading meant to you as a youngster. Is your concept still the same today? List for yourself the new ideas you have learned from reading this chapter.

Suggestion C

1. Think about and describe a school reading program that you have observed. Focus upon the following:

What is the basic philosophy?

What materials are used?

What is the teacher role? Student role?

Who assumes responsibility for what takes place?

How do youngsters function—in groups, teams, as a total class, or individually?

How is student achievement or progress evaluated?

2. Decide if this program meets the criteria discussed in the chapter. Talk over your findings with a fellow student.

3. What will be the components of *your* reading program?

Suggestion D

1. Survey several groups of children at the same grade level to determine their interests in reading. Find out the specific types of literature they enjoy or prefer, and their reasons for their preferences.

2. Analyze the similarities and differences in the interests of children in each group. How are they alike? How are they different?

3. Compare and contrast the group findings. Try to identify prior experiences that develop one's priorities and preferences.

4. Think of your own reading interests. How did they develop? What experiences have affected

your choices? Do you add to your personal repertoire of what you read? How do you decide
whether you will read or will not read a particular book?

Suggestion E

1. Focus upon children as they select books from a
library. Watch how they choose as they sort
through collections. Try to determine what criteria
or upon what basis they make their selections.

2. Think about the use of children's literature as a
major part of a reading program. What kinds of
experiences should teachers and librarians provide
for children? How can these books best be used as
a part of a program?

3. Locate and observe, if possible, classrooms
where reading programs are conducted with language experience and literature components only.
Also, arrange time to talk with the teacher about
the program.

Suggested readings

Looking first at fundamental purposes for reading,
Daniel and Lauren Resnick in "The Nature of Literacy" question the current "back to the basics"
movement saying that pedagogical practices from
the past offer little remedy for reading problems as
currently defined. Frank Smith in "Making Sense
of Reading—And of Reading Instruction" indicates that to learn to read children must know that
(1) print is meaningful, and (2) print is different
from speech. These two articles are part of a special issue of *Harvard Educational Review* called
"Reading, Language, and Learning." Postman
and Weingartner's *The School Book* is stimulating,
particularly the chapter on reading and Part II on
language and people. Malcolm Douglass edited
"A Little Revolution Now and Then" indicating
the need for changes, some "revolutionary," while
Goodman and Goodman write that "Learning to
Read Is Natural."

Hodges and Rudorf edited *Language and Learning
to Read: What Teachers Should Know about Language*,
which provides many cues for the classroom.
"Reading Is Only Incidentally Visual" by P. A.
Kolers challenges conventional wisdom. In "Conscious Comprehension: Reality Reading through
Artifacts" Potter and Hannemann emphasize the
similarity of inferring from reading and guessing

about an object. Along the same line Duane Tovey
wrote "The Psycholinguistic Guessing Game" and
Roger Shuy edited *Linguistic Theory: What Can It
Say About Reading?* Probably the simplest and most
clearly written statement of the process of reading
as seen by the psycholinguists is *Reading: Process
and Program* by Kenneth Goodman and Olive
Niles. Lundsteen's "On Developmental Relations
between Language-Learning and Reading" provides an excellent and extended analysis of problems children too often face in learning to read.

Certain commercial programs or systems for
teaching reading are attacked by Sam Sebesta in
"Tyrannosaurus Anonymous Met a Reader Autonomous"; and by Dale Johnson in "Skill Management Systems: Some Issues."

"Focus 2" of the March 1976 issue of *Language
Arts* deals with various aspects of psycholinguistics and reading. Goodman interprets instructional
issues in his "Effective Teachers of Reading Know
Language and Children," "Linguistic Insights
Which Teachers May Apply," and "Comprehension-Centered Reading." His article "A Linguistic Study of Cues and Miscues in Reading" is
an excellent introduction to this concept, while
Miscue Analysis: Applications to Reading Instruction
combines specific suggestions of several authors.

"The Role of Prediction in Reading" by Frank Smith emphasizes relevant implications for instruction. Documentation for the above approaches to reading is provided by Rose-Marie Weber's "First Graders' Use of Grammatical Context in Reading." Two other studies are relevant, Sara Rode's "Development of Phrase and Clause Boundary Reading in Children" and Virginia Mickish's "Children's Perception of Written Word Boundaries," both of which look at reading from the child's point of view.

The question of how—and when—phonics can be useful to children still attracts writers. Patrick Groff explains the "Fifteen Flaws of Phonics" and Carl Lefevre makes some of the same points in Chapter 4 of *Linguistics, English, and the Language Arts*. Sterl Artley in "Phonics Revisited" makes the point that reading is gaining meaning, not sounding out words. Frank Smith and Deborah Holmes reject letter identification as necessary for comprehension in their article, "The Independence of Letter, Word, and Meaning Identification in Reading."

For developing an understanding of the place and use of children's literature, the classic *Books*, *Children, and Men* by Paul Hazard is still basic. Lee Bennet Hopkins' *Books Are by People* and *More Books Are by More People* provide help in developing concepts of authorship. In helping teachers to locate and use materials for children's reading, the late May Hill Arbuthnot was a dependable source for years. Her *Children and Books* has been revised by Zena Sutherland. Also helpful are Francis Clarke Sayers' *Summoned by Books* and Part VI, "Literature: Reflections and Realities of Life and Language," in *A Forum for Focus* edited by Martha King, Robert Evans, and Patricia Cianciola. Patricia Cianciola and Jean Le Pere, in their *The Literary Time Line in American History*, relate fiction and nonfiction to periods or events in history. Virginia Witucke's *Poetry in the Elementary School* helps teachers find, evaluate, and use poetry. Sources of a wide range of materials are *Guide to Children's Magazines, Newspapers, Reference Books* by A.C.E.I., Nancy Larrick's "The Paperback Bonanza," and two articles in *Learning*, "Nonbooks: Rx for Bibliophobia" and "Getting Kids into Libraries—and Vice-Versa" provide ideas to stimulate and enhance library use; Anne Troy discusses "Literature for Content Area Learning."

Strategies for children's learning

Language experience extended

Purpose.   To demonstrate that the language experience approach to reading is appropriate with older students.

Appropriate level.   Grade four and beyond.

Participants.   All children.

Situation.   The basic procedures of the language experience approach to reading are to encourage children to express their thoughts, feelings, and ideas in writing and share them as material for their peers to read. Thus, by reading their own writing and the ideas expressed by their friends, as well as published books, periodicals, and newspapers, children increase their in-depth understanding of both reading and writing processes.

Teacher role

1. To provide opportunity for children to continue to record on paper their thoughts and feelings about the world they live in.

2. To help students understand the thoughts and feelings of their peers through reading their writings.

Procedures

1. Provide the environment, the atmosphere, and the opportunity for children to carry out the above procedures informally.

2. Set up situations for groups of children to discuss (a) books or stories they have all read, and (b) ideas they want to incorporate in their writing to improve it.

3. Set up situations for groups of children with similar interests to discuss their writings. While language experience emphasizes individuality, it also means that children write about what is important to them at a given time. Such topics as The Friday Sock Hop, Rock Music, The Rose Bowl, Arab-Israeli Conflicts may surface, as well as personal feelings about friends, school work, or a social situation.

4. Help children clarify their feelings by writing, and make this created expression available for individual and group reading. However, personal writing must never become group reading material without permission of the author.

5. Encourage children to experience various writing styles in published material. Discuss style with the group and suggest that when they find a style they especially like, they experiment with it, then try a different style. Explain the difference between directly imitating and adapting a style to their own use. Encourage them to try a variety of styles to find the one that seems most effective.

Evaluation. Are students continuing to put their ideas on paper? Is reading enhanced by the inclusion of material written by students? Are students better able to describe their thoughts and feelings on paper?

Recreating meaning

Purpose. To show children that the ability to recreate meaning depends on the ability to associate one's individual experiences with the language of the writer.

Appropriate level. Grade four and above.

Participants. All children.

Teacher role

1. To assist children with the understanding that in order to recreate meaning, that is, understand the meaning a writer has recorded, the reader must associate personal experiencing with language.

2. To provide opportunities for children to recreate meaning on this basis. (Note: This strategy is dependent on a thorough understanding of the concepts in this chapter.)

Procedures

1. In a small group, ask children to read a given selection in which the words and sentence structure are within the children's ability but the concepts and information are beyond them. Material from some vocational or professional field is an example. The ensuing discussion can bring out the lack of significant meaning the children were able to recreate. If someone is able to bring meaning to the selection, ask what experiences made that possible.

2. Then, ask the group to read a selection with many concepts and situations that most children have experienced firsthand. Now most of the group will be able to recreate meaning and discuss it. If some still cannot, try to discover what experiences they have not had that the others have.

3. Have a small group of children read a fairy tale or adventure story in which the setting is familiar but the action is beyond their personal experience. To what extent can children recreate meaning from this selection? How do they use vicarious experience? Vicarious experiences are useful to the extent that children have had relevant firsthand experiences that they can use as a basis for under-

standing. What experiences do children need to bring real and accurate meaning to science fiction?

Evaluation. Are children more able to recreate meaning in their reading in relation to their individual experiences? Does their language show their ability to make associations?

Prediction in reading

Purpose. To make children aware of the usefulness of prediction in reading as provided by normal redundancy.

Appropriate level. All levels including kindergarten.

Participants. All children.

Teacher role

1. To provide experiences to illustrate the usefulness of prediction.

2. To use prediction to help children who have difficulty in reading.

Procedures

1. In *kindergarten and first grade* before a child is reading, when children are using books with pictures and captions, ask them what they think the print means. If they approximate the printed statement, say, "Yes, it says_____" and read the actual wording.

When children recognize some of the words, such as the name of the object pictured, respond with, "Yes, it is a_____. What do you think it says about it?" Follow this general practice whenever the print is reasonably predictable. When they can read part of a statement, ask "What do you think it means?"

2. With *children who are reading* but do not recognize some words or phrases, ask them to read the whole sentence and see what they think it means. Refer to sentence meaning rather than word iden-

tification unless the unrecognized word is unpredictable with no cues to meaning.

3. Beginning about *fourth* grade, help children to become aware of what all have been doing for some time—predicting on the basis of linguistic and semantic cues—sounding like language and making sense. With material they have not read before, ask a small group to read the first page of a story to find out what it is about, then stop at the bottom of the page. If the page ends in the middle of a sentence, ask them to predict how the sentence will end. If the sentence is complete, ask what they think the next sentence might be. The second procedure is more difficult, of course, because syntactic cues are lacking. Then have children place a card part way down the next page and try to predict the end of a sentence. This activity can be exciting, and children will want to see how well they can predict. Success will be varied, but encourage all children to try.

4. Write sentences in each of which the ending of one word has been eliminated. Children then supply the ending needed to determine the word's use in the structure of the sentence, so the sentence makes sense and sounds like language.

5. Prepare a selection by leaving out a negative, changing a directional word (*up* to *down*, or *in* to *out*), or changing some other single word that changes the meaning of the selection. Ask children to read it and discover what is wrong. Most, if not all, should be able to locate the contradiction and thus recognize the normal redundancy of any extended writing. Emphasize that it is the meaning of the whole selection that is important, and the meaning of each sentence must make sense in terms of all the others. They need to use the normal redundancy as a check on meaning of the parts.

Evaluation. Do children think more about the meaning of their reading? Do they increase their reading speed? Is there any transfer to their writing of their greater awareness of syntax?

Two ways of reading for different purposes

Purpose. To show children how silent reading differs from oral reading.

Appropriate level. Grades three and up.

Participants. All children.

Teacher role

1. To provide experiences for children to differentiate between silent and oral reading skills.

2. To enable youngsters to understand the purpose of each more fully.

Procedures

1. Discuss the processes of silent reading. Help children understand those most useful. You might ask these questions: When reading silently—

> Do you read to understand the author's thoughts or do you sound in your head each individual word?
>
> Do you pay attention to every word?
>
> How important is each individual word?
>
> Does it really make any difference whether you can pronounce each word that you read silently?

2. Discuss the purposes and procedures for oral reading. You might ask these questions: When reading aloud—

> Do you listen for the ideas the words represent, or to the *sound* of the words?
>
> Do you pay attention to details?
>
> How important is pronouncing each word?
>
> How do you decide what interpretation to give by the way you use your voice?

3. Discuss reasons for reading orally, such as (a) sharing information the audience needs; (b) sharing a story or poem that others will enjoy; (c) providing information relevant to an ongoing discussion; (d) interpreting a piece of literature in which voice pitch, stress, and pauses are important.

Evaluation. Are the students able to differentiate between the skills of oral and silent reading? Are they increasingly able to read without subvocalizing? Do they always prepare if oral sharing is the purpose of the reading?

Selecting books

Purpose. To help children make an increasingly satisfying selection of books for their own reading.

Appropriate level. All levels, varied according to reading ability.

Participants. All children.

Teacher role

1. To assist children in developing awareness of their bases for choosing books.

2. To use this information in selecting a supply of books that permit satisfying choices.

Procedures

1. Work with the school librarian (where there is one) and/or public librarians to increase the supply of books needed and desired by children. Such books may be loaned to classrooms by school libraries or by local branch libraries in the neighborhood.

2. Discuss criteria for choosing books. One basis at all levels is the desire for more books about the content of ongoing projects.

In kindergarten and early first grade the bases for choice are simple. "Do I like the book?" "What kinds of books do I want more of?" The purpose is to make children aware of why and how they choose books to read.

During the next two years, children will develop other criteria, usually implicit unless brought to the level of awareness. The discussion can bring out special areas of interest: animal stories, fairy stories, funny stories, with an increasing list of individual interests.

From late third grade on through elementary school, the range of interests increases. Children begin to follow a favorite author. They also respond to differences in style of writing, even though they may not be able to explain preferences beyond "I just like to read those books."

3. Discuss other criteria for choosing books, including illustrations, easy or difficult reading, and whether the value of the content makes extra effort worthwhile. Children can become aware of illustrators as well as authors and know which ones they particularly like.

Children who have confidence in themselves as readers will usually balance the difficulty and value or usefulness of a book. They do not mind how hard they have to work to dig out of a book what they see as valuable. Over a period of time any one child's reading may vary from comic books to adult literature. Sixth graders as well as second graders can enjoy Dr. Seuss. It is extremely important that no child be told a book is too hard or too easy; the choice belongs to the child. Children who are not confident about their ability as readers need to feel it is all right to choose relatively easy books, for by this means they finally gain confidence and move on.

4. Another point of discussion is what children do when they go to the library or the book corner to choose a book. Their discussion of this point helps them think about it, and their sharing suggests a variety of procedures that others may adopt.

Evaluation. Are children more aware of why they choose a book? Are they increasingly satisfied with their choices? Are they more relaxed and confident about choosing whatever book appeals to them? Do they enjoy reading more?

LEARNING TO READ
NATURALLY

How does reading ability develop? It happens in many different ways and at different times and rates. Many kinds of experiences that happen to preschoolers increase their awareness of the meaningfulness of print. Some preschoolers are intrigued with big sister's or big brother's activities brought home from school. The younger children become willing pupils who permit older siblings to take on the teacher's role. Some parents or grandparents read to children from babyhood on. As the children look first at the pictures, but later at the print, they make associations from familiar stories: "That says, 'Come find me, Tom.'" In a variety of ways they acquire a store of familiar symbols related to thoughts: street signs, advertising signs, words and phrases on commercial packaging, television programs, and particularly TV commercials.

Probably no child in our present-day society comes to school without some implicit understanding about how print and meaning go together. Recognition of these relationships may be minimal and the children quite unaware of them. But some children are already reading material meaningfully within the level of the concepts they understand.

In this chapter we present procedures for developing children's reading competence based on the rationale of language experience—a natural way for children to learn to read—extended and confirmed by the recent research done by psycholinguists. We then outline ten stages of learning to read, explain the teacher's role for each stage, and consider the implications of the program for the child with a different dialect. The remainder of the chapter is devoted to various ways teachers can ensure continuing development to make reading more satisfying for children and children more efficient at gaining meaning from print.

What children bring to school

Awareness of what children bring to school enables us to start where they are in development and learning, rather than trying to teach what they already do well intuitively. The most important asset each child brings to school is a *facility with language*. The children can understand anything within their experience expressed in the language they have learned. They can initiate thoughts and respond to thoughts of others with adequate use of the language they have grown up with. These accomplishments are far more complex than learning a different form—a written form—of the code they already use.

Another valuable asset that each child brings to school is five or six years of *experiencing*. They have learned to read—to bring meaning to—many kinds of experience, some helpful and some harmful, but all bringing them information about their world and about themselves. Each one has developed relationships with people, ways of dealing with the physical world, awareness of animal life and what to expect from it. Each one has learned to recognize verbal and nonverbal cues that tell the child how to respond to the world and use it for his or her own developing purposes. Many of these cues are not consciously recognized but are available for the child's use intuitively.

A third factor that each child brings to school is a *self-concept*. Their success in school will be affected by the way they perceive themselves. We can expect children to be successful in most of their attempts if their experiences with people, with the world, and with reactions to their language have usually made them feel capable and accepted. But if their experiences have made them feel inadequate and not accepted, their chances of success are lessened.

All children are to some extent uncertain about how school will work out for them. If they have developed self-confidence, they expect new experiences to be happy and successful, and they soon feel comfortable in school. The more apprehensive children are likely to perceive much feedback as negative, which only increases their concern. In their uncertainty, they may be so filled with questions that they do not hear the teacher's directions. Thus, their lack of self-confidence, developed from previous experiences, sets the stage for further lack of success.

In order to follow the oft-repeated admonition, "Begin where the child is," we need some definite guidelines. First, since all children have experienced print, teachers need to take advantage of this experience. If children are encouraged to talk about it, they may become aware of other relevant experiences and dimly recognized relationships. Since the relationship of print and meaning is endless, such discussions should not be limited to the

first few months of school, which may be the most crucial, but can be continued for the rest of the individual's school experience at increasing levels of depth and complexity.

Awareness of previous experience with print is particularly important for children like Steve, who was good at baseball but thought he could not read. By leading him to talk about baseball, the teacher might have discovered that he was reading the sports page and helped him to recognize his reading ability. Then the teacher could have found exciting baseball stories for Steve to read instead of the material he was rejecting. With the teacher's encouragement, Steve could have recognized his successes and made real progress.

Children should be encouraged to talk about their experiences with the teacher, a group, or individual peers. In addition to the value of sharing, talking often clarifies experience. Feedback from such discussion gives the teacher a better basis for understanding and working with each child. The experience itself is not as important as what the experience means to the child—which is the significance of the term *experiencing*. The teacher cannot evaluate the experience without knowing what goes on within the child.

Second, the teacher should make use of the child's current stage of language development and provide opportunities to further it. It is crucial to use the child's own language skills when initiating and developing reading experiences. No one can read what he or she cannot understand when spoken. If children cannot see the relationship between their spoken thoughts and their reading experience, they see no purpose or value in reading, since it has so little meaning. Workbooks or ditto sheets that use other people's language may or may not have personal meaning for the child. The child may perform the task correctly without learning from it. Any learning that results is likely to be rote—without understanding—based on short-term memory, and useless to the child. These materials neither use nor develop the child's own language skills and seldom carry over usefully into reading.

Third, building feelings of self-worth may be even more important than making use of the child's experience and language skills. Children who are least advanced or hesitant to use their language abilities need extra encouragement and experience. The goal is never to undermine any child's self-confidence, but to build confidence at every opportunity.

When children are boastful, an adult's first reaction may be to "cut them down to size." We can avoid this damaging response if we understand the reason for boastfulness. Jack, a loud braggart, is working hard to convince himself and others that he is worthwhile. The negative feedback that he receives continues to make him doubt that he is a valuable person. He brags to call attention to any bit of evidence that enhances his self-worth. Negative comments reconfirm Jack's basic belief about his lack of competence and may result in resentment and resistance.

Confident people, who do not need to convince anyone, are more accurate in their self-evaluations. They know there are things they cannot do, but believe they will be able to develop these abilities at the appropriate time. Knowing that they are capable helps them to move ahead in their accomplishments, including the development of reading. Once children have experienced successful reading, their self-confidence in this area usually continues.

A program that uses children's natural learning

A reading program that is both logical and successful is built primarily on relatively recent awareness of the ease with which preschool children develop oral language merely by being in the presence of language and being able to participate in it. Despite the extremely complex nature of language, virtually all children develop oral language early and effectively. By comparison, learning to read is a much simpler task.

Then why do so many children have difficulty learning to read? Piaget helped to answer this question by distinguishing between the intuitive learning of the young child and the abstract learning that occurs later on. Perhaps we have been trying to teach reading through programs that depend on thought processes children are unable to use until they are seven, eight, or nine years old. An effective reading program must depend on the intuitive, preoperational, discovery learning of younger children.

The psychology of learning has established three additional principles: Children learn more easily what makes sense to them as a result of their own personal experience. Children learn more easily when they feel a commitment because they have chosen what they want to learn. Children learn most easily those things that bring feelings of success and increased confidence.

The most significant recent discovery established our understanding of the reading process itself. By studying what children actually do when they read, investigators learned that children depend intuitively on the structure of language. They are not merely naming words. For readers of any age, the flow of language must make sense and "sound like language." By listening to talk and to stories read aloud, children gain familiarity with many sentence patterns. Without direct instruction, even the least capable beginning readers implicitly use this structure in both talking and reading.

Educators have long recognized that children can read more easily when the material follows their own speech patterns. Nothing meets this criterion better than what the child says and writes. What peers write comes next in ease of reading. Years ago the general principle of differentiation in learning told us that children's awareness moves from the general to the particular, from the whole to recognition of its parts. Thus, the sentence as a complete thought is the unit of meaning and must be read as a whole by the beginning reader. Later, through writing, the child becomes aware of the separate words that make up the sentence, and finally of the letters that make up the words.

A perspective on pre-first graders and the teaching of reading

Pre-first graders need

Opportunities to express orally, graphically, and dramatically their feelings and responses to experiences.

and

Opportunities to interpret the language of others whether it is written, spoken, or nonverbal.

Teachers of pre-first graders need

Preparation which emphasizes developmentally appropriate language experiences for all pre-first graders, including those ready to read or already reading.

and

The combined efforts of professional organizations, colleges, and universities to help them successfully meet the concerns outlined in this document.

Concerns

1. Growing numbers of children are enrolled in pre-kindergarten and kindergarten classes in which highly structured pre-reading and reading programs are being used.

2. Decisions related to schooling, including the teaching of reading, are increasingly being made on economic and political bases instead of on our knowledge of young children and of how they best learn.

3. In a time of diminishing financial resources, schools often try to make "a good showing" on measures of achievement that may or may not be appropriate for the children involved. Such measures all too often dictate the content and goals of the program.

4. In attempting to respond to pressures for high scores on widely used measures of achievement, teachers of young children sometimes feel compelled to use materials, methods, and activities designed for older children. In so doing, they may impede the development of intellectual functions such as curiosity, critical thinking, and creative expression, and, at the same time, promote negative attitudes toward reading.

5. A need exists to provide alternative ways to teach and evaluate progress in pre-reading and reading skills.

6. Teachers of pre-first graders who are carrying out highly individualized programs without depending upon commercial readers and workbooks need help in articulating for themselves and the public what they are doing and why.

Recommendations

1. Provide reading experiences as an integrated part of the broader communication process that includes listening, speaking, and writing. A language experience approach is an example of such integration.

2. Provide for a broad range of activities both in scope and in content. Include direct experiences that offer opportunities to communicate in different settings with different persons.

3. Foster children's affective and cognitive development by providing materials, experiences, and opportunities to communicate what they know and how they feel.

4. Continually appraise how various aspects of each child's total development affects his/her reading development.

5. Use evaluation procedures that are developmentally appropriate for the children being assessed and that reflect the goals and objectives of the instructional program.

6. Insure feelings of success for all children in order to help them see themselves as persons who can enjoy exploring language and learning to read.

7. Plan flexibly in order to accommodate a variety of learning styles and ways of thinking.

8. Respect the language the child brings to school and use it as a base for language activities.

9. Plan activities that will cause children to become active participants in the learning process rather than passive recipients of knowledge.

10. Provide opportunities for children to experiment with language and simply to have fun with it.

11. Require that preservice and inservice teachers of young children be prepared in the teaching of reading in a way that emphasizes reading as an integral part of the language arts as well as the total curriculum.

12. Encourage developmentally appropriate language learning opportunities in the home.

This statement was developed by:

American Association of Elementary/Kindergarten/Nursery Educators

Association for Childhood Education International

Association for Supervision and Curriculum Development

International Reading Association

National Association for the Education of Young Children

National Association of Elementary School Principals

National Council of Teachers of English

Today the preschool child's world is filled with language. Written and oral language are combined on TV, and the child's incentive to read is increased by advertising, such as gift offers on cereal boxes. The need for a better understanding of how children learn to read became evident when more and more children began reading without instruction. At one time, educators assumed that such children fit a pattern: children of above average intelligence who come from well-educated families, speak standard English, and have been read to a great deal. Torrey was asked to study a child named John, whose story violated all of those criteria.

When John entered kindergarten at four years ten months, he had been reading and writing for some time. After two months in first grade, his reading level tested at 4.8, only slightly below fifth grade. His mother insisted that no one had read to him to any extent, and no one had taught him to read. He began by reading labels on food cans. John's IQ was 111, and his speech and that of his family, Black English. His father had eight years of schooling and his mother, ten years. Among the five children were an older brother and sister who had trouble with reading. John took great pleasure in reading to them stories that they could not read for themselves. John was fascinated by TV commercials, knew them by heart, and could write them as well as read them. He could sound out unrecognized words and used accurate intonation even in difficult sentences.

Torrey's conclusions are: (1) Reading is learned, not taught; (2) The key question is either "How does something I can say look in print?" or "What does that print say?"; and (3) High verbal ability and cultural privilege may be useful in stimulating reading, but neither is necessary (Torrey, 1969, p. 556).

Many classrooms have utilized these principles to help children learn to read. The same basic approach was used by Project Literacy, a national project that studied various procedures for producing a more effective literacy for children. The project established a program for a heterogeneous group of twenty-three first graders. A literate environment was provided by children's own stories, teacher's sentences, trade books, textbooks, messages from one child to another, bulletin board titles, work sheets, riddles, crossword puzzles, and stories composed by the staff. They allowed the children the full range of sampling necessary for reading in various situations. They also provided a tape recorder and an electric typewriter. No sharp demarcation was made between reading, listening, and writing, but these activities were interspersed among similar groups of children. "All learned to read; slow readers were reading comfortably at first grade level. Most were reading above grade level" (Robinson, 1966).

Developmental stages in learning to read naturally

Specifying developmental stages is difficult because children develop at different rates, and the order of accomplishment of developmental tasks may differ from child to child. Children are already at different stages when they come to school.

Some need help to extend their oral language skills, while others have moved through several stages in learning to read. Our ten stages of learning to read are therefore a generalization that no teacher should follow slavishly. The sequence that we suggest is likely to prove successful for most children, but not necessarily for all. No one can determine the sequence for any particular child. Some learn faster, some more slowly or in a different sequence. At any one time, members of the group will represent several stages.

Individual differences become more marked as the children progress. Any one child's progress and sequential development may vary from the ten stages, especially if reading development slows and the child is having problems. The child who has not "mastered" a certain stage may still carry out activities of succeeding stages if the child freely chooses to do so. No child should be denied the right to participate in self-chosen activities.

The teacher's role for each stage emphasizes purposes that teachers need to work toward. Procedures should be used selectively in a uniquely personal way with each child. The following stages illustrate the strength of individualized instruction and the procedures needed to carry it out.

1. *Children need to use oral language freely and informally with adults and peers before reading instruction begins*. The child's idiolect must be accepted—not "corrected"—and the child's thoughts, however expressed, should be treated with respect and interest.

Teacher role. Children may need encouragement to initiate, extend, and expand on talk. They need to listen with interest and attention to others, both peers and adults, and to respond. The better the oral communication and the more advanced its development, the more likely that reading will develop easily and smoothly.

Children need to feel as confident as possible about talking. So that they will not become self-conscious, accepting mispronunciations and dialects without comment will most easily allow them to adopt the more mature speech they hear. A child's difficulty with certain sounds may create problems for listeners, including teachers. Mary, who said "bah'l" instead of *barrel*, was told to say "bar-rel." She stamped her little foot in exasperation and replied, "I *did* say bah'l!" To Mary, there was no difference between her pronunciation—her intention—and the teacher's. When other children cannot understand, the teacher explains that Mary has her own way of talking, just as they each have their own ways. Listeners need to concentrate on meaning, rather than on differences in speech.

2. *Children need to develop familiarity with books and positive feelings about them.* Some children come to school with remembrances of many happy experiences with storytelling and books. These children naturally look to books for satisfaction and pleasure. However, many children, regardless of socioeconomic level, do not. Until storytelling is anticipated as pleasure and books become friends, there is a diminished chance of successful reading.

Teacher role. The teacher needs to read or tell a story to the children at least once every day—more often if many in the group have not experienced much story reading. Teachers need to build story time as an enjoyable experience for everyone to look forward to. They can create anticipation by occasionally stopping to ask, "What do you think happens next?" or "What do you suppose she did then?" This procedure permits active involvement with the narrative and confidence in their ability to predict.

Larrick (1976) suggests that children use wordless picture books as a basis for storytelling. Later on they can use similar books for writing stories. The teacher can use books as sources of information the children want, especially in areas of special interest. Books read for the teacher's own personal enjoyment and information can be shared with the group.

3. *Children need to discuss happenings both in small groups and with the total class.* Ideas from such a discussion continue children's language development and can often become the basis for a group story.

Teacher role. The teacher can ask if the children would like to write a story about an experience they have discussed. When the response is positive, the children can discuss, "What do we want to say first?" Such invitations bring forth statements from various children, which the teacher records on the board or on newsprint on an easel* just as the children say them. At the end of the story, they decide on a title. Then the teacher, running a hand from left to right under each line, reads the story with the children chiming in as they can. The children's comments or anyone's desire to read any part of it alone should be welcomed. If group stories are written frequently, more children will feel confident to read at least some part of them, and soon most children will be joining in, which contributes to their feeling of success and builds reading accomplishments.

4. *Children begin making up their own stories, dictating them, and seeing what they say written down.*

Teacher role. As children build with blocks and create with clay or paint, the teacher moves about the room and involves them one at a time in telling about their work. As they finish their projects, the teacher sits by an easel. In groups of four or five, children bring what they wish to share. Jimmy's picture is fastened to the easel, and he tells what he would like to say about it. His peers join in with questions or comments. Mrs. Thomas then asks, "What would you like written on your picture?" If Jimmy's reply would be more than one line, she listens and accepts, but then says, "What is the *one* most important thing you want me to write on your picture?" This question helps the child to focus his thinking on the key idea. It also results in a sentence short enough to be useful rather than confusing at this beginning-to-read stage.

*All writing for children is done in a good form of manuscript. Easel writing can be done with either a small group or a whole class clustered on the floor around the teacher. The easel, with newsprint attached, is placed to the left if the teacher is right-handed, to the right if left-handed, and facing the children.

The teacher writes the sentence in manuscript at the top or bottom of Jimmy's picture, wherever space is available. (After this procedure becomes familiar, children may make a double fold 1½ to 2 inches wide at the bottom of their papers before painting to ensure space to write.) With the group watching, Mrs. Thomas runs her hand from left to right under the sentence as she reads it. If any of the children wish to read it, they may, of course, but she does not ask them to. Minor changes that do not seriously distort the meaning are accepted without comment. A feeling of success is far more important at this point than "correctness." After all, it is thoughts we hope children will read, not just words.

Now it is the next child's turn. If Susie has brought her new puppy modeled in clay, she tells about it and identifies the one most important thought, which Mrs. Thomas writes on a blank piece of newsprint that Susie can display under her puppy. The same basic process is continued until each has had a turn to share, to organize the thoughts that each had in mind during the project, to see a sentence recorded and hear it read back *just as he or she said it*. Each has experienced "This is what I say, and this is what it looks like." Each has also experienced this happening with the others. Such opportunities three or four times a week for each child lead sooner or later to the next step.

5. *Children begin to recognize individual words.* From the first day on, a child may point to a word the teacher has written and say, "I know what that says."

Teacher role. Taking dictation from a child who is beginning to recognize words, the teacher says each word, writes it, then finishes by reading the entire sentence. Parents and teachers often assume that, from the beginning, children recognize the one-to-one relationship between a spoken word and a written word. But there are no "white spaces" between words in talking, and a common

word like *table* is seldom spoken by itself. A parent says, "Get down *offthetable*." Children sometimes ask, "How do you spell *onceuponatime*?"

Though teachers may be tempted, it would be a mistake to bring together all those children who have arrived at the stage of recognizing separate words. Closed groups separate friends who want to work together and undermine the self-confidence of the child who is excluded. In a mixed group, the more advanced children provide a nonthreatening stimulus for advancement and gain self-confidence by helping others.

6. *Children begin to recognize individual letters.* A child points out a recognized letter.

Teacher role. For the child who has recognized a letter, the teacher says each letter, writes it, says each word, then ends by saying the sentence as a whole. More and more often, the children want to read along.

7. *Children begin to write by copying their own dictation.* At any time, perhaps within the first few days, a child will say before the teacher starts to write the dictation, "I can write that."

Teacher role. "Would you like to write it?" If Alice agrees, the teacher writes the sentence in good manuscript on a strip of paper prepared in advance for this purpose. The strip of paper is the same size as the space left for writing on the children's pictures. Alice takes the strip and her picture to her table. She places the strip above the writing space on her picture so that she can copy the sentence directly below. So Alice begins her own writing.

8. *Children initiate writing their own stories.* After children have copied their dictation for a time, they will be ready to start writing their own stories.

Teacher role. Following the child's first attempt at independent writing, the teacher needs to recognize progress and ignore mistakes. If George has left out a word, reading the story to his friend, small group, or teacher will help him to recognize the omission. He can be given any help he asks for, but no other help *at this time*. He has made a great forward step, and it is essential that he feel good about it.

Soon children's writing is being put together in books, and the books are made available for all the children to read. At the least show of interest, the authors will read their books to a child who cannot read them yet. Writings can be displayed on bulletin boards and walls, along with charts of related words that the children have requested for their use. The room becomes a verbal environment where each word or group of words is embedded in its own meaningful context, not isolated. As materials, equipment, and activities available to children provide opportunities for exploration, discovery, and desired learning, the writing and reading continue.

Since no pressure is put on children to perform, they can move ahead when they feel confident and back off for a while when they do not. They do not see this as failure because they are carrying out their own decisions. No two children's learnings are exactly the same, but the range and diversity demonstrates what is possible. Forward steps are accomplished easily and naturally, as preschool learnings were, as success builds confidence and the desire for further learning.

9. *Children find satisfaction in published books.* Some children have read children's stories even before they came to school. Now others have started to read them, and many more enjoy picture books and "easy" books with many pictures. Some "read" the pictures and tell a story based on the illustrations. Gradually, in the context of the story that the teacher or another child reads aloud, words become familiar. When a child's reading does not make sense or sound like language, another child may be able to interpret. Here is an ideal learning situation: a desire to know, an emerging competence, and on-the-spot assistance

from a friend. When children have learned to turn to their peers for help, the teacher has time to do things only a teacher can do. Providing help to others increases the confidence of children.

Teacher role. From the very beginning the teacher has been providing a variety of picture books and easy reading books for the library corner. New books added from time to time have been displayed. From now on, it is especially important to bring in fresh reading material frequently, for instance, every Monday morning. Expectancy builds up as children look for the new materials.

10. *Children continue to progress, at their own rate and in their own sequence.* The more children read, the more accurate and extended is their writing. Likewise, the more the children write, the more closely does their reading follow the text, and the more their reading becomes silent reading. They are increasingly likely to tell their friends about what they have read, rather than read it to them, particularly when silent reading has been encouraged.

Teacher role. Working with individuals, small groups, and the large group, the teacher continues to provide for discussion, ask provocative questions, and encourage interpretation of children's stories and published books and pictures (Lee, 1968). The teacher continues to expect (not require) daily reading and writing and provides time for it. The day's schedule is flexible enough so that children can continue these activities by choice. When the children get personal satisfaction from them, reading and writing increase naturally as children develop competence. Other experiences going on in the classroom and resources of various sorts available to the children generate interest. When children are bored, they ask, "What can I write about?" When they are stimulated, they say, "I want to write about that!" In stories read by the teacher, the beauty, fun, and stimulation of children's literature continue to provide experience

Summary of the Ten Stages of Reading Development

Developmental stages	Rationale	Skills	Attitudes	Evaluation
1. Adequate use of oral language.	We can read only what we can talk about.	Improve speaking and listening skills through meaningful conversation and discussion.	More satisfaction and confidence in communicating with others.	Teacher awareness of increased language ability and communication. Keep audiotapes, recorded at intervals, of each child's conversation.
2. Familiarity with books.	Books are a source of satisfaction and interest.	Begin acquiring implicit guides to choosing books.	See books as both interesting and meeting needs.	Increase in time spent with books. More requests for teacher to read. Chosen books give satisfaction.
3. Discussion leads to group story.	A beginning experience of seeing "talk written down."	Able to contribute to discussion focused on a topic.	What we say can be put down and read back.	Increased interest in and involvement with group stories. Contributes regularly to discussion and story. Recognition of specific words or phrases indicates especially early development.
4. Children dictate own stories in small groups.	Experience own "talk written down."	Conceptualize a thought developed through action, express it so it communicates, and focus on the main idea.	Feeling of competence and achievement, desire to tell experiences.	Increased ability to report thoughts and experiences so they communicate and to identify a significant aspect.
5. Identifies known words.	Words significant to that child will be learned quickly.	Identify a concept as a single word sufficiently meaningful to be recognized.	Increased confidence that child can find success in school.	Rate of increase in number of words recognized in context.
6. Identifies known letters.	Familiarity with writing leads to identification of separate parts.	Ability to perceive and focus on individual letters and identify consistently.	Increased confidence that child can find success in school.	Rate of increase in number and consistency of recognizing letters.
7. Makes commitment to copy dictated story.	Pride in own stories leads to desire for greater involvement.	Begins handwriting competence by copying at close range.	Willing to make commitment to take on new tasks because of self-confidence.	Frequency of offering to copy own dictation after first commitment.

Summary of the Ten Stages of Reading Development (continued)

Developmental stages	Rationale	Skills	Attitudes	Evaluation
8. Writes own stories.	Confidence gained basis for further desired competence.	Puts together conceptualizing, verbalizing, and recording on paper.	Satisfaction and increased involvement, increased positive self-concept.	Willingness to attempt writing own stories. Frequency of writing.
Concurrently, a. "Reads back" own stories.	Knows context, experienced event and statement of it.	Uses syntactic and semantic skills to express thought of both child's own and peers' stories.	a. Satisfaction and pride in accomplishment and competence of recording—retrieving.	Reads the thought, if not all exact words.
b. "Reads" peers' stories.	Can identify with stories of peers—key thought leads to key words.		b. Increased satisfaction in extending competence to peers' stories.	Reads the thought, if not all exact words.
9. Finds satisfaction in printed books.	Begins to recognize familiar words and phrases. Uses pictures to identify context.	Can identify thought by pictures and words recognized. Uses syntactic and semantic cues.	Self-confidence increased. Positive feeling for books and other printed material increased.	More often chooses books, reports to others and/or teacher on something in a book. More often chooses books, discusses content beyond pictures; more often stays with book to finish it.
10. Writing increases accuracy of reading. Reading increases accuracy of writing.	Must pay attention to each word and letter in writing. Becomes more observant in reading. Identifies more words in reading, and recognizes when writing looks right.	Writes what he/she can say, using syntax and determiners. As more aware of these, can use them in reading. Reading suggests new thoughts, new ways of using them in writing.	Satisfaction from more confidence in own knowledge.	Increase in consistency between recorded and spoken words. Increase in correct spelling and expression in writing.

with the sound of written language, a sound that differs from spoken language. Books become friends that are sources of excitement and pleasure and stimulate ideas for children's writing. Teachers can begin individual reading conferences with children who are reading and with those who want to talk about charts or tell stories from picture books.

Children who speak a different dialect

Many educators have searched for the best way to teach reading to children who speak a dialect significantly different from standard English. Unless children can speak some version of the English language with considerable ease and fluency, teachers should not expect them to learn to read in English. Instead, they should help the children to develop oral fluency in the English language. To a large extent the procedures described in this chapter solve the problem of dialect and of familiarity of content. Therefore, we recommend that all children with different dialects should be involved in the same experiences as other children learning to read.

These procedures can be used with children from low economic areas, blacks, Puerto Ricans, Chicanos, Indians, and others, who benefit from reading and writing material in their own dialect, rather than trying to learn to read the standard English of commercial reading materials (Baratz and Shuy, 1969; Halliday, 1971). Teachers can accept writing in dialect up to the point where children are beginning to edit. Now teachers can raise questions gradually, calling attention to how people write in books. Of course, standard spelling has been used from the beginning when the dialect has varied in pronunciation only.

Acceptance by teachers and other students is equally important to these children. When children feel rejected by teachers, they tend to reject their teachers in turn. Such damaged relationships make effective teaching virtually impossible. Problems other than dialect prevent black children from reading as well as they can. These problems "are closely connected with conditions of life that keep people out of school and the conditions of schools that keep people from learning to read in spite of ostensible efforts to teach them" (Torrey, 1970, pp. 253–254). Torrey sees the different speech patterns functioning as a low-status stigma implying association with a rejected culture:

> Our traditional cultural and linguistic imperialism has been self-defeating not only because it has failed to acculturate its more divergent elements, but also because it has prevented our nation as a whole from appreciating the true richness of its diverse heritage (Torrey, 1970, p. 259).

When teachers understand that the idiolects children bring to school are legitimate, well-developed languages that express a wide range of thoughts and feelings—languages that are different rather than deficient—teachers will accept them. They will accept the children themselves, learn to appreciate some of their divergencies, and help them broaden and enrich their use of language. Teachers' acceptance is the key factor in developing the children's success in learning what the school offers, including learning to read.

Continuing children's progress

To ensure the child's ongoing interest, teachers need to provide challenging questions to stimulate thinking, problems of personal significance to solve, and new things to watch, see, and handle. The child needs a can-do approach to learning, bolstered by emphasis on continuing success and increased independence and self-direction. Drummond and McIntire (1976) found that children's attitudes toward school and themselves were extremely important in increasing reading ability.

Teachers can note what children still need to learn without treating the children's work negatively or implying that the children should be doing better. When two or three children need the same kind of help, they can be brought together to discuss the issue and help each other, under the teacher's guidance. These brief seminars enable teachers to catch potential problems early and keep children moving in their development. The teacher saves time by working with several children but avoids the total class approach that dictates the learning for those who need it and wastes the time of those who do not.

Gradually the children's reading is broadened to include materials in content areas. As children mature they need help in deepening comprehension in all types of reading. Such wider reading builds new concepts, ideas, and vocabulary, and develops comprehension. Nonfiction requires different reading skills from fiction. All children need to understand this difference and learn to modify their reading according to the material and their purposes.

Reading conferences Reading conferences provide the teacher with evidence of progress, extend children's thinking in relation to reading, and provide the child with specific positive feedback. They may be as short as one minute, or as long as fifteen minutes. If the demand for these conferences creates a time problem, the teacher can initiate a procedure for signing up for them. If the child wishes, the reading and writing conferences can be combined. When the child finds value in the conference and it increases self-confidence, the space for conference sign-up is seldom empty.

When a certain child has not had a conference for some time, the teacher can initiate conversation about material the child is reading to find out the child's understanding of it, then suggest that the child sign up to report on current reading when finished. Perhaps the child is reading without any problems, so feels no need for a conference. However, children who do not ask for conferences may not be reading. Perhaps reading is not satisfying because they cannot find the kind of material they want to read. If so, such material can be added to the room library. Sometimes children set their expectations too high or feel pressure from home or peers to read more advanced material than they

are ready for. If they are having trouble reading what they want to read, children should have conferences at the first opportunity to reassure them and to explore for materials they can handle and will enjoy reading.

A quiet, fairly secluded corner where teacher and child can sit together comfortably is a better place for a conference than the teacher's desk. But short, informal conferences can be held anywhere the child and teacher can talk. Any important information can be recorded later.

The teacher can nearly always find evidence of increasing understanding and competence in the reading process. It is essential to give the child specific feedback on progress, not global statements, either positive or negative. The teacher should avoid negative comments about not reading smoothly, carelessness, and not trying, and admonitions such as "read for comprehension," "read faster," "sound out the words." The child needs specific help, not pressure to do what the teacher wants, which creates anxiety and makes the child less able than before. Consistent comments of a negative sort prevent progress and can even stop a child's attempts to improve.

In the conference, questions to extend children's thinking vary depending on what the child has offered. They may inquire about the content of the reading. When a child has read a difficult or unusual phrase or word, one might say, "That was a special word [or phrase]. How did you know it?" or "How did you figure it out?" These questions help some children. If a child seems confused by a certain type of question, he or she is not ready for it, and the question should be reinterpreted or delayed.

Record keeping As soon as dictation of stories starts, the teacher needs to begin keeping individual reading records, which may be combined with records of the child's writing. Record indications of understanding and ability in reading. Note progress made in oral language—talking more comfortably with peers, telling more about activities engaged in, using more expanded speech and fewer mazes. An increase in requests to dictate titles or stories, more time spent with peers' stories and with books (within desirable limits), reading snatches of stories to peers, and asking for their help in reading are all indications of progress at this point.

If the child wishes to read to you orally and does it well, it is still necessary to check on his or her understanding of the meaning. If there is no comprehension problem, give the youngster recognition for real progress. If the child cannot discuss the meaning reasonably well, he or she is not reading but naming words. Note any indication of word calling: saying words with equal emphasis and pitch, saying words that make the sentence meaningless or not syntactically understandable. Such indicators show that the child needs immediate help to focus on gaining meaning.

Note any failure to correct, or attempt to correct, a miscue that either does not make sense or does not sound like language. As soon as it is clear that Sarah is not going to attempt a correction (when she has finished the story or stopped reading), question her about miscues that do not make sense or sound right. "I'm sorry, I don't think I understood what happened when_____." If the child said one thing and thought another, she may be able to explain the meaning. If she seems confused, ask her to tell about the story or topic of her reading. Her response will tell you how meaningful her reading has been.

When only a particular section has caused confusion, the teacher can suggest that she read it to herself to see if she can figure out the meaning. Sarah may see the problem immediately, or pinpoint the part that confused her. It may be a construction she does not understand, or a word or phrase to which she can bring no meaning. She needs help, and the cause of her confusion should be noted in the record.

If she can tell very little about the material read, the teacher may say something like this: "It can't be much fun reading something that doesn't make much sense to you. Would you like to choose a different book?" If Sarah agrees, then ask, "Is there anything you would especially like to read about? Maybe I can help you find something."

Freedom from assigned reading When children have been in a teacher-controlled situation for several years, they may have temporary problems in making good use of more freedom of choice. Many teachers are fearful that unless tasks are set, assignments made, certain so-called levels of reading required, children will stay at a minimum level. On the contrary, the rigidity of levels and prescribed "must do" tiny steps of progress often serve to keep the children at levels below their potential achievement. We have only to consider children's activities in an uncontrolled situation, such as after school, to observe their own continuous press for further accomplishment when they get satisfaction from the activity and have a measure of confidence that they can succeed.

If assigned reading has been too burdensome, children may retreat to far easier material. Even if this regression persists for some time, it is important not to comment. Any direct attempt to steer these children to more difficult reading is more likely to prolong their reluctance to move ahead. Eventually they will choose more advanced material because of boredom with the simpler concepts in the easier books, friends' recommendations of books, and involvement in interests and projects that require more information or suggest related materials.

Some children persist in choosing books that are too difficult for normal reading. They may want to bolster their self-concept as good readers. But perhaps they have never experienced comfortable reading since all assigned reading has been difficult for them. When these children notice that peers who read well enjoy "fun" books such as Dr. Seuss, they will decide it is not degrading to read easy books. We all need a wide variety of reading. Thus, children should not be told that a book they have chosen is too easy or too hard.

Jim had been in the first grade for two years, but as a second grader he still was not reading well. Yet one morning he chose a book on national parks that was difficult enough to be at a frustration level. When he asked for help with a word, the helper said, "Read the rest of the sentence and see if you can figure it out." Jim's oral reading was slow and irregular, but he made a successful try at the unfamiliar word. The helper asked, "How do you like reading that book?" Jim beamed and replied that his folks were planning a camping trip, and he wanted to learn about the parks they might visit. Jim was reading the book independently and getting something that he wanted from it. It was appropriate instructional material for he improved his recognition skills in response to the helper's question.

After lunch the teacher noticed that Jim was reading a much simpler book. Commenting on the change in books, Jim explained, "Yeah, now I'm resting." This incident clearly illustrates that he felt reading the book on parks was hard work, but it was satisfying because it provided information of value to him. If the book had been assigned, we can be sure he would not have persisted so long nor have gotten very much out of it. Teachers who limit the range of independent reading material would never have permitted him to try. Few people gain from new material all there is to be understood and reacted to. To prevent anyone from exploring material because of its difficulty cannot be condoned. Jim's struggles with the book on national parks helped him learn to read, but only because he chose it and had a definite purpose in reading it.

Developing reading skill

Children discover many important learnings on their own and do not need explanations. This extremely important fact is often ignored. In fact, explanations may be more hindrance than help. People of all ages learn implicitly and use their learning effectively but never verbalize it either to themselves or others. An explanation in someone else's terms may make children feel there is something further they must learn, instead of realizing that they are already using their own procedures effectively. Engaging in such explanations, especially with young children, may create confusion, disturb the operation of implicit understanding, and leave the individual less capable than before.

Therefore, it is important to find out partly through listening to children read, but mainly through talking with them about what they have read, which specific abilities they already use effectively and which they do not. If they understand what they read and feel comfortable about it, they are probably better left alone to gain greater precision gradually through much reading. As we are finding out, children learn to read by reading, especially when they get satisfaction from it. If children are bothered by some aspect of their reading or have consistent problems, then teachers may be able to expand the tools and cues children already use in getting meaning. As appropriate, teachers will help them expand and deepen their understanding of the meaning of the material.

Reading readiness

The term *reading readiness* was first used in relation to the child's stage of development as it affected the ability to learn to read. Educators developed reading readiness tests, which teachers gave to children entering school to predict each child's success in learning to read in the first grade. While such procedures were partially successful, test results were often used in unacceptable ways. Teachers often assigned children to classrooms or to groups within a classroom on the basis of the scores. Neither the reliability of test scores nor the relationship of scores with end-of-year success was high enough to make scores for individuals valid for such placement. Furthermore, we know that the teacher's expectancy of the child's success or failure could have increased the relationship of the test scores to the child's final accomplishment at year's end. Among the low scorers, low expectancy leads to low achievement!

Some schools are still giving such tests, but many have dropped them. Another test, essentially a reading readiness test, is used fairly extensively, especially in inner-city or ghetto schools, and particularly with bilinguals and children speaking a nonstandard dialect. The test's stated purpose is to identify "high-risk" children—that is, those children least likely to be successful in a regular school program. To the extent the self-fulfilling prophecy operates, children so identified will have problems. These children are grouped together with no peer models of successful experience or enthusiasm for school learning.

An outgrowth of the concept of readiness was the production of materials to help the child "get ready." These materials, as well as the tests, made explicit the skills and knowledge educators felt children should have in order to begin reading. By analyzing the tests and materials, one can get a reasonably good idea what their authors considered the reading process to be—word naming.

While the early and current use of the term *reading readiness* usually relates to the beginning reader, the idea has grown that readiness is a continuous process. Each person may be considered ready or not ready for any certain prescribed learning in any area. The issue is largely based on the concept of a particular and necessary sequence of learning. Since that concept is being questioned widely, the concept of readiness has lost some of its value. Also, when children can exercise choice in their learning, readiness is no longer an issue. They learn what they are ready to learn, because they select that which is meaningful to them!

Since all school children have achieved some of the prelearning needed to begin reading, the only realistic way to find out when a child will start to read is to provide that child with opportunities to begin reading, without pressure, and see what happens. Only if a child is to be placed in a pre-structured program does anyone need to know whether the child is "ready." The purpose of careful placement in a highly structured program would be to prevent failure because of the child's inability to meet requirements. Such early failure can do great damage by discouraging a child from

making further attempts at learning to read. Similarly, placing children in a prescribed program that is well below their current ability, may turn them away from any desire to read, at least at school.

A student in one of our classes was asked to tutor a boy during the spring of his first grade year. She selected a number of attractive library books written for beginners. She was talking with him about the pictures when he started reading the sentences under them. Surprised, she said, "Your teacher told me you couldn't read!" His indignant response was, "You don't think I'm going to read that baby stuff, do you?"

Engel (1976) believes teachers should develop the "I's" as a most effective way of developing interest and desire to read. The "I's" she suggests are image (self), initiative, imagination, inquisitiveness, industriousness, interaction, independence, and interest. The broad determiners of a child's readiness for reading are maturational factors, previous experiencing, the kind of reading program offered, and the teaching procedures used. Tests are investigating only certain factors such as visual discrimination, which may be useful in a certain type of reading program but seems to have relatively little importance for learning to read. The best predictors are those tasks that are most similar to the reading process itself (McGinitie, 1969). A number of studies of ways of building readiness have shown little if any positive effect (1) of instruction in specific cognitive skills and conceptual competence designed to develop abilities necessary to read and understand whole sentences and paragraphs and to make associations necessary to grasp a whole thought (Stank, 1973); (2) of training that rests heavily on transfer effects to reading skills (Pryzwansky, 1972); or (3) of training in auditory discrimination or word recognition (Dykstra, 1962).

Another study compared a kindergarten group receiving daily training in a basal reader program with a group of kindergartners provided with significant content materials, allowed to utilize language freely, and encouraged to develop a general reading readiness attitude, but with no

WRITTEN LANGUAGE: RECORDING AND RETRIEVING THOUGHTS

teacher expectancy of any specific learning. No difference was found between the groups on auditory discrimination and letter knowledge, despite the daily training in these factors in the basal reading group. Further, the informal conceptual language group had higher scores on visual discrimination of word forms, and more general readiness for reading according to readiness test scores at the end of kindergarten (O'Donnell, 1968).

The decision in advance that certain children are "high risk" candidates for learning to read, and subsequent treatment of them as such, cannot help but provide negative feedback. A far more positive approach, and one with more chance of success, is to assume that all children can and will learn to read. Children will do it in slightly different ways and in their own time. Then teachers provide the best learning situation they can, one with wide open opportunity and no pressure, one that allows operation of the child's natural desire to learn.

How children can use phonics

There is overwhelming evidence that many children learn to read well with no explicit instruction in phonics. When we realize how effectively all children discover how oral language works, through their experiencing, it is certainly possible and quite probable that they also discover how written language works. They cannot explain the first and, for the same reasons, cannot explain the second, but in neither case do they need it made explicit.

Many children learn the phonics they need in their own way through reading. Those who have already begun to read books and who have not yet discovered a sound-symbol relationship can be *led to figure it out*. This exploration may begin by seeing that many words that start with the same sound start with the same letter when written; or it may begin by discovering that many words that look alike at the beginning start with the same sound. Instead of working with word beginnings, children may work with words that rhyme, but

they need to realize there are many more exceptions with word endings. In some cases familiar sight words are used to assist the learner with other words that are phonetically similar. The child who knows *cat* and the sound that *b* represents (too often given as *buh*!) can read the word *bat*, but must always check to see that the sentence then makes sense and sounds like language. An effective use of the sound-symbol relationship for children learning to read in this type of program is to predict an unrecognized word from context and then look to see if the beginning letter or letters check out.

Children should be led to thinking about sound-symbol relationships within the context of what they are reading at that moment. Children should then be encouraged to make other similar discoveries on their own. When children find a way to help themselves get meaning they are striving for, that procedure will be significant to them. They will be able to use it and understand what they are doing. Often instruction or explanation by adults does *not* lead to understanding, nor to transfer to use in reading.

Phonic generalizations Phonic generalizations should be suggested to children only in reading conferences or small groups of children who need this kind of help. Unlike the simple sound-symbol relationship, generalizations would not be discussed in a reading situation. As children mature and their reading includes a more extensive vocabulary with contexts less relevant to their own experience, they may need and will be able to use more complex generalizations. By this time their thinking will be operational.

At this point it is important for the teacher to be aware that all phonic generalizations are not equally valuable. Working with primary grades, Clymer (1963) carried out research into the validity and consistency of the more important phonic rules. His study has been replicated by Bailey (1967), who extended it through grade six. They researched the same forty-five most commonly proposed generalizations. Clymer suggests that only eighteen of these are useful, while Bailey feels only six are simple to understand and apply, have few exceptions, and are applicable to large numbers of words.

One group of generalizations is useful only after children have learned to pronounce the words. These are rules that specify vowel sounds in accented syllables, and so help more with correct pronunciations of known words than with identifying unrecognized words. Because the application of a generalization to a new situation is still difficult for most fourth graders, Clymer raises the question of which generalizations primary children can apply in working out the pronunciation of unknown words.

Since the aim and purpose of phonics is helping children pronounce unknown words, those studies indicate the importance of careful selection of which rules to teach. We believe the following generalizations are usually helpful:

1. Words that look the same at the beginning often start the same way when spoken. Comparing an unrecognized word with one already known may provide the extra bit of needed information. One does not use this rule to "sound out" a word, but to check whether the word that seems to fit syntactically and semantically could be the word appearing in print, or to suggest a cue to an unrecognized word. This generalization is most useful when the child compares two words in which the first consonant and the following vowel have the same sounds. *Bat* can be compared to *band* but not to *barn, baby, bee, big, bone,* or *bun.*

2. Words rhyme when the last few letters are the same (*sent, bent,* and *rent*). This cue is less useful in reading but more useful in spelling in the beginning stages of writing or in writing first drafts.

3. Suffixes and prefixes are usually pronounced consistently. When suffixes in plurals and verb endings cause difficulties, children can be led to discover how they work. Problems with these endings are usually due to dialects that do not use these forms. In this case teachers should wait until children are mature and confident enough to accept the difference in dialects, then explain the suffixes so that children can make a conscious choice of which dialect to use.

At more advanced levels recognition of other suffixes and of prefixes can be helpful in both reading and writing. *Re-* as a prefix meaning *again* (*rewrite, retell*) and *un-* as a prefix meaning *not* (*until, unharmed*) are helpful both in clarifying meaning and in recognizing words. Children can learn to use prefixes in their writing to provide variety of expression. A group can play with other modifiers, making comparative and superlative forms (*short, shorter, shortest; happy, happier, happiest*). By manipulating such words, children can see how modifiers work. Children can also look for suffixes that change the use of words: *build, builder, building; drive, driving, driver, driven; beauty, beautiful, beautifully; satisfy, satisfaction, satisfactory.*

4. When monosyllables end in *e,* the first vowel is long and the *e* is silent. Perhaps the most consistent and most useful phonic generalization is the change in pronunciation between one-syllable words that differ only by the addition of a final silent *e.* Here again children can experiment by playing with words: *fin, fine; bit, bite; hat, hate; not, note; cut, cute.* When they can write and pronounce nonsense pairs, such as *hab, habe,* they really understand how the generalization works.

The relatively recent identification of the *schwa,* written ə, has had a significant effect on phonics as originally taught. It is the sound represented by *any* vowel in an unaccented syllable: the *a* in *ago,* the *e* in *agent,* the *i* in *sanity,* the *o* in *comply,* and the *u* in *focus.* The schwa has great effect on the use of phonics in reading and writing, for there is no way to identify such a vowel through sound. It also affects pronunciation. In the two previous sentences notice the use of *effect* and *affect*; the first is a noun and the second a verb, but there is no difference in their pronunciation. With the same pronunciation but different meaning, *effect* can also be a verb. When *affect* is a noun, however, the first syllable is accented, which changes the pronunciation of *a*. This example shows that the structure of the sentence, the syntactical and semantic cues, are the useful ones, for both pronunciation and meaning.

Structural analysis The division of words into syllables is another way of attacking unrecognized words. The idea is that when confronted with only one syllable at a time, the child can handle it. The concept is valid in some instances. However, English does not always follow the rules of syllabification any better than it follows the phonic rules. Also, dictionary identification of syllables does not consistently follow the separation of syllables as used in speech. For instance *joker* is divided *jok•er*, separating the suffix from the base *joke*, but pronouncing it as *jo'•ker*.

A rule that is consistent is that each syllable must have a vowel. Other sometimes helpful generalizations are that when a vowel is followed by a double consonant, syllables are broken between the consonants, but when the vowel is followed by a single consonant, the break is after the vowel. Then syllables ending in a vowel are called "open" syllables (in which case the vowel is long), and those ending in a consonant are "closed" (and the vowel is short). It does not take long to find exceptions to these generalizations. Examples are *val•en•tine*, which according to the rule should be *va•len•tine*. Also *de•nom•i•na•tor* by rule should be *de•no•mi•na•tor*, and thus pronounced differently.

Context clues

A reader can pronounce a word without knowing what it means. Whether or not the child is able to say the unknown word, meaning can be inferred from context clues. The reader simply reads on to look for clues in the normal redundancy and the general context, along with syntactical cues.

Specific cues may include a definition or description of what is referred to by the unknown word. Or the word may be one of a series, such as "millions, and billions, and *trillions* of cats." Modifying phrases and clauses or comparisons and contrasts are other clues to look for. Also helpful are familiar-word associations, such as "smoke goes up the *chimney*" or "the car's *engine* would not start." Any pattern within a sentence, paragraph, or selection is another help. Ames (1966) has classified some twelve contextual aids with examples. (See Appendix E.)

Streib (1976) finds that the difference between the ability of the educable mentally retarded and the average child to utilize context seems to be quantitative rather than qualitative. This finding has great implications for it means these retarded children can be encouraged to use context cues. Ehri (1976) finds that context-dependent words are especially hard to learn as isolated units.

Extending reading competence

As children continue writing and reading materials of their own choosing, basic control over these processes is attained relatively quickly, particularly when the attainment and expression of meaning, rather than the vocalizing of words, has been the thrust of the program. As they read longer selections, the context increasingly helps the child predict what comes next. The redundancy of all writing alerts readers to a miscue, sends them back to find their error, and helps them correct it.

In a program with self-selection of reading materials rather than teacher-assigned materials, children *want* to gain the meaning of what they read. Many educators have believed that children do not care about getting meaning from their reading and read only to fulfill the requirements of the teacher. This problem may occur in a traditional program, but virtually never do children in a free-selection program read unless they are doing it for enjoyment or to search for desired information, and in either case meaning is essential.

Learning to choose books

When children start choosing their own reading materials, they are likely to scan what is available and pick up whatever attracts them. With more experience, they begin to think what kind of material or type of book they want to read. If they have enjoyed a story, they may want to find similar fiction. When children are aware of authorship, they soon have favorite authors and begin to identify them by style and type of story.

Teachers can stimulate this awareness by: (1) discussing books in relation to their authors, (2) introducing material by different authors and characterizing their work, (3) sharing portions of books along with information about their authors, and (4) developing an awareness of individual authors as people with interests and concerns of their own. Helping children to think of authors as "ordinary people who write" enables them to identify with authors as they write their own stories.

Various guides help children learn to select content material. When a group or the total class is involved in a project, the teacher can bring a collection of appropriate materials into the classroom. Individuals interested in certain topics can learn to use book titles, tables of contents, and indexes in selecting relevant material. The next step is learning how to find such material in the library. School libraries have the responsibility of helping children feel competent in locating what they want. A child who feels at home, successful, and happy in the library has gone a long way toward becoming a lifelong reader.

Planning based on purpose

In order to achieve maximum comprehension, readers must be aware of the purposes for reading. When we know what we expect to get from our reading, we recognize the type of material we need and make our reading plans. The plan may be well thought out or implicitly assumed, but without any plan we would read all material in the same way—which is what many people do. By learning to plan their own reading, teachers can help children learn to read with purpose.

Among the *purposes* children can recognize are

(1) to follow the story line, (2) to search for a particular topic, (3) to get the author's point of view, (4) to find specific information, (5) to explore and enjoy the way a particular author develops characterization, or (6) to work through material to clarify new concepts. Instead of reading the same way to accomplish these very different purposes, the reader needs to scan, skim, read rapidly, read intensively, or in some cases stop, consider, and perhaps locate passages to reread.

Next, children need to *select the material* to read in terms of their purposes. If their purpose is enjoyment, they select some type of fiction or nonfiction in a field of special interest. When they desire more information about a topic, they select nonfiction from that area. When they are searching for something to read, they may recognize that a selection meets one of their continuing purposes.

Now that they have their purpose in mind and the materials at hand, they *choose appropriate reading skills*. Do they read rapidly to follow the story? Do they skim, scan, or sample to find what they want? Or do they read deeply and thoughtfully, perhaps reread, to digest the content?

The final step is *evaluation* of this particular reading session. Children need to ask themselves: Was the material relevant to my purpose? Do I need to continue with this material at another time? Do I search out other related materials by the same author on the same topic, or follow a new lead? Or on the other hand, have I satisfied my immediate purpose? Next time do I want to vary my purpose or my selection of material? Even more important, was my selection of reading skills effective? Did I waste time by too detailed reading, or did I try to read too rapidly? Do I understand what I read?

When children express interest in a particular topic, teachers can begin helping them learn to select materials in relation to their purposes. At first a few individual children may explain why they choose content materials instead of storybooks for their conferences. When several children are making such choices and more nonfiction books are brought into the room library, children can discuss the relationship of purposes and materials: One book provides an overall familiarity with the topic, and another is more detailed. When a few children contribute such ideas, others become aware of possibilities.

Deepening comprehension

The first level of comprehension is the literal meaning of the materials children read. Most of the questions teachers ask are of this nature: "Where did Billy go? What did his dog do? How did Nancy help Billy?" Such questions are helpful, first to ensure a literal understanding of the story, and second to refresh children's memory of the story line. But from the very beginning teachers need to ask questions about issues that are deeper than literal meaning. This deepening of comprehension is the teacher's most important responsibility.

Moving beyond literal meaning, teachers can ask children to think about how the character felt or how they would feel in the story situation. The next step is to consider what the happening in the story means. Very early in the reading process, children can draw inferences from material that is simple and clear. As children mature, they learn to "read between the lines." What is implied may be more important than what is stated. What was the author's purpose?

These questions lead to the next step, reading "behind the lines." What is the author's background? What can we find out about the author's experiences, enthusiasms, dedication? When was this material written, and what were the circumstances of the author's life at that time? Subtle implications of the story may reflect historical events and the mood of the country during that period.

If children are to develop full comprehension, they need significant material to read. The depth and richness of the material should reach each child at the growing edge of understanding, where growth can take place. Reading that is challenging is more stimulating and more fun than material that is superficial. If children feel free to lay aside reading that is too difficult, no harm can be done.

Reading flexibility When the emphasis is on meaning rather than naming words, many children develop a variety of reading procedures on their own, but others need help to acquire flexibility. Small groups of young children, using the same easily read material, can practice *skimming* to find where the material mentions a name or a subject. They then discuss how they found it.

A somewhat older group can *scan* several pages to discover the kind of information a book or periodical provides under each section heading. Again, children's discussion of the process they used to find information they wanted helps other children become aware of possibilities.

Intensive reading develops most frequently among children nine and above. For this purpose the children need to be sincerely interested in finding out more about their topic, and able to use a relatively high level of writing that contains detailed information. Discussion starts with what the group, a relatively small one, already knows about the topic. The children then read a paragraph or short section silently at normal reading speed. The teacher asks what the first sentence tells, and the content is listed on the board or a chart in a few key words. The meaning of each sentence is added in turn. At the end of the paragraph or section, the recorded ideas can be reviewed and summarized. The key words of the summary can then be recorded in a separate list. This procedure can be followed throughout the entire selection. Finally the teacher asks, "What do we know now about this topic that we did not know before?"

After children have learned to take the various steps on their own, they can modify this procedure to suit their individual needs and learning styles. Many will be able to accomplish their purposes in a single thoughtful reading without making notes. Others will prefer to make notes, and some may need to stay with the total process for some time. As individual children internalize the conscious use of an appropriate plan for reading—quick and informal or studied and written out—they can be left to their own way of working. Their independence permits the teacher to work more closely with those who still need help.

Understanding sentence structures One of the comprehension skills often needed, but seldom made explicit, is understanding a variety of sentence structures. Children have difficulty with sentence patterns unlike their own and those they are accustomed to hearing and reading. Research indicates that many upper-grade students have difficulty in recognizing sentence transformations with equivalent meanings, and also in identifying the kernel in a long sentence (Marcus, 1971).

The indirect object is one of the grammatical structures that causes problems. While 91 percent of the subjects in a research study correctly interpreted "She brought the cat a fish," only 74 percent understood "He brought the woman her son." Sentences with relative clauses cause trouble: In "The boy to whom she gave the rabbit climbed through a hole in the fence," only 59 percent correctly identified the kernels in both clauses. As various sentence patterns become more familiar, children can learn to clarify interpretations through discussion with the teacher, or with peers who have read the material.

Cues of relationship Another comprehension skill is recognizing cues that indicate relationships within a sentence, of one sentence to another, and of paragraphs within a selection. Children can become aware of sequences, both within a sentence and between sentences, and of the special linking words or phrases that enable the reader to follow the author's thinking. Many children need help to recognize the relationships indicated by *anaphoric forms*, which are words used as regular grammatical substitutes for preceding words or phrases. Examples are *it* and *do* in the sentence, "He likes it, and I do, too." Recognizing the referents for such words is essential for comprehension. Un-

derstanding the significance of such linkages is an important skill that some children pick up intuitively, but others do not.

One procedure that alerts readers to such linkages is "scrambled sentences." The teacher chooses a well-constructed paragraph and lists the sentences in random order. The children arrange the sentences in a meaningful sequence and explain how they decided on it. Other sequences would be possible by changing the wording. Children can analyze the changes that would be needed and explain how these changes signal linkages or relationships between ideas.

Writing is an even more valuable way of becoming aware of the linkages in language. Struggling to make thoughts clear, a child can learn to see the usefulness of transitions and linking words and phrases. When peers question the interrelationships of thoughts in a child's writing, the entire group can profit from the discussion.

Children can learn to recognize the purpose of a paragraph. They can identify the topic sentence, which may be at the beginning, at the end, or somewhere within the paragraph. They will then recognize the poorly written paragraph that lacks a consistent focus or purpose.

Function signals Function signals take the place of nonverbal cues that aid comprehension in face-to-face communication. Recognizing these devices increases the reader's comprehension. One example is the function signal that tells how the writer feels about the content. The verb *may* in sentences like "I may be able to go" indicates that the writer is uncertain. Similar expressions that compensate for the absence of tone of voice and facial expression are *it is possible*, *it is likely*, *it is certain*, and *it is necessary*. Lacking the feedback that is available in verbal communication, the writer uses another type of function signal to ensure that an unknown reader will understand the communication. Definitions and introductory statements are examples of this second type of function signal.

Maintaining contact with the reader is the function of phrases such as *in short*, *we may say*, or *in*

Reprinted by permission of the Chicago Tribune-New York News Syndicate.

other words. The redundancy of summaries serves the same purpose. The use of *we* and *you* increases identification with the reader. The direct involvement of the reader in thinking or acting increases understanding through the reader's own intracommunication.

Critical reading Young children can begin to read critically by making judgments about the value of the material they read. They can ask "Do I enjoy reading it?" and "Do I think it is worth reading?" From the very beginning children need to realize that reading is not an end in itself. When they enjoy what they read and gain value from it, they will become readers—not just people who know how to read.

Among older children critical reading involves making judgments about the reliability and validity of the material, its accuracy, fairness, and lack of bias. Both the writer and the reader have perceptions and beliefs based on experience. When the writer states a point of view and explains the rationale, readers have a basis to rethink their own beliefs. The reader can then decide how well the writer defends the position. Testing the writer's rationale against other points of view is a high-level reading-thinking skill.

Most advertising copywriters make statements without providing any rationale. Ads use attractive models to imply by association that the prod-

uct will improve the readers' health or make them lovable and sought after by people of importance. Many consumers lay aside their critical reading skills under the pressure of such persuasion. Children can be helped to identify the propaganda in advertising claims.

Of prime importance is the skill of reading to detect one's own bias and deal with it objectively. Readers may be so highly biased that they skip, deride, or ignore a point of view different from their own. They adopt the slogan "My mind's made up—don't confuse me with the facts." During busing for integration of schools, for example, children in a particular school may be unable to accept any positive information about the children being bused in.

When teachers generate discussion by asking pertinent questions, the need for critical reading skills becomes apparent to the children, and less direct instruction is needed. Since it is impossible to predict when a child will be ready for critical reading skills, teachers can provide opportunities for children to become aware of them as an integral part of reading. In order to make valid judgments, readers need the extended comprehension skills that develop over time as a result of thinking and experiencing. Although many people acquire critical reading skills without direct instruction, teachers must not take their acquisition for granted.

Reading for enjoyment of fiction The child's capacity to enjoy fiction can be enhanced by increasing awareness of the many factors to appreciate: the story line, character development, wording that stimulates visualization, the rhythm and flow of language, and techniques used to build the suspense that glues the reader to the story until the very end.

The author who understands human needs, desires, and motivations can enrich understanding by making characters live. Too often this aspect of good literature has not been introduced until the later years of high school or even until college. But preschoolers enjoy the characters they meet in stories, and talking about them in simple terms begins to build a deep and continuing appreciation.

Young children are not able to make a detailed analysis of the stories they hear or read. Nor should they feel they *ought to* state what they like about a story. But the opportunity to volunteer comments increases their awareness and their willingness to express feelings about what they have read. This exploration of reactions occurs when the teacher meets with a group who are reading the same book, and opens avenues for discussion. If the atmosphere is stimulating but comfortable, children will become lifelong readers.

Oral reading

Nearly all reading specialists disapprove of the common practice of "round-robin reading"—asking children who have read a story silently to take turns reading a page or a paragraph aloud in the reading circle (Hosey, 1977). In a program that stresses silent reading and reading to achieve meaning, any oral reading that occurs must serve a purpose. Occasionally children read aloud to themselves as an aid to concentration. Often they wish to share a selection with a teacher or a friend, but the chief purpose of oral reading is to share a written selection for the appreciation of a known audience.

Oral reading is more difficult than silent reading because it requires all the skills of silent reading plus the skills of oral interpretation. The first criterion of good oral presentation is conveying the "message" clearly. The group will establish other criteria and add to the list from time to time. One of the first is consideration of the audience, both in selection of the material and in its presentation. Readers can strive for a reasonable amount of eye-contact and pleasant speaking voices that can be heard by all members of the audience. Voices project better when the book or paper is held high enough so that the reader looks at the audience, rather than at the floor. A comfortable, natural reading position relaxes both the reader and the audience.

Since meaning is conveyed as much through intonation as through words, teachers need to be aware of it in children's reading from the beginning. As Lefevre (1968) has pointed out, intonation is not something one teaches, but that occurs naturally in speech from the earliest years. Only when a reader is encouraged to read meaning instead of words is he able to use his voice naturally to interpret that meaning. Encouragement might take the form of asking the child to look away from the book and tell you what it says. Or a group might play a story with each character producing the thoughts necessary to carry the story line. (Incidentally, this is a very useful procedure for evaluating the understanding of the material they have read.)

Natural intonation is hindered when children interpret oral reading as naming words. This occurs when teachers correct miscues and expect 100 percent accuracy in all oral reading. Neither is it helpful to tell children to "read with expression," for it provides no specific guidance.

Many teachers are reluctant to forgo routine oral reading in class. They ask, "How will we know that the children can read?" When reading is gaining meaning, oral reading does not provide the answer—but talking about what they have read silently can. Neither does oral reading indicate whether children have "prepared their lessons" because some can read better without any preparation than others who have preread the material several times. If they are not reading, they need to choose material that promises to be more interesting.

A successful oral reading experience before their peers can build the readers' self-confidence and self-esteem. A useful way of accomplishing it is to ask children to prepare something for oral reading once a month. The child may choose to read to a group of special friends, the whole class, or even children in another classroom. The reader accepts the responsibility for providing a valuable experience for the listeners and selects material with their interests or needs in mind. After selecting the material through silent reading, the child tries reading it aloud in a place where the audience cannot hear the selection—perhaps at home or in the hall at school. A particularly useful form of preparation is taping the material and listening to the tape. The selection can be recorded as often as necessary, until the child is satisfied. When children are ready they sign up on a list on the bulletin board and on the appointed day reap the rewards of their effort. Such an experience once a month has led to far more improvement in oral reading than reading around the circle every day.

Reading level

A child's reading level may be stated specifically as a score on a standardized test or more generally in terms of graded reading texts that the child can read. There are disadvantages to all standardized tests: The time limits discriminate between the one who reacts rapidly and the more deliberate student; extraneous factors, such as not feeling well, broken pencil points, and unrelated disturbances, affect results; and anxiety about the test is a handicap to some people. Because of its aura of authority and its precise numerical form, the test score often carries more weight than it should. Another disadvantage, usually not considered, is the low statistical reliability of an individual score. Most group tests provide a fairly accurate estimate of the groups' ability, but the score of any individual should be viewed with caution. Most teachers

have not had the technical training to recognize the significance of this factor.

To determine a child's reading level through graded books, teachers almost invariably have the child read aloud. This means that it is oral reading that is tested, rather than the thought-gaining process. The usual procedures call for the child to read a short selection from a teacher-selected reader with which the child is not familiar. The errors are counted: omitted words, added words, unrecognized words, miscalled words. The number of such errors indicates whether the material is at the independent, the instructional, or the frustration level for the child. Depending on the number of errors the child makes on the first selection, the teacher presents material of increasing or decreasing difficulty until the instructional level is indicated.

Let us look at this process in light of our current knowledge about reading. First, reading a short selection does not enable the child to predict by building a context for the thoughts. Second, miscue analysis shows that the better the readers understand the material, the more miscues they are likely to make. They may add, omit, or change order of words without change in meaning. When all "errors" are counted, the teacher may consider them reading at frustration level. Anxiety in the testing situation also may affect their performance.

Because all of these factors may make any designation false, and since an incorrect designation of reading level can do irreparable harm, we recommend that these measures not be used. What children gain from reading depends on their purposes, their familiarity with the concepts involved, and specific reading skills required by different types of material. Fiction and reference material require different reading skills. For this reason, the difficulty of the material may vary widely as the child changes purposes or gains more experience. Another type of material supposedly of equal difficulty may show a significantly different reading level for a particular child.

In the type of natural learning program compatible with current understanding of the development of reading competence, we see no need for using the concept of reading level in teaching. Authors of books and materials for children need to be aware of the directness and simplicity of statements, the level of abstraction, and sentence patterns consistent with those of the target audience. These factors should be kept reasonably consistent with the concept level, the complexity of ideas. Teachers also need to be aware of these factors as they select reading materials in all content areas for their classrooms. To estimate the concept level, they need to keep in mind the experiential backgrounds of children in their area.

If children select their own books and can decide to read them or return them whenever they wish, they usually read a wide variety in content and/or in level of difficulty over a period of time.

Vocabulary control in children's reading materials keeps the vocabulary in children's books so far below the child's own daily use of words that it makes the material seem unnatural, watered down, and babyish. Because of the necessity to build sentences, the writer uses a large proportion of structure words to content and action words, which makes the material more difficult to read. The actual, significant vocabulary control is within each child. When children are dictating their own first reading material, they will not use words or sentences that are not significant for them. When they begin reading printed material, they will choose and stay with that material that has meaning for them. Thus, there is no reason for the arbitrary vocabulary control used in most readers.

The development of children's vocabularies is a matter of normal life experiences. They constantly hear words they do not use. As these words acquire meaning, they add them to their repertoire just as they have done since babyhood. The more children read and the wider the selection of their books, the more different words they encounter and eventually begin to use. In introducing new concepts, teachers can emphasize words unfamiliar to the children, write them on the board, and encourage children to use them. All projects carried on both in and out of school introduce special terminology. Writing can encourage the use of a wider variety of words. "Exciting" words, synonyms and antonyms, and base words with all their derivatives can be listed on charts. The teacher's attitude of interest in different words and phrases encourages the children's interest. The least useful procedure is a vocabulary lesson in which an arbitrarily selected list of words is presented and discussed. Children need experience with the concepts before new words can be internalized.

Summary

The *natural way of learning to read* builds on what children already know and can do, on their natural ways of learning that are so successful in their preschool and out-of-school hours, on their implicit knowledge of language and how it works, and on each child's own background of experience. This way of learning is supported by recent research that provides a totally new way of understanding how children learn to read. The essential purpose of reading is to understand the author's thought. Children acquire meaning primarily through the structure of the language and secondarily by the specific words used. Therefore, as they look at written material, they seek cues to the content of the message.

By dictating and writing their own thoughts, children begin to recognize an ever increasing number of words-in-context. A key word or two within the structure of a familiar sentence enables the child to approximate the thought expressed. Success in this beginning provides desire and ability to continue. More approximations increase the number of recognized words and syntactic cues, bringing more success. Therefore, *approximations become closer to accurate reproductions as children continue to read*. Their intuitive sense of sound-symbol relationship is used and can be expanded as needed. When children seek meaning rather than sound, reading is exciting and holds a high priority with children. Development of more advanced skills for maturing readers has been explained.

Now that we have explored the fourth major aspect of the language arts, the interaction and interdependence of all of the aspects—listening, talking, writing, and reading—are well established. Teaching them as a unified whole seems to be of crucial importance.

Suggested learning experiences for prospective teachers

Suggestion A

1. Observe a first grade. Ask permission to read to the children a book you have selected for the purpose. (Select two or three so as to have at least one that is new to the children.)

2. Gather the children around you on the floor. You may sit either on the floor or on a chair, as seems most appropriate.

3. Show the book and introduce it to stimulate their interest in hearing it.

4. Read the story, paying attention to the use of your voice to interpret actions and feelings expressed in the story. Show pictures to the group.

5. After you are far enough into the story so that its context is clear, stop and ask children to predict the next word or words. If there is no immediate response, ask an appropriate question, such as "What do you think Bobby did?" or "What do you think they saw?"

6. Evaluate your reading and your choice of book by the interest and responses of the children. What did you learn?

Suggestion B

1. Observe a first grade. Ask permission to work with any child not yet reading.

2. Use something the child has made as a basis for conversation. Ask what is the one most important thing the child wants to say about this work. If it is a picture, ask the child's permission to put the sentence on the picture. Or write the sentence in good manuscript on another paper.

3. Read it aloud, then hand it to the child but do not ask the child to read it.

4. What did the child do with the written sentence?

5. Evaluate the experiences. What did you learn?

Suggestion C

1. Locate a story appropriate for most eight-year-olds.

2. List three or four what-does-it-say introductory questions.

3. List three or four questions about the feelings of the characters and the reader's projected feelings.

4. List two or three questions about inferences children can make from the story, what is meant or implied beyond what is directly stated.

5. List a question or two related to the author's own purpose in writing the story.

6. Look up information about the author. Share with the children information that shows the purpose behind the writing.

7. Ask a group of eight-year-olds to read the story out loud. Use the above questions and information.

8. Were responses different to different types of questions? Which questions were most valuable? Why?

Suggestion D

1. Observe in grade three or above. Ask permission to work with a group on syllabification.

2. Ask them to tell you what they know about syllables, and have them demonstrate on the chalkboard. Can someone in the group correct any misunderstandings?

3. Identify useful concepts the children are not aware of and ask questions to see if they can become aware of them.

4. Prepare in advance a list that includes both words that follow the rules and those that do not.

5. Bring out concepts of open and closed syllables. Use the terms *long* and *short vowels* only if the children use the terms. Otherwise note that in open syllables the vowel "says its name."

6. Make no comment about the pronunciation of vowels before *r*, for there is no other way to pronounce the vowel in such words.

7. Present several words, pronounced regularly, that are likely to be in the children's oral vocabulary but not in their writing, to see how well they can identify syllables.

8. Ask the group what they have learned, then ask yourself the same question.

Suggestion E

1. Observe in any classroom where children are reading. Ask permission to work with a group of from four to six children on context clues.

2. Locate material somewhat difficult for these children and provide several copies. The selection needs to be long enough so that the children can predict from the context what it is all about.

3. In preparation, list words in the middle and later parts that you feel children may not know or at least not recognize.

4. Ask children to read the selection silently. Indicate a word from your list by line and place in the line, and ask what the word is and what it means.

5. If all know the word, ask how they could have found out what it was if they had not known. If one or more do not know the word, ask the others not to tell what it is.

6. Ask those who do not know the word if they think it is the name of something, describes something, or gives some action. Can they identify its function in the sentence, and if so, how? By reading the whole sentence, leaving out that word, can they guess what it might be? Then how do they check their guesses?

7. Repeat this procedure for each of the words you have listed in your preparation. Are the children catching on to a way of identifying unrecognized words, or understanding the general meaning of words they have not heard before? The older children can use base units, prefixes, and suffixes to help in getting meaning where appropriate.

8. What have you learned from this experience?

Suggestion F

1. Observe in a classroom where children select at least some of the materials they read.

2. Watch a child selecting a book. Ask permission to discuss the selection with the child. Did the child select it quickly, after examining several books, or after a long process?

3. Ask why the child chose the book. Did the child have a specific purpose? If not, ask what kind of books or stories the child likes to read. Be alert to note fear of being unable to read some of the books.

4. If the child had a specific purpose in mind, how

was he or she using it to select a book? Was the child missing helpful cues?

5. Regardless of the basis of selection, is the child aware of flexibility of reading procedures? If this child were in your classroom, what could you do to improve her or his selection process and plan for reading?

6. If the first child you queried had no significant problems, check with other children and with those selecting periodicals or newspapers.

7. What have you learned that will enable you to help children select books and plan for reading them?

Suggestion G

1. Observe in a sixth grade. Ask permission to talk with one child at a time while they are reading silently.

2. Ask the child to tell you about what the book, story, or article says.

3. See if the child is also reading between the lines, by asking for the broader meaning, the inferences, and implications.

4. Check also to see if the child is reading behind the lines.

5. What does the child know about the author, why the author wrote it, and wrote it a certain way?

6. Check these concepts out with other children. How many are doing more than superficial read-

ing? Is there a difference between the way they read fiction and nonfiction?

7. What could you do in a classroom of your own to help children get more significance out of their reading?

8. What have you learned from this experience?

Suggestion H

1. Observe in a fourth grade. Ask permission to work with a small group on scanning and skimming.

2. Choose a book the children have not read in one of the content areas. Provide a copy for each child. In your preparation, identify concepts in the material.

3. In the group, ask the children to find one, two, or three places, as appropriate, where a certain concept is discussed. If some do not find them, let the others explain how they found them.

4. Ask the children how quickly they can find out what the material told them about this concept. For instance, if the concept were dams, what did it tell about dams? Their names and locations? Their uses? Problems concerning them?

5. Suggest another concept discussed in another section of the book, asking where does it tell about it, and what does it say. Are the children better able to scan? Can they skim or do they still need to read the whole thing to get answers?

6. What have you learned from this experience?

Suggested readings

The feeling of "I think I can!" can predict a child's accomplishment in reading, according to Wattenberg and Clifford in "Relation of Self-Concept to Beginning Achievement in Reading." Another factor is "Teacher Expectation: Prime Mover or Inhibitor?" as Braun, Neilson, and Dykstra describe many studies reporting the self-fulfilling prophecy. The value of reading to children is examined by Sandra McCormick in "Should You Read Aloud to Your Children?"

Goodman and Watson explain "A Reading Program to Live With: Focus on Comprehension," and Kenneth Goodman provides a basis for developing a reading program in "Orthography in a Theory of Reading Instruction." Sam Shohen gives positive results in "A Language Experience Approach to Reading Instruction," and Roach and Claryce Allen provide a wealth of appropriate activities in their *Language Experience Activities*. Joseph Rubin describes a program for more mature readers in his "The Stage Is Set—Language Experiences Begin!" In "Language Experience for Dialectically Different Black Learners" Leona Foerster analyzes problems and gives a rationale.

Goodman and Buck give their position in "Dialect Barriers to Reading Comprehension Revisited," while "Seven Fallacies: Reading Retardation and the Urban Disadvantaged Beginning Reader" by Cohen and Cooper suggests that the solution lies in "good pedagogy." Laffey and Shuy edited *Language Differences: Do They Interfere?* which contains articles dealing with the problem from many points of view. Other questions are raised by Yetta Goodman and Rudine Sims in their "Whose Dialect for Beginning Readers?" and Bernice Cullinan in *Black Dialects and Reading*.

The relatively recent miscue analysis is explained in Allen and Watson's *Findings of Research in Miscue Analysis: Classroom Implications*. The use of another relatively new technique is discussed by Neville and Pugh in "Context in Reading and Listening: Variations in Approach to Cloze Tasks." Adeline Gomberg in "Freeing Children to Take a Chance" suggests using cloze as a teaching tool for poor readers.

Two tongue-in-cheek articles that make some very useful points are Frank Smith's "Twelve Easy Ways to Make Learning to Read Difficult" and Victor Froese's "How to Cause Word-by-Word Reading." The development of reading ability throughout the curriculum gets help from "The Integrated Curriculum Revisited through Consumerism" by Alleman-Brooks and Fitzgerald. Knight and Hargis provide suggestions in their "Math Language Ability: Its Relationship to Reading in Math."

Special and/or more advanced types of reading are explored by several authors. Sara Lundsteen questions whether children respond to material on the basis of their maturity more than on the character of the material, in her "Levels of Meaning in Reading." Jane Hornburger gives suggestions for helping children in "Detecting and Dealing with Doublespeak." In the same booklet Francis Cacha suggests procedures and materials to use in combatting "Propaganda Techniques via Children's Literature." Elizabeth Parker gives help for "Teaching the Reading of Fiction: A Manual for Elementary School Teachers." Beth Atwood focuses on reading between and beyond the lines in her "Critical Reading: A Social Experience." John Dawkins clarifies a distinction in "Defining Fiction and Nonfiction." Ruth Carlson's book *Enrichment Ideas: Sparkling Fireflies* is packed with ways to encourage reading of literature to gain increased enjoyment and understanding.

Strategies for children's learning

I can read!

Purpose. To enable children to "read" on the first day of school.

Appropriate level. Sixes.

Participants. All children.

Situation. Children entering first grade often have high expectancies for learning to read, and many expect to read on the first day. It seems highly important not to disappoint them.

Teacher role

1. To present reading as something all can do, as understanding the meaning of what is written, and as dealing with thoughts.

2. Ensure that children gain the beginning of two concepts, that reading progresses from left to right, and that the print and oral expression fit together.

Procedures

1. Prepare a colorful chart with a simple repetitive nursery rhyme, illustrated with easily identifiable pictures. Make dittoed copies, one for each child.

2. Ask how many would like to learn to read something today.

3. Bring out the chart, have the children identify the pictures, and suggest we all read it together.

4. Run your hand under each line as you and the children say the nursery rhyme together. Do this at a slow-normal pace and with natural intonation.

5. Discuss the meaning of the rhyme with the children.

6. Repeat the reading as before, being sure the children are following your hand along the line from left to right.

7. Encourage volunteers to take your place at the chart and lead the reading. Be certain the child's hand follows the reading, line by line.

8. Hand out the dittoed copies and have the group "read" these following each line with hand or finger.

9. Suggest they may take these home to read to their families.

Awareness of print

Purpose. To help children become more aware of printed communication.

Appropriate level. Fives and sixes.

Participants. All children.

Situation. Most children have been surrounded by printed communication since infancy. Occasionally children in remote rural areas have not seen as much printed material. All children can gain from greater awareness.

Teacher role

1. To continuously bring printed or written material into the activities of the day, demonstrating their usefulness and identifying their meaning.

2. Show pleasure each time some child recognizes and identifies a sign, a phrase, or the meaning of something written.

3. Encourage children who are already reading to read things to children who are not yet reading for themselves.

Procedure

1. Write information on the chalkboard in good manuscript each day before children arrive.

2. Call their attention to it and read it to them, discussing with them the importance or implications of the information.

3. Choose a book to read to the children from the reading center where children have been exploring many picture books and easy storybooks. Sometimes a child will request a certain book from the collection.

4. Make name tags or cards for children to use for various purposes, like taking roll, choosing an activity, or forming groups.

5. On a field trip ask children to find all the signs and labels they can and tell about them when they get back. Then list the ones the children report and discuss their meaning and purpose.

6. Make group charts with the children for various purposes.

Evaluation. Are children becoming more aware of print? Are they more curious about what print "says"? Do they more frequently ask to have some printing read to them? Are they recognizing some words and phrases in their surroundings?

Children's dictation

Purpose. To take dictation from children as a basis for reading.

Appropriate level. Fives and sixes and occasionally older children.

Participants. All children who cannot yet write for themselves or for whom writing is still difficult.

Situation. There are basically two situations, (1) when a child has a relatively long story to tell, and (2) when the child, just getting started in reading, tells the main thought about a picture or other product. The first case is of necessity limited to a relatively few occasions unless extra help is available in the classroom. Taking dictation should occur almost daily, at least every other day.

Teacher role

1. To establish that, basically, reading is "talk written down."

2. To write what the child says. Spell conventionally all words spoken with a foreign or nonstandard accent. Do *not* correct elisions (*gonna*, etc.), poor usage, or words added unnecessarily (*nice of a day*).

Procedures

1. Gather a group before the easel when three, four, or five children have finished their products. Fasten a picture one of them has made to the easel and ask the artist to tell about it.

2. Encourage discussion about the content, the thoughts related to the picture.

3. Ask the child what you should write on the picture, and when necessary, ask the child to focus on one most important thought.

4. Write it in good manuscript exactly as the child says it, incorrect usage, dialect, and all. Individual words and letters may be verbalized depending on that child's development. It is essential that when it is read back by anyone, it must be in the child's own words. Otherwise the connection between talking, writing, and reading is broken.

5. Read the sentence running your hand under it from left to right.

Evaluation. Does the child identify someone's reading of the sentence as what he or she said? Do the others in the group?

Developing oral reading

Purpose. To develop oral reading facility.

Appropriate level. Sevens and older.

Participants. All who are reading adequately silently.

Situation. Most sixes and some sevens are not ready for a prepared audience situation, but nearly all sevens will be ready before the end of the year. Since oral reading is quite different from silent reading, special plans should be made for it. The teacher will be reading to children once or twice a day, and children's reading can take off from that.

Teacher role

1. To set up the situation as an opportunity, not a requirement.

2. To help children with any problems they have in carrying out the plan.

3. To conduct the discussion and evaluation following the reading.

Procedures

1. Start with a child who reads well, interpreting meaning through intonation, and who has asked to read a story to you. Ask whether the story is one the other children would like to hear. If so, suggest reading it to the group, and ask the child to take time to go over it once more to be sure there will be no problems.

2. Set aside sufficient time for the child to read the selection and the rest of the group to react to it.

3. Encourage the group to discuss and evaluate as they are learning to do, telling what they particularly like and then giving constructive suggestions if they have any.

4. Suggest that others may read to the group when they are ready, by signing up on a special chart.

5. Raise the question of how anyone gets ready. Accept these or similar steps and put them on a chart:

    a. Select something you feel you can read well.

    b. Select something you think the other children have not heard but would like to hear.

c. Read it over again to yourself, then aloud, where your audience cannot hear you.

d. When satisfied, sign your name on the chart.

These procedures enable every child to read to the group. Some children, unsure of themselves, may prefer to read to a small group of friends. After one or two successes, these children may be ready for the larger group. In discussion with the children, set a limit to the length of the reading and agree that no one has a second turn until everyone else has had a turn, unless no one else is ready.

6. After children are familiar with the procedures, suggest taping the reading. Begin with a self-confident child who volunteers.

7. Keep a record of the times children read to a group and of specific items that come out in the evaluation.

8. Note children who do not offer to read. Work with them individually, suggesting possible materials and building their confidence.

Evaluation. Are children offering to read to the group more often and making better preparation for it? Is children's oral reading becoming more fluent, better interpreted through intonation, and more enjoyable for both reader and listeners? Are children becoming more aware of what needs to be considered in selecting, preparing, presenting, and evaluating oral reading? Are all of the children participating with little or no extra encouragement?

In evaluation conferences with children, play recordings of early reading and current reading. Ask the child to identify points of progress.

Effects of intonation

Purpose. To help children be more aware of the effects of intonation, including pitch, stress, and juncture.

Appropriate level.   Eights and older.

Participants.   All children.

Situation.   Experimenting with various intonation patterns is perhaps the clearest way for children to understand the effects. The typical sentence "What are you doing?" can be either a question or an exclamation, and has four distinct meanings as each word is emphasized in turn.

A humorous sentence that emphasizes the effect of altering pauses is the old saying, credited to the Siamese, "Oh wa tagoo Siam!"

Teacher role

1. To help children learn to interpret meaning more effectively through their oral reading.

2. To reflect to the children when intonation is needed or when it misinterprets what they are reading.

Procedures.   Encourage children who are preparing for oral reading presentations to try different intonations. Which words should be stressed? Where should the tone of voice be raised or lowered to give a pleasing, natural rhythm to speech? Where should the pauses be? At punctuation marks, but anywhere else? A somewhat exaggerated intonation can be acceptable for a while and in most cases will moderate naturally before long.

Evaluation.   Are children improving in their control of intonation? Are they recognizing cues for voice changes and pacing? Are listeners showing awareness of intonation by their comments? Do they interpret meaning better?

Understanding books

Purpose.   To understand plot, characters, and theme of a book through discussion.

Appropriate level.   Nines and older.

Participants.   Those who have read the book.

Situation.   In any classroom where children

choose their reading, a number of children will read the same book, perhaps because of its attractive title, format, or pictures, or because children recommend it to one another.

Teacher role

1. To set up and/or make it possible for children to set up groups to discuss a book they have read.

2. In the beginning, explore one aspect with the children, helping them recognize cues to identify the story line, character development, or author's purpose.

3. Give children responsibility for increasing awareness. With added maturity and experience, they can carry more and more of the responsibility.

4. Continue to call their attention to significant aspects in the stories you read to the group.

Procedures

1. Set up a small group discussion—or set up procedures for children to set up such a group—of children who have read a certain book.

2. Develop with the children questions that may be considered, such as:

> Did you find it easy to follow the story plot? Did the plot seem real? Could it have happened? Did you enjoy it? Why or why not?

> How did the author build the characters? Was it similar to or different from the way other authors we have read did it? Did you think they seemed real?

> What do you think the author wanted to get across in the book?

> Why did the author use this particular setting and situation? What do we know about the author's life?

> When you are dealing with a particular book, questions will be more specific, and additional questions will be asked.

Evaluation. Do children feel such group discussions, with or without the teacher, are helpful? Do they ask for them? Does deeper understanding show up in their discussions at the conference? In making recommendations of books to others, do they show broader appreciations? Do they begin to use new understanding in writing their own stories?

Reading flexibility

Purpose. To help children develop flexibility in reading.

Appropriate level. Nines and older.

Participants. All children.

Situation. When children first start to read, they tend to read everything the same way. (Some adults still do!) Material is read for different purposes, some for recreation, some for study, some for locating certain specific pieces of information, and so on. It is important therefore that children learn early to identify their purpose for reading and how to read in relation to that purpose.

Teacher role

1. To involve the children's thoughts in relation to different purposes.

2. To help children understand and experience different kinds of reading for different purposes.

3. To raise questions on points the children are failing to consider.

Procedure A. Scanning and skimming.

1. Give each child in the group (small group or class) a book unfamiliar to them, initially a new text and later a group of library books dealing with the same general topic.

2. Tell them that since these new books could be useful, they need to know what is in them.

3. Ask them to suggest how they might find out in the next few minutes. Keep suggestions coming with "and what else?" When contradictory ideas are suggested, ask the group to evaluate them.

4. Give them a reasonable amount of time, then open a discussion of what the book (if each had the same text) or books (if they were a variety of books) contained.

5. Ask them to evaluate the usefulness of the procedures used, and identify and record the ones they would use another time.

Procedure B. Locate information.

1. Identify a situation requiring locating specific information. The group could be a committee studying a particular aspect of a broader topic involving the entire group.

2. Bring into the classroom a variety of books dealing with the general subject under study as well as those on that particular aspect.

3. Suggest committee members go through the books quickly to find which ones and what pages supply needed information.

4. After a short time return to the group, inquire about their success, and ask what procedures they are using. Ask each one to explain the procedures that were most successful. If you note something else they might try, ask if they have thought of it.

5. Raise the issue of how they will need to read the relevant portions.

6. Follow up, when necessary, with procedures for note-taking, including recording the reference.

Procedure C. (A follow-up of B)

1. Ask children to take their notes, made previously, and the book they were using, and find the place or places dealing with the topic.

2. Ask them how they will get all the information they need now that they know where to find it. Conduct a discussion of study reading and how it differs from other kinds of reading.

3. Give them a reasonable amount of time and then return to the group. Have them report on what they have learned. Be alert to contradictory information, and ask those reporting it to recheck. It may be a case of misreading, of misinterpretation, or an actual difference in the facts stated. Follow this up with Procedure D.

Procedure D.   (A follow-up of C)

1. Alert children to the possibility of contradictory information in different published materials. As a part of their critical reading, suggest they always follow up on any significant discrepancy.

2. Raise the question of whether there is a reasonable explanation, such as widely different publication dates, reference to different areas, indications that different factors were taken into consideration, and the like.

3. When there is a real contradiction, suggest that children write to each publisher, explain the problem, and ask for an explanation.

Procedure E.   Recreational reading.

1. Ask children to think about how they read when they read for fun.

2. List on a chart the characteristics of recreational reading the children suggest in their discussion.

3. Ask them which, if any, they use when they skim, scan, study, or read critically.

4. List the characteristics of each kind of reading on separate charts. Suggest they look these over after they have determined their purpose for reading but before they start to read.

Evaluation.   Are children becoming more able to use varied procedures as they read for various purposes? Do children bring up questions or express ideas related to the question of flexibility in reading? As they vary their style, are they reading more effectively?

The purpose of diagnosing and evaluating reading competence is to provide a better basis for helping children read more effectively, appreciatively, and usefully. In the past, most emphasis has been placed on finding weaknesses, rather than identifying aspects of reading with which children were having success. When successes are not identified, the evaluation is unbalanced. Identifying successes encourages children to tackle needed learning with more confidence, indicates what each child sees as important, and suggests the procedures by which that particular child learns best. These individual successes also prevent us from trying to teach all children the whole range of competencies, including those they have already learned. Such teaching is at best a waste of time and at worst a source of confusion that may erode the abilities children already have.

Since all diagnosis is evaluative and most evaluation is diagnostic, we will discuss these two processes together. We will describe diagnostic tools ranging from standardized achievement tests, which are generally misleading, to the relatively recent *Reading Miscue Inventory*, which seems to provide solid assistance. We will examine the causes of reading problems and some old and new approaches to remediation. Finally, we will suggest procedures that serve evaluative and diagnostic functions.

Tools for diagnosis and evaluation

Since the 1930s, standardized achievement tests have been a means of evaluating children's school learning. Most of these tests purport to measure accomplishment in the skill areas of reading, spelling, and mathematics; some broaden into language usage and a few into the content fields. In reading, they attempt to measure comprehension and to diagnose skills that have been considered necessary for learning to read.

Comprehension tests usually consist of a series of paragraphs, each followed by multiple choice questions calculated to determine whether the reader understands the meaning of the selection. The *Silent Reading Diagnostic Test* has eight parts: Words in Isolation, Words in Context, Visual Structural Analysis, Syllabification, Word Synthesis, Beginning Sounds, Ending Sounds, and Vowel and Consonant Sounds (Bond, Barlow, Hoyt, 1970).

Teachers in schools that routinely give standardized reading tests need to be aware of test makers' understanding of the reading process and the skills they consider necessary for effective reading. Virtually all such tests use short paragraphs, although there is much evidence that the reader needs relatively long selections to read most effectively. Children can save time—and so answer more items—by reading the questions first and then skimming the paragraph to find the answers. Equally effective readers who follow directions score lower.

Since there are many constraints on test makers, they realize they must make some compromises. Each published test must be appropriate for children over a wide age-grade range, in all sections of a country with no national curriculum, where states have only suggested guidelines, and where school districts are increasingly permitting schools or teachers to promote learning in their own ways. So different goals and expectations lead to different learning. Content and wording of tests must accommodate a wide variety of regional differences.

How *reliable* are these comprehension tests? In other words, if the same child took the same test again, would the results be the same? Probably not. Most tests require at least one hundred cases to have their average score dependable within a relatively few points. Although the average score for three or four classrooms together is quite reliable, it is less reliable for any one classroom and quite undependable for a single child. A child's score could easily vary from half a grade to a full grade, and under certain circumstances considerably more.

When diagnostic tests depend on subtests for their diagnostic ability, each subtest is limited to a much smaller number of responses. In order to be considered reliable, a test should include at least one hundred items, but a diagnostic test may have as few as eight or ten.

Thus, it is extremely important that teachers view individual test scores with considerable skepticism. Scores can be an indication if they seem consistent with other information on the child— but they are just one more bit of evidence.

How *valid* are standardized reading tests? In other words, does the test test what it purports to test? These instruments certainly do not test reading as it is used in life or the skills that are important in gaining meaning. Excellent readers can score low on such tests. The greatest weakness of such tests is their failure to help in identifying problems with either syntactic or semantic cues and their use in the language process. These tests are not valid because they are not testing reading.

The weakness of standardized tests can be illustrated by the story of a nine-year-old boy who could read adult literature but nevertheless was given a D in reading. His mother pointed out that he consistently read the newspapers and adult books. The teacher responded, "Well, I don't know all he is reading, but *he doesn't know his phonics!*" In other words, the teacher was saying that a child must know all the skills that are *supposed* to help him learn to read—whether he needs them or not!

Goodman (1974) sees standardized reading tests as "anchors against progress." Naylor (1972) found that general reading scores masked a large degree of individual variability, and that students grouped by levels did not demonstrate similar performance in subskills within groups. Many teachers hold to the traditional patterns of teaching—the patterns tests are built on—for fear that if they teach differently, their children will not score high enough on the tests. But the better children read, by whatever method, the higher they will score on a comprehension test, the only type of test that has any validity as a test of reading. If teachers want to test phonics and structural analysis, that is their decision, but direct measurement of such skills should be no part of a reading score.

Some people want a single number that seems to give a "definite" description of the child's reading ability. Such numbers make it easier to compare one child with another: "My child is a better reader than your child. She got a 5.4 grade score, and your child scored 5.1." If they only knew, the chances are excellent that on another similar test, the scores could well be reversed. And after all, the only result of comparing one child with another is to make the higher scorer feel superior and to "put down" the lower, which certainly does not help either child. The teacher will continue to help both children by selecting whatever procedures the other diagnostic means indicate. Pushing the slower child is counterproductive, and when a child is making faster than average progress, there is still room for growth.

No single number can express an evaluation of any child's reading competence, and it is simplistic to believe it can. Such competence is extremely complex and probably cannot be made explicit by any means. By the time the many aspects have been explored, changes have undoubtedly occurred in those first evaluated. So if standardized tests are not useful, how can teachers evaluate children's reading and diagnose their needs?

The cloze test

The most useful paper-and-pencil test of reading, by far, is the cloze test, which also has a good potential for diagnosis. A cloze test is any selection for reading in which words have been omitted from the original text in a regular fashion and blanks have been substituted. A reader then fills in each blank with a word that fits semantically and syntactically. Any word that meets these two qualifications is considered correct.

A teacher can, for instance, type a story of at least 250 words but leave a blank for every fifth word. The blanks should all be the same length and long enough for the child to write in a suitable word. When such a story is typed on a ditto mat, copies can be made available for all those for whom the test is appropriate. The test is not timed, allowing for different reading speeds.

The teacher needs to consider each paper carefully to decide whether words that vary from the original text are acceptable at that point in the sentence. When they are not, identifying the cue for the error can identify a child's problem, especially if that type of error is persistent. Has the

child used only the word or two preceding the blank as a cue to the missing word? Is the child's word related to the meaning but not in a form that fits the structure of the sentence? Or does the word fit syntactically but not make sense? When it seems impossible to understand why the child inserted a particular word, the teacher should get his or her explanation. Perhaps a word was unknown or misinterpreted.

If the words filled in do not fit syntactically, or semantically, or both, and are not related to meaning, then the child either is not getting the meaning or does not understand that all reading must make sense. On the other hand, if the words do not have the needed structural form, the child is not using the syntax of the sentence or is not aware that all reading must sound like language.

A number of cloze tests may be prepared at different levels of difficulty of structure and concepts. The text that is chosen should be unfamiliar and slightly difficult for the children who use the test. The excerpt should start at the beginning of a story or article so that the context can build quickly. Records are most useful if they note the percentage of blanks filled acceptably, the percentage semantically unacceptable, and the percentage syntactically unacceptable.

Observation

Observation of what children do, and how well they do it, has been the backbone of the evaluation program since early times. Objective measures were designed because some teachers were influenced by personal feelings, both positive and negative, about various children. Since these measures have proved inadequate, educators have advocated procedures to make observations more objective.

When observations of children are recorded, teachers need to record the child's specific behavior, not the teacher's on-the-spot, judgmental reaction to it. For instance, Betty's record might read, "Mon. asked for words ЦН II (seven times). Tues. asked for words ЦН. Wed. asked for words

III. Thurs. asked for words IIII. Fri. asked for words III." This type of record is far more helpful than a weekly comment that "Betty is too dependent on me to tell her words. She needs to develop more independence." The actual tally of words Betty requested tells us that she apparently is gaining independence. Having been bothered all week telling her words, the teacher has not realized that the number of requests decreased.

Broader factors for teachers to observe are the extent that major objectives are being achieved. Does each child show increased enjoyment in reading? Is each child's choice of material to read becoming more satisfying, increasingly inclusive of a range of types, of depth, and of breadth? Is each child's evaluation of material read becoming increasingly valid? These questions do not assume any particular stage of progress, but data that indicate change can be very useful over a period of time.

Randolph (1972) shares an "Observation Sheet to Determine the Frequency of Occurrence of Behaviors Exhibiting Enjoyment, Depth, and Breadth of Reading." The following behaviors are rated *Has Never Occurred, Occurred Once or Twice, Occurred Occasionally, Occurred Frequently.*

Behaviors

The pupil reads at least one book a month of his own choosing.

The pupil of his own volition visits the library two or three times a week to browse and read.

The pupil voluntarily visits a bookstore (or book area in another store) at least two or three times a month to browse or purchase a book (mainly older children).*

The pupil is building a personal library which includes a variety of selections (if financially able or if the school makes book clubs, for example, scholastic paperbacks, available).

The pupil reads book "blurbs" and reviews.

*Material in parentheses is ours.

One-fourth of the pupil's leisure time is spent in reading.

The pupil has a book, a magazine, or some other reading material accessible to read in case of a few spare minutes.

When given a choice of activities such as seeing a film, listening to a recording, or reading, the pupil chooses to read.

The pupil of his own volition shares ideas gleaned from personal reading with his peers, his teachers, or the librarian.

The pupil demonstrates a sensitivity to human feeling and actions by relating what happens in stories to similar situations in life and vice-versa.

The pupil voluntarily shares ideas from several different sources.

The pupil shares ideas from several different areas of reading such as science, history, art, or literature.

The pupil relates ideas gleaned from personal reading to a topic being discussed by comparing and contrasting, drawing conclusions or inferences, making predictions or evaluating.

If a teacher rated each child on this list of behaviors three or four times a year, the record might indicate programs and procedures the teacher could carry out after the first rating.

Another variable to observe is how children spend their reading time and their time for choosing reading material. When children are expected to read, do they quickly get their reading material and settle down in deep concentration? Or do they dally and find excuses for doing other things? Do they idly thumb through books with no apparent purpose in selecting? If this behavior varies from time to time, can any consistency be found to account for the variation? Do they check books out of the school or local library to read at home or use as resources on school projects? What are they reading at home?

If there is no payoff, people stop reading when not forced to. Finding out why children avoid reading is more important than requiring them to read. You can force a child to sit in front of an open book, but you cannot make the child read. The more adults pressure children to do a task they see as boring or threatening, the greater and more enduring will the children's resistance be. People must expect the experience to be valuable if they are going to read any particular material usefully. Therefore, teachers must help children find material in which they can see value. Such help may be in the form of exploring their immediate interests, encouraging them in projects they would like to carry out, and then making relevant material available or suggesting sources.

Teachers can use observation to evaluate silent reading. The following list suggests behaviors to observe while a child is reading silently for a significant period of time:

Is the child engrossed in the reading?

Is the child distracted by anything? By what?

How long does the child stay involved? Is this time generally increasing or decreasing?

Is there any lip movement? Does the child quietly voice words or phrases?

Does the child ask for assistance? If so, from whom? Does the child ask for help with a word or to understand an author's thoughts?

Are the requested words difficult to get from context?

Does the child occasionally laugh or show other feelings while reading silently?

How rapidly does the child turn pages? So slowly as to indicate subvocalizing each word? So fast as to indicate skimming? So irregularly as to imply selecting portions to read carefully?

What does each of these items tell us about children's silent reading? If Becky is easily distracted by normal classroom noises, she is prob-ably not deeply involved in her reading. If she looks up at many different noises, it might be useful for her to find a quiet spot for reading. Dick's subvocalization indicates a need for help in gaining meaning directly from print. If Harold asks for help frequently, the teacher might use a conference to discover the reason for his lack of independence and to help him find ways of helping himself. By using context more effectively, he can use what he already knows to help him with what he does not know.

The conference

We have already suggested various procedures for using the teacher-pupil reading conference for the purpose of instruction. The conference is used also for the purpose of evaluation with the child. The questions that the teacher asks will vary with the circumstances and the child's maturity. Follow-up questions depend on how the child responds. The following list illustrates the kinds of questions that might be asked:

How do you feel about the book, story, or article? (Begin with an open-ended question.)

What were some of the important things you got from it? (Information; exciting, funny, or adventurous story; understanding about what I want to do, or what I did, or a girl/boy like me.)

Sketch the main points in the story or article.

What kind of people are the characters? Do they seem like real people you might meet or have for friends?

Why do you think the author wrote this story?

How do you think the author felt about the people and the situation?

Try to get the child to initiate much of the information, and use the questions only to probe an aspect not discussed. During the conference be alert for many other insights into how the child is managing the reading process. From first grade on, many children can tell what bothers them when reading. When the teacher welcomes these comments and helps each child with respect, the child will continue to identify such problems and share them.

Does the child understand any unusual word? How? By content clues? How effectively are clues used? What might help increase this skill?

Is the child puzzled about some portion? What causes confusion? Is the cause syntactic or semantic?

What did the discussion of content reveal about thinking skills? Is the child reading critically, appreciatively, and with enjoyment?

A special kind of conference makes use of an *informal reading inventory*. Some inventories have been published, but the teacher can create one that is more effective by following this procedure: Select a series of materials at increasingly difficult concept levels. Mark selections of two or three pages at the beginning of a story, an article, a book, or a chapter. Begin with a selection that is relatively easy for the child and ask him or her to read silently until a "stop" is indicated. Then ask the reader to tell about the ideas in the material.

Raise questions if necessary to see whether the child is using higher-level thinking skills, organizing ideas, evaluating critically, making inferences, and applying ideas. If comprehension was adequate, move to the next more difficult selection and repeat the process. If comprehension was less than adequate ask the child to read the selection orally. Was lack of adequate word identification the problem? If not, what seemed to be? Then move to the selection at the next lower concept level and repeat the process. As long as comprehension is adequate, there is no point in oral reading, but reading aloud is useful whenever the reader does not understand important points. Usually the reading of two or three selections, if selected on the basis of the child's expected reading ability, is adequate to identify progress and some skills for the child to work on.

Miscue analysis

Teachers need to consider how both the language processes and the thought processes function in the reading act. The objective is not errorless reading regardless of meaning, but the ability to gain the most information and understanding from written material with minimum use of the three cuing systems, semantic, linguistic, and grapho-phonemic.

A *Reading Miscue Inventory* prepared by Yetta Goodman and Carolyn Burke (1972) provides rationale, explanations, and detailed instructions for carrying out a diagnosis of children's reading. Children are given new material to read orally without assistance. The teacher uses a copy of the story reproduced with lines spaced for note-taking. All miscues of any type are noted on the sheet for later analysis. When they have finished reading, children are asked to "tell me about the story," and their retelling is taped for later analysis and scoring. Following the retelling, the teacher asks questions about concepts that the child has reported, but does not provide any cues to additional concepts. These questions and answers also are taped.

Analysis involves consideration of dialect, intonation, graphic similarity, sound similarity, grammatical function, self-correction, grammatical acceptability, semantic acceptability, meaning change; no loss, partial loss, or total loss of comprehension; and strength, partial strength, weakness, or overcorrection of grammatical relationships. A profile is prepared and interpreted. (Recently the authors have simplified these procedures.)

To use the material, most teachers would need advance study, and classroom assistance during the time allotted to the inventory. As an alternative plan, one person might be designated to use the inventory with all children in a school or with those referred for solution of problems. However, the basic ideas can be used informally several times a year in teacher-pupil conferences within the normal time frame.

Suggested markings from *A Reading Miscue Inventory*

Substitution.   Write the incorrect word above the correct one.

head
He had heard a lot.

Omission.   Circle part omitted.

He took both pets down (to) town.

He worked (at home) every afternoon.

lib(r)ary

Insertion.   Write in the word added.

at
The boy hit ∧ the ball.

Reversal.   Indicate the transposition.

Where can I go, father?

No

Repetition.   Circle and underline.

Ǫ
David <u>helps</u> his father.

(A letter is written inside the circle to indicate the reason for the repetition.)

Self-correction.   Use the symbol C.

Ⓒ *helped*
David helps his father.

(Child first read *helped*, then corrected before finishing sentence.)

Abandoning correct form.   Use the symbol AC.

AC *in*
She ran into the store.

(Child first read correctly, then changed *into* to *in*.)

Unsuccessful correction.   Use the symbol UC.

UC 2. *hid*
1. *head*
He had heard a lot.

(Child first read *head*, then read *hid* and went on.)

Dialect.   Use the symbol d.

ⓓ *fahver*
to his father

Nonword.   Use the symbol $.

$ *crees*
the cries of many gulls.

Anticipating difficulty with a subsequent word.   Use the symbol A.

Ⓐ
Tony enjoyed doing chemistry experiments.

(Child read *Tony enjoyed* then repeated *enjoyed* while trying to figure out *chemistry*—note distance that eye is ahead of voice.)

Long pause.   Use the symbol /.

He went to buy/some candy for the party.

While the actual material must be new to the child, the general content and concepts should be familiar. The selection should be at least 250 words to permit the child to read enough so that context will be effective. Material producing an average of twenty-five miscues is of approximately the right difficulty. The teacher can indicate miscues on a thermofax copy of the story and use them to determine the child's needs.

Miscue analysis procedures are as follows: Mr. Wright asks Marian to read the story aloud. He explains that he will not be able to help her, so she must just do the best she can by herself. When she has finished he will ask her to tell the story. Then he starts a tape recorder to provide a record of Marian's reading and retelling for later evaluation.

Marian reads the story. Mr. Wright records miscues on his thermofax copy, and then asks her to tell what she has read. When she has finished he asks open-ended questions to elicit further information about the people, events, and specifics she has already mentioned. He may also question her about some of her more puzzling miscues. For instance, a boy was reading a story about a museum, which he consistently read as maximum. When questioned about what a maximum was, he said the word looked like museum but the story was about live animals and they don't keep live animals in museums!

Mr. Wright fully accepts whatever Marian offers. When it seems she has told all she remembers without direct prompting, he turns off the tape recorder and shows appreciation for her cooperation. Now he has the basis for a very useful evaluation.

In evaluating a child's reading performance, make a count of each of the miscues, that is, changes from the original. Indicate whether the miscue has graphic or sound similarity, whether the changes, including omissions, are grammatically and/or semantically acceptable, and whether the child's miscue changes the intended meaning significantly.

Obviously some miscues are more serious than others. If a child reads "The dog lay under the pine tree" when the copy says "The dog lay under the old pine tree," there is little distortion of meaning. However, a child who reads "The dog lay under the old pine three" is not getting much meaning. When a child read "He could see the white rabbit in the neighbor's yard" instead of "He could see a rabbit in the neighbor's yard," he was relating his reading to his own experience. But if he had read "He could see a robber in the neighbor's yard," the meaning would be seriously distorted even though the sentence is grammatically acceptable.

Self-correction is a positive factor, even when it is not successful. At least the reader recognizes that something does not fit. When most miscues are grammatically acceptable, the child understands that what is read must "sound like language," that reading is a part of the language process. When most are semantically acceptable, the child understands that reading is a part of the process of communicating meaning. Only rarely can a miscue satisfy both of the above criteria and still significantly change the meaning of the whole paragraph or selection. The indication of such miscues is that the reader is not getting the larger meaning, perhaps by paying close attention to saying the words, or that what the child said was different from what the child thought. Dialect differences, either in pronunciation or in grammatical structuring, are not negative indicators, but signs that the child is reading meaning.

From these data the teacher can derive a ratio of the number of miscues that changed the meaning significantly or made the sentence meaningless to those that made no significant difference in meaning. The teacher can record the ratio and compare it with this same ratio the next time the inventory is used. Miscues that make no significant difference indicate that the reader is probably decoding meaning, and from it encoding the thought. Miscues that make a significant difference, particularly those that make no sense at all, probably mean the child is just saying words.

In evaluating these miscues further, it is helpful to consider whether the miscue has graphic similarity or sound similarity to the original word. Did the reader mistake a word for another word that looks like it? Or was the reader responding to the sound associated with the letters? The predominance of either type of miscue tells the evaluator how a child usually attacks unrecognized words.

Omissions and additions have similar implications. Do they significantly change the meaning? If not, the reader is decoding meaning and then encoding it into oral language. When the reader adds nothing and omits nothing, except perhaps words too difficult to tackle, it indicates a word-by-word rendering of the material. So much attention may be given to this phase that the reader gets little meaning.

The second phase of the evaluation is analysis of the child's telling of the story. Was it nearly complete and accurate? Were most of the important factors reported, after some questioning, with a fair understanding? Or was the telling minimal with several misunderstandings? In judging the amount of facts and details given, a teacher needs to consider that child's usual way of talking. Some children are naturally more voluble than others. With a child who typically uses few words, the accuracy of what is told is of prime importance.

When evidence of comprehension provided by the retelling is combined with analysis of miscues, the significance of miscues is clearer, since comprehension is the goal. Some children make many miscues but understand very well, while some make few or none and understand very little. One teacher reported a girl read seven long pages without a miscue but could tell virtually nothing about what she had read. She obviously was putting practically all her attention on naming the words.

A research study found that when a child makes a high percentage of miscues that cause loss of meaning, most substitutions have high graphic similarity (Y. Goodman, 1972). The implication is that the child who does not understand the meaning tends to be a much more careful reader. This finding shows that it is not the *number* of mistakes but the *kind of mistake* that is significant.

Using either the full analysis or the simpler form, teachers may group children temporarily according to the needs indicated by the inventory. The material includes reading strategies for each major problem. The authors describe the essential difference between these strategies and the usual instruction in skills:

> To be fully effective, reading instruction, as well as the reading act itself, must be based on the ongoing interrelationship between the reader and the reading material. Reading instruction which makes use of the interrelated language systems can be said to focus on reading *strategies*. Such instruction can be opposed to that which makes reading *skills* its focus.
>
> Reading strategies are concerned with specific systems of the reading process as they function in relationship to the other ongoing systems.
>
> As soon as one system is entirely isolated from the others it loses the properties of the

whole. A person's ability to identify accurately the separate ingredients of a cake in no way indicates that he can combine these items in the needed combinations and quantities, and with the appropriate procedures, to produce a cake. Likewise, the way a person functions as he reads cannot be determined by examining his performance on a series of exercises related to isolated aspects of the reading process.

A skill is an isolated procedure which a person can accomplish with varying degrees of success. An example would be the ability to pronounce a list of words composed of common English spelling patterns. Such an ability, however, offers no assurance that the word will have any meaning to the reader once he has pronounced it. Nor does it provide for those vocabulary items that are not totally amenable to phonetic attack.

Opposed to this isolated attack on an individual word are the strategies which a group of readers used on the word *typical* when they met it within the context of a story concerning a "typical baby." Their most frequent initial pronunciation was *type-i-cal*. This initial attempt to deal with an unfamiliar word reflects the most effective use of English spelling patterns. There is no more that a reader can do without involving other language systems, as well as his own background knowledge.

A number of readers, for whom this was a new word, read through the entire story, repeating this initial pronunciation each of the thirteen times that the word appeared. Yet, later, when asked what was meant by the word, they said things such as, "Well, he was an ordinary baby" or "Just average." These readers had developed a useful concept in relation to the printed item *typical*, and even a functional pronunciation which fully adheres to English graphic/sound rules (Y. Goodman and Burke, 1972, pp. 95–96).

The analyses have provided windows into the strategies children use in reading. Strategies that work should be undisturbed while the teacher helps children develop strategies they still need. The *Reading Miscue Inventory Manual* suggests many helpful ideas.

When children are first starting to read and uncertain that they can, telling children words is supportive. Soon, however, teachers should ask what word they think it might be, or where else they might find it that could help them. The teacher supplies the unknown word when a child is frustrated to the point of giving up, or when the word defies any normal strategy for figuring out, and the child is unwilling not to know how it should be pronounced.

Far more useful is helping them develop independent strategies for gaining accurate understanding from their reading. When readers are depending solely or mainly on graphophonemic cues, they need help in using syntactic and semantic cues. When a child reading about a canary comes ''as close as *cannary* or *canries* and is still unable to produce the expected word, it should become obvious that the ability to sound out is not the needed skill. What is necessary is that the reader have some concept of canary as a type of bird'' (Y. Goodman and Burke, 1972, p. 100). The teacher might ask, ''What kind of thing do you think the author is talking about?'' If the child does not know, ask questions to encourage looking for cues before or after the troublesome word. When the child figures out it is a bird, the next question is ''What kind?''

Proficient readers are not able to pronounce correctly all the words they understand. Both our listening and reading vocabularies are larger than our speaking vocabularies. It is important for children to develop concepts for significant words or phrases whether or not they can say them.

Oral reading evaluation

In preparation for oral reading as an audience situation, the child becomes familiar with the meaning, the concepts, the structure, and any words that are unfamiliar. In evaluation, however, one important factor to note is intonation. Does the flow of language sound similar to natural talking? Does the intonation reflect the meaning of the material read?

Another factor to notice is pronunciation. The teacher can note any word mispronounced and call the child's attention to it at the end of the reading. Together they may check it in the dictionary. They may check with others in the group to find out if the mispronunciation is local or re-

gional. The teacher ignores changes caused by dialect unless the child has expressed the desire to develop the standard dialect. After a child has made such a commitment, the teacher needs to provide accurate feedback, which is more effective during preparation than following the presentation. Obviously, the child's reading is never interrupted with a correction.

Causes of reading problems

When children do not read as well as they can, the causes must be determined before significant help can be given. Children may read poorly because they have a mistaken idea about what reading is. Most children have little difficulty when reading procedures from the very beginning have been based on the understanding that reading is a thinking, meaningful process. If children have been taught that reading is naming words, they need to learn more constructive habits and procedures. The following are some common causes of reading problems.

Children have not learned procedures for helping themselves. These procedures can be carried out through a series of questions: (1) What word would make sense in the context of the whole sentence, paragraph, or story? (2) What word would make it sound like normal language? (3) Do words you have tried start the way the first letter or two of the unknown word indicate? (4) If not, what word that makes sense and sounds like language do the letters suggest? (5) Does the word seem important to the meaning? If so, ask someone what the word is. If not—if it is just someone's name, for instance—just ignore it.

In the beginning, before children have developed phonics skills, they may realize that the word they need was used in a story by one of their peers, in a book in the reading corner, or on a chart, or even in their own word bank. Finding it somewhere may uncover other context clues for identifying the word. Appropriate strategies help to develop this ability.

What the child is expected to read is of no interest. Self-selection from a well-chosen room library and use of the school library solves the problem of not wanting to read what is assigned. When children do the choosing, they want to find out what the material can tell them. They are more likely to use their strategies for identification of unknown words.

The child sees no reason for learning to read. Children's feelings about reading should be explored with respect. Perhaps the material that they value is not usually found in the classroom but could be made available. Until they see some reason for learning to read, and until they make the necessary commitment, pressure will lead to negative results.

The child is "turned-off" by school and avoids school activities. Children who are indifferent to school present the greatest indictment against traditional mass education, which is still largely prevalent today. Many of these children are capable of normal or even superior progress. They have a fine sense of self, know what is significant and valuable to them, and refuse to spend time and energy on activities that are not.

Great harm has been done by the mistaken idea that, in order to be "fair," schools must teach every child the same way and require the same activities of all. It has been said, "There is nothing so unfair as the equal treatment of unequals." Teachers must realize that it is equal *opportunity* that is important. When they really understand that each individual has a unique learning style, interests, concerns, purposes, and perceptions, teachers can no longer accept practices that attempt to force all children into the same mold.

Turned-off children need to be turned on. Along with their peers, they need to become involved in activities that each has selected because of its personal importance. Even if the selection of the turned-off child does not "fit" the established curriculum, enthusiastic learning is justification for the introduction of any reasonable and productive activity. When the teacher-child relationship is

good, the child may be influenced by the teacher's enthusiasm and suggestions. Otherwise, it may be better for the teacher not to suggest.

The sooner children can be permitted and encouraged to be self-reliant, the more effective persons they will become, and the greater will be their own development and learning. When this type of self-direction and responsibility has been established in classrooms, children's capabilities and learning can be tremendous. For greatest growth the home and community environment must also be encouraging, but the school alone can accomplish much. The freedom to learn what children see as important to them, in the way and with materials they feel most useful, will prevent the human waste of the "turned-off" students.

A variety of other problems have been proposed as reasons children have trouble learning to read. Two of the most significant are emotional problems that absorb the child's time and energy, and dialect differences that reach into all areas of communication. Some of the other factors discussed below become problems only when all children are expected to learn in the same way and at approximately the same rate.

Emotional problems

Two kinds of emotional problems interfere with progress in learning to read: problems derived from the child's life circumstances, and problems growing out of the reading situation itself. When personal problems in or out of school demand most of the child's attention, obviously the child cannot devote adequate attention to learning. While emotional problems can affect all school activities, the areas most likely to be affected critically are those that provide the child the least satisfaction and distraction from these worries.

Once a reading problem has developed, teachers' efforts to help may increase the child's anxiety. When children find themselves continually corrected, placed in a group where less is expected of them, or where they are receiving negative feedback on their reading, they may quite naturally begin to avoid reading. The more they avoid, the more the negative feedback, the less they progress, and a vicious circle is established. A study found that the severely disabled reader showed significantly higher avoidance attitudes toward reading (Leeds, 1971). A program similar to a traditional remedial reading program brought the strongest avoidance reaction of any among the primary grade disabled readers. When shown a picture of a child reading in an empty classroom, they perceived it as punitive.

The study also showed that poor readers were characterized by a high degree of dependency. They evidently had been convinced there was nothing they could do to help themselves, that only the teacher knew the answers. Obviously their earlier experiences in reading had broken down rather than built up their self-confidence.

Children with language differences

When miscue analysis indicates certain children's problems are mostly related to their natural speech, any attempt at change needs careful evaluation. In the early years at school, these children's speech should be accepted without comment in reading as well as in talking. When these children decide they wish to add the standard dialect to their speech and writing, they need help and encouragement. Until then, teachers need to accept their dialect as long as the children prefer it. Through such acceptance of their dialect and with encouragement to add the predominant local dialect, before these children leave elementary school most will have become aware of the social and economic value of speaking the dialect accepted by the majority of people in the community where they live.

Children labeled slow learners Children labeled slow learners are not always less capable of learning than other children. Many extraneous factors create early behavior seen as failure by some

schools. In some cases children are confused by inadequate instruction. When teachers respond to their behavior as failure, often the child's self-concept is damaged so that lack of success is more likely.

Evelyn very nearly became one of these mislabeled children. Evelyn had started first grade in the fall with the other six-year-olds. When she had not read a word by mid-January, her teacher, Mrs. Wall, thought Evelyn was mentally retarded. Mrs. Wall was enrolled in an evening class that was developing the talking-writing-reading approach to reading, and she began to use these procedures in her first grade class. By late March Evelyn was not only reading but was among the most advanced readers in her class.

Many teachers in special education classes are now actively searching for mislabeled children. When the teachers provide improved learning situations, including positive expectations, many of these children move ahead and are soon returned to regular classrooms.

A small percentage of children have more than normal difficulty with school learning for a variety of reasons. There is no evidence whatsoever that these children all learn in one way. Like other children, they are individuals, each with abilities, experiences, and accomplishments. They learn what they perceive as valuable to them, what makes sense to them, and what is relevant to their experiences.

Typical remedial procedures have used a great deal of drill, usually on isolated elements, such as letters, sounds, and words. These procedures make learning more meaningless and hence more difficult. Learning the sounds of letters, and then sounding out words requires a fairly advanced ability for applying generalizations, a characteristic these children are least apt to have.

With the current emphasis on mainstreaming, fewer children will be placed in separate classes. When all dimensions of individual differences are increased, it becomes even more important that teachers provide opportunities for all children to choose among available materials and procedures and to become more self-directing and responsible for their own learning.

Performance IQ vs. verbal IQ

Differences in the ways children think and learn are demonstrated by intelligence tests that score performance and verbal ability separately. A performance test asks children to respond by doing things, while a verbal test asks them to respond in words. Children who score significantly higher on performance are likely to be slow in learning to talk and are often hard to understand. In reading they may show a deficiency in relating sounds to letters. Sounding letters is not necessary in learning to read, but the lack of verbal fluency is likely to be a problem. As these children continue to develop their ability to speak clearly and use language well, they can also develop the ability to read, if they have not experienced pressure or failure. Writing may be even more important for those who learn better by doing than by verbalizing.

Perception

Do some children perceive letters or words as different from what others see? No one ever knows or can know how objects look to another person. In this sense perception is a completely private phenomenon. Some researchers use *reversals* to document their belief that children perceive figures differently. When a child is attempting to reproduce a figure, letter, or word, he or she must perceive the original figure and the drawing to be the same. Then why do some children draw figures or print letters in reverse (*d* for *b*, for example)?

The most logical explanation is that the adult expectation is exact reproduction in the same direction, while the child's expectation concerns only the general shape. It is quite reasonable to suppose that the child may be unaware of the exactness *and direction* that adults have taken for

granted through long years of experience. By making an issue of it, adults are quite likely prolonging the child's problem. If the child is given the opportunity to watch people write, most reversal problems disappear on their own.

Dyslexia

Dyslexia is a term that has lost useful meaning. By derivation it means ''does not read,'' and this is the way it is generally used today. Originally the term was used to refer to any type of brain damage that prevented a child from learning to read. As minimal brain damage is difficult or even impossible to identify, all sorts of reading difficulties began to be labeled dyslexia. The teacher of a child not reading well felt less responsible when the nonreader was said to be ''dyslexic.''

While some groups still use the term, most educators realize it is a catchall term that cannot point the way to any specific help for the child. In many cases the term refers to mirror writing (reversing letters and numbers) or to success in learning something one day but not being able to remember it the next. Many specific reading errors have been classified under this umbrella term. The child considered dyslexic may not be able to distinguish figure from ground. The inability to distinguish a figure from its background is an example of the type of optical illusion all people experience at times (two faces or two vases?). A child who has had little experience with printed material may easily have this illusion with print. In these cases, the problem is not due to brain damage, but to lack of experience.

Another difficulty that some say indicates dyslexia is an inadequate copying of designs, like diamonds. Drawing is another learned accomplishment. Given extremely complex figures, anyone might have difficulty making a recognizable reproduction. The young child must learn eye-hand coordination in order to draw, but physical coordination and ability to learn to read have no necessary relationship. Leo was a boy whose lack

Which is the figure and which the background?

M. C. Escher, Vlakvulling I. *Reprinted by permission of the Escher Foundation, Haags Gemeentemuseum, The Hague.*

and confusion on the part of the child. Ignoring the "errors" but providing experience in related skills in such a way as to develop the child's feelings of competence and self-confidence is more likely to succeed.

However, there certainly are children with brain damage, extensive to minimal. Teachers can accept these children as they are, try to discover which learning procedures are most effective, and recognize each success. When they choose their own learning tasks, they are more likely to choose those that permit them to feel successful. One dyslexia clinic found success in using the talking-dictating-writing way of learning to read, which took pressure off the children and made reading more meaningful. When these and similar procedures do not significantly increase learning, medical help is probably needed.

Eyedness and handedness

For a while many believed that left-handed children had more trouble learning to read than right-handers. At that time, most teachers insisted that all children write with their right hands. Since using the left hand was the natural way for these children to write, retraining was usually long and frustrating. The child naturally saw the teacher's attempts as criticism, which made self-acceptance more difficult, which in turn got in the way of learning.

When schools began testing for eyedness (which eye was dominant), the theory developed that when children were right-handed and left-eyed or vice-versa, they were likely to have trouble with reading. This hypothesis was based on studies of children who had been referred to a clinic for diagnosis of reading problems. However, when a large group of six-year-olds were tested for eyedness and handedness before being taught to read, those who later failed showed no more mixed dominance than did those who succeeded in reading (de Hirsch, 1966). The selection of clinic cases evidently had distorted the picture.

of coordination affected his speech and his walk, and made his writing almost illegible. Although his IQ was "listed" at 45, his favorite activity during recess was to find a bench and read to the younger children. His reading was so good many children stopped their play and sat spellbound listening.

One explanation for the persistence of the above problem behavior is adults' continual correction of children. Their errors are consistently called to their attention, and they learn what they attend to, the "errors" in this case. Correction creates anxiety

Remedial reading

A consistent pattern for remedial reading has been encouraged and supported by federal funds, and specialists have been trained to carry out the program. These teachers use varied procedures with children retarded in reading who are assigned to such programs. The most common practice is to use games and "easy" materials and emphasize the teaching and testing of phonics in various forms. Let's examine what this approach means to a child.

Of course, the child is aware that almost everybody else in the class is reading. When children are sent out of their classrooms to a special program, they infer that their teacher has decided they have little ability to read and has given up trying to help them. At the remedial reading center, the teacher and most of the fellow students are strangers. The teacher gives them a variety of materials focusing on word identification. If there are many children, a different teacher may give them instruction in phonics. Since they have already had phonics in every classroom they have been in, and since they have always failed when trying to deal with it, they again approach it with feelings of "I can't." Such feelings may be strong enough to prevent them from taking in what the teacher is trying to explain. They complete their work sheets without any real understanding, even if they happen to pick up a cue as to how to identify the right answers.

If the teacher gives them a book, it is probably one they have tried to read before without success. Their previous teachers had combed the textbook shelves for appropriate material, and only so many "easy" books are available. If the book is part of a basal series with a controlled low vocabulary, the stories and sentences do not sound like the language that children hear every day. Often the games and procedures do not make sense because they seem to have no relationship to the books the teacher wants the child to read.

On the plus side, the new teachers give children attention on a one-to-one basis and do not get too upset with them. Since none of the students can read well, no one has to stumble through a page while more fluent readers become restless and bored. The teacher stays with one procedure long enough so that the children can devise some cues of their own as to how to respond correctly. Also, in the remedial reading room they find some games they have not seen before.

There are many excellent remedial reading teachers, and there are better programs that do not follow the common pattern. The better current programs put the reading specialist in the classroom to work with "problem readers" and anyone else who asks for help. The specialist helps the regular classroom teacher to understand the roots of the various problems and suggests ways of dealing with them.

The reading consultant approaches each child as an individual. Methods and procedures that Peter has used unsuccessfully are identified and discarded because they are not useful to this child at this time. Because of the close relationship of oral language to reading, opportunities are expanded for Peter to carry on conversations with both peers and adults. For example, he might discuss the book he has chosen to read with a child who has read and enjoyed it. The teachers listen to him with interest and respond appropriately. They encourage him to write about the subject of his enthusiasm. The relationship between thinking, talking, reading, and writing is a point of special emphasis.

The consultant and the teacher do everything possible to increase Peter's confidence in himself to learn and particularly to learn to read. They eliminate negative feedback in his reading and work with his parents to do the same. They give recognition to all evidences of constructive learning. They may be able to gain added insights and understanding of Peter through the special services of the school. Beyond these procedures, ways of helping him further are determined as they would be with any child at any time: Start from where children are in their learning and help them learn in the way *they* can learn best on the basis of *their* perceptions. When more help is needed, teaching what has not yet been learned is more helpful than obvious reteaching. When teachers build or rebuild self-confidence early enough, they avoid many more serious problems.

Summary

The foremost objectives for the reading program are (1) that children can understand and react to continually broadening and increasingly complex materials; (2) that they read with increasing satisfaction and initiative; and (3) that they find and use strategies and procedures that increase their ability to understand what they read.

When these are the main objectives, teachers should not rely on standardized tests to evaluate reading. Instead we have suggested using a cloze test, observation, and the teacher-child reading conference for evaluation. Miscue analysis, a relatively recent procedure, is a useful approach to diagnosis and evaluation. We proposed and developed simplified, informal procedures that teachers can use in their regular teaching: learners' selection of materials to read, including trade books both fiction and nonfiction, newspapers, magazines, or comic books; recognition of any and all success; building up self-confidence throughout each day by recognition of accomplishment in any area of learning; replacing any criticism with constructive suggestions; removing whatever the reader may feel as pressure; and involving the child in classroom activities that he or she sees as exciting and interesting.

Suggested learning experiences for prospective teachers

Suggestion A

1. Locate copies of standardized reading tests in a library, learning materials center, or an office of the public schools.

2. Note the number of responses on each subtest, then on the entire test. Are there enough to anticipate the results would be reliable? If the manual for the test is available, do the authors give the reliability of each subtest? Of the total test?

3. Would you consider the score on each of the subtests to be reliable enough for diagnosis? Check the grade level equivalent for several of the subtest scores. What difference would one point make in grade level? Two points?

4. Answer some of the items in each test. What did you do mentally to get the answer? Is this a commonly needed skill in reading for meaning?

Can you see ways test-wise children could avoid the expected thought process?

5. Do you feel the test is valid as a test of reading extended material for meaning?

Suggestion B

1. Go through the material below and fill in the blanks with one word each.

Our schools are in _____. Public confidence in educational _____ of all varieties is _____ eroded. A fundamental question, _____ unformed and unuttered, hovers _____ above the endless debate _____ a dozen or more _____ educational issues. The question, _____ stated is, "What is _____ to happen to education _____ the seventies?" Will the _____ be identified, in the _____ sweep of history of _____ United States, as the _____ in which formal schooling _____ and dwindled as a

_____ force in the life _____ the nation, or was _____ and renewed?

The final _____ to that question, of _____ , is not at all _____ . We shall simply have _____ await the course of _____ and the passage of _____ before judgment can be _____ . Nevertheless, all signs point _____ the likelihood that the _____ will feature a reordering _____ educational priorities in the _____ . If this prediction turns _____ to be a valid _____ , then we are, indeed, _____ a revolutionary era.

One _____ read the many sharp _____ that contribute to the _____ disenchantment with education as _____ of concern, if not _____ , from a people already _____ into the process of _____ how to cope with _____ staggering changes that confront _____ as a country. The _____ call to account for _____ successes and failures of _____ school is prodding us _____ attempting to newly define _____ freshly redefine the purpose _____ function of education in _____ society.

2. How difficult was it? Were you able to fill all the blanks? Compare your filled-in words with those of your classmates. Were some different but acceptable?

3. Type out a cloze test using material appropriate for a child you have been talking with. Ask permission to use the test with the child, or perhaps with a group of children.

4. Go over the paper or papers, deciding on the acceptability of words that differ from the original material. Indicate the percentage of words acceptable, the percentage unacceptable semantically, and the percentage unacceptable syntactically.

5. With or without the help of the child, can you identify the cue that caused the unacceptable response?

6. Has the use of the cloze test given you new insights into the cues the child uses in reading and his or her concept of the purpose of reading?

Suggestion C

1. Ask permission to interview a child in fifth or sixth grade.

2. Using the Randolph Observation Sheet items, explore the child's independent and self-initiated activities related to reading. In a classroom of your own, many of the items could be observed directly, and others would come out in discussions.

3. How well does the child say he or she likes to read? What is your reaction after discussing the various items?

4. Which items from the Observation Sheet do you feel are most significant?

5. Are there others you would add that came out in the discussion?

Suggestion D

1. Ask permission to observe a group reading silently. Were they reading assigned material or material of their own choosing?

2. Observe in relation to the items suggested in the chapter for evaluating silent reading. Pick from three to six children whom you feel you can observe effectively and record results.

3. Were there significant differences in behavior among the children? Was each child's behavior consistent throughout the period of observation? If inconsistent, how did it change? Did you find out or can you guess why it changed? Did the way the material was selected make a difference?

4. Were there behaviors not listed that you noticed and felt were significant? If so add them to the list.

5. In a classroom of your own, could you observe these behaviors and record them for a few children at a time so that all could be checked at least once a month?

Suggestion E

1. Obtain permission to use miscue analysis with a child above first grade whose reading is about average for the group.

2. Select material that is slightly difficult and unfamiliar to the child and prepare a copy on which you can note the miscues.

3. Study the instructions in this chapter for indicating the child's reading behavior.

4. Obtain a tape recorder and a blank cassette. If the child is not familiar with the use of the recorder, have him or her experiment with it, talking with the microphone at rest as close as convenient but not where it will interfere. Then play back the tape. Adjust volume as necessary. Keep the recorder going the entire time of the reading, retelling, and questioning for clarification.

5. Carry out the child's reading and retelling, then question to expand on the retelling without giving additional cues.

6. Carry out the analysis as suggested in the text. Select activities useful in the child's further development of reading competence.

7. Analyze your own questions or comments to note if you gave any cues the child had not already mentioned. If so, decide how you could have avoided giving cues and still have accomplished your purpose.

Suggestion F

1. Make a plan for the use of miscue analysis in a classroom of your own. In light of the discussion in Chapter 10, plan some activities that would help children with what they had not yet learned. You can use your experience in Suggestion E as a basis.

Suggested readings

"The Assessment Controversy" is the topic of the whole issue of *Social Policy* for September-October 1977. There are differences in opinions but also threads of agreement. "Documenting Teaching and Learning" by Vito Perrone is immediately relevant for teachers. Fagan, Cooper, and Jensen in *Measures for Research and Evaluation in the English Language Arts* discuss more than seventy instruments. Among articles on standardized testing are Jack McGarvey's "Standardized Tests: Five Steps to Change," Vito Perrone's "On Standardized Testing and Evaluation," Kenneth Goodman's "Testing in Reading: A General Critique," and Edmund Farrell's "The Vice/Vise of Standardized Testing: National Depression by Quantification."

Yetta Goodman raises the question "Reading Diagnosis: Qualitative or Quantitative?" William Page edits *Help for the Reading Teacher: New Directions in Research* to help teachers observe students' reading and translate these observations into an evaluation of reading performance. Another advocate of observation rather than standardized testing is Jeannette Miccinati in "Watch, Listen, and Record." Kenneth and Yetta Goodman in "Learning about Psycholinguistic Processes by Analyzing Oral Reading" also explain an alternative to testing.

A number of articles focus on the wide variety of ways cloze tests can be used in instruction, diagnosis, and evaluation. Two helpful articles are "The Cloze Procedure: A Multi-Purpose Classroom Tool" by Bartnick and Lopardo and "Using the Cloze Technique" by John Pikulski. Mary Gove in "Using the Cloze Procedure in a First Grade Classroom" shows that it can be used at that level in any program. Two articles apply the procedure with children using the language experience approach. Balyeat and Norman wrote "LEA-Cloze-Comprehension Test" saying it was particularly useful with dialectally different children, and Genevieve Lopardo wrote "LEA-Cloze Reading Material for the Disabled Reader." From the more technical standpoint J. R. Bormuth wrote "Comparable Cloze and Multiple-Choice Comprehension Test Scores" concluding that a fifty-item deletion test provides a reliable score for most purposes in reading.

Strategies for children's learning

Many of the strategies in Chapters 9 and 10 can be used with emphasis on noting progress since first used, or noting specific problems of individual children.

A cloze test

Purpose. To discover how well children can use the meaning and the structure of a selection to supply missing words.

Appropriate level. Eight-year-olds and older.

Participants. All children, with material suited to their reading competence.

Situation. The child's use of context, both semantic and syntactic, to read the thoughts expressed in writing can become evident incidentally. The cloze test is a way to focus on this ability.

Teacher role

1. To prepare a copy of appropriate material for each child.

2. To explain and illustrate the procedure the first time children experience the activity.

3. To analyze the results for each child and discuss them at the child's conference.

Procedures

1. Prepare selections at several concept levels as described in the chapter.

2. The first time the process is used, discuss it with the children. On a chart or chalkboard, write sentences with every fifth word omitted and have the group suggest words to fill in the blanks.

3. When children suggest unacceptable words, have the group decide why they cannot be accepted. Discuss whether the problem was semantic or syntactic, using the phrases "make sense" and "sound like language" with younger children.

4. Give the cloze test. Set no time limit but see that children keep on working independently.

5. When papers are completed, go over them at the earliest opportunity and indicate unacceptable words filled in. Analyze each child's paper to indicate: (a) Child should try again with simpler material; (b) child should try more advanced material; (c) child needs help in the structuring of language; (d) child is not getting meaning from reading and needs more emphasis on meaning.

6. Conduct individual conferences with each child to set specific purposes to work toward.

Evaluation. Did this procedure identify needs? Did it identify progress or lack of it? Did it pinpoint a group who need more help in language structure? In getting meaning from material? Do such tests given later indicate progress? Which needs have or have not been met?

Observation and interview

Purpose. To understand children's overall reading attitudes, habits, and procedures.

Appropriate level. Some items at all levels, increasing with maturity and experience.

Participants. All children who are reading.

Situation. Reading may occur during any of children's waking hours. Of particular significance are reading activities that they initiate and those they include voluntarily stemming from classroom experiences. Teachers should take these activities into consideration in evaluating children's reading.

Teacher role

1. Set up procedures for becoming aware of children's attitudes and use of reading outside of the specific classroom reading program.

2. Keep these records relatively current.

Procedures

1. Set up a means of recording children's demonstrated reading attitudes, habits, and procedures on a continuing basis.

2. Select items appropriate to the maturity of the group either from Randolph's Observation Sheet or modifications of it. Add any items that seem to give useful information.

3. Make entries as information is available incidentally.

4. In the reading conferences include questions relevant to items with no recent notations.

5. Plan experiences that broaden and increase

children's use of reading as a means of enriching other activities either in or out of school.

6. Use these records in evaluation with the child at regular intervals.

Evaluation. Do these records provide information supplemental to the usual reading assessment? The main purpose of learning to read is to use practical and recreational reading in life situations. Do this record and resultant experiences increase the child's wider use of reading?

Observing silent reading

Purpose. To obtain another basis for evaluating children's silent reading.

Appropriate level. All levels.

Participants. All those who are reading.

Situation. Many teachers feel their evaluation of children's silent reading is difficult or inadequate.

Teacher role

1. Set up means of recording children's silent reading behavior that is indicative of comprehension and attitudes.

2. Observe both systematically and incidentally children's silent reading behavior and record it.

Procedures

1. Set up a system for recording children's behavior noted while they are reading silently. Select items from those given in Chapter 11 and add any that seem useful. Items should focus on the child's obvious concentration and enjoyment and also on those behaviors (such as consistent subvocalizing or asking for words easily identified from context) that may be diagnostic of problems.

2. Make and date notations when these behaviors become obvious or change either for better or

worse. When notations are lacking or not recent, plan systematic observation of these children.

3. Review these notations with the child at any reading conference, particularly at periodic evaluation conferences.

4. Plan reading experiences in light of needs and the child's expressed feelings about reading.

Evaluation. Do these records help to evaluate children's silent reading competence and attitudes? Do they provide another dimension when evaluating with a child? Do they indicate help children need?

Miscue analysis

Purpose. To evaluate and diagnose problems in children's reading.

Appropriate level. Most seven-year-olds and above.

Participants. All who are reading.

Situation. Since reading is a complex language process, evaluation of reading should be based on language processes, communicating meaning through the structure of language.

Teacher role

1. To prepare needed materials.

2. To use them with individuals to identify progress and diagnose needs.

Procedures

1. Select and prepare materials appropriate for the range of general reading competence of children in the classroom.

2. Provide a tape recorder and a blank cassette for recording each child's oral reading and retelling of the selection.

3. Make notes on your copy as the child reads.

4. Ask the child to retell the thoughts in the material. Question as necessary for expansion and elaboration, but do *not* introduce any content not already mentioned by the child. Make no comment about the correctness of the child's statements.

5. Later play the tape to check your notes. Note misconceptions, omissions of important points, and extensions or interpretations the child made that indicate thinking skills.

6. Determine, if possible, causes of any miscues that do not adequately interpret the meaning or that are syntactically inappropriate. Ignore changes due to the child's natural speech patterns or dialect.

7. Plan learning experiences indicated, if any, confer with the child concerning the results, and mutually establish next steps and long-term goals.

Evaluation. Do the results of the miscue analysis provide guidance in planning needed experiences? When conducted again at a later time, does analysis show progress?

EPILOGUE—THE LANGUAGE ARTS PROGRAM IN ACTION

In this section we attempt to help teachers put together an integrated language arts program in an atmosphere most conducive to effective long-term learning that will make a constructive difference in children's lives at the moment and throughout the years to come. As a basis for a teacher's planning, some of the key elements are:

An informal classroom, where teachers and children live together comfortably, creates an environment easily translatable into life outside of school and makes learning more usable in life situations.

Establishing their own purposes, both immediate and long-term, with teacher guidance as necessary, helps children recognize what is important to them, and thus the commitment they make helps them complete the learning.

When children learn on their own as much as possible, and ask help from teacher or peer only when unable to proceed on their own, they develop independence and confidence in their own abilities.

Children progress most consistently when they are learning at their growing edge, not working with what they already know or what they are not yet ready to learn.

Working individually and in small groups, children make more effective use of their own time and the teacher's time, since no two children have the same background of experience or the same specific competencies at the same time.

When children make their own decisions, under guidance, about what they need to accomplish, they develop self-direction, responsibility, and efficient use of time for effective learning.

Children gain commitment and enthusiasm when they are permitted to choose learning materials and procedures from many that are available.

Children internalize learning by putting observations and concepts into their own words when they are given the opportunity to talk with other children about their activities, about interesting things available in the classroom, and about any problems they are having.

Children develop mutual respect and skill in resolving differences when they plan how they want to live together in the classroom and solve problems by discussing alternative solutions.

Because child-child communication is more effective than adult-child communication, children learn from each other when they are organized into classroom groups with a wide range of ability and achievement (unselected children of a one-year age range or preferably a two- or three-year range). This organization provides stimulation and prevents the destruction of self-esteem that is inherent in "ability" groups. Such classrooms emphasize the need for child-centered instruction.

PUTTING IT ALL TOGETHER

We have presented a child-centered program that integrates all the language arts skills. Its emphasis is on developing communication skills so that children can become more effective communicators in every area of the curriculum and outside of school as well. Essential elements of the program are self-direction, self-evaluation, and a sense of responsibility for oneself and one's own learning. The teacher provides a positive, accepting classroom environment in which children can develop self-confidence. The teacher's role is even more important in this program than in the traditional classroom, but it is a different role. Both teacher and students need time to change gradually from a teacher-directed classroom to one that depends largely on children's natural desire to learn.

In this chapter we suggest various ways the total language arts program can be organized and developed. If our procedures are different from those you are familiar with, you will need some sequential steps to put such a program into operation. The procedures recommended in this chapter, and those discussed in previous chapters, enable the teacher to create the total language program gradually and confidently over a period of time. Although optimum results can be obtained only through implementation of the total program, you can begin by selecting the procedures with which you feel most comfortable. Be certain, however, that all of your teaching efforts reflect confidence in the child's ability to learn and to assume responsibility, and that what one part of the program tells children about the way you perceive them does not cancel out the effect of another part.

The rationale

In a program that integrates all the language arts skills, each phase strengthens and further develops other phases. The child develops the ability to talk not only by listening, but also by reading and writing. The child's listening abilities improve as talking develops, and as the child takes in ideas through reading and expresses them in writing. Awareness of the structure of language, developed through the use of oral language, is essential for reading and writing. Expressing one's ideas in writing further increases reading ability. In fact, many children learn to read through writing. Spelling finds value in written communication, and successful spelling is based partly on becoming familiar with the appearance of words in print.

Integration within the language arts is only one step. The next step is improved communication throughout the entire curriculum. The reason for developing communication skills is to enhance the giving and receiving of thoughts, ideas, and information in all aspects of living. When we talk, listen, read, or write, it is inevitably about something. As the content of the whole curriculum becomes this "something," both language skills and understanding of content benefit. When both teachers and children become aware of using more effective communication, children gain a better understanding of ideas in all school materials. Although some time will be spent directly on the concepts and skills of language arts, all language arts activities should approximate the forms of communication that the child will use outside of school and throughout a lifetime.

A child-centered program

In "the little red schoolhouse," education was planned around each individual. As more and more children entered public schools, however, schools were organized by grades according to achievement level. Educators falsely assumed that all children in a grade should be able to learn the same things at the same time and in the same way. Children had to meet specific standards in order to "pass." One result was that in some schools a first grade class might include children from age five to age sixteen. When school people realized this policy was untenable, "social promotion" was instituted. Now thirty to forty children of approximately the same age but of widely differing accomplishment were placed in the same room, with teachers who had not learned to deal with individual differences. Gradually various schemes were developed to meet the need. Homogeneous grouping based on intelligence or achievement test scores took place all over the country, and children were segregated and labeled X, Y, and Z groups. When parents and children rebelled, educators realized that the plan was doing more harm than good, and it was dropped virtually everywhere. But the problem of diversity within the classroom still remains. In fact, as we understand more about children's learning, awareness of the problem increases.

When individualized instruction was first advocated, schools lacked suitable materials and teachers who were prepared to implement such a program. Some publishers saw a way to help. These were the publishers of children's literature. A few ventured out by providing a wide range of material, varied in difficulty, in content, and in type. These companies deserve credit for providing the basic material for individualized reading programs. Some material for this purpose is now available in all of the content areas, but much more is needed.

As individualized instruction became more widely accepted, commercial publishers tried to meet the need by supplying volumes of materials arranged sequentially in a packet for each child. The child was tested and plugged into the program at a point indicated by the test score. This was called IPI, Individually Prescribed Instruction. All children used the same material in the same way, except that the pace was different. Each child worked alone without the benefit of discussion with peers. This plan met some student needs— but it also created more problems.

The second factor slowing down the true individualizing of instruction is the lack of adequate help for students in teacher education programs to understand an individualized classroom. Far too many colleges preparing teachers and school administrators do not provide enough information or experience so that these educators can feel competent in implementing such a program. Perhaps college instructors themselves have not experienced enough individualized instruction to help their students.

Since a large majority of schools are still not meeting the individual needs of children and youth, parents are becoming more concerned. Their concern leads to establishing higher standards of achievement rather than encouraging more effective teaching procedures. When teachers feel threatened by parental and community pressure, they tighten authoritarian control, which may produce a temporary increase in scores on those few specifics that lend themselves to testing. In other words, when schools react defensively, they use force (requirements) with teachers, who naturally pass these requirements on to children.

Behavioral Objectives and *Accountability* are two movements that have developed in response to public concern over lack of competence in young people. The idea behind both movements is laudable. We all want learners to indicate their increasing competence through what they do, and certainly all educators need to be accountable. However, the implementation of these movements has been tragic. Neither of them has made use of all the information we now have on children's learning: the importance of the learner's recognition of the purpose and usefulness of learnings in their own lives; the personal involvement of the learner in what is to be learned; or the implications of the whole range of individual differences in children's learning. Instead, skills have been broken into bits and pieces that have little relevance to a child's life in the here and now. Behavioral objectives have been made minuscule by analytical adults who used an inappropriate theory of learning. Teachers feel pressure to work contrary to the way children learn best. They obtain superficial evidence of learning, only slightly relevant to the basic development of children's competence, for they are working *against* children's natural ways of learning.

There are two basic theories of learning. One considers how learning affects the life competencies of the learner, and how capable the individual has become at any stage of development. The other focuses on isolated skills and information that a learner can document by taking a paper-and-pencil test. In other words, how many items determined by a test-maker, can the learner mark correctly in a contrived situation not found elsewhere in his life? So teachers spend time drilling on unrelated specifics, so their students will pass a test, so that teachers will appear competent.

Teachers not under this type of threat—those who feel strong enough in their understanding of the long-term basic goals of education—work differently with children. They guide students toward increasingly effective living through development of a wide range of relevant and related abilities. The student has a part in developing purposes and procedures for learning.

When teachers realize the effectiveness of children's out-of-school learning, when they take advantage of children's natural desire and ability to learn, they are working *with* children. When the children are enthusiastic about school, are learning much that is significant to their immediate needs, and are becoming more competent citizens of a democracy, parents and citizens in general support their teachers and their schools. Our purpose is to provide teachers with the help they need to accomplish these ends.

Planning

In general, a teacher carries out two kinds of planning—planning *for* children and planning *with* children—on a continuing basis. Before school starts, the teacher begins making plans by learning as much as possible about the children. Their age range, for example, can be projected according to the grade they will be in. The socioeconomic level and ethnic character of the children can be inferred by driving, or preferably walking, through the area where they live. While walking, the teacher might even encounter some children who could be engaged in pleasant conversation. People at the school also can contribute information.

The teacher can then select children's books on the basis of this information. First identify all available sources of books, such as school library, public library, and county or state library. Some seventy-five to one hundred books, other than textbooks, can be available on the first day. The selection will focus on the age level of the children, but will include material for children up to two or three years older and younger as well. The collection will probably be mostly fiction but will include nonfiction material particularly relevant to the local area and to the generally recognized interests of children at this age. The teacher can shelve most of these books and display a few attractively. College courses in children's and adolescents' literature help teachers to select useful books.

The teacher can select in advance various materials that will stimulate pupil interaction: art materials such as paint; newsprint in 18″ × 24″, 12″ × 18″, and 9″ × 12″ sizes; lined 8″ × 11″ paper; colored art papers; ditto masters; and any other materials that meet the criterion.

Equipment should include tape recorders, at least two or three cassettes per child, and a file cabinet with folders. If no cabinet is available, a sturdy carton of the proper size and shape will serve the purpose. Also useful are a record player the children can use, toy telephones for primary children, and a walkie-talkie set for older students. A bulletin board can be used to reflect children's interests, activities, and concerns. Flowers and pictures help to create a pleasant atmosphere.

Survey the size and other physical conditions of the room and its furniture to explore its flexibility and possibilities for informal seating arrangements, small group work, and learning centers. Relegate the teacher's desk to an inconspicuous spot. Perhaps carpet a quiet corner for the children with discarded samples from a furniture store. An old rocking chair, bean bag chairs, or other comfortable seating presents an informal, relaxed atmosphere.

After children arrive, you begin planning for individuals on the basis of information you continue to collect. You can identify learning that children may be ready for but that has not yet been achieved by each one. As you note those specific needs that are the same for a number of children at the same time, your plan will include a period when this small group can work together.

As you come to know more about the children's reading abilities, tastes, and enthusiasms, you can select new books each week or two to introduce to the group and replace those no longer needed or used. You can locate new periodicals and bring in newspapers as you continually watch for any type of material relevant to any of the children's interests.

Keep in mind all the ways children can increase their understanding of what they read, and their ability to talk about it with increasing effectiveness. Plan activities such as creative dramatics, small group discussions about materials all members have read, and other strategies suggested throughout this book or gleaned from other sources. As opportunities for such activities become available, you can suggest one or more. When children choose an activity, you can make it possible for them to carry it out with as little direction as required.

Also keep in mind all situations that make writing a natural and valued activity. When children think of writing as a means of self-expression as well as a means of communicating over time and space, many previously unrecognized opportunities open up. Suggesting or reminding children of these possibilities at opportune moments can significantly increase the volume of writing they produce. Creating and extending the children's awareness of effective oral communication, both talking and listening, should be a part of your planning.

Planning with children

One of the most important teaching roles is to plan *with* children and assist them in planning for themselves. This process begins early in the year when the class formulates principles for living together in harmony. The better members of a group know each other and the more mutually supportive they are, the more effective each individual can be. Because this fact is especially true with children, the time you devote to beginning the process saves both teacher's and children's time during the year. You can develop the concepts that each of us makes mistakes, which we usually later regret, but that in spite of errors, each one is a worthy person deserving respect. We each need acceptance as we are, and support for changing whatever we want to change about ourselves. Together with the children, you can plan how best to accomplish these purposes.

The next important area of planning with children is determining what kind of an atmosphere they want to live in, what kinds of decisions they want to make, and what guidelines they want for their actions. Except for those whose main satisfaction has come from pleasing someone in authority, most children want to make their own decisions and are willing to pay the price of being responsible for them. Self-initiated responsibility makes possible more important areas of teacher-pupil planning.

Children need to know what to expect. When they plan ways of living together, they understand the principles and have more interest in following them. Whatever the age of the children, this is the first step in planning together. As children grow older, the plan can be more sophisticated and the rationale more explicit. The teacher's next step is to hold them to their agreements unless these agreements are changed by further teacher-pupil planning.

Agreements made by younger children might be: We will be nice to each other and help each other; we will take turns; we will not interrupt. A first grade teacher who uses this approach reports that she spends the first month holding children to their agreement and insisting that they solve their own problems. After that, cooperation goes smoothly for the rest of the year. When differences arise, the teacher asks, "What's the problem?" When the children have explained, she asks, "What do you think you can do about it?" The children talk over their problem in terms of their agreement, then offer a solution. The teacher then may say, "If you think you can do that, go ahead." She accepts any plan that will not damage property or endanger anyone's self-concept or physical being. If any harm might result from the children's plan, the teacher raises questions about possible consequences the children have not thought of.

After children get acquainted at the beginning of the year, children eight or nine years and older can hold discussions to recognize helpful and constructive actions by others in the group. Self-evaluation can take place the last fifteen minutes of the day, structured by the questions, "How did I do today?" "Is there something I can do to make tomorrow better?" Such activities make children more aware of constructive actions by others, of their own achievements, and of how behavior and learning might be enhanced—a continual "accent on the positive."

Self-direction is one of the essentials of a child-centered program and a high priority for living in today's world. Preschool children are self-directed much of the time. First graders are more willing to take responsibility than those who have been in school longer and have become accustomed to waiting for teacher direction. Many older children need to regain confidence in their own thinking.

Children begin to develop responsibility for their own learning at the beginning of the year when discussions revolve around what they want to learn and do this school year. Beginners will be general and rather vague, but their commitments can be made into charts and used as a takeoff point for more specific plans to come later. Older children will include more details. When enthusiasm wanes during the year, children under teacher guidance can reevaluate these commitments, add more specifics, and establish fresh purposes.

Plans are made once a day by the youngest, and once a week by the older children. These commitments should be specific and related to each child's needs and purposes of the moment. Younger children may include a chosen activity for which they have to wait their turn, what they will read and write, and what each one will do on a group project. The plan also should leave room for spontaneous activities.

At the beginning of the week older children list their intended accomplishments in each of the curriculum areas for that week. On Friday they evaluate what they have accomplished and how good their planning was. Did they plan for more or less than they completed? Was it the fault of the plan? Did unpredictable events interfere? Did they run into unexpected difficulties? Or was it just that they had a hard time keeping at it? In the last situation, what was the problem? Perhaps the child attempted inappropriate work, lacked needed understanding or skills, lost interest, saw no purpose for the work, or just "goofed off." Each child analyzes the week's accomplishment and makes guidelines for next week. Children's acknowledgement of their own lack of accomplishment is sufficient. Without negative comment, the child does not become defensive and so is able to make constructive plans for the following week.

After total group and individual planning, the teacher role changes. The teacher's time is spent helping an individual, working with a small group on some common need, talking with any child not totally involved in some activity, supporting each child's efforts, and showing interest with enthusiastic recognition of special accomplishments. In addition, the teacher conducts total group instruction when appropriate, makes the group aware of new materials, books, and other possible activities, and offers to hold small group learning sessions for which the children have identified a need.

Choosing specific learning activities is another important area for teacher-pupil planning. Children can discuss what they need to learn, in both competence and understanding, and what procedures seem most useful. The teacher raises questions concerning areas or procedures not perceived by the children. When there is a difference of opinion, each group can work in its own way and then compare the effectiveness of the two procedures. This type of planning can begin in a simple way as early as second grade, and by some children even in first grade. By the upper grades, children are assuming major responsibility for the results of their learning.

A first grader was having difficulty recognizing the word *the*. The teacher said, "Tommy, you really are having trouble reading that word. What do you think you could do to help you remember it?" Tommy thought a minute, then said with great determination, "I know. I'll go to the reading center and find every *the* on every page in every book. Then I bet I won't forget." Tommy used his own procedure and never forgot the word again. Can you imagine a teacher suggesting such a procedure, and what Tommy's response would have been?

Topics or focuses of class projects can be determined by the interest and concern that a teacher generates within the group. When children are excited about the topic they have had a part in choosing, far more is accomplished than when someone else has chosen it and assigned the various activities.

Organizing the classroom

Any classroom needs three types of organizations, the one-to-one, the temporary small group formed for a specific purpose, and the whole group working together. The procedures we suggest for setting up the classroom easily permit all three. Organization is emphasized each morning when the teacher and children plan the day together. Participation by even the youngest, who may be able to discuss possibilities rather than initiate ideas as older children can, will facilitate the way procedures are carried out.

During the start-of-the-day activities, children can participate in taking roll in various ways. Perhaps each child finds his or her name card and puts it in a designated pocket on the room chart. Some children can count those who want milk or lunches while others can count the money. Soon, with some children counting and others checking, they can be responsible for the whole operation.

Because the results are satisfying, the teacher's expectations grow as long as children are successful in carrying out responsibility. Occasionally a teacher expects too much, however, and needs to say, "You people have been so responsible, I forgot you aren't older than you are. Shall we wait awhile before you try to take responsibility for that?" Those who object may be able to continue the activity on a voluntary basis.

Teachers and children can establish together the general procedures for the day. Activities may vary widely from group to group. Some groups may want to start their writing first, while others may want a group sharing time. There will be quiet times, periods of moving about, times for conversation and noisier activities. Each child will know what resources are available, how material is to be used, and how and where to put it away. Because of the variety available, anyone can engage in constructive activity, which frees the teacher for individual conferences or small group sessions.

The purposes and procedures for conferences are made clear to children through discussion and planning. Children can make their conferences more useful when they are given an opportunity for questions and input, and they know that each is responsible for getting ready for a conference and signing up for it. Children should understand that a conference entails the following steps: (1) Child and teacher identify specific needs and purposes; (2) child and teacher make plans, with the child taking the initiative or selecting from the teacher's suggestions; (3) child and teacher plan next steps, decide when the next conference may be needed, and specify what the child needs to do to get ready for it. The child carries out the plan, then evaluates the accomplishment with the teacher.

Small groups are organized for specific purposes that cover the entire curriculum and range from specific skills to broad competencies to deeper understanding. The children called together have indicated lack of some specific ability and a readiness to acquire it. The teacher sets up small group procedures and provides the necessary materials. Children stay in the group only until their purpose is accomplished. After explanations and some work on the concept or skill, a child may demonstrate understanding and then leave the group to pursue other activities. Because of this *spin-off*, the teacher can focus more time and attention on children with different perceptions and those who need more help.

Total group meetings are held for a variety of purposes: First, they help to improve working relationships within the class. A discussion may be designed to deal with irritation or unhappiness among the children. Such sessions should concentrate on "how we can all work together to solve the problem." Second, the meeting may be held to evaluate progress—"How are we doing?" The group can confirm some procedures and decide to initiate others. Third, the group may come together to provide mutual support in order to build self-confidence and self-concept. Individuals can use these meetings to set or extend goals. Fourth, the class may meet to plan a group project, discuss its purposes and procedures, and select committees children would like to work on.

The class may meet also for total group instruction. The topic might be a concept that is new to all or almost all of the children, a class activity such as a visitor or a field trip, or participation in an all-school activity. Group instruction is helpful when it is not part of sequential learning of content that some children already know and others are not yet ready for. And finally, the total class may simply enjoy doing something together: sharing experiences, listening to a story, learning a new song or art technique, enjoying a performer, a film, or a play. In the total group children can share their products, interests, and activities and learn from those of their peers.

Learning centers

The teacher and children can plan what learning centers they need. They know they need a well-lighted space where children can select books and stay to read. A reading corner should have shelf space for the 100 to 200 books, including those in the various content areas, which would be available in the room at any one time. They need a display space for new books brought in to replace those taken back to libraries. Perhaps the children would like a soft carpet on the floor so they can lie on their stomachs to read. Bill says he thinks he can bring some shag carpet that his family has just replaced. Sarah thinks she could bring a little rocking chair. Phil offers to bring his bean bag chair.

The children also want a writing center. Here they need "first draft" and "final copy" paper, pencils, ball-point pens, a dictionary, and a thesaurus. The wall above the table is a good place for their word charts. They think the table should be big enough for three or four children to write at a time. Someone asks if they might have desk screens to set up so they will feel really private while they are first putting down their ideas. After they begin using the center, they display correct forms for business and personal letters, and illustrations of punctuation. Temporarily added are lists of special words related to recent experiences or ongoing projects. A little later they ask for some help in starting their writing. The teacher adds a box of Story Starters and a copy of *Slithery Snakes and Other Aids to Children's Writing* (Petty, 1967) for children who have trouble thinking of things to write.

The children decide the listening-talking and oral reading center should be in a far corner, since it will be one of the noisiest areas. If they are lucky enough to have an outside door to their room, in nice weather children can go outside to use the cassette recorder. At the listening center are the three tape recorders, a tape deck to play music, tapes accompanying books, or those that the teacher prepares for various purposes. Here, also, children record oral reading, both for practice so they can listen and improve, and for long-term evaluation over the year.

Next comes their science and math center. The children want it near the sink because they will need water for a number of experiments. Various kitchen utensils are brought in. Measuring spoons, cups, and containers are needed for quantitative measurement in math, as well as for science experiments. Scales for measuring weight, a

yardstick, and a steel tape for distances are added. The children will need paper and pencil for planning and recording experiments, and for writing them up to share with others. They will need some of this equipment to work out the real-life math problems they are to exchange with peers. Materials and equipment will be added or eliminated during the year as concerns and interests change.

In the social studies center, a globe and a world atlas are permanent equipment, along with a book rack to hold the most important books related to the current project. Children will borrow the school opaque projector to make enlarged maps they want to use. Planning calls for butcher paper and space on the wall to put strips of it up where they can work on it. If their murals are too long, they will ask permission to put them up in the hall outside their door. They need regular writing paper, too, to organize and summarize the results of their study.

The art center will be near the sink and far away from any carpets that could be damaged by spilled paints. The children request two double easels so four can paint at a time. There is only one, but Diane thinks her dad could make them another. The school supplies a variety of paints and brushes, and children bring baby food jars and frozen orange juice cans to mix the paints in. The art cupboard contains a supply of newsprint and finger-painting paper, scissors, crayons, finger paint, powdered paint, glue, colored chalk, charcoal, and water colors. There is a large work table where children can do finger painting, or work on carefully thought-out illustrations for their stories, books, and reports.

A day in a self-directed classroom

Each day in a child-centered classroom demonstrates the many ways that children are encouraged to use language when they direct their own activities. By 9 o'clock each morning the room is filled with happy, eager children conversing, or locating incomplete projects they expect to work on today, or submerged in the book they had to leave yesterday when it was time to go home. Sarah, who is group chairman for the week, goes to the spot near the flag and calls the group to order. They quickly take their places and she leads them in the salute to the flag. She calls on Ben, the lunch and milk chairman, to make a count and give a report. His assistant, Betty, takes her position at a table. While he asks for hands to be raised, she receives money due that day and gives a simple receipt. He reports and joins Betty at the table. They count those previously paid and those that paid today, then compare that total with the number who want hot lunches today. When their figures agree, Betty puts the money, a list of those who paid today, and the total amount paid, in an envelope in Mrs. Miller's desk drawer. Meanwhile, Sarah has asked the attendance chairman to check the roll. He checks, fills out the attendance form, and puts both the form and the order for milk and lunches, which Ben has just completed, under the clip just outside the door.

Sarah now calls on the book chairman, Lloyd, to conduct book sharing. Lloyd asks if anyone has a book they would like to share. Several indicate they do. One after another they come to the front, name the title, author, and illustrator of the book, and hold it up so all can see the cover and any especially significant pictures. Each tells the kind of book it is and just enough about it so others have an idea whether they might like to read it.

Mrs. Miller enters the room quietly and her presence is hardly noticed. She had been detained in the office by a telephone call from one of the parents, who reported commitment of enough other parents to assist with the field trip next week.

When the book sharing ends, Sarah asks if someone has a special report for the day. Alice brings a box up to the table. She tells of the family's trip up the canyon on the previous weekend and of the rocks they collected. She opens the box and holds it so all can see. She tells how she used a book from the city library to identify each rock, glued them all to a cardboard, and wrote the name under each one. Several children stand, trying to see better, then realize they are keeping those behind them from seeing, and ask Alice to pass the box around. Alice describes the area where the rocks were found and answers many questions from the other children.

Sarah thanks all those who helped this morning, then asks Mrs. Miller if she has anything to tell them. Mrs. Miller explains the phone call. Then Sarah says if there are no other announcements, they can go ahead with their work. Most take out their journals and start writing. A few get books from the reading center and start preparing for reading conferences.

Susan, Bob, Linda, and Ron have all had reading and writing conferences earlier in the week and had written in their journals before school started. Now they go to the social studies center, discuss the next steps in the project they are working on, decide what part each of them will be responsible for, then go to work.

Bill, whose name is at the top of the list for reading conferences, asks Mrs. Miller if they can have their conference now. She agrees, but Steve comes up and asks for information. Mrs. Miller asks where he has looked for it. He says he doesn't know where to look. She asks him to think what kind of information it is he wants. He thinks a minute, then says, "Oh, I bet I know where." He goes quickly to a set of reference books, searches, and with a broad grin signals across the room that he has found it. Mrs. Miller and Bill settle down to the conference. After about seven minutes, Bill goes back to his desk, feeling satisfied with his progress but planning how to improve his next reading.

One child after another comes to Mrs. Miller asking for help. When the information they need is difficult or impossible for them to find, she quickly gives the answer or refers them to someone who can help. When it is something they can find or need to think out, she asks questions. Some children need more help than others, but soon they go away pleased with themselves that they "figured it out" and with more assurance that they can succeed next time.

By now many have finished writing in their journals and are moving on to other things. Some are working on their math, and some are polishing stories they wrote earlier. Susan leans over and asks Alice whether to write *puppys* or *puppies*—neither one looks right to her. Alice isn't sure but asks Susan if she means "The puppies are hungry" or "I fixed the puppy's dinner." Susan responds, and Alice explains how she thinks it is, but suggests Susan look it up in the dictionary.

Randy, who has been moving around restlessly, asks if anyone minds if he puts on a record. Several say, "Okay, but keep the volume down." He puts on a quiet, melodious piece that reminds him of the wind in the woods on his grandfather's farm. He sits down and soon he is writing steadily.

Ron has taken his revised story to Ethel, who is checking writing this week for their newspaper. She returns it to him, says she likes the new title better, indicates a couple of misspelled words, and suggests he check the length of his sentences because some of them are not clear to her. He thanks her and sets to work.

Mrs. Miller has had two more reading conferences and a writing conference, and now she is moving around the room, exchanging a few words here and there with children who have questions or comments. Now she sees it is mid-morning and some children are moving restlessly or staring out the window. She suggests that they take a break, move around, get a drink. Nearly all follow her suggestion. Sally asks if they can sing the song they have been learning, and many excitedly agree. Mrs. Miller gives the starting pitch, and they burst into a rollicking song accompanied by movements. After about five minutes Mrs. Miller asks if they feel better. All agree, sit down, and tackle their work with fresh vigor.

Various children have been moving to one or another of the learning centers all morning, particularly the reading, writing, and math centers. Now a group moves to the science center and decides on an experiment they want to try. Since it involves water, they agree to do it on the sink

shelf. Two of them who spilled water all over the science center recently remember the terrible job they had cleaning up. Others checked their plans for the week and on this basis decided what they needed to do.

Mrs. Miller thinks this would be a good time to check with the group she worked with last week on context clues in reading. At this week's conferences, some were still having problems. She lists their names on one corner of the chalkboard and asks them to meet her in the reading corner. There the children tell what they have been able to do and where they are still having trouble. As they point out words they cannot identify, Mrs. Miller finds two who are not trying to think of synonyms when the first word they thought of that made sense in the sentence obviously was not the "right" word. She sets these two to thinking of what other word it might be in light of the whole paragraph. She realizes that the words are not spelled phonetically, but the first two letters should give a clue. The sentence that bothered Evelyn she has interpreted incorrectly, so she is looking for a noun rather than a verb. When Mrs. Miller changes the intonation to fit the meaning, Evelyn comes up with the needed word immediately. They talk about the necessity of reading the whole sentence, not just the part preceding an unknown word. The other two now know their missing words, and all talk about how helpful it is to read on and identify important unrecognized words in light of the paragraph or section.

Such a morning can happen after several months of developing a program in the middle grades. Teachers need to realize, however, that progress requires mutual respect, consistency of planning, and holding children calmly but firmly to their responsibilities and commitments.

Record keeping

Keeping significant records, an essential part of any profitable learning program, can be done in a variety of ways and is the shared responsibility of both teacher and children.

The extent of the records kept by children, of course, depends on their maturity. However, keeping track of their accomplishments is important for even the youngest. For example, it can reinforce their acceptance of responsibility for daily participation in certain activities. Record keeping begins even before children learn to write. One possibility is that the various learning-activity centers can be identified by colors, and each child can have name tags of each color. Upon completing work at a center, the child hangs a tag on a hook in that area. When all that child's tags have been hung, the child is free to become involved in any activity available. The teacher then has a record of each child's participation for that day. This procedure, which has many modifications, is only one of various possible means of recording.

As children develop their ability to write, they can keep other records. When they are keeping journals, each day's writing is dated. A section of those booklets can be used for keeping track of the books they have read. They may record their reactions, such as "good book," "I liked the part about the girl finding the lady's ring," or "Story does not make sense. I put it back." There can be space also for recording other responsibilities completed. As children mature they extend such recording, but never to the point that it becomes laborious. Their own record is a basis for self-evaluation when they complete it and look it over near the end of each day and each week.

A simpler means of children's record keeping provides evidence that is useful for evaluation over longer periods of time. A file drawer or an appropriate-sized carton can hold a file folder for each child. Their first writing in each of the curriculum areas is placed in their folders and remains there throughout the year. They add papers they are proud of. They may leave all papers in the folder or substitute a new one for any but the first. By comparing each new addition with work they did at the beginning of the term or year, they become aware of progress they might not recognize otherwise.

Record keeping can be simplified or made as comprehensive as the teacher or children desire. Records are most useful as a basis for teacher-child conferences. All such records serve two main purposes: (1) a basis for evaluation and hence modification of the total program, some part of the program, or the activities of individual children; (2) a regular reminder of the responsibilities children have accepted.

If some children are not keeping records or carrying out their assumed responsibilities, perhaps these children do not feel any commitment, but see the situation as further imposition of teacher control. In these cases it is important to back off and find out what the child feels is important. A readjustment, to focus on what children feel is valuable for them, can bring constructive effort and set the stage for inclusion of other areas when children recognize their value.

Teacher's record keeping

Teachers need a means of keeping records that is relatively simple so that it does not get shunted aside in the busy day. Two forms have proved useful: five-by-eight-inch file cards in a file box with an index card for each child, or a loose-leaf notebook with the child's name on a tab divider to make location easy. The teacher may keep separate cards or pages for each curriculum area, or record them all together by date. (Before planning their records, teachers should refer to specific suggestions in chapters on each of the language arts areas.)

The important information to record is not a "good-better-best" rating, but rather the specific learning noted and specific concepts or skills that are needed but have not yet been learned. On the basis of skills needed, small groups are brought together. Any agreements made between teacher and child should be recorded as reminders.

Recorded information should be made available

to the child in order to build trust and confidence in the teacher.

Evaluation

Evaluation is not necessarily concerned with grades, but with taking a realistic look at what we have learned, what we can do, how much better we can do it now than before, what we know, what it means to us, and what we need to learn next. Evaluation can give us renewed self-confidence, for there is always some way in which we have made progress when we consider all areas of learning. Such ongoing, formative evaluation procedures help all of us to move closer to our goals.

Records by both children and teachers, such as those suggested above, are particularly useful during evaluation conferences, especially those summative evaluation procedures occurring every few weeks. On the other hand, the daily evaluation that takes place informally provides much significant data for the record keeping.

Evaluation of children should include recognition of specific situations illustrating more effective listening and talking. It should note how children have used reading both for practical purposes and for pleasure, to broaden and enrich their lives, and should recognize improvement of communication in their writing. Evaluation recognizes that all aspects of communication, including the arts, help children learn more about themselves and the world they live in: natural, work-a-day, political, and social. But of at least equal importance, teachers need to evaluate the expansion and deepening of children's creativity and thinking, their increase in self-direction, and their acceptance of responsibility. All these are the basics.

When considering evaluation of children's learning, teachers should refer to "Criteria for all school evaluations" in Chapter 4 (pp. 103–105) and to specific criteria discussed in other chapters on each of the language arts areas.

Evaluation of the program

Evaluation of the ongoing program should be continuous as should all evaluation. The end of a year calls for an in-depth look at what really happened to the children in your care, what they accomplished on their way to becoming responsible, contributing citizens. How far have they moved toward confidence in their own thinking, in their ability to identify a problem and to solve it? How much more effective are they in establishing productive human relationships with a wide variety of peers and adults? How much more responsibility are they taking for their own actions, for their own learning, for initiating useful suggestions and activities, for needed assistance to others? How much more clearly and effectively are they able to talk with others, to write both for useful purposes and for their own satisfaction? How much better are they able to select what they listen to? How far have they progressed toward becoming lifelong readers? Input may include comments from parents, any or all school personnel, and the children themselves. Of course, the answer to each of these questions will vary with each individual, and each child needs to be considered on each issue for you to arrive at a complete picture.

For yourself, there are other questions: How much more able are you to listen to children, to what they really mean? How much more confidence have you developed in all children's abilities, to learn, to think, to be self-directive, to be responsible? How much more often do you raise challenging questions rather than make instructional statements? How effectively have you been able to integrate the various language arts, thus saving time and making learning more effective? How much have you been able to make the language arts skills an effective instrument for learning in the total school program?

Summary

Preparing the children in our schools for a constructive, productive life in society is our basic responsibility as teachers. To do this we must see that our children develop the basic skills, knowledge, thought processes, attitudes, and behaviors they need. In this book we have provided information and suggested procedures in the language arts that we believe are most useful in accomplishing these purposes. We further believe that the way teachers work with children must be effective for their purposes, else much effort goes for naught. We hope we can help teachers to develop lifelong learners and readers, people who can take the initiative and responsibility for developing effective working relationships with their peers, and use their skills and knowledge to make a better life for all in our troubled world today. These are the basics.

Suggested learning experiences for prospective teachers

Suggestion A

1. Reread the introduction and rationale for this book. Compare the various points made there with the procedures discussed in these chapters.

2. Which elements of the program do you feel you want to carry out? Which do you agree with but feel would be impossible for you to carry out? Why? Which do you disagree with? Why?

3. If you feel some procedures would be impossible for you to carry out, is it because of your inexperience? Remember we recommended that new teachers start with the parts of the program they feel comfortable with, and gradually add other phases as they can.

4. If you feel the situation you are going into would not permit some aspects of the program, plan to start within their limits. Follow school regulations, especially out of the classroom. However, under any circumstances, you will be establishing relationships with the children. You can show respect for them as individuals, confidence in them as learners, and expectation that they want to learn. You can solve or prevent many problems by planning with them how you can all live together most profitably and comfortably, and then calmly but firmly holding them and yourself to the agreements. Mutual courtesy, respect, truth, and appreciation are key elements. Planning learning experiences based on what we know about children's learning and the way concepts and skills are acquired, rather than on traditional procedures, can secure children's interest in learning. Happy, responsible children, who can demonstrate significant competence, provide the best insurance for a program.

5. You may disagree with some elements of the program. If so, it is important for you to understand clearly why you disagree, and to have a well-thought-out rationale for an alternative approach. The lack of any defensible rationale on the part of teachers, and the resultant unthinking conformity to existing procedures, is the main reason for the public's disenchantment with schooling.

Suggestion B

1. While your thinking about language arts is fresh in mind, write out ideas you would like to carry out in your own classroom.

2. In a loose-leaf notebook, set up a section for each of the areas, and include your ideas in it. Cross-reference ideas that involve more than one area, as most of them will.

3. Note ways to use content learnings, suggested in other classes, to develop both understandings in that field and language arts skills.

4. Start or continue a reference file of books, articles, and other materials to serve two main purposes: specific ideas for day-to-day use, and material to renew your faith in the things you really believe. The first is always handy in planning, and the second is a great pick-me-up after the "bad days" all teachers have all their teaching lives. Consistent implementation of a well-thought-out philosophy gradually diminishes the frequency of those "days you would like to forget," and greatly increases the rewarding ones.

Suggested readings

A most important reference for those who work with children in schools is the article by the respected educator and psychologist Carl Rogers, "Beyond the Watershed: And Where Now?" Other useful interpretations of current problems are Arthur Combs' *Educational Accountability: Beyond Behavioral Objectives*; Welch, Richards, and Richards' *Educational Accountability: A Humanistic Perspective*; and Rogers and Church's *Open Education: Critique and Assessment*.

Many authors talk about the teacher's role in the classroom. Tony Wagner in "Learning Democratically" suggests ways to develop competence, independence, cooperation, and rational authority, while Berman, in her *New Priorities in the Curriculum* emphasizes skills basic to human living. Steven Bossert in "Tasks, Group Management, and Teacher Control Behavior: A Study of Classroom Organization and Teacher Style" deals with recitation, class tasks, and multitask teaching. Ralph Larkin in "Contextual Influences on Teacher Leadership Styles" compares teacher-pupil relationships in team-teaching, nongrading, and self-contained classrooms. Haim Ginott in *Teacher and Child: A Book for Parents and Teachers*, a vivid and down-to-earth book, deals with everyday problems of the classroom. In "Teacher's Role in Life-Centering the Curriculum," Edward Olsen comments on the slogan "Back to the Basics":

"No, not backward—forward to the fundamentals of living." Aspy and Roebuck show the relationship of teachers' positive attitudes toward students to an increase in learning and a decrease in discipline problems, in their "From Humane Ideas to Humane Technology and Back Again Many Times." Peggy Fisher in "The Transformation of a New England Schoolmarm" tells delightfully how a stiff, ruler-slapping disciplinarian becomes a free-spirited open-classroom teacher.

The commercial distortion of the concept of individualization is made clear in Kipler and Randall's "Individualization: The Subversion of Elementary Schooling." On the other hand, Shiman, Culver, and Lieberman tell of a variety of ways they have used individualizing usefully in "Teachers on Individualization: The Way We Do It."

To give specific help, Kenneth and Rita Dunn described "60 Activities That Develop Student Independence"; the A.C.E.I. has produced a booklet, *Learning Centers: Children On Their Own*; and Lehane and Peete in "The Amazing Adventures of Erik Stonefoot" have explained their way of integrating science and language arts through use of the shared skills.

Various authors explain a way of working with children to help them develop competence, self-direction, autonomy, and responsibility—the basic needs of citizens in a democracy. John

Lembo in *When Learning Happens* describes ways to make learning natural and important. Silberman, Allender, and Yanoff in *The Psychology of Open Teaching and Learning: An Inquiry Approach* provide a wealth of how's and why's for a teaching-learning program. Melvin Silberman edited *The Experience of Schooling*, in which various authors examined the unintended consequences of widely accepted school practices and conditions. In Carl Rogers' *Freedom to Learn*, the prologue and various chapters raise significant issues.

Louise Despert in *The Inner Voices of Children* helps teachers understand the child's point of view. Barbara Blitz in *The Open Classroom: Making It Work* is especially helpful about ways to move into the open classroom gradually, with specific ideas about learning centers. Michael Maccoby in "The Three C's and Discipline for Freedom" tells how to develop children's ability to concentrate, think critically, and communicate clearly. Virgil Howes edited *Individualization of Instruction: A Teaching Strategy*, which includes chapters by authorities in various fields. Lillian and Virgil Logan in *Design for Creative Teaching* suggest specific ways to establish the climate and strategies for creative teaching. Goodlad, Klein, and others in *Looking behind the Classroom Door* report that most teachers fail to individualize instruction even though they may believe they are doing so. Charles Silberman in *Crisis in the Classroom* describes a three-year investigation of American public education that found schools "grim" and "joyless" places. Postman and Weingartner talk about ways to change traditional procedures quietly in their *The Soft Revolution*.

Strategies for children's learning

How to develop a strategy for a known group

As teachers begin to plan strategies for developing children's understanding and skills, they can follow the general procedures used in this text. Once they know the children, however, plans should be more specific as to purpose and include more alternative ways of learning in order to take into account the varied experiences and interests of the group. The number of decisions children make depends on the age of the children, their experience in decision-making, and their experience in the content area. For instance, planning next steps is easier in an area they have been working in than in an unfamiliar area. Procedures should be flexible enough so that each child can move to new learning based firmly on present understanding. Evaluation then recognizes growth in the direction of a defensible life-related goal. Each child's record will include a sentence or two reflecting specific changes in competence and increased independence and self-confidence.

Guidelines for developing strategies

1. Identify a specific need of a group of children for a concept or skill that they do not have but are ready for.

2. Record why they need the learning and how it will be used; this information will affect the procedures.

3. Identify your role in this learning. For what part will you give information and direct activity? For what part will you raise questions to encourage children's thinking and decision-making?

4. Plan procedures that: (a) involve the children; (b) clarify the purpose and modify it as necessary so it becomes their own purpose; (c) present or

arrange for them to obtain the content for developing the concept or skill; (d) involve children in planning ways the content can be used to meet specific needs of the group and of particular individuals; and (e) give them as much responsibility as possible for carrying out the plans.

5. Plan to discuss how children will know that they have learned what they planned to learn. Many ways are appropriate for evaluating success in steps along the way, but any evaluation of long-term learning should refer to its use in real-life situations.

APPENDIXES

Appendix A: Various grammars

Joseph M. Williams, in *The New English*, offers the following description of grammar.

The grammars that most of us studied in junior high were tradition-encrusted monuments built by the Greeks and Romans two thousand years ago and little changed since then. Though every other body of knowledge has changed, even theology, even how the Bible is to be read, many people still believe that a grammar is something handed down from the mountain top, fixed and eternally valid, not to be questioned. But every other field of knowledge has changed and progressed because curious minds began to think about the questions they had been asking and whether they might not ask new questions that might result in new and more interesting answers.

When we studied "grammar" in junior high, we probably spent most of our time learning either how to speak and write as our teachers thought an educated person should, or how to label parts of speech and diagram sentences. Actually, we were studying language in two very different ways: as *usage* and as *structure*.

In addition to studying grammar as something that tells us how to speak and write "correctly," we also study grammar as the systematic structure of the entire language. This other side of grammar, which is too often merely labeling parts of speech and diagramming sentences, comes closer to describing what all dialects of a language, indeed all human languages, share. Wherever we come from, whatever our background, we all use *nouns* and *verbs*; our sentences have *subjects* and *predicates*; all speakers of all dialects at all social levels of English use *indirect objects*.

So we can define *grammar* in two ways: We can mean what is accepted as "grammatical" by a particular group of speakers in a particular geographical-social context in the sense that someone would say, "He has good grammar." This involves only a very superficial difference between the ways certain educated and uneducated people talk and write. It ignores the other 99 percent of the language they have in common. It is purely a social distinction like wearing narrow or wide lapels when narrow lapels are in style.

By "grammar" we can also mean the general

structure of those sentences which all speakers share and so never notice, a question which concentrates on that other 99 percent.

But we can define "grammar" in yet a different way: We can also say that a "grammar" is the description, in our terms the *model*, that represents our ability to speak in a certain way. If we describe only social and geographical differences, we will have a thin "grammar," a very short description because the differences are relatively few. But if our "grammar," our description, tries to account for the entire language, we will have a very long description. Indeed, every language, even that spoken by the most primitive, illiterate tribe on earth, is so complicated that no grammar will ever describe any language fully.

One way of describing language that tries to model what we know about English, that does let us ask questions, is called a *transformational grammar*. There are other kinds of new grammars, but transformational grammar is the most highly developed of the new theories of language. And since it does try to represent in some way our abilities to judge sentences and interpret them, we will be as interested in the form of a transformational grammar as in any particular grammatical structure it describes.

Source: *Excerpts reprinted with the permission of Macmillan Publishing Co., Inc., from Joseph Williams,* The New English, *pp. 2–13, copyright 1970 by The Free Press, a division of Macmillan.*

Wayne Harsh in *Grammar Instruction Today*, explains three grammars.

Traditional grammar

As a result of the work of descriptive grammarians—and of descriptive linguists in the past twenty-five years—the system of traditional grammar taught today, though it retains much of the prescription and proscription for which it has been criticized, leans somewhat toward a realistic description of the language. In brief, it is a system of grammatical analysis which interprets a sentence according to meaning and according to the intention of the speaker (thus the categories: *declarative, interrogative, imperative, and exclamatory*), then proceeds to define the components of the sentence, both the syntactic units of clauses and phrases and the single word units of nouns, verbs, prepositions, etc. All definitions are based either on meaning (*a noun names a person, place, thing, concept, action*) or on function (*a preposition is a word which relates its object to the rest of the sentence*). Using meaning to describe and discuss the various forms of words (inflected forms such as *boy, boys; run, runs, ran, running*), traditional grammar lists the properties of nouns and verbs, generally following as closely as the English language permits the pattern of language analysis and the terminological designations used in discussing the classical languages. The traditional system, in addition to defining the parts of speech and the syntactic units of English, describes with great detail the function of these elements in a sentence: *e.g.*, a noun, or substantive, serves in the following syntactic functions: subject, object of a transitive verb, subjective complement of a linking verb, indirect object, objective complement, object of a preposition, appositive, noun of direct address. Traditional grammar tends to concern itself almost exclusively with the written language and until quite recently failed to take into consideration such functional varieties of language as formal written, formal spoken, colloquial, literary, and so forth.

Descriptive linguistics

If one disregards the numerous variations in definition methods and definition terminology, which are due in large part to the relative newness of applied linguistics, descriptive linguistics may be briefly summarized as follows: It is a discipline which considers grammar to be "the set of formal patterns in which the words of a language are arranged in order to convey larger meanings," or "the branch of linguistic science which is concerned with the description, analysis, and formalization of formal language patterns." Descriptive linguists postulate that English has a set of grammatical patterns unique to it alone, and that to convey meaning it uses word form, word order, function words, and intonation patterns. In analyzing these patterns the descriptive linguists proceed from form to meaning, identifying first the meaningful minimal sounds (phonemes), then meaningful minimal lexical units (morphemes), and ultimately proceeding to larger syntactic units (phrases, clauses, sentences). Descriptive linguists define the parts of speech used in English under the two general categories of form class words and function words. Form class words (nouns, verbs, adjectives, and adverbs) carry the primary lexical meaning and inflect or change form to indicate meaning. Function words (noun determiners, auxiliary verb forms, subordinators, prepositions) have little or no lexical meaning, do not change in form, and are in closed classes, not borrowing or adding new words; function words are important in indicating structural relationships and grammatical meaning.

Distinguishing between the spoken language and the written language, linguists stress the importance of speech patterns unique to an individual (*idiolect*) and to geographic regions or social classes (*dialects*.) They distinguish various levels of English usage, such as *standard* versus *sub-standard* or *illiterate*; and they classify various functional varieties of usage such as *formal spoken, colloquial, literary, slang*.

Generative grammar

In brief, generative grammar proposes to describe not just existing English sentences but all possible English sentences and to give an explanation of how we form or "generate" sentences. Using the notations of symbolic logic, generative grammar expresses in formulas the components of phrase structure which constitute simple (kernel) sentences (S → NP + VP) and the transformations which add elements to and rearrange the elements of the simple sentence (such transformations as Tr. Passive, Tr. Negative, etc.). It provides formulas for explaining even such complicated structures of present-day English as the periphrastic verb forms:

be + tense   V + ing
(The plane *was landing*.)

Modal + tense   have   V + ed
(The plane *should have landed*.)

have + tense   V + en
(John *has given* his friend the book.)

have + tense   be+ en   V + ing
(The water *had been dripping*.)

Generative grammar offers a basis for explaining the ambiguity of such constructions as "Flying planes can be dangerous," by explaining the underlying structures of such sentences. In describing the kernel sentences and the transformations which these kernel sentences undergo, generative grammar utilizes the techniques and terminology of both traditional grammar and descriptive linguistics.

Source: *Adapted from Wayne Harsh*, Grammar Instruction Today *(Davis, California: Davis Publications in English, University of California, at Davis, 1965.) pp. 5–14. Reprinted by permission of the author.*

Appendix B: Goals for listening

Sara Lundsteen, in *Listening: Its Impact on Reading and the Other Language Arts*, offers the following as goals and skills related to good listening.

General listening skills or goals

1. To remember significant details accurately.

2. To remember simple sequences of words and ideas.

3. To follow oral directions.

4. To understand denotative meanings of words.

5. To understand meanings of words from spoken context.

6. To listen, to answer, and to formulate simple questions.

7. To paraphrase a spoken message.

8. To understand connotative meanings of words.

9. To identify main ideas and to summarize (the who, what, when, where, why).

10. To listen for implications of significant details.

11. To listen for implications of main ideas.

12. To understand interrelationships among ideas expressed or implied and the organizational pattern of spoken materials well enough to predict what will probably come next.

13. To follow a sequence in: (a) plot development, (b) character development, (c) speaker's argument.

14. To impose structure on a spoken presentation, sometimes including note-taking, by: (a) realizing the purpose of the speaker, (b) remaining aware of personal motives in listening, (c) connecting and relating what is said later in the presentation with earlier portions, (d) detecting transitional words or phrases which refer the listener back or carry him along, (e) detecting the skeleton of main and supporting points and other interrelationships.

15. To connect the spoken material with previous experience.

16. To listen, to apply, and to plan action.

17. To listen, to imagine, and to extend for enjoyment and emotional response (includes appreciation for aesthetic, artistic, dialectic richness, felicity of phrasing, rhythmic flow).

Critical listening skills

1. To distinguish fact from fancy, according to criteria.

2. To judge validity and adequacy of main ideas, arguments, hypotheses.

3. To distinguish well-supported statements from opinion and judgment and to evaluate them.

4. To distinguish well-supported statements from irrelevant ones and to evaluate them; to sort relevant from irrelevant information.

5. To inspect, compare, and contrast ideas and arrive at some conclusion in regard to them, e.g., the appropriateness and appeal of one descriptive word over another.

6. To evaluate use of fallacies such as: (a) self-contradictions, (b) "skirting" the question at issue, (c) hasty or false generalization, (d) false analogy, (e) failure to present all choices, (f) appeal to ignorance.

7. To recognize and judge effects of devices the speaker may use to influence the listener, such as: (a) music, (b) loaded words, (c) voice intonation, (d) play on emotional and controversial issues, (e) propaganda, sales pressure, i.e., to identify affective loading in communication and evaluate it.

8. To detect and evaluate bias and prejudice of a speaker or point of view.

9. To evaluate the qualifications of the speaker.

10. To plan to evaluate ways in which the speaker's ideas might be applied in a new situation.

Source: *Sara W. Lundsteen*, Listening: Its Impact on Reading and the Other Language Arts, *pp. 52–53. Copyright ©1971 by the National Council of Teachers of English. Reprinted by permission.*

Carl Weaver, in *Human Listening: Process and Behavior*, offers the following suggestions for improving listening and talking.

What the listener can do to improve

Developing a desire to listen,

Increasing your capacity to listen,

You can reflect the message to the talker,

You must guess the talker's intent or purpose,

You should strive to bring the quality of your habitual listening up to the level of your optimal capacity,

You should try to determine whether your referents for the words of the talker are about the same as his,

You should try to determine your purpose in every listening situation,

You should become aware of your own biases and attitudes,

You should learn to use your spare time well as you listen,

You should analyze your listening errors,

You should pay attention to the process of cognitive structuring as it occurs and to the time it takes,

You should learn as much as you can about the process of listening.

Summary

Developing your ability to evaluate what you hear,

You should get the whole story before evaluating it,

You should be alert to mistaken causal relations,

You should ask yourself whether the speaker has done his homework well,

You should ask yourself whether the opinions you hear are sound,

You should judge how much the speaker's biases are affecting his message.

What the talker can do to help

You should try to empathize with your listener,

You should prepare your listener for your message,

You should time your message well,

If you want your listener to remember the outline of your message, make it clear,

You should keep your message moving,

You should stimulate your listeners,

You should be specific enough,

You should be clear,

You should take advantage of preliminary tuning whenever you can,

You should reduce the number and kinds of inferences your listener must make,

You should do what you can to prevent premature evaluation,

When you are trying to explain or describe some object or event, you should tell your listener what it is *not* as well as what it is,

You should be aware of your own biases,

You can attract and re-attract the listener's attention when it ebbs.

Source: *Carl Weaver*, Human Listening: Process and Behavior, *pp. 99, 125. Copyright ©1972 by The Bobbs-Merrill Co., Inc. Reprinted by permission.*

Appendix C: T-units from Hunt's *Grammatical Structures*

Kellogg W. Hunt, in *Grammatical Structures Written at Three Grade Levels*, defines T-units as an index of maturity.

The increase in mean clause length and the increase in the number of subordinate clauses add up to something worth noting. If it is true that (1) the average main clause written by successively older students has more subordinate clauses attached to it, and if, in addition, (2) those clauses are longer, then the total length of such a unit would of course increase as a result of the two subsidiary kinds of lengthening. This unit whose total length is being discussed contains, to repeat, one main clause with all the subordinate clauses attached to it. The number of subordinate clauses can, of course, be none.

The length of such a unit might turn out to be a good index of maturity. It might turn out to be an even better index than the two subsidiary factors because of the fact that an individual who was high in subordination index but low in clause length (or the reverse) would have those opposite tendencies moderated by this combining index.

A whole piece of writing could be sliced up into units of this sort, just as a rib pork roast is sliced off into chops. The person slicing need only be careful to cut where the joint comes instead of cutting into a chunk of solid bone. There should be no trouble deciding whether an expression, if it is intelligible at all, goes with the preceding main clause or the following. An *and* between two main clauses would always go with the second clause, beginning it just as coordinating conjunctions so often

begin the sentences of mature writers. A student's failure to put in periods where he should would not interfere with the slicing process unless the passage already was an unintelligible garble.

Here is a sample to be sliced up. It is printed just as the fourth grader wrote it, except that the spelling is corrected. It is a whole theme, punctuated as one sentence, 68 words long. This one fourth grade sentence is four times as long as the average twelfth grade sentence.

> I like the movie we saw about Moby Dick the white whale the captain said if you can kill the white whale Moby Dick I will give this gold to the one that can do it and it is worth sixteen dollars they tried and tried but while they were trying they killed a whale and used the oil for the lamps they almost caught the white whale.

That same theme sliced off into these unnamed units appears below. A capital letter now begins each unit and a period ends each one. A slant line indicates the beginning of each new clause. One unit begins with an *and*, and another with a *but*. Each unit is grammatically capable of being considered a sentence. In fact, these units are the shortest grammatically allowable sentences into which the theme could be segmented. If it were segmented into units any shorter, some fragment would be created.

1. I like the movie / we saw about Moby Dick, the white whale.

2. The captain said / if you can kill the white whale, Moby Dick, / I will give this gold to the one / that can do it.

3. And it is worth sixteen dollars.

4. They tried and tried.

5. But / while they were trying / they killed a whale and used the oil for the lamps.

6. They almost caught the white whale.

As segmented above, several units contain only a single clause—a main clause, of course—like a simple sentence. There are several multiclause units like complex sentences. In fact, the second unit is rather intricate, for within the main clause is embedded a noun clause and within it is both an adverbial if clause and an adjective clause. There are no units like compound sentences or compound-complex sentences, for such units must be cut into two or more parts so that each will contain only one main clause.

These units need a name. It would be simplest to call them "minimal sentences." However, the word "sentence" already has so many different meanings that misunderstanding would be certain to result. The word "sentence" has troubles enough already. A fresh, neutral sounding name would be better. These units might be christened "minimal terminable units," since they would be minimal as to length, and each would be grammatically capable of being terminated with a capital letter and a period. For short, the "minimal terminable unit" might be nicknamed a "T-unit." One would hesitate to use both initials and let it be nicknamed an "M T unit." So "T-unit" will be the name used for it in this investigation.

As a potential index of maturity, the unit has the advantage of preserving all the subordination achieved by a student, and all of his coordination between words and phrases and subordinate clauses.

Source: *Kellogg W. Hunt, Grammatical Structures Written at Three Grade Levels, Research Report No. 3, pp. 20–21. Copyright ©1965 by the National Council of Teachers of English. Reprinted by permission of the publisher and author.*

Table 1. Grammatical structures at two grade levels

| | Relative frequency in percent taking grade 12 performance as 100 percent | |
Name of variable	Grade 4	Grade 8
Clause to sentence length factors		
1. Mean sentence length	79	94
2. Use of and between T-units	470	175
3. Mean clause length	77	94
4. Ratio of subordinate to all clauses	55	72
5. Mean Length of T-units	60	80
6. T-units shorter than 9 words	445	209
7. Ratio of clauses per T-unit	77	85
8. Ratio of T-units per sentence	137	117
Subordinate clauses		
9. Noun clauses	79	67
10. Adjective clauses	46	68
Expansion of nominals		
11. Total of 3 commonest nominals (unmodified)	157	121
12. Adjectives as noun modifiers	60	98
13. Genitives as noun modifiers	78	81
14. Prepositional phrases as noun modifiers	42	72

Table 1. Grammatical structures at two grade levels (Continued)

Name of variable	Relative frequency in percent taking grade 12 performance as 100 percent	
	Grade 4	Grade 8
Nominalized verbs		
15. Infinitives as noun modifiers	24	51
16. Past participles as noun modifiers	81	80
17. Present participles as noun modifiers	47	120
18. Factive infinitivals	61	70
19. Gerunds	10	40
Complexity count for nominals		
20. Counts for "complexity" of nominals		
21. Counts given to nominals with counts of 2 or more		
22. Counts given to nominals with counts of 3 or more		
Verb auxiliary		
23. "Perfect forms (*have* + past participle)	35	87
24. "Progressive" forms (*be* + present participle)	262	262
25. Passives	27	77
26. Total of 6 modals	46	58
27. Occurrences of *can*	50	59
Main Verbs		
28. Intransitive verbs with complements of motion	428	263
29. Intransitive verbs	186	188
30. Use of BE as main verb	79	80
Nonclause adverbials related to verbs		
31. Noncomplement adverbials of motion	367	237
32. Noncomplement adverbials of time	298	216
33. All nonclause noncomplement adverbials	112	128
34. Adverbials of manner	55	84
Predicate adjectives		
35. Predicate adjectives	74	71
36. Prepositional phrase complements to adjectives	29	41

Source: Adapted from Kellogg W. Hunt, *Grammatical Structures Written at Three Grade Levels,* Research Report No. 3, pp. 146–147. Copyright © 1965 by the National Council of Teachers of English. Reprinted by permission of the publisher and author.

Appendix D: The usefulness of phonic generalizations

Clymer selected from teachers' manuals forty-five phonic generalizations that were stated specifically enough to aid or hinder in the pronunciation of a particular word. He compiled his 2,600-word list of all the words introduced in the four basic series from which the generalizations were drawn plus the *Gates Reading Vocabulary* for the primary grades. He then identified all words to which each generalization might apply and noted the number pronounced as the generalization claimed and the number of exceptions. From these data he obtained the percentage of utility for each generalization.

Clymer then identified eighteen generalizations

that he felt constituted a reasonable degree of application. He selected them on the basis of two criteria: that the word list must contain a minimum of twenty words to which the generalization might apply, and that the generalization must have at least 75 percent utility.

Emans conducted a comparable study using the same generalizations as Clymer used, but his word list was a random sample of 10 percent of the words beyond the primary level in the *Teacher's Word Book of 30,000 Words* (Thorndike and Large, 1944). This sample produced a list of 1,944 words. Other procedures in the study were similar to Clymer's but produced somewhat different conclusions. In other words, some generalizations that appear useful in the primary grades may not be in the upper elementary grades, and some not useful for primary, may be for the older children. Emans identified fifteen generalizations that constitute a reasonable degree of application.

Bailey also replicated Clymer's study, but for grades one through six, by using the same generalizations and the same procedures. She drew her word list of 5,773 words from eight widely used basal reading series. She used all the words in all the books with the following exceptions: words that appeared in only one of the series, place names, proper names, and foreign words. She found only six generalizations simple to understand and apply, applicable to large numbers of words, and having few exceptions.

The forty-five generalizations Clymer identified follow. Those marked with asterisks were found useful according to Clymer's criteria.

1. When there are two vowels side by side, the long sound of the first one is heard and the second is usually silent.

2. When a vowel is in the middle of a one-syllable word, the vowel is short (middle letter, one of the middle two letters in a word of four letters, and one vowel within a word of more than four letters).

3. If the only vowel letter is at the end of a word, the letter usually stands for a long sound.

4. When there are two vowels, one of which is final *e*, the first vowel is long and the *e* is silent.

*5. The *r* gives the preceding vowel a sound that is neither long nor short.

6. The first vowel is usually long and the second silent in the digraphs *ai, ea, oa,* and *ui*.

7. In the phonogram *ie*, the *i* is silent and the *e* has a long sound.

*8. Words having double *e* usually have the long *e* sound.

9. When words end with silent *e*, the preceding *a* or *i* is long.

*10. In *ay* the *y* is silent and gives *a* its long sound.

11. When the letter *i* is followed by the letters *gh*, the *i* usually stands for its long sound and the *gh* is silent.

12. When *a* follows *w* in a word, it usually has the sound *a* as in *was*.

13. When *e* is followed by *w*, the vowel sound is the same as represented by *oo*.

14. The two letters *ow* make the long *o* sound.

15. *W* is sometimes a vowel and follows the vowel digraph rule.

*16. When *y* is the final letter in a word, it usually has a vowel sound.

17. When *y* is used as a vowel in words, it sometimes has the sound of long *i*.

18. The letter *a* has the same sound (ô) when followed by *l, w,* and *u*.

19. When *a* is followed by *r* and final *e*, we expect to hear the sound heard in *care*.

*20. When *c* and *h* are next to each other, they make only one sound.

*21. *Ch* is usually pronounced as it is in *kitchen, catch,* and *chair*, not like *sh*.

*22. When c is followed by e or i, the sound of s is likely to be heard.

*23. When the letter c is followed by o or a, the sound of k is likely to be heard.

24. The letter g often has a sound similar to that of j in jump when it precedes the letter i or e.

*25. When ght is seen in a word, gh is silent.

26. When a word begins kn, the k is silent.

27. When a word begins with wr, the w is silent.

*28. When two of the same consonants are side by side, only one is heard.

*29. When a word ends in ck, it has the same last sound as in look.

*30. In most two-syllable words, the first syllable is accented.

*31. If a, in, re, ex, de, or be is the first syllable in a word, it is usually unaccented.

*32. In most two-syllable words that end in a consonant followed by y, the first syllable is accented and the last is unaccented.

33. One vowel letter in an accented syllable has its short sound.

34. When y or ey is seen in the last syllable that is not accented, the long sound of e is heard.

35. When -ture is the final syllable in a word, it is unaccented.

36. When -tion is the final syllable in a word, it is unaccented.

37. In many two- and three-syllable words, the final e lengthens the vowel in the last syllable.

38. If the first vowel sound in a word is followed by two consonants, the first syllable usually ends with the first of the two consonants.

39. If the first vowel sound in a word is followed by a single consonant, that consonant usually begins the second syllable.

*40. If the last syllable of a word ends in le, the consonant preceding the le usually begins the last syllable.

*41. When the first vowel element in a word is followed by th, ch, or sh, these symbols are not broken when the word is divided into syllables and may go with either the first or second syllable.

42. In a word of more than one syllable, the letter v usually goes with the preceding vowel to form a syllable.

43. When a word has only one vowel letter, the vowel sound is likely to be short.

*44. When there is one e in a word that ends in a consonant, the e usually has a short sound.

*45. When the last syllable is the sound r, it is unaccented.

Source: *Theodore Clymer, "The Utility of Phonic Generalizations in the Primary Grades,"* The Reading Teacher 16 *(January 1963): 256–258. Reprinted by permission of the International Reading Association and the author.*

Table 1 gives the total number of words to which each generalization might apply in each of the three studies (Number of Incidents) and the Percentage of Utility for each generalization. To find the number of exceptions, multiply the figure in the Number of Incidents column by the Percentage of Utility. Generalizations that each investigator found "useful" are marked with asterisks.

Let's consider some of the generalizations Bailey does not include and the other two studies do: Number 5 refers to the influence of r. Many have questioned the use of this factor with children. While the dictionary uses a symbol for a, e, and u preceding r, the difference in sound is so slight as to be indistinguishable by many adults as well as children. In number 5, the exceptions appear to be where the ee precedes r as in deer. However, the chances of a child not being able to identify a word because of a lack of this generalization is minis-

Table 1. Utility of phonic generalizations

Generalizations	Clymer gr. 1–3		Emans gr. 4–6		Bailey gr. 1–6	
	Number of incidents	Percent of utility	Number of incidents	Percent of utility	Number of incidents	Percent of utility
1.	686	45	480	18	1,732	34
2.	657	62	139	73	1,021	71
middle letter	275	69	54	81	430	78
one of middle two letters	326	59	73	71	478	68
one vowel	56	46	12	42	113	62
3.	31	74	3	33	38	76
4.	288	63	59	63	578	57
5.	618	78*	59	63	478	57
6.	271	66	93	58	497	60
ai	67	64	23	83	121	72
ea	152	66	37	62	259	55
oa	35	97	14	86	66	95
ui	17	6	19	0	51	10
7.	47	17	22	23	88	31
8.	87	98*	24	100*	171	87
9.	272	60	198	48	674	50
10.	46	78*	6	100	50	88
11.	31	71	3	100	35	71
12.	47	32	18	28	78	22
13.	26	35	7	14	35	40
14.	85	59	18	50	111	55
15.	125	40	36	31	180	38
16.	201	84*	270	98*	518	89
17.	199	15	326	4	59	11
18.	126	65	113	24	346	34
19.	10	90	2	100	24	96
20.	103	100*	53	100*	225	100*
21.	104	95*	52	67	225	87
22.	69	96*	88	90*	284	92*
23.	143	100*	151	100*	428	100*
24.	77	64	75	80*	216	78
25.	30	100*	3	100	40	100
26.	10	100	3	100	17	100
27.	8	100	4	100	17	100
28.	337	99*	300	91*	826	98*
29.	46	100*	9	100	80	100
30.	971	85*	530	75*	2,345	81
31.	99	87*	215	83*	398	84
32.	105	96*	57	100*	195	97*
33.	903	61	1,490	64	3,031	65
34.	157	0	269	1	449	0
35.	4	100	6	100	22	95
36.	5	100	85	100*	102	100
37.	114	46	227	42	430	46
38.	563	72	811	80*	1,689	78
39.	427	44	659	47	1,283	50
40.	64	97*	68	78*	211	93*
41.	30	100*	44	100*	74	100

Table 1. Utility of phonic generalizations (Continued)

Generalizations	Clymer gr. 1–3		Emans gr. 4–6		Bailey gr. 1–6	
	Number of incidents	Percent of utility	Number of incidents	Percent of utility	Number of incidents	Percent of utility
42.	73	73	91	40	184	65
43.	744	57	136	70	1,105	69
44.	112	76*	18	83	149	92
45.	197	95*	172	96*	761	79

*Generalizations described as useful in each of the three studies.

Source: Theodore Clymer, "The Utility of Phonic Generalizations in the Primary Grades," *The Reading Teacher* 16 (January 1963): 256–258; Robert Emans, "The Usefulness of Phonic Generalizations above the Primary Grades," *The Reading Teacher* 20 (February 1967): 421–423; and Mildred H. Bailey, "The Utility of Phonic Generalizations in Grades One through Six," *The Reading Teacher* 20 (February 1967): 415–417. Reprinted by permission of the International Reading Association and the authors.

cule. In number 16, the generalization is one to which there are virtually no alternatives, the exceptions being words like *repay* and *replay*. Bailey believes numbers 30 and 45 are difficult to interpret and apply, and number 41 is not needed. Since neither Clymer nor Emans attempted to determine which generalizations *should* be taught, Bailey made such suggestions on the basis of professional judgment and experience.

Emans also made modifications to some of the forty-five generalizations. The changes that he feels are useful are presented in Table 2.

Bailey (1968) made a further study of two vowels together in a word and gave some recommendations. Children need to learn that (1) *oi* and *ou* are diphthongs that signal their own consistent sounds; (2) *oo* usually has its own distinctive sounds; (3) *au* nearly always has the same sound as *a* in *call* and *raw*; *io* is usually found in the phonograms *-tion* and *-sion* and then is pronounced as short *u*; and (5) when *ia* and *ua* are found in words, usually both are pronounced. It is obvious from the data in Table 3 that the only other useful generalization is that when *oa* is found, it will nearly always be pronounced as a long *o*.

Table 2. Modifications of the original forty-five generalizations

Generalization	Percentage of utility
1. The letters *io* usually represent a short *u* sound as in *nation*.	86
2. The letters *oo* usually have the long double *o* sound as in *food* or the short double *o* sound as in *good*. They are more likely to have the double *o* sound as in *food*.	100
3. When a vowel is in the middle of a one-syllable word, the vowel is short except that it may be modified in words in which the vowel is followed by an *r*.	80
4. When the vowel is the middle letter of a one-syllable word, the vowel is short.	80
5. When the first vowel in a word is *a* and the second is *i*, the *a* is usually long and the *i* silent.	83
6. When the first vowel is *o* and the second is *a*, the *o* is usually long and the *a* is silent.	86
7. The vowel combination *ui* has a short *i* sound.	79

Table 2. Modifications of the original forty-five generalizations (Continued)

Generalization	Percentage of utility
8. The two letters *ow* make the long *o* sound or the *ou* sound as in *out*.	100
9. When *y* is used as a vowel, it most often has the sound of long *e*.	92
10. The letter *a* has the same sound (ô) when followed by *w* and *u*.	84
11. One vowel letter in an accented syllable has its short sound if it comes before the end of the syllable and its long sound if it comes at the end of the syllable.	78
12. One vowel letter in an accented syllable has its short sound if it comes before the end of the syllable and its long sound if it comes at the end of the syllable except when it is followed by an *r*.	92
13. When *y* or *ey* is seen in the last syllable that is not accented, the short sound of *i* is heard.	97
14. A -*tion* at the end of a four-syllable word indicates a secondary accent on the first syllable with a primary accent on the syllable preceding the -*tion*.	95
15. Taking into account the original rules 5, 28, 29, 31 and 41, if the first vowel sound in a word is followed by two consonants, the first syllable usually ends with the first of the two consonants.	96
16. Except in some words with a prefix, if the first vowel sound in a word is followed by a single consonant, that consonant begins the second syllable and the vowel sound in the first syllable will be long, or if the consonant ends the first syllable, the vowel sound will be short.	84
17. A beginning syllable ending with a consonant and containing a short vowel sound is likely to be accented.	95
18. When a word has only one vowel letter, the vowel sound is likely to be short unless the vowel letter is followed by an *r*.	78

Source: Robert Emans, "The Usefulness of Phonic Generalizations above the Primary Grades," *The Reading Teacher* 20 (February 1967), p. 424. Reprinted by permission of the International Reading Association and the author.

Table 3. Utility of the vowel digraph generalization when applied to twenty-five adjacent vowel combinations

Adjacent-vowel combinations	Number of incidents investigated	Number of conformations	Number of exceptions	Percentage of utility
aa	1	0	1 (bazaar)*	0
ae	1	0	1 (phaeton)	0
ai	118	84 (bait)*	34 (air)	71
ao	0	0	0	0
au	45	0	45 (caught)	0
ea	252	141 (peach)	111 (pear)	56
ee	166	145 (cheek)	21 (been)	87
ei	30	9 (ceiling)	21 (freight)	30
eo	13	1 (people)	12 (geography)	8
eu	4	0	4 (museum)	0
ia	45	0	45 (giant)	0
ie	86	6 (lie)	80 (friend)	7
ii	1	0	1 (taxiing)	0

Table 3. Utility of the vowel digraph generalization when applied to twenty-five adjacent vowel combinations (Continued)

Adjacent-vowel combinations	Number of incidents investigated	Number of conformations	Number of exceptions	Percentage of utility
io	178	0	178 (union)*	0
iu	7	0	7 (aquarium)	0
oa	66	63 (road)*	3 (cupboard)	95
oe	12	5 (toe)	7 (shoe)	42
oi	43	0	43 (boil)	0
oo	124	2 (door)	122 (cool)	2
ou	185	17 (four)	168 (fought)	9
ua	38	0	38 (equal)	0
ue	38	12 (continue)	26 (fuel)	32
ui	50	5 (nuisance)	45 (ruin)	10
uo	2	0	2 (buoy)	0
uu	1	0	1 (vacuum)	0
Totals 25	1,506	490	1,016	33

*Examples of words that conformed or were exceptions to the generalization.

Source: Mildred H. Bailey, "Utility of Vowel Digraph Generalizations in Grades One through Six," in J. Allen Figurel, ed., *Reading and Realism* (Newark, Del.: IRA, 1969), p. 656. Reprinted by permission of the International Reading Association and the author.

Table 4. New vowel digraph generalizations

New generalizations	Number of incidents investigated	Number of conformations	Number of exceptions	Percentage of utility
1. When two vowels are side by side, usually only one vowel sound is heard.	1,506	1,381 (juice)*	125 (idea)*	92
2. When *ai, ea, ee,* or *oa* is found in a word, usually only the long sound of the first vowel is heard.	602	433 (pail) (bead) (feel) (goat)	169 (pair) (steak) (been) (cupboard)	72

*Examples of words that conformed or were exceptions to the generalization.

Source: Mildred H. Bailey, "Utility of Vowel Digraph Generalizations in Grades One through Six," in J. Allen Figurel, ed., *Reading and Realism* (Newark, Del.: IRA, 1969), p. 657. Reprinted by permission of the International Reading Association and the author.

Appendix E: Context clues

Ames (1966) studied the ways in which readers use context clues to fill in omitted or unrecognized words in a selection. He asked graduate students to read paragraphs containing a nonsense word, identify the word that belonged in its place, and explain their reasoning. Although the materials are not useful for young children, the fourteen classifications of contexual aids can be used in a variety of ways either in direct instruction or in working with individuals or small groups in need of such help.

Table 1. Examples of the use of Class I contextual aids—clues derived from language experience or familiar expressions

Contextual situation	Reader's response
Let us *heag* (look) for a moment at the American automobile, the foundation of our entire economy and, maybe, even of our entire civilization.	*"look*. Let us do something for a moment and a phrase to introduce a discussion is 'let us look for a moment.'"
I wonder how much the security of the country is being safeguarded by the paunchy reservist who spends one evening a week at the Reserve center *thacing* (chewing) the fat with the boys, thereby escaping from the dishes at home.	*"chewing*. It is a common phrase or cliche—to chew the fat."

Source: All tables in this appendix are adapted from Wilbur S. Ames, "The Development of a Classification Scheme of Contextual Aids," *Reading Research Quarterly* 2 (Fall 1966) pp. 67–80. Reprinted by permission of the International Reading Association and the author.

Table 2. Examples of the use of Class II contextual aids—clues utilizing modifying phrases or clauses

Contextual situation	Reader's response
The Disney characters dominate the field, but there are others—Daffy Duck, Porky Pig, the energetic Bugs Bunny—with the same *whitors* (qualities) of shrewd and resilient poise.	*"characteristics*. The types of poise described following are characteristics the characters would have."
She ran but he caught up with her, knocked her down and *shoered* (slashed) her repeatedly with a knife.	*"stabbed*. Because of the word 'knife' and doing something with it. Slashed or cut too would fit just as well."
The Great Atlantic and Pacific Tea Co., operating on the *stialx* (theory) that all the housewife really wants is high quality at the lowest price, became the Goliath of the industry.	*"assumption*. What follows is an assumption that the company has used. A company would operate on such an assumption or theory."

Table 3. Examples of the use of Class III contextual aids—clues utilizing definition or description

Contextual situation	Reader's response
One towering worry is the problem of the professional *nodar* (donor). A few who sell blood—nurses, medical students, professors of rare types—have been carefully screened.	*"donor.* We're talking about blood and it makes sense from what has gone on before and what comes after that the professional donor is the problem. Donor is defined later in the next sentence."
Since 1951, the *bomps* (firms) have gone in the red with such policies in every year except two.	*"companies.* They issue the policies and would be the ones to lose money as the expression 'going in the red' implies so it must be *companies*."

Table 4. Examples of the use of Class IV contextual aids—clues provided by words connected or in series

Contextual situation	Reader's response
Under questioning, Kendricks broke down and *mespolded* (confessed) the policeman's murder.	*"confessed or admitted.* The police attempt to get confessions and when one 'breaks down,' he confesses. The idea of questioning and the term 'breaking down' were the big clues."
Looking through an index of all the slides (called "foils") in the box, the officer picked out a *lona* (nose), eyes, chin.	*"nose.* These three are the internal features of the face and nose completes the series."

Table 5. Examples of the use of Class V Contextual aids—comparison or contrast clues

Contextual situation	Reader's response
What will we do with all this spare time? Will it be a blessing or a *fome* (bane)?	"I can't come up with a word but it is something that is the opposite of a blessing. The 'or' gives me the idea of it being the opposite."
The draft was dropped after World War II, but *haitsmaged* (reinstated) in 1948, following a bitter nationwide debate.	*"reinstated.* It was dropped it says and then in 1948 it got brought back in. The word 'but' was a kind of clue."

Table 6.   Examples of the use of Class VI contextual aids—synonym clues

Contextual situation	Reader's response
They *telded* (wanted) piped-in music, but no "specials" announced over the loud-speakers. They wanted the candy put out of reach of children.	*"wanted* or *preferred*. They are making suggestions on what they would like in the store and so one of the things they prefer is piped-in music."
But he's got to have the *enopes* (ideas). And in the early stage of testing the ideas, you shouldn't be dependent on using computers.	*"ideas*. In the next sentence 'ideas' used and this is same word. He's got to have the ideas and then later talks about testing these and elaborating upon what he was talking thing."

Table 7.   Examples of the use of Class VII contextual aids—clues provided by the tone, setting, and mood of a selection.

Contextual situation	Reader's response
Maybe the space age does belong to us after all. Under the existing conditions, it is necessary for *obspedists* (astronauts) to be ambidextrous in order to manipulate all the keys and switches on their instrument panels from their strapped and cramped position.	*"astronauts*. Such things as 'space age,' 'cramped conditions' 'instrument panel' give clues to what kind of people are being referred to."
Not a single chair was to be seen, and my whole body was trembling from the *maodly* (deadly) chill that had entered my veins.	*"ungodly*. The 'ly' forced me to use something that had that adverbial descriptive character. The whole tone of the story and the word 'trembling' gave clue to *ungodly* or *deadly*. He is in a very frightening situation."

Table 8.   Examples of the use of Class VIII contextual aids—referral clues

Contextual situation	Reader's response
Knowing that women usually don't want anything they have to peel, shuck, scrape, chop or wash through three waters, Jenkins started doing these *swurts* (things) at the store.	*"things*. Just has to be a term for all these chores listed just before."
In the next 24 hours 290 babies will die, either at birth or before reaching their first birthday. This is 2½ times the number of lives that will be lost in auto accidents in the same *rugoul* (period), and exceeds the total claimed in a day by lung, breast and stomach cancer.	*"period*. Talks up here about before they reach their first birthday. Then they speak of a day or 24 hours giving me the idea of a period of time and the word 'same' refers back to this one period of time."

Table 9. Examples of the use of Class IX contextual aids—association clues

Contextual situation	Reader's response
"In our reader," my oldest child once snorted, "all the little boys wear short *nerns* (pants) and their names all end in 'y' and they're cute."	"*pants* or *trousers*. Word 'wear' tells me it is an article of clothing. And pants could be short."
The AMA Journal states that brutal physical punishment by parents is likely to be "a more frequent cause of death than such well-recognized diseases as leukemia, cystic fibrosis and *fomronan* (muscular) dystrophy."	"*muscular*. I think perhaps because of advertisement that is the only kind of dystrophy I know."

Table 10. Examples of the use of Class X contextual aids—clues derived from the main idea and supporting details paragraph organization

Contextual situation	Reader's response
However, I soon found a *spemgelan* (practical) use for it. I began storing orange juice in it, since it fitted nicely inside the refrigerator.	"*practical*. He wasn't going to use it for mixing cocktails so he is going to use it to store orange juice which is what I would consider a practical use for it."
Sales shot up. From 19 small stores, in which he grossed about three million dollars, Jenkins has *chatratted* (progressed) to 98 Publix stores, which last year grossed 215 million dollars.	"*catered* or *served*. He is selling these things to these stores. No, it is *increased* or *expanded* as he owns the stores. He has gone from a small number to a big one. Main point made, then comes evidence."

Table 11. Examples of the use of Class XI contextual aids—clues provided through the question-and-answer paragraph organization

Contextual situation	Reader's response
Now it's becoming interesting to ask, "How does the human brain do it?" And, for the first time, within the last year or two, we're *vocting* (getting) a real idea of that.	"*getting*. They are talking about being interested and wanting to know how the human brain is doing it and this is the first time we are getting an idea of that. For one thing the way it is positioned in the sentence—you need a verb there."
Is there any evidence that the traditional man of Stratford, a countryborn actor, had these qualifications? The answers to the first two questions have been "maybe" and to the third a clear "no"—although in fairness it must be said that there is no *greel* (proof) that he didn't have these qualifications.	"*evidence*. It say that the answer to the first two questions is 'maybe' and to the third 'no' and then she adds in reference to the third question which was whether there was any evidence that he had these qualifications, there is no evidence that he didn't. She has asked questions and then answered them."

Table 12. Examples of the use of Class XII contextual aids—preposition clues

Contextual situation	Reader's response
The modus operandi was to take a demolished car from a salvage yard, tow it to a desolate country spot and there knock it over an *igraldturt* (embankment) with an insured vehicle.	*"embankment.* It seemed to fit in with the 'desolate country spot' and they knock it over something with an insured vehicle and *embankment* would seem to fit. Rather than a house or a solid object."
Respectable folk in the middle and upper class would have been horrified at the idea of a pipe or a cigar between feminine *cits* (lips).	*"lips.* That is where you put a pipe or a cigar between."

Table 13. Examples of the use of Class XIII contextual aids—clues utilizing nonrestrictive clauses or appositive phrases

Contextual situation	Reader's response
In many big city hospitals, prenatal facilities are inadequate, and crowding is so severe that after delivery a mother's stay is limited to 24 hours— *mantly* (hardly) a sufficient period for her infant to "stabilize."	*"hardly.* The dash says he wants to get away from the main theme and make a point that this is not a sufficient period. *Hardly* could be the word to introduce this extra thought."
Las Vegas, which *larps* (misses) few other bets, has yet to provide a slot machine by which we can lose our money with our left hand as nature intended.	*"misses.* 'Few others' is the clue here and also 'yet'."

Table 14. Examples of the use of Class XIV contextual aids—clues derived from cause and effect pattern of paragraph and sentence organization

Contextual situation	Reader's response
Foremost, of course, drivers need to realize that by cheating the insurance companies, they are only pushing their own premiums *lorter* (higher).	*"higher.* Drivers need to realize that something is happening to their premiums and this is the type of thing that worries them. They don't worry if they are lower."
He reads not for fun but to improve his mind and render his conversation less *caxail* (boring).	*"monotonous.* It says he doesn't read just for fun but to improve his mind and to make his conversation less something. If he did read a lot then it would be less monotonous. The word 'less' gives me the idea of this being something negative."

Appendix F: Examples for determining grammatical acceptability, semantic acceptability, and meaning change

For ease of reference in the following examples, a miscue number is placed over the miscue, and is discussed below. Refer to page 298 for the meaning of other codes.

Andrew[1]
Andre didn't say a word, but it seemed that everyone

© *Sus* © *hoping*[2]
else was talking! His sister, ⌈Suzanne, ⌊was hopping

called[3]   *directly*[4]
around and calling to him. Men were shouting directions

@ *fahver* $ *crees*[5]
to his father, and the cries of many gulls added

©   *noisy*[6]
⌈to the noise.*

*From "Andre's Secret" by Marguerite De Angeli. American Adventures,
Book IV ©1963 American Book Company, p. 97.*

READER	TEXT	COLUMN 7*	COLUMN 8*	COLUMN 9*
1. Andrew	Andre	Y—This miscue occurs in a grammatically acceptable sentence within the text.	Y—This miscue occurs in a semantically acceptable sentence within the text.	N—There is no meaning change.
2. hoping	hopping	P—Only the portion of the sentence prior to and including the miscue is grammatically acceptable.	P—Only the portion of the sentence prior to and including the miscue is semantically acceptable.	Y—There is extensive meaning change.
3. called	calling	Y—This miscue occurs in a grammatically acceptable sentence within the text.	Y—This miscue occurs in a semantically acceptable sentence within the text.	P—There is minimal meaning change.
4. directly	directions	Y—This miscue occurs in a grammatically acceptable sentence within the text.	P—Only the portion of the sentence prior to and including the miscue is semantically acceptable.	P—There is minimal meaning change.

READER	TEXT	COLUMN 7*	COLUMN 8*	COLUMN 9*
5. $screes	cries	Y—This miscue occurs in a grammatically acceptable sentence within the text.	N—This miscue occurs in a sentence which is not semantically acceptable.	Y—There is extensive meaning change.
6. noisy	noise	N—This miscue occurs in a sentence which is not grammatically acceptable.	N—This miscue occurs in a sentence which is not semantically acceptable.	P—There is minimal meaning change.

*Column 7—Grammatical acceptability. Y is yes, P is partly, N is no.
*Column 8—Semantic acceptability.
*Column 9—Meaning change.

Source: *Yetta Goodman and Carolyn Burke,* Reading Miscue Inventory Manual: Procedure for Diagnosis and Evaluation *(New York: Macmillan, 1972), pp. 64–65. Reprinted by permission of Yetta Goodman.*

Appendix G: Useful commercial books and materials

Book sets

Benefic Press

   Dan Frontier Series

   Sailor Jack Series

   Space Science Fiction Series

   Sports Mystery Series. All high interest, low reading level.

   Oral Reading and Linguistic Series. 6 books, grades 1–6. Dramatic literary selections, stories, plays, poems, all styles of writing for silent reading, oral interpretation, individual or group.

Bowmar

   ABC Serendipity, by Albert G. Miller. 6 books of rhymes, puzzles, and word histories.

The Bowmar Reading Center. 5 small libraries for prereaders through third grade.

   Breakthrough Books, based on children's writing, 45 titles. *Lollipops*, 4 books. *Instant Readers*, 18 books. *Seven Silly Stories* and *Primary Reading Series*, 66 books.

Double Play Reading Series. Read aloud, read along, involves children in reading plays and acting them out; reading level 2.5 to 5.9.

Manipulative Books, by Beth Clure and Helen Raemsey. 2 sets, 8 books each, teacher's guide.

NFL Reading Kit, by Ron Kidd. 50 different stories, high interest, easy reading at 2.0 to 4.25 reading levels. Developed in connection with the National Football League. On cards with comprehension checks on the back. Teacher's guide.

Play the Game. High interest supplementary readers.

Search Books, by John McInnes and William Murray. 12 books on topics of high interest. Reading level 3–5.

The Young Adventurers Series. 6 books with posters.

Cypress Publishing Corporation. (Order from Unicorn.)

Classroom Cookery. Grades 2–9, 6 titles, teacher's guide.

Freddy Higginbottom. Grades 4–9, 6 titles, teacher's guide.

Seafarers Reading Chest. Grades K–5, 13 kits of 8 books with read-along cassettes. Seven of the 13 are professionally acclaimed books.

Reading Listening Library. Grades 3–9, 12, professionally acclaimed books with dramatization of high points on cassettes.

Educational Methods, Inc.

Jelly Jam. Reading and activity book (a white rabbit environmentalist). Supplemental reading material, primary science and social studies, grades 1–4.

Harr Wagner Publishing. (Available from Addison-Wesley.)

The Check and Flag Series. 8 books.

The Deep-Sea Adventure Series. 7 books.

The Jim Forest Readers. 6 books.

The Morgan Bay Mysteries. 8 books.

Plays, Inc.

Favorite Plays for Classroom Reading. Grades 5–8.

Thirty Plays for Classroom Reading, by Donald Durrell and Alice Crossley. Grades 4–6.

Both have instructions and require little group rehearsal. Many other books of plays and programs are for lower and upper elementary grades.

Scholastic Book Services and Magazines

Sprint Library. 7 libraries; 2 are five 32-page books; 2 are five 64-page books; 3 are five 96-page books. High interest, low reading levels mainly for fourth, fifth, and sixth grades. Teacher's guide.

Arrow Book Club. Grades 4–6, 8 book offers a year, 36 books to choose from.

Lucky Book Club. Grades 2–3, 6 book offers a year, 19 books to choose from.

See-Saw Books. K–1, 5 book offers a year, a 4-page newspaper at each offering describes materials offered. The See-Saw Club includes some recordings.

Five units of 100 paperbacks in two book cases:

Reading Up. Readability level from no-text to 4th grade.

Reaching Higher. Levels 2–5, emphasis on level 3.

Reaching Forward. Levels 2–junior high, emphasis on level 4.

Reaching Ahead. Levels 2–junior high, emphasis on level 5.

Reaching Beyond. Levels 2–junior high, emphasis on level 6.

Each book has a Conference Card.

Books with sound filmstrips and cassettes or records

BFA

Reading, Researching, and Reporting in Science

The Universe. 4 sound filmstrips, 8 books, 50 activity cards, skill book, and teacher's guide.

Bowmar

The Best in Children's Literature, Dr. Walter Loban and Lillian Watkins, eds. Four series: legends, myths, folklore, and fantasy. Many books with records or cassettes, teacher's guide.

Highway Holidays Series. 6 books with listening tapes by Jo Stanchfield.

History of the Early American West, by Ken and Ellen McGill. 3 books with sound filmstrips and records or cassettes.

Language/Communication Program, by Ed and Ruth Radlauer. Picture dictionaries, trophy books, study prints with accompanying records and teacher guides. For children 8–14. High interest, easy reading.

Language Stimulus Program, by Alec Allinson, Beverly Allinson, and John McInnes. Levels 3 to 8 roughly corresponding to grade levels, each with 8 stimulus books and 20 Satellite books and teacher's guide. Filmstrips and cassettes provide rich content to talk about and share.

The Monster Books, by Ellen Blance and Ann Cook. Sets I and II for beginning readers. 12 titles in each set. Teacher's guide. Also available in Spanish.

Reading Incentive Language Program, by Ed and Ruth Radlauer. Books, sound filmstrips, records. 20 titles. Easy reading, high interest—cars, dune buggies, motorcycles, etc.

The Ways of Animals, by Aileen Fisher. 10 books with sound filmstrips, cassettes, and teacher's guide.

The Ways of Plants, by Aileen Fisher. 10 books with sound filmstrips, cassettes, and teacher's guide.

Books on Social Studies and Science. 32 books, all beautifully illustrated. Grades 4–6 and above.

Cypress Publishing Corporation. (Order from Unicorn.)

Thunder, the Dinosaur. Books, 10 titles, teacher's guide.

Weather. 8 titles, teacher's guide.

Economics. 8 titles, teacher's guide.

To Love the Sea. 6 titles, teacher's guide.

Child's Storybook Library. Grades K–5, 20 titles and teacher's guide for each.

Holt, Rinehart and Winston

Sounds of Language Series, by Bill Martin, Jr. in collaboration with Peggy Brogan. Grades K–8. Fifteen books and accompanying cassettes.

The Owl Books, four groups. *The Kinder Owls, The Little Owls, The Young Owls*, and *The Wise Owls*, cassettes, by Bill Martin and Peggy Brogan.

The Satellite Books. 84 paperbacks for all children through grade 6. Streamlined manuals with open-ended guidance.

Little Nature Books. A "read aloud" series. 10 books with correlated cassettes to help children develop an awareness and understanding of natural cycles and use various modes of learning.

Houghton Mifflin

Booklets. 27 soft cover, grades 1–3, 4–5, 4–6. Some have cassettes.

National Geographic Society

America: Colonization to Constitution

The Revolutionary War, 200 pages. 5 sound filmstrips. Grades 5 and above.

Life in Rural America, 208 pages. 5 sound filmstrips. Grades 5 and above.

Books for Young Explorers. Preschool through 3rd grade. Set 5 includes *Camping Adventure, Wonders of the Desert World, The Playful Dolphins, Animals that Build Their Homes*. Similar titles in sets 1, 2, 3, and 4.

Books on Social Studies and Science. 32 books, all beautifully illustrated. Grades 4–6 and above.

Materials to encourage writing

Cypress Publishing Corporation. (Order from Unicorn.)

Make-A-Book Series. 3 books, illustrations only, for children to write the stories; 3 books have stories for children to illustrate. Children make covers and put their names as authors or illustrators.

Guidance Associates

Write A Story—Put Yourself in This Picture. Filmstrip.

There's Always a Story Inside You. Sound filmstrip, record, or cassette.

What If . . . cards. 30 cards, laminated.

The Write Now Wordshop Series. See It and Write; Hear It and Write; Write a Story; Write Lively Language; Write in Order.

Weston Woods

How a Picture Book Is Made, by Steven Kellogg. Filmstrip, cassette and printed text. First half tells of how he wrote a book, second half the production of the book.

Learning kits and games

Argus

Fuzzies (Communications). Filmstrip, cassette, and teacher's guide.

Bowmar

Gold Cup Reading Games, by Ed and Ruth Radlauer. 6 games to develop reading, dictionary use, and number skills.

Concept Media

Guess What? Idea book, 5 filmstrips, record, cassettes, magnifying blocks, poster. Uses listening, seeing, and other senses, descriptive language, reasoning, and imagining.

d.o.k. Publishers

Team Learning Kits. Grades 3–6. For teams of 4 children; can be used by individuals. Instructions, project outline for each member of team. A complete lesson plan for the book. 12 projects at each level.

Education Today

The Whole Learning Catalog. Ideas and suggestions for just about anything. Series of learning handbooks includes information, games, activities.

Educators Marketing Service

WFF'N PROOF Games: *WFF: The Beginner's Game of Logic; The Propaganda Game.*

Ginn & Co.

Can You Imagine? R. E. Myers and E. Paul Torrance. For primary grades.

The Learning Seed Co.

Creativity Kit. 63 slides and 40-minute cassette. Mind stretchers, creativity exercises, lateral thinking (by Edward de Bono), and other ideas, grades 5–6.

Persuasion Box, 43-frame filmstrip; *Propaganda Game Power to Persuade*, by Cirino; *The Claim Game*, and other ideas, 5–6.

Houghton Mifflin

Talk and Take Game. Move pieces on board by reading instructions.

Silly Syntar Game. 1–3, and 4–6, by manipulating sentence parts, learn to play options in sentence construction.

Cross Word Puzzles. 4–6, for vocabulary and spelling.

Card Decks. 5 for 1–3, 5 for 4–6, various games, vocabulary, and concepts for science, social studies, and mathematics.

Recordings and films

ACI Films, Inc.

3 sets of 4 sound filmstrips. Grades K–3, for beginning readers or for listening; stimulation for talking and writing.

Bowmar Listening Center, record sets, stories, songs, and poems for K–3.

Sing a Song of People, by Roberta McLaughlin and Lucille Wood. Music, art as background for learning social service concepts. 3 sound filmstrips and mini books, for listening and discussion.

World Cultures. Folk songs, recordings, and commentaries that relate important geographical areas to the lives and art of the people. Characteristic instrumentation. 12 sets, for listening and discussion.

Encyclopedia Britannica Educational Corporation

Magic Moments. Sound films, 5 Units of 4 each. *Let's Talk, Let's Do, Let's See, Let's Pretend, Let's Play,* from 2 to 8 minutes each film. Grades K–6, stimulus for talking and writing.

Good Apple

Imagination and Me. Building vocabulary, stimulating thinking. Record and teacher's guide.

H. Wilson Corporation

Developing Creativity Ability. Grades K–6.

Developing Language Arts Skills. Grades 4–6.

Wonderful World, Sound and Fancy, Creative Patterns, World of Sound, We Listen and Learn, Developing Creative Ability, Developing L.A. Skills. All for grades K–3.

Early Childhood Enrichment Program. 52 lessons, in various curriculum areas, for listening and discussion.

Resources for teachers

d.o.k. Publishers

Guidlines to Creative Dramatics, by Margaret S. Woods and Beryl Trethart. For ages 5, 6, and 7.

Wonderwork: Creative Experiences for the Young Child, by Margaret S. Woods. Plans for developing capacity for wonder. Primary grades.

Say It With Movement, by Linda Elefson. For all elementary grades. Develops communication through language of movement.

Turning Children On Through Creative Writing, by Mary Attea.

Motivating Readers. List of book titles in more than 320 subjects, graded by reading level.

Classroom Ideas for Encouraging Thinking and Feeling. Frank Williams, ed. Contains ideas useful for grades 1–9.

Developing Creativity in Children, by Charles E. Schaefer. For grades 4–9. To develop creative thinking, improve self-image and sense of worth.

Scamper, by Robert F. Eberle. A book of idea games played entirely within the imagination.

Imagination Express, by Gary Davis. For grades 3–9. For creative thinking, problem solving, and language skills.

Oakland Unified School District, Oakland, California. Educational Development and Services, Office of Community Relations.

Gung Hei Fat Choy. Provides suggestions for activities, art and construction, calligraphy, and recipes for implementing a Chinese New Year Theme, with additional references.

Children's magazines

Boys Life. Monthly. Articles, fiction, cartoons and special features. Boy Scouts of America, New Brunswick, N.J. 08902.

Children's Express. Reporters, writers, and associate editors are children, 7–17. Cheshire Communications Company, 375 Park Ave., New York, N.Y. 10019.

Children's Playmate, ages 3–8; *Child Life,* 7–11; *Jack & Jill,* ages 3–8. *Young World,* ages 1–14. 10 issues a year. Youth Publications, P.O. Box 5678, Indianapolis, In. 46206.

Cricket. K–6. Monthly during school year. 96 pages. Open Court Publishing Company, 1058 Eighth St., La Salle, Ill. 61301.

Kids Magazine. Entirely written and illustrated by children, 5 to 15. 6 issues a year, October through June. 48 color pages. P.O. Box 4099, Grand Central Station, New York, N.Y. 10017.

National Geographic *School Bulletin.* 16 pages, each week of school year. From third grade. National Geographic Society, 17th and M Streets, Washington, D.C. 20036.

National Geographic *World.* 36 pages. Monthly issues. May contain punchouts. From third grade. National Geographic Society, 17th and M Streets, Washington, D.C. 20036.

Ranger Rick's Nature Magazine. Monthly except June and September. From 8 years. National Wildlife Federation, 1412 16th Street, N.W., Washington, D.C. 20036.

Sprint. Biweekly. September through April, except Christmas holidays. High-interest, low reading level. For grades 4–6. Scholastic Spring Magazine, 902 Sylvan Ave., Englewood Cliffs, N.J., 07632.

Resources for children's use

Grosset and Dunlop, Inc.

The Clear and Simple Thesaurus Dictionary, by Wittels and Griesman.

Macmillan

Learning about Changes in Our Language with Ling Wis Tix and *Learning about Nouns with Ling Wis Tix;* others about other parts of speech. 6 color filmstrips.

MIT Press

Yellow Pages of Learning Resources, Richard Saul Wurman, ed. An alphabetical list of community resources shows where to look, what to look for and kinds of questions to ask; guidelines for interviews, investigations, field trips.

National Geographic

National Geographic Index. Vol. I (1888–1946), Vol. II (1947–1969) with 1970–75 supplement, for independent location of needed information.

Scott Foresman

Thorndike-Barnhart Beginning Dictionary. For grades 3–4.

In Other Words I, A Beginning Thesaurus, W. Cabell Green. For grades 3–4.

In Other Words II, a Junior Thesaurus, W. Cabell Green. For grades 5–6.

Thorndike-Barnhart Intermediate Dictionary. For grades 5–6.

J. C. Penney Company

An Introduction To Value Clarification. Forum magazine for background, 7 folders of strategies for value clarification, suggestions for use.

Scholastic

Kindle. For early primary and pre-primary. *How Do I Learn, Getting Along, Mixing In.* 5 sound filmstrips for each.

SRA

Focus on Self. 1, Awareness; 2, Responding; 3, Involvement. Filmstrips, story records, photoboards, and comprehensive teacher guide for each. Discussion program to help children develop improved communication and self-awareness.

Materials for self-awareness and perception

American Guidance Services

Duso Kits for K–1, for K–2, D–2 for 2–4. Kits with recordings. Developing understanding of self and others.

Toward Affective Development. 44 illustrations focusing on ways feelings are communicated; 93 full-color pictures for discussing probable feelings and actions; filmstrip, cassettes; feeling wheels; material for tasks of cooperating and sharing. A comprehensive manual.

Argus

Got To Be Me. For self-awareness in grades 1–6. 48 double-sided cards with open-ended sentences. Teacher's guide. Materials in both English and Spanish.

Making Sense of Our Lives. For self-expression and values clarification in grades 5 and above. Units of six exercises in each of *Learning About Myself, Expressing Feelings and Emotions, Self-Concept, Sensitivity to Others, Goals, Decision-Making,* and *Social Issues.* Many other small units with similar purposes.

Bowmar

Project Me. Flexible dramatic program for primary grades.

Body Image. I and II, 10 and 5 filmstrips and cassettes.

Let's Look For (visual perception). 5 filmstrips and cassettes.

How Are You Feeling Today? 6 filmstrips and cassettes.

Early Childhood Series. Pre K–3 language arts/social science books, records, sound filmstrips, study prints. Part I, About Myself; Part II, The World Around Me; Part III, I Talk—I Think—I Reason.

Houghton Mifflin

Interaction. 16-mm sound film, 20 minutes each for inservice and orientation programs for students.

A Pupil-Centered Classroom, Body English, Creative Dramatics, Do and Talk, Small Group Improvisation, Reading Activities, Small Group Writing, Story Theater, Small Group Discussion.

National Geographic

Many science sound filmstrips as a basis for listening, discussion and writing.

Q-Ed Productions

Economics for Primates. 4 filmstrips or recordings for discussion and value awareness.

The Toy Store. Having wants and being consumers.

The Doghouse. Using productive resources to produce goods and services.

The Breakfast. Specialization and interdependence.

The Garden. Choices and opportunities.

Scholastic Book Services and Magazines

Let's Start. Record collection, paperback book collection, book, record, and picture collection for PP–1.

Walt Disney

The Animal Box. 8-mm cartridges, story starters.

Publishers' addresses

ACI Films, Inc., 35 W. 45th St., New York, N.Y. 10036

Addison-Wesley Publishing Co., Inc., Sand Hill Rd., Menlo Park, Calif. 94025

American Guidance Service, Inc., Publishers Building, Circle Pines, Minn. 55014

Argus Communications, 7440 Natchez Ave., Niles, Ill. 60648

Benefic Press, 10300 W. Roosevelt Rd., Westchester, Ill. 60153

BFA Educational Media, 2211 Michigan Ave., Santa Monica, Calif. 90406

Bowmar, 622 Rodier Dr., Glendale, Calif. 91201, or 292 Madison Ave., New York, N.Y. 10017

Concept Media, 1500 Adams Ave., Costa Mesa, Calif. 92626

d.o.k. Publishers, Inc., 71 Radcliff Rd., Buffalo, N.Y. 14214, or 771 E. DeLavan Ave., Buffalo, N.Y. 14215

Doubleday & Company, Inc., 501 Franklin Ave., Garden City, N.Y. 11530

Educational Methods, Inc., 500 North Dearborn St., Chicago, Ill. 60610

Education Today Company, Inc., 530 University Ave., Palo Alto, Calif. 94301

Educators Marketing Service, South Point Plaza, Lansing, Mich. 48910

E. M. Hale and Co., Eau Claire, Wisc. 54702

Encyclopedia Britannica Educational Corporation, 425 N. Michigan Ave., Chicago, Ill. 60611

Ginn and Company, 191 Spring St., Lexington, Mass. 02173

Good Apple, Inc., Box 299, Carthage, Ill. 62321

Grosset and Dunlap, Inc., 51 Madison Ave., New York, N.Y. 10010

Guidance Associates, 757 Third Ave., New York, N.Y. 10017

Holt, Rinehart and Winston, Inc., 383 Madison Ave., New York, N.Y. 10017

Houghton Mifflin, 1900 S. Batania Ave., Geneva, Ill. 60134

H. Wilson Corporation, 555 W. Taft Dr., South Holland, Ill. 60473

J. C. Penney Company, Inc., Educational and Consumer Relations Department, 1310 Avenue of the Americas, New York, N.Y. 10019

The Learning Seed Co., 145 Brentwood Dr., Palatine, Ill. 60067

National Geographic Society, Box 2330, Washington, D.C. 20013

Plays, Inc., 8 Arlington St., Boston, Mass. 02116

Q-Ed Productions, Box 1608, Burbank, Calif. 91505

Random House School and Library Service, Inc., 457 Madison Ave., New York, N.Y. 10022

Scholastic Book Services and Magazines, 902 Sylvan Ave., Englewood Cliffs, N.J. 07632

Science Research Associates, 259 E. Erie St., Chicago, Ill. 60611

Unicorn Learning Products, 12620 S.W. First St., Box 763, Beaverton, Oreg. 97005

Weston Woods, Weston, Conn. 06880

REFERENCES

Aaronson, D., and Markowitz, N. "Immediate Recall of Normal and 'Compressed' Auditory Sequences." Paper presented at the meeting of the Eastern Psychological Association, Boston, 1967.

Adams, Raymond S., and Biddle, Bruce J. *Realities of Teaching*. New York: Holt, Rinehart and Winston, 1970.

Akron Public Schools. *Curriculum Handbook: Reading and Literature, Oral and Written Communication*. Akron, Ohio: Akron Public Schools, 1956.

Alleman-Brooks, Janet, and Fitzgerald, Sheila. "The Integrated Curriculum Revisited Through Consumerism." *Language Arts* 54 (1977):387–394.

Allen, David P., and Watson, Dorothy J., eds. *Findings of Research in Miscue Analysis: Classroom Implications*. National Council of Teachers of English, 1976. 252 pp.

Allen, Roach Van, and Allen, Claryce. *Language Experience Activities*. Boston: Houghton Mifflin, 1976. 276 pp.

Almy, Millie; Chittenden, Edward; and Miller, Paula. *Young Children's Thinking: Studies of Some Aspects of Piaget's Theory*. New York: Teachers College Press, 1966. 153 pp.

Ames, Wilbur S. "The Development of a Classification Scheme of Contextual Aids." *Reading Research Quarterly* 2 (Fall 1966):57–80.

Anastasiow, Nicholas J. "Cognition and Language." In *Language Differences: Do They Interfere?* edited by James L. Laffey and Roger Shuy, pp. 17–25. Newark, Del.: International Reading Association, 1973.

Anglin, J. M., and Miller, G. A. "The Role of Phase Structure in the Recall of Meaningful Verbal Material." *Psychonomic Science* 10 (1968):343–344.

Applegate, Mauree. *Freeing Children to Write*. New York: Harper and Row, 1963. 184 pp.

———. *When the Teacher Says, "Write a Poem."* Evanston, Ill.: Harper and Row, 1965.

Arbuthnot, May Hill, and Sutherland, Zena. *Children and Books*. Chicago: Scott, Foresman, 1972. 836 pp.

Archer, Alane, and Akert, Robin M. "How Well Do You Read Body Language?" *Psychology Today* 11 (October 1977):68–94.

Artley, A. Sterl. "Phonics Revisited." *Language Arts* 54 (1977):121–126.

Ashton-Warner, Sylvia. *Teacher*. New York: Simon and Schuster, 1963.

Aspy, D. N., and Roebuck, F. N. "From Humane Ideas to Humane Technology and Back Again Many Times." *Education* 95 (1974):163–171.

Association for Supervision and Curriculum Development. *Perceiving-Behaving-Becoming*. 1962 Yearbook. Washington, D.C.: ASCD, 1962. 253 pp.

Atwood, Beth S. "Critical Reading: A Social Experience." *Learning* 4 (1975):34–37.

Bailey, Mildred H. "The Utility of Phonic Generalizations in Grades One through Six." *The Reading Teacher* 20 (1967):413–418.

———. "Utility of Vowel Digraph Generalizations in Grades One through Six." *International Reading Association Conference Proceedings* 13, pt. 1 (1969):654–658.

Balyeat, Ralph, and Norman, Douglas. "LEA-Cloze-Comprehension Test." *Reading Teacher* 28 (1975):555–560.

Baratz, Joan C., and Shuy, Roger W., eds. *Teaching Black Children to Read*. Washington, D.C.: Center for Applied Linguistics, 1969. 219 pp.

Bartnick, Robert, and Lopardo, Genevieve S. "The Cloze Procedure: A Multi-Purpose Classroom Tool." *Reading Improvement* 13 (1976):113–117.

Berko, Jean. "The Child's Learning of English Morphology." *Word* 14 (1958):150–177.

Berman, Louise M. *New Priorities in the Curriculum*. Columbus, Ohio: Charles E. Merrill, 1968. 241 pp.

———. *From Thinking to Behaving*. New York: Teachers College Press, 1967. 73 pp.

Bernstein, Basil. *Class, Codes and Control*, vol. 1. London: Routledge and Kegan Paul, 1971. 238 pp.

———. "Language and Roles." In *Language Acquisition: Models and Methods*, edited by Renira Huxley and Elisabeth Ingram, pp. 67–71. London: Academic Press, 1971b.

Bingham, Alma, and Dusenbery, Bea. "A Second Look at Ten Writing Rules." *Media and Methods* 13 (March 1977):52–53.

Biondi, Angelo M., ed. *The Creative Process*. Buffalo, New York: d.o.k. Publishers, 1972. 74 pp.

Birdwhistell, Ray L. "Some Body Motion Elements Accompanying Spoken American English." In *Communication: Concepts and Perspectives*, edited by Lee Thayer, pp. 53–72. London: Macmillan, 1967.

Blitz, Barbara. *The Open Classroom: Making It Work*. Boston: Allyn and Bacon, 1973. 262 pp.

Bloom, Benjamin S., ed. *Taxonomy of Educational Objectives, Handbook I: Cognitive Domain*. New York: David McKay, 1956. 209 pp.

Bond, Guy L.; Barlow, Bruce; and Hoyt, Cyril J. *Silent Reading Diagnostic Tests*. Chicago: Lyons and Carnahan, 1970.

Bormuth, John R. "Comparable Cloze and Multiple-Choice Comprehension Test Scores." *Journal of Reading* 10 (1967):291–299.

Bormuth, John R.; Carr, Julian; Manning, John; and Pearson, David. "Children's Comprehension of Between—and Within—Sentence Syntactic Structures." *Journal of Educational Psychology* 61 (1970):349–357.

Bossert, Steven T. "Tasks, Group Management, and Teacher Control Behavior: A Study of Classroom Organization and Teacher Style." *School Review* 85 (1977):552–565.

Bracken, Dorothy K. "Developing an Effective Listening Program." *Nineteenth National Conference Yearbook*, Part II. Atlanta, Ga.: National Reading Conference, 1969.

Brandt, Sue R. *How to Write a Report*. New York: Franklin Watts, 1968.

Braun, Carl. "Teacher Expectation: Socio-Psychological Dynamics." *Review of Educational Research* 46 (1976):185–213.

Braun, Carl; Neilson, Allan R.; and Dykstra, Robert. "Teacher Expectation: Prime Mover or Inhibitor?" In *Reading Interaction*, edited by Leonard Courtney, pp. 40–48. Newark, Del.: International Reading Association, 1976.

Brearley, Molly, ed. *The Teaching of Young Children: Some Applications of Piaget's Learning Theory*. New York: Schocken Books, 1970.

Brearley, Molly, and Hitchfield, Elizabeth. *A Guide to Reading Piaget*. New York: Schocken Books, 1969. 169 pp.

Britton, James. *Language and Learning*. Baltimore: Penguin Books, 1970. 298 pp.

———. "The Student's Writing." In *Explorations in Children's Writing*, edited by Eldonna L. Evertts, pp. 21–74. Urbana, Ill.: National Council of Teachers of English, 1970.

Brooks, Charlotte K. *They Can Learn English*. Belmont, Calif.: Wadsworth, 1973. 174 pp.

Brown, Margaret E. "A Practical Approach to Analyzing Children's Talk in the Classroom." *Language Arts* 54 (1977):506–510.

Burling, Robbins. *English in Black and White*. New York: Holt, Rinehart and Winston, 1973. 178 pp.

Burrows, Alvina Treut; Jackson, Doris C.; and Saunders, Dorothy O. *They All Want to Write: Written English in the Elementary School*, 3d ed. New York: Holt, Rinehart and Winston, 1965. 281 pp.

Buswell, Guy T. *Non-Oral Reading: A Study of Its Use in the Chicago Public Schools*. Chicago: University of Chicago Press, 1945. 55 pp.

Byers, Paul, and Byers, Happie. "Nonverbal Communication and the Education of Children." In *Functions of Language in the Classroom*, edited by Courtney B. Cazden; Vera P. John; and Dell Hymes, pp. 3–31. New York: Teachers College Press, 1972.

Cacha, Francis. "Propaganda Techniques via Children's Literature." In *Teaching About Doublespeak*, edited by Daniel Dietrich, pp. 89–91. Urbana, Ill.: National Council of Teachers of English, 1976.

Capparell, Lorraine, and Suid, Murray. "Masks: The Great Put-On." *Learning* 4 (October 1975):28–31.

Carlson, Ruth Kearney. *Enrichment Ideas: Sparkling Fireflies*. Dubuque, Iowa: William C. Brown, 1970. 109 pp.

———. "Raising Self-Concepts of Disadvantaged Children Through Puppetry." *Elementary English* 47 (1970):349–355.

Carroll, John B. *Comprehension by 3rd, 6th and 7th Graders of Words Having Multiple Grammatical Functions*. Final Report. Princeton, New Jersey: Educational Testing Service, 1970. ERIC Ed 048 311.

———. "Language and Cognition." In *Language Differences: Do They Interfere?* edited by James L. Laffey and Roger Shuy, pp. 173–185. Newark, Del.: International Reading Association, 1973.

———. *Language, Thought and Reality: Selected Writings of Benjamin Lee Whorf*. New York: John Wiley, 1956. 278 pp.

Carroll, John B., and Freedle, Roy O., eds. *Language Comprehension and the Acquisition of Knowledge*. Washington, D.C.: V. H. Winston, 1972. 380 pp.

Cazden, Courtney B. *Child Language and Education*. New York: Holt, Rinehart and Winston, 1972. 314 pp.

Cazden, Courtney; John, Vera, P.; and Hymes, Dell. *Functions of Language in a Classroom*. New York: Teachers College Press, 1972. 394 pp.

Cheifetz, Dan. "Improvisation: A Basic Skill for Living." *Learning* 3 (May 1975):18–24.

Cherry, Colin. *On Human Communication*. Cambridge, Mass.: M.I.T. Press, 1966. 337 pp.

Chomsky, Carol. *The Acquisition of Syntax in Children from 5 to 10*. Research Monograph no. 57. Cambridge, Mass.: M.I.T. Press, 1969. 121 pp.

———. "Stages in Language Development and Reading Exposure." *Harvard Educational Review* 42 (1972):1–33.

Chomsky, Noam. *Aspects of a Theory of Syntax*. Cambridge, Mass.: M.I.T. Press, 1965. 251 pp.

———. "Language and the Mind." *Psychology Today* 2 (February 1968):48–51.

———. *Syntactic Structures*. The Hague: Mouton, 1957. 120 pp.

Cianciolo, Patricia J., and Le Pere, Jean. *The Literary Time Line in American History*. Garden City, N.Y.: Doubleday, 1969.

Ciardi, John. *You Read To Me, I'll Read To You*. Philadelphia: Lippincott, 1962.

Claiborne, Robert. "The Birth of Writing." *Emergence of Man Series*. New York: Time/Life Books, 1974.

Clapp, Ouida H. *On Righting Writing*. Urbana, Ill.: National Council of Teachers of English. 1975.

Clay, Marie M. "Reading Errors and Self-Correction Behavior." *British Journal of Educational Psychology* 39 (1969):47–56.

———. "A Syntactic Analysis of Reading Errors." *Journal of Verbal Learning and Verbal Behavior* 7 (1968):434.

Clymer, Theodore. "The Utility of Phonic Generalizations in the Primary Grades." *The Reading Teacher* 16 (1963):252–258.

Cohen, S. Alan, and Cooper,Thelma. "Seven Fallacies: Reading Retardation and the Urban Disadvantaged Beginning Reader." *The Reading Teacher* 26 (1972):38–45.

Cole, Henry P. "Process Education and Creative Development: Retrospect and Prospects." *Journal of Creative Behavior* 10 (1976):1–11.

Collins, Mary L. "The Effects of Training for Enthusiasm on the Enthusiasm Displayed by Preservice Elementary Teachers." Ed.D. dissertation, Syracuse University, 1976. ERIC Ed 129 773.

Combs, Arthur W. *Educational Accountability: Beyond Behavioral Objectives*. Washington, D.C.: Association for Supervision and Curriculum Development, 1972. 40 pp.

Cook, Jimmie E. "A Study in Critical Listening Using Eight to Ten Year Olds in an Analysis of Commercial Propaganda Emanating from Television." Ed.D. dissertation, West Virginia University, 1972. 242 pp.

———. "I Can't Believe I Ate the Whole . . ." *Elementary English* 5 (1974):1158–1161.

Cramer, Ronald L. "The Write Way to Teach Spelling." *Elementary School Journal* 76 (1976): 464–467.

Cullinan, Bernice E., ed. *Black Dialects and Reading*. Urbana, Ill.: National Council of Teachers of English, 1974.

Cullum, Albert. *Aesop in the Afternoon*. New York: Citation Press, 1972. 207 pp.

———. *Push Back the Desks*. New York: Citation Press, 1967. 223 pp.

———. *Shake Hands With Shakespeare*. New York: Citation Press, 1968. 320 pp.

Currell, D. *Puppetry for School Children*. Newton Center, Mass.: Branford, 1971.

Curwin, Richard L., and Curwin, Jeri. "Building Trust: A Starting Point for Clarifying Values." *Learning* 3 (Feb. 1975):30–36.

D'Angelo, Frank. *A Conceptual Theory of Rhetoric*. Cambridge, Mass.: Winthrop, 1975.

Darkatsh, Manuel. "Improving Oral Language Activities." *Reading Improvement* 12 (1975):220–221.

Dawkins, John. "Defining Fiction and Nonfiction for Students." *Language Arts* 54 (1977):127–129.

de Bono, Edward. *Children Solve Problems*. New York: Harper and Row, 1972. 227 pp.

de Hirsch, Katrina; Jansky, Jeannette J.; and Langford, William S. *Predicting Reading Failure*. New York: Harper and Row, 1966. 144 pp.

de Velliers, P. A. "Imagery and Theme in Recall of Connected Discourse." *Journal of Experimental Psychology* 103 (1974):263–268.

Despert, Louise. *The Inner Voices of Children*. New York: Simon and Schuster, 1975. 1962 pp.

De Stefano, Johanna S., ed. *Language, Society and Education: A Profile of Black English*. Worthington, Ohio: Charles A. Jones, 1973. 326 pp.

Dewey, John. *How We Think*. Boston: D. C. Heath, 1910. 224 pp.

Dieterich, Daniel, ed. *Teaching about Doublespeak*. Urbana, Ill.: National Council of Teachers of English, 1976. 218 pp.

Dinan, Linda L. "By the Time I'm Ten, I'll Probably Be Famous." *Language Arts* 54 (1977): 750–755.

Divone, Eileen. "Puppets, an Educational Experience." *School Arts* 77 (1977):50–51.

Dixon, Glen T. "Investigating Words in the Primary Grades." *Language Arts* 54 (1977):418–422.

Dixon, John. *Growth through English*, 3d ed. New York: Oxford University Press, 1975. 137 pp.

Douglass, Malcolm P., ed. "A Little Revolution Now and Then." In *Claremont Reading Conference 40th Yearbook*. Claremont, Calif.: Claremont Graduate School, 1976. 215 pp.

Drummond, Robert J., and McIntire, Walter G. "Cognitive, Affective and Attitudinal Predictors of Reading Achievement in 'Open' Classrooms." *Reading Improvement* 13 (1976):108–112.

Duckworth, Eleanore. "Piaget Rediscovered." *Journal of Research in Science Teaching* 2 (1964): 172–175.

———. "Piaget Takes a Teacher's Look." *Learning* 2 (November 1973):22–27.

Duke, Charles R. *Creative Dramatics and English Teaching*. Urbana, Ill.: National Council of Teachers of English, 1974. 180 pp.

Dunkeld, Colin, and Hatch, Lynda. "Building Spelling Confidence." *Elementary English* 52 (1975):225–229.

Dunn, Kenneth, and Dunn, Rita. "60 Activities that Develop Student Independence." *Learning* 2 (1974):73–77.

Dykstra, Robert. "The Relationship between Selected Reading Readiness Measures of Auditory Discrimination and Reading Achievement at the End of First Grade." Ph.D. dissertation, University of Minnesota, 1962.

Ebensen, Barbara J. *A Celebration of Bees: Helping Children Write Poetry*. Minneapolis: Winston Press, 1975.

Ehri, Linnea. "Word Learning in Beginning Readers and Prereaders: Effects of Form Class and Defining Contexts." *Journal of Educational Psychology* 68 (1976):832–842.

Emans, Robert. "The Usefulness of Phonic Generalizations above the Primary Grades." *The Reading Teacher* 20 (1967):419–425.

Engel, Rosalind. "Literature Develops Children's 'I's' for Reading." *Language Arts* 53 (1976): 892–898.

Epstein, Sam, and Epstein, Beryl. *The First Book of Words: Their Family History*. New York: Franklin Watts, 1954. 65 pp.

Evans, Richard I., ed. *Jean Piaget: The Man and His Ideas*. New York: E. P. Dutton, 1973. 189 pp.

Everle, Bob. "Does Creative Dramatics Really Square with Research Evidence?" *Journal of Creative Behavior* 8 (1974):177–182.

Evertts, Eldonna L., ed. *Explorations in Children's Writing*. Urbana, Ill.: National Council of Teachers of English, 1970. 122 pp.

Fagan, William T.; Cooper, Charles R.; and Jensen, Julie M. *Measures for Research and Evaluation in the English Language Arts*. Urbana, Ill.: National Council of Teachers of English, 1975. ERIC Ed 099 835.

Faix, Thomas L. "Listening as a Human Relations Art." *Elementary English* 52 (1975):409–413.

Farb, Peter. *Word Play: What Happens When People Talk*. New York: Alfred A. Knopf, 1974. 350 pp.

Farrell, Edmund. "The Vice/Vise of Standardized Testing: National Depreciation by Quantification." *Language Arts* 54 (1977):486–490.

Fast, Julius. *Body Language*. New York: Pocket Books, 1971. 183 pp.

Ferguson, Charles W. *The Abecedarian Book*. Boston: Little, Brown, 1964. 131 pp.

Fincher, Jack. *Human Intelligence*. New York: G. P. Putnam's Sons, 1976. 512 pp.

Fisher, Peggy. "The Transformation of a New England Schoolmarm." *Learning* 3 (1975):64–70.

Fitzgerald, James A. *The Teaching of Spelling*. Milwaukee: Bruce, 1951.

Fitzgerald, Sheila. "Teaching Discussion Skills and Attitudes." *Language Arts* 52 (1975):1094–1096.

"Focus 2: Handwriting: Writing Legibly." *Elementary English* 52 (1975):201–220.

"Focus 2: Psycholinguistics and Reading." *Language Arts* 53 (1976):287–328.

"Focus 3: Spelling: Encoding English." *Elementary English* 52 (1975):221–257.

Foerster, Leona M. "Language Experience for Dialectically Different Black Learners." *Elementary English* 51 (1974):193–197.

———. "Sinistral Power! Help for Left-Handed Children." *Elementary English* 52 (1975):213–215.

Frankel, Jack R. *Helping Students Think and Value: Strategies for Teaching the Social Studies*. Englewood Cliffs, N.J.: Prentice-Hall, 1973. 413 pp.

Freyberg, Joan T. "Increasing the Imaginative Play of Urban Disadvantaged Kindergarten Children through Systematic Training." In *The Child's World of Make-Believe*, edited by Jerome Singer, pp. 129–154. New York: Academic Press, 1973.

Friedman, Herbert L., and Johnson, Raymond D. *Time-Compressed Speech as an Educational Medium: Studies of Stimulus Characteristics and Individual Differences*. Final Report. Silver Spring, Md.: American Institutes for Research, 1969.

Froese, Victor. "How to Cause Word-by-Word Reading." *The Reading Teacher* 30 (1977):611–615.

Furth, Hans G., and Wachs, Harry. *Thinking Goes to School: Piaget's Theory in Practice*. New York: Oxford University Press, 1974. 297 pp.

Galin, David. "Educating Both Halves of the Brain." *Childhood Education* 53 (1976):17–20.

Gall, M. D. "The Use of Questions in Teaching." *Review of Educational Research* 40 (1970):707–721.

Galloway, Charles M. "Nonverbal Communication in Teaching." In *Teaching Vantage Points for Study*, edited by Ronald T. Hyman, pp. 70–77. Philadelphia: J. B. Lippincott, 1968.

———. *Silent Language in the Classroom*. Bloomington, Ind.: Phi Delta Kappa Educational Foundation, 1976, 33 pp.

———. *Teaching is Communicating: Nonverbal Language in the Classroom*. Bulletin no. 29. Washington, D.C.: Association of Teacher Educators, 1970.

Gardner, Howard. "Brain Damage: A Window on the Mind." *Saturday Review*, 9 August 1975, pp. 26–29.

Gergen, Kenneth J. *The Concept of Self*. New York: Holt, Rinehart and Winston, 1971. 110 pp.

"Getting Kids into Libraries—and Vice Versa." *Learning* 5 (April 1977):60–63.

Gillies, Emily. *Creative Dramatics for All Children*. Washington, D.C.: Association for Childhood Education International, 1973.

Ginott, Haim G. *Teacher and Child: A Book for Parents and Teachers*. New York: Avon Books, 1975.

Glasser, William. *Schools without Failure*. New York: Harper and Row, 1969. 235 pp.

Glaus, Marlene. *From Thoughts to Words*. Urbana, Ill.: National Council of Teachers of English, 1965.

Gomberg, Adeline Wishengrad. "Freeing Children to Take a Chance." *Reading Teacher* 29 (1975):455–457.

Goodlad, John, and Klein, M. Frances. *Looking behind the Classroom Door*. Worthington, Ohio: Charles A. Jones, 1974.

Goodman, Kenneth S. "Analysis of Oral Reading Miscues: Applied Psycholinguistics." *Reading Research Quarterly* 5 (1969):9–30.

———. "Comprehension-Centered Reading." In *Claremont Reading Conference 34th Yearbook*, pp. 125–135. Claremont, Calif.: Claremont Graduate School, 1970.

———. "Effective Teachers of Reading Know Language and Children." *Elementary English* 51 (1974):823–828.

———. "Linguistic Insights which Teachers May Apply." *Education* 88 (1968):313–316.

———. "A Linguistic Study of Cues and Miscues in Reading." *Elementary English* 42 (1965):639–643.

———, ed. *Miscue Analysis: Applications to Reading Instruction*. Urbana, Ill.: National Council of Teachers of English, 1973. 120 pp. ERIC Ed 080 973.

———. "Orthography in a Theory of Reading Instruction." *Elementary English* 49 (1972):1254–1261.

———. "Testing in Reading: A General Critique." In *Accountability and Reading Instruction: Critical Issues*, edited by Robert B. Ruddell, pp. 21–33. Urbana, Ill.: National Council of Teachers of English, 1973.

Goodman, Kenneth S., and Buck, Catherine. "Dialect Barriers to Reading Comprehension Revisited." *Reading Teacher* 27 (1973a):6–12.

Goodman, Kenneth S., and Burke, Carolyn L. *Theoretically Based Studies of Patterns of Miscues in Oral Reading Performance*. Final Report. Wayne State University, April 1973b. 459 pp. ERIC Ed 079 708.

Goodman, Kenneth S., and Goodman, Yetta. "Learning about Psycholinguistic Processes by Analyzing Oral Reading." *Harvard Educational Review* 47 (1977):317–333.

Goodman, K. S., and Goodman, Y. "Learning to Read Is Natural." In *Theory and Practice of Early Reading*, vol. 1, edited by L. B. Resnick and P. Weaver. Hillsdale, N.J.: Erlbaum Associates, 1978.

Goodman, Kenneth S., and Niles, Olive S. *Reading: Process and Program*. Urbana, Ill.: National Council of Teachers of English, 1970. 74 pp.

Goodman, Yetta. "Reading Diagnosis: Qualitative or Quantitative." *Reading Teacher* 26 (1972): 32–37.

Goodman, Yetta, and Burke, Carolyn. *Reading Miscue Inventory Manual: Procedure for Diagnosis and Evaluation*. New York: Macmillan, 1972. 133 pp.

Goodman, Yetta M., and Sims, Rudine. "Whose Dialect for Beginning Readers?" *Elementary English* 51 (1974):837–841.

Goodman, Yetta, and Watson, Dorothy J. "A Reading Program to Live With: Focus on Comprehension." *Language Arts* 54 (1977):868–879.

Gottlieb, Sybil. "Modeling Effects Upon Fantasy." In *The Child's World of Make-Believe*, edited by Jerome Singer, pp. 155–182. New York: Academic Press, 1973.

Gove, Mary K. "Using the Cloze Procedure in a First Grade Classroom." *Reading Teacher* 29 (1975):36–38.

Granger, Robert C. "The Nonstandard Speaking Child: Myths Past and Present." *Young Children* 31 (1976):478–485.

Green, Harry A. "Direct Versus Formal Methods in Elementary English." *Elementary English* 24 (1947):273–285.

Green, W. Cabell. *In Other Words: A Beginning Thesaurus*. New York: Lathrop, Lee and Sheppard, 1969.

Groff, Patrick. "Fifteen Flaws of Phonics." *Elementary English* 50 (1973):35–40.

Guide to Children's Magazines, Newspapers, Reference Books. Washington, D.C.: Association for Childhood Education, International, 1974. 12 pp.

Gumperz, John J., and Hernandez-Chevez, Eduardo. "Bilingualism, Bidialectualism, and Classroom Interaction." In *Functions of Language in the Classroom*, edited by Courtney Cazden; Vera P. John; and Dell Hymes, pp. 84–110. New York: Teachers College Press, 1972.

Hall, Edward T. *Beyond Culture*. Garden City, N.Y.: Anchor Press/Doubleday, 1977. 298 pp.

———. *The Hidden Dimension*. Garden City, N.Y.: Anchor Press/Doubleday, 1969.

———. *The Silent Language*, Greenwich, Conn.: Faucett Publications, 1959. 192 pp.

Hall, Mary Anne; Moretz, Sara A.; and Statom, Jodellano. "Writing before Grade One — A Study of Early Writers." *Language Arts* 53 (1976):582–585.

Halliday, M. A. K. *Explorations in the Functions of Language*. London: Edward Arnold, 1973. 140 pp.

———. "Language Acquisition and Initial Literacy." *Claremont Reading Conference 35th Yearbook*, Claremont, Calif.: Claremont Graduate School, 1971.

———. "Language Structure and Language Function." In *New Horizons in Linguistics*, edited by John Lyones, pp. 141–165. 1970.

———. "Learning How to Mean." In *Foundations of Language Development*, vol. 1, edited by Eric Lenneburg, pp. 239–265. New York: Academic Press, 1975.

———. *Learning How to Mean: Explorations in the Development of Language*. New York: Elsevier-North Holland Publishing Co., 1977.

———. "Relevant Models of Language." In "The State of Language." *Educational Review* 22.1. Birmingham, England: University of Birmingham Press, pp. 26–37. 1969.

Halpin, Glennelle, and Halpin, Gerald. "Special Paper for Beginning Handwriting: An Unjustified Practice?" *Journal of Educational Research* 69 (1976):267–269.

Hanna, Paul R.; Hanna, Jean S.; Hodges, Richard E.; and Rudorf, Erwin H., Jr. *Phoneme-Grapheme Correspondences as Cues to Spelling Improvement*. Washington, D.C.: U.S. Department of Health, Education and Welfare, 1966.

Hanna, Paul R.; Hodges, Richard E.; and Hanna, Jean S. *Spelling: Structure and Strategies*. Boston: Houghton Mifflin, 1971.

Hassid, Teri. "Children as Authors and Publishers." *Language Arts* 54 (1977):793–795.

Hayes, Eloise. "Expanding the Child's World through Drama and Movement." *Childhood Education* 47 (1971):361–367.

Hazard, Paul. *Books, Children and Men*. Boston: Horn Book, 1944.

Heller, Suzanne. *Misery*. New York: Paul S. Ericksson, 1964.

Hennings, Dorothy Grant. *Mastering Classroom Communication — What Interaction Analysis Tells the Teacher*. Pacific Palisades, Calif.: Goodyear, 1975. 193 pp.

———. *Smiles, Nods, and Pauses*. New York: Citation Press, 1974. 232 pp.

Hennings, Dorothy Grant, and Grant, Barbara M. *Content and Craft: Written Expression in the Elementary School*. Englewood Cliffs, N.J.: Prentice-Hall, 1973. 235 pp.

Henry, Mabel Wright. *Creative Experiences in Oral Language*. Urbana, Ill.: National Council of Teachers of English, 1967. 121 pp.

Hillocks, George, Jr. *Observing and Writing*. Urbana, Ill.: National Council of Teachers of English, 1975. 32 pp.

Hodges, Richard E., and Rudorf, E. Hugh, eds. *Language and Learning to Read: What Teachers Should Know About Language*. Boston: Houghton Mifflin, 1972.

Hopkins, Lee Bennett. *Books Are by People*. New York: Citation Press, 1969.

———. *More Books Are by More People*. New York: Citation Press, 1974.

Hopper, Robert W. "Expanding the Notion of Competence: Implications for Elementary Speech Programs." *The Speech Teacher* 20 (1971):29–35.

Hopper, Robert, and Naremore, Rita C. *Children's Speech: A Practical Introduction to Communication Development*. New York: Harper and Row, 1973.

Horn, Ernest. *Basic Writing Vocabulary*. Iowa City: University of Iowa Press, 1926.

Horn, Thomas D., ed. *Reading for the Disadvantaged: Problems of Linguistically Different Learners*. New York: Harcourt, Brace and World, 1970. 267 pp.

Hornburger, Jane M. "Detecting and Dealing with Doublespeak." In *Teaching About Doublespeak*, edited by Daniel Dietrich, pp. 118–119. Urbana, Ill.: National Council of Teachers of English, 1976.

Hosey, Joseph Gerard. "Oral Reading—Misused?" *Elementary School Journal* 77 (1977):218–220.

Howes, Virgil M., ed. *Individualization of Instruction: A Teaching Strategy*. New York: Macmillan, 1970. 241 pp.

Huey, Edmund Burke. *The Psychology and Pedagogy of Reading*. Cambridge, Mass.: M.I.T. Press, 1968. 469 pp.

Hunkins, Francis P. *Questioning Strategies and Techniques*. Boston: Allyn and Bacon, 1972. 146 pp.

Hunt, Kellogg W. *Grammatical Structures Written at Three Grade Levels*. Research Report no. 3. Urbana, Ill.: National Council of Teachers of English, 1965. 159 pp.

————. *Syntactic Maturity in School Children and Adults*. Society for Research in Child Development Monograph no. 134, vol. 35, no. 1. Chicago: University of Chicago Press, 1970. 67 pp.

Hymes, Dell. "Competence and Performance in Linguistic Theory." In *Language Acquisition: Models and Methods*, edited by Renira Huxley and Elisabeth Ingram, pp. 3–28. London: Academic Press, 1971.

————. "The Ethnography of Speaking." In *Anthropology and Human Behavior*, pp. 13–53. Washington, D.C.: Anthropological Society of Washington, 1962.

————. Introduction to *Functions of Language in the Classroom*, edited by Courtney B. Cazden; Vera P. John; and Dell Hymes. New York: Teachers College Press, 1972.

Isenbarger, Joan, and Smith, Veta. "How Would You Feel If You Had to Change Your Dialect? Using a Simulation Game to Show the Effects of Forcing Language Change." *Elementary English* 51 (1974):215–221.

Jackson, Jacqueline. *Turn Not Pale, Beloved Snail: A Book About Writing Among Other Things*. Boston: Little, Brown, 1974. 235 pp.

Jacobs, Gabriel H. L. *When Children Think: Using Journals to Encourage Creative Thinking*. New York: Teachers College Press, 1970. 65 pp.

Johnson, Dale D. "Skills Management Systems: Some Issues." *Language Arts* 54 (1977):511–516.

Johnson, David W. *Reaching Out: Interpersonal Effectiveness and Self-Actualization*. Englewood Cliffs, N.J.: Prentice-Hall, 1972. 269 pp.

Jones, Beverly J. "A Study of Oral Language Comprehension of Black and White, Middle and Lower Class, Pre-school Children Using Standard English and Black Dialect in Houston, Texas, 1972." Ed.D. dissertation, University of Houston. 1973.

Kachur, Donald S., and Goodall, Robert C. "Nonverbal Studies in the Classroom." *News, Notes and Quotes*, Newsletter of Phi Delta Kappa 21 (1977):3.

Kamii, Constance. "One Intelligence Indivisible." *Young Children* 30 (1975):228–238.

Kantor, Ken, and Perron, Jack. "Thinking and Writing: Creativity in the Modes of Discourse." *Language Arts* 54 (1977):742–749.

Kelley, Earl C. "The Fully Functioning Self." In *Perceiving, Behaving, Becoming: A New Focus for Education*, pp. 9–20. Washington, D.C.: Association for Supervision and Curriculum Development, 1962.

King, Martha L.; Evans, Robert; and Cianciola, Patricia. *A Forum for Focus: The Language Arts in the Elementary School*. Urbana, Ill.: National Council of Teachers of English, 1973. 390 pp.

Kipler, Karen, and Randall, Jill Weinick. "Individualization: The Subversion of Elementary Schooling." *The Elementary School Journal* 77 (1977):358–363.

Klausmeier, Herbert J.; Ghatala, Elizabeth Schwenn; and Frayer, Dorothy A. *Conceptual Learning and Development: A Cognitive View*. New York: Academic Press, 1974. 283 pp.

Klein, Marvin L. *Talk in the Language Arts Classroom*. Urbana, Ill.: National Council of Teachers of English, 1977. 67 pp.

Knapp, Mark L. *Nonverbal Communication in Human Interaction*. New York: Holt, Rinehart and Winston, 1972. 213 pp.

Knight, Lester N., and Hargis, Charles H. "Math Language Ability: Its Relationship to Reading in Math." *Language Arts* 54 (1977):423–428.

Koch, Carl, and Brazil, James M. *Strategies for Teaching the Composition Process*. Urbana, Ill.: National Council of Teachers of English, 1974. 108 pp.

Koch, Kenneth. *Rose, Where Did You Get That Red?: Teaching Great Poetry to Children*. New York: Random House, 1973. 360 pp.

———. *Wishes, Lies, and Dreams: Teaching Children to Write Poetry*. New York: Chelsea House, 1970. 309 pp.

Kohl, Herbert R. *Math, Writing, and Games in the Open Classroom*. New York: New York Review, 1974. 252 pp.

Kolers, P. A. "Reading Is Only Incidentally Visual." In *Psycholinguistics and the Teaching of Reading*, edited by Kenneth S. Goodman and J. T. Fleming, pp. 8–16. Newark, Del.: International Reading Association, 1969.

Kranyik, Margerie A. "The Construction and Evaluation of Two Methods of Listening Skill Instruction and Their Effect on Listening Comprehension of Children in Grade 1." Ed.D. dissertation, Boston University, 1972.

Krathwohl, David R.; Bloom, Benjamin S.; and Masia, Bertram B. *Taxonomy of Educational Objectives Handbook II: Affective Domain*. New York: David McKay, 1964. 283 pp.

Kuipers, Joan, and Riccio, Mary Lou. "From Graphomania to Graphophobia and Halfway Back." *Elementary English* 52 (1975):216–220.

LaBenne, Wallace D., and Greene, Bert I. *Educational Implications of Self-Concept Theory*. Pacific Palisades, Calif.: Goodyear, 1969. 134 pp.

Labov, William. "Academic Ignorance and Black Intelligence." In *Culture, Child, and School*, edited by Martin L. Maehr and William M. Stallings, pp. 63–81. Monterey, Calif.: Brooks/Cole, 1975.

———. *The Study of Nonstandard English*. Urbana, Ill.: National Council of Teachers of English, 1970.

Laffey, James L., and Shuy, Roger. *Language Differences: Do They Interfere?* Newark, Del.: International Reading Association, 1973. 185 pp.

Lamoreaux, Lillian, and Lee, Dorris M. *Learning to Read through Experience*. New York: Appleton-Century-Crofts, 1943.

Larkin, Ralph. "Contextual Influences on Teacher Leadership Styles." *Sociology of Education* 46 (1973):471–479.

Larrick, Nancy. *Somebody Turned on a Tap in These Kids: Poetry and Young People Today*. New York: Delacorte, 1971. 178 pp.

———. "Wordless Picture Books and the Teaching of Reading." *Reading Teacher* 29 (1976):743–746.

———. "The Paperback Bonanza." In *Reading Interaction*, edited by Leonard Courtney, pp. 101–105. Newark, Del.: International Reading Association, 1976.

Larson, Richard L., ed. *Children and Writing in the Elementary School: Theories and Techniques*. New York: Oxford University Press, 1975. 420 pp.

Lawson, Anton E., and Renner, John W. "Teaching for Thinking: A Piagetian Perspective." *Today's Education* 65 (1976):38–41.

Learning Centers: Children on Their Own. Washington, D.C.: Association for Childhood Educational International, 1970. 84 pp.

Lee, Dorris, M. "Do We Group in an Individualized Program?" *Childhood Education* 45 (1968):197–199.

Lee, Dorris M., and Allen, R. Van. *Learning to Read through Experience*. New York: Appleton-Century-Crofts, 1963. 146 pp.

Lee, Dorris May, and Lee, J. Murray. "The Spelling Load Is Too Heavy." *National Elementary Principal* 20 (1941):484–487.

Leeds, Donald S. "Emotional Factors and the Reading Process." *Journal of Reading Specialists* 10 (1971):246–259.

Lefevre, Carl A. *Linguistics, English, and the Language Arts*. Boston: Allyn and Bacon, 1970. 371 pp.

———. "A Multidisciplinary Approach to Language and to Reading: Some Projections." In *The Psycholinguistic Nature of the Reading Process*, edited by Kenneth S. Goodman, pp. 291–312. Detroit: Wayne State University, 1968.

Lehane, Stephen, and Peete, May. "The Amazing Adventures of Erik Stonefoot." *Language Arts* 54 (1977):395–400.

Lembo, John M. *When Learning Happens*. New York: Schocken Books, 1972. 205 pp.

Lenneburg, Eric M. "On Explaining Language." *Science* 164 (1969):635–643.

Lighthall, Fredrick F. *Anxiety as Related to Thinking and Forgetting*. Washington, D.C.: National Education Association, Association of Classroom Teachers, 1964. 30 pp.

Livingston, Myra Cohen. "But Is It Poetry? Part I." *The Horn Book Magazine* 51 (1975):571–580.

————. "But Is It Poetry? Part II." *The Horn Book Magazine* 52 (1976):24–31.

Loban, Walter. *Language Development: Kindergarten through Grade 12*. Urbana, Ill.: National Council of Teachers of English, 1976. 160 pp.

————. *The Language of Elementary School Children*. NCTE Research Report no. 1. Urbana, Ill.: National Council of Teachers of English, 1963. 92 pp.

————. *Problems in Oral English: Kindergarten through Grade Nine*. NCTE Research Report no. 5. Urbana, Ill.: National Council of Teachers of English, 1966. 79 pp.

Logan, Vivan M., and Logan, Virgil G. *Design for Creative Teaching*. Toronto: McGraw-Hill, 1971. 224 pp.

Longman, Harold. *What's Behind the Word?* New York: Coward, McCann and Geoghegan, 1968.

Lopardo, Genevieve S. "LEA-Cloze Reading Material for the Disabled Reader." *Reading Teacher* 29 (1975):42–44.

Lorton, Mary Baratta. *Workjobs: Activity-Centered Learning for Early Childhood Education*. Menlo Park, Calif.: Addison-Wesley, 1972. 255 pp.

Luft, Joseph. *Of Human Interaction*. Palo Alto, Calif.: National Press, 1969. 177 pp.

Lundgren, Emil Robert. *The Effects of Listening Training on Teacher Listening and Discussion Skills*. Stanford, Calif.: Stanford Center for Research and Development in Teaching, 1972. 87 pp.

Lundsteen, Sara W. "Critical Listening—Permanency and Transfer of Gains Made during an Experiment in the Fifth and Sixth Grades." *California Journal of Educational Research* 16 (1965):210–216.

————, ed. *Help for the Teacher of Written Composition (K-9)*. Urbana, Ill.: National Council of Teachers of English, 1976. 72 pp.

————. "Levels of Meaning in Reading." *The Reading Teacher* 28 (1974):268–272.

————. *Listening: Its Impact on Reading and the Other Language Arts*. Urbana, Ill.: National Council of Teachers of English, 1971. 135 pp. ERIC Ed 078 420.

————. "On Developmental Relations Between Language-Learning and Reading." *Elementary School Journal* 77 (1977):192–203.

————. "Teaching Abilities in Critical Listening in the Fifth and Sixth Grades." Ph.D. dissertation, University of California, Berkeley, 1963. 241 pp.

Lyons, John, ed. *New Horizons in Linguistics*, Baltimore: Penguin Books, 1970. 367 pp.

Maccoby, Michael. "The Three C's and Discipline for Freedom." *School Review* 79 (1971):227–242.

Madison, Ann B. "Read and Rock—A Special Kind of Reading Center." *Reading Teacher* 30 (1977):501–503.

Maehr, Martin L., and Stallings, William M., eds. *Culture, Child and School*. Monterey, Calif.: Brooks Cole, 1975. 279 pp.

Manolakes, George. "The Teaching of Spelling: A Pilot Study." *Elementary English* 52 (1975): 243–247.

Marcus, Albert. *Understanding Sentence Structures*. Paper presented at the Annual Meeting of the National Council of Teachers of English, 1971. 16 pp.

Martin, James G. "Temporal Word Spacing and the Perception of Ordinary, Anomalous, and Scrambled Strings." *Journal of Verbal Learning and Verbal Behavior* 7 (1968):154–157.

Mathews, Mitford M. *American Words*. New York: World, 1959. 246 pp.

Maxwell, Edward R. "Semantic Structures." Ph.D. dissertation, Northwestern University, 1972.

McCormick, Sandra. "Should You Read Aloud to Your Children?" *Language Arts* 54 (1977):139–143.

McDaniel, Ernest. *Manual for Observer Rating Scales*. West LaFayette, Ind.: Purdue Educational Research Center, Purdue University, 1974.

McGarvey, Jack. "Standardized Tests: Five Steps to Change." *Learning* 2 (1974):24–26.

McGinitie, Walter H. "Evaluating Readiness for Learning To Read: A Critical Review and Evaluation of Research." *Reading Research Quarterly* 4 (1969):396–410.

McNeill, David. "Developmental Psycholinguistics." In *The Genesis of Language*, edited by Frank Smith and George Miller, pp. 15–84. Cambridge, Mass.: M.I.T. Press, 1966.

McPhee, Angus. "Children's Writing." *CITF Newsletter* 5 (1971):14–26.

Mearns, Hughes. *Creative Power: The Education of Youth in the Creative Arts*. New York: Dover, 1958. 272 pp.

Mehrabian, Albert. *Silent Messages*. Belmont, Calif.: Wadsworth, 1971. 152 pp.

Miccinati, Jeannette. "Watch, Listen and Record." *Educational Leadership* 34 (1977):252–256.

Mickish, Virginia. "Children's Perception of Written Word Boundaries." *Journal of Reading Behavior* 6 (April 1974):19–22.

Millar, Dan P., and Millar, Frank E. *Messages and Myths: Understanding Interpersonal Communication*. New York: Alfred, 1976. 209 pp.

Moffet, James. *Teaching the Universe of Discourse*. Boston: Houghton Mifflin, 1968. 215 pp.

Monson, Jay A. "Is Spelling Spelled Rut, Routine, or Revitalized?" *Elementary English* 52 (1975): 223–224.

Montagu, Ashley. *Touching: The Human Significance of the Skin*. New York: Columbia University Press, 1971. 338 pp.

Morrison, Coleman, and Austin, Mary C. *The Torch Lighters Revisited*. Newark, Del.: International Reading Association, 1977. 104 pp.

Moss, Joy F. "A General Language Arts Program in an Informal Classroom." *Elementary School Journal* 75 (1975):238–250.

———. "Learning to Write by Listening to Literature." *Language Arts* 54 (1977):537–542.

Nash, William R., and Torrance, E. Paul. "Creative Reading and the Questioning Abilities of Young Children." *Journal of Creative Behavior* 8 (1974):15–19.

Nathan, Joe. "Can Kids Improve Their Community? You Bet." *Learning* 3 (January 1975):60–61.

Naylor, Marilyn J. "Reading Skill Variability within and among Fourth, Fifth and Sixth Grade Students Attaining the Same Reading Achievement Score." Ph.D. dissertation, University of Michigan, 1972.

Neville, Mary H., and Pugh, A. K. "Context in Reading and Listening: Variations in Approach to Cloze Tasks." *Reading Research Quarterly* 12 (1976):13–31.

Nilsen, Alleen Pace, and Greenwell, Ivie Johnson. "Good Luck! Bad Luck!" *Language Arts* 54 (1977):786–790.

"Nonbooks: Rx for Bibliophobia." *Learning* 4 (November 1975):92–94.

O'Bruba, William S. "Promoting Oral Communication As the Basis for Reading and Writing." *Reading Improvement* 11 (1974):43–44.

O'Donnell, Charles M. P. "A Pilot Study to Compare a Conceptual-Language Program with a Basal Reader Approach in Developing Readiness in the Kindergarten." Ed.D. dissertation, Syracuse University, 1968. 165 pp.

O'Donnell, Holly. "Are You Listening? Are You Listening?" *Language Arts* 52 (1975):1080–1084.

O'Hare, Frank. *Sentence-Combining: Improving Student Writing Without Formal Grammar Instruction*. Urbana, Ill.: National Council of Teachers of English. 1971. 108 pp.

Olmo, Barbara G. "Teaching Students to Ask Questions." *Language Arts* 52 (1975):1116–1119.

Olsen, Edward C. "Teacher's Role in Life-Centering the Curriculum." *Journal of Teacher Education* 28 (1977):17–18.

Page, W. D., ed. *Help for the Reading Teacher: New Directions in Research*. Urbana, Ill.: National Council of Teachers of English, 1975.

Parker, Elizabeth Ann. *Teaching the Reading of Fiction*. New York: Teachers College Press, 1969. 154 pp.

Parnes, Sydney. "Idea Stimulation Techniques." *Journal of Creative Behavior* 10 (1976):126–128.

Paul, Rhea. "Invented Spelling in Kindergarten." *Young Children* 31 (1976):195–200.

Pei, Mario. *All about Language*, rev. ed. Philadelphia: J. B. Lippincott, 1965. 508 pp.

———, ed. *Language Today: A Survey of Current Linguistic Thought*. New York: Funk and Wagnalls, 1967. 150 pp.

Perez, Samuel A. "Teaching the Art of Writing Personal Letters." *Language Arts* 54 (1977): 795–797.

Perfetti, Charles A. "Psychosemantics: Some Cognitive Aspects of Structural Meaning." *Psychological Bulletin* 78 (1972):241–259.

Perfetti, Charles A., and Goldman S. R., "Thematization and Sentence Retrieval." *Journal of Verbal Learning and Verbal Behavior* 13 (1974): 70–79.

Perrone, Vito. "Documenting Teaching and Learning." *Social Policy* 8 (Sept.–Oct., 1977): 45–51.

———. "On Standardized Testing and Evaluation." *Childhood Education* 53 (1976):9–16.

Peterson, Georgia L. "An Approach to Writing for Kindergartners." *Elementary English* 52 (1975): 89–91.

Petty, Walter T. *Slithery Snakes and Other Aids to Children's Writing*. New York: Appleton-Century-Crofts, 1967. 99 pp.

Pflaumer, Elizabeth M. "Listening: A Definition and Application." Paper read at Annual Convention, International Communication Association, Atlanta, Georgia, 1972. ERIC Ed 063 789.

Piaget, Jean. *The Child and Reality*. New York. Grossman, 1973a. 182 pp.

———. "Cognitive Development in Children: The Piaget Papers." In *Piaget Rediscovered: A Report of the Conference on Cognitive Studies and Curriculum Development*, edited by R. E. Ripple and V. N. Rockcastle, pp. 6–48. Ithaca, N.Y.: School of Education, Cornell University, 1964.

———. *The Language and Thought of the Child*. 3d ed. rev. London: Routledge and Kegan Paul, 1959. 288 pp.

———. *Science of Education and Psychology of the Child*. New York: Orion Press, 1970. 186 pp.

Piaget, Jean, with Duckworth, Eleanor. "Piaget Takes a Teacher's Look." *Learning* 2 (1973b): 22–27.

Piaget, Jean, and Inhelder, Bärbel. *The Psychology of the Child*. New York: Basic Books, 1969. 173 pp.

Pikulski, John J. "Using the Cloze Technique." *Language Arts* 53 (1976):317–318.

Pooley, Robert C. *The Teaching of English Usage*. Urbana, Ill.: National Council of Teachers of English, 1974. 241 pp.

Possien, Wilma M. *They All Need to Talk: Oral Communication in the Language Arts Program*. New York: Appleton-Century-Crofts, 1969. 119 pp.

Postman, Neil M., and Weingartner, Charles. *Linguistics: A Revolution in Teaching*. New York: Delacorte, 1966. 206 pp.

———. *The School Book*. New York: Delacorte, 1973. 308 pp.

———. *The Soft Revolution*. New York: Dell, 1969. 218 pp.

Potter, Rosemary Lee, and Hannemann, Charles E. "Conscious 'Comprehension': Reality Reading through Artifacts." *The Reading Teacher* 30 (1977):644–648.

Pryzwansky, W. B. "Effects of Perceptual-Motor Training and Manuscript Writing on Reading Readiness Skills in Kindergarten." *Journal of Educational Psychology* 63 (1972):110–115.

Pulaski, Mary Ann Spencer. "The Rich Rewards of Make Believe." *Psychology Today* 8 (January 1974):68–74.

Purkey, William Watson. *Self-Concept and School Achievement*. Englewood Cliffs, N.J.: Prentice-Hall, 1970. 86 pp.

Randolph, Huberta V. "Measuring the Unmeasurable." In *Evaluation in Reading*, pp. 32–35. Utah: International Reading Association, 1972. ERIC Ed 080 964.

Raths, Louis E.; Harmin, Merrill; and Simon, Sidney B. *Values and Teaching: Working with Values in the Classroom*. Columbus, Ohio: Charles E. Merrill, 1966. 275 pp.

Raths, Louis E.; Jonas, Arthur; Rothstein, Arnold; and Wassermann, Selma. *Teaching for Thinking: Theory and Application*. Columbus, Ohio: Charles E. Merrill, 1967. 348 pp.

Raymond, Anne F. "The Acquisition of Nonverbal Behaviors by Preservice Science Teachers and Their Application during Student Teaching." *Journal of Research in Science Teaching* 10 (1973):13–24.

Read, Charles. "Children's Judgment of Phonetic Similarities in Relation to English Spelling." *Language Learning* 23 (1973):17–38.

"Reading, Language, and Learning: A Special Issue." *Harvard Educational Review* 47 (1977):v–xii, 257–451.

Resnick, Daniel P., and Resnick, Lauren B. "The Nature of Literacy: An Historical Exploration." *Harvard Educational Review* 47 (1977):370–385.

Restak, Richard. "Jose Delgado: Exploring Inner Space." *Saturday Review*, 9 August 1975, pp. 21–25.

Robinson, Joanne A. *Summary of First Grade Study, 1965–66. Project Literacy*. n.d. 123 pp. OE-DHEW Report no. 13 R-5-0537-19. ERIC Ed 011 589.

Robinson, W. P. "Social Factors and Language Development in Primary School Children." In *Language Acquisition: Models and Methods*, edited by Renira Huxley and Elisabeth Ingram, pp. 49–63. London: Academic Press, 1971.

Rode, Sara S. "Development of Phrase and Clause Boundary Reading in Children." *Reading Research Quarterly* 10 (1974):124–142.

Rogers, Carl. "Beyond the Watershed: And Where Now?" *Educational Leadership* 34 (1977):620–631.

―――. *Freedom to Learn*. Columbus, Ohio: Charles E. Merrill, 1969. 358 pp.

Rogers, Minnie M. "The Effect of Speech Patterns on Listening Comprehension." Ed.D. dissertation, Ball State University, 1972.

Rogers, Richard DeVere. *A Study of the Effect of Practice on the Ability to Follow Directions*. Ed.D. dissertation, Arizona State University, 1969.

Rogers, Vincent R., and Church, Bud, eds. *Open Education: Critique and Assessment*. Washington, D.C.: Association for Supervision and Curriculum Development, 1975. 107 pp.

Rosen, Harold. "Written Language and the Sense of Audience." *Educational Research* 15 (1973): 177–187.

Rosenshine, Barak. "Enthusiastic Teaching: A Research Review." *School Review* 78 (1970): 449–514.

Rosenthal, Robert, and Jacobson, Lenore. *Pygmalion in the Classroom*. New York: Holt, Rinehart and Winston, 1968. 240 pp.

Roslier, Florence. "Sunrise, Sunset; Pretest, Retest." *Elementary English* 52 (1975):230–231.

Ross, Elinor P., and Roe, Betty D. "Creative Drama Builds Proficiency in Reading." *Reading Teacher* 30 (1977):383–387.

Rothwell, J. Dan, and Costigan, James I. *Interpersonal Communication: Influences and Alternatives*. Columbus, Ohio: Charles E. Merrill, 1975. 269 pp.

Rubin, Joseph. "The Stage Is Set—Language Experiences Begin!" *Reading Teacher* 22 (1969): 414–418.

Rubin, Louis J., ed. *Life Skills in School and Society*. Washington, D.C.: Association for Supervision and Curriculum Development, 1969. 166 pp.

Rukavina, Joanne L. "Beginner, Perpetual Beginner: Encouraging Children to Write." *Language Arts* 54 (1977):780–785.

Samples, Robert E. "Are You Teaching Only One Side of the Brain?" *Learning* 3 (Feb. 1975):24–28.

Sanders, Norris M. *Classroom Questions: What Kinds?* New York: Harper and Row, 1966. 176 pp.

Sayers, Francis Clarke. *Summoned by Books*. New York: Viking, 1965. 173 pp.

Schank, Roger C., and Wilks, Yorick. "The Goals of Linguistic Theory Revisited." Department of Defense, Advanced Research Projects Agency, 1973. 43 pp. ERIC Ed 681 282.

Schell, Leo M. "B+ in Composition: C− in Spelling." *Elementary English* 52 (1975):239–242.

Schulz, Charles. *Happiness Is a Warm Puppy*. San Francisco: Determined Productions, 1962.

Schwartz, Mimi. "Rewriting or Recopying: What Are We Teaching?" *Language Arts* 54 (1977): 756–759.

Schwebel, Milton, and Raph, Jane, eds. *Piaget in the Classroom*. New York: Basic Books, 1973. 305 pp.

Sebesta, Sam Leaton. "Tyrannosaurus Anonymous Met a Reader Autonomous." In *Claremont Reading Conference 36th Yearbook*, edited by Malcolm P. Douglass, pp. 44–49. Claremont, Calif.: Claremont Graduate School, 1972.

Sereno, Kenneth R., and Mortensen, C. David. *Foundations of Communication Theory*. New York: Harper and Row, 1970. 371 pp.

Shaftel, Fannie R., and Shaftel, George. *Role-Playing for Social Values*. Englewood Cliffs, N.J.: Prentice-Hall, 1967. 431 pp.

―――. *Role-Playing the Problem Story*. New York: National Conference of Christians and Jews, 1952. 78 pp.

Shanahan, Timothy. "Writing Marathons and Concept Development." *Language Arts* 54 (1977): 403–405.

Sheldon, Harry J. "Wanted: More Effective Teaching of Oral Communication." *Language Arts* 54 (1977):665–667.

Shiman, David A.; Culver, Carmen M.; and Lieberman, Ann. *Teachers on Individualization: The Way We Do It*. New York: McGraw-Hill, 1974. 212 pp.

Shohen, Sam. "A Language Experience Approach to Reading Instruction." In *Views on Elementary Reading Instruction*, edited by Thomas C. Barrett and Dale D. Johnson, pp. 43–48. Newark, Del.: International Reading Association, 1973.

Shultz, Thomas R., and Pilon, Robert. "Development of the Ability to Detect Linguistic Ambiguity." *Child Development* 44 (1973):728–733.

Shuy, Roger W. *Discovering American Dialects*. Urbana, Ill.: National Council of Teachers of English, 1967. 68 pp.

———, ed. *Linguistic Theory: What Can It Say about Reading?* Newark, Del.: International Reading Association, 1977, 195 pp.

———. "Sociolinguistics and Reading." Paper read at the International Reading Association Conference, 1974, in New Orleans, La. 22 pp. ERIC Ed 090 801.

Silberman, Charles E. *Crisis in the Classroom*. New York: Random House, 1970

Silberman, Melvin L.; Allender, Jerome S.; and Yanoff, Jay M., eds. *The Psychology of Open Teaching and Learning: An Inquiry Approach*. Boston: Little, Brown, 1972. 307 pp.

Simon, Marianne. "Chasing Killer Statements from the Classroom." *Learning* 4 (1975):79–80.

Simon, Sidney, and O'Rourke, Robert. "Every Child Has High Worth—Prove It." *Learning* 4 (1975):46–50.

Singer, Jerome. *The Child's World of Make-Believe*. New York: Academic Press, 1973. 294 pp.

Skinner, B. F. *Verbal Behavior*. New York: Appleton-Century-Crofts, 1957. 478 pp.

Slobin, Dan I. *Psycholinguistics*. Glenview, Ill.: Scott, Foresman, 1971. 148 pp.

Smith, Frank. *Comprehension and Learning*. New York: Holt, Rinehart and Winston, 1975a. 275 pp.

———. "Making Sense of Reading—And of Reading Instruction." *Harvard Educational Review* 47 (1977):386–395.

———. *Psycholinguistics and Reading*. New York: Holt, Rinehart and Winston, 1973. 211 pp.

———. "The Role of Prediction in Reading." *Elementary English* 52 (1975b):305–311.

———. "Twelve Easy Ways to Make Learning to Read Difficult." In *Psycholinguistics and Reading*, edited by Frank Smith. New York: Holt, Rinehart and Winston, 1973.

———. *Understanding Reading*. New York: Holt, Rinehart and Winston, 1971. 230 pp. (Revised 1978.)

Smith, Frank, and Holmes, Deborah L. "The Independence of Letter, Word, and Meaning Identification in Reading." *Reading Research Quarterly* 6 (1971):394–415.

Social Policy 4. "The Assessment Controversy" (September-October 1977):2–71.

Sommer, Robert. "Classroom Ecology." *Journal of Applied Behavioral Science* 33 (1967):489–503.

Spinrad, Deane. "How All the Children Began to Read." *Language Arts* 53 (1976):572–573.

Stallard, Charles K. "Writing Readiness: A Developmental View." *Language Arts* 54 (1977): 775–779.

Stammer, John D. "Target: The Basics of Listening." *Language Arts* 54 (1977):661–664.

Stanford, Gene, and Stanford, Barbara Dodds. *Learning Discussion Skills through Games*. New York: Citation Press, 1969. 75 pp.

Stank, Peggy L. "First Grade Follow-Up of Kidi-Prep." Bureau of Information Systems, Pennsylvania State Department of Education, 1973. 7 pp. ERIC Ed 087 526.

Steen, Arleen M. "The Effectiveness of Listening Lessons in the Kindergarten as Determined by the Listening Response Test." Ph.D. dissertation, University of Iowa, 1969.

Stegall, Carrie. "Nashery." *Language Arts* 57 (1977):767–774.

Streib, Rachel. "Context Utilization in Reading by Educable Mentally Retarded Children." *Reading Research Quarterly* 12 (1976):32–54.

Strickland, Dorothy S. "Expanding Language Power of Young Black Children: A Literature Approach." In *Better Reading in Urban Schools*, pp. 9–17. International Reading Association, 1972. ERIC Ed 066 720.

Strickland, Dorothy S. "A Program for the Linguistically Different Black Children." *Research in the Teaching of English* 7 (1973):79–86.

Strickland, Ruth G. "The Contribution of Structural Linguistics to the Teaching of Reading, Writing and Grammar in the Elementary School." *Bulletin of the School of Education* 40, 1. Bloomington, Ind.: Indiana University, 1964.

———. "Language in the Schools." In *The Learning of Language*, edited by Carroll E. Reed. New York: Appleton-Century-Crofts, 1971.

Suhor, Charles. "Linda's Rewrite." *Learning* 4 (1975):20–25.

Sulin, R. A., and Dooling, D. J. "Intrusion of a Thematic Idea in Retension of Prose." *Journal of Experimental Psychology* 103 (1974):255–262.

Sund, Robert B. "Growing through Sensitive Listening and Questioning." *Childhood Education* 51 (1974):68–71.

Taba, Hilda. *Teaching Strategies and Cognitive Functioning in Elementary School Children.* San Francisco: San Francisco State College, 1966. 275 pp.

Taba, Hilda; Levine, Samuel; and Elzey, Freeman F. *Thinking in Elementary School Children.* Cooperative Research Project no. 1574, San Francisco State College, 1964. Ann Arbor: University Microfilms, Inc., 1967. 207 pp.

Taylor, Jo Ellyn. "Making Sense: The Basic Skill in Reading." *Language Arts* 54 (1977):668–672.

Thompson, James J. *Beyond Words: Nonverbal Communication in the Classroom.* New York: Citation Press, 1973. 208 pp.

Thompson School District R2-J, Loveland, Colo. *A Program of Primary Auding Skills.* Final Evaluation Report. 1970. 26 pp. ERIC Ed 061 009.

Tiedt, Iris M. *Individualizing Writing in the Elementary Classroom.* Urbana, Ill.: National Council of Teachers of English, 1975. 25 pp.

Torrance, E. Paul. *Encouraging Creativity in the Classroom.* Dubuque, Iowa: William C. Brown, 1970. 133 pp.

Torrance, E. Paul, and Myers, R. E. *Creative Learning and Teaching.* New York: Dodd, Mead, 1970. 343 pp.

Torrey, Jane W. "Illiteracy in the Ghetto." *Harvard Education Review* 40 (1970):253–259.

———. "Learning To Read without a Teacher." *Elementary English* 46 (1969):550–556.

Tovey, Duane R. "The Psycholinguistic Guessing Game." *Language Arts* 53 (1976):319–322.

Treffinger, Donald J.; Speedie, Stuart M.; and Brunner, Wayne D. "Improving Children's Creative Problem Solving Ability: The Purdue Creativity Project." *Journal of Creative Behavior* 8 (1974):20–30.

Troy, Anne. "Literature for Content Area Learning." *Reading Teacher* 30 (1977):470–474.

Tutolo, Daniel J. "One Approach to Teaching Critical Listening." In *Teaching about Doublespeak*, edited by Daniel Dietrich, pp. 92–99. Urbana, Ill.: National Council of Teachers of English, 1976.

Venezky, Richard L. "English Orthography: Its Graphical Structure and Its Relation to Sound." *Reading Research Quarterly* 2 (1967):75–106.

Vernon, McCay. "Relationship of Thought, Language, and Non-Verbal Communication to Reading." In *Claremont Reading Conference 36th Yearbook*, edited by Malcolm P. Douglass, pp. 137–149. Claremont, Calif.: Claremont Graduate School, 1972.

Vygotsky, Lev Semenovich. *Thought and Language*, edited and translated by Eugenia Hanfmann and Gertrude Vakar. Cambridge, Mass.: M.I.T. Press, 1962. 168 pp.

Wagner, Tony. "Learning Democratically." *The English Journal* 66 (1977):33–37.

Wales, R. J., and Marshall, J. C. "The Organization of Linguistic Performance." In *Psychological Papers*, edited by J. Lyons and R. J. Wales. Edinburgh, Scotland: Edinburgh University Press, 1966.

Walshe, R. D. "A Model of the Writing Situation." *College Composition and Communication* 28 (1977):384–386.

Wattenberg, William W., and Clifford, Clare. "Relation of Self-Concepts to Beginning Achievement in Reading." *Child Development* 35 (1964):461–467.

Weaver, Carl H. *Human Listening: Process and Behavior.* Indianapolis, Ind.: Bobbs-Merrill, 1972. 170 pp.

Weaver, Richard L. "Humanistic Approach in Speech: Affective Behavioral Objectives." Paper presented at Annual Meeting of the Speech Association of the Eastern States, 1973, in New York. 13 pp. ERIC Ed 078 471.

Weber, Rose-Marie. "First Graders' Use of Grammatical Context in Reading." In *Basic Studies in Reading*, edited by Harry Levin and Joanna Williams, pp. 160–162. New York: Basic Books, 1970a.

———. "A Linguistic Analysis of First Grade Reading Errors." *Reading Research Quarterly* 5 (1970b):427–451.

Webster, Staten W. *Knowing and Understanding the Socially Disadvantaged: Ethnic Minority Groups*. Scranton, Pa.: Intext Educational Publishers, 1972.

Welch, I. David; Richards, Fred; and Richards, Anne Cohen, eds. *Educational Accountability: A Humanistic Perspective*. Fort Collins, Colo.: Shields, n.d. 255 pp.

Western Richard D. "A Defense of Kenneth Koch." *Language Arts* 54 (1977):763–766.

Wexler, Lillian. *Teacher, Save My Writings*. Washington, D.C.: American Association for Elementary, Kindergarten, Nursery Educators, National Education Association, 1975.

Wilcox, Leah M. "Literature: The Child's Guide to Creative Writing." *Language Arts* 54 (1977): 549–554.

Williams, Roger M. "Why Children Should Draw: The Surprising Link between Art and Learning." *Saturday Review*, 3 September 1977, pp. 10–16.

Willson, Irwin A. "Changes in Mean Levels of Thinking in Grades 1–8 through Use of an Interaction Analysis System Based on Bloom's Taxonomy." *Journal of Educational Research* 66 (1972):421–429.

Winterwood, W. Ross. "A Teacher's Guide to the Real Basics." *Language Arts* 54 (1977):625–630.

Wittels, Harriet, and Greisman, Joan. *The Clear and Simple Thesaurus Dictionary*. Grosset and Dunlop, n.d.

Witucke, Virginia. *Poetry in the Elementary School*. Dubuque, Iowa: William C. Brown, 1970. 115 pp.

Wood, Barbara S. "Implications of Psycholinguistics for Elementary Speech Programs." *Speech Teacher* 17 (1968):183–192.

Woods, Margaret S. "The Serious Business of Make-Believe." *Kindergarten Portfolio*. Washington, D.C.: Association for Childhood Education, International, 1970.

———. *Wonderwork: Creative Experiences for the Young Child*. Buffalo, N.Y.: d.o.k. Publishers, 1970. 25 pp.

Woods, Margaret S., and Trihart, Beryl. *Guidelines to Creative Dramatics*. Buffalo, N.Y.: d.o.k. Publishers, 1970. 22 pp.

Yamamoto, Kaoru. *The Child and His Image: Self-Concept in the Early Years*. Boston: Houghton Mifflin, 1972. 235 pp.

Zuck, Louis V. "Some Questions about the Teaching of Syllabication Rules." *Reading Teacher* 27 (1974):582–588.

INDEX

Elzey, Freeman F., 46
Emans, Robert, 343, 346–347
Embedding, 65, 186
Emotions, expressions of, 116
Encoding, 8, 240, 241
Engel, Rosalind, 270
English
    Black, 120–121
    formal, 118
Epstein, Beryl, 137
Epstein, Sam, 137
Equilibration, 37, 40
    accommodation, 37, 39
    assimilation, 37, 39
Evans, Richard I., 51
Evans, Robert, 51, 249
Everle, Bob, 160
Evertts, Eldonna L., 195
Expectancy as binding, 11, 13
Experience, 9, 10, 37, 88, 116, 128,
        133, 177, 178, 180, 181, 189, 203,
        211, 214, 239, 256, 257, 266, 280,
        303
Experiencing, 9, 75, 88, 175, 178, 231,
        256, 262
Evaluation, 44, 330
    of actions, 42
    children's, 102, 104
    of classroom program, 330
    of communication, 20–23
    conference, 102, 104, 134, 222
    criteria for, 103–105
    diagnosis and, 292
    of discussion, 149
    of handwriting, 219
    of language development, 73
    of learning, xx
    of listener, 20–21
    of listening, 99, 102–107
    from miscue analysis, 299–300
    of nonverbal communication,
        21–22
    of oral reading, 301
    of reading, 292–301
    self, 44, 221–222
    of speaker, 20
    of spelling competence, 217
    of talking, xx
    of teacher's nonverbal
        communication, 21–22
    of teacher's verbal
        communication, 20–21
    of thinking, 48
    of writing, 192, 220–222

Fagan, William T., 309
Faix, Thomas L., 26
Farb, Peter, 137
Farrell, Edmund, 309
Fast, Julius, 26
Feedback
    in evaluation, 104–105, 106
    on reading, 267
    on writing, 208–209

Feelings, 116–117, 209
    from experiencing, 9
    personal, 100, 116
    private, 116
Ferguson, Charles W., 137
Fiction, enjoying, 278
Fincher, Jack, 33, 40, 51
First drafts, 184, 192, 223
Fisher, Peggy, 332
Fitzgerald, James A., 213
Fitzgerald, Sheila, 137, 284
Flexibility in reading, 275–276, 283,
        289
Foerster, Leona M., 225, 284
Formal operations, 35, 37, 39
Fours to sevens, 35, 37, 133, 258
Frankel, Jack R., 51
Freedle, Roy O., 106
Freeing and binding statements,
        13–14
Freyberg, Joan T., 33
Friedman, Herbert L., 90–91
Froese, Victor, 284
Furth, Hans G., 51

Galin, David, 51
Gall, M. D., 51
Galloway, Charles M., 19, 21–22, 26
Gardner, Howard, 34
Generalization, 37, 42
Gergen, Kenneth J., 26
Gillies, Emily, 160
Ginott, Haim G., 332
Glasser, William, 148, 160
Glaus, Marlene, 160
Goldman, S. R., 41
Gomberg, Adeline W., 284
Goodall, Robert C., 23
Goodlad, John, xix, 333
Goodman, Kenneth S., 120, 233,
        238, 241, 242, 248, 284, 293, 309
Goodman, Yetta, 248, 284, 297, 300,
        301, 309
Gottlieb, Sybil, 33, 39, 40
Gove, Mary K., 310
Grammar, 67, 335–337, 340–342
    function of, 65, 211
    intuitive use of, 68, 123
    rules of, 123
    and structural linguistics, 68
    teaching of, 116
    traditional (formal), value of, 68,
        336
    transformational generative, 68,
        336–337
    in writing, 210–211
Granger, Robert C., 137
Grant, Barbara M., 195
Green, Harry A., 68
Green, W. Cabell, 195
Greene, Bert I., 26
Greenwell, Ivie J., 224
Greisman, Joan, 195
Groff, Patrick, 249

Group discussion, 158
    evaluation of, 149
    procedures for, 148–149
    roles in, 149
    skills of, 146–149
Grouping
    large, 148, 325
    small, 132, 148, 261, 266–267
Growing edge, 36, 37, 49
Guidelines
    for beginning reading, 258–259
    for developing writing, 191–192
    for learning, 317
    for oral sharing, 153–154
Gumperz, John J., 72

Haiku, 206
Hall, Mary Anne, 224
Hall, Edward T., 26
Halliday, M.A.K., 59, 66, 69, 77, 115,
        177, 266
Halpin, Gerald, 225
Halpin, Glennelle, 225
Handedness
    and eyedness, 305
    left, in writing, 219
Handwriting, 217–220
    cursive, 219
    italic, 218
    manuscript, 217–218
    materials for, 217
    problems in, 219–220
Hanna, Jean S., 225
Hanna, Paul R., 213, 225
Hannemann, Charles E., 248
Hargis, Charles H., 284
Harmin, Merrill, 51
Harsh, Wayne, 336–337
Hassid, Teri, 185
Hatch, Lynda, 224
Hayes, Eloise, 160
Hazard, Paul, 249
Heller, Suzanne, 207
Hennings, Dorothy Grant, 26, 160,
        195
Henry, Mabel Wright, 160
Hillocks, George, Jr., 195
Hitchfield, Elizabeth, 51
Hodges, Richard E., 225, 248
Holmes, Deborah L., 249
Home effect on language, 119–122
Hopkins, Lee Bennett, 249
Hopper, Robert W., 77, 116
Horn, Ernest, 212
Horn, Thomas D., 120
Hornburger, Jane M., 284
Hosey, Joseph G., 278
Howes, Virgil M., 333
Hoyt, Cyril J., 292
Huey, Edmund Burke, 238
Human relations, 116, 132
    and language, 71
    and listening, 100
    problems, 152

Renner, John W., 51
Reporting, 126–127, 166–167
  oral, 155–156, 167
  written, 204–205
Research
  on the brain, 32–34
  in evaluation of teachers'
    nonverbal communication,
    22–23
  in grammar, 211
  in language development, 64
  in listening, 89–95
  instructional, 238
  in reading, 238–242
  in reading readiness, 270–271
  in spelling, 213, 215
Resnick, Daniel P., 248
Resnick, Lauren B., 248
Resources, 180–181
Respect, 49, 126, 147, 153, 322
Response
  freeing and binding, 13, 14
  styles of, 14–15
  types of, 25
Responsibility, xx, 105, 147, 148,
  208, 323
  for polishing, 208
Restak, Richard, 34
Revising. See Polishing
Rewriting, 185. See also Polishing
Riccio, Mary Lou, 225
Richards, Anne C., 332
Richards, Fred, 332
Robinson, Joanne A., 128
Robinson, W. P., 128
Rode, Sara S., 249
Roe, Betty D., 160
Roebuck, F. N., 332
Rogers, Carl, 14, 25, 332, 333
Rogers, Minnie M., 93
Rogers, Richard D., 93
Rogers, Vincent R., 332
Role-playing, 151–153, 158, 163, 164
  in the curriculum, 152
  and human relations, 152
Rosen, Harold, 203, 204
Rosenshine, Barak, 20
Rosenthal, Robert, 131
Rosalier, Florence, 224
Ross, Elenor P., 160
Rote memory, 39, 40
Rothstein, Arnold, 46
Rothwell, J. Dan, 26
Rubin, Joseph, 284
Rubin, Louis J., 51
Rudorf, Erwin H., 248
Rukavina, Joanne L., 224

Samples, Robert E., 51
Sanders, Norris M., 51
Saunders, Dorothy O., 195
Sayers, Francis C., 249
Scanning, 275, 283
Schank, Roger C., 69

Schell, Leo M., 224
School's role
  in developing speech, 122–133
  in developing thinking, 46
  in improving listening, 95–102
Schulz, Charles, 207
Schwa, 272
Schwartz, Mimi, 195
Schwebel, Milton, 51
Sebesta, Sam L., 248
Selective attention, 90
Self-awareness, 15, 16, 44, 94
Self-concept, 129, 189, 256
  and awareness, 29
  and communication, 16–18, 71
  defined, 16
  development of, 16–18
  effect of, 17
  and learning, 20
Self-confidence, 11, 13, 16, 17, 88,
  96, 181, 279
  of children, as communicators, 74
  of children, as readers, 306
  and learning, 20
Self-development, continuing,
  94–95
Self-direction, 13, 16, 105, 147, 266,
  304, 323, 326–327
Self-doubt, as barrier to
  understanding, 6
Self-evaluation, 44, 104, 221–222, 323
  of listening, 105, 107
  of polishing, 221–222
  of reading, 296–297
  of talking, 157
  in teacher-child conference, 134,
    156, 191, 222, 296–297
  of writing, 221–222
Self-esteem, 104, 178, 279, 322
Self-fulfilling prophecy, 131
Self-selection, 37, 44
  of reading activities, 260
  of reading materials, 273, 280
Semantics, 66–67
Sensory motor stage, 35
Sentence
  complete, 59
  kernel, 186
  one-word, 59
  patterns, 62, 64
  scrambled, 276
  structure, 62, 68, 181
  tightening, 186–187
  unit of meaning, 243
Sequence
  in developing reading, 260
  in developing talking, 63, 133
  in learning, 270
  time, 37
Sereno, Kenneth R., 8
Sevens to nines, 37, 38, 123, 133, 271
Shaftel, Fannie R., 152, 160

Shaftel, George, 152–160
Shanahan, Timothy, 180
Sharing books, 245
Sharing time, 153–155
Sheldon, Harry J., 109
Shiman, David A., 332
Shohen, Sam, 284
Shultz, Thomas R., 66
Shuy, Roger, 71, 121, 137, 248, 266,
  284
Silberman, Charles E., 333
Silberman, Melvin L., 51, 333
Simon, Marianne, 26
Simon, Sidney B., 26, 51
Sims, Rudine, 284
Singer, Jerome, 33
Skills
  basic, defined, xx–xxi
  of discussion, 145, 146–149
  of listening, 92, 93, 94
  of reading, 233–235, 242–243,
    269–273
  of thinking, 43, 49, 88, 128, 132
Skimming, 275, 283
Skinner, B. F., 61
Slobin, Dan I., 77
Smith, Frank, 40, 51, 59, 187, 238,
  239, 240, 248, 249, 284
Smith, Veta, 137
Social interaction, 37
Sociolinguistics, 66, 115
Sommer, Robert, 20
Speech
  acceptable, 118
  appropriateness of, 118, 119
  beginnings of, 58
  elaborated, 73, 121–122
  through imitation, 61, 130
  of inner-city children, 119–120
  and reading, 257
  restricted, 72, 121–122, 128–129
  structuring of, 64
  unacceptable, 118
Speedie, Stuart M., 51
Spelling, 212–217, 224–228
  evaluation of, 217
  how learned, 215–216
  instructional patterns for, 213–214
  problems, 215
  programs, 212
  purpose of, 214, 215
  resources, 214
  selection of words, 214–215
  and vocabulary, 214
Stages of development
  of language, 63
  of listening, 87
  of reading, 260–265
  of talking, 133
  of thought, 34–35
  of writing, 175, 221
Stallard, Charles K., 195
Stallings, William M., 77